The Essential Originalist Papers

Brion McClanahan

RED MILL PUBLISHING

Red Mill Publishing

Contents

An American Citizen I by Tench Coxe

Editor's Introduction:

Most modern Americans would not recognize the name Tench Coxe, but he was an important member of Philadelphia society and a leading political figure in his State during the founding period. He served in the Continental Congress and represented Pennsylvania at the 1786 Annapolis Convention where Alexander Hamilton and James Madison proposed a convention of all the States to revise the Articles of Confederation. It was here that Coxe developed a working relationship with Hamilton, and this later led Washington to appoint Coxe as Assistant Secretary of the Treasury on September 11, 1789. Coxe, in fact, helped Hamilton draft his famous *Report on Manufacturers* in 1791. Washington later tapped Coxe to be revenue commissioner, and he held that office until he was sacked by John Adams. Coxe switched "parties" and became a "Democratic-Republican." He exacted revenge on Adams during the 1800 election by publishing a letter that Adams wrote in 1792 where he accused the Pinckney family of South Carolina of being self-interested double agents for the British. Thomas Jefferson rewarded Coxe with an appointment as "purveyor of public supplies." Yet, the Republicans never fully embraced Coxe and eventually labeled him "Mr. Facing Bothways" for his perceived political duplicity.

Coxe wrote the first public defense of the Constitution in September 1787, just nine days after the Philadelphia Convention wrapped up, in a series of essays published in the *Independent Gazetteer* under the pseudonym "An American Citizen." These essays contrasted the new American Constitution with that of the British model of government. In the first essay, Coxe recounted the events that led to the American War for Independence, and unlike many radicals who wanted to purge the British model from the American mind, Coxe argued that if American rights and liberties had been protected as per the British constitution, the War would have been avoided. He then stressed that the newly created American executive would differ both in form and substance from the British king and urged Americans to support the new Constitution because did not create an elected American king. This was one of the more important points proponents of the Constitution made during the ratification debates, most conspicuously by Hamilton in *Federalist No. 69*. Coxe presented the argument to the Pennsylvania public first.

An American Citizen I

September 26, 1787

By Tench Coxe of Pennsylvania

It is impossible for an honest and feeling mind, of any nation or country whatever, to be insensible to the present circumstances of America. Were I an East Indian, or a Turk, I should consider this singular situation of a part of my fellow creatures, as most curious and interesting. Intimately connected with the country, as a citizen of the Union, I confess it entirely engrosses my mind and feelings.

To take a proper view of the ground on which we stand, it may be necessary to recollect the manner in which the United States were originally settled and established. Want of charity in the religious systems of Europe and of justice in their political governments were the principal moving causes which drove the emigrants of various countries to the American continent. The Congregationalists, Quakers, Presbyterians and other British dissenters, the Catholics of England and Ireland, and the Huguenots of France, the German Lutherans, Calvinists, and Moravians, with several other societies, established themselves in the different colonies, thereby laying the ground of that catholicism in ecclesiastical affairs, which has been observable since the late Revolution. Religious liberty naturally promotes corresponding dispositions in matters of government. The constitution of England, as it stood on paper, was one of the freest at that time existing in the world, and the American colonies considered themselves as entitled to the fullest enjoyment of it. Thus when the ill-judged discussions of latter times in England brought into question the rights of this country, as it stood connected with the British Crown, we were found more strongly impressed with their importance and accurately acquainted with their extent, than the wisest and most learned of our brethren beyond the Atlantic. When the greatest names in Parliament insisted on the power of that body over the commerce of the colonies, and even the right to bind us in all cases whatsoever, America, seeing that it was only another form of tyranny, insisted upon the immutable truth, that taxation and representation are inseparable, and while a desire of harmony and other considerations induced her into an acquiescence in the commercial regulations of Great Britain, it was done from the declared necessity of the case, and with a cautious, full and absolute saving of our voluntary suspended rights. The Parliament was persevering, and America continued firm till hostilities and open war commenced, and finally the late Revolution closed the contest forever.

Tis evident from this short detail and the reflections which arise from it, that the quarrel between the United States and the Parliament of Great Britain did not arise so much from objections to the form of government, though undoubtedly a better one by far is now within our reach, as from a difference concerning certain important rights resulting from the essential principles of liberty, which the constitution preserved to all the subjects actually residing within the realm. It was not asserted by America that the people of the island of Great Britain were slaves, but that we, though possessed absolutely of the same rights, were not admitted to enjoy an equal degree of freedom.

When the Declaration of Independence completed the separation between the two countries, new governments were necessarily established. Many circumstances led to the adoption of the republican form, among which was the predilection of the people. In devising the frames of government it may have been difficult to avoid extremes opposite to the vices of that we had just rejected; nevertheless many of the state constitutions we have chosen are truly excellent. Our misfortunes have been, that in the first instance we adopted no national government at all, but were kept together by common danger only, and that in the confusions of a civil war we framed a federal constitution now universally admitted to be inadequate to the preservation of liberty, property, and the Union. The question is not then how far our state constitutions are good or otherwise–the object of our wishes is to amend and supply the evident and allowed errors and defects of the federal government. Let us consider awhile, that which is now proposed to us. Let us compare it with the so much boasted British form of government, and see how much more it favors the people and how completely it secures their rights, remembering at the same time that we did not dissolve our connection with that country so much on account of its constitution as the perversion and maladministration of it.

In the first place let us look at the nature and powers of the head of that country, and those of the ostensible head of our own.

The British king is the great bishop or supreme head of an established church, with an immense patronage annexed. In this capacity he commands a number of votes in the House of Lords, by creating bishops, who, besides their great incomes, have voted in that assembly, and are judges in the last resort. They have also many honorable and lucrative places to bestow, and thus from their wealth, learning, dignities, powers and patronage giver a great luster and an enormous influence to the Crown.

In America our President will not only be without these influencing advantages, but they will be in the possession of the people at large, to strengthen their hands in the event of a contest with him. All religious funds, honors and powers are in the gift of numberless, unconnected, disunited, and contending corporations, wherein the principle of perfect equality universally prevails. In short, danger from ecclesiastical tyranny, that longstanding and still remaining curse of the people–that sacrilegious engine of royal power in some countries, can be feared by no man in the United States. In Britain their king is for life. In America our President will always be one of the people at the end of four years. In that country the king is hereditary and may be an idiot, a knave, or a tyrant by nature, or ignorant from neglect of his education, yet cannot be removed, for "he can do no wrong." In America, as the President is to be one of the people at the end of his short term, so will he and his fellow citizens remember, that he was originally one of the people; and that he is created by their breath. Further, he cannot be an idiot, probably not a knave or a tyrant, for those whom nature makes so, discover it before the age of thirty-five, until which period he cannot be elected. It appears we have not admitted that he can do no wrong, but have rather presupposed he may and will sometimes do wrong, by providing for his impeachment, his trial, and his peaceable and complete removal.

In England the king has a power to create members of the upper house, who are judges in the highest court, as well as legislators. Our President not only cannot make members of the upper house, but their creation, like his own, is by the people through their representatives, and a member of assembly may and will be as certainly dismissed at the end of his year for electing a weak or wicked Senator, as for any other blunder or misconduct.

The king of England has legislative power, while our President can only use it when the other servants of the people are divided. But in all great cases affecting the national interests or safety, his modified and restrained power must give way to the sense of two-thirds of the legislature. In fact it amounts to no more, than a serious duty imposed upon him to request both houses to reconsider any matter on which he entertains doubts or feels apprehensions; and here the people have a strong hold upon him from his sole and personal responsibility.

The president of the upper house (or the chancellor) in England is appointed by the king, while our Vice President, who is chosen by the people through the Electors and the Senate, is not at all dependent on the President, but may exercise equal powers on some occasions. In all royal governments an helpless infant or an inexperienced youth may wear the crown. Our President must be matured by the experience of years, and being born among us, his character at thirty-five must be fully understood. Wisdom, virtue, and active qualities of mind and body can alone make him the first servant of a free and enlightened people.

Our President will fall very far short indeed of any prince in his annual income, which will not be hereditary, but the absolute allowance of the people passing through the hands of their other servants from year to year as it becomes necessary. There will be no burdens on the nation to provide for his heir or other branches of his family. Tis probably, from the state of property in America and other circumstances, that many citizens will exceed him in show and expense, those dazzling trappings of kingly rank and power. He will have no authority to make a treaty without two-thirds of the Senate, nor can he appoint ambassadors or other great officers without their approbation, which will remove the idea of patronage and influence, and of personal obligation and dependence. The appointment of even the inferior officers may be taken out of his hands by an act of Congress at any time; he can create no nobility or titles of honor, nor take away offices during good behavior. His person is not so much protected as that of a member of the House of Representatives; for he may be proceeded against like any other man in the ordinary course of law. He appoints no officer of the separate states. He will have no influence from placemen in the legislature, nor can he prorogue or dissolve it. He will have no power over the treasures of the state; and lastly, as he is created through the Electors by the people at large, he must ever look up to the support of his creators. From such a servant with powers so limited and transitory, there can be no danger, especially when we consider the solid foundations on which our national liberties are immovably fixed by the other provisions of this excellent Constitution. Whatever of dignity or authority he possesses is a delegated part of their majesty and their political omnipotence, transiently vested in him by the people themselves for their own happiness.

"State House Yard Speech" by James Wilson

Editor's Introduction:

James Wilson of Pennsylvania played a role in virtually every important political event in the early federal republic. He was born in Scotland and emigrated to the North American colonies in 1765 where, with various letters of recommendation, he was able to secure a teaching position at the University of Pennsylvania. He studied law under John Dickinson—arguably next to Benjamin Franklin the most important political figure in the State—and set up practice in Reading, Pennsylvania. He then moved to a fine home in Philadelphia and became involved in the brewing conflict between the colonies and the crown. He penned an anti-Parliament pamphlet in 1768 that echoed the "no taxation without representation" theme of the time.

Wilson was elected to the Second Continental Congress in 1775, in part because of his 1768 pamphlet, but like his legal mentor Dickinson, he refused to vote for independence. He later signed the Declaration of Independence after it became clear a break was inevitable. Still, a large portion of Pennsylvania society did not trust his commitment to the cause. His house was attacked in 1779 by a mob enflamed by rumors that Wilson and his cohorts were in fact closet monarchists sympathetic with the British. The "Battle of Fort Wilson" resulted in six deaths and almost twenty wounded, and for a time it tarnished his reputation.

Wilson remained a steadfast nationalist during this period. His belief in the necessity of a strong central government was driven to support a revision of the Articles of Confederation by the factious political atmosphere in Pennsylvania. He was sent as a delegate to the Philadelphia Convention in 1787 where he favored every nationalist innovation including the newly created executive branch. Wilson helped author the "Three Fifths Compromise" to the Constitution and had his fingerprints all over Article II of the document.

He signed the Constitution and then became one of its most vocal proponents during the ratification process. His "State House Yard" speech was the most important pro-Constitution document during the ratification period because of its contemporary influence. Delivered in October 1787, the speech defended the federal structure of the new government, countered those who believed the document annihilated the States, and claimed that a bill of rights was unnecessary because the powers granted to the central authority were limited by the text itself. These arguments became standard for the pro-Constitution men throughout the United States.

"State House Yard Speech"

James Wilson of Pennsylvania

October 6, 1787

Mr. Chairman and Fellow Citizens:

Having received the honor of an appointment to represent you in the late convention, it is perhaps my duty to comply with the request of many gentlemen whose characters and judgements I sincerely respect, and who have urged that this would be a proper occasion to lay before you any information which will serve to explain and elucidate the principles and arrangements of the constitution that has been submitted to the consideration of the United States. I confess that I am unprepared for so extensive and so important a disquisition; but the insidious attempts, which are clandestinely and industriously made to pervert and destroy the new plan, induce me the more readily to engage in its defence: and the impressions of four months constant attendance to the subject, have not been so easily effaced, as to leave me without an answer to the objections which have been raised.

It will be proper, however, to mark the leading discrimination between the State constitutions and the constitution of the United States. When the people established the powers of legislation under their separate governments, they invested their representatives with every right and authority which they did not in explicit terms reserve; and therefore upon every question respecting the jurisdiction of the House of Assembly, if the frame of government is silent, the jurisdiction is efficient and complete. But in delegating federal powers, another criterion was necessarily introduced, and the congressional power is to be collected, not from tacit implication, but from the positive grant expressed in the instrument of the union. Hence, it is evident, that in the former case everything which is not reserved is given; but in the latter the reverse of the proposition prevails, and everything which is not given is reserved. This distinction being recognized, will furnish an answer to those who think the omission of a bill of rights a defect in the proposed constitution; for it would have been superfluous and absurd to have stipulated with a federal body of our own creation, that we should enjoy those privileges of which we are not divested, either by the intention or the act that has brought the body into existence. For instance, the liberty of the press, which has been a copious source of declamation and opposition -- what control can proceed from the Federal government to shackle or destroy that sacred palladium of national freedom? If, indeed, a power similar to that which has been granted for the regulation of commerce had been granted to regulate literary publications, it would have been as necessary to stipulate that the liberty of the press should be preserved inviolate, as that the impost should be general in its operation. With respect likewise to the particular district of ten miles, which is to be made the seat of federal government, it will undoubtedly be proper to observe this salutary precaution, as there the legislative power will be exclusively lodged in the President, Senate, and House of Representatives of the United States. But this could not be an object with the Convention, for it must naturally depend upon a future compact to which the citizens immediately interested will, and ought to be, parties; and there is no reason to suspect that so popular a privilege will in that case be neglected. In truth, then, the proposed system possesses no influence whatever upon the press, and it would have been merely nugatory to have introduced a formal declaration upon the subject -- nay, that very declaration might have been construed to imply that some degree of power was given, since we undertook to define its extent.

Another objection that has been fabricated against the new constitution, is expressed in this disingenious form -- "The trial by jury is abolished in civil cases." I must be excused, my fellow citizens, if upon this point I take advantage of my professional experience to detect the futility of the assertion. Let it be remembered then, that the business of the Federal Convention was not local, but general -- not limited to the views and establishments of a single State, but co-extensive with the continent, and comprehending the views and establishments of thirteen independent sovereignties. When, therefore, this subject was in discussion, we were involved in difficulties which pressed on all sides, and no precedent could be discovered to direct our course. The cases open to a trial by jury differed in the different States. It was therefore impracticable, on that ground, to have made a general rule. The want of uniformity would have rendered any reference to the practice of the States idle and useless; and it could not with any propriety be said that, "The trial by jury shall be as heretofore," since there has never existed any federal system of jurisprudence, to which the declaration could relate. Besides, it is not in all cases that the trial by jury is adopted in civil questions; for cases depending in courts of admiralty, such as relate to maritime captures, and such as are agitated in courts of equity, do not require the intervention of that tribunal. How, then was the line of discrimination to be drawn? The Convention found the task too difficult for them, and they left the business as it stands, in the fullest confidence that no danger could possibly ensue, since the proceedings of the Supreme Court are to be regulated by the Congress, which is a faithful representation of the people; and the oppression of government is effectually barred, by declaring that in all criminal cases the trial by jury shall be preserved.

This constitution, it has been further urged, is of a pernicious tendency, because it tolerates a standing army in the time of peace. This has always been a topic of popular declamation; and yet I do not know a nation in the world which has not found it necessary and useful to maintain the appearance of strength in a season of the most profound tranquility. Nor is it a novelty with us; for under the present articles of confederation, Congress certainly possesses this reprobated power, and the exercise of that power is proved at this moment by her cantonments along the banks of the Ohio. But what would be our national situation were it otherwise? Every principle of policy must be subverted, and the government must declare war, before they are prepared to carry it on. Whatever may be the provocation, however important the object in view, and however necessary dispatch and secrecy may be, still the declaration must precede the preparation, and the enemy will be informed of your intention, not only before you are equipped for an attack, but even before you are fortified for a defence. The consequence is too obvious to require any further delineation, and no man who regards the dignity and safety of his country can deny the necessity of a military force, under the control and with the restrictions which the new constitution provides.

Perhaps there never was a charge made with less reasons than that which predicts the institution of a baneful aristocracy in the federal Senate. This body branches into two characters, the one legislative and the other executive. In its legislative character it can effect no purpose, without the co-operation of the House of Representatives, and in its executive character it can accomplish no object without the concurrence of the President. Thus fettered I do not know any act which the Senate can of itself perform, and such dependence necessarily precludes every idea of influence and superiority. But I will confess that in the organization of this body a compromise between contending interests is descernible; and when we reflect how various are the laws commerce, habits, population and extent of the confederated States, this evidence of mutual concession and accommodation ought rather to command a generous applause, than to excite jealousy and reproach. For my part, my admiration can only be equalled by my astonishment in beholding so perfect a system formed from such heterogeneous materials.

The next accusation I shall consider is that which represents the federal constitution, as not only calculated, but designedly framed, to reduce the State governments to mere corporations and eventually to annihilate them. Those who have employed the term corporation upon this occasion are not perhaps aware of its extent. In common parlance, indeed, it is generally applied to petty associations for the ease and convenience of a few individuals; but in its enlarged sense, it will comprehend the government of Pennsylvania, the existing union of the States, and even this projected system is nothing more than a formal act of incorporation. But upon what presence can it be alleged that it was designed to annihilate the State governments? For I will undertake to prove that upon their existence depends the existence of the Federal plan. For this purpose, permit me to call your attention to the manner in which the President, Senate and House of Representatives are proposed to be appointed. The President is to be chosen by electors, nominated in such manner as the legislature of each State may direct; so that if there is no legislature there can be no electors, and consequently the office of President cannot be supplied.

The Senate is to be composed of two Senators from each State, chosen by the Legislature; and, therefore, if there is no Legislature, there can be no Senate. The House of Representatives is to be composed of members chosen every second year by the people of the several States, and the electors in each State shall have the qualifications requisite for electors of the most numerous branch of the State Legislature; unless, therefore, there is a State Legislature, that qualification cannot be ascertained, and the popular branch of the federal constitution must be extinct. From this view, then, it is evidently absurd to suppose that the annihilation of the separate governments will result from their union; or, that having that intention, the authors of the new system would have bound their connection with such indissoluble ties. Let me here advert to an arrangement highly advantageous, for you will perceive, without prejudice to the powers of the Legislature in the election of Senators, the people at large will acquire an additional privilege in returning members to the House of Representatives; whereas, by the present confederation, it is the Legislature alone that appoints the delegates to Congress.

The power of direct taxation has likewise been treated as an improper delegation to the federal government; but when we consider it as the duty of that body to provide for the national safety, to support the dignity of the union, and to discharge the debts contracted upon the collected faith of the States for their common benefit, it must be acknowledged that those upon whom such important obligations are imposed, ought in justice and in policy to possess every means requisite for a faithful performance of their trust. But why should we be alarmed with visionary evils? I will venture to predict that the great revenue of the United States must, and always will, be raised by impost, for, being at once less obnoxious and more productive, the interest of the government will be best promoted by the accommodation of the people. Still, however, the objects of direct taxation should be within reach in all cases of emergency; and there is no more reason to apprehend oppression in the mode of collecting a revenue from this resource, than in the form of an impost, which by universal assent, is left to the authority of the federal government. In either case, the force of civil institutions will be adequate to the purpose; and the dread of military violence, which has been assiduously disseminated, must eventually prove the mere effusion of a wild imagination or a factious spirit. But the salutary consequences that must flow from thus enabling the government to receive and support the credit of the union, will afford another answer to the objections upon this ground. The State of Pennsylvania particularly, which has encumbered itself with the assumption of a great proportion of the public debt, will derive considerable relief and advantage, for, as it was the imbecility of the present confederation which gave rise to the funding law, that law must naturally expire, when a competent and energetic federal system shall be substituted -- the State will then be discharged from an extraordinary burthen, and the national creditor will find it to be his interest to return to his original security.

After all, my fellow-citizens, it is neither extraordinary or unexpected that the constitution offered to your consideration should meet with opposition. It is the nature of man to pursue his own interest in preference to the public good, and I do not mean to make any personal reflection when I add that it is the interest of a very numerous, powerful and respectable body to counteract and destroy the excellent work produced by the late convention. All the officers of government and all the appointments for the administration of justice and the collection of the public revenue which are transferred from the individual to the aggregate sovereignty of the States, will necessarily turn the stream of influence and emolument into a new channel. Every person, therefore, who enjoys or expects to enjoy a place of profit under the present establishment, will object to the proposed innovation; not, in truth, because it is injurious to the liberties of his country, but because it affects his schemes of wealth and consequence. I will confess, indeed, that I am not a blind admirer of this plan of government, and that there are some parts of it which, if my wish had prevailed, would certainly have been altered. But when I reflect how widely men differ in their opinions, and that every man (and the observation applies likewise to every State) has an equal pretension to assert his own, I am satisfied that anything nearer to perfection could not have been accomplished. If there are errors, it should be remembered that the seeds of reformation are sown in the work itself and the concurrence of two-thirds of the Congress may at any time introduce alterations and amendments. Regarding it, then, in every point of view, with a candid and disinterested mind, I am bold to assert that it is the best form of government which has ever been offered to the world.

A Citizen of Philadelphia by Pelatiah Webster

Editor's Introduction:

The libertarian economist and historian Lawrence Reed has called Pelatiah Webster the American Adam Smith and the first American economist. This is high praise, but Webster, like many other members of the founding generation, has been lost to time.

Born in Connecticut in 1726, Webster attended Yale and began a career as a minister before marrying and relocating the Philadelphia in 1755 to engage in commerce and finance. He quickly embraced the principles of "laissez faire" economics long before Adam Smith published his *Wealth of Nations*. Webster became one of the wealthiest men in the British North American colonies and when the break with the Crown occurred in 1776 actively supported the American cause. His proximity to the Continental Congress and friendships with some of the leading men in Pennsylvania politics led members of that body to seek his advice on financial matters. Webster penned several short essays on American finance and by 1783 was calling for a new governing document to replace the Articles of Confederation. This predated the Annapolis Convention by three years.

He believed the new Constitution would better protect the fledgling American financial system, but he also insisted that the new government, while creating a "supreme" central authority and vesting it with more powers than under the Articles of Confederation, did not annihilate the States nor reduce them to corporate powers. Webster aimed his essay at the writing of the New York "Antifederalist" Brutus who famously predicted that the central government under the Constitution would be too powerful to contain and would eventually result in a monarchy or aristocracy.

Webster's defense of the Constitution in Pennsylvania was as important as Wilson's. The ratification process was local, not "national," and as a well-respected man in his home State, Webster could be classified as one of the most important proponents of the document, equal to Alexander Hamilton in New York or James Madison in Virginia.

A Citizen of Philadelphia: The Weaknesses of Brutus Exposed

November 8, 1787

By Pelatiah Webster of Pennsylvania

The long piece signed Brutus, (which was first published in a New-York paper, and was afterwards copied into the Pennsylvania Packet of the 26th instant) is wrote in a very good stile; the language is easy, and the address is polite and insinuating: but the sentiments, I conceive, are not only unsound, but wild and chimerical; the dreary fears and apprehensions, altogether groundless; and the whole tendency of the piece, in this important crisis of our politics, very hurtful. I have therefore thought it my duty to make some animadversions on it; which I here offer, with all due deference, to the Author and to the Public.

His first question is, *Whether a confederated government is best for the United States?*

I answer, If Brutus, or any body else, cannot find any benefit resulting from the union of the Thirteen States; if they can do *without* as well as *with* the respectability, the protection, and the security, which the States might derive from that union, I have nothing further to say: but if that union is to be supported in any such manner as to afford respectability, protection, or security to the States, I say it must be done by an adequate government, and cannot be otherwise done.

This government must have a supreme power, *superior to and able to controul* each and all of its parts. 'Tis essential to all governments, that such a power be somewhere existing in it; and if *the place* where the proposed Constitution has fixed it, does not suit Brutus and his friends, I will give him leave to stow it away in any *other place that is better*: but I will not consent to have it *annihilated*; neither will I agree to have it *cramped and pinched* for room, so as to lessen its energy; for that will *destroy* both its nature and use.

The supreme power of government ought to be *full, definite, established,* and *acknowledged*. Powers of government too limited, or uncertain and disputed, have ever proved, like *Pandora's* box, a most fruitful source of quarrels, animosities, wars, devastation, and ruin, in all shapes and degrees, in all communities, states and kingdoms on earth.

Nothing tends more to the honour, establishment, and peace of society, than public decisions, grounded on principles of right, natural fitness and prudence; but when the powers of government are *too limited,* such decisions can't be made and enforced; so the mischief goes without a remedy: dreadful examples of which we have felt, in instances more than enough, for seven years past.

Further, where the powers of government are not *definite* but *disputed*, the administration dare not make decisions on the footing of impartial justice and right; but must temporize with the parties, lest they lose friends or make enemies: and of course the *righteous* go off injured and disgusted, and the *wicked* go grumbling to; for 'tis rare that any sacrifices of a court can satisfy a prevailing party in the state.

'Tis necessary in States, as well as in private families, that controversies should have a just, *speedy*, and effectual decision, that right may be done before the contention has time to grow up into habits of malignity, resentment, ill nature, and ill offices. If a controversy happens between two states, must it continue undecided, and daily increase, and be more and more aggravated, by the repeated insults and injuries of the contending parties, 'till they are ripe for the decision of the sword? or must the weaker states suffer, without remedy, the groundless demands and oppressions of their stronger neighbours, because they have no avenger, or umpire of their disputes?

Or shall we institute a supreme power with full and effectual authority to controul the animosities, and decide the disputes of these strong contending bodies? In the one proposed to us, we have perhaps every chance of a *righteous judgment*, that we have any reason to hope for; but I am clearly of opinion, that even a *wrongful decision*, would, in most cases, be preferable to the continuance of such destructive controversies.

I suppose that neither Brutus nor any of his friends would wish to see our government *embroiled abroad*; and therefore will admit it necessary to institute some federal authority, sufficient to punish *any individual or State*, who shall violate our treaties with foreign nations, insult their dignity, or abuse their citizens, and compel due reparation in all such cases.

I further apprehend, that Brutus is willing to have the *general* interest and *welfare* of the States well provided for and supported, and therefore will consent that there shall exist in the states, an authority to *do* all this *effectually*; but he seems grieved that Congress should be the judges of this general welfare of the states. If he will be kind enough to point out any other more suitable and proper judges, I will consent to have them admitted.

Indeed I begin to have hopes of Brutus, and think he may come right at last; for I observe (after all his fear and tremblings about the new government) the constitution he *defines and adopts,* is the very same as that which the federal convention have proposed to us, *viz.* "that the Thirteen States should continue thirteen confederated republics under the *direction and controul* of a supreme federal head, for certain defined national purposes, only." Where we may observe,

1. That the new Constitution leaves all the Thirteen States, complete republics, as it found them, but all confederated under the direction and controul of a federal head, for certain defined national purposes only, *i. e.* it leaves all the dignities, authorities, and internal police of each State in free, full, and perfect condition; unless when national purposes make the controul of them by the federal head, or authority, necessary to the general benefit.

2. These powers of controul by the federal head or authority, are *defined* in the new constitution, as minutely as may be, in their principle; and any detail of them which may become necessary, is committed to the wisdom of Congress.

3. It extends the controuling power of the federal head to no one case, to which the jurisdiction or power of definitive decision of any one state, can be competent. And,

> 4. In every such case, the controuling power of the federal head, is absolutely necessary to the support, dignity, and benefit of the national government, and the safety of individuals; neither of which can, by any possibility, be secured without it.

All this falls in pretty well with Brutus's sentiments; for he does not think that the new Constitution in *its present state* so very bad, but fears that it will not preserve its purity of institution; but if adopted, will immediately verge to, and terminate in *a consolidation*, *i. e.* a destruction of the state governments. For argument, he suggests the avidity of power natural to rulers; and the eager grasp with which they hold it when obtained; and their strong propensity to abuse their power, and encroach on the liberties of the people.

He dwells on the vast powers vested in Congress by the new Constitution, *i. e.* of levying taxes, raising armies, appointing federal courts, *&c.*; takes it for granted, that all these powers will be abused, and carried to an oppressive excess; and then harangues on the dreadful case we shall be in, when our *wealth* is all devoured by taxes, our *liberty* destroyed by the power of the army, and our *civil rights* all sacrificed by the unbounded power of the federal courts, *&c.*

And when he has run himself out of breath with this dreary declamation, he comes to the conclusion he set out with, *viz.* That the Thirteen States are too big for a republican government, which requires *small territory*, and can't be supported in *more extensive nations*; that in large states liberty will soon be swallowed up, and lost in the magnitude of power requisite in the government, *&c.*

If any conclusion at all can be drawn from this baseless assemblage of gloomy thoughts, I think it must be against *any union at all*; against *any kind of federal government*. For nothing can be plainer than this, *viz.* that *the union can't by any possibility be supported with success, without adequate and effectual powers of government?*

We must have *money* to support the union, and therefore the power of raising it must be lodged somewhere; we must have *a military force*, and of consequence the power of raising and directing it must exist; civil and criminal causes of national concern will arise, therefore there must be somewhere a power of appointing *courts* to hear and determine them.

These powers must be vested in Congress; for nobody pretends to wish to have them vested in any other body of men.

The Thirteen States have a territory very extensive, and inhabitants very numerous, and every day rapidly increasing; therefore the powers of government necessary to support their union must be great in proportion. If the ship is large the mast must be proportionately great, or it will be impossible to make her sail well. The federal powers must extend to every part of the federal territory, *i. e.* to the utmost limits of the Thirteen States, and to every part of them; and must carry with them, sufficient authority to secure the execution of them; and these powers must be vested in Congress, and the execution of them must be under their direction and controul.

These powers are *vast*, I know, and the trust is of the most *weighty kind* that can be committed to human direction; and the execution and administration of it will require the greatest *wisdom*, *knowledge*, *firmness*, and *integrity* in that august body; and I hope they will have all the *abilities and virtues* necessary to that important station, and will *perform their duty well*; but if they fail, the fault is in them, not in the constitution. The best constitution possible, even a divine one, badly administered, will make a bad government.

The members of Congress will be the best we can get; they will all of them derive their appointment from the States, and if the States are not wise enough to send *good and suitable* men, great *blame*, great *sin* will lie at their door. But I suppose nobody would wish to mend this fault by taking away the election of the people, and directing the appointment of Congress to be made in any other way.

When we have got the best that can be obtained, we ought to be quiet and cease complaining. 'Tis not in the power of human wisdom to do more; 'tis the fate of human nature *to be imperfect and to err;* and no doubt but Congress, with all their *dignity of station and character*, with all their *opportunities* to gain *wisdom and information*, with all their *inducements to virtue and integrity*, will err, and abuse or misapply their powers in more or less instances. I have no expectation that they will make *a court of angels*, or be anything more than *men*: 'tis probable many of them will be *insufficient* men, and some of them may be *bad* men.

The greatest wisdom, care, and caution, has been used in the *mode* of their appointment; in the *restraints and checks* under which they must act; in the numerous *discussions and deliberations* which all their acts must pass through, before they can receive the stamp of authority; in the terrors of *punishment* if they misbehave. I say, in *all these ways* the greatest care has been used to procure and form a good Congress.

The *dignity and importance* of their station and character will afford all the inducements to virtue and effort, which can influence a mind *capable* of their force.

Their own *personal reputation*, with the eyes of all the world on them,—the *approbation of their fellow citizens,* which every man in public station naturally wishes to enjoy,—and the *dread of censure and shame*, all contribute very forceable and strong inducements to noble, upright and worthy behavior.

The *particular interest* which every member of Congress has in every public order and resolution, is *another strong motive* to right action. For every act to which any member gives his sanction, if it be raising an *army*, levying a *tax*, instituting a *court*, or any other act to bind the *States*,—such act will equally bind *himself, his nearest connections, and his posterity*.

Another mighty influence to the noblest principle of action will be *the fear of God before their eyes*; for while they sit in the place of God, to give law, justice, and right to the States, they must be *monsters indeed* if they do not regard *his law*, and imitate *his character*.

If all this will not produce a Congress fit to be trusted, and worthy of the public confidence, I think we may give the matter up as impracticable. But still we must make ourselves as easy as we can, under a *mischief* which admits *no remedy*, and bear with patience an *evil* which can't be *cured*: for a government we must have; there is no safety without it; though we know it will be imperfect, we still must prefer it to anarchy or no government at all. 'Tis the height of folly and madness to reject a necessary convenience, because it is not a perfect good.

Upon this statement of facts and principles, (for the truth and reality of which, I appeal to every candid man,) I beg leave to remark,

1. That the federal Convention, in the constitution proposed to us, have exerted their utmost to produce *a Congress worthy of the public confidence*, who shall have abilities adequate to their important duty, and shall act under every possible inducement to execute it *faithfully*.

2. That this affords every chance which the nature of the thing will admit, of a wise and upright administration.

3. Yet all this notwithstanding, 'tis very possible that Congress *may err, may abuse, or misapply their powers*, which no precaution of human wisdom can prevent.

> 4. 'Tis *vain*, 'tis *childish*, 'tis *contentious* to object to a constitution thus framed and guarded, on pretence that the commonwealth may suffer by a bad administration of it; or to *withhold* the *necessary powers* of government, from the supreme rulers of it, least they should *abuse* or *misapply* those powers. This is an objection which will operate with equal force against every institution that can be made in this world, whether of policy, religion, commerce, or any other human concern, which can require regulations: for 'tis not possible to form any institution however necessary, wise and good, whose uses may not be lessened or destroyed by bad management.

If Brutus, or any body else, can point out any *checks, cautions,* or *regulations,* which have been hitherto omitted, which will make Congress more *wise,* more *capable,* more *diligent,* or more *faithful,* I am willing to attend to them. But to set Congress at the head of the government, and object to their being vested with full and sufficient power to manage all the great departments of it, appears to me *absurd*, quite *wild*, and *chimerical*: it would produce a plan which would destroy itself as it went along, would be a sort of counter position of contrary parts, and render it impossible for rulers to render those services, and secure those benefits to the States, which are the only great ends of their appointment.

The constitution under Brutus's corrections would stand thus, viz. Congress would have power to *raise money*, but must not direct the *quantity*, or *mode of levying* it; they might raise armies, but must not judge to the *number* of soldiers necessary, or direct their destination; they ought to provide for the *general welfare*, but must not be judges of what that welfare *consists in*, or in *what manner* 'tis to be provided for; they might controul the several States, for *defined national purposes*, but must not be judges of *what purposes* would come within that *definition, &c.*

Any body with half an eye, may see what sort of administration the constitution, thus corrected, would produce, *e. g.* it would require much greater trouble to leave the work *undone*, than would be necessary to get it *well done*, under a constitution of sufficient powers. If any one wishes to view more minutely this blessed operation, he may see a lively sample of it, in the last seven years practice of our federal government.

1. Brutus all along sounds his objections, and fears on *extreme cases* of abuse or misapplication of supreme powers, which may *possibly* happen, under the administration of a wild, weak, or wicked Congress; but 'tis easy to observe that all institutions are liable to *extremes*, but ought not *to be judged by them*; they do not often appear, and perhaps never may; but if they should happen in the cases supposed, (which God forbid) there is *a remedy pointed out, in the Constitution itself.*

'Tis not supposeable that such abuses could arise to any ruinous height, before they would affect the States so much, that at least *two-thirds* of them would unite in pursuing a remedy in the mode prescribed by the Constitution, which will always be liable to amendment, whenever any mischiefs or abuses appear in the government, which the Constitution in its present state, can't reach and correct.

1. Brutus thinks we can never be too much afraid of the *encroaching avidity of rulers*; but 'tis pretty plain, that however great the natural *lust of power in rulers may be*, the *jealousy of the people in giving it*, is about equal; these two opposite passions, will always operate in opposite directions to each

> other, and like *action and reaction* in natural bodies, will ever tend to a good ballance.

At any rate, the Congress can never *get* more power than the people will give, nor *hold* it any longer than they will *permit*; for should they assume tyrannical powers, and make incroachments on liberty without the consent of the people, they would soon attone for their temerity, with shame and disgrace, and probably with their heads.

But 'tis here to be noted, that all the danger does not arise from the extreme of power *in the rulers*; for when the ballance verges to the contrary extreme, and the power of the rulers becomes too much *limited and cramped*, all the nerves of government are weakened, and the administration must unavoidably sicken, and lose that energy which is absolutely necessary for the support of the State, and the security of the people. For 'tis a truth worthy of great attention, that laws are not made so much for the *righteous* as for the *wicked*; who never fail to shelter themselves from punishment, whenever they can, under the *defects of the law, and the weakness of government.*

I now come to consider the grand proposition which Brutus sets out with, concludes with, and interlards all along, and which seems to be the great gift of his performance, *viz. That a confederation of the Thirteen States into one great republic is not best for them*: and goes on to prove by a variety of arguments, *that a republican form of government is not compatible, and cannot be convenient to so extensive a territory as the said States possess*. He begins by taking one assumption for granted (for I can't see that his arguments prove it at all) *viz.* That the Constitution proposed will melt down and destroy the *jurisdiction* of the particular States, and *consolidate* them all into one great republic.

I can't see the least reason for this sentiment; nor the least tendency in the new Constitution to produce this effect. For the Constitution does not suffer the federal powers to controul in the least, or so much as to interfere in the internal policy, jurisdiction, or municipal rights of any particular State: except where great and manifest *national purposes and interests* make that controul necessary. It appears very evident to me, that *the Constitution gives an establishment, support, and protection* to the *internal* and *separate* police of each State, under the superintendency of the federal powers, which it could not possibly enjoy in an independent state. Under the confederation each State derives strength, firmness and permanency from its compact with the other States. Like a stave in a cask well bound with hoops, it stands *firmer*, is not so easily *shaken, bent*, or *broken*, as it would be were it set up by itself alone, without any connection with its neighbours.

There can be no doubt that each State will receive from the union great *support and protection* against the *invasions and inroads* of foreign enemies, as well as against *riots and insurrections* of their own citizens; and of consequence, the course of their internal administration will be secured by this means against any *interruption or embarrassment* from either of these causes.

They will also derive their share of benefit from the respectability of the union abroad, from the treaties and alliances which may be made with foreign nations, *&c.*

Another benefit they will receive from the controul of the supreme power of the union is this, *viz.* they will be restrained from making *angry, oppressive, and destructive laws*, from declaring *ruinous wars* with their neighbours, from fomenting *quarrels and controversies, &c.* all which ever *weaken* a state, tend to its fatal *disorder*, and often end in its dissolution. *Righteousness exalts* and strengthens *a nation*; but *sin is a reproach* and weakening of *any people*.

They will indeed have the privilege of oppressing *their own citizens* by bad laws or bad administration; but the moment the mischief extends beyond their own State, and begins to affect the citizens of other States strangers, or the national welfare,—the salutary controul of the supreme power will check the evil, and restore *strength and security*, as well as *honesty and right*, to the offending state.

It appears then very plain, that the natural effect and tendency of the supreme powers of the union is to give *strength*, *establishment, and permanency* to the internal police and jurisdiction of each of the particular States; not to *melt down and destroy*, but to *support and confirm* them all.

By what sort of assurance, then, can *Brutus* tell us that the new Constitution, *if executed, must certainly and infallibly terminate in a consolidation of the whole, into one great republic, subverting all the State authorities.* His only argument is, that the federal powers *may be corrupted, abused, and misapplied*, 'till this effect shall be produced. 'Tis true that the constitution, like every other on earth, committed to human management, *may be corrupted by a bad administration,* and be made to operate to the *destruction* of the very capital benefits and uses, which were the great end of its institution. The same argument will prove with equal cogency, that the constitution of each particular State, may be corrupted in practice, become tyranical and inimical to liberty. In short the argument proves *too much*, and therefore proves *nothing*: 'tis empty, childish, and futile, and a serious proposal of it, is, I conceive, an affront to the human understanding.

But after all, supposing this event should take place, and by some strange fatality, the several states should be melted down, and merged in the great commonwealth, in the form of counties, or districts; I don't see why *a commonwealth mode of government, would not be as suitable and convenient for the great State, as any other form whatever;*

I cannot see any sufficient ground or reason, for the position pretty often and boldly advanced, *that a republican form of government can never be suitable for any nation of extensive territory, and numerous population*: for if Congress can be chosen by the several States, though under the form and name of *counties, or election districts*, and be in every respect, instituted as directed by the new constitution, I don't see but we shall have as suitable a *national council*, as wise a *legislative*, and as strong and safe an *executive power*, as can be obtained under any form of government whatever; let our territory be ever so extensive or populous.

The most despotic monarch that can exist, must have his councils, and officers of state; and I can't see any one circumstance of their being appointed under a monarchy, that can afford any chance of their being any wiser or better, than ours may be. 'Tis true indeed, the despot may, if he pleases, act without any advice at all; but when he does so, I conceive it will be very rare that the nation will receive greater advantages from his unadvised edicts, than may be drawed from the deliberate acts and orders of our supreme powers. All that can be said in favour of *those*, is, that they will have less chance of delay, and more of secrecy, than *these*; but I think it probable, that the latter will be grounded on better information, and greater wisdom; will carry more weights and be better supported.

The Romans rose, from small beginnings, to a very great extent of territory, population, and wisdom; I don't think their constitution of government, was near so good as the one proposed to us, yet we find their power, strength, and establishment, were raised to their utmost height, under *a republican form of government*. Their State received very little acquisition of territory, strength, or wealth, after their government became imperial; but soon began to weaken and decay.

The *Carthagenians* acquired an amazing degree of strength, wealth, and extent of dominion, under *a republican form of government.* Neither *they* or *the Romans*, owed their dissolution to any causes arising from *that kind of government*: 'twas the *party rage*, animosity, and violence of their citizens, which destroyed them both; it weakened them, 'till *the one* fell under the power of their enemy, and was thereby reduced to ruin; *the other* changed their form of government, to a monarchy, which proved in the end, equally fatal to them.

The same causes, if they can't be restrained, will weaken or destroy any nation on earth, let their form of government be what it will; witness the *division and dissolution* of the Roman empire; the late *dismemberment of Poland*; the intestine divisions, rage, and wars of *Italy*, of *France*, of *Spain*, and of *England.*

No form of government can preserve a nation which can't controul the party rage of its own citizens; when any one citizen can rise *above the controul* of the laws, *ruin* draws near. 'Tis not possible for any nation on earth, to hold their strength and establishment, when the dignity of their government is lost, and this dignity will forever depend on the *wisdom* and *firmness* of the officers of government, aided and supported by the *virtue* and *patriotism* of their citizens.

On the whole, I don't see but that any form of government may be safe and practicable, where the controuling authority of the supreme powers, is strong enough to effect the ends of its appointment, and at the same time, sufficiently *checked* to keep it within due bounds, and limit it to the objects of its duty; and I think it appears, that the constitution proposed to us, has all these qualities in as great perfection, as any form we can devise.

But after all, the *grand secret of forming a good government,* is, *to put good men into the administration*: for *wild*, *vicious*, or *idle men*, will ever make a bad government, let its principles be ever so good;

but *grave, wise, and faithful men*, acting under a good constitution, will afford the best chances of security, peace, and prosperity, to the citizens, which can be derived from civil police, under the present disorders, and uncertainty of all earthly things.

FEDERALIST NO. 7 BY ALEXANDER HAMILTON

Editor's Introduction

Alexander Hamilton is the most conspicuous proponent of the Constitution today (due in large measure to his cult-like following on the left and right), but during the ratification process was just one of many voices insisting on its adoption by the States. In fact, the *Federalist* essays were only marginally effective in swinging votes toward ratification in New York where the Constitution only received three more "yeas" than "nays" in 1788 ratifying convention in Poughkeepsie.

Hamilton considered the document to be superior to the Articles of Confederation, and along with James Madison, was the driving force in calling a convention of all the States during the Annapolis Convention of 1786. Hamilton was a nationalist who thought the States presented obstacles to effective central government, and during the Philadelphia Convention of 1787, he argued for what amounted to an elected king and senators for life. The Constitution he defended in the *Federalist* did not match his desired political system, but he resolutely argued for its ratification.

The *Federalist* essays were first published in New York papers and later disseminated to other States and presses and were written by Hamilton, John Jay, and James Madison under the pseudonym "Publius," meaning "the people." It could have also referred to Publius Poplicola, one of the anti-monarchist founders of the Roman Republic in 509 B.C. Hamilton, however, never believed in popular government though he did favor a strong central authority for the purposes of commerce and defense. His experiences during the American War for Independence, his "foreign" background—Hamilton arrived in the British North American colonies as a teenager—and his close association with leading financiers and bankers like Robert Morris, colored his judgment of American government.

Federalist Number 7 is the first of three essays explaining the necessity of Union and the folly of "separate confederacies" in North America. In this essay he paints a horrific picture of war and violence should the Constitution be rejected by the States.

Federalist No. 7

November 17, 1787

By Alexander Hamilton of New York

To the People of the State of New York.It is sometimes asked, with an air of seeming triumph, what inducements could the States have, if disunited, to make war upon each other? It would be a full answer to this question to say--precisely the same inducements which have, at different times, deluged in blood all the nations in the world. But, unfortunately for us, the question admits of a more particular answer. There are causes of differences within our immediate contemplation, of the tendency of which, even under the restraints of a federal constitution, we have had sufficient experience to enable us to form a judgment of what might be expected if those restraints were removed.

Territorial disputes have at all times been found one of the most fertile sources of hostility among nations. Perhaps the greatest proportion of wars that have desolated the earth have sprung from this origin. This cause would exist among us in full force. We have a vast tract of unsettled territory within the boundaries of the United States. There still are discordant and undecided claims between several of them, and the dissolution of the Union would lay a foundation for similar claims between them all. It is well known that they have heretofore had serious and animated discussion concerning the rights to the lands which were ungranted at the time of the Revolution, and which usually went under the name of crown lands. The States within the limits of whose colonial governments they were comprised have claimed them as their property, the others have contended that the rights of the crown in this article devolved upon the Union; especially as to all that part of the Western territory which, either by actual possession, or through the submission of the Indian proprietors, was subjected to the jurisdiction of the king of Great Britain, till it was relinquished in the treaty of peace. This, it has been said, was at all events an acquisition to the Confederacy by compact with a foreign power. It has been the prudent policy of Congress to appease this controversy, by prevailing upon the States to make cessions to the United States for the benefit of the whole. This has been so far accomplished as, under a continuation of the Union, to afford a decided prospect of an amicable termination of the dispute. A dismemberment of the Confederacy, however, would revive this dispute, and would create others on the same subject. At present, a large part of the vacant Western territory is, by cession at least, if not by any anterior right, the common property of the Union. If that were at an end, the States which made the cession, on a principle of federal compromise, would be apt when the motive of the grant had ceased, to reclaim the lands as a reversion. The other States would no doubt insist on a proportion, by right of representation. Their argument would be, that a grant, once made, could not be revoked; and that the justice of participating in territory acquired or secured by the joint efforts of the Confederacy, remained undiminished. If, contrary to probability, it should be admitted by all the States, that each had a right to a share of this common stock, there would still be a difficulty to be surmounted, as to a proper rule of apportionment. Different principles would be set up by different States for this purpose; and as they would affect the opposite interests of the parties, they might not easily be susceptible of a pacific adjustment.

In the wide field of Western territory, therefore, we perceive an ample theatre for hostile pretensions, without any umpire or common judge to interpose between the contending parties. To reason from the past to the future, we shall have good ground to apprehend, that the sword would sometimes be appealed to as the arbiter of their differences. The circumstances of the dispute between Connecticut and Pennsylvania, respecting the land at Wyoming, admonish us not to be sanguine in expecting an easy accommodation of such differences. The articles of confederation obliged the parties to submit the matter to the decision of a federal court. The submission was made, and the court decided in favor of Pennsylvania. But Connecticut gave strong indications of dissatisfaction with that determination; nor did she appear to be entirely resigned to it, till, by negotiation and management, something like an equivalent was found for the loss she supposed herself to have sustained. Nothing here said is intended to convey the slightest censure on the conduct of that State. She no doubt sincerely believed herself to have been injured by the decision; and States, like individuals, acquiesce with great reluctance in determinations to their disadvantage.

Those who had an opportunity of seeing the inside of the transactions which attended the progress of the controversy between this State and the district of Vermont, can vouch the opposition we experienced, as well from States not interested as from those which were interested in the claim; and can attest the danger to which the peace of the Confederacy might have been exposed, had this State attempted to assert its rights by force. Two motives preponderated in that opposition: one, a jealousy entertained of our future power; and the other, the interest of certain individuals of influence in the neighboring States, who had obtained grants of lands under the actual government of that district. Even the States which brought forward claims, in contradiction to ours, seemed more solicitous to dismember this State, than to establish their own pretensions. These were New Hampshire, Massachusetts, and Connecticut. New Jersey and Rhode Island, upon all occasions, discovered a warm zeal for the independence of Vermont; and Maryland, till alarmed by the appearance of a connection between Canada and that State, entered deeply into the same views. These being small States, saw with an unfriendly eye the perspective of our growing greatness. In a review of these transactions we may trace some of the causes which would be likely to embroil the States with each other, if it should be their unpropitious destiny to become disunited.

The competitions of commerce would be another fruitful source of contention. The States less favorably circumstanced would be desirous of escaping from the disadvantages of local situation, and of sharing in the advantages of their more fortunate neighbors. Each State, or separate confederacy, would pursue a system of commercial policy peculiar to itself. This would occasion distinctions, preferences, and exclusions, which would beget discontent. The habits of intercourse, on the basis of equal privileges, to which we have been accustomed since the earliest settlement of the country, would give a keener edge to those causes of discontent than they would naturally have independent of this circumstance. *We should be ready to denominate injuries those things which were in reality the justifiable acts of independent sovereignties consulting a distinct interest.* The spirit of enterprise, which characterizes the commercial part of America, has left no occasion of displaying itself unimproved. It is not at all probable that this unbridled spirit would pay much respect to those regulations of trade by which particular States might endeavor to secure exclusive benefits to their own citizens. The infractions of these regulations, on one side, the efforts to prevent and repel them, on the other, would naturally lead to outrages, and these to reprisals and wars.

The opportunities which some States would have of rendering others tributary to them by commercial regulations would be impatiently submitted to by the tributary States. The relative situation of New York, Connecticut, and New Jersey would afford an example of this kind. New York, from the necessities of revenue, must lay duties on her importations. A great part of these duties must be paid by the inhabitants of the two other States in the capacity of consumers of what we import. New York would neither be willing nor able to forego this advantage. Her citizens would not consent that a duty paid by them should be remitted in favor of the citizens of her neighbors; nor would it be practicable, if there were not this impediment in the way, to distinguish the customers in our own markets. Would Connecticut and New Jersey long submit to be taxed by New York for her exclusive benefit? Should we be long permitted to remain in the quiet and undisturbed enjoyment of a metropolis, from the possession of which we derived an advantage so odious to our neighbors, and, in their opinion, so oppressive? Should we be able to preserve it against the incumbent weight of Connecticut on the one side, and the co-operating pressure of New Jersey on the other? These are questions that temerity alone will answer in the affirmative.

The public debt of the Union would be a further cause of collision between the separate States or confederacies. The apportionment, in the first instance, and the progressive extinguishment afterward, would be alike productive of ill-humor and animosity. How would it be possible to agree upon a rule of apportionment satisfactory to all? There is scarcely any that can be proposed which is entirely free from real objections. These, as usual, would be exaggerated by the adverse interest of the parties. There are even dissimilar views among the States as to the general principle of discharging the public debt. Some of them, either less impressed with the importance of national credit, or because their citizens have little, if any, immediate interest in the question, feel an indifference, if not a repugnance, to the payment of the domestic debt at any rate. These would be inclined to magnify the difficulties of a distribution. Others of them, a numerous body of whose citizens are creditors to the public beyond proportion of the State in the total amount of the national debt, would be strenuous for some equitable and effective provision. The procrastinations of the former would excite the resentments of the latter. The settlement of a rule would, in the meantime, be postponed by real differences of opinion and affected delays. The citizens of the States interested would clamour; foreign powers would urge for the satisfaction of their just demands, and the peace of the States would be hazarded to the double contingency of external invasion and internal contention.

Suppose the difficulties of agreeing upon a rule surmounted, and the apportionment made. Still there is great room to suppose that the rule agreed upon would, upon experiment, be found to bear harder upon some States than upon others. Those which were sufferers by it would naturally seek for a mitigation of the burden. The others would as naturally be disinclined to a revision, which was likely to end in an increase of their own incumbrances. Their refusal would be too plausible a pretext to the complaining States to withhold their contributions, not to be embraced with avidity; and the non-compliance of these States with their engagements would be a ground of bitter discussion and altercation. If even the rule adopted should in practice justify the equality of its principle, still delinquencies in payments on the part of some of the States would result from a diversity of other causes--the real deficiency of resources; the mismanagement of their finances; accidental disorders in the management of the government; and, in addition to the rest, the reluctance with which men commonly part with money for purposes that have outlived the exigencies which produced them, and interfere with the supply of immediate wants. Delinquencies, from whatever causes, would be productive of complaints, recriminations, and quarrels. There is, perhaps, nothing more likely to disturb the tranquillity of nations than their being bound to mutual contributions for any common object that does not yield an equal and coincident benefit. For it is an observation, as true as it is trite, that there is nothing men differ so readily about as the payment of money.

Laws in violation of private contracts, as they amount to aggressions on the rights of those States whose citizens are injured by them, may be considered as another probable source of hostility. We are not authorized to expect that a more liberal or more equitable spirit would preside over the legislations of the individual States hereafter, if unrestrained by any additional checks, than we have heretofore seen in too many instances disgracing their several codes. We have observed the disposition to retaliation excited in Connecticut in consequence of the enormities perpetrated by the Legislature of Rhode Island; and we reasonably infer that, in similar cases, under other circumstances, a war, not of *parchment*, but of the sword, would chastise such atrocious breaches of moral obligation and social justice.

The probability of incompatible alliances between the different States or confederacies and different foreign nations, and the effects of this situation upon the peace of the whole, have been sufficiently unfolded in some preceding papers. From the view they have exhibited of this part of the subject, this conclusion is to be drawn, that America, if not connected at all, or only by the feeble tie of a simple league, offensive and defensive, would, by the operation of such jarring alliances, be gradually entangled in all the pernicious labyrinths of European politics and wars; and by the destructive contentions of the parts into which she was divided, would be likely to become a prey to the artifices and machinations of powers equally the enemies of them all. *Divide et impera* (1) must be the motto of every nation that either hates or fears us.

Federalist No. 8 by Alexander Hamilton

Editor's Introduction

Hamilton continues to press the importance of Union in warding off disastrous civil wars and factionalism in *Federalist* Number 8. Hamilton also begins to address one of the principal concerns of the opposition, namely the ability for the general government to create a standing army. He reasons in this essay that standing armies would be more probable if the Constitution *were not* adopted as separate confederacies would constantly war over the control of North America. In other words, Hamilton reasons that the Constitution would more likely *prevent* a standing army than lead to the creation of a permanent military establishment.

Federalist No. 8

November 20, 1787

By Alexander Hamilton of New York

To the People of the State of New York.ASSUMING it therefore as an established truth that the several States, in case of disunion, or such combinations of them as might happen to be formed out of the wreck of the general Confederacy, would be subject to those vicissitudes of peace and war, of friendship and enmity, with each other, which have fallen to the lot of all neighboring nations not united under one government, let us enter into a concise detail of some of the consequences that would attend such a situation.

War between the States, in the first period of their separate existence, would be accompanied with much greater distresses than it commonly is in those countries where regular military establishments have long obtained. The disciplined armies always kept on foot on the continent of Europe, though they bear a malignant aspect to liberty and economy, have, notwithstanding, been productive of the signal advantage of rendering sudden conquests impracticable, and of preventing that rapid desolation which used to mark the progress of war prior to their introduction. The art of fortification has contributed to the same ends. The nations of Europe are encircled with chains of fortified places, which mutually obstruct invasion. Campaigns are wasted in reducing two or three frontier garrisons, to gain admittance into an enemy's country. Similar impediments occur at every step, to exhaust the strength and delay the progress of an invader. Formerly, an invading army would penetrate into the heart of a neighboring country almost as soon as intelligence of its approach could be received; but now a comparatively small force of disciplined troops, acting on the defensive, with the aid of posts, is able to impede, and finally to frustrate, the enterprises of one much more considerable. The history of war, in that quarter of the globe, is no longer a history of nations subdued and empires overturned, but of towns taken and retaken; of battles that decide nothing; of retreats more beneficial than victories; of much effort and little acquisition.

In this country the scene would be altogether reversed. The jealousy of military establishments would postpone them as long as possible. The want of fortifications, leaving the frontiers of one state open to another, would facilitate inroads. The populous States would, with little difficulty, overrun their less populous neighbors. Conquests would be as easy to be made as difficult to be retained. War, therefore, would be desultory and predatory. PLUNDER and devastation ever march in the train of irregulars. The calamities of individuals would make the principal figure in the events which would characterize our military exploits.

This picture is not too highly wrought; though, I confess, it would not long remain a just one. Safety from external danger is the most powerful director of national conduct. Even the ardent love of liberty will, after a time, give way to its dictates. The violent destruction of life and property incident to war, the continual effort and alarm attendant on a state of continual danger, will compel nations the most attached to liberty to resort for repose and security to institutions which have a tendency to destroy their civil and political rights. To be more safe, they at length become willing to run the risk of being less free.

The institutions chiefly alluded to are STANDING ARMIES and the correspondent appendages of military establishments. Standing armies, it is said, are not provided against in the new Constitution; and it is therefore inferred that they may exist under it. Their existence, however, from the very terms of the proposition, is, at most, problematical and uncertain. But standing armies, it may be replied, must inevitably result from a dissolution of the Confederacy. Frequent war and constant apprehension, which require a state of as constant preparation, will infallibly produce them. The weaker States or confederacies would first have recourse to them, to put themselves upon an equality with their more potent neighbors. They would endeavor to supply the inferiority of population and resources by a more regular and effective system of defense, by disciplined troops, and by fortifications. They would, at the same time, be necessitated to strengthen the executive arm of government, in doing which their constitutions would acquire a progressive direction toward monarchy. It is of the nature of war to increase the executive at the expense of the legislative authority.

The expedients which have been mentioned would soon give the States or confederacies that made use of them a superiority over their neighbors. Small states, or states of less natural strength, under vigorous governments, and with the assistance of disciplined armies, have often triumphed over large states, or states of greater natural strength, which have been destitute of these advantages. Neither the pride nor the safety of the more important States or confederacies would permit them long to submit to this mortifying and adventitious superiority. They would quickly resort to means similar to those by which it had been effected, to reinstate themselves in their lost pre-eminence. Thus, we should, in a little time, see established in every part of this country the same engines of despotism which have been the scourge of the Old World. This, at least, would be the natural course of things; and our reasonings will be the more likely to be just, in proportion as they are accommodated to this standard.

These are not vague inferences drawn from supposed or speculative defects in a Constitution, the whole power of which is lodged in the hands of a people, or their representatives and delegates, but they are solid conclusions, drawn from the natural and necessary progress of human affairs.

It may, perhaps, be asked, by way of objection to this, why did not standing armies spring up out of the contentions which so often distracted the ancient republics of Greece? Different answers, equally satisfactory, may be given to this question. The industrious habits of the people of the present day, absorbed in the pursuits of gain, and devoted to the improvements of agriculture and commerce, are incompatible with the condition of a nation of soldiers, which was the true condition of the people of those republics. The means of revenue, which have been so greatly multiplied by the increase of gold and silver and of the arts of industry, and the science of finance, which is the offspring of modern times, concurring with the habits of nations, have produced an entire revolution in the system of war, and have rendered disciplined armies, distinct from the body of the citizens, the inseparable companions of frequent hostility.

There is a wide difference, also, between military establishments in a country seldom exposed by its situation to internal invasions, and in one which is often subject to them, and always apprehensive of them. The rulers of the former can have a good pretext, if they are even so inclined, to keep on foot armies so numerous as must of necessity be maintained in the latter. These armies being, in the first case, rarely, if at all, called into activity for interior defense, the people are in no danger of being broken to military subordination. The laws are not accustomed to relaxations, in favor of military exigencies; the civil state remains in full vigor, neither corrupted, nor confounded with the principles or propensities of the other state. The smallness of the army renders the natural strength of the community an over-match for it; and the citizens, not habituated to look up to the military power for protection, or to submit to its oppressions, neither love nor fear the soldiery; they view them with a spirit of jealous acquiescence in a necessary evil, and stand ready to resist a power which they suppose may be exerted to the prejudice of their rights. The army under such circumstances may usefully aid the magistrate to suppress a small faction, or an occasional mob, or insurrection; but it will be unable to enforce encroachments against the united efforts of the great body of the people.

In a country in the predicament last described, the contrary of all this happens. The perpetual menacings of danger oblige the government to be always prepared to repel it; its armies must be numerous enough for instant defense. The continual necessity for their services enhances the importance of the soldier, and proportionably degrades the condition of the citizen. The military state becomes elevated above the civil. The inhabitants of territories, often the theatre of war, are unavoidably subjected to frequent infringements on their rights, which serve to weaken their sense of those rights; and by degrees the people are brought to consider the soldiery not only as their protectors, but as their superiors. The transition from this disposition to that of considering them masters, is neither remote nor difficult; but it is very difficult to prevail upon a people under such impressions, to make a bold or effectual resistance to usurpations supported by the military power.

The kingdom of Great Britain falls within the first description. An insular situation, and a powerful marine, guarding it in a great measure against the possibility of foreign invasion, supersede the necessity of a numerous army within the kingdom. A sufficient force to make head against a sudden descent, till the militia could have time to rally and embody, is all that has been deemed requisite. No motive of national policy has demanded, nor would public opinion have tolerated, a larger number of troops upon its domestic establishment. There has been, for a long time past, little room for the operation of the other causes, which have been enumerated as the consequences of internal war. This peculiar felicity of situation has, in a great degree, contributed to preserve the liberty which that country to this day enjoys, in spite of the prevalent venality and corruption. If, on the contrary, Britain had been situated on the continent, and had been compelled, as she would have been, by that situation, to make her military establishments at home coextensive with those of the other great powers of Europe, she, like them, would in all probability be, at this day, a victim to the absolute power of a single man. 'T is possible, though not easy, that the people of that island may be enslaved from other causes; but it cannot be by the prowess of an army so inconsiderable as that which has been usually kept up within the kingdom.

If we are wise enough to preserve the Union we may for ages enjoy an advantage similar to that of an insulated situation. Europe is at a great distance from us. Her colonies in our vicinity will be likely to continue too much disproportioned in strength to be able to give us any dangerous annoyance. Extensive military establishments cannot, in this position, be necessary to our security. But if we should be disunited, and the integral parts should either remain separated, or, which is most probable, should be thrown together into two or three confederacies, we should be, in a short course of time, in the predicament of the continental powers of Europe --our liberties would be a prey to the means of defending ourselves against the ambition and jealousy of each other.

This is an idea not superficial or futile, but solid and weighty. It deserves the most serious and mature consideration of every prudent and honest man of whatever party. If such men will make a firm and solemn pause, and meditate dispassionately on the importance of this interesting idea; if they will contemplate it in all its attitudes, and trace it to all its consequences, they will not hesitate to part with trivial objections to a Constitution, the rejection of which would in all probability put a final period to the Union. The airy phantoms that flit before the distempered imaginations of some of its adversaries would quickly give place to the more substantial forms of dangers, real, certain, and formidable.

This objection will be fully examined in its proper place, and it will be shown that the only natural precaution which could have been taken on this subject has been taken; and a much better one than is to be found in any constitution that has been heretofore framed in America, most of which contain no guard at all on this subject.

FEDERALIST NO. 9 BY ALEXANDER HAMILTON

Editor's Introduction:

Hamilton concludes his discussion on the merits of Union in *Federalist* No. 9 while concurrently evaluating the thoughts of the Baron de Montesquieu on the size and nature of republics. Critics of the Constitution frequently cited Montesquieu while claiming that a republic could not function over a territory as diverse and vast as the United States. Hamilton counters by suggesting that the republics in Montesquieu's work are much smaller than the States within the United States and still those function within a republican framework. He then pivots to a discussion of a "Confederate Republic." Hamilton insists that the United States, even under the Constitution, would still be classified as a "Confederate Republic," and that Montesquieu believed such a framework would be best suited to the interests and design of the United States.

Hamilton, then, takes one of the most important figures of the opposition and uses him to advance the side of ratification. This was an ingenious move designed to take the fire from the opposition. Most importantly, however, is Hamilton's insistence that the Constitution did not establish a consolidated or national government but a "Confederate Republic" with the States as important branch of the general system. Hamilton thus presents an argument for real federalism in a "federal" rather than consolidated or "national" government, a position virtually every proponent of the Constitution adopted in the months leading to ratification of the document.

Federalist No. 9

November 21, 1787

By Alexander Hamilton of New York

To the People of the State of New York.

A FIRM Union will be of the utmost moment to the peace and liberty of the States, as a barrier against domestic faction and insurrection. It is impossible to read the history of the petty republics of Greece and Italy without feeling sensations of horror and disgust at the distractions with which they were continually agitated, and at the rapid succession of revolutions by which they were kept in a state of perpetual vibration between the extremes of tyranny and anarchy. If they exhibit occasional calms, these only serve as short-lived contrast to the furious storms that are to succeed. If now and then intervals of felicity open to view, we behold them with a mixture of regret, arising from the reflection that the pleasing scenes before us are soon to be overwhelmed by the tempestuous waves of sedition and party rage. If momentary rays of glory break forth from the gloom, while they dazzle us with a transient and fleeting brilliancy, they at the same time admonish us to lament that the vices of government should pervert the direction and tarnish the lustre of those bright talents and exalted endowments for which the favored soils that produced them have been so justly celebrated.

From the disorders that disfigure the annals of those republics the advocates of despotism have drawn arguments, not only against the forms of republican government, but against the very principles of civil liberty. They have decried all free government as inconsistent with the order of society, and have indulged themselves in malicious exultation over its friends and partisans. Happily for mankind, stupendous fabrics reared on the basis of liberty, which have flourished for ages, have, in a few glorious instances, refuted their gloomy sophisms. And, I trust, America will be the broad and solid foundation of other edifices, not less magnificent, which will be equally permanent monuments of their errors.

But it is not to be denied that the portraits they have sketched of republican government were too just copies of the originals from which they were taken. If it had been found impracticable to have devised models of a more perfect structure, the enlightened friends to liberty would have been obliged to abandon the cause of that species of government as indefensible. The science of politics, however, like most other sciences, has received great improvement. The efficacy of various principles is now well understood, which were either not known at all, or imperfectly known to the ancients. The regular distribution of power into distinct departments; the introduction of legislative balances and checks; the institution of courts composed of judges holding their offices during good behavior; the representation of the people in the legislature by deputies of their own election: these are wholly new discoveries, or have made their principal progress towards perfection in modern times. They are means, and powerful means, by which the excellences of republican government may be retained and its imperfections lessened or avoided. To this catalogue of circumstances that tend to the amelioration of popular systems of civil government, I shall venture, however novel it may appear to some, to add one more, on a principle which has been made the foundation of an objection to the new Constitution; I mean the ENLARGEMENT of the ORBIT within which such systems are to revolve, either in respect to the dimensions of a single State or to the consolidation of several smaller States into one great Confederacy. The latter is that which immediately concerns the object under consideration. It will, however, be of use to examine the principle in its application to a single State, which shall be attended to in another place.

The utility of a Confederacy, as well to suppress faction and to guard the internal tranquillity of States, as to increase their external force and security, is in reality not a new idea. It has been practiced upon in different countries and ages, and has received the sanction of the most approved writers on the subject of politics. The opponents of the plan proposed have, with great assiduity, cited and circulated the observations of Montesquieu on the necessity of a contracted territory for a republican government. But they seem not to have been apprised of the sentiments of that great man expressed in another part of his work, nor to have adverted to the consequences of the principle to which they subscribe with such ready acquiescence.

When Montesquieu recommends a small extent for republics, the standards he had in view were of dimensions far short of the limits of almost every one of these States. Neither Virginia, Massachusetts, Pennsylvania, New York, North Carolina, nor Georgia can by any means be compared with the models from which he reasoned and to which the terms of his description apply. If we therefore take his ideas on this point as the criterion of truth, we shall be driven to the alternative either of taking refuge at once in the arms of monarchy, or of splitting ourselves into an infinity of little, jealous, clashing, tumultuous commonwealths, the wretched nurseries of unceasing discord, and the miserable objects of universal pity or contempt. Some of the writers who have come forward on the other side of the question seem to have been aware of the dilemma; and have even been bold enough to hint at the division of the larger States as a desirable thing. Such an infatuated policy, such a desperate expedient, might, by the multiplication of petty offices, answer the views of men who possess not qualifications to extend their influence beyond the narrow circles of personal intrigue, but it could never promote the greatness or happiness of the people of America.

Referring the examination of the principle itself to another place, as has been already mentioned, it will be sufficient to remark here that, in the sense of the author who has been most emphatically quoted upon the occasion, it would only dictate a reduction of the SIZE of the more considerable MEMBERS of the Union, but would not militate against their being all comprehended in one confederate government. And this is the true question, in the discussion of which we are at present interested.

So far are the suggestions of Montesquieu from standing in opposition to a general Union of the States, that he explicitly treats of a CONFEDERATE REPUBLIC as the expedient for extending the sphere of popular government, and reconciling the advantages of monarchy with those of republicanism.

"It is very probable," (says he(A)) "that mankind would have been obliged at length to live constantly under the government of a single person, had they not contrived a kind of constitution that has all the internal advantages of a republican, together with the external force of a monarchical government. I mean a CONFEDERATE REPUBLIC."

"This form of government is a convention by which several smaller *States* agree to become members of a larger *one*, which they intend to form. It is a kind of assemblage of societies that constitute a new one, capable of increasing, by means of new associations, till they arrive to such a degree of power as to be able to provide for the security of the united body."

"A republic of this kind, able to withstand an external force, may support itself without any internal corruptions. The form of this society prevents all manner of inconveniences."

"If a single member should attempt to usurp the supreme authority, he could not be supposed to have an equal authority and credit in all the confederate states. Were he to have too great influence over one, this would alarm the rest. Were he to subdue a part, that which would still remain free might oppose him with forces independent of those which he had usurped and overpower him before he could be settled in his usurpation."

"Should a popular insurrection happen in one of the confederate states the others are able to quell it. Should abuses creep into one part, they are reformed by those that remain sound. The state may be destroyed on one side, and not on the other; the confederacy may be dissolved, and the confederates preserve their sovereignty."

"As this government is composed of small republics, it enjoys the internal happiness of each; and with respect to its external situation, it is possessed, by means of the association, of all the advantages of large monarchies.'"

I have thought it proper to quote at length these interesting passages, because they contain a luminous abridgment of the principal arguments in favor of the Union, and must effectually remove the false impressions which a misapplication of other parts of the work was calculated to make. They have, at the same time, an intimate connection with the more immediate design of this paper; which is, to illustrate the tendency of the Union to repress domestic faction and insurrection.

A distinction, more subtle than accurate, has been raised between a *confederacy* and a *consolidation* of the States. The essential characteristic of the first is said to be, the restriction of its authority to the members in their collective capacities, without reaching to the individuals of whom they are composed. It is contended that the national council ought to have no concern with any object of internal administration. An exact equality of suffrage between the members has also been insisted upon as a leading feature of a confederate government. These positions are, in the main, arbitrary; they are supported neither by principle nor precedent. It has indeed happened, that governments of this kind have generally operated in the manner which the distinction taken notice of, supposes to be inherent in their nature; but there have been in most of them extensive exceptions to the practice, which serve to prove, as far as example will go, that there is no absolute rule on the subject. And it will be clearly shown in the course of this investigation that as far as the principle contended for has prevailed, it has been the cause of incurable disorder and imbecility in the government.

The definition of a *confederate republic* seems simply to be "an assemblage of societies," or an association of two or more states into one state. The extent, modifications, and objects of the federal authority are mere matters of discretion. So long as the separate organization of the members be not abolished; so long as it exists, by a constitutional necessity, for local purposes; though it should be in perfect subordination to the general authority of the union, it would still be, in fact and in theory, an association of states, or a confederacy. The proposed Constitution, so far from implying an abolition of the State governments, makes them constituent parts of the national sovereignty, by allowing them a direct representation in the Senate, and leaves in their possession certain exclusive and very important portions of sovereign power. This fully corresponds, in every rational import of the terms, with the idea of a federal government.

In the Lycian confederacy, which consisted of twenty-three *cities* or republics, the largest were entitled to *three* votes in the *common council*, those of the middle class to *two*, and the smallest to *one*. The *common council* had the appointment of all the judges and magistrates of the respective *cities*. This was certainly the most, delicate species of interference in their internal administration; for if there be any thing that seems exclusively appropriated to the local jurisdictions, it is the appointment of their own officers. Yet Montesquieu, speaking of this association, says: "Were I to give a model of an excellent Confederate Republic, it would be that of Lycia." Thus we perceive that the distinctions insisted upon were not within the contemplation of this enlightened civilian; and we shall be led to conclude, that they are the novel refinements of an erroneous theory.

1. *Spirit of Laws, Vol. I., Book IX., Chap. I.*

A Countryman II by Roger Sherman

Editor's Introduction:

Roger Sherman of Connecticut was one of the most important members of the founding generation, and perhaps no man carried more weight in his State than the "Old Atlas." Sherman played a vital role in the Philadelphia Convention and helped draft the "Connecticut Compromise," a move that allowed for equal representation of the States in the Senate, a key provision that maintained the "federal republic" as under the Articles of Confederation.

Sherman was a true self-made man who earned his place in Connecticut society through honesty, hard work, and patriotism. His honesty led Thomas Jefferson to remark that he never heard Sherman say a foolish thing in his life and by default forced both his peers and his constituents to trust his judgement on most matters, including the merits of the new Constitution.

Sherman was also partly responsible for the "Three-Fifths Compromise" to the Constitution. This agreement between Connecticut and South Carolina ensured that the South would support the document—as would slave trading Northerners—if for no other reason than Southerners could block the possibility of federal taxes on slaves.

His "Countryman" essays displayed Sherman's Spartan use of language and his ability to effectively throttle the opposition. Sherman used less than two thousand words in each essay and still punched as hard as Hamilton in the *Federalist*. In "A Countryman II," Sherman insisted that the people of Connecticut had nothing to fear from the Constitution, for while it opened the possibility that the general government could abuse its authority, it would be comprised of the same caliber of men that represented Connecticut, and Connecticut was never in danger of being politically repressed. Sherman classified his opposition as mere "rabble."

A Countryman II

November 22, 1787

By Roger Sherman of Connecticut

To the People *of* Connecticut.

It is fortunate that you have been but little distressed with that torrent of impertinence and folly with which the newspaper politicians have overwhelmed many parts of our country.

It is enough that you should have heard, that one party has seriously urged, that we should adopt the *New Constitution* because it has been approved by *Washington* and *Franklin*,: and the other, with all the solemnity of apostolic address to *Men, Brethren, Fathers, Friends, and Countrymen*,, have urged that we should reject, as dangerous, every clause thereof, because that *Washington* is more used to command as a soldier, than to reason as a politician—*Franklin* is *old*—others are *young*—and *Wilson* is *haughty*. You are too well informed to decide by the opinion of others, and too independent to need a caution against undue influence.

Of a very different nature, tho' only one degree better than the other reasoning, is all that sublimity of *nonsense* and *alarm*, that has been thundered against it in every shape of *metaphoric terror*, on the subject of a *bill of rights, the liberty of the press, rights of conscience, rights of taxation and election, trials in the vicinity, freedom of speech, trial by jury, and a standing army.* These last are undoubtedly important points, much too important to depend on mere paper protection. For, guard such privileges by the strongest expressions, still if you leave the legislative and executive power in the hands of those who are or may be disposed to deprive you of them- you are but slaves. Make an absolute monarch – give him the supreme authority, and guard as much as you will by bills of right, your liberty of the press, and trial by jury; he will find means either to take them from you, or to render them useless.

The only real security that you can have for all your important rights must be in the nature of your government. If you suffer any man to govern you who is not strongly interested in supporting your privileges, you will certainly lose them. If you are about to trust your liberties with people whom it is necessary to bind by stipulation, that they shall not keep a standing army, your stipulation is not worth even the trouble of writing. No bill of rights ever yet bound the supreme power longer than the *honey moon* of a new married couple, unless the *rulers were interested* in preserving the rights; and in that case they have always been ready enough to declare the rights and to preserve them when they were declared.- The famous English *Magna Charta* is but an act of parliament, which every subsequent parliament has had just as much constitutional power to repeal and annul, as the parliament which made it had to pass it at first. But the security of the nation has always been, that their government was so formed, that at least *one branch* of their legislature must be strongly interested to preserve the rights of the nation.

You have a bill of rights in Connecticut (i.e.)your legislature many years since enacted that the subjects of this state should enjoy certain privileges. Ever assembly since that time could, by the same authority, enact that the subjects should enjoy none of those privileges; and the only reason that it has not long since been so enacted, is that your legislature were as strongly interested in preserving those rights as any of the subjects; and this is your only security that it shall not be so enacted at the next session of assembly: and it is security enough.

Your General Assembly under your present constitution are supreme. They may keep troops on foot in the most profound peace, if they think proper. They have heretofore abridged the trial by jury in some causes, and they can again in all. They can restrain the press, and may lay the most burdensome taxes if they please, and who can forbid? But still the people are perfectly safe that not one of these events shall take place so longs as the members of the General Assembly are as much interested, and interested in the same manner as the other subjects.

On examining the new proposed constitution, there can not be a question, but that there is authority enough lodged in the proposed federal Congress, if abused, to do the greatest injury. And it is perfectly idle to object to it, that there is no bill of rights, or to propose to add to it a provision that a trial by jury shall in no case be omitted, or to patch it up by adding a stipulation in favor of the press, or to guard it by removing the paltry objection to the right of Congress to regulate the time and manner of elections.

If you can not prove by the best of all evidence, viz., by the *interest of the rulers,*, that this authority will not be abused, or at least, that those powers are not more likely to be abused by the Congress, than by those who now have the same powers, you must by no means adopt the constitution: -No, not with all the bills of rights and all the stipulations in favor of the people that can be made.

But if the members of Congress are to be interested just as you and I are, and just as the members of our present legislatures are interested, we shall be just as safe, with even supreme power, (if that were granted) in Congress, as in the General Assembly. If the members of Congress can take no improper step which will not affect them as much as it does us, we need not apprehend that they will usurp authorities not given them to injure that society of which they are a part.

The sole question, (so far as any apprehension of tyranny and oppression is concerned) ought to be, how are Congress formed? how far are them members interested to preserve your rights? How far have you a control over them? –Decide this, and then all the questions about their power may be dismissed for the amusement of those politicians whose business it is to catch flies, or may occasionally furnish subjects for *George Bryan's POMPOSITY*, or the declamations of *Cato- An Old Whig-Son of Liberty-Brutus- Brutus Junior- An Officer of the Continental Army, -the more contemptible Timoleon,- and the residue of that rabble of writers.*

Federalist No. 10 by James Madison

Editor's Introduction:

James Madison's reputation as the "Father of the Constitution" has been buttressed, in part, by his participation in the *Federalist* essays. He was a last-minute addition. John Jay left the project after scribbling a handful of essays, and Hamilton needed an ally to complete the daunting task of persuading a reluctant New York public to embrace the new Constitution. He turned to his friend from Virginia. Madison ultimately hammered out nearly thirty of the eighty-five total essays, the first being *Federalist* No. 10.

Madison was one of the foremost members of the Philadelphia Convention in 1787 and kept a copious journal of its proceedings. But unlike Hamilton, who packed his bags and bolted the Convention when events did not favor his views, Madison followed through on his promise to help craft a governing document that, at least on paper, improved the central government. "Little Jemmy" was a sickly bookworm with a sharp intellect but little social grace who feared the political power of men like Patrick Henry in his home State. He proposed a national government in Philadelphia only to be rebuffed by most of the delegates at the Convention. He never waivered in his belief in the necessity of a strong central authority though he eventually attempted to sell the Constitution as written, meaning a federal republic with limited powers delegated by the people of the States.

Federalist No 10 is more than an essay aimed at persuading wavering delegates about the merits of the Constitution; it is a statement of political philosophy. Madison warned against the evils of "faction," which he defined as "a number of citizens, whether amounting to a majority or a minority of the whole, who are united and actuated by some common impulse of passion, or of interest, adversed to the rights of other citizens, or to the permanent and aggregate interests of the community." Of course, he had Patrick Henry and every other powerful local politician on his mind when penning these words. Madison thought "a well constructed Union" would curtail the power of these big fish in small ponds and eventually render them impotent. He was wrong on one account. While the Constitution did undercut State leaders like Henry, John Hancock in Massachusetts, or George Clinton in New York, it allowed for the rise of large coalitions of factions—political parties—to emerge and dominate the general government. The modern Democrat Party is little more than a collection of minority factions with a common goal of centralized power. The Constitution, rather than retarding factions in America, made them possible.

Federalist No. 10

November 22, 1787

By James Madison of Virginia

To the People of the State of New York:

AMONG the numerous advantages promised by a well constructed Union, none deserves to be more accurately developed than its tendency to break and control the violence of faction. The friend of popular governments never finds himself so much alarmed for their character and fate, as when he contemplates their propensity to this dangerous vice. He will not fail, therefore, to set a due value on any plan which, without violating the principles to which he is attached, provides a proper cure for it. The instability, injustice, and confusion introduced into the public councils, have, in truth, been the mortal diseases under which popular governments have everywhere perished; as they continue to be the favorite and fruitful topics from which the adversaries to liberty derive their most specious declamations. The valuable improvements made by the American constitutions on the popular models, both ancient and modern, cannot certainly be too much admired; but it would be an unwarrantable partiality, to contend that they have as effectually obviated the danger on this side, as was wished and expected. Complaints are everywhere heard from our most considerate and virtuous citizens, equally the friends of public and private faith, and of public and personal liberty, that our governments are too unstable, that the public good is disregarded in the conflicts of rival parties, and that measures are too often decided, not according to the rules of justice and the rights of the minor party, but by the superior force of an interested and overbearing majority. However anxiously we may wish that these complaints had no foundation, the evidence, of known facts will not permit us to deny that they are in some degree true. It will be found, indeed, on a candid review of our situation, that some of the distresses under which we labor have been erroneously charged on the operation of our governments; but it will be found, at the same time, that other causes will not alone account for many of our heaviest misfortunes; and, particularly, for that prevailing and increasing distrust of public engagements, and alarm for private rights, which are echoed from one end of the continent to the other. These must be chiefly, if not wholly, effects of the unsteadiness and injustice with which a factious spirit has tainted our public administrations.

By a faction, I understand a number of citizens, whether amounting to a majority or a minority of the whole, who are united and actuated by some common impulse of passion, or of interest, adversed to the rights of other citizens, or to the permanent and aggregate interests of the community.

There are two methods of curing the mischiefs of faction: the one, by removing its causes; the other, by controlling its effects.

There are again two methods of removing the causes of faction: the one, by destroying the liberty which is essential to its existence; the other, by giving to every citizen the same opinions, the same passions, and the same interests.

It could never be more truly said than of the first remedy, that it was worse than the disease. Liberty is to faction what air is to fire, an aliment without which it instantly expires. But it could not be less folly to abolish liberty, which is essential to political life, because it nourishes faction, than it would be to wish the annihilation of air, which is essential to animal life, because it imparts to fire its destructive agency.

The second expedient is as impracticable as the first would be unwise. As long as the reason of man continues fallible, and he is at liberty to exercise it, different opinions will be formed. As long as the connection subsists between his reason and his self-love, his opinions and his passions will have a reciprocal influence on each other; and the former will be objects to which the latter will attach themselves. The diversity in the faculties of men, from which the rights of property originate, is not less an insuperable obstacle to a uniformity of interests. The protection of these faculties is the first object of government. From the protection of different and unequal faculties of acquiring property, the possession of different degrees and kinds of property immediately results; and from the influence of these on the sentiments and views of the respective proprietors, ensues a division of the society into different interests and parties.

The latent causes of faction are thus sown in the nature of man; and we see them everywhere brought into different degrees of activity, according to the different circumstances of civil society. A zeal for different opinions concerning religion, concerning government, and many other points, as well of speculation as of practice; an attachment to different leaders ambitiously contending for pre-eminence and power; or to persons of other descriptions whose fortunes have been interesting to the human passions, have, in turn, divided mankind into parties, inflamed them with mutual animosity, and rendered them much more disposed to vex and oppress each other than to co-operate for their common good. So strong is this propensity of mankind to fall into mutual animosities, that where no substantial occasion presents itself, the most frivolous and fanciful distinctions have been sufficient to kindle their unfriendly passions and excite their most violent conflicts. But the most common and durable source of factions has been the various and unequal distribution of property. Those who hold and those who are without property have ever formed distinct interests in society. Those who are creditors, and those who are debtors, fall under a like discrimination. A landed interest, a manufacturing interest, a mercantile interest, a moneyed interest, with many lesser interests, grow up of necessity in civilized nations, and divide them into different classes, actuated by different sentiments and views. The regulation of these various and interfering interests forms the principal task of modern legislation, and involves the spirit of party and faction in the necessary and ordinary operations of the government.

No man is allowed to be a judge in his own cause, because his interest would certainly bias his judgment, and, not improbably, corrupt his integrity. With equal, nay with greater reason, a body of men are unfit to be both judges and parties at the same time; yet what are many of the most important acts of legislation, but so many judicial determinations, not indeed concerning the rights of single persons, but concerning the rights of large bodies of citizens? And what are the different classes of legislators but advocates and parties to the causes which they determine? Is a law proposed concerning private debts? It is a question to which the creditors are parties on one side and the debtors on the other. Justice ought to hold the balance between them. Yet the parties are, and must be, themselves the judges; and the most numerous party, or, in other words, the most powerful faction must be expected to prevail. Shall domestic manufactures be encouraged, and in what degree, by restrictions on foreign manufactures? are questions which would be differently decided by the landed and the manufacturing classes, and probably by neither with a sole regard to justice and the public good. The apportionment of taxes on the various descriptions of property is an act which seems to require the most exact impartiality; yet there is, perhaps, no legislative act in which greater opportunity and temptation are given to a predominant party to trample on the rules of justice. Every shilling with which they overburden the inferior number, is a shilling saved to their own pockets.

It is in vain to say that enlightened statesmen will be able to adjust these clashing interests, and render them all subservient to the public good. Enlightened statesmen will not always be at the helm. Nor, in many cases, can such an adjustment be made at all without taking into view indirect and remote considerations, which will rarely prevail over the immediate interest which one party may find in disregarding the rights of another or the good of the whole.

The inference to which we are brought is, that the *causes* of faction cannot be removed, and that relief is only to be sought in the means of controlling its *effects*.

If a faction consists of less than a majority, relief is supplied by the republican principle, which enables the majority to defeat its sinister views by regular vote. It may clog the administration, it may convulse the society; but it will be unable to execute and mask its violence under the forms of the Constitution. When a majority is included in a faction, the form of popular government, on the other hand, enables it to sacrifice to its ruling passion or interest both the public good and the rights of other citizens. To secure the public good and private rights against the danger of such a faction, and at the same time to preserve the spirit and the form of popular government, is then the great object to which our inquiries are directed. Let me add that it is the great desideratum by which this form of government can be rescued from the opprobrium under which it has so long labored, and be recommended to the esteem and adoption of mankind.

By what means is this object attainable? Evidently by one of two only. Either the existence of the same passion or interest in a majority at the same time must be prevented, or the majority, having such coexistent passion or interest, must be rendered, by their number and local situation, unable to concert and carry into effect schemes of oppression. If the impulse and the opportunity be suffered to coincide, we well know that neither moral nor religious motives can be relied on as an adequate control. They are not found to be such on the injustice and violence of individuals, and lose their efficacy in proportion to the number combined together, that is, in proportion as their efficacy becomes needful.

From this view of the subject it may be concluded that a pure democracy, by which I mean a society consisting of a small number of citizens, who assemble and administer the government in person, can admit of no cure for the mischiefs of faction. A common passion or interest will, in almost every case, be felt by a majority of the whole; a communication and concert result from the form of government itself; and there is nothing to check the inducements to sacrifice the weaker party or an obnoxious individual. Hence it is that such democracies have ever been spectacles of turbulence and contention; have ever been found incompatible with personal security or the rights of property; and have in general been as short in their lives as they have been violent in their deaths. Theoretic politicians, who have patronized this species of government, have erroneously supposed that by reducing mankind to a perfect equality in their political rights, they would, at the same time, be perfectly equalized and assimilated in their possessions, their opinions, and their passions.

A republic, by which I mean a government in which the scheme of representation takes place, opens a different prospect, and promises the cure for which we are seeking. Let us examine the points in which it varies from pure democracy, and we shall comprehend both the nature of the cure and the efficacy which it must derive from the Union.

The two great points of difference between a democracy and a republic are: first, the delegation of the government, in the latter, to a small number of citizens elected by the rest; secondly, the greater number of citizens, and greater sphere of country, over which the latter may be extended.

The effect of the first difference is, on the one hand, to refine and enlarge the public views, by passing them through the medium of a chosen body of citizens, whose wisdom may best discern the true interest of their country, and whose patriotism and love of justice will be least likely to sacrifice it to temporary or partial considerations. Under such a regulation, it may well happen that the public voice, pronounced by the representatives of the people, will be more consonant to the public good than if pronounced by the people themselves, convened for the purpose. On the other hand, the effect may be inverted. Men of factious tempers, of local prejudices, or of sinister designs, may, by intrigue, by corruption, or by other means, first obtain the suffrages, and then betray the interests, of the people. The question resulting is, whether small or extensive republics are more favorable to the election of proper guardians of the public weal; and it is clearly decided in favor of the latter by two obvious considerations:

In the first place, it is to be remarked that, however small the republic may be, the representatives must be raised to a certain number, in order to guard against the cabals of a few; and that, however large it may be, they must be limited to a certain number, in order to guard against the confusion of a multitude. Hence, the number of representatives in the two cases not being in proportion to that of the two constituents, and being proportionally greater in the small republic, it follows that, if the proportion of fit characters be not less in the large than in the small republic, the former will present a greater option, and consequently a greater probability of a fit choice.

In the next place, as each representative will be chosen by a greater number of citizens in the large than in the small republic, it will be more difficult for unworthy candidates to practice with success the vicious arts by which elections are too often carried; and the suffrages of the people being more free, will be more likely to centre in men who possess the most attractive merit and the most diffusive and established characters.

It must be confessed that in this, as in most other cases, there is a mean, on both sides of which inconveniences will be found to lie. By enlarging too much the number of electors, you render the representatives too little acquainted with all their local circumstances and lesser interests; as by reducing it too much, you render him unduly attached to these, and too little fit to comprehend and pursue great and national objects. The federal Constitution forms a happy combination in this respect; the great and aggregate interests being referred to the national, the local and particular to the State legislatures.

The other point of difference is, the greater number of citizens and extent of territory which may be brought within the compass of republican than of democratic government; and it is this circumstance principally which renders factious combinations less to be dreaded in the former than in the latter. The smaller the society, the fewer probably will be the distinct parties and interests composing it; the fewer the distinct parties and interests, the more frequently will a majority be found of the same party; and the smaller the number of individuals composing a majority, and the smaller the compass within which they are placed, the more easily will they concert and execute their plans of oppression. Extend the sphere, and you take in a greater variety of parties and interests; you make it less probable that a majority of the whole will have a common motive to invade the rights of other citizens; or if such a common motive exists, it will be more difficult for all who feel it to discover their own strength, and to act in unison with each other. Besides other impediments, it may be remarked that, where there is a consciousness of unjust or dishonorable purposes, communication is always checked by distrust in proportion to the number whose concurrence is necessary.

Hence, it clearly appears, that the same advantage which a republic has over a democracy, in controlling the effects of faction, is enjoyed by a large over a small republic,--is enjoyed by the Union over the States composing it. Does the advantage consist in the substitution of representatives whose enlightened views and virtuous sentiments render them superior to local prejudices and schemes of injustice? It will not be denied that the representation of the Union will be most likely to possess these requisite endowments. Does it consist in the greater security afforded by a greater variety of parties, against the event of any one party being able to outnumber and oppress the rest? In an equal degree does the increased variety of parties comprised within the Union, increase this security. Does it, in fine, consist in the greater obstacles opposed to the concert and accomplishment of the secret wishes of an unjust and interested majority? Here, again, the extent of the Union gives it the most palpable advantage.

The influence of factious leaders may kindle a flame within their particular States, but will be unable to spread a general conflagration through the other States. A religious sect may degenerate into a political faction in a part of the Confederacy; but the variety of sects dispersed over the entire face of it must secure the national councils against any danger from that source. A rage for paper money, for an abolition of debts, for an equal division of property, or for any other improper or wicked project, will be less apt to pervade the whole body of the Union than a particular member of it; in the same proportion as such a malady is more likely to taint a particular county or district, than an entire State.

In the extent and proper structure of the Union, therefore, we behold a republican remedy for the diseases most incident to republican government. And according to the degree of pleasure and pride we feel in being republicans, ought to be our zeal in cherishing the spirit and supporting the character of Federalists.

Speech Before the Pennsylvania Ratifying Convention by James Wilson

Editor's Introduction:

James Wilson spoke more than any other man at the Pennsylvania Ratifying Convention in November and December 1787. It could be argued that he almost single-handedly secured its ratification in that State. The Ratifying Convention offered the opportunity for long-form defense of the document, something newspaper essays or extemporaneous speeches failed to provide.

Wilson focused most of his efforts in this speech on defining the nature of the new government. He compared the benefits and burdens of monarchy, aristocracy, and democracy and concluded that the new Constitution combined the best aspects of democracy with the restraints of a federal government. To Wilson, the new Constitution maintained the federal republic while expanding its powers so that it could operate on individuals as well as States. As a result, the people would be represented in the Congress through the House of Representatives, and the general government would be charged with the preservation of American liberty through effective, though limited, powers. This was the same theme he championed during the "State House Yard" speech in October. If nothing else, Wilson followed a cogent and consistent line of reasoning in defending the document during ratification.

Speech Before the Pennsylvania Ratifying Convention
November 26, 1787
By James Wilson of Pennsylvania

Mr. WILSON. The system proposed, by the late Convention, for the government of the United States, is now before you. Of that Convention I had the honor to be a member. As I am the only member of that body who has the honor to be also a member of this, it may be expected that I should prepare the way for the deliberations of this assembly, by unfolding the difficulties which the late Convention were obliged to encounter; by pointing out the end which they proposed to accomplish; and by tracing the general principles which they have adopted for the accomplishment of that end.

To form a good system of government for a single city or state, however limited as to territory, or inconsiderable as to numbers, has been thought to require the strongest efforts of human genius. With what conscious diffidence, then, must the members of the Convention have revolved in their minds the immense undertaking which was before them. Their views could not be confined to a small or a single community, but were expanded to a great number of states; several of which contain an extent of territory, and resources of population, equal to those of some of the most respectable kingdoms on the other side of the Atlantic. Nor were even these the only objects to be comprehended within their deliberations. Numerous states yet unformed, myriads of the human race, who will inhabit regions hitherto uncultivated, were to be affected by the result of their proceedings. It was necessary, therefore, to form their calculations on a scale commensurate to a large portion of the globe.

For my own part, I have been often lost in astonishment at the vastness of the prospect before us. To open the navigation of a single river was lately thought, in Europe, an enterprise equal to imperial glory. But could the commercial scenes of the Scheldt be compared with those that, under a good government, will be exhibited on the Hudson, the Delaware, the Potomac, and the numerous other rivers, that water and are intended to enrich the dominions of the United States?

The difficulty of the business was equal to its magnitude. No small share of wisdom and address is requisite to combine and reconcile the jarring interests that prevail, or seem to prevail, in a single community. The United States contain already thirteen governments mutually independent. Those governments present to the Atlantic a front of fifteen hundred miles in extent. Their soil, their climates, their productions, their dimensions, their numbers, are different. In many instances, a difference, and even an opposition, subsists among their interests; and a difference, and even an opposition, is imagined to subsist in many more. An apparent interest produces the same attachment as a real one, and is often pursued with no less perseverance and vigor. When all these circumstances are seen, and attentively considered, will any member of this honorable body be surprised that such a diversity of things produced a proportionate diversity of sentiment? Will he be surprised that such a diversity of sentiment rendered a spirit of mutual forbearance and conciliation indispensably necessary to the success of the great work? And will he be surprised that mutual concessions and sacrifices were the consequences of mutual forbearance and conciliation? When the springs of opposition were so numerous and strong, and poured forth their waters in courses so varying, need we be surprised that the stream formed by their conjunction was impelled in a direction somewhat different from that which each of them would have taken separately?

I have reason to think that a difficulty arose in the minds of some members of the Convention from another consideration — their ideas of the temper and disposition of the people for whom the Constitution is proposed. The citizens of the United States, however different in some other respects, are well known to agree in one strongly-marked feature of their character — a warm and keen sense of freedom and independence. This sense has been heightened by the glorious result of their late struggle against all the efforts of one of the most powerful nations of Europe. It was apprehended, I believe, by some, that a people so highly spirited would ill brook the restraints of an efficient government. I confess that this consideration did not influence my conduct. I knew my constituents to be high-spirited, but I knew them also to possess sound sense. I knew that in event they would be best pleased with that system of government which would be best, to promote their freedom and happiness. I have also often revolved this subject in my mind. I have supposed one of my constituents to ask me why I gave such a vote on a particular question. I have always thought it would be a satisfactory answer to say, Because I judged, upon the best consideration I could give, that such a vote was right, I have thought that it would be a very poor compliment to my constituents to say, that, in my opinion, such a vote would have been proper, but that I supposed a contrary one would be more agreeable to those who sent me to the Convention. I could not, even in idea, expose myself to such a retort, as, upon the last answer, might have been justly made to me — Pray, sir, what reasons have you for supposing that a right vote would displease your constituents? Is this the proper return for the high confidence they have placed in you? If they have given cause for such a surmise, it was by choosing a representative who could entertain such an opinion of them. I was under no apprehension that the good people of this state would behold with displeasure the brightness of the rays of delegated power, when it only proved the superior splendor of the luminary of which those rays were only the reflection.

A very important difficulty arose from comparing the extent of the country to be governed with the kind of government which it would be proper to establish in it. It has been an opinion, countenanced by high authority, "that the natural property of small states is to be governed as a republic; of middling ones, to be subject to a monarchy; and of large empires, to be swayed by a despotic prince; — and that the consequence is, that, in order to preserve the principles of the established government, the state must be supported in the extent it has acquired; and that the spirit of the state will alter in proportion as it extends or contracts its limits." (*Montesquieu*, b. 8, c. 20.) This opinion seems to be supported, rather than contradicted, by the history of the governments in the old world. Here, then, the difficulty appeared in full view. On one hand, the United States contain an immense extent of territory; and, according to the foregoing opinion, a despotic government is best adapted to that extent. On the other hand, it was well known, that, however the citizens of the United States might with pleasure submit to the legitimate restraints of a republican constitution, they would reject with indignation the fetters of despotism. What, then, was to be done? The idea of a confederate republic presented itself. This kind of constitution has been thought to have "all the internal advantages of a republican together with the external force of a monarchical government." (*Mont.* b. 9, c. 1, 2. *Paley*, 199, 202.)

Its description is "a convention, by which several states agree to become members of a larger one, which they intend to establish. It is a kind of assemblage of societies that constitute a *new one*, capable of increasing by means of further association." — (*Montesquieu*, b. 9, c. 1.) The *expanding* quality of such government is peculiarly fitted for the United States, the greatest part of whose territory is yet uncultivated.

But while this form of government enabled us to surmount the difficulty last mentioned, it conducted us to another, of which I am now to take notice. It left us almost without precedent or guide, and, consequently, without the benefit of that instruction which, in many cases, may be derived from the constitution, and history, and experience, of other nations. Several associations have frequently been called by the name of *confederate states*, which have not, in propriety of language, deserved it. The Swiss cantons are connected only by alliances. The United Netherlands are, indeed, an assemblage of societies; but this assemblage constitutes no *new one*, and therefore it does not correspond with the full definition of a confederate republic. The Germanic body is composed of such disproportioned and discordant materials, and its structure is so intricate and complex, that little useful knowledge can be drawn from it. Ancient history discloses, and barely discloses, to our view, some confederate republics — the Achaean league, the Lycian confederacy, and the Amphictyonic council. But the facts recorded concerning their constitutions are so few and general, and their histories are so unmarked and defective, that no satisfactory information can be collected from them concerning many particular circumstances, from an accurate discernment and comparison of which, alone, legitimate and practical inferences can be made from one constitution to another. Besides, the situation and dimensions of those confederacies, and the state of society, manners, and habits, in them, were so different from those of the United States, that the most correct descriptions could have supplied but a very small fund of applicable remark. Thus, in forming this system, we were deprived of many advantages which the history and experience of other ages and other countries would, in other cases, have afforded us.

Permit me to add, in this place, that the science even of government itself seems yet to be almost in its state of infancy. Governments, in general, have been the result of force, of fraud, and accident. After a period of six thousand years has elapsed since the creation, the United States exhibit to the world the first instance, as far as we can learn, of a nation, unattacked by external force, unconvulsed by domestic insurrections, assembling voluntarily, deliberating fully, and deciding calmly, concerning that system of government under which they would wish that they and their posterity should live. The ancients, so enlightened on other subjects, were very uninformed with regard to this. They seem scarcely to have had any idea of any other kinds of governments than the three simple forms designed by the epithets *monarchical, aristocratical*, and *democratical*. I know that much and pleasing ingenuity has been exerted, in modern times, in drawing entertaining parallels between some of the ancient constitutions and some of the mixed governments that have since existed in Europe. But I much suspect that, on strict examination, the instances of resemblance will be found to be few and weak; to be suggested by the improvements which, in subsequent ages, have been made in government, and not to be drawn immediately from the ancient constitutions themselves, as they were intended and understood by those who framed them. To illustrate this, a similar observation may be made on another subject. Admiring critics have fancied that they have discovered in their favorite *Homer* the seeds of all the improvements in philosophy and in the sciences made since his time. What induces me to be of this opinion is, that *Tacitus* — the profound politician Tacitus — who lived towards the latter end of those ages which are now denominated *ancient*, who undoubtedly had studied the constitutions of all the states and kingdoms known before and in his time, and who certainly was qualified, in an uncommon degree, for understanding the full force and operation of each of them, considers, after all he had known and read, a mixed government, composed of the three simple forms, as a thing rather to be wished than expected. And he thinks that, if such a government could even be instituted, its duration could not be long. One thing is very certain — that the doctrine of representation in government was altogether unknown to the ancients. Now, the knowledge and practice of this doctrine is, in my opinion, essential to every system that can possess the qualities of freedom, wisdom, and energy.

It is worthy of remark, and the remark may, perhaps, excite some surprise, that representation of the people is not, even at this day, the sole principle of any government in Europe. Great Britain boasts — and she may well boast — of the improvement she has made in politics by the admission of representation; for the improvement is important as far as it goes; but it by no means goes far enough. Is the executive power of Great Britain founded on representation? This is not pretended. Before the revolution, many of the kings claimed to reign by divine right, and others by hereditary right; and even at the revolution, nothing further was effected or attempted than the recognition of certain parts of an original contract, (*Blackstone*, 233,) supposed, at some former remote period, to have been made between the king and the people. A contract seems to exclude, rather than to imply, delegated power. The judges of Great Britain are appointed by the crown. The judicial authority, therefore, does not depend upon representation, even in its most remote degree. Does representation prevail in the legislative department of the British government? Even here it does not predominate, though it may serve as a check. The legislature consists of three branches — the king, the lords, and the commons. Of these, only the latter are supposed by the constitution to represent the authority of the people. This short analysis clearly shows to what a narrow corner of the British constitution the principle of representation is confined. I believe it does not extend farther, if so far, in any other government in Europe. For the American states were reserved the glory and the happiness of diffusing this vital principle throughout the constituent parts of government. Representation is the chain of communication between the people and those to whom they have committed the exercise of the powers of government. This chain may consist of one or more links, but in all cases it should be sufficiently strong and discernible.

To be left without guide or precedent was not the only difficulty in which the Convention were involved, by proposing to their constituents a plan of a confederate republic. They found themselves embarrassed with another, of peculiar delicacy and importance. I mean that of drawing a proper line between the national government and the governments of the several states. It was easy to discover a proper and satisfactory principle on the subject. Whatever object of government is confined, in its operation and effects, within the bounds of a particular state, should be considered as belonging to the government of that state; whatever object of government extends, in its operation or effects, beyond the bounds of a particular state, should be considered as belonging to the government of the United States. But though this principle be sound and satisfactory, its application to particular cases would be accompanied with much difficulty, because, in its application, room must be allowed for great discretionary latitude of construction of the principle. In order to lessen or remove the difficulty arising from discretionary construction on this subject, an enumeration of particular instances, in which the application of the principle ought to take place, has been attempted with much industry and care. It is only in mathematical science that a line can be described with mathematical precision. But I flatter myself that, upon the strictest investigation, the enumeration will be found to be safe and unexceptionable, and accurate, too, in as great a degree as accuracy can be expected in a subject of this nature. Particulars under this head will be more properly explained, when we descend to the minute view of the enumeration which is made in the proposed Constitution.

After all, it will be necessary that, on a subject so peculiarly delicate as this, much prudence, much candor, much moderation, and much liberality, should be exercised and displayed both by the federal government and by the governments of the several states. It is to be hoped that those virtues in government will be exercised and displayed, when we consider that the powers of the federal government and those of the state governments are drawn from sources equally pure. If a difference can be discovered between them, it is in favor of the federal government, because that government is founded on a representation of the *whole* Union; whereas the government of any particular state is founded only on the representation of a part, inconsiderable when compared with the whole. Is it not more reasonable to suppose that the counsels of the whole will embrace the interest of every part, than that the counsels of any part will embrace the interests of the whole?

I intend not, sir, by this description of the difficulties with which the Convention were surrounded, to magnify their skill or their merit in surmounting them, or to insinuate that any predicament in which the Convention stood should prevent the closest and most cautious scrutiny into the performance which they have exhibited to their constituents and to the world. My intention is of far other and higher aim — to evince, by the conflicts and difficulties which must arise from the many and powerful causes which I have enumerated, that it is hopeless and impracticable to form a constitution which, in every part, will be acceptable to every citizen, or even to every government, in the United States; and that all which can be expected is, to form such a constitution as, upon the whole, is the best that can possibly be obtained. Man and perfection! — a state and perfection! — an assemblage of states and perfection! Can we reasonably expect, however ardently we may wish, to behold the glorious union?

I can well recollect, though I believe I cannot convey to others, the impression which, on many occasions, was made by the difficulties which surrounded and pressed the Convention. The great undertaking sometimes seemed to be at a stand; at other times, its motion seemed to be retrograde. At the conclusion, however, of our work, many of the members expressed their astonishment at the success with which it terminated.

Having enumerated some of the difficulties which the Convention were obliged to encounter in the course of their proceedings, I shall next point out the end which they proposed to accomplish. Our wants, our talents, our affections, our passions, all tell us that we were made for a state of society. But a state of society could not be supported long or happily without some civil restraint. It is true that, in a state of nature, any one individual may act uncontrolled by others; but it is equally true that, in such a state, every other individual may act uncontrolled by him. Amidst this universal independence, the dissensions and animosities between interfering members of the society would be numerous and ungovernable. The consequence would be, that each member, in such a natural state, would enjoy less liberty, and suffer more interruption, than he would in a regulated society. Hence the universal introduction of governments of some kind or other into the social state. The liberty of every member is increased by this introduction; for each gains more by the limitation of the freedom of every other member, than he loses by the limitation of his own. The result is, that civil government is necessary to the perfection and happiness of man. In forming this government, and carrying it into execution, it is *essential* that the *interest* and *authority* of the whole community should be binding in every part of it.

The foregoing principles and conclusions are generally admitted to be just and sound with regard to the nature and formation of single governments, and the duty of submission to them. In some cases, they will apply, with much propriety and force, to states already formed. The advantages and necessity of civil government among individuals in society, are not greater or stronger than, in some situations and circumstances, are the advantages and necessity of a federal government among states. A natural and very important question now presents itself — Is such the situation, are such the circumstances, of the United States? A proper answer to this question will unfold some very interesting truths.

The United States may adopt any one of four different systems. They may become consolidated into one government, in which the separate existence of the states shall be entirely absolved. They may reject any plan of union or association, and act as separate and unconnected states. They may form two or more confederacies. They may unite in one federal republic. Which of these systems ought to have been formed by the Convention? To support, with vigor, a single government over the whole extent of the United States, would demand a system of the most unqualified and the most unremitted despotism. Such a number of separate states, contiguous in situation, unconnected and disunited in government, would be, at one time, the prey of foreign force, foreign influence, and foreign intrigue; at another, the victims of mutual rage, rancor, and revenge. Neither of these systems found advocates in the late Convention. I presume they will not find advocates in this. Would it be proper to divide the United States into two or more confederacies? It will not be unadvisable to take a more minute survey of this subject. Some aspects under which it may be viewed are far from being, at first sight, uninviting. Two or more confederacies would be each more compact and more manageable than a single one extending over the same territory. By dividing the United States into two or more confederacies, the great collision of interests apparently or really different and contrary in the *whole extent* of their dominion, would be broken, and, in a great measure, disappear, in the several parts. But these advantages, which are discovered from certain points of view, are greatly overbalanced by inconveniences that will appear on a more accurate examination. Animosities, and perhaps wars, would arise from assigning the extent, the limits, and the rights, of the different confederacies. The expenses of governing would be multiplied by the number of federal governments. The danger resulting from foreign influence and mutual dissensions, would not, perhaps, be less great and alarming in the instance of different confederacies, than in the instance of different though more numerous unassociated states.

These observations, and many others that might be made on the subject, will be sufficient to evince that a division of the United States into a number of separate confederacies would probably be an unsatisfactory and an unsuccessful experiment. The remaining system which the American states may adopt, is a union of them under one confederate republic. It will not be necessary to employ much time, or many arguments, to show that this is the most eligible system that can be proposed. By adopting this system, the vigor and decision of a wide-spreading monarchy may be joined to the freedom and beneficence of a contracted republic. The extent of territory, the diversity of climate and soil, the number, and greatness, and connection, of lakes and rivers with which the United States are intersected and almost surrounded, — all indicate an enlarged government to be fit and advantageous for them. The principles and dispositions of their citizens indicate that, in this government, liberty shall reign triumphant. Such, indeed, have been the general opinions and wishes entertained since the era of independence. If those opinions and wishes are as well founded as they have been general, the late Convention were justified in proposing to their constituents *one* confederate republic, as the best system of a national government for the United States.

In forming this system, it was proper to give minute attention to the interest of all the parts; but there was a duty of still higher import — to feel and to show a predominating regard to the superior interests of the whole. If this great principle had not prevailed, the plan before us would never have made its appearance. The same principle that was so necessary in forming it, is equally necessary in our deliberations, whether we should reject or ratify it.

I make these observations with a design to prove and illustrate this great and important truth — that, in our decisions on the work of the late Convention, we should not limit our views and regards to the state of Pennsylvania. The aim of the Convention was to form a system of good and efficient government, on the more extensive scale of the United States. In this, and in every other instance, the work should be judged with the same spirit with which it was performed. A principle of duty, as well as candor, demands this.

We have remarked that civil government is necessary to the perfection of society; we now remark that civil liberty is necessary to the perfection of civil government. Civil liberty is natural liberty itself, divested of only that part which, placed in the government, produces more good and happiness to the community than if it had remained in the individual. Hence it follows that civil liberty, while it resigns a part of natural liberty, retains the free and generous exercise of all the human faculties, so far as it is compatible with the public welfare.

In considering and developing the nature and end of the system before us, it is necessary to mention another kind of liberty, which has not yet, as far as I know, received a name. I shall distinguish it by the appellation of *federal liberty*. When a single government is instituted, the individuals of which it is composed surrender to it a part of their natural independence, which they before enjoyed as men, When a confederate republic is instituted, the communities of which it is composed surrender to it a part of their political independence, which they before enjoyed as states. The principles which directed, in the former case, what part of the natural liberty of the man ought to be given up, and what part ought to be retained, will give similar directions in the latter case. The states should resign to the national government that part, and that part only, of their political liberty, which, placed in that government, will produce more good to the whole than if it had remained in the several states. While they resign this part of their political liberty, they retain the free and generous exercise of all their other faculties, as states, so far as it is compatible with the welfare of the general and superintending confederacy.

Since *states*, as well as *citizens*, are represented in the Constitution before us, and form the objects on which that Constitution is proposed to operate, it was necessary to notice and define *federal* as well as *civil* liberty.

These general reflections have been made in order to introduce, with more propriety and advantage, a practical illustration of the end proposed to be accomplished by the late Convention.

It has been too well known — it has been too severely-felt — that the present Confederation is inadequate to the government, and to the exigencies, of the United States. The great struggle for Liberty in this country, should it be unsuccessful, will probably be the last one which she will have for her existence and prosperity in any part of the globe. And it must be confessed that this struggle has, in some of the stages of its progress, been attended with symptoms that foreboded no fortunate issue. To the iron hand of Tyranny, which was lifted up against her, she manifested, indeed, an intrepid superiority. She broke in pieces the fetters which were forged for her, and showed that she was unassailable by force. But she was environed with dangers of another kind, and springing from a very different source. While she kept her eye steadily fixed on the efforts of oppression, licentiousness was secretly undermining the rock on which she stood.

Need I call to your remembrance the *contrasted* scenes of which we have been witnesses? On the glorious conclusion of our conflict with Britain, what high expectations were formed concerning us by others! What high expectations did we form concerning ourselves! Have those expectations been realized? No. What has been the cause? Did our citizens lose their perseverance and magnanimity? No. Did they become insensible of resentment and indignation at any high-handed attempt that might have been made to injure or enslave them? No. What, then, has been the cause? The truth is, we dreaded danger only on one side: this we manfully repelled. But, on another side, danger, not less formidable but more insidious, stole in upon us; and our unsuspicious tempers were not sufficiently attentive either to its approach or to its operations. Those whom foreign strength could not overpower, have well nigh become the victims of internal anarchy.

If we become a little more particular, we shall find that the foregoing representation is by no means exaggerated. When we had baffled all the menaces of foreign power, we neglected to establish among ourselves a government that would insure domestic vigor and stability. What was the consequence? The commencement of peace was the commencement of every disgrace and distress that could befall a people in a peaceful state. Devoid of *national power*, we could not prohibit the extravagance of our importations, nor could we derive a revenue from their excess. Devoid of national *importance*, we could not procure, for our exports, a tolerable sale at foreign markets. Devoid of national *credit*, we saw our public securities melt in the hands of the holders, like snow before the sun. Devoid of national *dignity*, we could not, in some instances, perform our treaties, on our part; and, in other instances, we could neither obtain nor compel the performance of them, on the part of others. Devoid of national *energy*, we could not carry into execution our own resolutions, decisions, or laws.

Shall I become more particular still? The tedious detail would disgust me. The years of languor are now over. We have felt the dishonor with which we have been covered — we have seen the destruction with which we have been threatened. We have penetrated to the causes of both, and when we have once discovered them, we have begun to search for the means of removing them. For the confirmation of these remarks, I need not appeal to an enumeration of facts. The proceedings of Congress, and of the several states, are replete with them. They all point out the weakness and insufficiency as the cause, and an *efficient* general government as the only cure, of our political distempers.

Under these impressions, and with these views, was the late Convention appointed; and under these impressions, and with these views, the late Convention met.

We now see the great end which they proposed to accomplish. It was to frame, for the consideration of their constituents, one federal and national constitution — a constitution that would produce the advantages of good, and prevent the inconveniences of bad government — a constitution whose beneficence and energy would pervade the whole Union, and bind and embrace the interests of every part — a constitution that would insure peace, freedom, and happiness, to the states and people of America.

We are now naturally led to examine the means by which they proposed to accomplish this end. This opens more particularly to our view the discussion before us. But, previously to our entering upon it, it will not be improper to stale some general and leading principles of government, which will receive particular application in the course of our investigations.

There necessarily exists, in every government, a power from which there is no appeal, and which, for that reason, may be termed supreme, absolute, and uncontrollable. Where does this power reside? To this question writers on different governments will give different answers. Sir William Blackstone will tell you, that in Britain the power is lodged in the British Parliament; that the Parliament may alter the form of the government; and that its power is absolute, without control. The idea of a constitution, limiting and superintending the operations of legislative authority, seems not to have been accurately understood in Britain. There are, at least, no traces of practice conformable to such a principle. The British constitution is just what the British Parliament pleases. When the Parliament transferred legislative authority to Henry VIII., the act transferring could not, in the strict acceptation of the term, be called unconstitutional.

To control the power and conduct of the legislature, by an overruling constitution, was an improvement in the science and practice of government reserved to the American states.

Perhaps some politician, who has not considered with sufficient accuracy our political systems, would answer that, in our governments, the supreme power was vested in the constitutions. This opinion approaches a step nearer to the truth, but does not reach it. The truth is, that, in our governments, the supreme, absolute, and uncontrollable power *remains* in the people. As our constitutions are superior to our legislatures, so the people are superior to our constitutions. Indeed, the superiority, in this last instance, is much greater; for the people possess over our constitutions control in *act*, as well as right.

The consequence is, that the people may change the constitutions whenever and however they please. This is a right of which no positive institution can ever deprive them.

These important truths, sir, are far from being merely speculative. We, at this moment, speak and deliberate under their immediate and benign influence. To the operation of these truths we are to ascribe the scene, hitherto unparalleled, which America now exhibits to the world — a gentle, a peaceful, a voluntary, and a deliberate transition from one constitution of government to another. In other parts of the world, the idea of revolutions in government is, by a mournful and an indissoluble association, connected with the idea of wars, and all the calamities attendant on wars. But happy experience teaches us to view such revolutions in a very different light — to consider them only as progressive steps in improving the knowledge of government, and increasing the happiness of society and mankind.

Oft have I marked, with silent pleasure and admiration, the force and prevalence, through the United States, of the principle that the supreme power resides in the people, and that they never part with it. It may be called the *panacea* in politics. There can be no disorder in the community but may here receive a radical cure. If the error be in the legislature, it may be corrected by the constitution; if in the constitution, it may be corrected by the people. There is a remedy, therefore, for every distemper in government, if the people are not wanting to themselves; if they are wanting to themselves, there is no remedy. From their power, as we have seen, there is no appeal; of their error there is no superior principle of correction.

There are three simple species of government — monarchy, where the supreme power is in a single person; aristocracy, where the supreme power is in a select assembly, the members of which either fill up, by election, the vacancies in their own body, or succeed to their places in it by inheritance, property, or in respect of some *personal* right or qualification; a republic or democracy, where the people at large *retain* the supreme power, and act either collectively or by representation.

Each of these species of government has its advantages and disadvantages.

The advantages of a *monarchy* are, strength, despatch, secrecy, unity of counsel. Its disadvantages are, tyranny, expense, ignorance of the situation and wants of the people, insecurity, unnecessary wars, evils attending elections or successions.

The advantages of *aristocracy* are, wisdom, arising from experience and education. Its disadvantages are, dissensions among themselves, oppression to the lower orders.

The advantages of *democracy* are, liberty, equality, cautious and salutary laws, public spirit, frugality, peace, opportunities of exciting and producing abilities of the best citizens. Its disadvantages are, dissensions, the delay and disclosure of public counsels, the imbecility of public measures, retarded by the necessity of a numerous consent.

A government may be composed of two or more of the simple forms above mentioned. Such is the British government. It would be an improper government for the United States, because it is inadequate to such an extent of territory, and because it is suited to an establishment of different orders of men. A more minute comparison between some parts of the British constitution, and some parts of the plan before us, may perhaps find a proper place in a subsequent period of our business.

What is the nature and kind of that government which has been proposed for the United States by the late Convention? In its principle, it is purely democratical. But that principle is applied in different forms, in order to obtain the advantages, and exclude the inconveniences, of the simple modes of government.

If we take an extended and accurate view of it, we shall find the streams of power running in different directions, in different dimensions, and at different heights — watering, adorning, and fertilizing, the fields and meadows through which their courses are led; but if we trace them, we shall discover that they all originally flow from one abundant fountain.

In this Constitution, *all authority is derived from the people.*

Fit occasions will hereafter offer for particular remarks on the different parts of the plan. I have now to ask pardon of the house for detaining them so long.

A Landholder IV by Oliver Ellsworth

Editor's Introduction:

If Roger Sherman was the most respected statesman in Connecticut, Oliver Ellsworth may have been a close second. Ellsworth, along with Sherman and Oliver Wolcott (his father-in-law), led the charge for ratification in the Nutmeg State. Both Ellsworth and Sherman participated in the Philadelphia Convention, and both placed their stamp on the Connecticut Compromise and the Three-Fifths Compromise, but Ellsworth, more than Sherman, led the public charge for ratification through the press.

Ellsworth served in the Continental Congress during the American War for Independence and for four years was a judge on the Connecticut Supreme Court. He became convinced that the Articles of Confederation were incapable of maintaining the Union and supported strengthening the central government. Yet Ellsworth believed that the States should still be represented and challenged the creation of a "national government" during the Philadelphia Convention. He preferred to keep the name "United States" and insisted on equal representation in at least one branch of the legislature. During his life,

Ellsworth was a staunch defender of a "federal" rather than "national" republic, and he even supported secession in 1794.

After the Constitution was ratified in 1788, Connecticut sent him to the United States Senate and George Washington later appointed him to the United States Supreme Court where he served as Chief Justice from 1796 until 1800 where he was succeeded by John Marshall.

Ellsworth's "Landholder" essays directly attacked some of the leading opponents of the Constitution, including Elbridge Gerry of Massachusetts and George Mason of Virginia. In this essay, Ellsworth sought to reassure the public that the Constitution did not create a consolidated government and that the States, and the people thereof, retained control over the system through fair and adequate representation. As he wrote in the conclusion, "State representation and government is the very basis of the congressional power proposed."

A Landholder IV

November 26, 1787

By Oliver Ellsworth of Connecticut

Remarks on the objections made by the Hon. ELBRIDGE GERRY, to the new constitution.

To the Landholders and Farmers.

To censure a man for an opinion in which he declares himself honest, and in a matter of which all men have a right to judge, is highly injurious; at the same time, when the opinions even of honourable men are submitted to the people, a tribunal before which the meanest citizen hath a right to speak, they must abide the consequences of public stricture. We are ignorant whether the honorable gentlemen possesses state dignities or emoluments which will be endangered by the new system, or hath motives of personality to prejudice his mind and throw him into the opposition; or if it be so, do not wish to evade the objections by such a charge. As a member of the general

Convention, and deputy of a great state, this honorable person hath a right to speak and be heard. It gives us pleasure to know the extent of what may be objected or even surmised, by one whose situation was the best to spy danger, and mark the defective parts of the constitution, if any such there be. Mr. Gerry, tho' in the character of an objector, tells us "he was fully convinced that to preserve the union an efficient government was indispensibly necessary, and that it would be difficult to make proper amendments to the old articles of confederation" therefore by his own concession there was an indispensible necessity of a system, in many particulars entirely new. He tells us further "that if the people reject this altogether, anarchy may ensue" and what situation can be pictured more awful than a total dissolution had better be risked than to fall back into that state of rude violence, in which every man's hand is against his neighbour, and there is no judge to decide between them or power of justice to control. But we hope to show that there are no such alarming defects in the proposed structure of government, and that while a public force is created, the liberties of the people have every possible guard.

Several of the honorable Gentleman's objections are expressed in such vague and indecisive terms, that they rather deserve the name of insinuations, and we know not against what particular parts of the system they are pointed. Others are explicit, and if real deserve serious attention. His first objection is "that there is no adequate provision for a representation of the people". This must have respect either to the number of representatives, or to the manner in which they are chosen. The proper number to constitute a safe representation is a matter of judgement, in which honest and wise men often disagree. Were it possible for all the people to convene and give their personal assent, some would think this the best mode of making laws, but in the present instance it is impracticable. The state representation is composed of one or two from every town and district, which composes an assembly not so large as to be unwieldy in acting nor so expensive as to burden the people. But if so numerous a representation were made from every part of the United States with our present population, the new Congress would consist of three thousand men; with the population of Great Britain to which we may arrive in a half century, of ten thousand; and with the population of France, which we shall probably equal in a century and a half, of thirty thousand.

Such a body of men might be an army to defend the country in case of foreign invasion, but not a legislature, and the expense to support them would equal the whole national revenue. By the proposed constitution the new Congress will consist of nearly one hundred men. When our population is equal to Great Britain of three hundred men, and when equal to France of nine hundred. Plenty of Lawgivers! why any gentlemen should wish for more is inconceivable.

Considering the immense territory of America, the objection with many will be on the other side; that when this whole is populated it will constitute a legislature unmanagable by its members. Convention foreseeing this danger, have so worded the article, that if the people should at any time judge necessary, they may diminish the representation.

As the state legislature have to regulate the internal policy, of every town and neighborhood, it is convenient enough to have one or two men, particularly acquainted with every small district of country, its interests, parties, and passions. But the federal legislature can take cognizance only of national questions and interests, which in their very nature are general, and for this purpose five or ten honest and wise men are chosen from each state men who have had previous experience in state legislation, will be more competent than a hundred. From an acquaintance with their own state legislatures, they will always know the sense of the people at large, and the expence of supporting such a number will be as much as we ought to incur.

If the Hon. gentleman, in saying "there is no adequate provision for a representation of the people" refers to the manner of choosing them, a reply to this is naturally blended with his second objection "that they have no security for the right of election" it is impossible to conceive what greater security can be given, by any form of words, than we here find.

The federal representatives are to be chosen by the people. Every freeman is an elector. The same qualifications which enable you to vote for state representatives, give you federal voice. It is a right you cannot loose [sic], unless you first annihilate the state legislature, and declare yourselves incapable of electing, which is a degree of infatuation improbable as a second deluge to drown the world.

Your own assemblies are to regulate the formalities of this choice, and unless they betray you, you cannot be betrayed. But perhaps it may be said, Congress have a power to control this formality as to the time and place of electing, and we allow they have: But this objections which at first looks frightful was designed as a guard to the privileges of the electors. Even state assemblies may have their madness and passion, this tho' not probable is still possible.

We have a recent instance in the state of Rhode Island, where a desperate junto are governing, contrary to the sense of a great majority of the people. It may be the case in any other state, and should it ever happen, that the ignorance or rashness of the state assemblies, in a fit of jealousy should deny you this sacred right, the deliberate justice of the continent, is enabled to interpose, and restore you a federal voice. This right is therefore more inviolably guarded than it can be by the government of your state, for it is guaranteed by the whole empire. Tho' out of the order in which the Hon. Gentleman proposes his doubts, I wish here to notice some opinions which he makes. The proposed plan among others he tells us involves these questions "whether the several state government, shall be altered as in effect to be dissolved? Whether in lieu of the state governments the national constitution now proposed shall be substituted?" I wish for sagacity to see on what these questions are founded. No alteration in the state governments is even proposed, but they are to remain identically the same that they now are. Some powers are to be given into the hands of your federal representatives, but these powers are all in their nature general, such as must be exercised by the whole or not at all, and such as are absolutely necessary; or your commerce, the price of your commodities, your riches and your safety will be the sport of every foreign adventurer. Why are we told of the dissolution of our state governments, when by this plan they are indissolubly linked. They must stand or fall, live or die together. The national legislature consists of two houses, a senate and a house of Representative. The senate is to be chosen by the assemblies of the particular states; so that if the assemblies are dissolved, the senate dissolves with them. The national representatives are to be chosen by the same electors, and under the same qualifications, as choose state representatives; so that if the state representation be dissolved, the national representation is gone of course.

State representation and government is the very basis of the congressional power proposed. This is the most valuable link in the chain of connexion, and affords double security for the rights of the people. Your liberties are pledged to you by your own state, and by the power of the whole empire. You have a voice in the government of your own state, and in the government of the whole. Were not the gentleman on whom the remarks are made very honourable, and the eminence of office raised above a suspicion of cunning, we should think he had, in this instance, insinuated merely to alarm the fears of the people. His other objections will be mentioned in some future number of the

Landholder.

Federalist No. 14 by James Madison

Editor's Introduction:

James Madison's *Federalist* No. 14 is one of the finest expositions on the "federal republic" written in the ratification period. Gone are his designs for a "national government" at the Philadelphia Convention where the States were considered hindrances to effective central authority. In fact, Madison stated in *Federalist* No. 14 that they were indispensable for the "self-preservation" of the general authority due to their influence over local matters. But the Union, in Madison's opinion, would secure these thirteen "primitive states" by ensuring adequate defense and commerce, something the Articles of Confederation failed to provide. Notice that Madison attempted to sell the Constitution on its common points of interest—commerce and defense—while shoring up the argument that the States would still be an integral part of the system. These were the key arguments for ratification. If the public could be convinced that the Constitution maintained the federal republic while strengthening the few, delegated, and defined powers of the central authority, the document was sure to sail through the State ratifying conventions.

Federalist No. 14

November 30, 1787

By James Madison of Virginia

To the People of the State of New York:

WE HAVE seen the necessity of the Union, as our bulwark against foreign danger, as the conservator of peace among ourselves, as the guardian of our commerce and other common interests, as the only substitute for those military establishments which have subverted the liberties of the Old World, and as the proper antidote for the diseases of faction, which have proved fatal to other popular governments, and of which alarming symptoms have been betrayed by our own. All that remains, within this branch of our inquiries, is to take notice of an objection that may be drawn from the great extent of country which the Union embraces. A few observations on this subject will be the more proper, as it is perceived that the adversaries of the new Constitution are availing themselves of the prevailing prejudice with regard to the practicable sphere of republican administration, in order to supply, by imaginary difficulties, the want of those solid objections which they endeavor in vain to find.

The error which limits republican government to a narrow district has been unfolded and refuted in preceding papers. I remark here only that it seems to owe its rise and prevalence chiefly to the confounding of a republic with a democracy, applying to the former reasonings drawn from the nature of the latter. The true distinction between these forms was also adverted to on a former occasion. It is, that in a democracy, the people meet and exercise the government in person; in a republic, they assemble and administer it by their representatives and agents. A democracy, consequently, will be confined to a small spot. A republic may be extended over a large region.

To this accidental source of the error may be added the artifice of some celebrated authors, whose writings have had a great share in forming the modern standard of political opinions. Being subjects either of an absolute or limited monarchy, they have endeavored to heighten the advantages, or palliate the evils of those forms, by placing in comparison the vices and defects of the republican, and by citing as specimens of the latter the turbulent democracies of ancient Greece and modern Italy. Under the confusion of names, it has been an easy task to transfer to a republic observations applicable to a democracy only; and among others, the observation that it can never be established but among a small number of people, living within a small compass of territory.

Such a fallacy may have been the less perceived, as most of the popular governments of antiquity were of the democratic species; and even in modern Europe, to which we owe the great principle of representation, no example is seen of a government wholly popular, and founded, at the same time, wholly on that principle. If Europe has the merit of discovering this great mechanical power in government, by the simple agency of which the will of the largest political body may be concentrated, and its force directed to any object which the public good requires, America can claim the merit of making the discovery the basis of unmixed and extensive republics. It is only to be lamented that any of her citizens should wish to deprive her of the additional merit of displaying its full efficacy in the establishment of the comprehensive system now under her consideration.

As the natural limit of a democracy is that distance from the central point which will just permit the most remote citizens to assemble as often as their public functions demand, and will include no greater number than can join in those functions; so the natural limit of a republic is that distance from the centre which will barely allow the representatives to meet as often as may be necessary for the administration of public affairs. Can it be said that the limits of the United States exceed this distance? It will not be said by those who recollect that the Atlantic coast is the longest side of the Union, that during the term of thirteen years, the representatives of the States have been almost continually assembled, and that the members from the most distant States are not chargeable with greater intermissions of attendance than those from the States in the neighborhood of Congress.

That we may form a juster estimate with regard to this interesting subject, let us resort to the actual dimensions of the Union. The limits, as fixed by the treaty of peace, are: on the east the Atlantic, on the south the latitude of thirty-one degrees, on the west the Mississippi, and on the north an irregular line running in some instances beyond the forty-fifth degree, in others falling as low as the forty-second. The southern shore of Lake Erie lies below that latitude. Computing the distance between the thirty-first and forty-fifth degrees, it amounts to nine hundred and seventy-three common miles; computing it from thirty-one to forty-two degrees, to seven hundred and sixty-four miles and a half. Taking the mean for the distance, the amount will be eight hundred and sixty-eight miles and three-fourths. The mean distance from the Atlantic to the Mississippi does not probably exceed seven hundred and fifty miles. On a comparison of this extent with that of several countries in Europe, the practicability of rendering our system commensurate to it appears to be demonstrable. It is not a great deal larger than Germany, where a diet representing the whole empire is continually assembled; or than Poland before the late dismemberment, where another national diet was the depositary of the supreme power. Passing by France and Spain, we find that in Great Britain, inferior as it may be in size, the representatives of the northern extremity of the island have as far to travel to the national council as will be required of those of the most remote parts of the Union.

Favorable as this view of the subject may be, some observations remain which will place it in a light still more satisfactory.

In the first place it is to be remembered that the general government is not to be charged with the whole power of making and administering laws. Its jurisdiction is limited to certain enumerated objects, which concern all the members of the republic, but which are not to be attained by the separate provisions of any. The subordinate governments, which can extend their care to all those other subjects which can be separately provided for, will retain their due authority and activity. Were it proposed by the plan of the convention to abolish the governments of the particular States, its adversaries would have some ground for their objection; though it would not be difficult to show that if they were abolished the general government would be compelled, by the principle of self-preservation, to reinstate them in their proper jurisdiction.

A second observation to be made is that the immediate object of the federal Constitution is to secure the union of the thirteen primitive States, which we know to be practicable; and to add to them such other States as may arise in their own bosoms, or in their neighborhoods, which we cannot doubt to be equally practicable. The arrangements that may be necessary for those angles and fractions of our territory which lie on our northwestern frontier, must be left to those whom further discoveries and experience will render more equal to the task.

Let it be remarked, in the third place, that the intercourse throughout the Union will be facilitated by new improvements. Roads will everywhere be shortened, and kept in better order; accommodations for travelers will be multiplied and meliorated; an interior navigation on our eastern side will be opened throughout, or nearly throughout, the whole extent of the thirteen States. The communication between the Western and Atlantic districts, and between different parts of each, will be rendered more and more easy by those numerous canals with which the beneficence of nature has intersected our country, and which part finds it so little difficult to connect and complete.

A fourth and still more important consideration is, that as almost every State will, on one side or other, be a frontier, and will thus find, in regard to its safety, an inducement to make some sacrifices for the sake of the general protection; so the States which lie at the greatest distance from the heart of the Union, and which, of course, may partake least of the ordinary circulation of its benefits, will be at the same time immediately contiguous to foreign nations, and will consequently stand, on particular occasions, in greatest need of its strength and resources. It may be inconvenient for Georgia, or the States forming our western or northeastern borders, to send their representatives to the seat of government; but they would find it more so to struggle alone against an invading enemy, or even to support alone the whole expense of those precautions which may be dictated by the neighborhood of continual danger. If they should derive less benefit, therefore, from the Union in some respects than the less distant States, they will derive greater benefit from it in other respects, and thus the proper equilibrium will be maintained throughout.

I submit to you, my fellow-citizens, these considerations, in full confidence that the good sense which has so often marked your decisions will allow them their due weight and effect; and that you will never suffer difficulties, however formidable in appearance, or however fashionable the error on which they may be founded, to drive you into the gloomy and perilous scene into which the advocates for disunion would conduct you. Hearken not to the unnatural voice which tells you that the people of America, knit together as they are by so many cords of affection, can no longer live together as members of the same family; can no longer continue the mutual guardians of their mutual happiness; can no longer be fellow citizens of one great, respectable, and flourishing empire. Hearken not to the voice which petulantly tells you that the form of government recommended for your adoption is a novelty in the political world; that it has never yet had a place in the theories of the wildest projectors; that it rashly attempts what it is impossible to accomplish. No, my countrymen, shut your ears against this unhallowed language. Shut your hearts against the poison which it conveys; the kindred blood which flows in the veins of American citizens, the mingled blood which they have shed in defense of their sacred rights, consecrate their Union, and excite horror at the idea of their becoming aliens, rivals, enemies. And if novelties are to be shunned, believe me, the most alarming of all novelties, the most wild of all projects, the most rash of all attempts, is that of rendering us in pieces, in order to preserve our liberties and promote our happiness. But why is the experiment of an extended republic to be rejected, merely because it may comprise what is new? Is it not the glory of the people of America, that, whilst they have paid a decent regard to the opinions of former times and other nations, they have not suffered a blind veneration for antiquity, for custom, or for names, to overrule the suggestions of their own good sense, the knowledge of their own situation, and the lessons of their own experience? To this manly spirit, posterity will be indebted for the possession, and the world for the example, of the numerous innovations displayed on the American theatre, in favor of private rights and public happiness. Had no important step been taken by the leaders of the Revolution for which a precedent could not be discovered, no government established of which an exact model did not present itself, the people of the United States might, at this moment have been numbered among the melancholy victims of misguided councils, must at best have been laboring under the weight of some of those forms which have crushed the liberties of the rest of mankind. Happily for America, happily, we trust, for the whole human race, they pursued a new and more noble course. They accomplished a revolution which has no parallel in the annals of human society. They reared the fabrics of governments which have no model on the face of the globe. They formed the design of a great Confederacy, which it is incumbent on their successors to improve and perpetuate. If their works betray imperfections, we wonder at the fewness of them. If they erred most in the structure of the Union, this was the work most difficult to be executed; this is the work which has been new modelled by the act of your convention, and it is that act on which you are now to deliberate and to decide.

Federalist No. 15 by Alexander Hamilton

Editor's Introduction:

Hamilton followed Madison's pro-federalism essay with two installments in the *Federalist* that nearly undermined every argument other proponents made in favor of a federal republic. Hamilton wildly asserted that the United States had reached the "last stage of national humiliation" by clinging to the Articles of Confederation and its outmoded model of revenue collection and military preparation. The culprit? In Hamilton's mind the method of enforcement in the Articles. States could not be compelled to support Congressional legislation under the Articles unless by force, whereas because the new Constitution acted on individuals, revenue collection—taxes—and overall compliance would be much more effective, though Hamilton insisted that, "It is essential to the idea of a law, that it be attended with a sanction; or, in other words, a penalty or punishment for disobedience." While other proponents of the document pointed out that the Constitution would operate on individuals rather than States, Hamilton's forceful presentation of the matter certainly stoked fears of an oppressive central authority that could bypass any State check on usurpation of powers. In retrospect, the ability for the general government to act on individuals has opened the door to a slew of dubious taxes and regulations.

Federalist No. 15

December 1, 1787

By Alexander Hamilton of New York

To the People of the State of New York.

IN THE course of the preceding papers, I have endeavored, my fellow-citizens, to place before you, in a clear and convincing light, the importance of Union to your political safety and happiness. I have unfolded to you a complication of dangers to which you would be exposed, should you permit that sacred knot which binds the people of America together be severed or dissolved by ambition or by avarice, by jealousy or by misrepresentation. In the sequel of the inquiry through which I propose to accompany you, the truths intended to be inculcated will receive further confirmation from facts and arguments hitherto unnoticed. If the road over which you will still have to pass should in some places appear to you tedious or irksome, you will recollect that you are in quest of information on a subject the most momentous which can engage the attention of a free people, that the field through which you have to travel is in itself spacious, and that the difficulties of the journey have been unnecessarily increased by the mazes with which sophistry has beset the way. It will be my aim to remove the obstacles from your progress in as compendious a manner as it can be done, without sacrificing utility to despatch.

In pursuance of the plan which I have laid down for the discussion of the subject, the point next in order to be examined is the "insufficiency of the present Confederation to the preservation of the Union." It may perhaps be asked what need there is of reasoning or proof to illustrate a position which is not either controverted or doubted, to which the understandings and feelings of all classes of men assent, and which in substance is admitted by the opponents as well as by the friends of the new Constitution. It must in truth be acknowledged that, however these may differ in other respects, they in general appear to harmonize in this sentiment, at least, that there are material imperfections in our national system, and that something is necessary to be done to rescue us from impending anarchy. The facts that support this opinion are no longer objects of speculation. They have forced themselves upon the sensibility of the people at large, and have at length extorted from those, whose mistaken policy has had the principal share in precipitating the extremity at which we are arrived, a reluctant confession of the reality of those defects in the scheme of our federal government, which have been long pointed out and regretted by the intelligent friends of the Union.

We may indeed with propriety be said to have reached almost the last stage of national humiliation. There is scarcely anything that can wound the pride or degrade the character of an independent nation which we do not experience. Are there engagements to the performance of which we are held by every tie respectable among men? These are the subjects of constant and unblushing violation. Do we owe debts to foreigners and to our own citizens contracted in a time of imminent peril for the preservation of our political existence? These remain without any proper or satisfactory provision for their discharge. Have we valuable territories and important posts in the possession of a foreign power which, by express stipulations, ought long since to have been surrendered? These are still retained, to the prejudice of our interests, not less than of our rights. Are we in a condition to resent or to repel the aggression? We have neither troops, nor treasury, nor government.(a) Are we even in a condition to remonstrate with dignity? The just imputations on our own faith, in respect to the same treaty, ought first to be removed. Are we entitled by nature and compact to a free participation in the navigation of the Mississippi? Spain excludes us from it. Is public credit an indispensable resource in time of public danger? We seem to have abandoned its cause as desperate and irretrievable. Is commerce of importance to national wealth? Ours is at the lowest point of declension. Is respectability in the eyes of foreign powers a safeguard against foreign encroachments? The imbecility of our government even forbids them to treat with us. Our ambassadors abroad are the mere pageants of mimic sovereignty. Is a violent and unnatural decrease in the value of land a symptom of national distress? The price of improved land in most parts of the country is much lower than can be accounted for by the quantity of waste land at market, and can only be fully explained by that want of private and public confidence, which are so alarmingly prevalent among all ranks, and which have a direct tendency to depreciate property of every kind. Is private credit the friend and patron of industry? That most useful kind which relates to borrowing and lending is reduced within the narrowest limits, and this still more from an opinion of insecurity than from the scarcity of money. To shorten an enumeration of particulars which can afford neither pleasure nor instruction, it may in general be demanded, what indication is there of national disorder, poverty, and insignificance that could befall a community so peculiarly blessed with natural advantages as we are, which does not form a part of the dark catalogue of our public misfortunes?

This is the melancholy situation to which we have been brought by those very maxims and councils which would now deter us from adopting the proposed Constitution; and which, not content with having conducted us to the brink of a precipice, seem resolved to plunge us into the abyss that awaits us below. Here, my countrymen, impelled by every motive that ought to influence an enlightened people, let us make a firm stand for our safety, our tranquillity, our dignity, our reputation. Let us at last break the fatal charm which has too long seduced us from the paths of felicity and prosperity.

It is true, as has been before observed that facts, too stubborn to be resisted, have produced a species of general assent to the abstract proposition that there exist material defects in our national system; but the usefulness of the concession, on the part of the old adversaries of federal measures, is destroyed by a strenuous opposition to a remedy, upon the only principles that can give it a chance of success. While they admit that the government of the United States is destitute of energy, they contend against conferring upon it those powers which are requisite to supply that energy. They seem still to aim at things repugnant and irreconcilable; at an augmentation of federal authority, without a diminution of State authority; at sovereignty in the Union, and complete independence in the members. They still, in fine, seem to cherish with blind devotion the political monster of an *imperium in imperio*. This renders a full display of the principal defects of the Confederation necessary, in order to show that the evils we experience do not proceed from minute or partial imperfections, but from fundamental errors in the structure of the building, which cannot be amended otherwise than by an alteration in the first principles and main pillars of the fabric.

The great and radical vice in the construction of the existing Confederation is in the principle of LEGISLATION for STATES or GOVERNMENTS, in their CORPORATE or COLLECTIVE CAPACITIES, and as contradistinguished from the INDIVIDUALS of which they consist. Though this principle does not run through all the powers delegated to the Union, yet it pervades and governs those on which the efficacy of the rest depends. Except as to the rule of appointment, the United States has an indefinite discretion to make requisitions for men and money; but they have no authority to raise either, by regulations extending to the individual citizens of America. The consequence of this is, that though in theory their resolutions concerning those objects are laws, constitutionally binding on the members of the Union, yet in practice they are mere recommendations which the States observe or disregard at their option.

It is a singular instance of the capriciousness of the human mind, that after all the admonitions we have had from experience on this head, there should still be found men who object to the new Constitution, for deviating from a principle which has been found the bane of the old, and which is in itself evidently incompatible with the idea of GOVERNMENT; a principle, in short, which, if it is to be executed at all, must substitute the violent and sanguinary agency of the sword to the mild influence of the magistracy.

There is nothing absurd or impracticable in the idea of a league or alliance between independent nations for certain defined purposes precisely stated in a treaty regulating all the details of time, place, circumstance, and quantity; leaving nothing to future discretion; and depending for its execution on the good faith of the parties. Compacts of this kind exist among all civilized nations, subject to the usual vicissitudes of peace and war, of observance and non-observance, as the interests or passions of the contracting powers dictate. In the early part of the present century there was an epidemical rage in Europe for this species of compacts, from which the politicians of the times fondly hoped for benefits which were never realized. With a view to establishing the equilibrium of power and the peace of that part of the world, all the resources of negotiation were exhausted, and triple and quadruple alliances were formed; but they were scarcely formed before they were broken, giving an instructive but afflicting lesson to mankind, how little dependence is to be placed on treaties which have no other sanction than the obligations of good faith, and which oppose general considerations of peace and justice to the impulse of any immediate interest or passion.

If the particular States in this country are disposed to stand in a similar relation to each other, and to drop the project of a general DISCRETIONARY SUPERINTENDENCE, the scheme would indeed be pernicious, and would entail upon us all the mischiefs which have been enumerated under the first head; but it would have the merit of being, at least, consistent and practicable. Abandoning all views towards a confederate government, this would bring us to a simple alliance offensive and defensive; and would place us in a situation to be alternate friends and enemies of each other, as our mutual jealousies and rivalships, nourished by the intrigues of foreign nations, should prescribe to us.

But if we are unwilling to be placed in this perilous situation; if we still will adhere to the design of a national government, or, which is the same thing, of a superintending power, under the direction of a common council, we must resolve to incorporate into our plan those ingredients which may be considered as forming the characteristic difference between a league and a government; we must extend the authority of the Union to the persons of the citizens, --the only proper objects of government.

Government implies the power of making laws. It is essential to the idea of a law, that it be attended with a sanction; or, in other words, a penalty or punishment for disobedience. If there be no penalty annexed to disobedience, the resolutions or commands which pretend to be laws will, in fact, amount to nothing more than advice or recommendation. This penalty, whatever it may be, can only be inflicted in two ways: by the agency of the courts and ministers of justice, or by military force; by the COERCION of the magistracy, or by the COERCION of arms. The first kind can evidently apply only to men; the last kind must of necessity, be employed against bodies politic, or communities, or States. It is evident that there is no process of a court by which the observance of the laws can, in the last resort, be enforced. Sentences may be denounced against them for violations of their duty; but these sentences can only be carried into execution by the sword. In an association where the general authority is confined to the collective bodies of the communities, that compose it, every breach of the laws must involve a state of war; and military execution must become the only instrument of civil obedience. Such a state of things can certainly not deserve the name of government, nor would any prudent man choose to commit his happiness to it.

There was a time when we were told that breaches, by the States, of the regulations of the federal authority were not to be expected; that a sense of common interest would preside over the conduct of the respective members, and would beget a full compliance with all the constitutional requisitions of the Union. This language, at the present day, would appear as wild as a great part of what we now hear from the same quarter will be thought, when we shall have received further lessons from that best oracle of wisdom, experience. It at all times betrayed an ignorance of the true springs by which human conduct is actuated, and belied the original inducements to the establishment of civil power. Why has government been instituted at all? Because the passions of men will not conform to the dictates of reason and justice, without constraint. Has it been found that bodies of men act with more rectitude or greater disinterestedness than individuals? The contrary of this has been inferred by all accurate observers of the conduct of mankind; and the inference is founded upon obvious reasons. Regard to reputation has a less active influence, when the infamy of a bad action is to be divided among a number than when it is to fall singly upon one. A spirit of faction, which is apt to mingle its poison in the deliberations of all bodies of men, will often hurry the persons of whom they are composed into improprieties and excesses, for which they would blush in a private capacity.

In addition to all this, there is, in the nature of sovereign power, an impatience of control, that disposes those who are invested with the exercise of it, to look with an evil eye upon all external attempts to restrain or direct its operations. From this spirit it happens, that in every political association which is formed upon the principle of uniting in a common interest a number of lesser sovereignties, there will be found a kind of eccentric tendency in the subordinate or inferior orbs, by the operation of which there will be a perpetual effort in each to fly off from the common centre. This tendency is not difficult to be accounted for. It has its origin in the love of power. Power controlled or abridged is almost always the rival and enemy of that power by which it is controlled or abridged. This simple proposition will teach us how little reason there is to expect, that the persons intrusted with the administration of the affairs of the particular members of a confederacy will at all times be ready, with perfect good-humor, and an unbiased regard to the public weal, to execute the resolutions or decrees of the general authority. The reverse of this results from the constitution of human nature.

If, therefore, the measures of the Confederacy cannot be executed without the intervention of the particular administrations, there will be little prospect of their being executed at all. The rulers of the respective members, whether they have a constitutional right to do it or not, will undertake to judge of the propriety of the measures themselves. They will consider the conformity of the thing proposed or required to their immediate interests or aims; the momentary conveniences or inconveniences that would attend its adoption. All this will be done; and in a spirit of interested and suspicious scrutiny, without that knowledge of national circumstances and reasons of state, which is essential to a right judgment, and with that strong predilection in favor of local objects, which can hardly fail to mislead the decision. The same process must be repeated in every member of which the body is constituted; and the execution of the plans, framed by the councils of the whole, will always fluctuate on the discretion of the ill-informed and prejudiced opinion of every part. Those who have been conversant in the proceedings of popular assemblies; who have seen how difficult it often is, where there is no exterior pressure of circumstances, to bring them to harmonious resolutions on important points, will readily conceive how impossible it must be to induce a number of such assemblies, deliberating at a distance from each other, at different times, and under different impressions, long to co-operate in the same views and pursuits.

In our case, the concurrence of thirteen distinct sovereign wills is requisite, under the Confederation, to the complete execution of every important measure that proceeds from the Union. It has happened as was to have been foreseen. The measures of the Union have not been executed; the delinquencies of the States have, step by step, matured themselves to an extreme, which has, at length, arrested all the wheels of the national government, and brought them to an awful stand. Congress at this time scarcely possess the means of keeping up the forms of administration, till the States can have time to agree upon a more substantial substitute for the present shadow of a federal government. Things did not come to this desperate extremity at once. The causes which have been specified produced at first only unequal and disproportionate degrees of compliance with the requisitions of the Union. The greater deficiencies of some States furnished the pretext of example and the temptation of interest to the complying, or to the least delinquent States. Why should we do more in proportion than those who are embarked with us in the same political voyage? Why should we consent to bear more than our proper share of the common burden? These were suggestions which human selfishness could not withstand, and which even speculative men, who looked forward to remote consequences, could not, without hesitation, combat. Each State, yielding to the persuasive voice of immediate interest or convenience, has successively withdrawn its support, till the frail and tottering edifice seems ready to fall upon our heads, and to crush us beneath its ruins.

(a) "I mean for the Union."

Federalist No. 16 by Alexander Hamilton

Editor's Introduction:

This essay in the *Federalist* was one of the more aggressive pronouncements of federal power in the series and in stark contrast to more subdued and veiled discussions of "national" supremacy by other writers. Hamilton squarely denied the ability of a State to counteract the authority of the general government in the new Constitution and outlined the role of a standing army to snuff potential "insurrection" in its cradle, though he admitted that combinations opposed to the general authority for the purpose of "revolutions or dismemberments" would be too difficult to guard against on paper. He hoped that all conflict within the Union would be handled by the proper "magistrates," meaning judges, and that bloodshed would be avoided through judicial review of federal legislation. It must be noted that "judicial review" is not an explicit power in the Constitution, but that both proponents and opponents of the document hoped it would be used to squash unconstitutional *federal* legislation, but not as a legislative hammer to create new laws out of thin air.

Federalist No. 16

December 4, 1787

By Alexander Hamilton of New York

To the People of the State of New York:

THE tendency of the principle of legislation for States, or communities, in their political capacities, as it has been exemplified by the experiment we have made of it, is equally attested by the events which have befallen all other governments of the confederate kind, of which we have any account, in exact proportion to its prevalence in those systems. The confirmations of this fact will be worthy of a distinct and particular examination. I shall content myself with barely observing here, that of all the confederacies of antiquity, which history has handed down to us, the Lycian and Achaean leagues, as far as there remain vestiges of them, appear to have been most free from the fetters of that mistaken principle, and were accordingly those which have best deserved, and have most liberally received, the applauding suffrages of political writers.

This exceptionable principle may, as truly as emphatically, be styled the parent of anarchy: It has been seen that delinquencies in the members of the Union are its natural and necessary offspring; and that whenever they happen, the only constitutional remedy is force, and the immediate effect of the use of it, civil war.

It remains to inquire how far so odious an engine of government, in its application to us, would even be capable of answering its end. If there should not be a large army constantly at the disposal of the national government it would either not be able to employ force at all, or, when this could be done, it would amount to a war between parts of the Confederacy concerning the infractions of a league, in which the strongest combination would be most likely to prevail, whether it consisted of those who supported or of those who resisted the general authority. It would rarely happen that the delinquency to be redressed would be confined to a single member, and if there were more than one who had neglected their duty, similarity of situation would induce them to unite for common defense. Independent of this motive of sympathy, if a large and influential State should happen to be the aggressing member, it would commonly have weight enough with its neighbors to win over some of them as associates to its cause. Specious arguments of danger to the common liberty could easily be contrived; plausible excuses for the deficiencies of the party could, without difficulty, be invented to alarm the apprehensions, inflame the passions, and conciliate the good-will, even of those States which were not chargeable with any violation or omission of duty. This would be the more likely to take place, as the delinquencies of the larger members might be expected sometimes to proceed from an ambitious premeditation in their rulers, with a view to getting rid of all external control upon their designs of personal aggrandizement; the better to effect which it is presumable they would tamper beforehand with leading individuals in the adjacent States. If associates could not be found at home, recourse would be had to the aid of foreign powers, who would seldom be disinclined to encouraging the dissensions of a Confederacy, from the firm union of which they had so much to fear. When the sword is once drawn, the passions of men observe no bounds of moderation. The suggestions of wounded pride, the instigations of irritated resentment, would be apt to carry the States against which the arms of the Union were exerted, to any extremes necessary to avenge the affront or to avoid the disgrace of submission. The first war of this kind would probably terminate in a dissolution of the Union.

This may be considered as the violent death of the Confederacy. Its more natural death is what we now seem to be on the point of experiencing, if the federal system be not speedily renovated in a more substantial form. It is not probable, considering the genius of this country, that the complying States would often be inclined to support the authority of the Union by engaging in a war against the non-complying States. They would always be more ready to pursue the milder course of putting themselves upon an equal footing with the delinquent members by an imitation of their example. And the guilt of all would thus become the security of all. Our past experience has exhibited the operation of this spirit in its full light. There would, in fact, be an insuperable difficulty in ascertaining when force could with propriety be employed. In the article of pecuniary contribution, which would be the most usual source of delinquency, it would often be impossible to decide whether it had proceeded from disinclination or inability. The pretense of the latter would always be at hand. And the case must be very flagrant in which its fallacy could be detected with sufficient certainty to justify the harsh expedient of compulsion. It is easy to see that this problem alone, as often as it should occur, would open a wide field for the exercise of factious views, of partiality, and of oppression, in the majority that happened to prevail in the national council.

It seems to require no pains to prove that the States ought not to prefer a national Constitution which could only be kept in motion by the instrumentality of a large army continually on foot to execute the ordinary requisitions or decrees of the government. And yet this is the plain alternative involved by those who wish to deny it the power of extending its operations to individuals. Such a scheme, if practicable at all, would instantly degenerate into a military despotism; but it will be found in every light impracticable. The resources of the Union would not be equal to the maintenance of an army considerable enough to confine the larger States within the limits of their duty; nor would the means ever be furnished of forming such an army in the first instance. Whoever considers the populousness and strength of several of these States singly at the present juncture, and looks forward to what they will become, even at the distance of half a century, will at once dismiss as idle and visionary any scheme which aims at regulating their movements by laws to operate upon them in their collective capacities, and to be executed by a coercion applicable to them in the same capacities. A project of this kind is little less romantic than the monster-taming spirit which is attributed to the fabulous heroes and demi-gods of antiquity.

Even in those confederacies which have been composed of members smaller than many of our counties, the principle of legislation for sovereign States, supported by military coercion, has never been found effectual. It has rarely been attempted to be employed, but against the weaker members; and in most instances attempts to coerce the refractory and disobedient have been the signals of bloody wars, in which one half of the confederacy has displayed its banners against the other half.

The result of these observations to an intelligent mind must be clearly this, that if it be possible at any rate to construct a federal government capable of regulating the common concerns and preserving the general tranquillity, it must be founded, as to the objects committed to its care, upon the reverse of the principle contended for by the opponents of the proposed Constitution. It must carry its agency to the persons of the citizens. It must stand in need of no intermediate legislations; but must itself be empowered to employ the arm of the ordinary magistrate to execute its own resolutions. The majesty of the national authority must be manifested through the medium of the courts of justice. The government of the Union, like that of each State, must be able to address itself immediately to the hopes and fears of individuals; and to attract to its support those passions which have the strongest influence upon the human heart. It must, in short, possess all the means, and have aright to resort to all the methods, of executing the powers with which it is intrusted, that are possessed and exercised by the government of the particular States.

To this reasoning it may perhaps be objected, that if any State should be disaffected to the authority of the Union, it could at any time obstruct the execution of its laws, and bring the matter to the same issue of force, with the necessity of which the opposite scheme is reproached.

The plausibility of this objection will vanish the moment we advert to the essential difference between a mere NON-COMPLIANCE and a DIRECT and ACTIVE RESISTANCE. If the interposition of the State legislatures be necessary to give effect to a measure of the Union, they have only NOT TO ACT, or to ACT EVASIVELY, and the measure is defeated. This neglect of duty may be disguised under affected but unsubstantial provisions, so as not to appear, and of course not to excite any alarm in the people for the safety of the Constitution. The State leaders may even make a merit of their surreptitious invasions of it on the ground of some temporary convenience, exemption, or advantage.

But if the execution of the laws of the national government should not require the intervention of the State legislatures, if they were to pass into immediate operation upon the citizens themselves, the particular governments could not interrupt their progress without an open and violent exertion of an unconstitutional power. No omissions nor evasions would answer the end. They would be obliged to act, and in such a manner as would leave no doubt that they had encroached on the national rights. An experiment of this nature would always be hazardous in the face of a constitution in any degree competent to its own defense, and of a people enlightened enough to distinguish between a legal exercise and an illegal usurpation of authority. The success of it would require not merely a factious majority in the legislature, but the concurrence of the courts of justice and of the body of the people. If the judges were not embarked in a conspiracy with the legislature, they would pronounce the resolutions of such a majority to be contrary to the supreme law of the land, unconstitutional, and void. If the people were not tainted with the spirit of their State representatives, they, as the natural guardians of the Constitution, would throw their weight into the national scale and give it a decided preponderancy in the contest. Attempts of this kind would not often be made with levity or rashness, because they could seldom be made without danger to the authors, unless in cases of a tyrannical exercise of the federal authority.

If opposition to the national government should arise from the disorderly conduct of refractory or seditious individuals, it could be overcome by the same means which are daily employed against the same evil under the State governments. The magistracy, being equally the ministers of the law of the land, from whatever source it might emanate, would doubtless be as ready to guard the national as the local regulations from the inroads of private licentiousness. As to those partial commotions and insurrections, which sometimes disquiet society, from the intrigues of an inconsiderable faction, or from sudden or occasional ill humors that do not infect the great body of the community the general government could command more extensive resources for the suppression of disturbances of that kind than would be in the power of any single member. And as to those mortal feuds which, in certain conjunctures, spread a conflagration through a whole nation, or through a very large proportion of it, proceeding either from weighty causes of discontent given by the government or from the contagion of some violent popular paroxysm, they do not fall within any ordinary rules of calculation. When they happen, they commonly amount to revolutions and dismemberments of empire. No form of government can always either avoid or control them. It is in vain to hope to guard against events too mighty for human foresight or precaution, and it would be idle to object to a government because it could not perform impossibilities.

A Landholder VI by Oliver Ellsworth

Editor's Introduction:

Ellsworth turned his attention to George Mason's objections to the Constitution in "A Landholder VI." Both Ellsworth and Mason attended the Philadelphia Convention, and according to Ellsworth, Mason supported most of the proceedings, that is until he could not get the Convention to insert language prohibiting "navigation laws." Ellsworth insinuated that Mason's objections were, in fact, sectionally driven and dangerous to Union. Navigation laws are better known as protective tariffs, and Mason, like other Southerners, feared that such power would be abused by the commercial States at the expense of the producing States of the South. He was right, but Ellsworth chastised Mason for favoring agriculture over commerce, when at the time nearly eighty percent of the American population were farmers, North and South. Mason was clearly being a true "nationalist" opposed to the sectionally driven policies of New England at this point.

Ellsworth additionally considered a bill of rights unnecessary because the power to abridge speech or the press was not delegated to the general government, the president's powers—though necessary for energy and vigor—were to be limited by the document, the judicial power to be corralled to federal questions only by the language of the Constitution, and ex post facto laws to be illegal.

A Landholder VI

December 10, 1787

By Oliver Ellsworth of Connecticut

He that is first in his own cause seemeth just; but his neighbor cometh and searcheth him.

To the Landholders and Farmers:

The publication of Col. Mason's reasons for not signing the new Constitution, has extorted some truths that would otherwise in all probability have remained unknown to us all. His reasons, like Mr. Gerry's, are most of them *ex post facto*, have been revised in New York by R. H. L. and by him brought into their present artful and insidious form. The factious spirit of R. H. L., his implacable hatred to General Washington, his well-known intrigues against him in the late war, his attempts to displace him and give the command of the American army to General Lee, is so recent in your minds it is not necessary to repeat them. He is supposed to be the author of most of the scurrility poured out in the New-York papers against the new constitution.

Just at the close of the Convention, whose proceedings in general were zealously supported by Mr. Mason, he moved for a clause that no navigation act should ever be passed but with the consent of two-thirds of both branches; urging that a navigation act might otherwise be passed excluding foreign bottoms from carrying American produce to market, and throw a monopoly of the carrying business into the hands of the eastern states who attend to navigation, and that such an exclusion of foreigners would raise the freight of the produce of the southern states, and for these reasons Mr. Mason would have it in the power of the southern states to prevent any navigation act.

This clause, as unequal and partial in the extreme to the southern states, was rejected; because it ought to be left on the same footing with other national concerns, and because no state would have a right to complain of a navigation act which should leave the carrying business equally open to them all. Those who preferred cultivating their lands would do so; those who chose to navigate and become carriers would do that. The loss of this question determined Mr. Mason against the signing the doings of the convention, and is undoubtedly among his reasons as drawn for the southern states; but for the eastern states this reason would not do. It would convince us that Mr. Mason preferred the subjects of every foreign power to the subjects of the United States who live in New-England; even the British who lately ravaged Virginia— that Virginia, my countrymen, where your relations lavished their blood—where your sons laid down their lives to secure to her and us the freedom and independence in which we now rejoice, and which can only be continued to us by a firm, equal and effective union. But do not believe that the people of Virginia are all thus selfish: No, there is a Washington, a Blair, a Madison and a Lee, (not R. H. L.) and I am persuaded there is a majority of liberal, just and federal men in Virginia, who, whatever their sentiments may be of the new constitution, will despise the artful injustice contained in Col. Mason's reasons as published in the Connecticut papers.

The President of the United States has no council, etc., says Col. Mason. His proposed council would have been expensive— they must constantly attend the president, because the president constantly acts. This council must have been composed of great characters, who could not be kept attending without great salaries, and if their opinions were binding on the president his responsibility would be destroyed—if divided, prevent vigor and dispatch—if not binding, they would be no security. The states who have had such councils have found them useless, and complain of them as a dead weight. In others, as in England, the supreme executive advises when and with whom he pleases; if any information is wanted, the heads of the departments who are always at hand can best give it, and from the manner of their appointment will be trustworthy. Secrecy, vigor, dispatch and responsibility, require that the supreme executive should be one person, and unfettered otherwise than by the laws he is to execute.

There is no Declaration of Rights. Bills of Rights were introduced in England when its kings claimed all power and jurisdiction, and were considered by them as grants to the people. They are insignificant since government is considered as originating from the people, and all the power government now has is a grant from the people. The constitution they establish with powers limited and defined, becomes now to the legislator and magistrate, what originally a bill of rights was to the people. To have inserted in this constitution a bill of rights for the states would suppose them to derive and hold their rights from the federal government, when the reverse is the case.

There is to be no ex post facto laws. This was moved by Mr Gerry and supported by Mr. Mason, and is exceptional only as being unnecessary; for it ought not to be presumed that government will be so tyranical, and opposed to the sense of all modern civilians, as to pass such laws: if they should, they would be void.

The general Legislature is restrained from prohibiting the further importation of slaves for twenty odd years. But every state legislature may restrain its own subjects; but if they should not, shall we refuse to confederate with them? their consciences are their own, tho' their wealth and strength are blended with ours. Mr. Mason has himself about three hundred slaves, and lives in Virginia, where it is found by prudent management they can breed and raise slaves faster than they want them for their own use, and could supply the deficiency in

Georgia and South Carolina; and perhaps Col. Mason may suppose it more humane to breed than import slaves—those imported having been bred and born free, may not so tamely bear slavery as those born slaves, and from their infancy inured to it; but his objections are not on the side of freedom, nor in compassion to the human race who are slaves, but that such importations render the United States weaker, more vulnerable, and less capable of defence. To this I readily agree, and all good men wish the entire abolition of slavery, as soon as it can take place with safety to the public, and for the lasting good of the present wretched race of slaves. The only possible step that could be taken towards it by the convention was to fix a period after which they should not be imported.

There is no declaration of any kind to preserve the Liberty of the press, etc. Nor is liberty of conscience, or of matrimony, or of burial of the dead; it is enough that congress have no power to prohibit either, and can have no temptation. This objection is answered in that the states have all the power originally, and congress have only what the states grant them.

The judiciary of the United States is so constructed and extended as to absorb and destroy the judiciaries of the several states; thereby rendering law as tedious, intricate and expensive, and justice as unattainable by a great part of the community, as in England; and enable the rich to oppress and ruin the poor. It extends only to objects and cases specified, and wherein the national peace or rights, or the harmony of the states is concerned, and not to controversies between citizens of the same state (except where they claim under grants of different states); and nothing hinders but the supreme federal court may be held in different districts, or in all the states, and that all the cases, except the few in which it has original and not appellate jurisdiction, may in the first instance be had in the state courts and those trials be final except in cases of great magnitude; and the trials be by jury also in most or all the causes which were wont to be tried by them, as congress shall provide, whose appointment is security enough for their attention to the wishes and convenience of the people. In chancery courts juries are never used, nor are they proper in admiralty courts, which proceed not by municipal laws, which they may be supposed to understand, but by the civil law and law of nations.

Mr. Mason deems the president and senate's power to make treaties dangerous, because they become laws of the land. If the president and his proposed council had this power, or the president alone, as in England and other nations is the case, could the danger be less?—or is the representative branch suited to the making of treaties, which are often intricate, and require much negotiation and secrecy? The senate is objected to as having too much power, and bold unfounded assertions that they will destroy any balance in the government, and accomplish what usurpation they please upon the rights and liberties of the people; to which it may be answered, they are elective and rotative, to the mass of the people; the populace can as well balance the senatorial branch there as in the states, and much better than in England, where the lords are hereditary, and yet the commons preserve their weight; but the state governments on which the constitution is built will forever be security enough to the people against aristocratic usurpations:—The danger of the constitution is not aristrocracy or monarchy, but anarchy.

I intreat you, my fellow citizens, to read and examine the new constitution with candor—examine it for yourselves: you are, most of you, as learned as the objector, and certainly as able to judge of its virtues or vices as he is. To make the objections the more plausible, they are called *The objections of the Hon. George Mason, etc.*—They may possibly be his, but be assured they were not those made in convention, and being directly against what he there supported in one instance ought to caution you against giving any credit to the rest; his violent opposition to the powers given congress to regulate trade, was an open decided preference of all the world to you. A man governed by such narrow views and local prejudices, can never be trusted; and his pompous declaration in the House of Delegates in Virginia that no man was more federal than himself, amounts to no more than this, "Make a federal government that will secure Virginia all her natural advantages, promote all her interests regardless of every disadvantage to the other states, and I will subscribe to it."

It may be asked how I came by my information respecting Col. Mason's conduct in convention, as the doors were shut? To this I answer, no delegate of the late convention will contradict my assertions, as I have repeatedly heard them made by others in presence of several of them, who could not deny their truth. Whether the constitution in question will be adopted by the United States in our day is uncertain; but it is neither aristocracy or monarchy can grow out of it, so long as the present descent of landed estates last, and the mass of the people have, as at present, a tolerable education; and were it ever so perfect a scheme of freedom, when we become ignorant, vicious, idle, and regardless of the education of our children, our liberties will be lost—we shall be fitted for slavery, and it will be an easy business to reduce us to obey one or more tyrants.

Speech in the Pennsylvania Ratifying Convention by Thomas McKean

Editor's Introduction:

Two men in the founding period played leading roles in both Pennsylvania and Delaware—John Dickinson and Thomas McKean—and both favored the ratification of the Constitution. McKean served as a delegate from Delaware to the Stamp Act Congress in 1765 and both the First and Second Continental Congresses where he helped draft the Articles of Confederation. He was eventually elected president of that body. He also served as governor of both Delaware and Pennsylvania and as Chief Justice of the Pennsylvania Supreme Court. One grandson would serve as Prime Minister of Spain and another as an admiral in the Confederate Navy during the War for Southern Independence.

McKean was a firebrand with a hot Scottish temper who fiercely supported independence in 1776. He enlisted in the Pennsylvania militia during the War and helped defend New York and New Jersey in 1776 and 1777. More importantly, McKean ardently favored the equality of the States in any proposed Union (he pushed this position while a member of the Stamp Act Congress), which makes his defense of the Constitution that much more important.

In this speech, he pinpointed ten arguments leveled against the Constitution and systematically refuted each, but he spent the most energy on reassuring the people of Pennsylvania that the general government's powers would be limited by the language of the document and so defined that they could never be abused. This was an important line of defense and a common theme in nearly every speech or public document in favor of ratification.

Speech in the Pennsylvania Ratifying Convention

December 10, 1787

By Thomas McKean of Pennsylvania

THOMAS MCKEAN: Sir, you have under your consideration a matter of very great weight and importance, not only to the present generation but to posterity; for where the rights and liberties of the people are concerned, there certainly it is fit to proceed with the utmost caution and regard. You have done so hitherto. The power of this Convention, being derived from the people of Pennsylvania, by a positive and voluntary grant, cannot be extended further than what this positive grant hath conveyed. You have been chosen by the people, for the sole purpose of "assenting to and ratifying the Constitution, proposed for the future government of the United States, with respect to their general and common concerns," or of rejecting it. It is a sacred trust; and, as on the one hand, you ought to weigh well the innovations it will create in the governments of the individual states and the dangers which may arise by its adoption; so upon the other hand, you ought fully to consider the benefits it may promise and the consequences of a rejection of it. You have hitherto acted strictly conformably to your delegated power; you have agreed, that a single question can come before you; and it has been accordingly moved, that you resolve, "to assent to and ratify this Constitution." Three weeks have been spent in hearing the objections that have been made against it, and it is now time to determine whether they are of such a nature as to overbalance any benefits or advantages that may be derived to the State of Pennsylvania by your accepting it.

Sir, I have as yet taken up but little of your time; notwithstanding this, I will endeavor to contract what occurs to me on the subject. And in what I have to offer, I shall observe this method: I will first consider the arguments that have been used against this Constitution, and then give my reasons why I am for the motion. The arguments against the Constitution are, I think, chiefly these. First. That the elections of Representatives and Senators are not frequent enough to insure responsibility to their constituents. Second. That one Representative for thirty thousand persons is too few. Third. The Senators have a share in the appointment of certain officers and are to be the judges on the impeachment of such officers. This is blending the executive with the legislative and judicial departments, and is likely to screen the offenders impeached, because of the concurrence of a majority of the Senate in their appointment. Fourth. That the Congress may by law deprive the electors of a fair choice of their Representatives, by fixing improper times, places, and modes of election. Fifth. That the powers of Congress are too large, particularly in laying internal taxes and excises, because they may lay excessive taxes and leave nothing for the support of the state governments. In raising and supporting armies, and that the appropriation of money for that use, should not be for so long a term as two years. In calling forth the militia on necessary occasions; because they may call them from one end of the continent to the other, and wantonly harrass them; besides they may coerce men to act in the militia, whose consciences are against bearing arms in any case. In making all laws which shall be necessary and proper for carrying into execution the foregoing powers, and all other powers vested by this Constitution in the government of the United States, or in any department or officer thereof. And in declaring, that this Constitution, and the laws of the United States which shall be made in pursuance thereof, and all treaties made, or which shall be made, under the authority of the United States, shall be the supreme law of the land. That migration or importation of such persons, as any of the states shall admit, shall not be prohibited prior to 1808, nor a tax or duty imposed on such importation exceeding ten dollars for each person. Sixth. That the whole of the executive power is not lodged in the President alone, so that there might be one responsible person. That he has the sole power of pardoning offenses against the United States, and may therefore pardon traitors for treasons committed in consequence of his own ambitious and wicked projects or those of the Senate. That the Vice President is a useless officer, and being an executive officer, is to be President of the Senate, and in case of a division is to have the casting voice. Seventh. The judicial power shall be vested in one Supreme Court. An objection is made, that the compensation for the services of the judges shall not be diminished during their continuance in office, and this is contrasted with the compensation to the President, which is to be neither increased nor diminished during the period for which he shall have been elected. But that of the judges may be increased, and the judge may hold other offices of a lucrative nature, and his judgment be thereby warped. That in all the cases enumerated, except where the Supreme Court has original jurisdiction, "they shall have appellate jurisdiction, both as to law and facts, with such exceptions, and under such regulations as the congress shall make." From hence is inferred that the trial by jury is not secured. That they have jurisdiction between citizens of different states. Eighth. That there is no bill or declaration of rights in this Constitution. Ninth. That this is a consolidation of the several states, and not a confederation. Tenth. It is an aristocracy and was intended to be so by the framers of it.

The first objection that I heard advanced against this Constitution, I say, sir, was that the elections of Representatives and Senators are not frequent enough to insure responsibility to their constituents. This is a subject that most men differ about, but there are more considerations than that of mere responsibility. By this system the House of Representatives is composed of persons chosen every second year by the people of the several states; and the Senators every six years by the legislatures. Whether the one or the other of these periods are of too long duration is a question to which various answers will be given; some persons are of opinion that three years in the one case, and seven in the other, would be a more eligible term than that adopted in this Constitution. In Great Britain, we find the House of Commons elected for seven years; the House of Lords is perpetual; and the king never dies. The Parliament of Ireland is octennial; in various other parts of the British dominions, the house of representatives are during the royal pleasure, and have been continued twenty years; this, sir, is a term undoubtedly too long. In a single state, I think annual elections most proper, but then there ought to be more branches in the legislature than one. An annual legislature possessed of supreme power may be properly termed an annual despotism—and, like an individual, they are subject to caprice, and act as party spirit or spleen dictates; hence that instability to our laws, which is the bane of republican governments. The framers of this Constitution wisely divided the legislative department between two houses subject to the qualified negative of the President of the United States, the this government embraces only enumerated powers. In a single state, annual elections may be proper, the more so, when the legislative powers extend to all cases; but in such an extent of country as the United States, and when the powers are circumscribed, there is not that necessity, nor are the objects of the general government of that nature as to be acquired immediately by every capacity. To combine the various interests of thirteen different states requires more extensive knowledge than is necessary for the legislature of any one of them; two years are therefore little enough, for the members of the House of Representatives to make themselves fully acquainted with the views, the habits, and interests of the United States. With respect to the Senate, when we consider the trust reposed in them, we cannot hesitate to pronounce, the period assigned to them is short enough; they possess, in common with the House of Representatives, legislative power; with its concurrence they also have power to declare war; they are joined with the President in concluding treaties; it therefore behooves them to be conversant with the politics of the nations of the world and the dispositions of the sovereigns, and their ministers; this requires much reading and attention. And believe me, the longer a man bends his study to any particular subject, the more likely he is to be master of it. Experience and practice will assist genius and education. I therefore think the time allowed, under this system, to both houses to be extremely proper. This objection has been made repeatedly, but it can only have weight with those who are not at the pains of thinking on the subject. When anything, sir, new or great is done, it is very apt to create a ferment among those out of doors who, as they cannot always enter into the depth and wisdom of councils, are too apt to censure what they do not understand; upon a little reflection and experience, the people often find that to be a singular blessing which at first they deemed a curse.

Second. "That one Representative for thirty thousand persons is too few. "There will be, sir, sixty-five in the House of Representatives and twenty-six in the Senate, in all ninety-one, who, together with the

President, are to make laws in the several particular matters entrusted to them, and which are all enumerated and expressed. I think the number sufficient at the present, and in three years time, when a census or actual enumeration must take place, they will be increased, and in less than twenty-five years they will be more than double. With respect to this, different gentlemen in the several states will differ, and at last the opinion of the majority must govern.

Third. "The Senators have a share in the appointment of certain officers, and are to be the judges on the impeachment of such officers. This is blending the executive with the legislative and judicial departments, and is likely to screen the offenders impeached because of the concurrence of a majority of the Senate in their appointment. "The President is to nominate to office, and with the advice and consent of the Senate appoint officers, so that he is the responsible person, and when any such impeachment shall be tried, it is more than probable, that not one of the Senate, who concurred in the appointment, will be a Senator, for the seats of a third part are to be vacated every two years, and of all in six. As to the Senators having a share in the executive power, so far as to the appointment of certain officers, I do not know where this restraint on the President could be more safely lodged. Some may think a privy councillor might have been chosen by every state, but this could little mend the matter if any, and it would be a considerable additional expense to the people. Nor need the Senate be under any necessity of sitting constantly, as has been alleged, for there is an express provision made to enable the President to fill up all vacancies that may happen during their recess; the commissions to expire at the end of the next sessions. As to impeachments, the objection is much stronger against the Supreme Executive Council of Pennsylvania. The House of Lords in Great Britain are judges in the last resort in all civil causes and besides have the power of trying impeachments. On the trial of impeachments the Senators are to be under the sanction of an oath or affirmation besides the other ties upon them to do justice; and the bias is more likely to be against the officer accused, than in his favor, for there are always more persons disobliged than the contrary when an office is given away, and the expectants of office are more numerous than the possessors.

Fourth. "That the Congress may by law deprive the electors of a fair choice of their Representatives by fixing improper times, places and modes of election. "Every House of Representatives are of necessity to be the judges of the elections, returns, and qualifications of its own members. It is therefore their province, as well as duty, to see, that they are fairly chosen, and are the legal members; for this purpose, it is proper they should have it in their power to provide that the times, places, and manner of election should be such as to insure free and fair elections. Annual congresses are expressly secured; they have only a power given to them to take care that the elections shall be at convenient and suitable times and places, and conducted in a proper manner; and I cannot discover why we may not entrust these particulars to the representatives of the United States with as much safety as to those of the individual states. In some states the electors vote viva voce, in others by ballot; they ought to be uniform, and the elections held on the same day throughout the United States to prevent corruption or undue influence. Why are we to suppose that Congress will make a bad use of this power, more than the representatives in the several states?

It is said "that the powers of Congress, under this Constitution are too large, particularly in laying internal taxes and excises, because they may lay excessive taxes and leave nothing for the support of the state governments." Sir, no doubt but you will discover, on consideration, the necessity of extending these powers to the government of the

Union. If they have to borrow money, they are certainly bound in honor and conscience to pay the interest, until they pay the principal, as well to the foreign as to the domestic creditor; it therefore becomes our duty to put it in their power to be honest. At present, sir, this is not the case, as experience has fully shown. Congress have solicited and required the several states to make provision for these purposes; has one state paid its quota? I believe not one of them; and what has been the result? Foreigners have been compelled to advance money, to enable us to pay the interest due them on what they furnished to Congress during the late war. I trust, we have had experience enough to convince us that Congress ought no longer to depend upon the force of requisition. I heard it urged, that Congress ought not to be authorized to collect taxes until a state had refused to comply with this requisition. Let us examine this position.

The engagements entered into by the general government render it necessary that a certain sum shall be paid in one year; notwithstanding this, they must not have power to collect it until the year expires, and then it is too late. Or is it expected that Congress would borrow the deficiency? Those who lent us in our distress have little encouragement to make advances again to our government; but give the power to Congress to lay such taxes as may be just and necessary, and public credit will revive. Yet, because they have the power to lay taxes and excise, does it follow that they must? For my part, I hope it may not be necessary; but if it is, it is much easier for the citizens of the United States to contribute their proportion, than for a few to bear the weight of the whole principal and interest of the domestic debt; and there is perfect security on this head, because the regulation must equally affect every state, and the law must originate with the immediate Representatives of the people, subject to the investigation of the state representatives. But is the abuse an argument against the use of power? I think it is not; and, upon the whole, I think this power wisely and securely lodged in the hands of the general government; though on the first view of this work, I was of opinion they might have done without it; but, sir, on reflection, I am satisfied that it is not only proper, but that our political salvation may depend upon the exercise of it.

The next objection is against "the power of raising and supporting armies, and the appropriation of money for that use should not be for so long a term as two years." Is it not necessary that the authority superintending the general concerns of the United States should have the power of raising and supporting armies? Are we, sir, to stand defenseless amidst conflicting nations? Wars are inevitable, but war cannot be declared without the consent of the immediate Representatives of the people; there must also originate the law which appropriates the money for the support of the army, yet they can make no appropriation for a longer term than two years; but does it follow that because they may make appropriations for that period, that they must or even will do it? The power of raising and supporting armies is not only necessary, but is enjoyed by the present Congress, who also judge of the expediency or necessity of keeping them up. In England there is a standing army, though in words it is engaged but for one year. Yet is it not kept constantly up? Is there a year that Parliament refuses to grant them supplies? Though this is done annually, it might be done for any longer term. Are not their officers commissioned for life, and when they exercise this power with so much prudence, shall the representatives of this country be suspected the more, because they are restricted to two years?

It is objected that the powers of Congress are too large, because "they have the power of calling forth the militia on necessary occasions, and may call them from one end of the continent to the other and wantonly harrass them; besides they may coerce men to act in the militia, whose consciences are against bearing arms in any case." It is true, by this system, power is given to Congress to organize, arm, and discipline the militia, but everything else is left to the state governments; they are to officer and train them. Congress have also the power of calling them forth, for the purpose of executing the laws of the Union, suppressing insurrections, and repelling invasions; but can it be supposed they would call them in such case from Georgia to New Hampshire? Common sense must oppose the idea.

Another objection was taken from these words of the Constitution: "to make all laws which shall be necessary and proper for carrying into execution the foregoing powers, and all other powers vested by this Constitution in the government of the United States, or in any department, or officer thereof." And in declaring "that this Constitution, and the laws of the United States which shall be made in pursuance thereof, and all treaties made, or which shall be made, under the authority of the United States, shall be the supreme law of the land." This has at last been conceded, that though it is explicit enough, yet it gives to Congress no further powers than those already enumerated. Those that first said it gave to Congress the power of superseding the state governments cannot persist in it; for no person can, with a tolerable face, read the clauses over and infer that such may be the consequence.

Provision is made that Congress shall have power to prohibit the importation of slaves after the year 1808, but the gentlemen in opposition accuse this system of a crime, because it has not prohibited them at once. I suspect those gentlemen are not well acquainted with the business of the diplomatic body, or they would know that an agreement might be made, that did not perfectly accord with the will and pleasure of any one person. Instead of finding fault with what has been gained, I am happy to see a disposition in the United States to do so much.

The next objections have been against the executive power; it is complained of, "because the whole of the executive power is not lodged in the President alone, so that there might be one responsible person; he has the sole powers of pardoning offenses against the United States, and may therefore pardon traitors for treasons committed in consequence of his own ambitious or wicked projects or those of the Senate. "Observe the contradiction, sir, in these two objections; one moment the system is blamed for not leaving all executive authority to the President alone, the next it is censured for giving him the sole power to pardon traitors. I am glad to hear these objections made, because it forebodes an amendment in that body in which amendment is necessary. The President of the United States must nominate to all offices, before the persons can be chosen; he here consents and becomes liable. The Executive Council of Pennsylvania appoint officers by ballot, which effectually destroys responsibility. He may pardon offense, and hence it is inferred that he may pardon traitors for treason committed in consequence of his own ambitious and wicked projects. The Executive Council of Pennsylvania can do the same. But the President of the United States may be impeached before the Senate and punished for his crimes. "The Vice President is an useless officer." Perhaps the government might be executed without him, but there is a necessity of having a person to preside in the Senate to continue a full representation of each state in that body. The chancellor of England is a judicial officer, yet he sits in the House of Lords.

The next objection is against the judicial department. The judicial power shall be vested in one Supreme Court. An objection is made that the compensation for the services of the judges shall not be diminished during their continuance in office, and this is contrasted with the compensation of the President, which is to be neither increased nor diminished during the period for which he shall be elected. But that of the judges may be increased, and the judges may hold other offices of a lucrative nature, and his judgment be thereby warped. Do gentlemen not see the reason why this difference is made? Do they not see that the President is appointed but for four years, whilst the judges may continue for life, if they shall so long behave themselves well? In the first case, little alteration can happen in the value of money; but in the course of a man's life, a very great one may take place from the discovery of silver and gold mines and the great influx of those metals; in which case an increase of salary may be requisite. A security that their compensation shall not be lessened, nor they have to lookup to every session for salary, will certainly tend to make those officers more easy and independent.

"The judges may hold other offices of a lucrative nature." This part of the objection reminds me of the scheme that was fallen upon in Pennsylvania to prevent any person from taking up large tracts of land. A law was passed restricting the purchaser to a tract not exceeding three hundred acres; but all the difference it made was that the land was taken up by several patents, instead of one, and the wealthy could procure, if they chose it, three thousand acres. What, though the judges could hold no other office, might they not have brothers, children and other relations, whom they might wish to see placed in the offices forbidden to themselves? I see no apprehensions that may be entertained on this account. That in all cases enumerated, except where the Supreme Court has original jurisdiction, "they shall have appellate jurisdiction both as to law and fact, with such exceptions and under such regulations as the Congress shall make." From this is inferred, that the trial by jury is not secured; and an objection is set up to the system, because they have jurisdiction between citizens of different states. Regulations, under this head, are necessary, but the Convention would form no one that would have suited each of the United States. It has been a subject of amazement to me to hear gentlemen contend that the verdict of a jury shall be without revision in all cases. Juries are not infallible because they are twelve in number. When the law is so blended with the fact, as to be almost inseparable, may not the decision of a jury be erroneous? Yet notwithstanding this, trial by jury is the best mode that is known. Appellate jurisdiction, sir, is known in the common law, and causes are removed from inferior courts by writ of error into some court of appeal. It is said that the lord chancellor, in all cases, sends down to the lower courts when he wants to determine a fact, but that opinion is not well-founded, because he determines nineteen out of twenty without the intervention of any jury. The power to try causes between citizens of different states was thought by some gentlemen invidious; but I apprehend they must see the necessity of it, from what has been already said by my honorable colleague [James Wilson].

"That there is no bill or declaration of rights in this Constitution." To this I answer, such a thing has not been deemed essential to liberty excepting in Great Britain, where there is a king and an House of Lords quite distinct with respect to power and interest from the rest of the people; or in Poland, the Pacta Conventa, which the king signs before he is crowned, and in six states of the American United States. Again, because it is unnecessary, for the powers of Congress, being derived from the people in the mode pointed out by this Constitution, and being therein enumerated and positively granted, can be no other than what this positive grant conveys. With respect to executive officers, they have no manner of authority, any of them, beyond what is, by positive grant and commission, delegated to them.

"That this is a consolidation of the several states and not a confederation. "To this I answer, the name is immaterial—the thing unites the several states and makes them like one in particular instances and for particular purposes, which is what is ardently desired by most of the sensible men in this country. I care not, whether it is called a consolidation, confederation, or national government, or by what other name, if it is a good government and calculated to promote the blessings of liberty, tranquility and happiness.

"It is an aristocracy and was intended to be so by the framers of it." Here again, sir, the name is immaterial, if it is a good system of government for the general and common concerns of the United States. But after the definition which has already been given of an aristocratic government, it becomes unnecessary to repeat arguments to prove that this system does not establish an aristocracy.

There have been some other small objections to, or rather criticisms on this work, which I rest assured the gentlemen who made them will, on reflection, excuse me in omitting to notice them. Many parts of this Constitution have been wrested and tortured, in order to make way for shadowy objections, which must have been observed by every auditor. Some other things were said with acrimony; they seemed to be personal; I heard the sound, but it was inarticulate. I can compare it to nothing better than the feeble noise occasioned by the working of small beer. It holds in argument as well as nature, that *destructio unius est generatio alterius*—the refutation of an argument begets a proof. The objections to this Constitution having been answered, and all done away, it remains pure and unhurt, and this alone is a forcible argument of its goodness. President, I am sure nothing can prevail with me to give my vote for ratifying this Constitution, but a conviction from comparing the arguments on both sides, that the not doing it is liable to more inconvenience and danger than the doing it.

I. If you do it, you strengthen the government and people of these United States, and will thereby have the wisdom and assistance of all the states. II. You will settle, establish,. and firmly perpetuate our independence, by destroying the vain hopes of all its enemies, both at home and abroad. III. You will encourage your allies to join with you; nay to depend, that what hath been stipulated or shall hereafter be stipulated and agreed upon will be punctually performed, and other nations will be induced to enter into treaties with you. IV. It will have a tendency to break our parties and divisions, and by that means, lay a firm and solid foundation for the future tranquility and happiness of the United States in general, and of this state in particular. V. It will invigorate your commerce and encourage shipbuilding.VI. It will have a tendency not only to prevent any other nation from making war upon you, but from offering you any wrong or even insult. In short, the advantages that must result from it are obviously so numerous and important, and have been so fully and ably pointed out by others, that it appears to be unnecessary to enlarge on this head. Upon the whole, sir, the law has been my study from my infancy, and my only profession. I have gone through the circle of office, in the legislative, executive, and judicial departments of government; and from all my study, observation, and experience, I must declare, that from a full examination and due consideration of this system, it appears to me the best the world has yet seen. I congratulate you on the fair prospect of its being adopted, and am happy in the expectation of seeing accomplished, what has been long my ardent wish—that you will hereafter have a SALUTARY PERMANENCY, in magistracy and STABILITY IN THE LAWS.

Federalist No. 23 by Alexander Hamilton

Editor's Introduction:

Hamilton returned to similar theme from *Federalist* No. 15 in this essay, namely the benefits of Union in resisting external and internal strife. While not as forceful as the aforementioned essay, *Federalist* No. 23 nevertheless focused on the dangers a weak central government created: invasion and insurrection. And while this essay did not focus on the commercial or political benefits of Union, it also foreshadowed a position Hamilton would use to justify the constitutionality of the Bank of the United States in 1791. Hamilton argued in *Federalist* No. 23 that the Constitution allowed for the ends to justify the means for it was "impossible to foresee or define the extent and variety of national exigencies, or the correspondent extent and variety of the means which may be necessary to satisfy them." In other words, he was teeing up implied powers, though he insisted in other essays that the powers of the new government were so defined that there would never be a hint of abuse. Regardless, this is the most important public statement during the ratification process supporting a "loose construction" of the Constitution, a position that was the exception rather than the rule. Hamilton also suggested that if opponents of the document were correct that the Union was built on incompatible things, it would be better to separate than force warring interests into a national body.

Federalist No. 23

December 18, 1787

By Alexander Hamilton of New York

To the People of the State of New York:

THE necessity of a Constitution, at least equally energetic with the one proposed, to the preservation of the Union, is the point at the examination of which we are now arrived.

This inquiry will naturally divide itself into three branches the objects to be provided for by the federal government, the quantity of power necessary to the accomplishment of those objects, the persons upon whom that power ought to operate. Its distribution and organization will more properly claim our attention under the succeeding head.

The principal purposes to be answered by union are these: the common defense of the members; the preservation of the public peace as well against internal convulsions as external attacks; the regulation of commerce with other nations and between the States; the superintendence of our intercourse, political and commercial, with foreign countries.

The authorities essential to the common defense are these: to raise armies; to build and equip fleets; to prescribe rules for the government of both; to direct their operations; to provide for their support. These powers ought to exist without limitation, BECAUSE IT IS IMPOSSIBLE TO FORESEE OR DEFINE THE EXTENT AND VARIETY OF NATIONAL EXIGENCIES, OR THE CORRESPONDENT EXTENT AND VARIETY OF THE MEANS WHICH

MAY BE NECESSARY TO SATISFY THEM. The circumstances that endanger the safety of nations are infinite, and for this reason no constitutional shackles can wisely be imposed on the power to which the care of it is committed. This power ought to be coextensive with all the possible combinations of such circumstances; and ought to be under the direction of the same councils which are appointed to preside over the common defense.

This is one of those truths which, to a correct an unprejudiced mind, carries its own evidence along with it; and may be obscured, but cannot be made plainer by argument or reasoning. It rests upon axioms as simple as they are universal; the MEANS ought to be proportioned to the END; the persons, from whose agency the attainment of any END is expected, ought to possess the MEANS by which it is to be attained.

Whether there ought to be a federal government intrusted with the care of the common defense, is a question in the first instance, open for discussion; but the moment it is decided in the affirmative, it will follow, that that government ought to be clothed with all the powers requisite to complete execution of its trust. And unless it can be shown that the circumstances which may affect the public safety are reducible within certain determinate limits; unless the contrary of this position can be fairly and rationally disputed, it must be admitted, as a necessary consequence, that there can be no limitation of that authority which is to provide for the defense and protection of the community, in any matter essential to its efficacy that is, in any matter essential to the FORMATION, DIRECTION, or SUPPORT of the NATIONAL FORCES.

Defective as the present Confederation has been proved to be, this principle appears to have been fully recognized by the framers of it; though they have not made proper or adequate provision for its exercise. Congress have an unlimited discretion to make requisitions of men and money; to govern the army and navy; to direct their operations. As their requisitions are made constitutionally binding upon the States, who are in fact under the most solemn obligations to furnish the supplies required of them, the intention evidently was that the United States should command whatever resources were by them judged requisite to the "common defense and general welfare." It was presumed that a sense of their true interests, and a regard to the dictates of good faith, would be found sufficient pledges for the punctual performance of the duty of the members to the federal head.

The experiment has, however, demonstrated that this expectation was ill-founded and illusory; and the observations, made under the last head, will, I imagine, have sufficed to convince the impartial and discerning, that there is an absolute necessity for an entire change in the first principles of the system; that if we are in earnest about giving the Union energy and duration, we must abandon the vain project of legislating upon the States in their collective capacities; we must extend the laws of the federal government to the individual citizens of America; we must discard the fallacious scheme of quotas and requisitions, as equally impracticable and unjust. The result from all this is that the Union ought to be invested with full power to levy troops; to build and equip fleets; and to raise the revenues which will be required for the formation and support of an army and navy, in the customary and ordinary modes practiced in other governments.

If the circumstances of our country are such as to demand a compound instead of a simple, a confederate instead of a sole, government, the essential point which will remain to be adjusted will be to discriminate the OBJECTS, as far as it can be done, which shall appertain to the different provinces or departments of power; allowing to each the most ample authority for fulfilling the objects committed to its charge.

Shall the Union be constituted the guardian of the common safety? Are fleets and armies and revenues necessary to this purpose? The government of the Union must be empowered to pass all laws, and to make all regulations which have relation to them. The same must be the case in respect to commerce, and to every other matter to which its jurisdiction is permitted to extend. Is the administration of justice between the citizens of the same State the proper department of the local governments? These must possess all the authorities which are connected with this object, and with every other that may be allotted to their particular cognizance and direction. Not to confer in each case a degree of power commensurate to the end, would be to violate the most obvious rules of prudence and propriety, and improvidently to trust the great interests of the nation to hands which are disabled from managing them with vigor and success.

Who is likely to make suitable provisions for the public defense, as that body to which the guardianship of the public safety is confided; which, as the centre of information, will best understand the extent and urgency of the dangers that threaten; as the representative of the WHOLE, will feel itself most deeply interested in the preservation of every part; which, from the responsibility implied in the duty assigned to it, will be most sensibly impressed with the necessity of proper exertions; and which, by the extension of its authority throughout the States, can alone establish uniformity and concert in the plans and measures by which the common safety is to be secured? Is there not a manifest inconsistency in devolving upon the federal government the care of the general defense, and leaving in the State governments the EFFECTIVE powers by which it is to be provided for? Is not a want of co-operation the infallible consequence of such a system? And will not weakness, disorder, an undue distribution of the burdens and calamities of war, an unnecessary and intolerable increase of expense, be its natural and inevitable concomitants? Have we not had unequivocal experience of its effects in the course of the revolution which we have just accomplished?

Every view we may take of the subject, as candid inquirers after truth, will serve to convince us, that it is both unwise and dangerous to deny the federal government an unconfined authority, as to all those objects which are intrusted to its management. It will indeed deserve the most vigilant and careful attention of the people, to see that it be modeled in such a manner as to admit of its being safely vested with the requisite powers. If any plan which has been, or may be, offered to our consideration, should not, upon a dispassionate inspection, be found to answer this description, it ought to be rejected. A government, the constitution of which renders it unfit to be trusted with all the powers which a free people OUGHT TO DELEGATE TO ANY GOVERNMENT, would be an unsafe and improper depositary of the NATIONAL INTERESTS. Wherever THESE can with propriety be confided, the coincident powers may safely accompany them. This is the true result of all just reasoning upon the subject. And the adversaries of the plan promulgated by the convention ought to have confined themselves to showing, that the internal structure of the proposed government was such as to render it unworthy of the confidence of the people. They ought not to have wandered into inflammatory declamations and unmeaning cavils about the extent of the powers. The POWERS are not too extensive for the OBJECTS of federal administration, or, in other words, for the management of our NATIONAL INTERESTS; nor can any satisfactory argument be framed to show that they are chargeable with such an excess. If it be true, as has been insinuated by some of the writers on the other side, that the difficulty arises from the nature of the thing, and that the extent of the country will not permit us to form a government in which such ample powers can safely be reposed, it would prove that we ought to contract our views, and resort to the expedient of separate confederacies, which will move within more practicable spheres. For the absurdity must continually stare us in the face of confiding to a government the direction of the most essential national interests, without daring to trust it to the authorities which are indispensible to their proper and efficient management. Let us not attempt to reconcile contradictions, but firmly embrace a rational alternative.

I trust, however, that the impracticability of one general system cannot be shown. I am greatly mistaken, if any thing of weight has yet been advanced of this tendency; and I flatter myself, that the observations which have been made in the course of these papers have served to place the reverse of that position in as clear a light as any matter still in the womb of time and experience can be susceptible of. This, at all events, must be evident, that the very difficulty itself, drawn from the extent of the country, is the strongest argument in favor of an energetic government; for any other can certainly never preserve the Union of so large an empire. If we embrace the tenets of those who oppose the adoption of the proposed Constitution, as the standard of our political creed, we cannot fail to verify the gloomy doctrines which predict the impracticability of a national system pervading entire limits of the present Confederacy.

FEDERALIST NO. 24 BY ALEXANDER HAMILTON

Editor's Introduction:

This essay focused on the prospect of a standing army in the new federal republic. Hamilton deflected the arguments of his opponents by centering his defense on the ability for the legislature to control the military. Hamilton would dedicate several essays to the executive branch in future installments of the *Federalist*, but here he reassured the public that the president lacked the power to call up the army and that Congress alone controlled both the purse and the sword. He also considered a small standing army to be an appropriate and necessary deterrent to hostile forces on the frontier, a theme other writers would emphasize when trying to encourage support for a stronger central authority. This was born from experience. The American War for Independence may have officially ended in 1783, but the British and Spanish maintained fortifications along the wild American frontier and often encouraged Indian tribes to attack American settlements. Hamilton called these "savage tribes" the "natural enemies" of the United States. "National Security" drove many Americans to support the Constitution in 1787 and 1788.

Federalist No. 24

December 19, 1787

By Alexander Hamilton of New York

To the People of the State of New York:

To THE powers proposed to be conferred upon the federal government, in respect to the creation and direction of the national forces, I have met with but one specific objection, which, if I understand it right, is this, that proper provision has not been made against the existence of standing armies in time of peace; an objection which, I shall now endeavor to show, rests on weak and unsubstantial foundations.

It has indeed been brought forward in the most vague and general form, supported only by bold assertions, without the appearance of argument; without even the sanction of theoretical opinions; in contradiction to the practice of other free nations, and to the general sense of America, as expressed in most of the existing constitutions. The proprietory of this remark will appear, the moment it is recollected that the objection under consideration turns upon a supposed necessity of restraining the LEGISLATIVE authority of the nation, in the article of military establishments; a principle unheard of, except in one or two of our State constitutions, and rejected in all the rest.

A stranger to our politics, who was to read our newspapers at the present juncture, without having previously inspected the plan reported by the convention, would be naturally led to one of two conclusions: either that it contained a positive injunction, that standing armies should be kept up in time of peace; or that it vested in the EXECUTIVE the whole power of levying troops, without subjecting his discretion, in any shape, to the control of the legislature.

If he came afterwards to peruse the plan itself, he would be surprised to discover, that neither the one nor the other was the case; that the whole power of raising armies was lodged in the LEGISLATURE, not in the EXECUTIVE; that this legislature was to be a popular body, consisting of the representatives of the people periodically elected; and that instead of the provision he had supposed in favor of standing armies, there was to be found, in respect to this object, an important qualification even of the legislative discretion, in that clause which forbids the appropriation of money for the support of an army for any longer period than two years a precaution which, upon a nearer view of it, will appear to be a great and real security against the keeping up of troops without evident necessity.

Disappointed in his first surmise, the person I have supposed would be apt to pursue his conjectures a little further. He would naturally say to himself, it is impossible that all this vehement and pathetic declamation can be without some colorable pretext. It must needs be that this people, so jealous of their liberties, have, in all the preceding models of the constitutions which they have established, inserted the most precise and rigid precautions on this point, the omission of which, in the new plan, has given birth to all this apprehension and clamor.

If, under this impression, he proceeded to pass in review the several State constitutions, how great would be his disappointment to find that TWO ONLY of them (i) contained an interdiction of standing armies in time of peace; that the other eleven had either observed a profound silence on the subject, or had in express terms admitted the right of the Legislature to authorize their existence.

Still, however he would be persuaded that there must be some plausible foundation for the cry raised on this head. He would never be able to imagine, while any source of information remained unexplored, that it was nothing more than an experiment upon the public credulity, dictated either by a deliberate intention to deceive, or by the overflowings of a zeal too intemperate to be ingenuous. It would probably occur to him, that he would be likely to find the precautions he was in search of in the primitive compact between the States. Here, at length, he would expect to meet with a solution of the enigma. No doubt, he would observe to himself, the existing Confederation must contain the most explicit provisions against military establishments in time of peace; and a departure from this model, in a favorite point, has occasioned the discontent which appears to influence these political champions.

If he should now apply himself to a careful and critical survey of the articles of Confederation, his astonishment would not only be increased, but would acquire a mixture of indignation, at the unexpected discovery, that these articles, instead of containing the prohibition he looked for, and though they had, with jealous circumspection, restricted the authority of the State legislatures in this particular, had not imposed a single restraint on that of the United States. If he happened to be a man of quick sensibility, or ardent temper, he could now no longer refrain from regarding these clamors as the dishonest artifices of a sinister and unprincipled opposition to a plan which ought at least to receive a fair and candid examination from all sincere lovers of their country! How else, he would say, could the authors of them have been tempted to vent such loud censures upon that plan, about a point in which it seems to have conformed itself to the general sense of America as declared in its different forms of government, and in which it has even superadded a new and powerful guard unknown to any of them? If, on the contrary, he happened to be a man of calm and dispassionate feelings, he would indulge a sigh for the frailty of human nature, and would lament, that in a matter so interesting to the happiness of millions, the true merits of the question should be perplexed and entangled by expedients so unfriendly to an impartial and right determination. Even such a man could hardly forbear remarking, that a conduct of this kind has too much the appearance of an intention to mislead the people by alarming their passions, rather than to convince them by arguments addressed to their understandings.

But however little this objection may be countenanced, even by precedents among ourselves, it may be satisfactory to take a nearer view of its intrinsic merits. From a close examination it will appear that restraints upon the discretion of the legislature in respect to military establishments in time of peace, would be improper to be imposed, and if imposed, from the necessities of society, would be unlikely to be observed.

Though a wide ocean separates the United States from Europe, yet there are various considerations that warn us against an excess of confidence or security. On one side of us, and stretching far into our rear, are growing settlements subject to the dominion of Britain. On the other side, and extending to meet the British settlements, are colonies and establishments subject to the dominion of Spain. This situation and the vicinity of the West India Islands, belonging to these two powers create between them, in respect to their American possessions and in relation to us, a common interest. The savage tribes on our Western frontier ought to be regarded as our natural enemies, their natural allies, because they have most to fear from us, and most to hope from them. The improvements in the art of navigation have, as to the facility of communication, rendered distant nations, in a great measure, neighbors. Britain and Spain are among the principal maritime powers of Europe. A future concert of views between these nations ought not to be regarded as improbable. The increasing remoteness of consanguinity is every day diminishing the force of the family compact between France and Spain. And politicians have ever with great reason considered the ties of blood as feeble and precarious links of political connection. These circumstances combined, admonish us not to be too sanguine in considering ourselves as entirely out of the reach of danger.

Previous to the Revolution, and ever since the peace, there has been a constant necessity for keeping small garrisons on our Western frontier. No person can doubt that these will continue to be indispensable, if it should only be against the ravages and depredations of the Indians. These garrisons must either be furnished by occasional detachments from the militia, or by permanent corps in the pay of the government. The first is impracticable; and if practicable, would be pernicious. The militia would not long, if at all, submit to be dragged from their occupations and families to perform that most disagreeable duty in times of profound peace. And if they could be prevailed upon or compelled to do it, the increased expense of a frequent rotation of service, and the loss of labor and disconcertion of the industrious pursuits of individuals, would form conclusive objections to the scheme. It would be as burdensome and injurious to the public as ruinous to private citizens. The latter resource of permanent corps in the pay of the government amounts to a standing army in time of peace; a small one, indeed, but not the less real for being small. Here is a simple view of the subject, that shows us at once the impropriety of a constitutional interdiction of such establishments, and the necessity of leaving the matter to the discretion and prudence of the legislature.

In proportion to our increase in strength, it is probable, nay, it may be said certain, that Britain and Spain would augment their military establishments in our neighborhood. If we should not be willing to be exposed, in a naked and defenseless condition, to their insults and encroachments, we should find it expedient to increase our frontier garrisons in some ratio to the force by which our Western settlements might be annoyed. There are, and will be, particular posts, the possession of which will include the command of large districts of territory, and facilitate future invasions of the remainder. It may be added that some of those posts will be keys to the trade with the Indian nations. Can any man think it would be wise to leave such posts in a situation to be at any instant seized by one or the other of two neighboring and formidable powers? To act this part would be to desert all the usual maxims of prudence and policy.

If we mean to be a commercial people, or even to be secure on our Atlantic side, we must endeavor, as soon as possible, to have a navy. To this purpose there must be dock-yards and arsenals; and for the defense of these, fortifications, and probably garrisons. When a nation has become so powerful by sea that it can protect its dock-yards by its fleets, this supersedes the necessity of garrisons for that purpose; but where naval establishments are in their infancy, moderate garrisons will, in all likelihood, be found an indispensable security against descents for the destruction of the arsenals and dock-yards, and sometimes of the fleet itself.

(i) This statement of the matter is taken from the printed collection of State constitutions. Pennsylvania and North Carolina are the two which contain the interdiction in these words: "As standing armies in time of peace are dangerous to liberty, THEY OUGHT NOT to be kept up." This is, in truth, rather a CAUTION than a PROHIBITION. New Hampshire, Massachusetts, Delaware, and Maryland have, in each of their bills of rights, a clause to this effect: "Standing armies are dangerous to liberty, and ought not to be raised or kept up WITHOUT THE CONSENT OF THE LEGISLATURE"; which is a formal admission of the authority of the Legislature. New York has no bills of rights, and her constitution says not a word about the matter. No bills of rights appear annexed to the constitutions of the other States, except the foregoing, and their constitutions are equally silent. I am told, however that one or two States have bills of rights which do not appear in this collection; but that those also recognize the right of the legislative authority in this respect.

Federalist No. 28 by Alexander Hamilton

Editor's Introduction:

Federalist No. 28 reasonably considered the possibility of separate confederacies in North America as a counterweight to the prospect of force to put down "seditions and insurrections." Hamilton wondered why opponents failed to understand that any government might eventually have to resort to force to prevent internal strife, though he suggested that in the event any government became abusive or destructive, the people had an "original right of self-defense" to preserve their liberty and independence. Hamilton considered the structure of the Union to be pivotal for security, as both the States and the central authority would work in concert to prevent invasion while the relative isolation of the United States would offer a deterrent to European meddling. Moreover, legislative control of the military placed the full power of the general government in the hands of the people, and Hamilton argued that was the surest and safest check on government tyranny.

Federalist No. 28

December 26, 1787

By Alexander Hamilton of New York

To the People of the State of New York:

THAT there may happen cases in which the national government may be necessitated to resort to force, cannot be denied. Our own experience has corroborated the lessons taught by the examples of other nations; that emergencies of this sort will sometimes arise in all societies, however constituted; that seditions and insurrections are, unhappily, maladies as inseparable from the body politic as tumors and eruptions from the natural body; that the idea of governing at all times by the simple force of law (which we have been told is the only admissible principle of republican government), has no place but in the reveries of those political doctors whose sagacity disdains the admonitions of experimental instruction.

Should such emergencies at any time happen under the national government, there could be no remedy but force. The means to be employed must be proportioned to the extent of the mischief. If it should be a slight commotion in a small part of a State, the militia of the residue would be adequate to its suppression; and the national presumption is that they would be ready to do their duty. An insurrection, whatever may be its immediate cause, eventually endangers all government. Regard to the public peace, if not to the rights of the Union, would engage the citizens to whom the contagion had not communicated itself to oppose the insurgents; and if the general government should be found in practice conducive to the prosperity and felicity of the people, it were irrational to believe that they would be disinclined to its support.

If, on the contrary, the insurrection should pervade a whole State, or a principal part of it, the employment of a different kind of force might become unavoidable. It appears that Massachusetts found it necessary to raise troops for repressing the disorders within that

State; that Pennsylvania, from the mere apprehension of commotions among a part of her citizens, has thought proper to have recourse to the same measure. Suppose the State of New York had been inclined to re-establish her lost jurisdiction over the inhabitants of Vermont, could she have hoped for success in such an enterprise from the efforts of the militia alone? Would she not have been compelled to raise and to maintain a more regular force for the execution of her design? If it must then be admitted that the necessity of recurring to a force different from the militia, in cases of this extraordinary nature, is applicable to the State governments themselves, why should the possibility, that the national government might be under a like necessity, in similar extremities, be made an objection to its existence? Is it not surprising that men who declare an attachment to the Union in the abstract, should urge as an objection to the proposed Constitution what applies with tenfold weight to the plan for which they contend; and what, as far as it has any foundation in truth, is an inevitable consequence of civil society upon an enlarged scale? Who would not prefer that possibility to the unceasing agitations and frequent revolutions which are the continual scourges of petty republics?

Let us pursue this examination in another light. Suppose, in lieu of one general system, two, or three, or even four Confederacies were to be formed, would not the same difficulty oppose itself to the operations of either of these Confederacies? Would not each of them be exposed to the same casualties; and when these happened, be obliged to have recourse to the same expedients for upholding its authority which are objected to in a government for all the States? Would the militia, in this supposition, be more ready or more able to support the federal authority than in the case of a general union? All candid and intelligent men must, upon due consideration, acknowledge that the principle of the objection is equally applicable to either of the two cases; and that whether we have one government for all the States, or different governments for different parcels of them, or even if there should be an entire separation of the States, there might sometimes be a necessity to make use of a force constituted differently from the militia, to preserve the peace of the community and to maintain the just authority of the laws against those violent invasions of them which amount to insurrections and rebellions.

Independent of all other reasonings upon the subject, it is a full answer to those who require a more peremptory provision against military establishments in time of peace, to say that the whole power of the proposed government is to be in the hands of the representatives of the people. This is the essential, and, after all, only efficacious security for the rights and privileges of the people, which is attainable in civil society.(i)

If the representatives of the people betray their constituents, there is then no resource left but in the exertion of that original right of self-defense which is paramount to all positive forms of government, and which against the usurpations of the national rulers, may be exerted with infinitely better prospect of success than against those of the rulers of an individual state. In a single state, if the persons intrusted with supreme power become usurpers, the different parcels, subdivisions, or districts of which it consists, having no distinct government in each, can take no regular measures for defense. The citizens must rush tumultuously to arms, without concert, without system, without resource; except in their courage and despair. The usurpers, clothed with the forms of legal authority, can too often crush the opposition in embryo. The smaller the extent of the territory, the more difficult will it be for the people to form a regular or systematic plan of opposition, and the more easy will it be to defeat their early efforts. Intelligence can be more speedily obtained of their preparations and movements, and the military force in the possession of the usurpers can be more rapidly directed against the part where the opposition has begun. In this situation there must be a peculiar coincidence of circumstances to insure success to the popular resistance.

The obstacles to usurpation and the facilities of resistance increase with the increased extent of the state, provided the citizens understand their rights and are disposed to defend them. The natural strength of the people in a large community, in proportion to the artificial strength of the government, is greater than in a small, and of course more competent to a struggle with the attempts of the government to establish a tyranny. But in a confederacy the people, without exaggeration, may be said to be entirely the masters of their own fate. Power being almost always the rival of power, the general government will at all times stand ready to check the usurpations of the state governments, and these will have the same disposition towards the general government. The people, by throwing themselves into either scale, will infallibly make it preponderate. If their rights are invaded by either, they can make use of the other as the instrument of redress. How wise will it be in them by cherishing the union to preserve to themselves an advantage which can never be too highly prized!

It may safely be received as an axiom in our political system, that the State governments will, in all possible contingencies, afford complete security against invasions of the public liberty by the national authority. Projects of usurpation cannot be masked under pretenses so likely to escape the penetration of select bodies of men, as of the people at large. The legislatures will have better means of information. They can discover the danger at a distance; and possessing all the organs of civil power, and the confidence of the people, they can at once adopt a regular plan of opposition, in which they can combine all the resources of the community. They can readily communicate with each other in the different States, and unite their common forces for the protection of their common liberty.

The great extent of the country is a further security. We have already experienced its utility against the attacks of a foreign power. And it would have precisely the same effect against the enterprises of ambitious rulers in the national councils. If the federal army should be able to quell the resistance of one State, the distant States would have it in their power to make head with fresh forces. The advantages obtained in one place must be abandoned to subdue the opposition in others; and the moment the part which had been reduced to submission was left to itself, its efforts would be renewed, and its resistance revive.

We should recollect that the extent of the military force must, at all events, be regulated by the resources of the country. For a long time to come, it will not be possible to maintain a large army; and as the means of doing this increase, the population and natural strength of the community will proportionably increase. When will the time arrive that the federal government can raise and maintain an army capable of erecting a despotism over the great body of the people of an immense empire, who are in a situation, through the medium of their State governments, to take measures for their own defense, with all the celerity, regularity, and system of independent nations? The apprehension may be considered as a disease, for which there can be found no cure in the resources of argument and reasoning.

(i) Its full efficacy will be examined hereafter.

Federalist No. 32 by Alexander Hamilton

Editor's Introduction:

Hamilton addressed the claim that States would lose their taxing power should the Constitution be ratified in this installment of the *Federalist*. He made two important arguments in this essay: 1) the States retained their "sovereignty" except in three cases where they "EXCLUSIVELY" delegated that authority to the general government: where the Constitution gave exclusive jurisdiction to the general government; where the Constitution prohibited certain powers to the States; and where the State authority would be "CONTRADICTORY" and "REPUGNANT" to the welfare of the Union. 2) Hamilton insisted the States would have concurrent powers of taxation and that this power would be properly used to support and maintain the State governments. Hamilton continued to press that the Constitution maintained a federal republic and did not annihilate the State governments.

Federalist No. 32

January 2, 1788

By Alexander Hamilton of New York

To the People of the State of New York:

ALTHOUGH I am of opinion that there would be no real danger of the consequences which seem to be apprehended to the State governments from a power in the Union to control them in the levies of money, because I am persuaded that the sense of the people, the extreme hazard of provoking the resentments of the State governments, and a conviction of the utility and necessity of local administrations for local purposes, would be a complete barrier against the oppressive use of such a power; yet I am willing here to allow, in its full extent, the justness of the reasoning which requires that the individual States should possess an independent and uncontrollable authority to raise their own revenues for the supply of their own wants. And making this concession, I affirm that (with the sole exception of duties on imports and exports) they would, under the plan of the convention, retain that authority in the most absolute and unqualified sense; and that an attempt on the part of the national government to abridge them in the exercise of it, would be a violent assumption of power, unwarranted by any article or clause of its Constitution.

An entire consolidation of the States into one complete national sovereignty would imply an entire subordination of the parts; and whatever powers might remain in them, would be altogether dependent on the general will. But as the plan of the convention aims only at a partial union or consolidation, the State governments would clearly retain all the rights of sovereignty which they before had, and which were not, by that act, EXCLUSIVELY delegated to the United States. This exclusive delegation, or rather this alienation, of State sovereignty, would only exist in three cases: where the Constitution in express terms granted an exclusive authority to the Union; where it granted in one instance an authority to the Union, and in another prohibited the States from exercising the like authority; and where it granted an authority to the Union, to which a similar authority in the States would be absolutely and totally CONTRADICTORY and REPUGNANT. I use these terms to distinguish this last case from another which might appear to resemble it, but which would, in fact, be essentially different; I mean where the exercise of a concurrent jurisdiction might be productive of occasional interferences in the POLICY of any branch of administration, but would not imply any direct contradiction or repugnancy in point of constitutional authority. These three cases of exclusive jurisdiction in the federal government may be exemplified by the following instances: The last clause but one in the eighth section of the first article provides expressly that Congress shall exercise "EXCLUSIVE LEGISLATION" over the district to be appropriated as the seat of government. This answers to the first case. The first clause of the same section empowers Congress "TO LAY AND COLLECT TAXES, DUTIES, IMPOSTS AND EXCISES"; and the second clause of the tenth section of the same article declares that, "NO STATE SHALL, without the consent of Congress, LAY ANY IMPOSTS OR DUTIES ON IMPORTS OR EXPORTS, except for the purpose of executing its inspection laws." Hence would result an exclusive power in the Union to lay duties on imports and exports, with the particular exception mentioned; but this power is abridged by another clause, which declares that no tax or duty shall be laid on articles exported from any State; in consequence of which qualification, it now only extends to the DUTIES ON IMPORTS. This answers to the second case. The third will be found in that clause which declares that Congress shall have power "to establish an UNIFORM RULE of naturalization throughout the United States." This must necessarily be exclusive; because if each State had power to prescribe a DISTINCT RULE, there could not be a UNIFORM RULE.

A case which may perhaps be thought to resemble the latter, but which is in fact widely different, affects the question immediately under consideration. I mean the power of imposing taxes on all articles other than exports and imports. This, I contend, is manifestly a concurrent and coequal authority in the United States and in the individual States. There is plainly no expression in the granting clause which makes that power EXCLUSIVE in the Union. There is no independent clause or sentence which prohibits the States from exercising it. So far is this from being the case, that a plain and conclusive argument to the contrary is to be deduced from the restraint laid upon the States in relation to duties on imports and exports. This restriction implies an admission that, if it were not inserted, the States would possess the power it excludes; and it implies a further admission, that as to all other taxes, the authority of the States remains undiminished. In any other view it would be both unnecessary and dangerous; it would be unnecessary, because if the grant to the Union of the power of laying such duties implied the exclusion of the States, or even their subordination in this particular, there could be no need of such a restriction; it would be dangerous, because the introduction of it leads directly to the conclusion which has been mentioned, and which, if the reasoning of the objectors be just, could not have been intended; I mean that the States, in all cases to which the restriction did not apply, would have a concurrent power of taxation with the Union. The restriction in question amounts to what lawyers call a NEGATIVE PREGNANT that is, a NEGATION of one thing, and an AFFIRMANCE of another; a negation of the authority of the States to impose taxes on imports and exports, and an affirmance of their authority to impose them on all other articles. It would be mere sophistry to argue that it was meant to exclude them ABSOLUTELY from the imposition of taxes of the former kind, and to leave them at liberty to lay others SUBJECT TO THE CONTROL of the national legislature. The restraining or prohibitory clause only says, that they shall not, WITHOUT THE CONSENT OF CONGRESS, lay such duties; and if we are to understand this in the sense last mentioned, the Constitution would then be made to introduce a formal provision for the sake of a very absurd conclusion; which is, that the States, WITH THE CONSENT of the national legislature, might tax imports and exports; and that they might tax every other article, UNLESS CONTROLLED by the same body. If this was the intention, why not leave it, in the first instance, to what is alleged to be the natural operation of the original clause, conferring a general power of taxation upon the Union? It is evident that this could not have been the intention, and that it will not bear a construction of the kind.

As to a supposition of repugnancy between the power of taxation in the States and in the Union, it cannot be supported in that sense which would be requisite to work an exclusion of the States. It is, indeed, possible that a tax might be laid on a particular article by a State which might render it INEXPEDIENT that thus a further tax should be laid on the same article by the Union; but it would not imply a constitutional inability to impose a further tax. The quantity of the imposition, the expediency or inexpediency of an increase on either side, would be mutually questions of prudence; but there would be involved no direct contradiction of power. The particular policy of the national and of the State systems of finance might now and then not exactly coincide, and might require reciprocal forbearances. It is not, however a mere possibility of inconvenience in the exercise of powers, but an immediate constitutional repugnancy that can by implication alienate and extinguish a pre-existing right of sovereignty.

The necessity of a concurrent jurisdiction in certain cases results from the division of the sovereign power; and the rule that all authorities, of which the States are not explicitly divested in favor of the Union, remain with them in full vigor, is not a theoretical consequence of that division, but is clearly admitted by the whole tenor of the instrument which contains the articles of the proposed Constitution. We there find that, notwithstanding the affirmative grants of general authorities, there has been the most pointed care in those cases where it was deemed improper that the like authorities should reside in the States, to insert negative clauses prohibiting the exercise of them by the States. The tenth section of the first article consists altogether of such provisions. This circumstance is a clear indication of the sense of the convention, and furnishes a rule of interpretation out of the body of the act, which justifies the position I have advanced and refutes every hypothesis to the contrary.

Federalist No. 33 by Alexander Hamilton

Editor's Introduction:

Hamilton focused on the "sweeping clauses" of the Constitution in *Federalist* No. 33. Opponents of the document claimed that the "Necessary and Proper Clause" and the "Supremacy Clause" exposed that the Constitution would foist a national, consolidated government on the existing Union of States. Hamilton scoffed at this notion and insisted that only the powers made "IN PURSUANCE" of the Constitution would be supreme and that included those laws which would be "NECESSARY and PROPER" for executing the powers the document expressly delegated to the central government. If the Congress should exceed its delegated authority, Hamilton thought the people of the States would have the power to check the usurpation. He did not explain how this would be accomplished, but it is important to note that proponents of the document, even nationalists like Hamilton, believed that the people of the States would have recourse to check unconstitutional federal acts.

Federalist No. 33

January 2, 1788

By Alexander Hamilton of New York

To the People of the State of New York:

THE residue of the argument against the provisions of the Constitution in respect to taxation is ingrafted upon the following clause. The last clause of the eighth section of the first article of the plan under consideration authorizes the national legislature "to make all laws which shall be NECESSARY and PROPER for carrying into execution THE POWERS by that Constitution vested in the government of the United States, or in any department or officer thereof"; and the second clause of the sixth article declares, "that the Constitution and the laws of the United States made IN PURSUANCE THEREOF, and the treaties made by their authority shall be the SUPREME LAW of the land, any thing in the constitution or laws of any State to the contrary notwithstanding."

These two clauses have been the source of much virulent invective and petulant declamation against the proposed Constitution. They have been held up to the people in all the exaggerated colors of misrepresentation as the pernicious engines by which their local governments were to be destroyed and their liberties exterminated; as the hideous monster whose devouring jaws would spare neither sex nor age, nor high nor low, nor sacred nor profane; and yet, strange as it may appear, after all this clamor, to those who may not have happened to contemplate them in the same light, it may be affirmed with perfect confidence that the constitutional operation of the intended government would be precisely the same, if these clauses were entirely obliterated, as if they were repeated in every article. They are only declaratory of a truth which would have resulted by necessary and unavoidable implication from the very act of constituting a federal government, and vesting it with certain specified powers. This is so clear a proposition, that moderation itself can scarcely listen to the railings which have been so copiously vented against this part of the plan, without emotions that disturb its equanimity.

What is a power, but the ability or faculty of doing a thing? What is the ability to do a thing, but the power of employing the MEANS necessary to its execution? What is a LEGISLATIVE power, but a power of making LAWS? What are the MEANS to execute a LEGISLATIVE power but LAWS? What is the power of laying and collecting taxes, but a LEGISLATIVE POWER, or a power of MAKING LAWS, to lay and collect taxes? What are the proper means of executing such a power, but NECESSARY and PROPER laws?

This simple train of inquiry furnishes us at once with a test by which to judge of the true nature of the clause complained of. It conducts us to this palpable truth, that a power to lay and collect taxes must be a power to pass all laws NECESSARY and PROPER for the execution of that power; and what does the unfortunate and calumniated provision in question do more than declare the same truth, to wit, that the national legislature, to whom the power of laying and collecting taxes had been previously given, might, in the execution of that power, pass all laws NECESSARY and PROPER to carry it into effect? I have applied these observations thus particularly to the power of taxation, because it is the immediate subject under consideration, and because it is the most important of the authorities proposed to be conferred upon the Union. But the same process will lead to the same result, in relation to all other powers declared in the Constitution. And it is EXPRESSLY to execute these powers that the sweeping clause, as it has been affectedly called, authorizes the national legislature to pass all NECESSARY and PROPER laws. If there is any thing exceptionable, it must be sought for in the specific powers upon which this general declaration is predicated. The declaration itself, though it may be chargeable with tautology or redundancy, is at least perfectly harmless.

But SUSPICION may ask, Why then was it introduced? The answer is, that it could only have been done for greater caution, and to guard against all caviling refinements in those who might hereafter feel a disposition to curtail and evade the legitimate authorities of the Union. The Convention probably foresaw, what it has been a principal aim of these papers to inculcate, that the danger which most threatens our political welfare is that the State governments will finally sap the foundations of the Union; and might therefore think it necessary, in so cardinal a point, to leave nothing to construction. Whatever may have been the inducement to it, the wisdom of the precaution is evident from the cry which has been raised against it; as that very cry betrays a disposition to question the great and essential truth which it is manifestly the object of that provision to declare.

But it may be again asked, Who is to judge of the NECESSITY and PROPRIETY of the laws to be passed for executing the powers of the Union? I answer, first, that this question arises as well and as fully upon the simple grant of those powers as upon the declaratory clause; and I answer, in the second place, that the national government, like every other, must judge, in the first instance, of the proper exercise of its powers, and its constituents in the last. If the federal government should overpass the just bounds of its authority and make a tyrannical use of its powers, the people, whose creature it is, must appeal to the standard they have formed, and take such measures to redress the injury done to the Constitution as the exigency may suggest and prudence justify. The propriety of a law, in a constitutional light, must always be determined by the nature of the powers upon which it is founded. Suppose, by some forced constructions of its authority (which, indeed, cannot easily be imagined), the Federal legislature should attempt to vary the law of descent in any State, would it not be evident that, in making such an attempt, it had exceeded its jurisdiction, and infringed upon that of the State? Suppose, again, that upon the pretense of an interference with its revenues, it should undertake to abrogate a land tax imposed by the authority of a State; would it not be equally evident that this was an invasion of that concurrent jurisdiction in respect to this species of tax, which its Constitution plainly supposes to exist in the State governments? If there ever should be a doubt on this head, the credit of it will be entirely due to those reasoners who, in the imprudent zeal of their animosity to the plan of the convention, have labored to envelop it in a cloud calculated to obscure the plainest and simplest truths.

But it is said that the laws of the Union are to be the SUPREME LAW of the land. But what inference can be drawn from this, or what would they amount to, if they were not to be supreme? It is evident they would amount to nothing. A LAW, by the very meaning of the term, includes supremacy. It is a rule which those to whom it is prescribed are bound to observe. This results from every political association. If individuals enter into a state of society, the laws of that society must be the supreme regulator of their conduct. If a number of political societies enter into a larger political society, the laws which the latter may enact, pursuant to the powers intrusted to it by its constitution, must necessarily be supreme over those societies, and the individuals of whom they are composed. It would otherwise be a mere treaty, dependent on the good faith of the parties, and not a government, which is only another word for POLITICAL POWER AND SUPREMACY. But it will not follow from this doctrine that acts of the large society which are NOT PURSUANT to its constitutional powers, but which are invasions of the residuary authorities of the smaller societies, will become the supreme law of the land. These will be merely acts of usurpation, and will deserve to be treated as such. Hence we perceive that the clause which declares the supremacy of the laws of the Union, like the one we have just before considered, only declares a truth, which flows immediately and necessarily from the institution of a federal government. It will not, I presume, have escaped observation, that it EXPRESSLY confines this supremacy to laws made PURSUANT TO THE CONSTITUTION; which I mention merely as an instance of caution in the convention; since that limitation would have been to be understood, though it had not been expressed.

Though a law, therefore, laying a tax for the use of the United States would be supreme in its nature, and could not legally be opposed or controlled, yet a law for abrogating or preventing the collection of a tax laid by the authority of the State, (unless upon imports and exports), would not be the supreme law of the land, but a usurpation of power not granted by the Constitution. As far as an improper accumulation of taxes on the same object might tend to render the collection difficult or precarious, this would be a mutual inconvenience, not arising from a superiority or defect of power on either side, but from an injudicious exercise of power by one or the other, in a manner equally disadvantageous to both. It is to be hoped and presumed, however, that mutual interest would dictate a concert in this respect which would avoid any material inconvenience. The inference from the whole is, that the individual States would, under the proposed Constitution, retain an independent and uncontrollable authority to raise revenue to any extent of which they may stand in need, by every kind of taxation, except duties on imports and exports. It will be shown in the next paper that this CONCURRENT JURISDICTION in the article of taxation was the only admissible substitute for an entire subordination, in respect to this branch of power, of the State authority to that of the Union.

Speech Before the Connecticut Ratifying Convention by Oiver Ellsworth

Editor's Introduction:

Connecticut opened its ratifying convention on January 3, 1788. Four States had already ratified the document—Delaware, Pennsylvania, New Jersey, and Georgia—and proponents of the document in the Nutmeg State hoped to quickly follow suit. Like Pennsylvania, Connecticut had a robust opposition to the Constitution, though also like Pennsylvania, the majority constantly tried to stifle dissent either through suppressing opposition views in the press or through intimidation. The leading political figures in the State rallied around ratification. This included Roger Sherman and Oliver Ellsworth, but also men like Oliver Wolcott and Samuel Huntington. Ellsworth had already engaged the public through his Landholder essays, but now that he was elected to the ratifying convention, he had the opportunity to openly explain the merits of the new document. His January 4 speech in favor of the Constitution outlined the benefits of union and the necessity of a "coercive" power for the central authority. He did not explain what type of "coercive" power existed in the new government, and he whined about New England's burden in financing the War for American Independence and the reluctance of other States to pay their fair share toward the maintenance of the general government. George Washington complained loudly during the War that New Englanders were driven by money and little else. Ellsworth certainly supported that generalization in this speech, but more than anything, his conclusion that the Constitution corrected the deficiencies of the Article of Confederation had the greatest impact on the minds of the ratifiers in Connecticut.

Speech Before the Connecticut Ratifying Convention
January 4, 1788
By Oliver Ellsworth of Connecticut

Mr. Ellsworth opened the Debates of the day, in a Speech the substance of which is as follows:

Mr. President. It is observable, that there is no preface to the proposed Constitution; but it evidently presupposes two things; one is the necessity of a federal government, the other is the inefficiency of the old articles of confederation. A Union is necessary for the purposes of national defence. United, we are strong; divided we are weak. It is easy for hostile nations to sweep off a number of separate states one after another. Witness the states in the neighbourhood of ancient Rome. They were successively subdued by that ambitious city; which they might have conquered with the utmost ease, if they had been United. Witness the Canaanitish nations, whose divided situation rendered them an easy prey. Witness England, which, when divided into a number of separate states, was twice conquered by an inferior force. Thus it always happens to small states, and to great ones, if divided. Or if to avoid this, they connect themselves with some powerful state, their situation is not much better. This shows us the necessity of our combining our whole force; and, as to national purposes, becoming one state.

A Union, Sir, is likewise necessary considered with relation to economy. Small States have enemies as well as great ones. They must provide for their defence. The expense of it, which would be moderate for a large kingdom, would be intolerable to a petty State. The Dutch are wealthy, but they are one of the smallest of the European nations, and their taxes are higher than in any other country of Europe. Their taxes amount to forty shillings per head, when those of England do not exceed half that sum.

We must unite, in order to preserve peace among ourselves. If we are divided, what is to hinder wars from breaking out among the states? States, as well as individuals, are subject to ambition, to avarice, to those jarring passions which disturb the peace of society. What is to check these? If there is a parental hand over the whole, this, and nothing else, can restrain the unruly conduct of the members.

Union is necessary to preserve commutative justice between the states. If divided, what is to hinder the large states from oppressing the small? What is to defend us from the ambition and rapacity of New York, when she has spread over that vast territory, which she claims and holds? Do we not already see in her the seeds of an overbearing ambition? On our other side there is a large and powerful State. Have we not already begun to be tributaries? If we do not improve the present critical time, if we do not unite, shall we not be like Issachar of old, a strong ass crouching down between two burdens? New Jersey and Delaware have seen this, and have adopted the constitution unanimously.

A more energetic system is necessary. The present is merely advisory. It has no coercive power. Without this, government is ineffectual, or rather is no government at all. But it is said, such a power is not necessary. States will not do wrong. They need only to be told their duty, and they will do it. I ask, Sir, what warrant is there for this assertion? Do not States do wrong? Whence come wars? One of two hostile nations must be in the wrong. But it is said, among sister States this can never be presumed. But do we not know, that when friends become enemies, their enmity is the most virulent? The seventeen provinces of the Netherlands were once confederated; they fought under the same banner. Antwerp, hard pressed by Philip, applied to the other states for relief. Holland, a rival in trade, opposed, and prevented the needed succours. Antwerp was made a sacrifice. I wish I could say, there were no seeds of similar injustice springing up among us. Is there not in one of our states injustice too barefaced for eastern despotism? That state is small; it does little hurt to any but itself. But it has a spirit, which would make a tophet of the universe. But some will say, we formerly did well, without any union. I answer, our situation is materially changed. While Great Britain held her authority, she awed us. She appointed governors and councils for the American provinces. She had a negative upon our laws. But now, our circumstances are so altered, that there is no arguing what we shall be from what we have been.

It is said, that other confederacies have not had the principle of coercion. Is this so? Let us attend to those confederacies which have resembled our own. Sometime before Alexander, the Grecian States confederated together. The Amphyctionic council, consisting of Deputies from these States, met at Delphos; and had authority to regulate the general interests of Greece. This Council did enforce its decrees by coercion. The Beotians once infringed upon a decree of the Amphyctions. A heavy mulct was laid upon them. They refused to pay it. Upon that, their whole territory was confiscated. They were then glad to compound the matter. After the death of Alexander, the Achean League was formed. The decrees of this confederacy were enforced by dint of arms. The f£tolian league was formed by some other Grecian cities in opposition to the Achean; and there was no peace between them, till they were conquered, and reduced to a Roman province. They were then all obliged to sit down in peace under the same yoke of despotism.

How is it with respect to the principle of coertion in the Germanic body? In Germany there are about three hundred principalities and republics; deputies from these meet annually in the general Diet to make regulations for the empire. But the execution of those is not left voluntarily with the members. The empire is divided into ten circles; over each of which a superintendant is appointed, with the rank of a major general. It is his duty to execute the decrees of the empire with a military force.

The confederation of the Swiss Cantons has been considered as an example. But their circumstances are far different from ours. They are small republics, about twenty miles square, situated among the Alps, and inaccessible to hostile attacks. They have nothing to tempt an invasion. Till lately, they had neither commerce, nor manufactures. They were merely a set of herdsmen. Their inaccessibleness has availed them. Four hundred of those mountainers defeated 15,000 Austrians, who were marching to subdue them. They spend the ardour of youth in foreign service; they return old, and disposed for tranquility. Between some of the Cantons and France, there has long subsisted a defensive treaty. By this treaty, France is to be a mediator to settle differences between the Cantons. If any one is obstinate, France is to compel a submission to reasonable terms.

The Dutch Republic is an example that merits attention. The form of their constitution, as it is on paper, admits not of coertion. But necessity has introduced it in practice. This coercive power is the influence of the stadtholder, an officer originally unknown to their constitution. But they have been necessitated to appoint him, in order to set their unwieldy machine of government in motion. He is commander in chief of their navy, and of their army consisting of 40, or 50 regiments. He appoints the officers of the land and naval forces. He resides in the states general, and in the states of every province; and by means of this, he has a great opportunity to influence the elections and decisions. The province of Holland have ever been opposed to the appointment of a stadtholder; because, by their wealth and power, being equal to all the other provinces, they possess the weight and influence of the stadtholder, when that office is vacant. Without such an influence, their machine of government would no more move, than a ship without wind, or a clock without weights.

But to come nearer home, Mr. President, have we not seen and felt the necessity of such a coercive power? What was the consequence of the want of it during the late war, particularly towards the close? A few states bore the burden of the war. While we, and one or two more of the states, were paying 80 or 100 dollars per man to recruit the continental army, the regiments of some states had scarcely men enough to wait on their officers. Since the close of the war, some of the states have done nothing towards complying with the requisitions of Congress; others, who did something at first, seeing that they were left to bear the whole burden, have become equally remiss. What is the consequence? To what shifts have we been driven? We have been driven to the wretched expedient of negotiating new loans in Europe to pay the interest of the foreign debt. And what is still worse, we have even been obliged to apply these new loans to the support of our own civil government at home.

Another ill consequence of this want of energy is that treaties are not performed. The treaty of peace with Great Britain was a very favourable one for us. But it did not happen perfectly to please some of the states: and they would not comply with it. The consequence is, Britain charges us with the breach, and refuses to deliver up the forts on our northern quarter.

Our being tributaries to our sister states is a consequence of the want of a federal system. The state of New York raises 60 or 80,000 a year by impost. Connecticut consumes about one third of the goods upon which this impost is laid; and consequently pays one third of this sum to New York. If we import by the medium of Massachusetts, she has an impost, and to her we pay a tribute. If this is done, when we have the shadow of a national government, what shall we not suffer, when even that shadow is gone?

If we go on as we have done, what is to become of the foreign debts? Will foreign nations forgive us this debt, because we neglect to pay? or will they levy it by reprisals as the laws of nations authorize them? Will our weakness induce Spain to relinquish the exclusive navigation of the Mississippi, or the territory which she claims on the east side of that river? Will our weakness induce the British to give up the Northern posts? If a war breaks out, and our situation invites our enemies to make war, how are we to defend ourselves? Has Government the means to enlist a man, or buy an ox? or shall we rally the remainder of our old army? The European nations, I believe to be not friendly to us. They were pleased to see us disconnected from Great Britain; they are pleased to see us disunited among ourselves. If we continue so, how easy it is for them to canton us out among them, as they did the Kingdom of Poland? But supposing this is not done, if we suffer the union to expire, the least that can be expected is that the European powers will form alliances, some with one State and some with another, and play the States off one against another, and that we shall be involved in all the labyrinths of European politics. But I do not wish to continue the painful recital: enough has been said to shew, that a power in the general government to enforce the decrees of the union, is absolutely necessary.

The Constitution before us is a complete system of legislative, judicial, and executive power. It was designed to supply the defects of the former system; and I believe, upon a full discussion, it will be found calculated to answer the purposes for which it was designed.

Speech Before the Connecticut Ratifying Convention by Samuel Huntington and Oliver Wolcott

Editor's Introduction:

Neither Samuel Huntington nor Oliver Wolcott are considered great men of the founding generation, but both were leading men of the Connecticut political class. Huntington was Governor of Connecticut when the ratifying convention met in January 1788 and he was succeeded by Wolcott in 1796, the Lieutenant Governor during Huntington's entire tenure in office. Both men served in the Second Continental Congress and along with Roger Sherman voted for independence in 1776. Huntington later served as president of the Continental Congress and held that position when the Articles of Confederation were ratified in 1781. Huntington concurrently served as Chief Justice of the Connecticut Supreme Court and Lieutenant Governor from 1784-1785. Perhaps only Roger Sherman had more political clout than Huntington in Connecticut. Huntington presided over the ratifying convention and his speech in favor of the document, though brief, undoubtedly moved many men to support the document.

Wolcott served as major general of the Connecticut militia during the American War for Independence and for a brief period as Governor of Connecticut after Huntington's death in 1796. Like Huntington, Wolcott died in office in 1797. His military career lacked success and other than a short stint as Commissioner of Indian Affairs, he never held a prominent "national" position.

Both Huntington and Wolcott delivered their speeches on the final day of the convention. Like Ellsworth, both stressed the need for a federal "coercive" principle though neither thought that the power would be used to destroy the State governments. In fact, Wolcott called the States the "pillars" upon which the entire system was built. Both believed that the liberties of the people of Connecticut would be well guarded by a stronger Union and both argued that the Articles of Confederation were woefully inadequate to preserve the hard-fought independence of the American States. These were common arguments from proponents of the document across the United States. Connecticut ratified the document on January 9, 1788 by a vote of 128-40.

Speech Before the Connecticut Ratifying Convention

January 9, 1788

By Samuel Huntington and Oliver Wolcott of Connecticut

SAMUEL HUNTINGTON: Upon the general discussion of the subject, His Excellency Governor Samuel Huntington expressed himself nearly as follows. Mr. President, I do not rise to detain this Convention for any length of time. The subject has been so fully discussed that very little can be added to what has been already offered. I have heard and attended with pleasure to what has been said upon this subject. The importance of it merited a full and ample discussion. It does not give me pain, but pleasure, to hear the sentiments of those gentlemen who differ from me. It is not to be expected from human nature that we should all have the same opinion. The best way to learn the nature and effects of different systems of government is not from theoretical dissertations, but from experience from what has actually taken place among mankind. From this latter source of information, it is that mankind have obtained a more complete knowledge of the nature of government than they had in ages past.

It is an established truth that no nation can exist without a coercive power, a power to enforce the execution of its political regulations. There is such a love of liberty implanted in the human breast that no nation ever willingly gave up its liberty. If they lose this inestimable birthright of man, it is from a want not of will but of the proper means to support it. If we look into history, we shall find that the common avenue through which tyranny has entered in, and enslaved nations who were once free, has been their not supporting government. The great secret of preserving liberty is to lodge the supreme power so as to be well supported and not abused. If this could only be effected, no nation would ever lose its liberty. The history of mankind clearly shows that it is dangerous to entrust the supreme power in the hands of one man. The same source of knowledge proves that it is not only inconvenient but dangerous to liberty for the people of a large community to attempt to exercise in person the supreme authority. Hence arises the necessity that the people should act by their representatives; but this method, so necessary for the support of civil liberty, is an improvement of modern times. Liberty however is not so well secured as it ought to be when the supreme power is lodged in one body of representatives. There ought to be two branches of the legislature, that the one may be a check upon the other. It is difficult for the people at large to know when the supreme power is verging towards abuse and to apply the proper remedy.

But if the government be properly balanced, it will possess a renovating principle by which it will be able to right itself. The constitution of the British nation affords us great light upon the subject of government. Learned men in other countries have admired it, but they thought it too finespun to prove beneficial in practice. But a long trial has now shown its excellence; and the difficulties which that nation now experiences arise not from their constitution but from other circumstances. The Author of Nature has given to mankind a certain degree of insight into futurity. As far as we can see a probability that certain events will happen, so far we do well to provide and guard. But we may attempt to go too far; it is in vain to think of providing against every possible contingency.

The happiness of civil society depends not merely upon their constitution of government but upon a variety of circumstances. One constitution may suit one particular nation exceedingly well; when a different one would suit another nation in different circumstances. Even among the American states there is such a difference in sentiments, habits, and customs that a government which would be very suitable for one might not be agreeable to another.

I am fully of opinion that the great council of the Union must have a controlling power with respect to matters of national concern. There is at present an extreme want of power in the national government; and it is my opinion that this Constitution does not give too much. As to the subject of representation, at first view it appears small; but upon the whole, the purposes of the Union could not be so well answered by a greater number. It is impracticable to have the numbers of the representation as great, and the times of electing as frequent, as they are in our state governments. Nor is this necessary for the security of liberty. It is sufficient if the choice of Representatives be so frequent that they must depend upon the people, and that an inseparable connection be kept up between the electors and elected.

The state governments, I think, will not be endangered by the powers vested by this Constitution in the general government. While I have attended in Congress, I have observed that the members were quite as strenuous advocates for the rights of their respective states as for those of the Union. I doubt not but this will continue to be the case, and hence I infer that the general government will not have the disposition to encroach upon the states. But still the people themselves must be the chief support of liberty. While the great body of the freeholders are acquainted with the duties which they owe to their God, to themselves, and to men, they will remain free. But if ignorance and depravity should prevail, they will inevitably lead to slavery and ruin.

Upon the whole view of this Constitution, I am in favor of it and think it bids fair to promote our national prosperity. This is a new event in the history of mankind. Heretofore, most governments have been formed by tyrants and imposed on mankind by force. Never before did a people, in time of peace and tranquility, meet together by their representatives and, with calm deliberation, frame for themselves a system of government. This noble attempt does honor to our country. While I express my sentiments in favor of this Constitution, I candidly believe that the gentlemen who oppose it are actuated by principles of regard to the public welfare. If we will exercise mutual candor for each other, and sincerely endeavor to maintain our liberties, we may long continue to be a free and happy people.

OLIVER WOLCOTT: Mr. President, I do not expect to throw any new light upon a subject which has been so fully discussed. Yet I cannot content myself without giving my opinion more explicitly than by a silent vote. It is generally agreed that the present Confederation is inadequate to the exigencies of our national affairs. We must therefore adopt this plan of government or some other, or risk the consequences of disunion.

As the present Articles of Confederation are inadequate, we ought to consider whether this Constitution be as good as can be agreed on by so many different states or whether it be a dangerous system; whether it secures the liberties of the people or whether its tendency be unfavorable to the rights of a free people. I have given it all the consideration in my power. I have a considerable time since made up my mind upon it; and I think it my duty to give my voice in favor of adopting it. It is founded upon the election of the people. If it varies from the former system, or if it is to be altered hereafter, it must be with the consent of the people. This is all the security in favor of liberty which can be expected. Mankind may become corrupt and give up the cause of freedom, but I believe that love of liberty which prevails among the people of this country will prevent such a direful calamity. This Constitution effectually secures the states in their several rights. It must secure them for its own sake, for they are the pillars which uphold the general system. The Senate, a constituent branch of the general legislature without whose assent no public act can be made, are appointed by the states and will secure the rights of the several states.

The other branch of the legislature, the Representatives, are to be elected by the people at large. They will therefore be the guardians of the rights of the great body of the citizens. So well guarded is this Constitution throughout that it seems impossible that the rights either of the states or of the people should be destroyed.

I do not see the necessity of such a test as some gentlemen wish for. The Constitution enjoins an oath upon all the officers of the United States. This is a direct appeal to that God who is the Avenger of Perjury. Such an appeal to Him is a full acknowledgment of His being and providence. An acknowledgment of these great truths is all that the gentlemen contend for. For myself, I should be content either with or without that clause in the Constitution which excludes test laws. Knowledge and liberty are so prevalent in this country that I do not believe that the United States would ever be disposed to establish one religious sect and lay all others under legal disabilities. But as we know not what may take place hereafter, and any such test would be exceedingly injurious to the rights of free citizens, I cannot think it altogether superfluous to add a clause which secures us from the possibility of such oppression. I shall only add that I give my assent to this Constitution and am happy to see the states in a fair way to adopt a system which will protect their rights and promote their welfare.

Speech Before the Massachusetts Ratifying Convention by Fisher Ames

Editor's Introduction:

Fisher Ames has been described as the most eloquent orator in the early federal period. He unfortunately never spared with John Randolph of Roanoke, a contest that would have surpassed any of the great debates of in American history. Ames rose to prominence precisely because he could outwit nearly every political opponent. He had only briefly served in the Massachusetts government when he was sent to the Massachusetts ratifying convention in January 1788. The Convention opened on January 9 and at first appeared as if the opponents of the document held the upper hand. With men like Samuel Adams and John Hancock opposed to ratification, it took a nearly Herculean effort by Ames and other proponents to persuade them to support the new Constitution.

Ames reluctantly accepted the necessity of a proposed bill of rights, but his January 9 speech did not address that objection to the document. Rather, Ames focused his attention on the contention that biennial elections would be a detriment to liberty and good government. Ames argued that the size and extent of the federal republic made annual elections impossible. He also thought that the limited powers of the general government made annual elections unnecessary. This is an important point. Ames implicitly conceded that the central government's powers were confined to certain enumerated objects and that all other powers not delegated to the center were retained by the people of the States.

While Ames was a committed Federalist during his political career, he was always more interested in the well being of Massachusetts and issuing warns against the dangers of democracy than any lofty nationalist rhetoric, so much so that Ames fervently supported the secessionist sentiments of the Essex Junto during the early federal period.

Speech Before the Massachusetts Ratifying Convention

January 15, 1788

By Fisher Ames of Massachusetts

Mr. AMES: I do not regret, Mr. President, that we are not unanimous upon this question. I do not consider the diversity of sentiment which prevails as an impediment in our way to the discovery of truth. In order that we may think alike upon this subject at last, we shall be compelled to discuss it by ascending to the principles upon which the doctrine of representation is grounded.

Without premeditation, in a situation so novel, and awed by the respect which I feel for this venerable assembly, I distrust extremely my own feelings, as well as my competency to prosecute this inquiry. With the hope of an indulgent hearing, I will attempt to proceed. I am sensible, sir, that the doctrine of frequent elections has been sanctioned by antiquity, and is still more endeared to us by our recent experience and uniform habits of thinking. Gentlemen have expressed their zealous partiality for it. They consider this as a leading question in the debate, and that the merits of many other parts of the Constitution are involved in the decision. I confess, sir, and I declare that my zeal for frequent elections is not inferior to their own. I consider it as one of the first securities for popular liberty, in which its very essence may be supposed to reside. But how shall we make the best use of this pledge and instrument of our safety?

A right principle, carried to an extreme, becomes useless. It is apparent that a declaration for a very short term, as for a single day, would defeat the design of representation. The election, in that case, would not seem to the people to be of any importance, and the person elected would think as lightly of his appointment. The other extreme is equally to be avoided. An election for a very long term of years, or for life, would remove the member too far from the control of the people, would be dangerous to liberty, and in fact repugnant to the purposes of the delegation. The truth, as usual, is placed somewhere between the extremes, and I believe is included in this proposition: The term of election must be so long, that the representative may understand the interest of the people, and yet so limited, that his fidelity may be secured by a dependence upon their approbation.

Before I proceed to the application of this rule, I cannot forbear to premise some remarks upon two opinions, which have been suggested.

Much has been said about the people divesting themselves of power, when they delegate it to representatives; and that all representation is to their disadvantage, because it is but an image, a copy, fainter and more imperfect than the original, the people, in whom the light of power is primary and unborrowed, which is only reflected by their delegates. I cannot agree to either of these opinions. The representation of the people is something more than the people. I know, sir, but one purpose which the people can effect without delegation, and that is to destroy a government. That they cannot erect a government, is evinced by our being thus assembled on their behalf. The people must govern by a majority, with whom all power resides. But how is the sense of this majority to be obtained? It has been said that a pure democracy is the best government for a small people who assemble in person. It is of small consequence to discuss it, as it would be inapplicable to the great country we inhabit. It may be of some use in this argument, how ever, to consider, that it would be very burdensome, subject to faction and violence; decisions would often be made by surprise, in the precipitancy of passion, by men who either understand nothing or care nothing about the subject; or by interested men, or those who vote for their own indemnity. It would be a government not by laws, but by men.

Such were the paltry democracies of Greece and Asia Minor, so much extolled, and so often proposed as a model for our imitation. I desire to be thankful that our people (said Mr. Ames) are not under any temptation to adopt the advice. I think it will not be denied that the people are gainers by the election of representatives. They may destroy, but they cannot exercise, the powers of government in person, but by their servants they govern: they do not renounce their power; they do not sacrifice their rights; they become the true sovereigns of the country when they delegate that power, which they cannot use themselves to their trustees.

I know, sir, that the people talk about the liberty of nature, and assert that we divest ourselves of a portion of it when we enter into society. This is declamation against matter of fact. We cannot live without society; and as to liberty, how can I be said to enjoy that which another may take from me when he pleases? The liberty of one depends not so much on the removal of all restraint from him, as on the due restraint upon the liberties of others. Without such restraint, there can be no liberty. Liberty is so far from being endangered or destroyed by this, that it is extended and secured. For I said that we do not enjoy that which another may take from us. But civil liberty cannot be taken from us, when any one may please to invade it; for we have the strength of the society on our side.

I hope, sir, that these reflections will have some tendency to remove the ill impressions which are made by proposing to divest the people of their power.

That they may never be divested of it, I repeat that I am in favor of frequent elections. They who commend annual elections are desired to consider, that the question is, whether biennial elections are a defect in the Constitution; for it does not follow, because annual elections are safe, that biennial are dangerous; for both may be good. Nor is there any foundation for the fears of those, who say that if we, who have been accustomed to choose for one year only, now extend it to two, the next stride will be to five or seven years, and the next for term of life; for this article, with all its supposed defects, is in favor of liberty. Being inserted in the Constitution, it is not subject to be repealed by law. We are sure that it is the worst of the case. It is a fence against ambitious encroachments, too high and too strong to be passed. In this respect, we have greatly the advantage of the people of England, and of all the world. The law which limits their Parliaments is liable to be repealed.

I will not defend this article by saying that it was a matter of compromise in the federal Convention. It has my entire approbation as it stands. I think that we ought to prefer, in this article, biennial elections to annual; and my reasons for this opinion are drawn from these sources: —

From the extent of the country to be governed;

The objects of their legislation;

And the more perfect security of our liberty.

It seems obvious that men who are to collect in Congress from this great territory, perhaps from the Bay of Fundy, or from the banks of the Ohio, and the shore of Lake Superior, ought to have a longer term in office, than the delegates of a single state, in their own legislature. It is not by riding post to and from Congress that a man can acquire a just knowledge of the true interests of the Union. This term of election is inapplicable to the state of a country as large as Germany, or as the Roman empire in the zenith of its power.

If we consider the objects of their delegation, little doubt will remain. It is admitted that annual elections may be highly fit for the state legislature. Every citizen grows up with a knowledge of the local circumstances of the state. But the business of the federal government will be very different. The objects of their power are few and national. At least two years in office will be necessary to enable a man to judge of the trade and interests of the state which he never saw. The time, I hope, will come, when this excellent country will furnish food, and freedom, (which is better than food, which is the food of the soul,) for fifty millions of happy people. Will any man say that the national business can be understood in one year?

Biennial elections appear to me, sir, an essential security to liberty. These are my reasons: —

Faction and enthusiasm are the instruments by which popular governments are destroyed. We need not talk of the power of an aristocracy. The people, when they lose their liberties, are cheated out of them. They nourish factions in their bosoms, which will subsist so long as abusing their honest credulity shall be the means of acquiring power. A democracy is a volcano, which conceals the fiery materials of its own destruction. These will produce an eruption, and carry desolation in their way. The people always mean right; and, if time is allowed for reflection and information, they will do right. I would not have the first wish, the momentary impulse of the public mind, become law; for it is not always the sense of the people, with whom I admit that all power resides. On great questions, we first hear the loud clamors of passion, artifice, and faction. I consider biennial elections as a security that the sober, second thought of the people shall be law. There is a calm review of public transactions, which is made by the citizens who have families and children, the pledges of their fidelity. To provide for popular liberty, we must take care that measures shall not be adopted without due deliberation. The member chosen for two years will feel some independence in his seat. The factions of the day will expire before the end of his term.

The people will be proportionably attentive to the merits of a candidate. Two years will afford opportunity to the member to deserve well of them, and they will require evidence that he has done it.

But, sir, the representatives are the grand inquisition of the Union. They are, by impeachment, to bring great offenders to justice. One year will not suffice to detect guilt, and to pursue it to conviction; therefore they will escape, and the balance of the two branches will be destroyed, and the people oppressed with impunity. The senators will represent the sovereignty of the states. The representatives are to represent the people. The offices ought to bear some proportion in point of importance. This will be impossible if they are chosen for one year only.

Will the people, then, blind the eyes of their own watchmen? Will they bind the hands which are to hold the sword for their defence? Will they impair their own power by an unreasonable jealousy of themselves?

For these reasons, I am clearly of opinion that the article is entitled to our approbation as it stands; and as it has been demanded, why annual elections were not preferred to biennial, permit me to retort the question, and to inquire, in my turn, what reason can be given, why, if annual elections are good, biennial elections are not better?

The inquiry in the latter part of Mr. Ames's speech being directed to the Hon. Mr. Adams, that gentleman said, he only made the inquiry for information, and that he had heard sufficient to satisfy himself of its propriety.

Federalist No. 39 by James Madison

Editor's Introduction:

Historians consider *Federalist* No. 39 to be one of the most important essays in the collection. Madison engaged in a round of political philosophy in this installment, one that leaves the impression that he was attempting to work through his own conceptions of the true nature of the new Constitution. In the process, Madison advanced a type of Frankenstein government, one that was not wholly national or wholly federal, one that divided sovereignty between the general government and the States, and one that would leave the entire question of supreme power balancing on a razor's edge. Madison insisted the general government would be supreme in three areas while the States would hold the advantage in four. That means the States, as other writers acknowledged, would be the primary agents in the new government, but Madison concluded that the Constitution was neither national nor federal "but a composition of both." This confusing supposition would form the basis of the entire conflict leading to the War in 1861 and still contributes to our political tensions in modern America. Madison's disjointed partly federal and partly national government opened the door to competing factions, the very thing he warned against in *Federalist* No. 10.

Federalist No. 39

January 16, 1788

By James Madison of Virginia

To the People of the State of New York:

THE last paper having concluded the observations which were meant to introduce a candid survey of the plan of government reported by the convention, we now proceed to the execution of that part of our undertaking.

The first question that offers itself is, whether the general form and aspect of the government be strictly republican. It is evident that no other form would be reconcilable with the genius of the people of America; with the fundamental principles of the Revolution; or with that honorable determination which animates every votary of freedom, to rest all our political experiments on the capacity of mankind for self-government. If the plan of the convention, therefore, be found to depart from the republican character, its advocates must abandon it as no longer defensible.

What, then, are the distinctive characters of the republican form? Were an answer to this question to be sought, not by recurring to principles, but in the application of the term by political writers, to the constitution of different States, no satisfactory one would ever be found. Holland, in which no particle of the supreme authority is derived from the people, has passed almost universally under the denomination of a republic. The same title has been bestowed on Venice, where absolute power over the great body of the people is exercised, in the most absolute manner, by a small body of hereditary nobles. Poland, which is a mixture of aristocracy and of monarchy in their worst forms, has been dignified with the same appellation. The government of England, which has one republican branch only, combined with an hereditary aristocracy and monarchy, has, with equal impropriety, been frequently placed on the list of republics. These examples, which are nearly as dissimilar to each other as to a genuine republic, show the extreme inaccuracy with which the term has been used in political disquisitions.

If we resort for a criterion to the different principles on which different forms of government are established, we may define a republic to be, or at least may bestow that name on, a government which derives all its powers directly or indirectly from the great body of the people, and is administered by persons holding their offices during pleasure, for a limited period, or during good behavior. It is ESSENTIAL to such a government that it be derived from the great body of the society, not from an inconsiderable proportion, or a favored class of it; otherwise a handful of tyrannical nobles, exercising their oppressions by a delegation of their powers, might aspire to the rank of republicans, and claim for their government the honorable title of republic. It is SUFFICIENT for such a government that the persons administering it be appointed, either directly or indirectly, by the people; and that they hold their appointments by either of the tenures just specified; otherwise every government in the United States, as well as every other popular government that has been or can be well organized or well executed, would be degraded from the republican character. According to the constitution of every State in the Union, some or other of the officers of government are appointed indirectly only by the people. According to most of them, the chief magistrate himself is so appointed. And according to one, this mode of appointment is extended to one of the co-ordinate branches of the legislature. According to all the constitutions, also, the tenure of the highest offices is extended to a definite period, and in many instances, both within the legislative and executive departments, to a period of years. According to the provisions of most of the constitutions, again, as well as according to the most respectable and received opinions on the subject, the members of the judiciary department are to retain their offices by the firm tenure of good behavior.

On comparing the Constitution planned by the convention with the standard here fixed, we perceive at once that it is, in the most rigid sense, conformable to it. The House of Representatives, like that of one branch at least of all the State legislatures, is elected immediately by the great body of the people. The Senate, like the present Congress, and the Senate of Maryland, derives its appointment indirectly from the people. The President is indirectly derived from the choice of the people, according to the example in most of the States. Even the judges, with all other officers of the Union, will, as in the several States, be the choice, though a remote choice, of the people themselves, the duration of the appointments is equally conformable to the republican standard, and to the model of State constitutions The House of Representatives is periodically elective, as in all the States; and for the period of two years, as in the State of South Carolina. The Senate is elective, for the period of six years; which is but one year more than the period of the Senate of Maryland, and but two more than that of the Senates of New York and Virginia. The President is to continue in office for the period of four years; as in New York and Delaware, the chief magistrate is elected for three years, and in South Carolina for two years. In the other States the election is annual. In several of the States, however, no constitutional provision is made for the impeachment of the chief magistrate. And in Delaware and Virginia he is not impeachable till out of office. The President of the United States is impeachable at any time during his continuance in office. The tenure by which the judges are to hold their places, is, as it unquestionably ought to be, that of good behavior. The tenure of the ministerial offices generally, will be a subject of legal regulation, conformably to the reason of the case and the example of the State constitutions.

Could any further proof be required of the republican complexion of this system, the most decisive one might be found in its absolute prohibition of titles of nobility, both under the federal and the State governments; and in its express guaranty of the republican form to each of the latter.

"But it was not sufficient," say the adversaries of the proposed Constitution, "for the convention to adhere to the republican form. They ought, with equal care, to have preserved the FEDERAL form, which regards the Union as a CONFEDERACY of sovereign states; instead of which, they have framed a NATIONAL government, which regards the Union as a CONSOLIDATION of the States." And it is asked by what authority this bold and radical innovation was undertaken? The handle which has been made of this objection requires that it should be examined with some precision.

Without inquiring into the accuracy of the distinction on which the objection is founded, it will be necessary to a just estimate of its force, first, to ascertain the real character of the government in question; secondly, to inquire how far the convention were authorized to propose such a government; and thirdly, how far the duty they owed to their country could supply any defect of regular authority.

First. In order to ascertain the real character of the government, it may be considered in relation to the foundation on which it is to be established; to the sources from which its ordinary powers are to be drawn; to the operation of those powers; to the extent of them; and to the authority by which future changes in the government are to be introduced.

On examining the first relation, it appears, on one hand, that the Constitution is to be founded on the assent and ratification of the people of America, given by deputies elected for the special purpose; but, on the other, that this assent and ratification is to be given by the people, not as individuals composing one entire nation, but as composing the distinct and independent States to which they respectively belong. It is to be the assent and ratification of the several States, derived from the supreme authority in each State, the authority of the people themselves. The act, therefore, establishing the Constitution, will not be a NATIONAL, but a FEDERAL act.

That it will be a federal and not a national act, as these terms are understood by the objectors; the act of the people, as forming so many independent States, not as forming one aggregate nation, is obvious from this single consideration, that it is to result neither from the decision of a MAJORITY of the people of the Union, nor from that of a MAJORITY of the States. It must result from the UNANIMOUS assent of the several States that are parties to it, differing no otherwise from their ordinary assent than in its being expressed, not by the legislative authority, but by that of the people themselves. Were the people regarded in this transaction as forming one nation, the will of the majority of the whole people of the United States would bind the minority, in the same manner as the majority in each State must bind the minority; and the will of the majority must be determined either by a comparison of the individual votes, or by considering the will of the majority of the States as evidence of the will of a majority of the people of the United States. Neither of these rules have been adopted. Each State, in ratifying the Constitution, is considered as a sovereign body, independent of all others, and only to be bound by its own voluntary act. In this relation, then, the new Constitution will, if established, be a FEDERAL, and not a NATIONAL constitution.

The next relation is, to the sources from which the ordinary powers of government are to be derived. The House of Representatives will derive its powers from the people of America; and the people will be represented in the same proportion, and on the same principle, as they are in the legislature of a particular State. So far the government is NATIONAL, not FEDERAL. The Senate, on the other hand, will derive its powers from the States, as political and coequal societies; and these will be represented on the principle of equality in the Senate, as they now are in the existing Congress. So far the government is FEDERAL, not NATIONAL. The executive power will be derived from a very compound source. The immediate election of the President is to be made by the States in their political characters. The votes allotted to them are in a compound ratio, which considers them partly as distinct and coequal societies, partly as unequal members of the same society. The eventual election, again, is to be made by that branch of the legislature which consists of the national representatives; but in this particular act they are to be thrown into the form of individual delegations, from so many distinct and coequal bodies politic. From this aspect of the government it appears to be of a mixed character, presenting at least as many FEDERAL as NATIONAL features.

The difference between a federal and national government, as it relates to the OPERATION OF THE GOVERNMENT, is supposed to consist in this, that in the former the powers operate on the political bodies composing the Confederacy, in their political capacities; in the latter, on the individual citizens composing the nation, in their individual capacities. On trying the Constitution by this criterion, it falls under the NATIONAL, not the FEDERAL character; though perhaps not so completely as has been understood. In several cases, and particularly in the trial of controversies to which States may be parties, they must be viewed and proceeded against in their collective and political capacities only. So far the national countenance of the government on this side seems to be disfigured by a few federal features. But this blemish is perhaps unavoidable in any plan; and the operation of the government on the people, in their individual capacities, in its ordinary and most essential proceedings, may, on the whole, designate it, in this relation, a NATIONAL government.

But if the government be national with regard to the OPERATION of its powers, it changes its aspect again when we contemplate it in relation to the EXTENT of its powers. The idea of a national government involves in it, not only an authority over the individual citizens, but an indefinite supremacy over all persons and things, so far as they are objects of lawful government. Among a people consolidated into one nation, this supremacy is completely vested in the national legislature. Among communities united for particular purposes, it is vested partly in the general and partly in the municipal legislatures. In the former case, all local authorities are subordinate to the supreme; and may be controlled, directed, or abolished by it at pleasure. In the latter, the local or municipal authorities form distinct and independent portions of the supremacy, no more subject, within their respective spheres, to the general authority, than the general authority is subject to them, within its own sphere. In this relation, then, the proposed government cannot be deemed a NATIONAL one; since its jurisdiction extends to certain enumerated objects only, and leaves to the several States a residuary and inviolable sovereignty over all other objects. It is true that in controversies relating to the boundary between the two jurisdictions, the tribunal which is ultimately to decide, is to be established under the general government. But this does not change the principle of the case. The decision is to be impartially made, according to the rules of the Constitution; and all the usual and most effectual precautions are taken to secure this impartiality. Some such tribunal is clearly essential to prevent an appeal to the sword and a dissolution of the compact; and that it ought to be established under the general rather than under the local governments, or, to speak more properly, that it could be safely established under the first alone, is a position not likely to be combated.

If we try the Constitution by its last relation to the authority by which amendments are to be made, we find it neither wholly NATIONAL nor wholly FEDERAL. Were it wholly national, the supreme and ultimate authority would reside in the MAJORITY of the people of the Union; and this authority would be competent at all times, like that of a majority of every national society, to alter or abolish its established government. Were it wholly federal, on the other hand, the concurrence of each State in the Union would be essential to every alteration that would be binding on all. The mode provided by the plan of the convention is not founded on either of these principles. In requiring more than a majority, and principles. In requiring more than a majority, and particularly in computing the proportion by STATES, not by CITIZENS, it departs from the NATIONAL and advances towards the FEDERAL character; in rendering the concurrence of less than the whole number of States sufficient, it loses again the FEDERAL and partakes of the NATIONAL character.

The proposed Constitution, therefore, is, in strictness, neither a national nor a federal Constitution, but a composition of both. In its foundation it is federal, not national; in the sources from which the ordinary powers of the government are drawn, it is partly federal and partly national; in the operation of these powers, it is national, not federal; in the extent of them, again, it is federal, not national; and, finally, in the authoritative mode of introducing amendments, it is neither wholly federal nor wholly national.

FEDERALIST NO. 40 BY JAMES MADISON

Editor's Introduction:

Madison's *Federalist* No. 40 directly confronted the argument that the Philadelphia Convention exceeded its authority by drafting a new Constitution for the United States. He considered this a foolish critique because history proved that the men who attended the Convention were under directions from the United States Congress to improve the central government and were not confined to proposing amendments. More interesting, Madison made the argument that the powers of the Constitution, rather than being new powers, were simply "the expansion of principles which are found in the articles of Confederation." This is important. If the Constitution maintained the Union as under the Articles, and proponents argued consistently that it did, and the powers of the central government under the Constitution were merely an augmentation of the powers of the original central authority, then the Constitution could not be considered a vehicle for consolidation.

Federalist No. 40

January 18, 1788

By James Madison of Virginia

To the People of the State of New York:

THE SECOND point to be examined is, whether the convention were authorized to frame and propose this mixed Constitution. The powers of the convention ought, in strictness, to be determined by an inspection of the commissions given to the members by their respective constituents. As all of these, however, had reference, either to the recommendation from the meeting at Annapolis, in September, 1786, or to that from Congress, in February, 1787, it will be sufficient to recur to these particular acts. The act from Annapolis recommends the "appointment of commissioners to take into consideration the situation of the United States; to devise SUCH FURTHER PROVISIONS as shall appear to them necessary to render the Constitution of the federal government ADEQUATE TO THE EXIGENCIES OF THE UNION; and to report such an act for that purpose, to the United States in Congress assembled, as when agreed to by them, and afterwards confirmed by the legislature of every State, will effectually provide for the same. "The recommendatory act of Congress is in the words following:

"WHEREAS, There is provision in the articles of Confederation and perpetual Union, for making alterations therein, by the assent of a Congress of the United States, and of the legislatures of the several States; and whereas experience hath evinced, that there are defects in the present Confederation; as a mean to remedy which, several of the States, and PARTICULARLY THE STATE OF NEW YORK, by express instructions to their delegates in Congress, have suggested a convention for the purposes expressed in the following resolution; and such convention appearing to be the most probable mean of establishing in these States A FIRM NATIONAL GOVERNMENT:

"Resolved, That in the opinion of Congress it is expedient, that on the second Monday of May next a convention of delegates, who shall have been appointed by the several States, be held at Philadelphia, for the sole and express purpose OF REVISING THE ARTICLES OF CONFEDERATION, and reporting to Congress and the several legislatures such ALTERATIONS AND PROVISIONS THEREIN, as shall, when agreed to in Congress, and confirmed by the States, render the federal Constitution ADEQUATE TO THE EXIGENCIES OF GOVERNMENT AND THE PRESERVATION OF THE UNION.

"From these two acts, it appears, 1st, that the object of the convention was to establish, in these States, A FIRM NATIONAL GOVERNMENT; 2d, that this government was to be such as would be ADEQUATE TO THE EXIGENCIES OF GOVERNMENT and THE PRESERVATION OF THE UNION; 3d, that these purposes were to be effected by ALTERATIONS AND PROVISIONS IN THE ARTICLES OF CONFEDERATION, as it is expressed in the act of Congress, or by SUCH FURTHER PROVISIONS AS SHOULD APPEAR NECESSARY, as it stands in the recommendatory act from Annapolis; 4th, that the alterations and provisions were to be reported to Congress, and to the States, in order to be agreed to by the former and confirmed by the latter. From a comparison and fair construction of these several modes of expression, is to be deduced the authority under which the convention acted. They were to frame a NATIONAL GOVERNMENT, adequate to the EXIGENCIES OF GOVERNMENT, and OF THE UNION; and to reduce the articles of Confederation into such form as to accomplish these purposes.

There are two rules of construction, dictated by plain reason, as well as founded on legal axioms. The one is, that every part of the expression ought, if possible, to be allowed some meaning, and be made to conspire to some common end. The other is, that where the several parts cannot be made to coincide, the less important should give way to the more important part; the means should be sacrificed to the end, rather than the end to the means.

Suppose, then, that the expressions defining the authority of the convention were irreconcilably at variance with each other; that a NATIONAL and ADEQUATE GOVERNMENT could not possibly, in the judgment of the convention, be affected by ALTERATIONS and PROVISIONS in the ARTICLES OF CONFEDERATION; which part of the definition ought to have been embraced, and which rejected? Which was the more important, which the less important part? Which the end; which the means? Let the most scrupulous expositors of delegated powers; let the most inveterate objectors against those exercised by the convention, answer these questions. Let them declare, whether it was of most importance to the happiness of the people of America, that the articles of Confederation should be disregarded, and an adequate government be provided, and the Union preserved; or that an adequate government should be omitted, and the articles of Confederation preserved. Let them declare, whether the preservation of these articles was the end, for securing which a reform of the government was to be introduced as the means; or whether the establishment of a government, adequate to the national happiness, was the end at which these articles themselves originally aimed, and to which they ought, as insufficient means, to have been sacrificed.

But is it necessary to suppose that these expressions are absolutely irreconcilable to each other; that no ALTERATIONS or PROVISIONS in THE ARTICLES OF THE CONFEDERATION could possibly mould them into a national and adequate government; into such a government as has been proposed by the convention? No stress, it is presumed, will, in this case, be laid on the TITLE; a change of that could never be deemed an exercise of ungranted power. ALTERATIONS in the body of the instrument are expressly authorized. NEW PROVISIONS therein are also expressly authorized. Here then is a power to change the title; to insert new articles; to alter old ones. Must it of necessity be admitted that this power is infringed, so long as a part of the old articles remain? Those who maintain the affirmative ought at least to mark the boundary between authorized and usurped innovations; between that degree of change which lies within the compass of ALTERATIONS AND FURTHER PROVISIONS, and that which amounts to a TRANSMUTATION of the government. Will it be said that the alterations ought not to have touched the substance of the Confederation? The States would never have appointed a convention with so much solemnity, nor described its objects with so much latitude, if some SUBSTANTIAL reform had not been in contemplation. Will it be said that the FUNDAMENTAL PRINCIPLES of the Confederation were not within the purview of the convention, and ought not to have been varied? I ask, What are these principles? Do they require that, in the establishment of the Constitution, the States should be regarded as distinct and independent sovereigns? They are so regarded by the Constitution proposed.

Do they require that the members of the government should derive their appointment from the legislatures, not from the people of the States? One branch of the new government is to be appointed by these legislatures; and under the Confederation, the delegates to Congress MAY ALL be appointed immediately by the people, and in two States are actually so appointed. Do they require that the powers of the government should act on the States, and not immediately on individuals? In some instances, as has been shown, the powers of the new government will act on the States in their collective characters. In some instances, also, those of the existing government act immediately on individuals. In cases of capture; of piracy; of the post office; of coins, weights, and measures; of trade with the Indians; of claims under grants of land by different States; and, above all, in the case of trials by courts-marshal in the army and navy, by which death may be inflicted without the intervention of a jury, or even of a civil magistrate; in all these cases the powers of the Confederation operate immediately on the persons and interests of individual citizens.

Do these fundamental principles require, particularly, that no tax should be levied without the intermediate agency of the States? The Confederation itself authorizes a direct tax, to a certain extent, on the post office. The power of coinage has been so construed by Congress as to levy a tribute immediately from that source also. But pretermitting these instances, was it not an acknowledged object of the convention and the universal expectation of the people, that the regulation of trade should be submitted to the general government in such a form as would render it an immediate source of general revenue? Had not Congress repeatedly recommended this measure as not inconsistent with the fundamental principles of the Confederation? Had not every State but one; had not New York herself, so far complied with the plan of Congress as to recognize the PRINCIPLE of the innovation? Do these principles, in fine, require that the powers of the general government should be limited, and that, beyond this limit, the States should be left in possession of their sovereignty and independence? We have seen that in the new government, as in the old, the general powers are limited; and that the States, in all unenumerated cases, are left in the enjoyment of their sovereign and independent jurisdiction.

The truth is, that the great principles of the Constitution proposed by the convention may be considered less as absolutely new, than as the expansion of principles which are found in the articles of Confederation. The misfortune under the latter system has been, that these principles are so feeble and confined as to justify all the charges of inefficiency which have been urged against it, and to require a degree of enlargement which gives to the new system the aspect of an entire transformation of the old. In one particular it is admitted that the convention have departed from the tenor of their commission. Instead of reporting a plan requiring the confirmation OF THE LEGISLATURES OF ALL THE STATES, they have reported a plan which is to be confirmed by the PEOPLE, and may be carried into effect by NINE STATES ONLY. It is worthy of remark that this objection, though the most plausible, has been the least urged in the publications which have swarmed against the convention. The forbearance can only have proceeded from an irresistible conviction of the absurdity of subjecting the fate of twelve States to the perverseness or corruption of a thirteenth; from the example of inflexible opposition given by a MAJORITY of one sixtieth of the people of America to a measure approved and called for by the voice of twelve States, comprising fifty-nine sixtieths of the people an example still fresh in the memory and indignation of every citizen who has felt for the wounded honor and prosperity of his country. As this objection, therefore, has been in a manner waived by those who have criticised the powers of the convention, I dismiss it without further observation.

The THIRD point to be inquired into is, how far considerations of duty arising out of the case itself could have supplied any defect of regular authority. In the preceding inquiries the powers of the convention have been analyzed and tried with the same rigor, and by the same rules, as if they had been real and final powers for the establishment of a Constitution for the United States. We have seen in what manner they have borne the trial even on that supposition. It is time now to recollect that the powers were merely advisory and recommendatory; that they were so meant by the States, and so understood by the convention; and that the latter have accordingly planned and proposed a Constitution which is to be of no more consequence than the paper on which it is written, unless it be stamped with the approbation of those to whom it is addressed. This reflection places the subject in a point of view altogether different, and will enable us to judge with propriety of the course taken by the convention. Let us view the ground on which the convention stood.

It may be collected from their proceedings, that they were deeply and unanimously impressed with the crisis, which had led their country almost with one voice to make so singular and solemn an experiment for correcting the errors of a system by which this crisis had been produced; that they were no less deeply and unanimously convinced that such a reform as they have proposed was absolutely necessary to effect the purposes of their appointment. It could not be unknown to them that the hopes and expectations of the great body of citizens, throughout this great empire, were turned with the keenest anxiety to the event of their deliberations. They had every reason to believe that the contrary sentiments agitated the minds and bosoms of every external and internal foe to the liberty and prosperity of the United States.

They had seen in the origin and progress of the experiment, the alacrity with which the PROPOSITION, made by a single State (Virginia), towards a partial amendment of the Confederation, had been attended to and promoted. They had seen the LIBERTY ASSUMED by a VERY FEW deputies from a VERY FEW States, convened at Annapolis, of recommending a great and critical object, wholly foreign to their commission, not only justified by the public opinion, but actually carried into effect by twelve out of the thirteen States. They had seen, in a variety of instances, assumptions by Congress, not only of recommendatory, but of operative, powers, warranted, in the public estimation, by occasions and objects infinitely less urgent than those by which their conduct was to be governed.

They must have reflected, that in all great changes of established governments, forms ought to give way to substance; that a rigid adherence in such cases to the former, would render nominal and nugatory the transcendent and precious right of the people to "abolish or alter their governments as to them shall seem most likely to effect their safety and happiness," since it is impossible for the people spontaneously and universally to move in concert towards their object; and it is therefore essential that such changes be instituted by some INFORMAL AND UNAUTHORIZED PROPOSITIONS, made by some patriotic and respectable citizen or number of citizens.

They must have recollected that it was by this irregular and assumed privilege of proposing to the people plans for their safety and happiness, that the States were first united against the danger with which they were threatened by their ancient government; that committees and congresses were formed for concentrating their efforts and defending their rights; and that CONVENTIONS were ELECTED in THE SEVERAL STATES for establishing the constitutions under which they are now governed; nor could it have been forgotten that no little ill-timed scruples, no zeal for adhering to ordinary forms, were anywhere seen, except in those who wished to indulge, under these masks, their secret enmity to the substance contended for. They must have borne in mind, that as the plan to be framed and proposed was to be submitted TO THE PEOPLE THEMSELVES, the disapprobation of this supreme authority would destroy it forever; its approbation blot out antecedent errors and irregularities. It might even have occurred to them, that where a disposition to cavil prevailed, their neglect to execute the degree of power vested in them, and still more their recommendation of any measure whatever, not warranted by their commission, would not less excite animadversion, than a recommendation at once of a measure fully commensurate to the national exigencies.

Had the convention, under all these impressions, and in the midst of all these considerations, instead of exercising a manly confidence in their country, by whose confidence they had been so peculiarly distinguished, and of pointing out a system capable, in their judgment, of securing its happiness, taken the cold and sullen resolution of disappointing its ardent hopes, of sacrificing substance to forms, of committing the dearest interests of their country to the uncertainties of delay and the hazard of events, let me ask the man who can raise his mind to one elevated conception, who can awaken in his bosom one patriotic emotion, what judgment ought to have been pronounced by the impartial world, by the friends of mankind, by every virtuous citizen, on the conduct and character of this assembly?

Or if there be a man whose propensity to condemn is susceptible of no control, let me then ask what sentence he has in reserve for the twelve States who USURPED THE POWER of sending deputies to the convention, a body utterly unknown to their constitutions; for Congress, who recommended the appointment of this body, equally unknown to the Confederation; and for the State of New York, in particular, which first urged and then complied with this unauthorized interposition?

But that the objectors may be disarmed of every pretext, it shall be granted for a moment that the convention were neither authorized by their commission, nor justified by circumstances in proposing a Constitution for their country: does it follow that the Constitution ought, for that reason alone, to be rejected? If, according to the noble precept, it be lawful to accept good advice even from an enemy, shall we set the ignoble example of refusing such advice even when it is offered by our friends?

The prudent inquiry, in all cases, ought surely to be, not so much FROM WHOM the advice comes, as whether the advice be GOOD. The sum of what has been here advanced and proved is, that the charge against the convention of exceeding their powers, except in one instance little urged by the objectors, has no foundation to support it; that if they had exceeded their powers, they were not only warranted, but required, as the confidential servants of their country, by the circumstances in which they were placed, to exercise the liberty which they assume; and that finally, if they had violated both their powers and their obligations, in proposing a Constitution, this ought nevertheless to be embraced, if it be calculated to accomplish the views and happiness of the people of America. How far this character is due to the Constitution, is the subject under investigation.

Federalist No. 41 by James Madison

Editor's Introduction:

Federalist No. 41 launched Madison's inquiry into two "important questions." The first centered on the "sum or quantity of power" in the general government and the second on the "particular structure" of power. The first question addressed the pressing issue of federalism, namely if the powers of the central authority under the Constitution would be either "unnecessary or improper" or "dangerous" to the States. To answer this question, Madison condensed the powers of the general government into six categories, and he focused this essay and the next several in the series on answering these "important questions." In this essay, Madison focused almost entirely on the Constitution's power to protect the Union from "foreign danger." This was both a military and economic question, and Madison thought that the powers of the general government under the new Constitution were both proper and necessary for the security of the Union.

Federalist No. 41

January 19, 1788

By James Madison of Virginia

To the People of the State of New York:

THE Constitution proposed by the convention may be considered under two general points of view. The FIRST relates to the sum or quantity of power which it vests in the government, including the restraints imposed on the States. The SECOND, to the particular structure of the government, and the distribution of this power among its several branches.

Under the FIRST view of the subject, two important questions arise:

1. Whether any part of the powers transferred to the general government be unnecessary or improper?

2. Whether the entire mass of them be dangerous to the portion of jurisdiction left in the several States?

Is the aggregate power of the general government greater than ought to have been vested in it? This is the FIRST question. It cannot have escaped those who have attended with candor to the arguments employed against the extensive powers of the government, that the authors of them have very little considered how far these powers were necessary means of attaining a necessary end. They have chosen rather to dwell on the inconveniences which must be unavoidably blended with all political advantages; and on the possible abuses which must be incident to every power or trust, of which a beneficial use can be made.

This method of handling the subject cannot impose on the good sense of the people of America. It may display the subtlety of the writer; it may open a boundless field for rhetoric and declamation; it may inflame the passions of the unthinking, and may confirm the prejudices of the misthinking: but cool and candid people will at once reflect, that the purest of human blessings must have a portion of alloy in them; that the choice must always be made, if not of the lesser evil, at least of the GREATER, not the PERFECT, good; and that in every political institution, a power to advance the public happiness involves a discretion which may be misapplied and abused. They will see, therefore, that in all cases where power is to be conferred, the point first to be decided is, whether such a power be necessary to the public good; as the next will be, in case of an affirmative decision, to guard as effectually as possible against a perversion of the power to the public detriment.

That we may form a correct judgment on this subject, it will be proper to review the several powers conferred on the government of the Union; and that this may be the more conveniently done they may be reduced into different classes as they relate to the following different objects:

1. Security against foreign danger;
2. Regulation of the intercourse with foreign nations;
3. Maintenance of harmony and proper intercourse among the States;
4. Certain miscellaneous objects of general utility;
5. Restraint of the States from certain injurious acts;
6. Provisions for giving due efficacy to all these powers.

The powers falling within the FIRST class are those of declaring war and granting letters of marque; of providing armies and fleets; of regulating and calling forth the militia; of levying and borrowing money. Security against foreign danger is one of the primitive objects of civil society. It is an avowed and essential object of the American Union. The powers requisite for attaining it must be effectually confided to the federal councils. Is the power of declaring war necessary? No man will answer this question in the negative. It would be superfluous, therefore, to enter into a proof of the affirmative. The existing Confederation establishes this power in the most ample form. Is the power of raising armies and equipping fleets necessary? This is involved in the foregoing power. It is involved in the power of self-defense. But was it necessary to give an INDEFINITE POWER of raising TROOPS, as well as providing fleets; and of maintaining both in PEACE, as well as in war? The answer to these questions has been too far anticipated in another place to admit an extensive discussion of them in this place. The answer indeed seems to be so obvious and conclusive as scarcely to justify such a discussion in any place. With what color of propriety could the force necessary for defense be limited by those who cannot limit the force of offense? If a federal Constitution could chain the ambition or set bounds to the exertions of all other nations, then indeed might it prudently chain the discretion of its own government, and set bounds to the exertions for its own safety.

How could a readiness for war in time of peace be safely prohibited, unless we could prohibit, in like manner, the preparations and establishments of every hostile nation? The means of security can only be regulated by the means and the danger of attack. They will, in fact, be ever determined by these rules, and by no others. It is in vain to oppose Constitutional barriers to the impulse of self-preservation. It is worse than in vain; because it plants in the Constitution itself necessary usurpations of power, every precedent of which is a germ of unnecessary and multiplied repetitions. If one nation maintains constantly a disciplined army, ready for the service of ambition or revenge, it obliges the most pacific nations who may be within the reach of its enterprises to take corresponding precautions.

The fifteenth century was the unhappy epoch of military establishments in the time of peace. They were introduced by Charles VII. of France. All Europe has followed, or been forced into, the example. Had the example not been followed by other nations, all Europe must long ago have worn the chains of a universal monarch. Were every nation except France now to disband its peace establishments, the same event might follow. The veteran legions of Rome were an overmatch for the undisciplined valor of all other nations and rendered her the mistress of the world. Not the less true is it, that the liberties of Rome proved the final victim to her military triumphs; and that the liberties of Europe, as far as they ever existed, have, with few exceptions, been the price of her military establishments. A standing force, therefore, is a dangerous, at the same time that it may be a necessary, provision. On the smallest scale it has its inconveniences. On an extensive scale its consequences may be fatal. On any scale it is an object of laudable circumspection and precaution.

A wise nation will combine all these considerations; and, whilst it does not rashly preclude itself from any resource which may become essential to its safety, will exert all its prudence in diminishing both the necessity and the danger of resorting to one which may be inauspicious to its liberties. The clearest marks of this prudence are stamped on the proposed Constitution. The Union itself, which it cements and secures, destroys every pretext for a military establishment which could be dangerous. America united, with a handful of troops, or without a single soldier, exhibits a more forbidding posture to foreign ambition than America disunited, with a hundred thousand veterans ready for combat.

It was remarked, on a former occasion, that the want of this pretext had saved the liberties of one nation in Europe. Being rendered by her insular situation and her maritime resources impregnable to the armies of her neighbors, the rulers of Great Britain have never been able, by real or artificial dangers, to cheat the public into an extensive peace establishment. The distance of the United States from the powerful nations of the world gives them the same happy security. A dangerous establishment can never be necessary or plausible, so long as they continue a united people. But let it never, for a moment, be forgotten that they are indebted for this advantage to the Union alone. The moment of its dissolution will be the date of a new order of things. The fears of the weaker, or the ambition of the stronger States, or Confederacies, will set the same example in the New, as Charles VII. did in the Old World. The example will be followed here from the same motives which produced universal imitation there. Instead of deriving from our situation the precious advantage which Great Britain has derived from hers, the face of America will be but a copy of that of the continent of Europe. It will present liberty everywhere crushed between standing armies and perpetual taxes.

The fortunes of disunited America will be even more disastrous than those of Europe. The sources of evil in the latter are confined to her own limits. No superior powers of another quarter of the globe intrigue among her rival nations, inflame their mutual animosities, and render them the instruments of foreign ambition, jealousy, and revenge. In America the miseries springing from her internal jealousies, contentions, and wars, would form a part only of her lot. A plentiful addition of evils would have their source in that relation in which Europe stands to this quarter of the earth, and which no other quarter of the earth bears to Europe. This picture of the consequences of disunion cannot be too highly colored, or too often exhibited. Every man who loves peace, every man who loves his country, every man who loves liberty, ought to have it ever before his eyes, that he may cherish in his heart a due attachment to the Union of America, and be able to set a due value on the means of preserving it.

Next to the effectual establishment of the Union, the best possible precaution against danger from standing armies is a limitation of the term for which revenue may be appropriated to their support. This precaution the Constitution has prudently added. I will not repeat here the observations which I flatter myself have placed this subject in a just and satisfactory light. But it may not be improper to take notice of an argument against this part of the Constitution, which has been drawn from the policy and practice of Great Britain. It is said that the continuance of an army in that kingdom requires an annual vote of the legislature; whereas the American Constitution has lengthened this critical period to two years. This is the form in which the comparison is usually stated to the public: but is it a just form? Is it a fair comparison? Does the British Constitution restrain the parliamentary discretion to one year? Does the American impose on the Congress appropriations for two years? On the contrary, it cannot be unknown to the authors of the fallacy themselves, that the British Constitution fixes no limit whatever to the discretion of the legislature, and that the American ties down the legislature to two years, as the longest admissible term.

Had the argument from the British example been truly stated, it would have stood thus: The term for which supplies may be appropriated to the army establishment, though unlimited by the British Constitution, has nevertheless, in practice, been limited by parliamentary discretion to a single year. Now, if in Great Britain, where the House of Commons is elected for seven years; where so great a proportion of the members are elected by so small a proportion of the people; where the electors are so corrupted by the representatives, and the representatives so corrupted by the Crown, the representative body can possess a power to make appropriations to the army for an indefinite term, without desiring, or without daring, to extend the term beyond a single year, ought not suspicion herself to blush, in pretending that the representatives of the United States, elected FREELY by the WHOLE BODY of the people, every SECOND YEAR, cannot be safely intrusted with the discretion over such appropriations, expressly limited to the short period of TWO YEARS? A bad cause seldom fails to betray itself. Of this truth, the management of the opposition to the federal government is an unvaried exemplification.

But among all the blunders which have been committed, none is more striking than the attempt to enlist on that side the prudent jealousy entertained by the people, of standing armies. The attempt has awakened fully the public attention to that important subject; and has led to investigations which must terminate in a thorough and universal conviction, not only that the Constitution has provided the most effectual guards against danger from that quarter, but that nothing short of a Constitution fully adequate to the national defense and the preservation of the Union, can save America from as many standing armies as it may be split into States or Confederacies, and from such a progressive augmentation, of these establishments in each, as will render them as burdensome to the properties and ominous to the liberties of the people, as any establishment that can become necessary, under a united and efficient government, must be tolerable to the former and safe to the latter.

The palpable necessity of the power to provide and maintain a navy has protected that part of the Constitution against a spirit of censure, which has spared few other parts. It must, indeed, be numbered among the greatest blessings of America, that as her Union will be the only source of her maritime strength, so this will be a principal source of her security against danger from abroad. In this respect our situation bears another likeness to the insular advantage of Great Britain. The batteries most capable of repelling foreign enterprises on our safety, are happily such as can never be turned by a perfidious government against our liberties.

The inhabitants of the Atlantic frontier are all of them deeply interested in this provision for naval protection, and if they have hitherto been suffered to sleep quietly in their beds; if their property has remained safe against the predatory spirit of licentious adventurers; if their maritime towns have not yet been compelled to ransom themselves from the terrors of a conflagration, by yielding to the exactions of daring and sudden invaders, these instances of good fortune are not to be ascribed to the capacity of the existing government for the protection of those from whom it claims allegiance, but to causes that are fugitive and fallacious.

If we except perhaps Virginia and Maryland, which are peculiarly vulnerable on their eastern frontiers, no part of the Union ought to feel more anxiety on this subject than New York. Her seacoast is extensive. A very important district of the State is an island. The State itself is penetrated by a large navigable river for more than fifty leagues. The great emporium of its commerce, the great reservoir of its wealth, lies every moment at the mercy of events, and may almost be regarded as a hostage for ignominious compliances with the dictates of a foreign enemy, or even with the rapacious demands of pirates and barbarians. Should a war be the result of the precarious situation of European affairs, and all the unruly passions attending it be let loose on the ocean, our escape from insults and depredations, not only on that element, but every part of the other bordering on it, will be truly miraculous.

In the present condition of America, the States more immediately exposed to these calamities have nothing to hope from the phantom of a general government which now exists; and if their single resources were equal to the task of fortifying themselves against the danger, the object to be protected would be almost consumed by the means of protecting them. The power of regulating and calling forth the militia has been already sufficiently vindicated and explained. The power of levying and borrowing money, being the sinew of that which is to be exerted in the national defense, is properly thrown into the same class with it. This power, also, has been examined already with much attention, and has, I trust, been clearly shown to be necessary, both in the extent and form given to it by the Constitution.

I will address one additional reflection only to those who contend that the power ought to have been restrained to external taxation by which they mean, taxes on articles imported from other countries. It cannot be doubted that this will always be a valuable source of revenue; that for a considerable time it must be a principal source; that at this moment it is an essential one. But we may form very mistaken ideas on this subject, if we do not call to mind in our calculations, that the extent of revenue drawn from foreign commerce must vary with the variations, both in the extent and the kind of imports; and that these variations do not correspond with the progress of population, which must be the general measure of the public wants. As long as agriculture continues the sole field of labor, the importation of manufactures must increase as the consumers multiply. As soon as domestic manufactures are begun by the hands not called for by agriculture, the imported manufactures will decrease as the numbers of people increase.

In a more remote stage, the imports may consist in a considerable part of raw materials, which will be wrought into articles for exportation, and will, therefore, require rather the encouragement of bounties, than to be loaded with discouraging duties. A system of government, meant for duration, ought to contemplate these revolutions, and be able to accommodate itself to them. Some, who have not denied the necessity of the power of taxation, have grounded a very fierce attack against the Constitution, on the language in which it is defined. It has been urged and echoed, that the power "to lay and collect taxes, duties, imposts, and excises, to pay the debts, and provide for the common defense and general welfare of the United States," amounts to an unlimited commission to exercise every power which may be alleged to be necessary for the common defense or general welfare. No stronger proof could be given of the distress under which these writers labor for objections, than their stooping to such a misconstruction. Had no other enumeration or definition of the powers of the Congress been found in the Constitution, than the general expressions just cited, the authors of the objection might have had some color for it; though it would have been difficult to find a reason for so awkward a form of describing an authority to legislate in all possible cases. A power to destroy the freedom of the press, the trial by jury, or even to regulate the course of descents, or the forms of conveyances, must be very singularly expressed by the terms "to raise money for the general welfare.

"But what color can the objection have, when a specification of the objects alluded to by these general terms immediately follows, and is not even separated by a longer pause than a semicolon? If the different parts of the same instrument ought to be so expounded, as to give meaning to every part which will bear it, shall one part of the same sentence be excluded altogether from a share in the meaning; and shall the more doubtful and indefinite terms be retained in their full extent, and the clear and precise expressions be denied any signification whatsoever? For what purpose could the enumeration of particular powers be inserted, if these and all others were meant to be included in the preceding general power? Nothing is more natural nor common than first to use a general phrase, and then to explain and qualify it by a recital of particulars.

But the idea of an enumeration of particulars which neither explain nor qualify the general meaning, and can have no other effect than to confound and mislead, is an absurdity, which, as we are reduced to the dilemma of charging either on the authors of the objection or on the authors of the Constitution, we must take the liberty of supposing, had not its origin with the latter. The objection here is the more extraordinary, as it appears that the language used by the convention is a copy from the articles of Confederation. The objects of the Union among the States, as described in article third, are "their common defense, security of their liberties, and mutual and general welfare. " The terms of article eighth are still more identical: "All charges of war and all other expenses that shall be incurred for the common defense or general welfare, and allowed by the United States in Congress, shall be defrayed out of a common treasury," etc. A similar language again occurs in article ninth. Construe either of these articles by the rules which would justify the construction put on the new Constitution, and they vest in the existing Congress a power to legislate in all cases whatsoever.

But what would have been thought of that assembly, if, attaching themselves to these general expressions, and disregarding the specifications which ascertain and limit their import, they had exercised an unlimited power of providing for the common defense and general welfare? I appeal to the objectors themselves, whether they would in that case have employed the same reasoning in justification of Congress as they now make use of against the convention. How difficult it is for error to escape its own condemnation!

Speech Before the Massachusetts Ratifying Convention by Fisher Ames and Rufus King

Editor's Introduction:

Like Fisher Ames, Rufus King was a young and energetic member of the Massachusetts Ratifying Convention. He had barely served a couple of terms in the Massachusetts legislature when he was sent to the Philadelphia Convention of 1787. Here, he was counted among the nationalists, but he consistently favored compromise to preserve the Union, including over issues of slavery. King personally opposed slavery and worked throughout his life for gradual emancipation, but he always considered the institution to be a political and economic issue that would eventually be snuffed out. Shortly after the ratification of the Constitution, King packed up and moved to New York where he was almost immediately elected to the United States Senate. He served in that body twice, and both times he left after being appointed as the United States Minister to Great Britain.

King, like Ames, also favored secession at one point in his political career. While in the Senate in 1794, King and Oliver Ellsworth of

Connecticut cornered John Taylor of Caroline (Virginia) in the Senate cloak room and pressed for a dissolution of the Union. Neither favored being in a Union where the interests of New England and the "Eastern States" were continually sacrificed for those of the South.

These two speeches on the Senate highlight that real argument against ratification of the Constitution, both in Massachusetts and the other States at large, centered on the potential consolidation of the United States into a "national" unitary State. Ames insisted the Senate "represented the sovereignty of the states" and said that "too much provision cannot be made against a consolidation," while King suggested that the Senate preserved the "equality of the States." Every man in favor of the Constitution made similar statements during the ratification process and often sold the Senate as the key to the entire document. If the Senate preserved the "sovereignty" and "equality" of the States, then men who claimed the Constitution consolidated the United States had little room for argument.

Speech Before the Massachusetts Ratifying Convention
January 19, 1788
By Fisher Ames and Rufus King of Massachusetts

Mr. AMES observed, that an objection was made against the Constitution, because the senators are to be chosen for six years. It has been said, that they will be removed too far from the control of the people, and that, to keep them in proper dependence, they should be chosen annually. It is necessary to premise, that no argument against the new plan has made a deeper impression than this, that it will produce a consolidation of the states. This is an effect which all good men will deprecate. For it is obvious, that, if the state powers are to be destroyed, the representation is too small. The trust, in that case, would be too great to be confided to so few persons. The objects of legislation would be so multiplied and complicated, that the government would be unwieldy and impracticable. The state governments are essential parts of the system, and the defence of this article is drawn from its tendency to their preservation. The senators represent the sovereignty of the states; in the other house, individuals are represented. The Senate may not originate bills. It need not be said that they are principally to direct the affairs of wars and treaties. They are in the quality of ambassadors of the states, and it will not be denied that some permanency in their office is necessary to a discharge of their duty. Now, if they were chosen yearly, how could they perform their trust? If they would be brought by that means more immediately under the influence of the people, then they will represent the state legislatures less, and become the representatives of individuals. This belongs to the other house. The absurdity of this, and its repugnancy to the federal principles of the Constitution, will appear more fully, by supposing that they are to be chosen by the people at large. If there is any force in the objection to this article, this would be proper. But whom, in that case, would they represent? — Not the legislatures of the states, but the people. This would totally obliterate the federal features of the Constitution. What would become of the state governments, and on whom would devolve the duty of defending them against the encroachments of the federal government? A consolidation of the states would ensue, which, it is conceded, would subvert the new Constitution, and against which this very article, so much condemned, is our best security. Too much provision cannot be made against a consolidation. The state governments represent the wishes, and feelings, and local interests, of the people. They are the safeguard and ornament of the Constitution; they will protract the period of our liberties; they will afford a shelter against the abuse of power, and will be the natural avengers of our violated rights.

A very effectual check upon the power of the Senate is provided. A third part is to retire from office every two years. By this means, while the senators are seated for six years, they are admonished of their responsibility to the state legislatures. If one third new members are introduced, who feel the sentiments of their states, they will awe that third whose term will be near expiring. This article seems to be an excellence of the Constitution, and affords just ground to believe that it will be, in practice as in theory, a federal republic.

Mr. KING said, as the Senate preserved the equality of the states, their appointment is equal. To the objection to this branch, that it is chosen for too long a period, he observed, if the principle of classing them is considered, although it appears long, it will not be found so long as it appears. One class is to serve two years, another four years, and another six years; the average, therefore, is four years. The senators, said Mr. K., will have a powerful check in those men who wish for their seats, who will watch their whole conduct in the general government, and will give the alarm in case of misbehavior. And the state legislatures, if they find their delegates erring, can and will instruct them. Will not this be a check? When they hear the voice of the people solemnly dictating to them their duty, they will be bold men indeed to act contrary to it. These will not be instructions sent them in a private letter, which can be put in their pockets; they will be public instructions, which all the country will see, and they will be hardy men indeed to violate them. The honorable gentleman said, the powers to control the Senate are as great as ever was enjoyed in any government; and that the members, therefore, will be found not to be chosen for too long a time. They are, says he, to assist the executive in the designation and appointment of officers; and they ought to have time to mature their judgments. If for a shorter period, how can they be acquainted with the rights and interests of nations, so as to form advantageous treaties?

To understand these rights is the business of education. Their business being naturally different, and more extensive, than the other branch, they ought to have different qualifications; and their duration is not too long for a right discharge of their duty.

Speech Before the Massachusetts Ratifying Convention by Rufus King and Thomas Dawes

Editor's Introduction:

Thomas Dawes, IV was barely thirty when the people of Massachusetts sent him to the State ratifying convention in 1788. His father was a notable member of Massachusetts society who served with distinction during the American War for Independence and later as an architect helped construction portions of Harvard and other landmark buildings in Boston. Dawes was a commercially minded man, and like other New Englanders, favored the Constitution because of the potential benefits to his section and State. He would later be sent to the Massachusetts Supreme Court.

These two speeches underscore the importance the people of Massachusetts placed on the commercial aspects of the new Constitution. King explained that the document would force the States to comply with congressional requisitions of money, a problem under the Articles of Confederation. Shay's Rebellion clearly weighed on every man in Massachusetts. That tax revolt was spurred by a hike in taxes after the War so that the State could cover its debt. King complained that other States had not paid their fair share and thus the Constitution would spread the burdens of Union equally among the constituent parts. Dawes considered money being sent from the Southern States to Great Britain through shipping to be "New England" money and thought the economic benefits of the new Constitution alone should move men to vote for ratification.

Speech Before the Massachusetts Ratifying Convention
January 21, 1788
By Rufus King and Thomas Dawes, IV of Massachusetts

Mr. KING. Mr. President, it is painful for me to obtrude my sentiments on the Convention so frequently. However, sir, I console myself with the idea that my motives are as good as those of more able gentlemen, who have remained silent. Sir, this is a very important clause, and of the highest consequence to the future fortune of the people of America. It is not my intention to go into any elaborate discussion of the subject. I shall only offer those considerations which have influenced my mind in favor of the article, in the hope that it may tend to reconcile gentlemen to it. It shall not be with a view of exhibiting any particular knowledge of mine; for such is not my intention. Hitherto we have considered the construction of the general government. We now come, sir, to the consideration of the powers with which that government shall be clothed. The introduction to this Constitution is in these words: "We, the people," &c. The language of the Confederation is, "We, the states," &c. The latter is a mere federal government of states. Those, therefore, that assemble under it, have no power to make laws to apply to the individuals of the states confederated; and the attempts to make laws for collective societies necessarily leave a discretion to comply with them or not. In no instance has there been so frequent deviation from first principles, as in the neglect or refusal to comply with the requisitions of general governments for the collection of moneys.

In the ancient governments, this has been the principal defect. In the United Provinces of the Netherlands, it has been conspicuously so. A celebrated political writer — I mean John Dewitt, formerly pensioner of Holland — said that, in the confederacy of 1570, though the articles were declared equally binding on the several provinces, yet any one had it in its power to comply with the requisitions of the generality or not; and some provinces, taking advantage of this discretionary power, never paid any thing. During forty years of war with Spain, the province of Holland paid fifty-eight parts of a hundred of all the expenses thereof. Two or three of the provinces never so much as passed a resolution to pay any thing; and Dewitt says that two of them paid not a single guilder. What was the consequence? In one instance, Holland compelled a neighboring province to comply with the requisitions, by marching a force into it. This was a great instance of usurpation, made in the time of a war. The Prince of Orange, and the generality, found that they could not continue the war in this manner. What was to be done? They were obliged to resort to the expedient of doubling the ordinary requisitions on the states. Some of the provinces were prevailed upon to grant these requisitions fully, in order to induce Holland to do the same. She, seeing the other states appearing thus forward, not only granted the requisitions, but paid them. The others did not. Thus was a single province obliged to bear almost the whole burdens of the war; and, one hundred years after, the accounts of this war were unsettled. What was the reason? Holland had but one voice in the States-General. That voice was feeble when opposed by the rest.

This fact is true. The history of our own country is a melancholy proof of a similar truth. Massachusetts has paid while other states have been delinquent. How was the war carried on with the paper money? Requisitions on the states for that money were made. Who paid them? Massachusetts and a few others. A requisition of 29,000,000 dollars were quoted on Massachusetts, and it was paid. This state has paid in her proportion of the old money. How comes it, then, that gentlemen have any of this money by them? Because the other states have shamefully neglected to pay their quotas. Do you ask for redress? You are scoffed at. The next requisition was for 11,000,000 of dollars, 6,000,000 of which were to be paid in facilities, the rest in silver money, for discharging the interest of the national debt. If the legislatures found a difficulty in paying the hard money, why did they not pay the paper? But 1,200,000 dollars have been paid. And six states have not paid a farthing of it.

After mentioning another requisition, equally disregarded, Mr. King said, two states have not paid a single farthing from the moment they signed the Confederation to this day, if my documents are to be depended on, and they are open to the inspection of all. Now, sir, what faith is to be put in requisitions on the states, for moneys to pay our domestic creditors, and discharge our foreign debts, for moneys lent us in the day of difficulty and distress? Sir, experience proves, as well as any thing can be proved, that no dependence can be placed on such requisitions. What method, then, can be devised to compel the delinquent states to pay their quotas? Sir, I know of none. Laws, to be effective, therefore, must not be laid on states, but upon individuals. Sir, it has been objected to the proposed Constitution, that the power is too great, and by this Constitution is to be sacred. But if the want of power is the defect in the old Confederation, there is a fitness and propriety in adopting what is here proposed, which gives the necessary power wanted. Congress now have power to call for what moneys, and in what proportion, they please; but they have no authority to compel a compliance therewith. It is an objection in some gentlemen's minds, that Congress should possess the power of the purse and the sword. But, sir, I would ask, whether any government can exist, or give security to the people, which is not possessed of this power. The first revenue will be raised from the impost, to which there is no objection, the next from the excise; and if these are not sufficient, direct taxes must be laid. To conclude, sir, if we mean to support an efficient federal government, which, under the old Confederation, can never be the case, the proposed Constitution is, in my opinion, the only one that can be substituted.

Mr. DAWES said, he thought the powers in the paragraph under debate should be fully vested in Congress. We have suffered, said he, for want of such authority in the federal head. This will be evident if we take a short view of our agriculture, commerce, and manufactures. Our agriculture has not been encouraged by the imposition of national duties on rival produce; nor can it be, so long as the several states may make contradictory laws. This has induced our farmers to raise only what they wanted to consume in their own families; I mean, however, after raising enough to pay their own taxes; for I insist that, upon the old plan, the land has borne the burden; for, as Congress could not make laws, whereby they could obtain a revenue, in their own way, from impost or excise, they multiplied their requisition on the several states. When a state was thus called on, it would perhaps impose new duties on its own trade, to procure money for paying its quota of federal demands. This would drive the trade to such neighboring states as made no such new impositions; thus the revenue would be lost with the trade, and the only resort would be a direct tax.

As to commerce, it is well known that the different states now pursue different systems of duties in regard to each other. By this, and for want of general laws of prohibition through the Union, we have not secured even our own domestic traffic that passes from state to state. This is contrary to the policy of every nation on earth. Some nations have no other commerce. The great and flourishing empire of China has but little commerce beyond her own territories; and no country is better circumstanced than we for an exclusive traffic from state to state; yet even in this we are rivalled by foreigners — by those foreigners to whom we are the least indebted. A vessel from Roseway or Halifax finds as hearty a welcome with its fish and whalebone at the southern ports, as though it was built, navigated, and freighted from Salem or Boston. And this must be the case, until we have laws comprehending and embracing alike all the states in the Union.

But it is not only our coasting trade — our whole commerce is going to ruin. Congress has not had power to make even a trade law, which shall confine the importation of foreign goods to the ships of the producing or consuming country. If we had such a law, we should not go to England for the goods of other nations; nor would British vessels be the carriers of American produce from our sister states. In the states southward of the Delaware, it is agreed that three fourths of the produce are exported, and three fourths of the returns are made, in British bottoms. It is said that, for exporting timber, one half the property goes to the carrier; and of the produce in general, it has been computed that, when it is shipped for London from a southern state, to the value of one million of dollars, the British merchant draws from that sum three hundred thousand dollars under the names of freight and charges. This is money which belongs to the New England states, because we can furnish the ships as well as, and much better than, the British. Our sister states are willing that we should receive these benefits, and that they should be secured to us by national laws; but until this is done, their private merchants will, no doubt, for the sake of long credit, or some other such temporary advantage, prefer the ships of foreigners; and yet we have suffered these ignominious burdens, rather than trust our own representatives with power to help us; and we call ourselves free and independent states! We are independent of each other, but we are slaves to Europe. We have no uniformity in duties, imposts, excises, or prohibitions. Congress has no authority to withhold advantages from foreigners, in order to obtain advantages from them. By the 9th of the old articles, Congress may enter into treaties and alliances under certain provisoes; but Congress cannot pledge that a single state shall not render the whole treaty of commerce a nullity.

Our manufactures are another great subject, which has received no encouragement by national duties on foreign manufactures, and they never can by any authority in the Confederation. It has been said that no country can produce manufactures until it be overstocked with inhabitants. It is true that the United States have employment, except in the winter, for their citizens in agriculture — the most respectable employment under heaven; but it is now to be remembered, that, since the old Confederation, there is a great emigration of foreign artisans hither, some of whom are left here by the armies of the last war, and others who have more lately sought the new world, from hopes of mending their condition; these will not change their employments. Besides this, the very face of our country leads to manufactures. Our numerous falls of water, and places for mills, where paper, snuff, gunpowder, iron works, and numerous other articles, are prepared, — these will save us immense sums of money, that would otherwise go to Europe. The question is, Have these been encouraged? Has Congress been able, by national laws, to prevent the importation of such foreign commodities as are made from such raw materials as we ourselves raise? It is alleged that the citizens of the United States have contracted debts within the last three years, with the subjects of Great Britain, for the amount of near six millions of dollars, and that consequently our lands are mortgaged for that sum. So Corsica was once mortgaged to the Genoese merchants for articles which her inhabitants did not want, or which they could not have made themselves; and she was afterwards sold to a foreign power. If we wish to encourage our own manufactures, to preserve our own commerce, to raise the value of our own lands, we must give Congress the powers in question.

The honorable gentleman from Norton, last speaking, says, that, if Congress will have the power of laying and collecting taxes, they will use the power of the sword. I hold the reverse to be true. The doctrine of requisitions, or of demands upon a whole state, implies such a power; for surely a whole state, a whole community, can be compelled only by an army; but taxes upon an individual imply only the use of a collector of taxes. That Congress, however, will not apply to the power of direct taxation, unless in cases of emergency, is plain; because, as thirty thousand inhabitants will elect a representative, eight tenths of which electors perhaps are yeomen, and holders of farms, it will be their own faults if they are not represented by such men as will never permit the land to be injured by unnecessary taxes.

Speech Before the Massachusetts Ratifying Convention by James Bowdoin

Editor's Introduction:

James Bowdoin and John Hancock had much in common. Both men were prominent merchants in Massachusetts who were initially lukewarm to colonial agitation against the Crown; both men were politically ambitions and counted among their colleagues leading men on both sides of the Atlantic; both men were well respected by the people of Massachusetts; both attended the same church in Boston. Perhaps because of this, they were almost always political rivals who quarreled over even the most insignificant details. Bowdoin called Hancock a "foppish demagogue." Hancock was elected first governor of Massachusetts, Bowdoin the second, and was then again succeeded by Hancock. Hancock opposed the Constitution without a bill of rights, Bowdoin supported it without amendments.

Bowdoin was less of a populist than the gregarious Hancock, but his description of the Boston Massacre of 1770 dominated the interpretation of the event. He was also interested in science and education and maintained a long friendship with Benjamin Franklin. Bowdoin served in the Massachusetts General Court throughout the colonial period.

Bowdoin's speech in favor of the Constitution preceded the compromise between the opponents and proponents over a bill of rights. Bowdoin declared that the entire Constitution was a declaration of rights and like other proponents did not think a separate bill of rights necessary. His speech offered a full summary of the various arguments for the Constitution, most importantly that the general government would not abuse its powers because Americans were firmly dedicated to the spirit of liberty and would oppose such usurpations of power.

After proponents agreed to support the document with amendments, Massachusetts ratified the Constitution on February 6, 1788 by a vote of 187-168, making it the sixth State to ratify the document.

Speech Before the Massachusetts Ratifying Convention

January 23, 1788

By James Bowdoin of Massachusetts

Hon. Mr. BOWDOIN. Mr. President, on the subject of government, which admits of so great a variety in its parts and combinations, a diversity of opinions is to be expected; and it was natural to suppose that, in this Convention, respectable for its numbers, but much more so for the characters which compose it, there would be a like diversity concerning the federal Constitution, that is now the subject of our consideration.

In considering it, every gentleman will reflect how inadequate to the purposes of the Union the Confederation has been. When the plan of the Confederation was formed, the enemy were invading us; and this inspired the several states with such a spirit of union and mutual defence, that a mere requisition or recommendation of Congress was sufficient to procure the needful aids, without any power of coercion; and for that reason, among others, no such power was given by the

Confederation. But since that reason had ceased, and the idea of danger being removed by the peace, the requisitions of Congress have, in most of the states, been little regarded, notwithstanding they solemnly pledged their faith to comply with them.

This non-compliance has compelled Congress to increase the foreign debt of the Union, by procuring further loans to pay the interest and instalments due on former loans; and in that way to preserve the public faith, which had been pledged to foreign powers. It has compelled them, in order to prevent the consequences of a breach of faith, as relative to those powers, to enter repeatedly into those ruinous negotiations, by which "the United States jointly, and each of them in particular, together with all their lands, chattels, revenues, and products, and also the imposts and taxes already laid and raised in the same, or in time to come to be laid and raised, are for the whole," mortgaged for the repayment of those loans by instalments, and for the payment of the interest on them annually. These debts must be paid, bona fide, according to contract, or be further increased by procuring, if procurable, further loans; which, ruinous as the measure is, must be continued, unless the states empower Congress to raise money for the discharging those debts. It will not be in the power of the United States, and I am sure it will not be in their inclination, to rid themselves of those debts in the same base and ignominious manner in which a faction, in one of them, are endeavoring to get rid of theirs. To the same cause (a non-compliance with congressional requisitions) are owing the repeated but necessary breaches of public faith in regard to the payment of the federal domestic debt. And hence, as relative to the joint consolidated debt, the inefficiency of the public finances, and the bankrupt state of the federal treasury, which can never be remedied without empowering Congress to levy adequate duties and taxes. Without such a power, the accumulating debt will never be paid, but by a forcible collection, which our foreign creditors know how, and are able to apply, if, unhappily, it should be necessary. The several loans, which by contract are to be paid by instalments, will, in case of the failure of any of the stipulated payments, become, the whole of them, immediately payable; and any of the property of any of the states, whether public or private, that can be most easily come at, will, in that case, be seized and applied for that purpose.

This mode of reimbursement, or reprisal, will be upon the trade and navigation of the United States; and in proportion as ours of this state may be larger and more extensive than the trade and navigation of other states, we shall be the greatest sufferers. This ruin of our trade will involve in it not only the ruin of the mercantile part of the state, and of the numerous body of mechanics dependent upon it, but will most essentially affect every other class of citizens, and operate most extensively to the injury of the commonwealth.

These are some of the consequences, certain and infallible, that will flow from the denial of that power to Congress. Shall we then, we of this state, who are so much interested in this matter, deny them that power — a power so essential to our political happiness?

But if we attend to our trade, as it is at present, we shall find that the miserable state of it is owing to a like want of power in Congress. Other nations prohibit our vessels from entering their ports, or lay heavy duties on our exports carried thither; and we have no retaliating or regulating power over their vessels and exports, to prevent it. Hence a decrease of our commerce and navigation, and the duties and revenue arising from them. Hence an insufficient demand for the produce of our lands, and the consequent discouragement of agriculture. Hence the inability to pay debts, and particularly taxes, which by that decrease are enhanced. And hence, as the necessary result of all these, the emigration of our inhabitants. If it be asked, How are these evils, and others that might be mentioned, to be remedied? the answer is short — By giving Congress adequate and proper power. Whether such power be given by the proposed Constitution, it is left with the Conventions from the several states, and with us, who compose one of them, to determine.

In determining on this question, every gentleman will, doubtless, consider the importance of cultivating a spirit of union among ourselves, and with the several states. This spirit procured our emancipation from British tyranny; and the same spirit, by uniting us in the necessary means, must secure to us our dear-bought, blood-purchased liberty and independence, and deliver us from evils which, unless remedied, must end in national ruin. The means for effecting these purposes are within our reach; and the adoption of the proposed Constitution will give us the possession of them. Like all other human productions, it may be imperfect; but most of the imperfections imputed to it are ideal and unfounded, and the rest are of such a nature that they cannot be certainly known but by the operations of the Constitution; and if, in its operation, it should in any respect be essentially bad, it will be amended in one of the modes prescribed by it. I say, will be amended, because the Constitution is constructed on such principles, that its bad effects, if any such should arise from it, will injure the members of Congress equally with their constituents; and, therefore, both of them must be equally induced to seek for, and effectuate, if possible, the requisite amendments.

There have been many objections offered against the Constitution; and of these the one most strongly urged has been, the great power vested in Congress. On this subject, I beg leave to make a few general observations, which ought to be attended to, as being applicable to every branch of that power.

It may, therefore, be observed, that the investiture of such power, so far from being an objection, is a most cogent reason for accepting the Constitution. The power of Congress, both in the legislative and executive line, is the power of the people, collected through a certain medium, to a focal point, at all times ready to be exerted for the general benefit, according as circumstances or exigencies may require. If you diminish or annihilate it, you diminish or annihilate the means of your own safety and prosperity; which means, if they were to be measured like mathematical quantities, would be in exact proportion, as the power is greater or less. But this is not the case; for power that does not reach, or is inadequate to the object, is worse than none. An exertion of such power would increase the evil it was intended to remove, and at the same time create a further evil, which might be a very great one — the expense of a fruitless exertion.

If we consider the objects of the power, they are numerous and important; and as human foresight cannot extend to many of them, and all of them are in the womb of futurity, the quantum of the power cannot be estimated. Less than the whole, as relative to federal purposes, may, through its insufficiency, occasion the dissolution of the Union, and a subjugation or division of it among foreign powers. Their attention is drawn to the United States; their emissaries are watching our conduct, particularly upon the present most important occasion; and if we should be so unhappy as to reject the federal Constitution proposed to us, and continue much longer our present weak, unenergetic federal government, their policy will probably induce them to plan a division or partition of the states among themselves, and unite their forces to effect it.

But, however that may be, this is certain — that the respectability of the United States among foreign nations, our commerce with them on the principles of reciprocity, and our forming beneficial treaties with them on those principles, their estimation of our friendship and fear of losing it, our capacity to resent injuries, and our security against interior as well as foreign attacks, must be derived from such a power. In short, the commercial and political happiness, the liberty and property, the peace, safety, and general welfare, both internal and external, of each and all the states, depend on that power; which, as it must be applied to a vast variety of objects, and to cases and exigencies beyond the ken of human prescience, must be very great; and which cannot be limited without endangering the public safety.

It will be, and has been said, this great power may be abused, and, instead of protecting, may be employed by Congress in oppressing, their constituents. A possibility of abuse, as it may be affirmed of all delegated power whatever, is by itself no sufficient reason for withholding the delegation. If it were a sufficient one, no power could be delegated; nor could government of any sort subsist. The possibility, however, should make us careful, that, in all delegations of importance, like the one contained in the proposed Constitution, there should be such checks provided as would not frustrate the end and intention of delegating the power, but would, as far as it could be safely done, prevent the abuse of it; and such checks are provided in the Constitution. Some of them were mentioned the last evening by one of my worthy colleagues; but I shall here exhibit all of them in one view.

The two capital departments of government, the legislative and executive, in which the delegated power resides, consisting of the President, Vice-President, Senate and Representatives, are directly, and by the respective legislatures and delegates, chosen by the people.

The President, and also the Vice-President, when acting as President, before they enter on the execution of the office, shall each "solemnly swear or affirm, that he will faithfully execute the office of President of the United States, and will, to the best of his ability, preserve, protect, and defend, the Constitution of the United States."

"The senators and representatives before mentioned, and the members of the state legislatures, and all executive and judicial officers, both of the United States and of the several states, shall be bound, by oath or affirmation, to support this Constitution."

"The President and Vice-President, and all civil officers of the United States, shall be removed from office, on impeachment for, and conviction of, treason, bribery, or other high crimes or misdemeanors."

"No senator or representative shall, during the time for which he was elected, be appointed to any civil office, which shall have been created, or the emoluments whereof shall have been increased, during such time; and no person holding any office under the United States shall be a member of either house, during his continuance in office."

"No title of nobility shall be granted by the United States, or by any particular state; and no person holding any office of profit or trust under the United States shall, without the consent of the Congress, accept of any present, emolument, office, or title, of any kind whatever, from any king, prince, or foreign state."

"The United States shall guaranty to every state in this Union a republican form of government, and shall protect each of them against invasion and domestic violence."

To these great checks may be added several other very essential ones, as, the negative which each house has upon the acts of the other; the disapproving power of the President, which subjects those acts to a revision by the two houses, and to a final negative, unless two thirds of each house shall agree to pass the returned acts, notwithstanding the President's objections; the printing the journals of each house, containing their joint and respective proceedings; and the publishing, from time to time, a regular statement and account of receipts and expenditures of all public money, none of which shall be drawn from the treasury but in consequence of appropriations made by law.

All these checks and precautions, provided in the Constitution, must, in a great measure, prevent an abuse of power, at least in all flagrant instances, even if Congress should consist wholly of men who were guided by no other principle than their own interest. Under the influence of such checks, this would compel them to a conduct which, in the general, would answer the intention of the Constitution. But the presumption is, — and, if the people duly attend to the objects of their choice, it would be realized, — that the President of the United States and the members of Congress would, for the most part, be men, not only of ability, but of a good moral character; in which case, an abuse of power is not to be apprehended, nor any error in the government, but such as every human institution is subject to.

There is a further guard against the abuse of power, which, though not expressed, is strongly implied in the federal Constitution, and, indeed, in the constitution of every government founded on the principles of equal liberty; and that is, that those who make the laws, and particularly laws for the levying of taxes, do, in common with their fellow-citizens, fall within the power and operation of those laws.

As, then, the individuals in Congress will all share in the burdens they impose, and be personally affected by the good or bad laws they make for the Union, they will be under the strongest motives of interest to lay the lightest burdens possible, and to make the best laws, or such laws as shall not unnecessarily affect either the property or the personal rights of their fellow-citizens.

With regard to rights, the whole Constitution is a declaration of rights, which primarily and principally respect the general government intended to be formed by it. The rights of particular states, or private citizens, not being the object or subject of the Constitution, they are only incidentally mentioned. In regard to the former, it would require a volume to describe them, as they extend to every subject of legislation, not included in the powers vested in Congress; and, in regard to the latter, as all governments are founded on the relinquishment of personal rights in a certain degree, there was a clear impropriety in being very particular about them. By such a particularity the government might be embarrassed, and prevented from doing what the private, as well as the public and general, good of the citizens and states might require.

The public good, in which private is necessarily involved, might be hurt by too particular an enumeration; and the private good could suffer no injury from a deficient enumeration, because Congress could not injure the rights of private citizens without injuring their own, as they must, in their public as well as private character, participate equally with others in the consequences of their own acts. And by this most important circumstance, in connection with the checks above mentioned, the several states at large, and each citizen in particular, will be secured, as far as human wisdom can secure them, against the abuse of the delegated power.

In considering the Constitution, we shall consider it, in all its parts, upon those general principles which operate through the whole of it, and are equivalent to the most extensive bill of rights that can be formed.

These observations, which are principally of a general nature, but will apply to the most essential parts of the Constitution, are, with the utmost deference and respect, submitted to your candid consideration; with the hope that, as they have influenced my own mind decidedly in favor of the Constitution, they will not be wholly unproductive of a like influence on the minds of the gentlemen of the Convention.

If the Constitution should be finally accepted and established, it will complete the temple of American liberty, and, like the keystone of a grand and magnificent arch, be the bond of union to keep all the parts firm and compacted together. May this temple, sacred to liberty and virtue, sacred to justice, the first and greatest political virtue, and built upon the broad and solid foundation of perfect union, be dissoluble only by the dissolution of nature; and may this Convention have the distinguished honor of erecting one of its pillars on that lasting foundation!

Federalist No. 42 by James Madison

Editor's Introduction:

Madison continued his inquiry into the nature and character of federal power in *Federalist* No. 42. This essay covered federal objectives two and three from *Federalist* No. 41, namely the regulation of commerce and the power to maintain harmony and proper interaction among the State governments. Both issues were considered defects under the Articles of Confederation as States could levy tariffs against other States while ignoring federal trade agreements with foreign powers. But as Madison explained, even in *Federalist* No. 41, the regulation of commerce could extend to the power to make treaties and to conduct a proper foreign intercourse with other nations. These were collective powers the States could not undertake on their own authority. Madison also considered the prohibition on State powers to "coin" money and a uniform rule of naturalization to be a solid benefit for the entire Union, the first because it would destroy paper money and the second because States needed cogency on the issue of citizenship.

January 22, 1788

By James Madison of Virginia

To the People of the State of New York:

THE SECOND class of powers, lodged in the general government, consists of those which regulate the intercourse with foreign nations, to wit: to make treaties; to send and receive ambassadors, other public ministers, and consuls; to define and punish piracies and felonies committed on the high seas, and offenses against the law of nations; to regulate foreign commerce, including a power to prohibit, after the year 1808, the importation of slaves, and to lay an intermediate duty of ten dollars per head, as a discouragement to such importations. This class of powers forms an obvious and essential branch of the federal administration. If we are to be one nation in any respect, it clearly ought to be in respect to other nations. The powers to make treaties and to send and receive ambassadors, speak their own propriety. Both of them are comprised in the articles of Confederation, with this difference only, that the former is disembarrassed, by the plan of the convention, of an exception, under which treaties might be substantially frustrated by regulations of the States; and that a power of appointing and receiving "other public ministers and consuls," is expressly and very properly added to the former provision concerning ambassadors.

The term ambassador, if taken strictly, as seems to be required by the second of the articles of Confederation, comprehends the highest grade only of public ministers, and excludes the grades which the United States will be most likely to prefer, where foreign embassies may be necessary. And under no latitude of construction will the term comprehend consuls. Yet it has been found expedient, and has been the practice of Congress, to employ the inferior grades of public ministers, and to send and receive consuls. It is true, that where treaties of commerce stipulate for the mutual appointment of consuls, whose functions are connected with commerce, the admission of foreign consuls may fall within the power of making commercial treaties; and that where no such treaties exist, the mission of American consuls into foreign countries may PERHAPS be covered under the authority, given by the ninth article of the Confederation, to appoint all such civil officers as may be necessary for managing the general affairs of the United States. But the admission of consuls into the United States, where no previous treaty has stipulated it, seems to have been nowhere provided for.

A supply of the omission is one of the lesser instances in which the convention have improved on the model before them. But the most minute provisions become important when they tend to obviate the necessity or the pretext for gradual and unobserved usurpations of power. A list of the cases in which Congress have been betrayed, or forced by the defects of the Confederation, into violations of their chartered authorities, would not a little surprise those who have paid no attention to the subject; and would be no inconsiderable argument in favor of the new Constitution, which seems to have provided no less studiously for the lesser, than the more obvious and striking defects of the old. The power to define and punish piracies and felonies committed on the high seas, and offenses against the law of nations, belongs with equal propriety to the general government, and is a still greater improvement on the articles of Confederation. These articles contain no provision for the case of offenses against the law of nations; and consequently leave it in the power of any indiscreet member to embroil the Confederacy with foreign nations.

The provision of the federal articles on the subject of piracies and felonies extends no further than to the establishment of courts for the trial of these offenses. The definition of piracies might, perhaps, without inconveniency, be left to the law of nations; though a legislative definition of them is found in most municipal codes. A definition of felonies on the high seas is evidently requisite. Felony is a term of loose signification, even in the common law of England; and of various import in the statute law of that kingdom. But neither the common nor the statute law of that, or of any other nation, ought to be a standard for the proceedings of this, unless previously made its own by legislative adoption. The meaning of the term, as defined in the codes of the several States, would be as impracticable as the former would be a dishonorable and illegitimate guide. It is not precisely the same in any two of the States; and varies in each with every revision of its criminal laws. For the sake of certainty and uniformity, therefore, the power of defining felonies in this case was in every respect necessary and proper.

The regulation of foreign commerce, having fallen within several views which have been taken of this subject, has been too fully discussed to need additional proofs here of its being properly submitted to the federal administration. It were doubtless to be wished, that the power of prohibiting the importation of slaves had not been postponed until the year 1808, or rather that it had been suffered to have immediate operation. But it is not difficult to account, either for this restriction on the general government, or for the manner in which the whole clause is expressed. It ought to be considered as a great point gained in favor of humanity, that a period of twenty years may terminate forever, within these States, a traffic which has so long and so loudly upbraided the barbarism of modern policy; that within that period, it will receive a considerable discouragement from the federal government, and may be totally abolished, by a concurrence of the few States which continue the unnatural traffic, in the prohibitory example which has been given by so great a majority of the Union. Happy would it be for the unfortunate Africans, if an equal prospect lay before them of being redeemed from the oppressions of their European brethren! Attempts have been made to pervert this clause into an objection against the Constitution, by representing it on one side as a criminal toleration of an illicit practice, and on another as calculated to prevent voluntary and beneficial emigrations from Europe to America. I mention these misconstructions, not with a view to give them an answer, for they deserve none, but as specimens of the manner and spirit in which some have thought fit to conduct their opposition to the proposed government.

The powers included in the THIRD class are those which provide for the harmony and proper intercourse among the States. Under this head might be included the particular restraints imposed on the authority of the States, and certain powers of the judicial department; but the former are reserved for a distinct class, and the latter will be particularly examined when we arrive at the structure and organization of the government. I shall confine myself to a cursory review of the remaining powers comprehended under this third description, to wit: to regulate commerce among the several States and the Indian tribes; to coin money, regulate the value thereof, and of foreign coin; to provide for the punishment of counterfeiting the current coin and secureties of the United States; to fix the standard of weights and measures; to establish a uniform rule of naturalization, and uniform laws of bankruptcy, to prescribe the manner in which the public acts, records, and judicial proceedings of each State shall be proved, and the effect they shall have in other States; and to establish post offices and post roads. The defect of power in the existing Confederacy to regulate the commerce between its several members, is in the number of those which have been clearly pointed out by experience.

To the proofs and remarks which former papers have brought into view on this subject, it may be added that without this supplemental provision, the great and essential power of regulating foreign commerce would have been incomplete and ineffectual. A very material object of this power was the relief of the States which import and export through other States, from the improper contributions levied on them by the latter. Were these at liberty to regulate the trade between State and State, it must be foreseen that ways would be found out to load the articles of import and export, during the passage through their jurisdiction, with duties which would fall on the makers of the latter and the consumers of the former. We may be assured by past experience, that such a practice would be introduced by future contrivances; and both by that and a common knowledge of human affairs, that it would nourish unceasing animosities, and not improbably terminate in serious interruptions of the public tranquillity.

To those who do not view the question through the medium of passion or of interest, the desire of the commercial States to collect, in any form, an indirect revenue from their uncommercial neighbors, must appear not less impolitic than it is unfair; since it would stimulate the injured party, by resentment as well as interest, to resort to less convenient channels for their foreign trade. But the mild voice of reason, pleading the cause of an enlarged and permanent interest, is but too often drowned, before public bodies as well as individuals, by the clamors of an impatient avidity for immediate and immoderate gain. The necessity of a superintending authority over the reciprocal trade of confederated States, has been illustrated by other examples as well as our own. In Switzerland, where the Union is so very slight, each canton is obliged to allow to merchandises a passage through its jurisdiction into other cantons, without an augmentation of the tolls. In Germany it is a law of the empire, that the princes and states shall not lay tolls or customs on bridges, rivers, or passages, without the consent of the emperor and the diet; though it appears from a quotation in an antecedent paper, that the practice in this, as in many other instances in that confederacy, has not followed the law, and has produced there the mischiefs which have been foreseen here. Among the restraints imposed by the Union of the Netherlands on its members, one is, that they shall not establish imposts disadvantageous to their neighbors, without the general permission.

The regulation of commerce with the Indian tribes is very properly unfettered from two limitations in the articles of Confederation, which render the provision obscure and contradictory. The power is there restrained to Indians, not members of any of the States, and is not to violate or infringe the legislative right of any State within its own limits. What description of Indians are to be deemed members of a State, is not yet settled, and has been a question of frequent perplexity and contention in the federal councils. And how the trade with Indians, though not members of a State, yet residing within its legislative jurisdiction, can be regulated by an external authority, without so far intruding on the internal rights of legislation, is absolutely incomprehensible. This is not the only case in which the articles of Confederation have inconsiderately endeavored to accomplish impossibilities; to reconcile a partial sovereignty in the Union, with complete sovereignty in the States; to subvert a mathematical axiom, by taking away a part, and letting the whole remain.

All that need be remarked on the power to coin money, regulate the value thereof, and of foreign coin, is, that by providing for this last case, the Constitution has supplied a material omission in the articles of Confederation. The authority of the existing Congress is restrained to the regulation of coin STRUCK by their own authority, or that of the respective States. It must be seen at once that the proposed uniformity in the VALUE of the current coin might be destroyed by subjecting that of foreign coin to the different regulations of the different States.

The punishment of counterfeiting the public securities, as well as the current coin, is submitted of course to that authority which is to secure the value of both. The regulation of weights and measures is transferred from the articles of Confederation, and is founded on like considerations with the preceding power of regulating coin.

The dissimilarity in the rules of naturalization has long been remarked as a fault in our system, and as laying a foundation for intricate and delicate questions. In the fourth article of the Confederation, it is declared "that the FREE INHABITANTS of each of these States, paupers, vagabonds, and fugitives from justice, excepted, shall be entitled to all privileges and immunities of FREE CITIZENS in the several States; and THE PEOPLE of each State shall, in every other, enjoy all the privileges of trade and commerce," etc. There is a confusion of language here, which is remarkable. Why the terms FREE INHABITANTS are used in one part of the article, FREE CITIZENS in another, and PEOPLE in another; or what was meant by superadding to "all privileges and immunities of free citizens," "all the privileges of trade and commerce," cannot easily be determined. It seems to be a construction scarcely avoidable, however, that those who come under the denomination of FREE INHABITANTS of a State, although not citizens of such State, are entitled, in every other State, to all the privileges of FREE CITIZENS of the latter; that is, to greater privileges than they may be entitled to in their own State: so that it may be in the power of a particular State, or rather every State is laid under a necessity, not only to confer the rights of citizenship in other States upon any whom it may admit to such rights within itself, but upon any whom it may allow to become inhabitants within its jurisdiction. But were an exposition of the term "inhabitants" to be admitted which would confine the stipulated privileges to citizens alone, the difficulty is diminished only, not removed. The very improper power would still be retained by each State, of naturalizing aliens in every other State. In one State, residence for a short term confirms all the rights of citizenship: in another, qualifications of greater importance are required. An alien, therefore, legally incapacitated for certain rights in the latter, may, by previous residence only in the former, elude his incapacity; and thus the law of one State be preposterously rendered paramount to the law of another, within the jurisdiction of the other.

We owe it to mere casualty, that very serious embarrassments on this subject have been hitherto escaped. By the laws of several States, certain descriptions of aliens, who had rendered themselves obnoxious, were laid under interdicts inconsistent not only with the rights of citizenship but with the privilege of residence. What would have been the consequence, if such persons, by residence or otherwise, had acquired the character of citizens under the laws of another State, and then asserted their rights as such, both to residence and citizenship, within the State proscribing them? Whatever the legal consequences might have been, other consequences would probably have resulted, of too serious a nature not to be provided against. The new Constitution has accordingly, with great propriety, made provision against them, and all others proceeding from the defect of the Confederation on this head, by authorizing the general government to establish a uniform rule of naturalization throughout the United States. The power of establishing uniform laws of bankruptcy is so intimately connected with the regulation of commerce, and will prevent so many frauds where the parties or their property may lie or be removed into different States, that the expediency of it seems not likely to be drawn into question. The power of prescribing by general laws, the manner in which the public acts, records and judicial proceedings of each State shall be proved, and the effect they shall have in other States, is an evident and valuable improvement on the clause relating to this subject in the articles of Confederation. The meaning of the latter is extremely indeterminate, and can be of little importance under any interpretation which it will bear. The power here established may be rendered a very convenient instrument of justice, and be particularly beneficial on the borders of contiguous States, where the effects liable to justice may be suddenly and secretly translated, in any stage of the process, within a foreign jurisdiction. The power of establishing post roads must, in every view, be a harmless power, and may, perhaps, by judicious management, become productive of great public conveniency. Nothing which tends to facilitate the intercourse between the States can be deemed unworthy of the public care.

A Freeman I by Tench Coxe

Editor's Introduction:

Tench Coxe's "A Freeman" series was published after Pennsylvania ratified the Constitution but in response to the minority report from the Pennsylvania Ratifying Convention. Why pen a defense of the Constitution after it was ratified? To ensure that opponents of the document understood that the Constitution did not consolidate or eliminate the State governments. The fact that Coxe published it after ratification lends to a stronger point about "originalism." This public proclamation that the States were the foundation of the government and the most important leg undergirding the structure of the general government proves that even after the Constitution was ratified this remained the most pressing problem for the United States. All other issues were components of the larger picture, namely State versus federal power. Coxe's ninth point about the limitation of federal powers is the most important part of the document and conclusively proves that under an original understanding of the Constitution, most of what the federal government does today is unconstitutional.

A Freeman I

January 23, 1788

By Tench Coxe of Pennsylvania

To the MINORITY of the CONVENTION of *Pennsylvania*

Gentlemen, The great question which at this time engages the attention of the United States calls for the fairest and most dispassionate discussion. Mistakes in taking up the subject must lead to erroneous conclusions, and men of pure intentions, both among yourselves and the people at large, should misconceptions have arisen, may continue avers to the system, after it has received the *fiat* of all the conventions. Well intended attempts to throw light upon the interesting subject cannot, therefore, be unpleasing to you. Without further introduction, then, I will proceed to a point of considerable importance in itself and in its consequences, on which I conceive your opinions have been erroneously formed, and on which I earnestly hope we shall finally concur.

The consolidation of the United States into one government by the operation of the proposed constitution (in contradistinction from a confederacy) appears to you to be the consequence of the system, and the intention of its framers. This is the point of the difference which I mean to treat of, and for the present I shall confine my observations to it alone.

Were the parts of the federal government which you have particularized as much of the nature of consolidation as you seem to suppose, real nature and design, and the state sovereignties, would indeed be finally annihilated. The appearances which have misled you I shall remark on in the course of these papers, and I shall endeavour to exhibit clear and permanent marks and lines of *separate sovereignty*, which must ever distinguish and circumscribe each of the several states, and *prevent their annihilation* by the federal government, or any of its operations.

When the people of America dissolved their connexion with the crown of Britain, they found themselves separated from all the world, but a few powerless colonies, the principal of which indeed they expected to induce into their measures. The crown having been merely a centre of *union*, the act of independence dissolved the political ties that had formerly existed among the states, and it was attended with no absolute confederacy; but many circumstances conspired to render some new form of connexion desirable and necessary. We wished not to continue distinct bodies of people, but to form a respectable nation. The remains of our ancient governments kept us in the form of thirteen political bodies, and from a variety of just and prudent considerations, we determined to enter into an indissoluble and perpetual *union*. Though a confederacy of sovereign states was the mode of connexion which was wisely desired and actually adopted, yet in that feeble and inadequate bond of union to which we assented, articles strongly partaking of the nature of consolidation are observable.

We see, for example, that the free inhabitants of each state were rendered, to all intents and purposes, *free citizens of all the rest*. Persons fleeing from justice in one state were to be *delivered up* by any other in which they might take *refuge*, contrary to the laws prevailing among *distinct* sovereignties, whereby the jurisdiction of one state pervaded the territories of all the rest, to the effectual length of trial, condemnation and punishment. The right to judge of *the sums that should be expended for the use of the nation* lies, even under the old confederation, *solely* with Congress, and after the demand is fixed by them, and formally make, the states are *bound*, as far as they can be bound by any compact, to pay their respective quotas into the federal treasury, by which the power of the purse is fully given to them; nor can the states *constitutionally* refuse to comply. It is very certain that there is not in the present federal government vigor enough to carry *this actually delegated* power into execution; yet, if Congress has possessed energy sufficient to have done it, there is no doubt but they would have been justifiable in the measure, though the season of invasion was unfavorable for internal contests.

We shall also find, that *the right to raise armies and build navies* is also vested in Congress by the present confederation, and they are to be the sole judges of the occasion, and the force required. The state, therefore, that refuses to fulfil the requisitions of Congress on either of these articles, acts *unconstitutionally*. It appears, then, that it was thought necessary at the time of forming the old federal constitution, that Congress should have what is termed "*the powers of the purse and the sword*." That constitution contained a delegation of them, because the framers of it saw that those powers were necessary to *the perpetuity and efficiency* of the union, and to obtain the desirable ends of it. It is certainly very true, that the means provided to enable Congress to apply those powers, which the constitution vested in them, were so liable to opposition, interruption and delay, that the clauses containing them became a mere dead letter. This however was not expected or desired by any of the states at the time, and their subsequent defaults are *infringements* of the letter and spirit of the confederation. On these circumstances I entreat your most dispassionate and candid consideration. I beg leave to remark, however, that as in the present constitution they are only *appearances* of consolidation, irrefragably contradicted by other facts and circumstances, so also are the facts and observations in your address *merely appearances* of a consolidation, which I hope to demonstrate does not exist. The matter will be better understood by proceeding to those points which shew, that, as under the old so under the new federal constitution, the thirteen United

States were *not intended* to be, and really *are not consolidated*, in such manner as to *absorb or destroy* the sovereignties of the several states. In order to [have] a perfect understanding of each other, it may be proper to observe here, that by your term *consolidation* I understand you mean *the final annihilation of separate state government or sovereignty, by the nature and operations of the proposed constitution*. Among the proofs you adduce of such consolidation being the *intention* of the late convention, is the expression of "We the People." Tho' this is a mere form of words, it will be well to see what expressions are to be found in the constitution in opposition to this, and indicative of the intentions of the convention, before we consider those things, which, as I conceive, secure the states from a possibility of losing their respective sovereignties.

First, then, tho' the convention propose that it should be the act of the people, yet it is in their capacities as citizens of *the several members of our confederacy* for they are expressly declared to be "the people of *the United States*" to which idea the expression is *strictly* confined, and the *general* term of *America*, which is constantly used in speaking of us *as a nation*, is carefully omitted: a pointed view was evidently had to our *existing union*. But we must see at once, that the reason of "*the People*" being mentioned was, that alterations of several constitutions were to be effected, which the convention well knew could be done by no authority but that of "*the people*," either determining themselves *in their several states*, or delegating adequate powers to their *state conventions*. Had the federal convention meant to exclude the idea of "*union*," that is, of *several and separate* sovereignties joining in a confederacy, they would have said, we *the people of America*; for union necessarily involves the idea of component states, which complete consolidations exclude. But the severalty of the states is frequently recognized in the most distinct manner in the course of the constitution. The representatives are to be inhabitants of *the state* they represent each *state* is to have a representative the militia officers are to be appointed by the *several states* and many other instances will be found in reading the constitutions. These, however, are all mere expressions, and I should not have introduced them, but to overbalance the words you have mentioned by a superior weight of the same kind. Let us, then, proceed to evidences against consolidation, of more force than the mere forms of words.

It will be found, on a careful examination, that many things, which are indispensably necessary to the existence and good order of society, cannot be performed by the federal government, but will require *the agency and powers* of the state legislatures or sovereignties, with their various appurtenances and appendages.

1st. Congress, under all the powers of the proposed constitution, can neither train the militia, nor appoint the officers thereof.

2dly. They cannot fix the qualifications of electors of representatives, or of the electors of the electors of the President or Vice-President.

3dly. In case of a vacancy in the senate or the house of representatives, they cannot issue a writ for a new election, nor take any of the measures necessary to obtain one.

4thly. They cannot appoint a judge, constitute a court, or in any other way interfere in determining offences against the criminal law of the states, nor can they in any way interfere in the determinations of civil causes between citizens of the same state, which will be innumerable and highly important.

5thly. They cannot elect a President, a Vice-President, a Senator, or a federal representative, without all of which their own government must remain *suspended*, and universal *Anarchy must ensue*.

6thly. They cannot determine the place of chusing senators, because that would be derogatory to *the sovereignty* of the state legislatures, who are to elect them.

7thly. They cannot enact laws for the inspection of the produce of the country, a matter of the utmost importance to the commerce of the *several* states, and the honor of *the whole*.

8thly. They cannot appoint or commission *any state officer*, legislative, executive or judicial.

9thly. They cannot interfere with the openings of rivers and canals; the making or regulation of roads, except post roads; building bridges; erecting ferries; establishment of state seminaries of learning; libraries; literary, religious, trading or manufacturing societies; erecting or regulating the police of cities, towns or boroughs; creating new state offices; building light houses, public wharves, county gaols, markets, or other public buildings; making sale of state lands, and other state property; receiving or appropriating the incomes of state buildings and property; executing the state laws; altering the criminal law; nor can they do any other matter or thing appertaining to the internal affairs of any state, whether legislative, executive or judicial, civil or ecclesiastical.

10thly. They cannot interfere with, alter or amend the constitution of any state, which, it is admitted, now is, and, from time to time, will be more or less necessary in most of them.

The proper investigation of this subject will require more of your time than I can take the liberty of engaging at present. I shall therefore leave what I have now written to your honest and cool reflection.

Federalist No. 44 by James Madison

Editor's Introduction:

If historians did not know Madison wrote *Federalist* No. 44, its authorship could easily be subscribed to Hamilton. Why? Because Madison used the same logic Hamilton relied upon when defending the constitutionality of the Bank of the United States in 1791, namely that any legislative act was constitutional if the ends justified the means. This is interesting because Madison would walk back such a broad explanation of "implied powers" in the next two essays in the *Federalist*, but his defense of the "necessary and proper clause" and "supremacy clause" opened the door to a "loose construction" interpretation of the Constitution.

Madison used *Federalist* No. 44 to defend Article I, Section 10 of the Constitution, the portion of the document that prohibited States from engaging in "injurious acts." These prohibitions corresponded to a positive grant of power to the general government, for example the States could not coin money whereas the general government could mint coins. The Constitution made ex-post facto laws, bills of attainder, and laws "impairing the obligation of contracts" illegal and thus protected rights long established under English common law.

Federalist No. 44

January 25, 1788

By James Madison of Virginia

To the People of the State of New York:

A FIFTH class of provisions in favor of the federal authority consists of the following restrictions on the authority of the several States:

1. "No State shall enter into any treaty, alliance, or confederation; grant letters of marque and reprisal; coin money; emit bills of credit; make any thing but gold and silver a legal tender in payment of debts; pass any bill of attainder, ex-post-facto law, or law impairing the obligation of contracts; or grant any title of nobility.

"The prohibition against treaties, alliances, and confederations makes a part of the existing articles of Union; and for reasons which need no explanation, is copied into the new Constitution. The prohibition of letters of marque is another part of the old system, but is somewhat extended in the new. According to the former, letters of marque could be granted by the States after a declaration of war; according to the latter, these licenses must be obtained, as well during war as previous to its declaration, from the government of the United States. This alteration is fully justified by the advantage of uniformity in all points which relate to foreign powers; and of immediate responsibility to the nation in all those for whose conduct the nation itself is to be responsible. The right of coining money, which is here taken from the States, was left in their hands by the Confederation, as a concurrent right with that of Congress, under an exception in favor of the exclusive right of Congress to regulate the alloy and value. In this instance, also, the new provision is an improvement on the old. Whilst the alloy and value depended on the general authority, a right of coinage in the particular States could have no other effect than to multiply expensive mints and diversify the forms and weights of the circulating pieces. The latter inconveniency defeats one purpose for which the power was originally submitted to the federal head; and as far as the former might prevent an inconvenient remittance of gold and silver to the central mint for recoinage, the end can be as well attained by local mints established under the general authority.

The extension of the prohibition to bills of credit must give pleasure to every citizen, in proportion to his love of justice and his knowledge of the true springs of public prosperity. The loss which America has sustained since the peace, from the pestilent effects of paper money on the necessary confidence between man and man, on the necessary confidence in the public councils, on the industry and morals of the people, and on the character of republican government, constitutes an enormous debt against the States chargeable with this unadvised measure, which must long remain unsatisfied; or rather an accumulation of guilt, which can be expiated no otherwise than by a voluntary sacrifice on the altar of justice, of the power which has been the instrument of it. In addition to these persuasive considerations, it may be observed, that the same reasons which show the necessity of denying to the States the power of regulating coin, prove with equal force that they ought not to be at liberty to substitute a paper medium in the place of coin. Had every State a right to regulate the value of its coin, there might be as many different currencies as States, and thus the intercourse among them would be impeded; retrospective alterations in its value might be made, and thus the citizens of other States be injured, and animosities be kindled among the States themselves. The subjects of foreign powers might suffer from the same cause, and hence the Union be discredited and embroiled by the indiscretion of a single member. No one of these mischiefs is less incident to a power in the States to emit paper money, than to coin gold or silver. The power to make any thing but gold and silver a tender in payment of debts, is withdrawn from the States, on the same principle with that of issuing a paper currency.

Bills of attainder, ex-post-facto laws, and laws impairing the obligation of contracts, are contrary to the first principles of the social compact, and to every principle of sound legislation. The two former are expressly prohibited by the declarations prefixed to some of the State constitutions, and all of them are prohibited by the spirit and scope of these fundamental charters. Our own experience has taught us, nevertheless, that additional fences against these dangers ought not to be omitted. Very properly, therefore, have the convention added this constitutional bulwark in favor of personal security and private rights; and I am much deceived if they have not, in so doing, as faithfully consulted the genuine sentiments as the undoubted interests of their constituents. The sober people of America are weary of the fluctuating policy which has directed the public councils. They have seen with regret and indignation that sudden changes and legislative interferences, in cases affecting personal rights, become jobs in the hands of enterprising and influential speculators, and snares to the more-industrious and less informed part of the community. They have seen, too, that one legislative interference is but the first link of a long chain of repetitions, every subsequent interference being naturally produced by the effects of the preceding. They very rightly infer, therefore, that some thorough reform is wanting, which will banish speculations on public measures, inspire a general prudence and industry, and give a regular course to the business of society. The prohibition with respect to titles of nobility is copied from the articles of Confederation and needs no comment.

1. "No State shall, without the consent of the Congress, lay any imposts or duties on imports or exports, except what may be absolutely necessary for executing its inspection laws, and the net produce of all duties and imposts laid by any State on imports or exports, shall be for the use of the treasury of the United States; and all such laws shall be subject to the revision and control of the Congress. No State shall, without the consent of Congress, lay any duty on tonnage, keep troops or ships of war in time of peace, enter into any agreement or compact with another State, or with a foreign power, or engage in war unless actually invaded, or in such imminent danger as will not admit of delay. "The restraint on the power of the States over imports and exports is enforced by all the arguments which prove the necessity of submitting the regulation of trade to the federal councils. It is needless, therefore, to remark further on this head, than that the manner in which the restraint is qualified seems well calculated at once to secure to the States a reasonable discretion in providing for the conveniency of their imports and exports, and to the United States a reasonable check against the abuse of this discretion. The remaining particulars of this clause fall within reasonings which are either so obvious, or have been so fully developed, that they may be passed over without remark.

The SIXTH and last class consists of the several powers and provisions by which efficacy is given to all the rest.

1. Of these the first is, the "power to make all laws which shall be

> necessary and proper for carrying into execution the foregoing powers, and all other powers vested by this Constitution in the government of the United States, or in any department or officer thereof.

"Few parts of the Constitution have been assailed with more intemperance than this; yet on a fair investigation of it, no part can appear more completely invulnerable. Without the SUBSTANCE of this power, the whole Constitution would be a dead letter. Those who object to the article, therefore, as a part of the Constitution, can only mean that the FORM of the provision is improper. But have they considered whether a better form could have been substituted? There are four other possible methods which the Constitution might have taken on this subject. They might have copied the second article of the existing Confederation, which would have prohibited the exercise of any power not EXPRESSLY delegated; they might have attempted a positive enumeration of the powers comprehended under the general terms "necessary and proper"; they might have attempted a negative enumeration of them, by specifying the powers excepted from the general definition; they might have been altogether silent on the subject, leaving these necessary and proper powers to construction and inference.

Had the convention taken the first method of adopting the second article of Confederation, it is evident that the new Congress would be continually exposed, as their predecessors have been, to the alternative of construing the term "EXPRESSLY" with so much rigor, as to disarm the government of all real authority whatever, or with so much latitude as to destroy altogether the force of the restriction. It would be easy to show, if it were necessary, that no important power, delegated by the articles of Confederation, has been or can be executed by Congress, without recurring more or less to the doctrine of CONSTRUCTION or IMPLICATION. As the powers delegated under the new system are more extensive, the government which is to administer it would find itself still more distressed with the alternative of betraying the public interests by doing nothing, or of violating the Constitution by exercising powers indispensably necessary and proper, but, at the same time, not EXPRESSLY granted.

Had the convention attempted a positive enumeration of the powers necessary and proper for carrying their other powers into effect, the attempt would have involved a complete digest of laws on every subject to which the Constitution relates; accommodated too, not only to the existing state of things, but to all the possible changes which futurity may produce; for in every new application of a general power, the PARTICULAR POWERS, which are the means of attaining the OBJECT of the general power, must always necessarily vary with that object, and be often properly varied whilst the object remains the same.

Had they attempted to enumerate the particular powers or means not necessary or proper for carrying the general powers into execution, the task would have been no less chimerical; and would have been liable to this further objection, that every defect in the enumeration would have been equivalent to a positive grant of authority. If, to avoid this consequence, they had attempted a partial enumeration of the exceptions, and described the residue by the general terms, NOT NECESSARY OR PROPER, it must have happened that the enumeration would comprehend a few of the excepted powers only; that these would be such as would be least likely to be assumed or tolerated, because the enumeration would of course select such as would be least necessary or proper; and that the unnecessary and improper powers included in the residuum, would be less forcibly excepted, than if no partial enumeration had been made. Had the Constitution been silent on this head, there can be no doubt that all the particular powers requisite as means of executing the general powers would have resulted to the government, by unavoidable implication. No axiom is more clearly established in law, or in reason, than that wherever the end is required, the means are authorized; wherever a general power to do a thing is given, every particular power necessary for doing it is included. Had this last method, therefore, been pursued by the convention, every objection now urged against their plan would remain in all its plausibility; and the real inconveniency would be incurred of not removing a pretext which may be seized on critical occasions for drawing into question the essential powers of the Union. If it be asked what is to be the consequence, in case the Congress shall misconstrue this part of the Constitution, and exercise powers not warranted by its true meaning, I answer, the same as if they should misconstrue or enlarge any other power vested in them; as if the general power had been reduced to particulars, and any one of these were to be violated; the same, in short, as if the State legislatures should violate the irrespective constitutional authorities. In the first instance, the success of the usurpation will depend on the executive and judiciary departments, which are to expound and give effect to the legislative acts; and in the last resort a remedy must be obtained from the people who can, by the election of more faithful representatives, annul the acts of the usurpers.

The truth is, that this ultimate redress may be more confided in against unconstitutional acts of the federal than of the State legislatures, for this plain reason, that as every such act of the former will be an invasion of the rights of the latter, these will be ever ready to mark the innovation, to sound the alarm to the people, and to exert their local influence in effecting a change of federal representatives. There being no such intermediate body between the State legislatures and the people interested in watching the conduct of the former, violations of the State constitutions are more likely to remain unnoticed and unredressed.

1. "This Constitution and the laws of the United States which shall be made in pursuance thereof, and all treaties made, or which shall be made, under the authority of the United States, shall be the supreme law of the land, and the judges in every State shall be bound thereby, any thing in the constitution or laws of any State to the contrary notwithstanding. "The indiscreet zeal of the adversaries to the Constitution has betrayed them into an attack on this part of it also, without which it would have been evidently and radically defective. To be fully sensible of this, we need only suppose for a moment that the supremacy of the State constitutions had been left complete by a saving clause in their favor. In the first place, as these constitutions invest the State legislatures with absolute sovereignty, in all cases not excepted by the existing articles of Confederation, all the authorities contained in the proposed Constitution, so far as they exceed those enumerated in the Confederation, would have been annulled, and the new Congress would have been reduced to the same impotent condition with their predecessors. In the next place, as the constitutions of some of the States do not even expressly and fully recognize the existing powers of the Confederacy, an express saving of the supremacy of the former would, in such States, have brought into question every power contained in the proposed Constitution.

In the third place, as the constitutions of the States differ much from each other, it might happen that a treaty or national law, of great and equal importance to the States, would interfere with some and not with other constitutions, and would consequently be valid in some of the States, at the same time that it would have no effect in others. In fine, the world would have seen, for the first time, a system of government founded on an inversion of the fundamental principles of all government; it would have seen the authority of the whole society every where subordinate to the authority of the parts; it would have seen a monster, in which the head was under the direction of the members.

1. "The Senators and Representatives, and the members of the several State legislatures, and all executive and judicial officers, both of the United States and the several States, shall be bound by oath or affirmation to support this Constitution. "It has been asked why it was thought necessary, that the State magistracy should be bound to support the federal Constitution, and unnecessary that a like oath should be imposed on the officers of the United States, in favor of the State constitutions. Several reasons might be assigned for the distinction. I content myself with one, which is obvious and conclusive. The members of the federal government will have no agency in carrying the State constitutions into effect. The members and officers of the State governments, on the contrary, will have an essential agency in giving effect to the federal Constitution. The election of the President and Senate will depend, in all cases, on the legislatures of the several States. And the election of the House of Representatives will equally depend on the same authority in the first instance; and will, probably, forever be conducted by the officers, and

according to the laws, of the States.

2. Among the provisions for giving efficacy to the federal powers might be added those which belong to the executive and judiciary departments: but as these are reserved for particular examination in another place, I pass them over in this. We have now reviewed, in detail, all the articles composing the sum or quantity of power delegated by the proposed Constitution to the federal government, and are brought to this undeniable conclusion, that no part of the power is unnecessary or improper for accomplishing the necessary objects of the Union. The question, therefore, whether this amount of power shall be granted or not, resolves itself into another question, whether or not a government commensurate to the exigencies of the Union shall be established; or, in other words, whether the Union itself shall be preserved.

Federalist No. 45 by James Madison

Editor's Introduction:

If Madison helped establish "loose construction" in *Federalist* No. 44, then *Federalist* No. 45 developed the "compact theory" of the Constitution, or more accurately the "compact fact" as proponents of the document more often defended the Constitution using language Madison conspicuously used in January 1788. After again defending the necessity of the central government for peace and security, he reasoned that the real danger to the Constitution would be the State governments and not be an oppressive central government. This warning aside, Madison reasoned that, "The powers reserved to the several States will extend to all the objects which, in the ordinary course of affairs, concern the lives, liberties, and properties of the people, and the internal order, improvement, and prosperity of the State." In other words, the central authority had narrowly limited powers that did not extend beyond the enumerated powers delegated to it by the Constitution and were confined primarily to commerce and defense. That the States had more power in this government than even Madison wanted when he arrived in Philadelphia in 1787 is unquestionably true, but Madison realized that opponents of the document were chipping away at the Constitution by shining a light on its centralizing tendencies. Madison hoped by explaining the "federalism" contained in the document these so-called "anti-federalists" could be silenced.

Federalist No. 45

January 26, 1788

By James Madison of Virginia

To the People of the State of New York:

HAVING shown that no one of the powers transferred to the federal government is unnecessary or improper, the next question to be considered is, whether the whole mass of them will be dangerous to the portion of authority left in the several States. The adversaries to the plan of the convention, instead of considering in the first place what degree of power was absolutely necessary for the purposes of the federal government, have exhausted themselves in a secondary inquiry into the possible consequences of the proposed degree of power to the governments of the particular States. But if the Union, as has been shown, be essential to the security of the people of America against foreign danger; if it be essential to their security against contentions and wars among the different States; if it be essential to guard them against those violent and oppressive factions which embitter the blessings of liberty, and against those military establishments which must gradually poison its very fountain; if, in a word, the Union be essential to the happiness of the people of America, is it not preposterous, to urge as an objection to a government, without which the objects of the Union cannot be attained, that such a government may derogate from the importance of the governments of the individual States? Was, then, the American Revolution effected, was the American Confederacy formed, was the precious blood of thousands spilt, and the hard-earned substance of millions lavished, not that the people of America should enjoy peace, liberty, and safety, but that the government of the individual States, that particular municipal establishments, might enjoy a certain extent of power, and be arrayed with certain dignities and attributes of sovereignty? We have heard of the impious doctrine in the Old World, that the people were made for kings, not kings for the people. Is the same doctrine to be revived in the New, in another shape that the solid happiness of the people is to be sacrificed to the views of political institutions of a different form?

It is too early for politicians to presume on our forgetting that the public good, the real welfare of the great body of the people, is the supreme object to be pursued; and that no form of government whatever has any other value than as it may be fitted for the attainment of this object. Were the plan of the convention adverse to the public happiness, my voice would be, Reject the plan. Were the Union itself inconsistent with the public happiness, it would be, Abolish the Union. In like manner, as far as the sovereignty of the States cannot be reconciled to the happiness of the people, the voice of every good citizen must be, Let the former be sacrificed to the latter. How far the sacrifice is necessary, has been shown. How far the unsacrificed residue will be endangered, is the question before us. Several important considerations have been touched in the course of these papers, which discountenance the supposition that the operation of the federal government will by degrees prove fatal to the State governments. The more I revolve the subject, the more fully I am persuaded that the balance is much more likely to be disturbed by the preponderancy of the last than of the first scale.

We have seen, in all the examples of ancient and modern confederacies, the strongest tendency continually betraying itself in the members, to despoil the general government of its authorities, with a very ineffectual capacity in the latter to defend itself against the encroachments. Although, in most of these examples, the system has been so dissimilar from that under consideration as greatly to weaken any inference concerning the latter from the fate of the former, yet, as the States will retain, under the proposed Constitution, a very extensive portion of active sovereignty, the inference ought not to be wholly disregarded. In the Achaean league it is probable that the federal head had a degree and species of power, which gave it a considerable likeness to the government framed by the convention. The Lycian Confederacy, as far as its principles and form are transmitted, must have borne a still greater analogy to it. Yet history does not inform us that either of them ever degenerated, or tended to degenerate, into one consolidated government. On the contrary, we know that the ruin of one of them proceeded from the incapacity of the federal authority to prevent the dissensions, and finally the disunion, of the subordinate authorities. These cases are the more worthy of our attention, as the external causes by which the component parts were pressed together were much more numerous and powerful than in our case; and consequently less powerful ligaments within would be sufficient to bind the members to the head, and to each other.

In the feudal system, we have seen a similar propensity exemplified. Notwithstanding the want of proper sympathy in every instance between the local sovereigns and the people, and the sympathy in some instances between the general sovereign and the latter, it usually happened that the local sovereigns prevailed in the rivalship for encroachments. Had no external dangers enforced internal harmony and subordination, and particularly, had the local sovereigns possessed the affections of the people, the great kingdoms in Europe would at this time consist of as many independent princes as there were formerly feudatory barons. The State government will have the advantage of the Federal government, whether we compare them in respect to the immediate dependence of the one on the other; to the weight of personal influence which each side will possess; to the powers respectively vested in them; to the predilection and probable support of the people; to the disposition and faculty of resisting and frustrating the measures of each other. The State governments may be regarded as constituent and essential parts of the federal government; whilst the latter is nowise essential to the operation or organization of the former. Without the intervention of the State legislatures, the President of the United States cannot be elected at all. They must in all cases have a great share in his appointment, and will, perhaps, in most cases, of themselves determine it. The Senate will be elected absolutely and exclusively by the State legislatures. Even the House of Representatives, though drawn immediately from the people, will be chosen very much under the influence of that class of men, whose influence over the people obtains for themselves an election into the State legislatures. Thus, each of the principal branches of the federal government will owe its existence more or less to the favor of the State governments, and must consequently feel a dependence, which is much more likely to beget a disposition too obsequious than too overbearing towards them.

On the other side, the component parts of the State governments will in no instance be indebted for their appointment to the direct agency of the federal government, and very little, if at all, to the local influence of its members. The number of individuals employed under the Constitution of the United States will be much smaller than the number employed under the particular States. There will consequently be less of personal influence on the side of the former than of the latter. The members of the legislative, executive, and judiciary departments of thirteen and more States, the justices of peace, officers of militia, ministerial officers of justice, with all the county, corporation, and town officers, for three millions and more of people, intermixed, and having particular acquaintance with every class and circle of people, must exceed, beyond all proportion, both in number and influence, those of every description who will be employed in the administration of the federal system. Compare the members of the three great departments of the thirteen States, excluding from the judiciary department the justices of peace, with the members of the corresponding departments of the single government of the Union; compare the militia officers of three millions of people with the military and marine officers of any establishment which is within the compass of probability, or, I may add, of possibility, and in this view alone, we may pronounce the advantage of the States to be decisive. If the federal government is to have collectors of revenue, the State governments will have theirs also. And as those of the former will be principally on the seacoast, and not very numerous, whilst those of the latter will be spread over the face of the country, and will be very numerous, the advantage in this view also lies on the same side.

It is true, that the Confederacy is to possess, and may exercise, the power of collecting internal as well as external taxes throughout the States; but it is probable that this power will not be resorted to, except for supplemental purposes of revenue; that an option will then be given to the States to supply their quotas by previous collections of their own; and that the eventual collection, under the immediate authority of the Union, will generally be made by the officers, and according to the rules, appointed by the several States. Indeed it is extremely probable, that in other instances, particularly in the organization of the judicial power, the officers of the States will be clothed with the correspondent authority of the Union. Should it happen, however, that separate collectors of internal revenue should be appointed under the federal government, the influence of the whole number would not bear a comparison with that of the multitude of State officers in the opposite scale. Within every district to which a federal collector would be allotted, there would not be less than thirty or forty, or even more, officers of different descriptions, and many of them persons of character and weight, whose influence would lie on the side of the State. The powers delegated by the proposed Constitution to the federal government are few and defined. Those which are to remain in the State governments are numerous and indefinite. The former will be exercised principally on external objects, as war, peace, negotiation, and foreign commerce; with which last the power of taxation will, for the most part, be connected.

The powers reserved to the several States will extend to all the objects which, in the ordinary course of affairs, concern the lives, liberties, and properties of the people, and the internal order, improvement, and prosperity of the State. The operations of the federal government will be most extensive and important in times of war and danger; those of the State governments, in times of peace and security. As the former periods will probably bear a small proportion to the latter, the State governments will here enjoy another advantage over the federal government. The more adequate, indeed, the federal powers may be rendered to the national defense, the less frequent will be those scenes of danger which might favor their ascendancy over the governments of the particular States. If the new Constitution be examined with accuracy and candor, it will be found that the change which it proposes consists much less in the addition of NEW POWERS to the Union, than in the invigoration of its ORIGINAL POWERS. The regulation of commerce, it is true, is a new power; but that seems to be an addition which few oppose, and from which no apprehensions are entertained. The powers relating to war and peace, armies and fleets, treaties and finance, with the other more considerable powers, are all vested in the existing Congress by the articles of Confederation. The proposed change does not enlarge these powers; it only substitutes a more effectual mode of administering them.

The change relating to taxation may be regarded as the most important; and yet the present Congress have as complete authority to REQUIRE of the States indefinite supplies of money for the common defense and general welfare, as the future Congress will have to require them of individual citizens; and the latter will be no more bound than the States themselves have been, to pay the quotas respectively taxed on them. Had the States complied punctually with the articles of Confederation, or could their compliance have been enforced by as peaceable means as may be used with success towards single persons, our past experience is very far from countenancing an opinion, that the State governments would have lost their constitutional powers, and have gradually undergone an entire consolidation. To maintain that such an event would have ensued, would be to say at once, that the existence of the State governments is incompatible with any system whatever that accomplishes the essential purposes of the Union.

Federalist No. 46 by James Madison

Editor's Introduction:

Federalist No. 46 continued Madison's discussion of allegiance in the United States, specifically, would Americans have more loyalty to their State or to the general government. His answer would probably surprise modern Americans. In fact, Madison sounded more like Robert E. Lee in this essay than Abraham Lincoln. He reasoned that Americans would feel more comfortable with their State and local officials by reason of family connections and community than that of a general government comprised of mostly alien representatives from different States and regions, and that because of this, State governments would maintain the affections and allegiances of the people over a federal government with limited authority. And if Madison suggested "implied powers" in *Federalist* No. 44, he foreshadowed his participation in the Virginia and Kentucky Resolutions of 1798 in *Federalist* No. 46. He argued that should the general government overstep its authority, the people of the States would quickly organize to crush these usurpations in the cradle. Madison argued that he intended his Virginia Resolves to open a conversation with other States on an appropriate response to the Sedition Act while concurrently insisting that the State could act as a hedge to protect the people against unconstitutional power. Reading *Federalist* No. 46 provides the same impression.

Federalist No. 46

January 29, 1788

By James Madison of Virginia

To the People of the State of New York:

RESUMING the subject of the last paper, I proceed to inquire whether the federal government or the State governments will have the advantage with regard to the predilection and support of the people. Notwithstanding the different modes in which they are appointed, we must consider both of them as substantially dependent on the great body of the citizens of the United States. I assume this position here as it respects the first, reserving the proofs for another place. The federal and State governments are in fact but different agents and trustees of the people, constituted with different powers, and designed for different purposes. The adversaries of the Constitution seem to have lost sight of the people altogether in their reasonings on this subject; and to have viewed these different establishments, not only as mutual rivals and enemies, but as uncontrolled by any common superior in their efforts to usurp the authorities of each other. These gentlemen must here be reminded of their error. They must be told that the ultimate authority, wherever the derivative may be found, resides in the people alone, and that it will not depend merely on the comparative ambition or address of the different governments, whether either, or which of them, will be able to enlarge its sphere of jurisdiction at the expense of the other.

Truth, no less than decency, requires that the event in every case should be supposed to depend on the sentiments and sanction of their common constituents. Many considerations, besides those suggested on a former occasion, seem to place it beyond doubt that the first and most natural attachment of the people will be to the governments of their respective States. Into the administration of these a greater number of individuals will expect to rise. From the gift of these a greater number of offices and emoluments will flow. By the superintending care of these, all the more domestic and personal interests of the people will be regulated and provided for. With the affairs of these, the people will be more familiarly and minutely conversant. And with the members of these, will a greater proportion of the people have the ties of personal acquaintance and friendship, and of family and party attachments; on the side of these, therefore, the popular bias may well be expected most strongly to incline. Experience speaks the same language in this case. The federal administration, though hitherto very defective in comparison with what may be hoped under a better system, had, during the war, and particularly whilst the independent fund of paper emissions was in credit, an activity and importance as great as it can well have in any future circumstances whatever. It was engaged, too, in a course of measures which had for their object the protection of everything that was dear, and the acquisition of everything that could be desirable to the people at large.

It was, nevertheless, invariably found, after the transient enthusiasm for the early Congresses was over, that the attention and attachment of the people were turned anew to their own particular governments; that the federal council was at no time the idol of popular favor; and that opposition to proposed enlargements of its powers and importance was the side usually taken by the men who wished to build their political consequence on the prepossessions of their fellow-citizens. If, therefore, as has been elsewhere remarked, the people should in future become more partial to the federal than to the

State governments, the change can only result from such manifest and irresistible proofs of a better administration, as will overcome all their antecedent propensities. And in that case, the people ought not surely to be precluded from giving most of their confidence where they may discover it to be most due; but even in that case the State governments could have little to apprehend, because it is only within a certain sphere that the federal power can, in the nature of things, be advantageously administered. The remaining points on which I propose to compare the federal and State governments, are the disposition and the faculty they may respectively possess, to resist and frustrate the measures of each other. It has been already proved that the members of the federal will be more dependent on the members of the State governments, than the latter will be on the former.

It has appeared also, that the prepossessions of the people, on whom both will depend, will be more on the side of the State governments, than of the federal government. So far as the disposition of each towards the other may be influenced by these causes, the State governments must clearly have the advantage. But in a distinct and very important point of view, the advantage will lie on the same side. The prepossessions, which the members themselves will carry into the federal government, will generally be favorable to the States; whilst it will rarely happen, that the members of the State governments will carry into the public councils a bias in favor of the general government. A local spirit will infallibly prevail much more in the members of Congress, than a national spirit will prevail in the legislatures of the particular States.

Every one knows that a great proportion of the errors committed by the State legislatures proceeds from the disposition of the members to sacrifice the comprehensive and permanent interest of the State, to the particular and separate views of the counties or districts in which they reside. And if they do not sufficiently enlarge their policy to embrace the collective welfare of their particular State, how can it be imagined that they will make the aggregate prosperity of the Union, and the dignity and respectability of its government, the objects of their affections and consultations? For the same reason that the members of the State legislatures will be unlikely to attach themselves sufficiently to national objects, the members of the federal legislature will be likely to attach themselves too much to local objects. The States will be to the latter what counties and towns are to the former. Measures will too often be decided according to their probable effect, not on the national prosperity and happiness, but on the prejudices, interests, and pursuits of the governments and people of the individual States. What is the spirit that has in general characterized the proceedings of Congress? A perusal of their journals, as well as the candid acknowledgments of such as have had a seat in that assembly, will inform us, that the members have but too frequently displayed the character, rather of partisans of their respective States, than of impartial guardians of a common interest; that where on one occasion improper sacrifices have been made of local considerations, to the aggrandizement of the federal government, the great interests of the nation have suffered on a hundred, from an undue attention to the local prejudices, interests, and views of the particular States.

I mean not by these reflections to insinuate, that the new federal government will not embrace a more enlarged plan of policy than the existing government may have pursued; much less, that its views will be as confined as those of the State legislatures; but only that it will partake sufficiently of the spirit of both, to be disinclined to invade the rights of the individual States, or the preorgatives of their governments. The motives on the part of the State governments, to augment their prerogatives by defalcations from the federal government, will be overruled by no reciprocal predispositions in the members. Were it admitted, however, that the Federal government may feel an equal disposition with the State governments to extend its power beyond the due limits, the latter would still have the advantage in the means of defeating such encroachments. If an act of a particular State, though unfriendly to the national government, be generally popular in that State and should not too grossly violate the oaths of the State officers, it is executed immediately and, of course, by means on the spot and depending on the State alone. The opposition of the federal government, or the interposition of federal officers, would but inflame the zeal of all parties on the side of the State, and the evil could not be prevented or repaired, if at all, without the employment of means which must always be resorted to with reluctance and difficulty.

On the other hand, should an unwarrantable measure of the federal government be unpopular in particular States, which would seldom fail to be the case, or even a warrantable measure be so, which may sometimes be the case, the means of opposition to it are powerful and at hand. The disquietude of the people; their repugnance and, perhaps, refusal to co-operate with the officers of the Union; the frowns of the executive magistracy of the State; the embarrassments created by legislative devices, which would often be added on such occasions, would oppose, in any State, difficulties not to be despised; would form, in a large State, very serious impediments; and where the sentiments of several adjoining States happened to be in unison, would present obstructions which the federal government would hardly be willing to encounter. But ambitious encroachments of the federal government, on the authority of the State governments, would not excite the opposition of a single State, or of a few States only. They would be signals of general alarm. Every government would espouse the common cause. A correspondence would be opened. Plans of resistance would be concerted. One spirit would animate and conduct the whole. The same combinations, in short, would result from an apprehension of the federal, as was produced by the dread of a foreign, yoke; and unless the projected innovations should be voluntarily renounced, the same appeal to a trial of force would be made in the one case as was made in the other. But what degree of madness could ever drive the federal government to such an extremity. In the contest with Great Britain, one part of the empire was employed against the other. The more numerous part invaded the rights of the less numerous part. The attempt was unjust and unwise; but it was not in speculation absolutely chimerical. But what would be the contest in the case we are supposing? Who would be the parties? A few representatives of the people would be opposed to the people themselves; or rather one set of representatives would be contending against thirteen sets of representatives, with the whole body of their common constituents on the side of the latter.

The only refuge left for those who prophesy the downfall of the State governments is the visionary supposition that the federal government may previously accumulate a military force for the projects of ambition. The reasonings contained in these papers must have been employed to little purpose indeed, if it could be necessary now to disprove the reality of this danger. That the people and the States should, for a sufficient period of time, elect an uninterupted succession of men ready to betray both; that the traitors should, throughout this period, uniformly and systematically pursue some fixed plan for the extension of the military establishment; that the governments and the people of the States should silently and patiently behold the gathering storm, and continue to supply the materials, until it should be prepared to burst on their own heads, must appear to every one more like the incoherent dreams of a delirious jealousy, or the misjudged exaggerations of a counterfeit zeal, than like the sober apprehensions of genuine patriotism.

Extravagant as the supposition is, let it however be made. Let a regular army, fully equal to the resources of the country, be formed; and let it be entirely at the devotion of the federal government; still it would not be going too far to say, that the State governments, with the people on their side, would be able to repel the danger. The highest number to which, according to the best computation, a standing army can be carried in any country, does not exceed one hundredth part of the whole number of souls; or one twenty-fifth part of the number able to bear arms. This proportion would not yield, in the United States, an army of more than twenty-five or thirty thousand men. To these would be opposed a militia amounting to near half a million of citizens with arms in their hands, officered by men chosen from among themselves, fighting for their common liberties, and united and conducted by governments possessing their affections and confidence. It may well be doubted, whether a militia thus circumstanced could ever be conquered by such a proportion of regular troops. Those who are best acquainted with the last successful resistance of this country against the British arms, will be most inclined to deny the possibility of it. Besides the advantage of being armed, which the Americans possess over the people of almost every other nation, the existence of subordinate governments, to which the people are attached, and by which the militia officers are appointed, forms a barrier against the enterprises of ambition, more insurmountable than any which a simple government of any form can admit of. Notwithstanding the military establishments in the several kingdoms of Europe, which are carried as far as the public resources will bear, the governments are afraid to trust the people with arms. And it is not certain, that with this aid alone they would not be able to shake off their yokes. But were the people to possess the additional advantages of local governments chosen by themselves, who could collect the national will and direct the national force, and of officers appointed out of the militia, by these governments, and attached both to them and to the militia, it may be affirmed with the greatest assurance, that the throne of every tyranny in Europe would be speedily overturned in spite of the legions which surround it.

Let us not insult the free and gallant citizens of America with the suspicion, that they would be less able to defend the rights of which they would be in actual possession, than the debased subjects of arbitrary power would be to rescue theirs from the hands of their oppressors. Let us rather no longer insult them with the supposition that they can ever reduce themselves to the necessity of making the experiment, by a blind and tame submission to the long train of insidious measures which must precede and produce it. The argument under the present head may be put into a very concise form, which appears altogether conclusive. Either the mode in which the federal government is to be constructed will render it sufficiently dependent on the people, or it will not. On the first supposition, it will be restrained by that dependence from forming schemes obnoxious to their constituents. On the other supposition, it will not possess the confidence of the people, and its schemes of usurpation will be easily defeated by the State governments, who will be supported by the people. On summing up the considerations stated in this and the last paper, they seem to amount to the most convincing evidence, that the powers proposed to be lodged in the federal government are as little formidable to those reserved to the individual States, as they are indispensably necessary to accomplish the purposes of the Union; and that all those alarms which have been sounded, of a meditated and consequential annihilation of the State governments, must, on the most favorable interpretation, be ascribed to the chimerical fears of the authors of them.

Federalist No. 47 by James Madison

Editor's Introduction:

Madison opened a lengthy discussion of separation of powers in *Federalist* No. 47. One common charge against the Constitution centered on an allegedly dangerous blending of the executive, legislative, and judicial powers, primarily through the Senate. Madison used examples from various State constitutions to illustrate that this was a common practice, not just in Great Britain where powers bled between branches more easily, but in various American States as well. No one raised a whisper against it until the Constitution was presented to the States for ratification. He concluded, "What I have wished to evince is, that the charge brought against the proposed Constitution, of violating the sacred maxim of free government, is warranted neither by the real meaning annexed to that maxim by its author, nor by the sense in which it has hitherto been understood in America."

Federalist No. 47

January 30, 1788

By James Madison of Virginia

To the People of the State of New York:

HAVING reviewed the general form of the proposed government and the general mass of power allotted to it, I proceed to examine the particular structure of this government, and the distribution of this mass of power among its constituent parts. One of the principal objections inculcated by the more respectable adversaries to the Constitution, is its supposed violation of the political maxim, that the legislative, executive, and judiciary departments ought to be separate and distinct. In the structure of the federal government, no regard, it is said, seems to have been paid to this essential precaution in favor of liberty. The several departments of power are distributed and blended in such a manner as at once to destroy all symmetry and beauty of form, and to expose some of the essential parts of the edifice to the danger of being crushed by the disproportionate weight of other parts. No political truth is certainly of greater intrinsic value, or is stamped with the authority of more enlightened patrons of liberty, than that on which the objection is founded.

The accumulation of all powers, legislative, executive, and judiciary, in the same hands, whether of one, a few, or many, and whether hereditary, self-appointed, or elective, may justly be pronounced the very definition of tyranny. Were the federal Constitution, therefore, really chargeable with the accumulation of power, or with a mixture of powers, having a dangerous tendency to such an accumulation, no further arguments would be necessary to inspire a universal reprobation of the system. I persuade myself, however, that it will be made apparent to every one, that the charge cannot be supported, and that the maxim on which it relies has been totally misconceived and misapplied. In order to form correct ideas on this important subject, it will be proper to investigate the sense in which the preservation of liberty requires that the three great departments of power should be separate and distinct. The oracle who is always consulted and cited on this subject is the celebrated Montesquieu. If he be not the author of this invaluable precept in the science of politics, he has the merit at least of displaying and recommending it most effectually to the attention of mankind. Let us endeavor, in the first place, to ascertain his meaning on this point. The British Constitution was to Montesquieu what Homer has been to the didactic writers on epic poetry. As the latter have considered the work of the immortal bard as the perfect model from which the principles and rules of the epic art were to be drawn, and by which all similar works were to be judged, so this great political critic appears to have viewed the Constitution of England as the standard, or to use his own expression, as the mirror of political liberty; and to have delivered, in the form of elementary truths, the several characteristic principles of that particular system. That we may be sure, then, not to mistake his meaning in this case, let us recur to the source from which the maxim was drawn.

On the slightest view of the British Constitution, we must perceive that the legislative, executive, and judiciary departments are by no means totally separate and distinct from each other. The executive magistrate forms an integral part of the legislative authority. He alone has the prerogative of making treaties with foreign sovereigns, which, when made, have, under certain limitations, the force of legislative acts. All the members of the judiciary department are appointed by him, can be removed by him on the address of the two Houses of Parliament, and form, when he pleases to consult them, one of his constitutional councils. One branch of the legislative department forms also a great constitutional council to the executive chief, as, on another hand, it is the sole depositary of judicial power in cases of impeachment, and is invested with the supreme appellate jurisdiction in all other cases. The judges, again, are so far connected with the legislative department as often to attend and participate in its deliberations, though not admitted to a legislative vote. From these facts, by which Montesquieu was guided, it may clearly be inferred that, in saying "There can be no liberty where the legislative and executive powers are united in the same person, or body of magistrates," or, "if the power of judging be not separated from the legislative and executive powers," he did not mean that these departments ought to have no PARTIAL AGENCY in, or no CONTROL over, the acts of each other. His meaning, as his own words import, and still more conclusively as illustrated by the example in his eye, can amount to no more than this, that where the WHOLE power of one department is exercised by the same hands which possess the WHOLE power of another department, the fundamental principles of a free constitution are subverted. This would have been the case in the constitution examined by him, if the king, who is the sole executive magistrate, had possessed also the complete legislative power, or the supreme administration of justice; or if the entire legislative body had possessed the supreme judiciary, or the supreme executive authority.

This, however, is not among the vices of that constitution. The magistrate in whom the whole executive power resides cannot of himself make a law, though he can put a negative on every law; nor administer justice in person, though he has the appointment of those who do administer it. The judges can exercise no executive prerogative, though they are shoots from the executive stock; nor any legislative function, though they may be advised with by the legislative councils. The entire legislature can perform no judiciary act, though by the joint act of two of its branches the judges may be removed from their offices, and though one of its branches is possessed of the judicial power in the last resort. The entire legislature, again, can exercise no executive prerogative, though one of its branches constitutes the supreme executive magistracy, and another, on the impeachment of a third, can try and condemn all the subordinate officers in the executive department. The reasons on which Montesquieu grounds his maxim are a further demonstration of his meaning. "When the legislative and executive powers are united in the same person or body," says he, "there can be no liberty, because apprehensions may arise lest THE SAME monarch or senate should ENACT tyrannical laws to EXECUTE them in a tyrannical manner. " Again: "Were the power of judging joined with the legislative, the life and liberty of the subject would be exposed to arbitrary control, for THE JUDGE would then be THE LEGISLATOR. Were it joined to the executive power, THE JUDGE might behave with all the violence of AN OPPRESSOR. " Some of these reasons are more fully explained in other passages; but briefly stated as they are here, they sufficiently establish the meaning which we have put on this celebrated maxim of this celebrated author.

If we look into the constitutions of the several States, we find that, notwithstanding the emphatical and, in some instances, the unqualified terms in which this axiom has been laid down, there is not a single instance in which the several departments of power have been kept absolutely separate and distinct. New Hampshire, whose constitution was the last formed, seems to have been fully aware of the impossibility and inexpediency of avoiding any mixture whatever of these departments, and has qualified the doctrine by declaring "that the legislative, executive, and judiciary powers ought to be kept as separate from, and independent of, each other AS THE NATURE OF A FREE GOVERNMENT WILL ADMIT; OR AS IS CONSISTENT WITH THAT CHAIN OF CONNECTION THAT BINDS THE WHOLE FABRIC OF THE CONSTITUTION IN ONE INDISSOLUBLE BOND OF UNITY AND AMITY. " Her constitution accordingly mixes these departments in several respects. The Senate, which is a branch of the legislative department, is also a judicial tribunal for the trial of impeachments. The President, who is the head of the executive department, is the presiding member also of the Senate; and, besides an equal vote in all cases, has a casting vote in case of a tie. The executive head is himself eventually elective every year by the legislative department, and his council is every year chosen by and from the members of the same department. Several of the officers of state are also appointed by the legislature. And the members of the judiciary department are appointed by the executive department. The constitution of Massachusetts has observed a sufficient though less pointed caution, in expressing this fundamental article of liberty. It declares "that the legislative department shall never exercise the executive and judicial powers, or either of them; the executive shall never exercise the legislative and judicial powers, or either of them; the judicial shall never exercise the legislative and executive powers, or either of them. " This declaration corresponds precisely with the doctrine of Montesquieu, as it has been explained, and is not in a single point violated by the plan of the convention. It goes no farther than to prohibit any one of the entire departments from exercising the powers of another department. In the very Constitution to which it is prefixed, a partial mixture of powers has been admitted. The executive magistrate has a qualified negative on the legislative body, and the Senate, which is a part of the legislature, is a court of impeachment for members both of the executive and judiciary departments. The members of the judiciary department, again, are appointable by the executive department, and removable by the same authority on the address of the two legislative branches. Lastly, a number of the officers of government are annually appointed by the legislative department.

As the appointment to offices, particularly executive offices, is in its nature an executive function, the compilers of the Constitution have, in this last point at least, violated the rule established by themselves. I pass over the constitutions of Rhode Island and Connecticut, because they were formed prior to the Revolution, and even before the principle under examination had become an object of political attention. The constitution of New York contains no declaration on this subject; but appears very clearly to have been framed with an eye to the danger of improperly blending the different departments. It gives, nevertheless, to the executive magistrate, a partial control over the legislative department; and, what is more, gives a like control to the judiciary department; and even blends the executive and judiciary departments in the exercise of this control. In its council of appointment members of the legislative are associated with the executive authority, in the appointment of officers, both executive and judiciary. And its court for the trial of impeachments and correction of errors is to consist of one branch of the legislature and the principal members of the judiciary department.

The constitution of New Jersey has blended the different powers of government more than any of the preceding. The governor, who is the executive magistrate, is appointed by the legislature; is chancellor and ordinary, or surrogate of the State; is a member of the Supreme Court of Appeals, and president, with a casting vote, of one of the legislative branches. The same legislative branch acts again as executive council of the governor, and with him constitutes the Court of Appeals. The members of the judiciary department are appointed by the legislative department and removable by one branch of it, on the impeachment of the other. According to the constitution of Pennsylvania, the president, who is the head of the executive department, is annually elected by a vote in which the legislative department predominates. In conjunction with an executive council, he appoints the members of the judiciary department, and forms a court of impeachment for trial of all officers, judiciary as well as executive. The judges of the

Supreme Court and justices of the peace seem also to be removable by the legislature; and the executive power of pardoning in certain cases, to be referred to the same department. The members of the executive council are made EX-OFFICIO justices of peace throughout the State. In Delaware, the chief executive magistrate is annually elected by the legislative department. The speakers of the two legislative branches are vice-presidents in the executive department. The executive chief, with six others, appointed, three by each of the legislative branches constitutes the Supreme Court of Appeals; he is joined with the legislative department in the appointment of the other judges. Throughout the States, it appears that the members of the legislature may at the same time be justices of the peace; in this State, the members of one branch of it are EX-OFFICIO justices of the peace; as are also the members of the executive council. The principal officers of the executive department are appointed by the legislative; and one branch of the latter forms a court of impeachments. All officers may be removed on address of the legislature.

Maryland has adopted the maxim in the most unqualified terms; declaring that the legislative, executive, and judicial powers of government ought to be forever separate and distinct from each other. Her constitution, notwithstanding, makes the executive magistrate appointable by the legislative department; and the members of the judiciary by the executive department. The language of Virginia is still more pointed on this subject. Her constitution declares, "that the legislative, executive, and judiciary departments shall be separate and distinct; so that neither exercise the powers properly belonging to the other; nor shall any person exercise the powers of more than one of them at the same time, except that the justices of county courts shall be eligible to either House of Assembly." Yet we find not only this express exception, with respect to the members of the inferior courts, but that the chief magistrate, with his executive council, are appointable by the legislature; that two members of the latter are triennially displaced at the pleasure of the legislature; and that all the principal offices, both executive and judiciary, are filled by the same department. The executive prerogative of pardon, also, is in one case vested in the legislative department.

The constitution of North Carolina, which declares "that the legislative, executive, and supreme judicial powers of government ought to be forever separate and distinct from each other," refers, at the same time, to the legislative department, the appointment not only of the executive chief, but all the principal officers within both that and the judiciary department. In South Carolina, the constitution makes the executive magistracy eligible by the legislative department. It gives to the latter, also, the appointment of the members of the judiciary department, including even justices of the peace and sheriffs; and the appointment of officers in the executive department, down to captains in the army and navy of the State. In the constitution of Georgia, where it is declared "that the legislative, executive, and judiciary departments shall be separate and distinct, so that neither exercise the powers properly belonging to the other," we find that the executive department is to be filled by appointments of the legislature; and the executive prerogative of pardon to be finally exercised by the same authority. Even justices of the peace are to be appointed by the legislature. In citing these cases, in which the legislative, executive, and judiciary departments have not been kept totally separate and distinct, I wish not to be regarded as an advocate for the particular organizations of the several State governments. I am fully aware that among the many excellent principles which they exemplify, they carry strong marks of the haste, and still stronger of the inexperience, under which they were framed. It is but too obvious that in some instances the fundamental principle under consideration has been violated by too great a mixture, and even an actual consolidation, of the different powers; and that in no instance has a competent provision been made for maintaining in practice the separation delineated on paper. What I have wished to evince is, that the charge brought against the proposed Constitution, of violating the sacred maxim of free government, is warranted neither by the real meaning annexed to that maxim by its author, nor by the sense in which it has hitherto been understood in America. This interesting subject will be resumed in the ensuing paper.

A Freeman II by Tench Coxe

Editor's Introduction:

In the first installment of "A Freeman," Coxe discussed how the powers of the general government were confined to those delegated to it by the Constitution and could not extend to most functions of government. In "A Freeman II," he turned this argument on its head, arguing "Having seen what Congress *cannot do*, let us now proceed to examine what the state governments *must or may do*." This included almost every necessary internal governmental policy. In other words, Coxe concluded that the States could not and would not be annihilated because "they are so requisite to our system, *that they could not be dispensed with*." These essays support the claim that the Constitution continued the federal republic as under the Articles of Confederation and that the States possessed expansive powers while those of the general government were limited and defined.

A Freeman II

January 30, 1788

By Tench Coxe of Pennsylvania

To the MINORITY of the CONVENTION of *Pennsylvania*

Gentlemen, The principal object of my last paper was to point out a variety of instances, in which *the agency and power of the state governments* are absolutely *necessary* to *the existence* of civil society, and to *the execution* of the federal constitution itself. I therein shewed that certain important matters, which must be done from time to time, cannot be attempted or performed by the general government. Here, then, we find, not only that the state powers will not be annihilated, but that they are so requisite to our system, *that they cannot be dispensed with.*

Having seen what Congress *cannot do*, let us now proceed to examine what the state governments *must or may do.*

First, then each state can appoint every officer of its own militia, and can train the same, by which it will be sure of a powerful military support attached to, and even part of itself, wherein no citizen of any other state can be a private centinel, much less have influence or command.

2dly. Every regulation relating to religion, or the property of religious bodies, must be made by the state governments, since no powers affecting those points are contained in the constitution.

3dly. The state legislatures and constitutions must determine the qualifications of the electors for both branches of the federal government; and here let us remember to adhere firmly within our respective commonwealths to *genuine republican principles*. Wisdom, on this point which lies entirely in our hands, will pervade the whole system, and will *be a never failing antidote* to aristocracy, oligarchy and monarchy.

4thly. Regulating the law of descents, and forbidding the entail of landed estates, are exclusively in the power of the state legislatures. A perfect equality, at least among the males, and possibly among the females, should be established, not only in the strict line of descent, but in the most remote collateral branches. If a man *omits* to make a will, the public should distribute his property *equally* among those who have *equal* pretensions, and who are able to render *equal* services to the community. By these means, poverty and extreme riches would be avoided, and a republican spirit would be given to our laws, not only without a violation of private rights, but consistently with the principles of justice and sound policy. This power with that mentioned under the last head, if exercised with wisdom and virtue, will preserve the freedom of the states beyond any other means.

5thly. The elections of the President, Vice President, Senators and Representatives, are exclusively in the hands of the states, even as to filling vacancies. The smallest interference of Congress is not permitted, either in prescribing the qualifications of electors, or in determining what persons may or may not be elected.

The clause which enables the federal legislature to make regulations on this head, permits them only to say at what time in the two years the house of representatives shall be chosen, at what time in the six years the Senate shall be chosen, and at what time in the four years the President shall be elected; but these elections, by other provisions in the constitution, *must take place every two, four and six years*, as is declared in the several clauses respectively.

6thly. The states elect, appoint and commission all their own officers, without any possible interference of the federal government.

7thly. The states can alter and amend their several constitutions, provided they do not make them aristocratical, oligarchic or monarchical–for the federal constitution restrains them from any alterations that are not *really republican*. That is, the sovereignty of the people is never to be infringed or destroyed.

8thly. The states have the power to erect corporations for literary, religious, commercial, or other purposes, which the federal government cannot prevent.

9thly. Every state can always give its dissent to federal bills, as each has *a vote* in the Senate secured by the constitution. Hence it appears, that the state governments are not only intended to remain in force within their respective jurisdictions, but they are always to be known to, and have their voices, *as states*, in the federal councils.

10thly. The states not only elect all their own officers, but they have *a check*, by their delegates to the Senate, on the appointment of *all federal officers.*

11thly. The states are to hold *separate territorial rights*, and the domestic jurisdiction thereof, exclusively of any interference of the federal government.

12thly. The states will regulate and administer the criminal law, *exclusively of Congress*, so far as it regards *mala in se*, or real crimes; such as murder, robbery, &c. They will also have a certain and large part of the jurisdiction, with respect to *mala prohibita*, or matters which are *forbidden* from political considerations, though not in themselves immoral; such as unlicenced public houses, nuisances, and many other things of the like nature.

13thly. The states are to determine all the innumerable disputes about property lying within their respective territories between their own citizens, such as titles and boundaries of lands, debts by assumption, note, bond, or account, mercantile contracts, &c. *none of which can ever be cognizable by any department of the federal government.*

14thly. The several states can create corporations civil and religious; prohibit or impose duties on the importation of slaves into their own ports; establish seminaries of learning; erect boroughs, cities and counties; promote and establish manufactures; licence taverns; alter the criminal law; constitute new courts and offices; establish ferries; erect public buildings; sell, lease and appropriate the proceeds and rents of *their lands*, and of every other species of *state property*; establish poor houses, hospitals, and houses of employment; regulate the police; and many other things of the utmost importance to the happiness of their respective citizens. In short, besides the particulars enumerated, every thing of a domestic nature must or can be done by them.

In addition to this enumeration of the powers and duties of the state governments, we shall find many other instances under the constitution, which require or imply the existence or continuance of the sovereignty and severalty of the states.–The following are some of them:–

All process against criminals and many other law proceedings will be brought by and run in the name of *that commonwealth*, in which the offence or event has taken place.

The senate will be representatives of the several *state sovereignties*.

Every state must send *its own* citizens to the senate and to the house of representatives. No man can go thither, but from the state of which he is a complete *citizen*, and to which, if they choose, he shall be *sworn to be faithful*.

No state shall on any pretence be without *an equal voice* in the senate.

Any state may repel invasions or *commence a war* under emergent circumstances, without waiting for the consent of Congress.

The electors of the President and Vice-President must not nominate more than one person *of the state to which they belong*: so *careful* is the federal constitution *to preserve the rights of the states*.

In case of an equality of votes in the election of the President or Vice-President, a casting voice is given to *the states* from a due attention to their *sovereignty* in appointing the ostensible head of the federal government.

The President of the United States may require written communications from *the governors of the states.*

Provision is made for adjusting differences between *two states*–or *one state* and the citizens of *another. New states* may be admitted into *the union*. As all *the territory* of each state is *already* in the *union*, it is clear that any district will stand on different ground *when erected into a state*, from what it did when it composed a number of counties, or a part of an already existing member of the confederacy.

Two states may not become *one* without the consent of Congress, which proved clearly that the convention held *the severalty* of the states *necessary*. This is directly opposed to your idea, *that consolidation was intended*. *Each state* and the federal justiciary are to give faith and credit to the records and proceedings of *every other state.*

The states have, in the federal constitution, a guarantee of *a separate republican form of government.*

Two thirds of *the states* in the proposed confederacy can call a convention.

Three fourths of those *states* can alter the constitution.

From this examination of the proposed constitution for the United States, I trust it will appear, that though there are some parts of it, which, taken separately, look a little like consolidation, yet there are many others of a nature, which proves, that no such thing was intended, and that it cannot ever take place.

It is but since the middle of the present century, that the principles and practice of free governments have been well understood, political science having been much slower in its progress than any other branch. Perhaps this has been caused by the greater degree of passion, to which, from its nature, this department of knowledge is subjected. The principles on which free sovereignties ought to confederate is quite a new question, and a new case. It is difficult to take it up at once in the proper way. One circumstance has exceedingly obscured the subject, and hid the truth from the eyes of many of us. Most of the states being in the possession of free governments, have looked for the same forms in *a confederating instrument*, which they have justly esteemed in their several *social compacts*. Recommending this distinction as necessary to be taken home to your minds when you examine the great subject before you, I shall cease to trespass on your time.

Remarks on the Proposed Plan of a Federal Government by Alexander Contee Hanson

Editor's Introduction:

Maryland had not yet ratified the Constitution when Alexander Contee Hanson, writing as Aristides, published his "Remarks on the Proposed Plan of a Federal Government" in January 1788. Hanson was a prominent member of the Old Line State. His father, John Hanson, served as the first president of Congress under the Articles of Confederation and was regarded as a stalwart patriot. Alexander Contee Hanson served as George Washington's secretary for a brief period in 1776 but fell ill and had to return to Maryland. He was eventually appointed Judge of the General Court and commissioned to participate in the process of condensing the laws of Maryland. He did almost all the work and as a result they are typically referred to as "Hanson's Laws."

Hanson wrote well and penned several pamphlets on economics and politics following the war under the pseudonym Aristides. He despised paper currency and argued for its eradication and defended Annapolis as the permanent seat of government for the United States (a document he considered his finest essay), but his pamphlet arguing for the ratification of the Constitution was perhaps his most important. Hanson was appointed Chancellor of Maryland in 1789 and served in that position until his death in 1806. His son would eventually become a United States Senator, and the Hanson family is still active in Maryland politics.

"Remarks on the Proposed Plan of a Federal Government" covered most of the contentious issues surrounding ratification. The most cited section of the document concerned a proposed bill of rights. Hanson opposed adding such a document to the Constitution, for like other opponents of the proposal, he feared that some liberties would be omitted, and the powers of the general government illegally enlarged. Hanson defended the powers of the States under the new Constitution and while he had some issues with the document believed it to be the best that could be produced. While Hanson is not well known today, his contribution to orginialism cannot be overlooked.

Remarks on the Proposed Plan of a Federal Government

January 31, 1788

By Alexander Contee Hanson (Aristides) of Maryland

IT is my intention, with all possible plainness, to examine the proposed plan of a Federal Government. Its enemies and its advocates have laid particular stress on the names, wherewith it is subscribed. As one side would obtain your implicit assent, by a reference to characters, and as the other would defeat measures by exciting your jealousy of men, permit me, in the first place, to make some general observations on the persons who composed the late memorable convention.

In general, they had been distinguished by their talents and services. They were not principally the men to whom the idea of the convention first suggested itself, and it is notorious that, in general, they accepted their appointments with reluctance. It would seem, however, according to some vague insinuations, that, no sooner did they find themselves convened, than their natures changed; and fatally have they combined for the destruction of your liberties. Now this altogether shocks my faith. I should sooner imagine that the sacredness of the trust, the unparalleled grandeur of the occasion, and the fellowship of the great and good, might have elevated the soul of the most abandoned wretch, had it been possible for such to obtain a seat in that illustrious assemblage.

If those, who would inspire suspicion and distrust, can suggest any precise idea, it must be this, that the members of the convention will be elected into the first federal congress, and there combining again will compose a body capable of bearing down all opposition to their own aggrandisement.

By their scheme, however, thus deeply concerted, the house of representatives is to be chosen by the people once in two years; and if they have acted so as to warrant any reasonable apprehension of their designs, it will be easy at any time, to prevent their election. The truth is, that very few of them either wish to be elected, or would consent to serve, either in that house, or in the senate. I have exercised my imagination to devise in what manner they or any other men, supposing them to bear full sway in both houses, could erect this imaginary fabric of power. I request any person to point out any law, or system of laws, that could be possibly contrived for that purpose, obtain the final assent of each branch, and be carried into effect, contrary to the interests and wishes of a free, intelligent, prying people, accustomed to the most unbounded freedom of inquiry. To begin by an attempt to restrain the press, instead of promoting their designs, would be the most effectual thing to prevent them.

I am apprized of the almost universal disposition for the increase and abuse of authority. But if we are to withhold power because there is a possibility of its perversion, we must abolish government, and submit to those evils, which it was intended to prevent. The perfection of political science consists chiefly in providing mutual checks amongst the several departments of power, preserving at the same time, the dependance of the greatest on the people. I speak with reference to a single government. The necessity of another species of government, for the mutual defence and protection of these American states, no man of sense and honesty, that I know of, has ever yet denied.

The convention had the above principle constantly in their view. They have contrived, that it shall be extremely difficult, if not altogether impracticable, for any person to exceed or abuse his lawful authority. There is nothing in their plan like the cloathing of individuals with power, for their own gratification. Every delegation, and every advantage that may be derived to individuals, has a strict reference to the general good.

To examine their constitution, by article and section, would be a painful and needless undertaking. I shall endeavor to answer such objections, as I have already heard, to anticipate others; to point out some advantages not generally known ; and to correct certain errors, with respect to construction. When the convention was appointed, I much feared that the numerous seeds, and principles of discord amongst the states, would, for ever, prevent them from agreeing to any efficient system whatever. I apprehended, the dispute about representation would be the rock, on which the vessel containing all our hopes would be dashed. When, therefore, I discerned that equitable compromise between the larger and lesser states, my anxiety was instantly removed, and my soul enlightened by a sudden ray.

How then was I, some months after, disgusted at the repetition, of the arguments respecting the inequality of representatives in the first branch. We were told, that the minority in convention reasoned on first principles, that, as all men, in a state of nature, are equal with respect to rights, so also are equal all separate and distinct states;–that, when individuals form a free government, they must all have equal suffrage, either in framing laws by themselves, or in choosing representatives, although one man be ten times stronger, richer, or wiser than another; so also, when several states unite, for common convenience, they must meet on terms of perfect equality, although one be ten times more wealthy, expensive and populous than another;-that, under our present compact, the states are equal, and that no injury has resulted from the equality.

To these arguments, we may imagine, was opposed something like the following: "You talk of first principles, and, at the same time, would let 180,000 free inhabitants of Maryland have no more to do in the choice of representatives than only 30,000 inhabitants of Delaware. Do you propose, that these 30,000 shall bear an equal part of burdens and impositions? As to no injury having resulted from the equality, as you call it, under the articles of confederation, we think the reverse; and that this pretended equality was a poison, which pervaded all our affairs."

The anticipation of arguments like these had raised those apprehensions of an irreconcilable difference. It were needless to repeat more. Had an angel been the umpire, he could propose no expedient more equitable and more politic, not only as a compromise, but to establish such a decided difference between the two branches of congress, as will make them, indeed, two distinct bodies, operating by way of mutual balance and check.

By this expedient, is safety secured to the lesser states, as completely as if the senate were the only legislative body. It is possible (if such a thing can be devised) that, from the inequality in the first branch, propositions will be made to give the larger states some advantage over the lesser; but the equality in the senate will, forever, preclude its adoption. It is well worthy of remark, that not more than three of the thirteen are, at present, deemed larger states, in the peculiar sense of the word. There is no reason for supposing, in the federal, like a state, legislature, the senate will be intimidated or overawed, by the more numerous branch. A demagogue may declaim, rave, menace and foam, with as little impression as the roaring billows produce upon the solid beach. Were it not for this equality in one, and inequality in the other, a jealousy might be entertained of too perfect a coincidence of sentiment.

The convention has been censured for an excess of its authority. But with no other power was it invested, than is possessed by every free citizen of the states. Its office was to advise, and no further has it proceeded. Had it been even invested with full powers to amend the present compact, their proposed plan would not have exceeded their trust. Amendment, in parliamentary language, means either addition, or diminution, or striking out the whole, and substituting some- thing in its room. The convention were not limited. The states did not tell them, this article must stand, this must be struck out, and this may be altered. The avowed object of a convention was to consult on the additional power necessary to be vested in congress. But the members of this convention perceiving, from the experience of these states, from the history of ancient and modern states, and, I may add, from the principles of human nature, that the same body of men ought not to make and execute laws; and that one body alone ought not to do the first, have separated the executive, so far as was proper, from the legislative; and this last they have divided into two branches, composed of different materials, distinct from, and totally independent of, each other.

The house of representatives is to be the immediate choice of the people, and one man is to represent 30,000 souls. In an affair of so much importance, and in districts containing so many suffrages, it is not to be supposed, that a worthless character will succeed by those arts, which have, sometimes, prevailed in county elections. It is to be expected, that, in general, the people will choose men of talents and character. Were they even so inclined, they can choose none but of ripe age, who have been, at least, seven years citizens of the United States, and, at the time of election, residents of the respective state. Whatever laws shall be proposed, or assented to by these men, are to bind themselves, their children, and their connections. If a single man, or a party, shall propose a measure, calculated to promote private interest, at the expense of public good, is it conceivable, that the whole house will be brought into the measure? Suppose it should. The measure cannot be adopted into a law, without the concurrence of another house, consisting of men still more select, possessing superior qualifications of residence and age, and equally bound by the laws. After gaining the assent of the senate, the bill must be submitted to the objections of the president. He is not in any manner dependent on the legislature, which can, in no manner, punish him, except for some crime known to the laws. He is elected by persons chosen for that special purpose. He receives a compensation, which cannot be diminished or increased, during his continuance in office. The term of his commission is limited to four years, unless he shall have acted so as to merit the people's favour. From the mode of his election, it is impossible he can intrigue to advantage; and, from the nature of other things, he will never succeed by bribery and corruption. Like any other individual, he is liable to punishment. Finally, at the expiration of his office, he returns into the mass of the people.

In spite of all these circumstances, an idea is gone forth amongst the enemies of the plan, and they labour to impress it on your minds, that whatever power may be exercised by these delegates of the people, will be used contrary to the interests of their constituents. This is a supposition, so repulsive to my mind, that I wonder any man of the least generosity, or reflection, can possibly adopt it. The assembly of Maryland, with respect to internal regulations, is almost omnipotent. And yet, is there a man who supposes the assembly would, intentionally, pass laws injurious to the people? Why then should we distrust the federal assembly, chosen for a short term, bound by the same ties, and selected on account of their talents and patriotism?

But, say the objectors, although we might probably confide with safety in congress, it is not consistent with prudence, without a manifest necessity, to empower any men to do us an injury.

Whenever the proposed plan delegates authority, which you imagine might safely be denied, be assured, that a little reflection will suggest abundant reason for granting it. At the same time you may be convinced, that, as some powers were not intended to be exercised, so they never will be exercised, without absolute necessity.

I have been amused by the writings of an avowed friend to the plan. "Let no man," says he, "think of proposing amendments. Should each person object, and should his objections prevail, not a title of the system will be left. You are to accept the whole, or reject the whole." After speaking in this very sensible way, he advises the states to reject, with unanimity and firmness, the following provision.

"Art. I, sect. 4. The times, places, and manner of holding elections for senators and representatives, shall be prescribed in each state, by the legislature thereof; *but the congress may, at any time, by law, make or alter such regulations, except as to the places of choosing senators.*"

Can this writer imagine, that congress will presume to use this power, without the occurrence of some one or more of the cases, the contemplation whereof induced the convention to create it. These are the cases of invasion by a foreign power; of neglect, or obstinate refusal, in a state legislature; of the prevalance of a party, prescribing so as to suit a sinister purpose, or injure the general government. Others might perhaps occur in the convention. But these may suffice to evince the propriety of such a power in the federal head. It was never meant, that congress should at any time interfere, unless on the failure of a state lagislature, or to alter such regulations as may be obviously improper. The exercise of this power must at all times be so very invidious, that congress, will not venture upon it without some very cogent and substantial reason. Let congress, even officiously, exert every power given by this clause, the representatives must still be chosen by the people, and the senate by the state legislatures. The provision cannot by any possibility admit of a different construction.

Should the bare appointment to congress have the magic to pervert the tempers and principles of men, I perceive not the temptation for abusing this, or any other of their powers. There are bad men to be found at times, in every numerous assembly. But, under all circumstances, I predict, that, in congress, their party will be small. Should there be thither sent the most prostituted character, that ever acted, like a pest, to his own state; should he possess talents superior to the rest, I should have little dread of his influence, unless I could suppose, that a majority of like characters may be chosen. Even then, I repeat it—they will be under no temptation sufficient to influence a sensible mind; and no man of ripe age was ever yet wicked for the sake of wickedness alone.

You have heard, that, by the privilege of nominating persons to office, the president will find the congress obsequious enough to pass any laws, he shall think fit to propose. It is incumbent on the authors of this suggestion to show some interest in the president, inducing him to propose prejudicial measures. I have remarked, that under the constitution, his salary can be neither augumented nor curtailed, during his commission; and, to change the constitution, is not in the power of congress. Should he, however, devise, and endeavour to procure, some dangerous act of the body, can we conceive, that this lure will be powerful enough to corrupt a majority in each house. No member can be appointed to an office, created, or of which the profits shall be increased, during the time for which he was elected. And the expectation of such, as may fall vacant, within four years, will hardly corrupt even the smallest number, that can, in any possible case, be a majority, in the two houses. To make the members of each house ineligible to any other office whatever, would be even impolitic, on account of its precluding these states from the services perhaps of its best men. And it would be unjust to deny men the possibility of benefits, which might be attained by others less deserving.

In ascertaining and defining this obvious principle, the convention evidently pursued this obvious principle, that all things, which concern the union in general, should be regulated by the federal head; and that each state legislature should regulate those things, which concern only its own internal government, together with the separate interests of its citizens. The enemies of the proposed constitution have deemed it material to shew, that such a one never existed before. It dees not indeed agree with definitions in books, taken from the Amphyctyonic council, the United Netherlands, or the Helvetic body. They would therefore infer, that it is wrong. This mode of reasoning deserves not a serious refutation. The convention examined those several constitutions, if such a thing they can be called. It found them either woefully defective, as to their own particular object, or inapplicable to ours. Peradventure, our own articles of confederation, in theory, appear more perfect than any of them. These articles were made according to rule; the legislative and executive authorities being vested in one assembly. The extreme caution of its framers to secure the independence of the several states, on account of its principle, was much to be commended. But experience having fully demonstrated this constitution to be inadequate to the purposes for which it was framed, and a general conviction of its defects having occasioned the convention, it is astonishing, that attempts are now made to prefer still a theory, not founded on the nature of things, but derived merely from a few deplorable examples. If two branches in a state legislature be proper, why, in the name of common sense, are they not so in a confederate legislature ?—Many instances of hasty unadvised proceedings of congress, as a legislature, have by other writers been adduced; and so long as mankind shall remain under the influence of passion or interest, there will be such proceedings in every numerous assembly of men.

It is universally, by good writers, agreed, that where any one political body possesses *full* powers, legislative and executive, whether it be a single man, or a select few, or a numerous assembly, it matters not ;-the government must, in a short time, become despotic. That in a free government, therefore, the legislative and executive ought to be ever distinct and separate, is a position in the Maryland declaration of rights. This hackneyed principle, has been urged, with great confidence, against constituting the senate a council to the president. It has been urged too, even by the men who would have the whole power of the federal government centered in a single assembly. I mean the men who insist that the convention ought to have done no more than advise in what manner the powers of the present congress should be increased. Let us understand the principle in its proper extent. It does not follow, that a body, whose assent is required, in making laws, but who cannot, by themselves, do any legislative act, may not be a fit council to the supreme executive magistrate, deriving his authority, like them, from the people, in no manner dependent on them, or the immediate of the people, for any private advantage, and possessed of no share in legislation, except that of offering his advice.

The objection to this part of the constitution, I confess, at first, appeared formidable. The reasons which I now conjecture to have influenced the convention, did not then occur. But I have long adhered to a maxim, which I warmly recommend to others—never to condemn, absolutely, even within myself, any one kind, until I can hit upon some other kind which I *conceive* better. As no human institution can possess absolute perfection, it is an easy matter to espy some fault or defect in almost everything, which the wit of man can contrive, or at least, to reason plausibly against it. But this faculty of finding faults is by no means sufficient to constitute the politician or statesman. I deliberated what kind of council might be preferable, under all circumstances, to the senate. The plainest thing in nature! Exclaims he, who solves all difficulties at once. Why not appoint a body to act as council and nothing else?

One reason, and that not very unpopular, is the great additional expence. However, this reason I deem the lightest of all; and the general proposition involves a great variety of other considerations.

It is essential to a council, that the members be free, as possible, from all bias, or improper influence. This separate and distinct council must be elected by the people, or by special electors; by the legislature, or by one of its branches; or by some department; or by the president.

That the people should either make laws to bind themselves, or elect persons, without whose consent, no laws shall be made, is essential to their freedom. But universal experience forbids, that they should immediately choose persons for the execution of the laws. Shall the legislature then, or the senate, or the house of representatives, have this appointment? A council thus chosen would be dependent on its electors; and it would be the same thing in many respects, as if the legislature should execute its own laws. Can you believe, that a council, chosen annually, or once in two or three years, would dare to pursue, in all cases, the dictates of its own judgment, contrary to the known will of those, who will soon have an opportunity of removing them? Would they not be emulous to please leading men; and there not be opened, at every period of election, a fine field for intrigue and cabal? There would be one way only of rendering a council, thus chosen, independent of their electors; and that is, the choosing them for life, with salaries, not to be augmented or diminished.

Against choosing an executive for life the reasons are weighty indeed. Should they then hold their commissions during good behaviour, there must be some tribunal to determine on that good behaviour; and what body it can be, except the congress, would be difficult to decide. Besides good behaviour in a member of council is not determinable, like that of a judge, which has relation to the laws, and things universally known. In the office of the former, there is much left to discretion, that I cannot conceive with what propriety he can hold it on the condition of good behaviour. There can be no sure criterion, and the decision must therefore unavoidably depend on the discretion or mere opinion of his judges, founded on no established principles whatever.

A council, chosen by the president himself, would probably consist of creatures devoted to his will. I can discern no reason, wherefore any officer of the government should make the appointment. There remains then only the people's choosing electors, and placing the council of the president on the same footing with himself. Here occurs the objection of expence; and here again would arise the controversy respecting equality of representation.

The senate, will, in all human likelihood, consist of the most important characters, men of enlightened minds, mature in judgment, independent in their circumstances, and not deriving their principal subsistence from their pay, as probably would the members of a board, distinct and separate from all other public employments.

I am not, therefore, barely reconciled to the article in question. It commands my warmest admiration, and entire applause.

Is there any power improperly trusted to that select assembly, in which all the states have equal interest, and to which they will assuredly make a determined point of sending their best men? It is this equality, almost as much as any other circumstance, which recommends it as an executive council. The senate are to try impeachments. By their advice only, may the president make treaties, appoint ambassadors, ministers, counsels, judges of the supreme court, and officers, not otherwise provided for in the constitution. Let us reflect, whether these things could be better done, by any other body, and whether it be proper for any one man (suppose even the saviour of his country to be immortal) to have the appointment of all those important officers. It has always appeared to me, that neither one man, nor many men, should possess this transcendant authority, in a republic. A single man, in high power, if he always means right, can with difficulty discern the true characters of men. Continual efforts are made to impose on his judgment. But, indeed, a single man *generally* confers by favour. In a large assembly there is perhaps equal partiality; and elections are conducted by intrigue and cabal. A select assembly is open to direct application; and although each may be supposed to entertain his partialities, he cannot recommend his favourites, without pointing out their essential qualifications and becoming, in some measure, responsible for their conduct. It is here, that characters are most fairly investigated, and appointments are most deliberately made. I appeal to universal experience, whether these remarks be not founded on fact, and whether the most judicious appointments have not been made by small select assemblies. I confess, that the number of the senators for this purpose only is excessive. But I can confidently rely on the extraordinary selection to compensate for the excess.

The power of the president is alarming peculiarly to that class, who cannot bear to view others in possession of that fancied blessing, to which, alas! they must themselves aspire in vain. They tell you, this supreme magistrate, although he be called the modest name of president, and elected for only four years, will, in every essential, be an emperor, king, or stadtholder at least; and that his dignity in a few years, will become hereditary. Let us examine the foundation of this alarming prediction.

Before this appointment can be *entailed*, and before even the term can be enlarged, the constitution must be changed, by consent of the people. By what method, then, shall the president effect this alteration? Every citizen in the union will be a censor on his conduct. Not even his person is particularly protected; and the means of oppression are little in his power. Let the jealousy of the people once take the alarm, and, at the expiration of his term, he is dismissed, as inevitably as light succeeds to darkness. The election of a president is not carried on in a single assembly, where the several arts of corruption may be essayed. He is elected by persons chosen on the same day, in thirteen different assemblies, in thirteen different states. An elective monarchy has long been severely reprobated. But had the countries, where it prevailed, enjoyed regulations like these, they would perhaps, at this time, be preferred to the rules of hereditary succession, which have so often placed fools and tyrants on the throne.

It seems, however, that the president may possibly be continued for life. He may so, provided he deserve it. If not, he retires to obscurity, without even the consolation of having produced any of the convulsions, attendant usually on grand revolutions. Should he be wicked or frantic enough to make the attempt, he atones for it, with the certain loss of wealth, liberty or life.

I return to the powers of congress. They are almost universally admitted to be proper for a federal head, except only the *sweeping clause*, and the power of raising fleets and armies, without any stint or limitation, in time of peace. The clause runs thus:— ART. I, sec. 8, par. the last. "To make all laws, which shall be necessary and be proper for carrying into execution the foregoing powers, and all other powers vested by this constitution, in the government of the United States, or in any department or officer thereof."

It is apprehended, that this *sweeping clause* will afford pretext, for freeing congress from all constitutional restraints.

I will not here again insist on the pledge we enjoy, in the common interest, and sure attachment of the representatives and senate; setting aside the little probability of a majority in each branch lying under the same temptation. Consider the import of the words.

I take the construction of these words to be precisely the same, as if the clause had preceded further and said, "No act of congress shall be valid, unless it have relation to the foregoing powers, and be necessary and proper for carrying them "into execution." But say the objectors, "The congress, being itself to judge of the necessity and propriety, may pass any act, which it may deem *expedient*, for any other purpose." This objection applies with equal force to each particular power, defined by the constitution; and, if there were a bill of rights, congress might be said to be the judge of that also. They may reflect however, that every judge in the union, whether of federal or state appointment, (and some persons would say every jury) will have a right to reject any act, handed to him as a law, which he may conceive repugnant to the constitution.

It may nevertheless strike you at first view, that a provision, so obviously apt to excite distrust, might have well been omitted. So indeed it might, were there a possibility of providing every thing, necessary and proper, for carrying into effect the various powers, intended to be conferred. Without this general clause, it were easy to suppose cases, wherein a particular clause might be incompetent to its own purpose.

For want of some plain and obvious distinctions, there has been vented so much senseless clamour against standing armies, that they are become a political bugbear. A limited monarch, with the means of maintaining, at all times, an army devoted to his will, might soon trample on the natural and civil rights of his subjects. Could the present congress find means of augmenting the force, which it now maintains, which of you, on that account, would experience the slightest anxiety? Which of all the European powers is destitute of an army? Which of them if they were free, could be secure of remaining so without a standing force? I might go further, and demand, whether any of them have lost their liberties, by means of a standing army? The troops, continually kept up in Great Britain, are formidable to its neighbors, and yet no rational Englishman apprehends the destruction of his rights. It is true, that he knows, these troops cannot be maintained, without the consent of his representatives, annually obtained. But the necessity of an army he readily conceives; and the number he leaves to the discretion of parliament. Ought then an American to have greater fears of a president, than an Englishman has of his king? Or may he not trust his representatives and the senate, with as much confidence, as the Englishman reposes in the commons and lords?

Let the federal head be constituted as it may, there can be no perfect security, without both a land force, and naval armament. It is impossible to say how much will, at all times of peace, be sufficient. We have the same security against the abuse of this, as of any other authority. The expenses of an army might indeed raise fears of a different kind,-that we shall not be able to maintain force enough for the most proper occasion.

Suppose a limitation in time of peace. What then is to be done on the prospect of a war? Should you make the distinction between profound peace and a *threatened* war, who is there, but congress, to determine on the exigency? If you make no distinction, then it will be expedient to declare war, at the instant in which the danger shall be conceived, in order that it may be lawful to prepare for only a just defence. In fine, I consider this grand objection, as a mere pretext for terrifying you, like children, with spectres and hobgoblins. It may be material here to remark, that although a well regulated militia has ever been considered as the true defence of a free republic, there are always honest purposes, which are not to be answered by a militia. If they were, the burthen of the militia would be so great, that a free people would, by no means, be willing to sustain it. If indeed it be possible in the nature of things, that congress shall, at any future period, alarm us by an improper augmentation of troops, could we not, in that case, depend on the militia, which is ourselves. In such a case it would be ridiculous to urge that the federal government, is invested with a power over the whole militia of the union. Even when congress shall exercise this power, on the most proper occasions, it is provided in the constitution, that each state shall officer and train its own militia.

The objections against the judiciary are probably more sincere. The article has been generally misconceived, or misrepresented; and after bestowing much attention, I am not certain that I fully comprehend it. I am, however, at length satisfied, that no rational construction can be given to this part of the proposed plan, either to warrant a rejection of the whole, or to place matters on a worse footing, than they are at present.

The judiciary power is to be vested in one supreme court, fixed at the seat of government, with the ease and convenience of the people, the congress may hereafter appoint inferior courts in each of the states. The jurisdiction of this supreme court is to be partly original, and partly appellate. With respect to the extent of either, there can be no possible doubt, as there is neither ambiguity nor uncertainty in the relative expressions.

The original jurisdiction of the supreme court extends:–

1. To all cases, in which may be concerned an ambassador, any public minister, or a consul.

2. To all cases whatever, in which a state may be a party. —This second division may be branched into I. Cases between the United States, and one or more of the individual states. 3. Cases between two or more states. 3. Cases between a state and its own citizens. 4. Cases between a state, and the citizens of another state. 5. Cases between a state, and a foreign state. 6. Cases between a state, and the citizens, or subjects of a foreign state.

The appellate jurisdiction of the supreme court extends:–

1. To all cases whatever between parties of every kind, in law and equity, arising under this constitution, and the laws of congress, passed agreeably thereto, and to treaties already, or hereafter to be, made.

2. To all cases of admiralty or maritime jurisdiction.

3. To all cases, in which the United States shall be a party.

4. To all cases between citizens of different states.

5. To all cases between citizens of the same state, claiming lands under the grants of different states.

6. To all cases between citizens of a state, and foreign states, or their citizens or subjects.

One doubt arising on the judiciary article is, whether in these cases of appellate jurisdiction, the appeal lies both from the state courts, and the inferior federal courts, or only from the former, or only from the latter.

Another doubt is, whether the inferior courts are to be branches of the supreme court, constituted for convenience, and having equal jurisdiction, both original and appellate, with the supreme court, or whether the inferior courts are to be confined to an *original* jurisdiction in those cases, wherein the supreme court has *appellate* jurisdiction.

I shall not presume to decide absolutely on the genuine construction of an article, which is said to have caused much private debate and perplexity. I am however fully persuaded, that, as the article speaks of an original and appellate jurisdiction, of a supreme court, and inferior courts; and, as there is no intimation of appeals from the several state tribunals, the inferior federal courts are intended to have original jurisdiction in all cases, wherein the supreme court has appellate jurisdiction; and the appeal lies only from them. I can, almost, with confidence, maintain, that, as there is no express clause, or necessary implication, to oust the jurisdiction of state courts, an action, after the adoption of the plan, may be instituted in any court, having, at this time, a jurisdiction. And if an action be brought in a state court, I do not, at present, perceive, that it can, in any manner, be transferred to the supreme or inferior federal court.

According then to the best of my judgment the affair stands thus. The supreme federal court will have an exclusive original jurisdiction in all cases relative to the rights of ambassadors, other ministers, and consuls; because, as I humbly conceive, the several state governments have at this time nothing to do with these cases. With respect to the cases, in which a state may be party, the supreme federal court, and the several state courts, will have, I conceive, concurrent original jurisdiction, *provided a state may, at this time, institute an action in its own name, in the courts of another state.* The inferior federal courts, and the state courts, will, I conceive, have concurrent original jurisdiction in all the enumerated cases wherein an appeal lies to the supreme court, *except only the cases created by or under the proposed constitution, in which, as they do not now exist, the inferior federal courts will have exclusive jurisdiction.* From the state inferior courts, I further apprehend, that an appeal will lie, in all cases, to their own high courts of appeal, as heretofore.

A choice of jurisdictions has been ever esteemed a valuable right, even where there are both of the same kind. The purpose of extending so far the jurisdiction of the federal judiciary, is to give every assurance to the general government, of a faithful execution of its laws, and to give citizens, states, and foreigners, an assurance of the impartial administration of justice. Without the salutary institution, the federal government might frequently be obstructed, and its servants want protection. It is calculated not as an engine of oppression, but to secure the blessings of peace and good order. The provisions respecting different states, their citizens, and foreigners, if not absolutely necessary, are much to be applauded. The human mind is so framed, that the slightest circumstance may prevent the most upright and well known tribunal from giving complete satisfaction ; and there may happen a variety of cases, where the distrust and suspicion may not be altogether destitute of a just foundation.

On these principles, an appeal as to fact is no less proper, than the appeal from judges of law. A jury, whose legal qualifications are only property and ripe age, may more probably incur the imputation of weakness, partiality, or undue influence. But in regard to appeals, it is very material to remark, that congress is to make such regulations and exceptions, as upon mature deliberation, it shall think proper. And indeed, before such regulations and exceptions shall be made, the manner of appeal will not be ascertained. Is it then to be presumed, that, in making regulations and exceptions, this appellate jurisdiction shall be calculated as an engine of oppression, or to serve only the purpose of vexation and delay.

As the rod of Aaron once swallowed up the rods of the Egyptian *magi*, so also is it feared, that these federal courts, will, at length, swallow up the state tribunals. A miracle, in one case, is as necessary, as in the other.

But let not the officers of state courts be overmuch alarmed! The causes, which, by possibility, may be instituted in the federal courts bear no comparison to the rest. In the course of ten years, not one action, that I know of, in Maryland, has concerned either another state, or an ambassador, consul, or other minister. It is hoped, that actions by foreigners, will, in a few years, become much rarer than at any time heretofore, and these may still be determined in the state courts.

A gentleman, as it is conjectured, in the law department of a neighboring state, has been pleased to infer, that fictions, similar to those in the king's bench and exchequer of England, will be contrived, to draw causes into the federal courts. He seems not aware, that, even in England, the established fictions of law are not of modern date.

They were ingenious devices, to remedy defects in the common law, *without the aid of parliament.* The fundamental principle however, with respect to their adoption, was, that they *consist with equity, and be requisite for the advancement of justice.* Now every man, who would establish over his cause a jurisdiction in a federal court, must shew, that such cause comes under the description of the constitution. If he do not, there will be wanting that equity, which is the support of legal fiction. But can any man seriously imagine, that fiction will be permitted, to give the judges a power of legislation, denied to congress itself? Wherefore should the judges, holding their commissions during good behaviour, be guilty of such gross falsehood, perjury, and breach of trust? Would there not be a general revolt against such barefaced impudent innovations. Away then with your trumpery of fictions! Accuse not the illustrious members of the convention of having in their contemplation such sophistry, pettifogging and chicane! But another fear is, that whatever actions may be instituted in the federal courts will there seek an admission, on account of a more speedy decision. That man alone, "on whose brow shame is ashamed to sit," will avow his opposition to a more speedy administration of justice.

The institution of the trial by jury has been sanctified by the experience of ages. It has been recognised by the constitution of every state in the union. It is deemed the birthright of Americans; and it is imagined, that liberty cannot subsist without it. The proposed plan expressly adopts it, for the decision of all criminal accusations, except impeachment; and is silent with respect to the determination of facts in civil cases.

The inference, hence drawn by many, is not warranted by the premises. By recognising the jury trial in criminal cases, the constitution effectually provides, that it shall prevail, so long as the constitution itself shall remain unimpaired and unchanged. But, from the great variety of civil cases, arising under this plan of government, it would be unwise and impolitic to say aught about it, in regard to these. Is there not a great variety of cases, in which this trial is taken away in each of the states? Are there not many more cases, where it is denied in England? For the convention to ascertain in what cases it shall prevail, and in what others it may be expedient to prefer other modes was impracticable. On this subject a future congress is to decide; and I see no foundation under Heaven for the opinion that congress will despise the known prejudices and inclination of their countrymen. A very ingenious writer of Philadelphia has mentioned the objections without deigning to refute that, which he conceives to have originated in "sheer malice."

I proceed to attack the whole body of anti-federalists in their strong hold. The proposed constitution contains no bill of rights.

Consider again the nature and intent of a federal republic. It consists of an assemblage of distinct states, each completely organized for the protection of its own citizens, and the whole consolidated, by express compact, under one head, for the general welfare and common defence.

Should the compact authorize the sovereign, or head to do all things it may think necessary and proper, then there is no limitation to its authority; and the liberty of each citizen in the union has no other security, than the sound policy, good faith, virtue, and perhaps proper interests, of the head.

When the compact confers the aforesaid general power, making nevertheless some special reservations and exceptions, then is the citizen protected further, so far as these reservations and exceptions shall extend.

But, when the compact ascertains and defines the power delegated to the federal head, then cannot this government, without manifest usurpation, exert any power not expressly, or by *necessary* implication, conferred by the compact.

This doctrine is so obvious and plain, that I am amazed any good man should deplore the omission of a bill of rights.

When we were told, that the celebrated Mr. Wilson had advanced this doctrine in effect, it was said, Mr. Wilson would not dare to speak thus to a CONSTITUTIONALIST. With talents inferior to that gentleman's, I will maintain the doctrine against any CONSTITUTIONALIST who will condescend to enter the lists, and behave like a gentleman.

It is, however, the idea of another most respectable character, that, as a bill of rights could do no harm, and might quiet the minds of many good people, the convention would have done well to indulge them. With all due deference, I apprehend, that a bill of rights might not be this innocent quieting instrument. Had the convention entered on the work, they must have comprehended within it everything, which the citizens of the United States claim as a natural or a civil right. An omission of a single article would have caused more discontent, than is either felt or pretended, on the present occasion. A multitude of articles might be the source of infinite controversy, by clashing with the powers intended to be given. To be full and certain, a bill of rights might have cost the convention more time, than was expended on their other work. The very appearance of it might raise more clamour than its omission,--I mean from those who study pretexts for condemning the whole fabric of the constitution. —

"What (might they say) did these exalted spirits imagine, that the natural rights of mankind depend on their gracious concession. If indeed they possessed that tyrannic, sway, which, the kings of England had once usurped, we might humbly thank them for their *magna charta*, defective as it is. As that is not the case, we will not suffer it to be understood, that their new-fangled federal head shall domineer with the powers not excepted by their precious bill of rights. What? if the owner of 1,000 acres of land thinks proper to fell one half, is it necessary to take a release from the vendee of the other half? Just as necessary is it for the people to have a grant of their natural rights from a government which derives everything it has, from the grant of the people."

The restraints laid on the state legislatures will tend to secure domestic tranquility, more than all the bills, or declarations, of rights, which human policy could devise. It is very justly asserted, that the plan contains an avowal of many rights. It provides that no man, shall suffer by ex post facto laws or bills of attainder. It declares, that gold and silver only shall be a tender for specie debts; and that no law shall impair the obligation of a contract.

I have here perhaps touched a string, which secretly draws together many of the foes to the plan. Too long have we sustained evils, resulting from injudicious emissions of paper, and from the operation of tender laws. To bills of credit as they are now falsely called, may we impute the entire loss of confidence between men. Hence it is, that specie has, in a great degree, ceased its proper office, and been confined to speculations, baneful to the public, and enriching a few enterprising sharp-sighted men, at the expence not only of the ignorant, slothful, and needy, but of their country's best benefactors. Hence chiefly are the bankruptcies throughout America, and the disreputable ruinous state of our commerce. Hence is it principally, that America hath lost its credit abroad, and American faith become a proverb. The convention plainly saw, that nothing short of a renunciation of the right to emit bills of credit could produce that grand consummation of policy, the RESTORATION OF PUBLIC AND PRIVATE FAITH.

Were it possible for the nations abroad to suppose Great Britain would emit bills on the terms whereon they have issued in America, how soon would the wide arch of that mighty empire tumble into ruins? In no other country in the universe has prevailed the idea of supplying, by *promissory notes*, the want of coin, for commerce and taxes. In America, indeed, they have heretofore served many valuable purposes. It is this consideration, which has so powerfully attached to them many well meaning honest citizens; and they talk of gratitude to paper money, as if it were a sensible benefactor, entitled to the highest rank and distinction; and as if, to abandon it, would be a deadly sin. But when everything demonstrates the season to be past; when the credit of America, in all places, depends on the security she shall give to contracts, it would be madness in the states to be tenacious of their right. So long as Europe shall believe we regard not justice, gratitude and honour, so long will America labour under the disadvantages of an individual, who attempts to make good his way through the world with a blasted reputation. To the man, who shall say, "it is of no consequence to consult national honour," I only answer thus, "If thy soul be so narrow and depraved, as to believe this, it were a needless attempt to cure thee of thy error."

On this subject there is no necessity for enlarging, to the people of my native state; their conduct on a recent occasion having acquired them great and deserved applause. Is it necessary to enlarge on the propriety of giving more efficient powers to a federal head? At this moment, congress is little more than a name, without power to effect a single thing, which is the object of a confederate republic. Reflect on the recent period, when, in a sister state, a numerous body of her frantic citizens appeared armed for the destruction of a government, framed by the people. When that unhappy state was devoted to the miseries of a civil war, did congress even dare to interpose? Conscious of its inability to protect, it could only await the result, in silence and in terror. It indeed ventured to *make application* to the states for a small body of troops, under the poor pretext of another, and a necessary, destination. But, notwithstanding the universal contagion of the alarm, did the states, on *that* occasion, comply with the *requisition*? Suppose even an invasion by a foreign power, in what manner could congress provide for its own defence? In the contemptible light in which America has lately stood, is it reasonable to expect she will be suffered to remain long in peace? The distance between the two continents is the only circumstance on which we can rely. All Europe is now in suspence; and the result of your deliberations will instruct her in the part she shall act.

With amazement, her nations contemplate a scene, of which the world is too young to furnish a parallel. We assembled our sages, patriots, and statesmen, to consult what mode of government is capable of producing the greatest sum of general good, with the least mixture of general, and partial evil. Not that each individual in this august assembly was expected to offer a system; but that the product of their joint wisdom should be referred to the several states, to be adopted, or rejected, as the great body of the people shall determine on a free and full deliberation.

As the occasion was unparalleled so also is the plan, which, after many months of painful investigation, is submitted, with an unanimity, also unparalleled.

If there be any man, who approves the great outlines of the plan, and, at the same time, would reject it, because he views some of the minute parts as imperfect, he should reflect, that, if the states think as he does, an alteration may be hereafter effected, at leisure. When the convention determined, that the whole should be received, or the whole fail, they did not on an arrogant conceit of their own infallibility, but on the soundest principles of policy and common sense. Were each state legislature, or convention, to take it up, article by article, and section by section, with the liberty of adopting some, and rejecting the rest, in all probability, so small a part would be approved by nine states, on the narrow view which each has of the subject, and attached as each is to its own supposed interest, that, in its mutilated condition, it would be worse than the present confederation. For thirteen different assemblies, in that way, to approve so much of any plan whatever, as might merit the name of system, the convention well knew to be impossible. Were there any one body of men, invested with full power, in behalf of the whole United States, to consider, and amend the plan, then would it be proper to debate it by sections, in the same manner as it was originally debated.

With a view to defeat totally the plan, another general convention is proposed; not with the power of giving a finishing hand to a constitution; but *again* to consider objections, to strike out, to add, and *again* to make their report to the several states.

In this way, there can never be an end. We must at last return to this, that whatever is agreed on, by the assembly appointed to propose, must be either adopted in the whole, or in the whole rejected.

The idea of a new convention is started by some men, with the vain expectation of having amendments made to suit a particular state, or to advance their own selfish views. Were this fatal idea adopted, I should bid a last adieu to that elevated hope, which now inspires me, of living under the happiest form of government which the sun ever beheld. Recollect again and again, that almost every state in the union made a determined point of delegating its first characters to this grand convention. Reflect upon the time spent in the arduous work, and the sacrifices which those distinguished persons made to their country. Should the same men be deputed again, would they not, think you, with the same unanimity, subscribe and recommend the same plan. So far as I have been informed, those members, who, in the progression of the plan, had opposed certain parts, and yet afterwards subscribed cheerfully to the whole, have, with the candour which becomes them, acknowledged their errors in debate. Even an illustrious character, who was of the minority, consisting only of three, I have been told, has since regretted his refusal.

Suppose then a second convention, with a different choice of delegates. These too would either speedily subscribe, or they might propose some other system, to be debated, paragraph by paragraph, in thirteen different assemblies; and then there would be the same probability of a mutilated plan ; or they would propose something, to be adopted or rejected in the whole; and there would be the same necessity of another convention. Besides, as the second convention, if it consist of different men, must *inevitably* be inferior to the first, there is little probability that their work will be superior. Never again, in an assembly constituted as that was, will there be found the same liberality of sentiment, "the same spirit of amity, and the same mutual deference and concession."

If it be contended, that the second, being possessed of the various objections from the several states, must be better able to determine, I would ask, what conduct this second convention should adopt? Are they to take the proposed plan, and strike out every thing objected to by nine states? Or may they likewise adopt and recommend the entire plan. In short, to appoint a second convention, merely to consult and propose, would be the most absurd expedient, that ever, in a matter of this amazing magnitude, was proposed. Does any man then entertain the thought of another kind of convention, invested with full powers to consult, amend, adopt, and confirm? A scheme like this was never yet, I trust, in agitation. But, if it were, I would propose this single question. Whether is it better to amend, before it be tried, that plan, which may be termed the result of the wisdom of America, or leave it to be amended, at leisure, as mature experience shall direct.

Although a very great variety of ostensible objections have been publicly offered, the real and sincere objections are hardly ever disclosed in private. There is a class, opposed to the union of *thirteen different states*, and the reason they assign, is the vast extent of our territory. Let us consider well their objection.

To consolidate the whole thirteen states into a single organization, was out of the convention's contemplation, for two unanswerable reasons. In the first place, they were satisfied, that not one of the states would renounce its sovereignty. In the next place, they considered, that, in a single government, with a great extent of territory, the advantages are most unequally diffused. As the extreme parts are scarcely sensible of its protection, so are they scarcely under its domination. It is generally agreed, that a great extended nation can long continue under no *single* form of government, except a despotism into which, either a republic, or a limited monarchy, will be certain to degenerate. And hence, if I understand the man who styles himself a Centinel, he insinuates, that, if these states will persist in remaining under one head, they must soon fall under the dominion of a despot. But, my fellow-citizens, in a confederate republic, consisting of distinct states, completely organized within themselves, and each of no greater extent than is proper for a republican form, almost all the blessings of government are equally diffused. Its protection extends to the remotest corner, and there every man is under restraint of laws.

A true federal republic is always capable of accession by the peaceable and friendly admission of new single states. *Its true size is neither greater nor less than that, which may comprehend all the states, which, by their contiguity, may become enemies, unless united under one common head, capable of reconciling all their differences.* Such a government as this, excels any single government, extending over the same territory, as a band of brothers is superior to a band of slaves, or as thirteen common men, for the purposes of agriculture, would be superior to a giant, enjoying strength of body equal to them all.

The idea of a balance has long influenced the politics of Europe. But how much superior to this almost impracticable balance would be a general league, constituting a kind of federal republic, consisting of all the independent powers of Europe, for preventing the impositions and encroachments of one upon another! A true and perfect confederate government, however, in her situation, is not to be attained ; although the great soul of HENRY THE FOURTH is said to have conceived the idea.

Shall America then form one grand federal republic? Or shall she, after experiencing the benefits of even an imperfect union, and when a union the most perfect is requisite for her permanent safety;-shall she, in this situation, divide into thirteen contemptible single governments, exposed to every insult and wrong from abroad, and watching each other's motions, with all the captiousness of jealous rivals? Or shall she divide into two or more federal republics, actuated by the same malignant dispositions. In either of these cases, after struggling through infinite toils, difficulty, and danger, should the thirteen single states be, at last, delivered from foreign foes, they will fall upon each other; and no man can predict, what forms of government, or division of territory, shall finally obtain - Two or three federal republics might possibly retain their independence. But they would be in the same situation, with respect to each other, as France, England, and Spain, scarcely ever free from war; practicing the arts of dissimulation and intrigue; in vain striving to impose, by endless negotiation ; and, after all, relying only on the immense naval and land forces, which they continually maintain.

Let us then, my countrymen, embrace those blessings which Providence is ready to shower on us. Open and extend your views. Let the prospect comprehend the present and future generations, yourselves, your children, your relatives, your fellow-citizens, dwellers on the same continent, and inhabitants of the whole terraqueous globe.

With the prospect of my country's future glory, presented to my glowing imagination, it is difficult to resist the strong impulse of enthusiasm. But it is neither *my* talent, nor desire, to mislead. I wish only to impress the genuine advantages of the proposed plan; and, if possible, to rouse every man from that supineness, into which he is lulled by the present deceitful calm. To acquit themselves, like men, when visible danger assails; and, when it is repelled, to sink like savages, into indolence, is said to be characteristic of Americans. I am not, however, one of those, who imagine a necessity for embracing almost any scheme, which the convention might have devised, for giving to the union more efficient powers. Had the plan, they have proposed, contained the seeds of much, though distant, evil, perhaps a *faithful patriot* might address you thus:

"Let us not, my friends, in a fit of unmanly apprehension, betray that immense charge, with which Americans, at this day are entrusted! Let us confide in the *wisdom of our great men*, with the assistance of Heaven, to establish yet our safety and happiness. Let us, in the meantime, sustain all our evils, with resignation and firmness. Let us hope, that no foreign power, or lawless internal combinations, shall do us a mighty injury! Let us be frugal, economical, industrious! Let us suspend the cruel collection of debts! Let commerce continue to droop! Let us awhile submit even to infamy; and turn a callous ear to the indignant reproaches of our late faithful and affectionate servants, friends and benefactors."

To this purpose might a man plausibly declaim; provided the proposed plan contained many and great faults; provided it were not calculated to promote the general good, without violating the *just rights* of a single individual; and provided it were not the best, which, under all circumstances, could be reasonably expected. It was the parting declaration of the American NESTOR, to his exalted fellow-labourers, that "he would subscribe, because he thought it good, and because he did not know, but it was the best that could be contrived." My own declaration, which would be the same, were I now standing on the verge of eternity, is, that if the whole matter were left to my discretion, I would not change a single part. On reflection, I was pleased with the conduct of the Virginia and Maryland assemblies, in appointing distant days for the meeting of their state conventions. Not that I greatly admired the supposed motive; but because I sincerely wished every man might have time to comprehend and weigh the plan, before the ultimate decision of these two states should be pronounced. The longer it is contemplated, after it is understood, the greater, I am persuaded, will be the approbation of those, who wish the public good, and to whose private views and expectations, nothing, which tends to promote that good, can be greatly detrimental.

But alas! My fellow citizens, on the adoption of this fatal plan, and when every part of the great complicated machine shall be put in motion, the lustre of our state assemblies will be diminished by the superior splendour of the federal head. This single consideration, although many hesitate to avow it, will cause more opposition, than all the rest united. Weigh well the objection. If ever it be material to inquire, by whom reasons are adduced, it is on this peculiar occasion.

From the objection itself, may perhaps be discerned the danger we are opposed to, from the secret views and selfish considerations of the objector.

What at this moment to the nations abroad is the state of Maryland. The poor member of a defenceless system of petty republics. In what light is she viewed by her sister states? Whatever rank she now possesses, will remain after the great alteration of the system. They will all rise or fall in the proportion which now exists. What then are the powers an individual state will lose? She will no longer be able to deny congress that, which congress, at this moment, has a right to demand. She will have no power to enter into a treaty, alliance, or confederation. She shall, in time of war, grant no letters of marque and reprisal. She shall coin no money, emit no bills of credit, nor make any thing but gold and silver a tender in payment of debts. She shall pass no bill of attainder, or ex post facto law, or law impairing the obligation of a contract. She shall grant no title of nobility. She shall not, *without consent of congress*, lay any duty on imports or exports, except what may be necessary for executing her inspection laws. She shall not, *without consent of congress*, lay any duty on tonnage, keep troops or ships of war, in time of peace; enter into any agreement, or compact, with another state, or with a foreign power; or engage in war, unless actually invaded, or in such imminent danger, as will not admit of delay. Of the several powers, from which an individual state is thus restrained, some are improper to be used at all ; others belong not even now to the individual states; and the rest are strictly proper for only the federal head. The aversion from ceding them to congress, is just as reasonable as in a state of nature would be the reluctance of an individual to relinquish any of his natural rights, upon entering into a state of society. The principle, on which, at length, he surrenders, is the necessity of every one's making a cession of some rights, to enable the sovereign to protect the rest. Each state is fully sensible, that she cannot protect herself; and yet she would enjoy the advantages of an union, without making the necessary contributions. To discern how preposterous is the idea, requires not more than a moment's reflection.

For the honour of my countrymen, I hope this extreme reluctance to surrender power is confined to those, whose ambition, or private interest, would have all things subservient to the omnipotence of assembly. In the few years that the state constitutions have endured, has not every one seen pregnant proofs of the vain love of domination? Has he not also seen decisive marks of overbearing secret influence? Where are the instances of exalted patriotism. But I forbear. Far from me is the wish to cast wantonly one stinging or disagreeable reflection. The subject naturally required the general remark, and I hope, this short hint may be excused.

Is there a possible advantage to be derived to the public, from a single state's exercising powers proper only for the federal head; suppose even each state should use them properly and alike; which, in the nature of things, is not to be expected. If there be men, who delight in parliamentary warfare; who choose a fair wide field for displaying their talents; who wish to see every servant of the public prostrate before them ; whose ears soothed by humble supplication; they may still enjoy rich sources of gratification. Are not the regulations of property, the regulations of the penal law, the protection of the weak, the promotion of useful arts, the whole internal government of their respective republics; are not these the main objects of every wise and honest legislature? Are not these things still in their power; and, whilst free from invasion or injuries abroad, are not these almost the only things, in which sovereignty is exercised?

That the state legislatures will soon "drop out of sight," is an idea most extravagant and absurd; because, in addition to the importance of their duties, the very existence of the congress depends upon them. That they will, at least, dwindle into something like city corporations, is an apprehension, founded on no better principle. May the Ruler of the universe inspire them with wisdom to discharge those numerous and extensive duties, which they will find remaining. To do this, as they ought, will be far preferable to the breaking all useful national measures, and marring the concerns of a continent. To do this, as they ought, will afford more true pleasure to a good mind, than the carrying, by consummate eloquence and address, the most interesting federal measure, which cannot be contrived by an enlightened honest politician, in a state assembly, possessing all its darling sovereignties!

You have been assured, that, soon as this fatal plan shall succeed, an host of rapacious collectors will invade the land ; that they will wrest from you the hard product of your industry, turn out your children from their dwellings, perhaps commit your bodies to a jail : and your own immediate representatives will have no power to relieve you. This is the mere phrenzy of declamation, the ridiculous conjuration of spectres and hobgobblins!

To the five per cent. impost most of the states have more than once given their assent. This is the only tax which congress wishes immediately to impose. Of the imposition of assessment, capitation, or direct taxes of any kind, the congress entertains no idea at present; and although it be proper for the federal head to possess this power in reserve, nothing but some unforeseen disaster will ever drive them to such ineligible expedients. Setting aside the immediate advantages of revived credit and trade, and the increased value of your property and labour, you will be delivered, in a great measure, from that load of direct taxation, which has been so unequally borne, and produced so little substantial good.

Permit me to demand, what mighty benefit has resulted from the exercise of those sovereign rights, that, in general, you should be loth to resign them. Has not a perpetual clamour been kept up (it matters not whether justly or otherwise) concerning the enormous impositions on the people? And what are the advantages derived to the people of the respective states, to the union, or to meritorious individuals? Has not the far greater part of a state's internal expences been owing to the extreme length of sessions? Have not these sessions been consumed in disgusting altercation, and in passing laws, serving to little better purpose, than to swell the statute book, encourage a negligence of duty, and obstruct the administration of justice?

To trace each real and ostensible objection up to its proper course, would be a task equally invidious, irksome and unnecessary. The characters of the principal advocates and opponents are well known. To him who declines not a public avowal of his sentiments, some credit is due, for his candour; and he is entitled to your patient attention. But, he that prefers a secret corner, for dealing forth his objections, and expositions, should be heard with caution and distrust. It is in a land of slavery alone, where truth shuns the open day.— Each side has imputed to the other illiberal and selfish motives. Consider then the particular interests of each; and bear this in your minds, that an interest may be either honourable and praiseworthy, or directly the reverse.

You have been told that the proposed plan was calculated peculiarly for the rich. In all governments, not merely despotic, the wealthy must, in most things, find an advantage, from the possession of that, which is too much the end and aim of mankind. In the proposed plan, there is nothing like a discrimination in their favour. How this amazing objection is to be supported, I am at a loss to conjecture. Is it a just cause of reproach, that the constitution effectually secures property.

Or would the objectors introduce a general scramble. In eligibility to office, in suffrage, and in every other civil right, men are all on terms of perfect equality. And yet, notwithstanding this just equality, each man is to pay taxes in proportion to his ability, or his expences.

A still more surpassing objection remains to be considered. "This new constitution, so much bepraised, and admired, will commence in a moderate aristocracy. To a corrupt and oppressive one the transition is easy, and inevitable, unless some Caesar, or a Cromwell, in their stead, shall make a seizure of their liberties. As to the house of representatives, they will either be insignificant spectators of the contest between the president and the senate, or their weight will be thrown in to one of the scales."

No man, indeed, has exactly used these words; but they contain the sum and scope of several recent publications.

In the course of my remarks, I have already said enough to expose the futility of certain objections, which are ushered to the world, under the auspices of a pair of honourable names. Notwithstanding the care and pomposity, with which they are circulated, it is not worth while to draw invidious comparison. One gentleman, whose name is thus *freely* used, I think, calls the house of representatives a mere shred, or rag of representation. Does he consider the distinction between the objects of a confederate republic, and of a single government? It is a poor return for that singular respect which the convetion paid to the majesty of the people, in contriving, that congress shall not only be a representation of states, as heretofore, but also an immediate representation of the people. Were 5, 10, or even 20,000, the ratio proposed, then peradventure the honourable objector might clamour about the expence of a mobbish legislature.

The fact is, that the new government, constructed on the broad basis of equality, mutual benefits, and national good, is not calculated to secure a single state all her natural advantages at the expence of the natural and acquired advantages of her respectable brethren of New England.

His real objection against constituting the senate an executive council arises, I conceive, from the equality of representation. As to the trite maxim, that the legislative and executive ought ever to be distinct and separate, I would, in addition to my foregoing observations on this head, refer him to Montesquieu's chapter on the English government. I could wish, the writings of that great man, and of Judge Blackstone, so often either copied, or cited for conclusive authority, were better understood. Should a second, or a third convention, be obtained, the aforesaid honourable gentlemen can never be *fully* indulged in their main object of a proportionate representation.

The examples of a genuine aristocracy are rare. They were founded in times of profound ignorance, and when the mass of property was in the hands of a few, whilst the rest pined in want and wretchedness. One European aristocratic government, if such it can be called, has grown out of the original defective form, the offspring of necessity, and commenced amidst the horrors of a civil war. Although the people of that country fought, and intended, to be free, their compact of government never was complete; they did not attend to the principle of rotation, and checks; and a genuine representation did never there prevail.

An aristocracy can perhaps subsist with only a moderate extent of territory and population. But it is a farce to talk of an aristocracy; when there are two branches, so differently formed ; when the members of each are chosen for a reasonable term; and when their reappointment depends on the good opinion of their countrymen. It is not in nature, that a man with the least portion of *common* sense can believe the people of America will consent to such a deplorable change in their constitution, as shall confine all power to a few noble families, or that, without their consent, the change will be effected, by internal policy, or force.

Whilst mankind shall believe freedom to be better than slavery; whilst our lands shall be generally distributed, and not held by a few insolent barons, on the debasing terms of vassalage; whilst we shall teach our children to read and write; whilst the liberty of the press, that grand palladium, which tyrants are compelled to respect, shall remain; whilst a spark of public love shall animate even a small part of the people; whilst even self-love shall be the general ruling principle; so long will it be impossible for an aristocracy to arise from the proposed plan.—Should Heaven, in its wrath, inflict blindness on the people of America; should they reject this fair offer of permanent safety and happiness; to predict what species of government shall at last spring from disorder, is beyond the short reach of political foresight.

Believe me, my fellow citizens, that no overweening self conceit, no vain ambition, no restless meddling spirit, has produced this address. Long had I waited to see this vast question treated, as it deserves; and the publication disseminated in my native state. Many judicious observations had appeared in newspapers and handbills. But no publication, that I have seen, has gone fully into the merits, considered the objections, and explained that, which is doubtful and obscure. On this account I, at length, made the attempt. That my performance is equal to my wishes, I can by no means believe. I have, however, a consolation in reflecting, that it will be difficult for any man to demonstrate, that, in this business, I have a particular interest. In many of my remarks, I have been anticipated by writings, which I have seen; and I have collected materials, wherever I could find them. Could I be convinced, that I have said nothing, which had not before been said or thought by thousands, the reflection would yield far less mortification than pleasure.

Federalist No. 48 by James Madison

Editor's Introduction:

Madison continued his discussion of separation of powers in *Federalist* No. 48, one of the six most cited documents among legal scholars of the last one-hundred fifty years. Madison worried about "parchment barriers" and argued that unless more stringent safeguards were added to written constitutions, the tendency of the legislative to overwhelm the other branches of government would be too difficult to overcome. The same could be said for the executive branch. He cited both the constitutions of Virginia and Pennsylvania to illustrate that separation of powers needed a more robust safeguard than those contained in these two American constitutions.

Federalist No. 48

February 1, 1788

By James Madison of Virginia

To the People of the State of New York:

IT WAS shown in the last paper that the political apothegm there examined does not require that the legislative, executive, and judiciary departments should be wholly unconnected with each other. I shall undertake, in the next place, to show that unless these departments be so far connected and blended as to give to each a constitutional control over the others, the degree of separation which the maxim requires, as essential to a free government, can never in practice be duly maintained. It is agreed on all sides, that the powers properly belonging to one of the departments ought not to be directly and completely administered by either of the other departments. It is equally evident, that none of them ought to possess, directly or indirectly, an overruling influence over the others, in the administration of their respective powers. It will not be denied, that power is of an encroaching nature, and that it ought to be effectually restrained from passing the limits assigned to it. After discriminating, therefore, in theory, the several classes of power, as they may in their nature be legislative, executive, or judiciary, the next and most difficult task is to provide some practical security for each, against the invasion of the others.

What this security ought to be, is the great problem to be solved. Will it be sufficient to mark, with precision, the boundaries of these departments, in the constitution of the government, and to trust to these parchment barriers against the encroaching spirit of power? This is the security which appears to have been principally relied on by the compilers of most of the American constitutions. But experience assures us, that the efficacy of the provision has been greatly overrated; and that some more adequate defense is indispensably necessary for the more feeble, against the more powerful, members of the government. The legislative department is everywhere extending the sphere of its activity, and drawing all power into its impetuous vortex. The founders of our republics have so much merit for the wisdom which they have displayed, that no task can be less pleasing than that of pointing out the errors into which they have fallen. A respect for truth, however, obliges us to remark, that they seem never for a moment to have turned their eyes from the danger to liberty from the overgrown and all-grasping prerogative of an hereditary magistrate, supported and fortified by an hereditary branch of the legislative authority. They seem never to have recollected the danger from legislative usurpations, which, by assembling all power in the same hands, must lead to the same tyranny as is threatened by executive usurpations. In a government where numerous and extensive prerogatives are placed in the hands of an hereditary monarch, the executive department is very justly regarded as the source of danger, and watched with all the jealousy which a zeal for liberty ought to inspire. In a democracy, where a multitude of people exercise in person the legislative functions, and are continually exposed, by their incapacity for regular deliberation and concerted measures, to the ambitious intrigues of their executive magistrates, tyranny may well be apprehended, on some favorable emergency, to start up in the same quarter. But in a representative republic, where the executive magistracy is carefully limited; both in the extent and the duration of its power; and where the legislative power is exercised by an assembly, which is inspired, by a supposed influence over the people, with an intrepid confidence in its own strength; which is sufficiently numerous to feel all the passions which actuate a multitude, yet not so numerous as to be incapable of pursuing the objects of its passions, by means which reason prescribes; it is against the enterprising ambition of this department that the people ought to indulge all their jealousy and exhaust all their precautions. The legislative department derives a superiority in our governments from other circumstances. Its constitutional powers being at once more extensive, and less susceptible of precise limits, it can, with the greater facility, mask, under complicated and indirect measures, the encroachments which it makes on the co-ordinate departments. It is not unfrequently a question of real nicety in legislative bodies, whether the operation of a particular measure will, or will not, extend beyond the legislative sphere.

On the other side, the executive power being restrained within a narrower compass, and being more simple in its nature, and the judiciary being described by landmarks still less uncertain, projects of usurpation by either of these departments would immediately betray and defeat themselves. Nor is this all: as the legislative department alone has access to the pockets of the people, and has in some constitutions full discretion, and in all a prevailing influence, over the pecuniary rewards of those who fill the other departments, a dependence is thus created in the latter, which gives still greater facility to encroachments of the former. I have appealed to our own experience for the truth of what I advance on this subject. Were it necessary to verify this experience by particular proofs, they might be multiplied without end. I might find a witness in every citizen who has shared in, or been attentive to, the course of public administrations. I might collect vouchers in abundance from the records and archives of every State in the Union. But as a more concise, and at the same time equally satisfactory, evidence, I will refer to the example of two States, attested by two unexceptionable authorities.

The first example is that of Virginia, a State which, as we have seen, has expressly declared in its constitution, that the three great departments ought not to be intermixed. The authority in support of it is Mr. Jefferson, who, besides his other advantages for remarking the operation of the government, was himself the chief magistrate of it. In order to convey fully the ideas with which his experience had impressed him on this subject, it will be necessary to quote a passage of some length from his very interesting "Notes on the State of Virginia," p. 195. "All the powers of government, legislative, executive, and judiciary, result to the legislative body. The concentrating these in the same hands, is precisely the definition of despotic government. It will be no alleviation, that these powers will be exercised by a plurality of hands, and not by a single one. One hundred and seventy-three despots would surely be as oppressive as one. Let those who doubt it, turn their eyes on the republic of Venice. As little will it avail us, that they are chosen by ourselves. An ELECTIVE DESPOTISM was not the government we fought for; but one which should not only be founded on free principles, but in which the powers of government should be so divided and balanced among several bodies of magistracy, as that no one could transcend their legal limits, without being effectually checked and restrained by the others. For this reason, that convention which passed the ordinance of government, laid its foundation on this basis, that the legislative, executive, and judiciary departments should be separate and distinct, so that no person should exercise the powers of more than one of them at the same time. BUT NO BARRIER WAS PROVIDED BETWEEN THESE SEVERAL POWERS. The judiciary and the executive members were left dependent on the legislative for their subsistence in office, and some of them for their continuance in it. If, therefore, the legislature assumes executive and judiciary powers, no opposition is likely to be made; nor, if made, can be effectual; because in that case they may put their proceedings into the form of acts of Assembly, which will render them obligatory on the other branches. They have accordingly, IN MANY instances, DECIDED RIGHTS which should have been left to JUDICIARY CONTROVERSY, and THE DIRECTION OF THE EXECUTIVE, DURING THE WHOLE TIME OF THEIR SESSION, IS BECOMING HABITUAL AND FAMILIAR.

"The other State which I shall take for an example is Pennsylvania; and the other authority, the Council of Censors, which assembled in the years 1783 and 1784. A part of the duty of this body, as marked out by the constitution, was "to inquire whether the constitution had been preserved inviolate in every part; and whether the legislative and executive branches of government had performed their duty as guardians of the people, or assumed to themselves, or exercised, other or greater powers than they are entitled to by the constitution." In the execution of this trust, the council were necessarily led to a comparison of both the legislative and executive proceedings, with the constitutional powers of these departments; and from the facts enumerated, and to the truth of most of which both sides in the council subscribed, it appears that the constitution had been flagrantly violated by the legislature in a variety of important instances. A great number of laws had been passed, violating, without any apparent necessity, the rule requiring that all bills of a public nature shall be previously printed for the consideration of the people; although this is one of the precautions chiefly relied on by the constitution against improper acts of legislature. The constitutional trial by jury had been violated, and powers assumed which had not been delegated by the constitution. Executive powers had been usurped. The salaries of the judges, which the constitution expressly requires to be fixed, had been occasionally varied; and cases belonging to the judiciary department frequently drawn within legislative cognizance and determination. Those who wish to see the several particulars falling under each of these heads, may consult the journals of the council, which are in print. Some of them, it will be found, may be imputable to peculiar circumstances connected with the war; but the greater part of them may be considered as the spontaneous shoots of an ill-constituted government.

It appears, also, that the executive department had not been innocent of frequent breaches of the constitution. There are three observations, however, which ought to be made on this head: FIRST, a great proportion of the instances were either immediately produced by the necessities of the war, or recommended by Congress or the commander-in-chief; SECONDLY, in most of the other instances, they conformed either to the declared or the known sentiments of the legislative department; THIRDLY, the executive department of Pennsylvania is distinguished from that of the other States by the number of members composing it. In this respect, it has as much affinity to a legislative assembly as to an executive council. And being at once exempt from the restraint of an individual responsibility for the acts of the body, and deriving confidence from mutual example and joint influence, unauthorized measures would, of course, be more freely hazarded, than where the executive department is administered by a single hand, or by a few hands.

The conclusion which I am warranted in drawing from these observations is, that a mere demarcation on parchment of the constitutional limits of the several departments, is not a sufficient guard against those encroachments which lead to a tyrannical concentration of all the powers of government in the same hands.

Federalist No. 51 by James Madison

Editor's Introduction:

Madison concluded his discussion of "separation of powers" by explaining the benefits of the proposed Constitution. Maintaining the independency of the separate branches of government was difficult but not impossible. Madison suggested that the Constitution kept "each other in their proper places" by ensuring each branch had the means of protecting itself from the other. But Madison argued that the ultimate safeguard for the "separation of powers" could be found in the uniquely American creation of federalism. This prevented factions both among citizens and in the government from seizing power and establishing a legislative, executive, or judicial tyranny.

Federalist No. 51

February 6, 1788

By James Madison of Virginia

To the People of the State of New York:

TO WHAT expedient, then, shall we finally resort, for maintaining in practice the necessary partition of power among the several departments, as laid down in the Constitution? The only answer that can be given is, that as all these exterior provisions are found to be inadequate, the defect must be supplied, by so contriving the interior structure of the government as that its several constituent parts may, by their mutual relations, be the means of keeping each other in their proper places. Without presuming to undertake a full development of this important idea, I will hazard a few general observations, which may perhaps place it in a clearer light, and enable us to form a more correct judgment of the principles and structure of the government planned by the convention.

In order to lay a due foundation for that separate and distinct exercise of the different powers of government, which to a certain extent is admitted on all hands to be essential to the preservation of liberty, it is evident that each department should have a will of its own; and consequently should be so constituted that the members of each should have as little agency as possible in the appointment of the members of the others. Were this principle rigorously adhered to, it would require that all the appointments for the supreme executive, legislative, and judiciary magistracies should be drawn from the same fountain of authority, the people, through channels having no communication whatever with one another. Perhaps such a plan of constructing the several departments would be less difficult in practice than it may in contemplation appear. Some difficulties, however, and some additional expense would attend the execution of it. Some deviations, therefore, from the principle must be admitted. In the constitution of the judiciary department in particular, it might be inexpedient to insist rigorously on the principle: first, because peculiar qualifications being essential in the members, the primary consideration ought to be to select that mode of choice which best secures these qualifications; secondly, because the permanent tenure by which the appointments are held in that department, must soon destroy all sense of dependence on the authority conferring them.

It is equally evident, that the members of each department should be as little dependent as possible on those of the others, for the emoluments annexed to their offices. Were the executive magistrate, or the judges, not independent of the legislature in this particular, their independence in every other would be merely nominal. But the great security against a gradual concentration of the several powers in the same department, consists in giving to those who administer each department the necessary constitutional means and personal motives to resist encroachments of the others. The provision for defense must in this, as in all other cases, be made commensurate to the danger of attack. Ambition must be made to counteract ambition. The interest of the man must be connected with the constitutional rights of the place. It may be a reflection on human nature, that such devices should be necessary to control the abuses of government. But what is government itself, but the greatest of all reflections on human nature? If men were angels, no government would be necessary. If angels were to govern men, neither external nor internal controls on government would be necessary. In framing a government which is to be administered by men over men, the great difficulty lies in this: you must first enable the government to control the governed; and in the next place oblige it to control itself.

A dependence on the people is, no doubt, the primary control on the government; but experience has taught mankind the necessity of auxiliary precautions. This policy of supplying, by opposite and rival interests, the defect of better motives, might be traced through the whole system of human affairs, private as well as public. We see it particularly displayed in all the subordinate distributions of power, where the constant aim is to divide and arrange the several offices in such a manner as that each may be a check on the other that the private interest of every individual may be a sentinel over the public rights. These inventions of prudence cannot be less requisite in the distribution of the supreme powers of the State. But it is not possible to give to each department an equal power of self-defense. In republican government, the legislative authority necessarily predominates. The remedy for this inconveniency is to divide the legislature into different branches; and to render them, by different modes of election and different principles of action, as little connected with each other as the nature of their common functions and their common dependence on the society will admit. It may even be necessary to guard against dangerous encroachments by still further precautions. As the weight of the legislative authority requires that it should be thus divided, the weakness of the executive may require, on the other hand, that it should be fortified.

An absolute negative on the legislature appears, at first view, to be the natural defense with which the executive magistrate should be armed. But perhaps it would be neither altogether safe nor alone sufficient. On ordinary occasions it might not be exerted with the requisite firmness, and on extraordinary occasions it might be perfidiously abused. May not this defect of an absolute negative be supplied by some qualified connection between this weaker department and the weaker branch of the stronger department, by which the latter may be led to support the constitutional rights of the former, without being too much detached from the rights of its own department? If the principles on which these observations are founded be just, as I persuade myself they are, and they be applied as a criterion to the several State constitutions, and to the federal Constitution it will be found that if the latter does not perfectly correspond with them, the former are infinitely less able to bear such a test.

There are, moreover, two considerations particularly applicable to the federal system of America, which place that system in a very interesting point of view. First. In a single republic, all the power surrendered by the people is submitted to the administration of a single government; and the usurpations are guarded against by a division of the government into distinct and separate departments. In the compound republic of America, the power surrendered by the people is first divided between two distinct governments, and then the portion allotted to each subdivided among distinct and separate departments. Hence a double security arises to the rights of the people. The different governments will control each other, at the same time that each will be controlled by itself. Second. It is of great importance in a republic not only to guard the society against the oppression of its rulers, but to guard one part of the society against the injustice of the other part. Different interests necessarily exist in different classes of citizens. If a majority be united by a common interest, the rights of the minority will be insecure.

There are but two methods of providing against this evil: the one by creating a will in the community independent of the majority that is, of the society itself; the other, by comprehending in the society so many separate descriptions of citizens as will render an unjust combination of a majority of the whole very improbable, if not impracticable. The first method prevails in all governments possessing an hereditary or self-appointed authority. This, at best, is but a precarious security; because a power independent of the society may as well espouse the unjust views of the major, as the rightful interests of the minor party, and may possibly be turned against both parties. The second method will be exemplified in the federal republic of the United States. Whilst all authority in it will be derived from and dependent on the society, the society itself will be broken into so many parts, interests, and classes of citizens, that the rights of individuals, or of the minority, will be in little danger from interested combinations of the majority.

In a free government the security for civil rights must be the same as that for religious rights. It consists in the one case in the multiplicity of interests, and in the other in the multiplicity of sects. The degree of security in both cases will depend on the number of interests and sects; and this may be presumed to depend on the extent of country and number of people comprehended under the same government. This view of the subject must particularly recommend a proper federal system to all the sincere and considerate friends of republican government, since it shows that in exact proportion as the territory of the Union may be formed into more circumscribed Confederacies, or States oppressive combinations of a majority will be facilitated: the best security, under the republican forms, for the rights of every class of citizens, will be diminished: and consequently the stability and independence of some member of the government, the only other security, must be proportionately increased. Justice is the end of government. It is the end of civil society. It ever has been and ever will be pursued until it be obtained, or until liberty be lost in the pursuit. In a society under the forms of which the stronger faction can readily unite and oppress the weaker, anarchy may as truly be said to reign as in a state of nature, where the weaker individual is not secured against the violence of the stronger; and as, in the latter state, even the stronger individuals are prompted, by the uncertainty of their condition, to submit to a government which may protect the weak as well as themselves; so, in the former state, will the more powerful factions or parties be gradually induced, by a like motive, to wish for a government which will protect all parties, the weaker as well as the more powerful.

It can be little doubted that if the State of Rhode Island was separated from the Confederacy and left to itself, the insecurity of rights under the popular form of government within such narrow limits would be displayed by such reiterated oppressions of factious majorities that some power altogether independent of the people would soon be called for by the voice of the very factions whose misrule had proved the necessity of it. In the extended republic of the United States, and among the great variety of interests, parties, and sects which it embraces, a coalition of a majority of the whole society could seldom take place on any other principles than those of justice and the general good; whilst there being thus less danger to a minor from the will of a major party, there must be less pretext, also, to provide for the security of the former, by introducing into the government a will not dependent on the latter, or, in other words, a will independent of the society itself. It is no less certain than it is important, notwithstanding the contrary opinions which have been entertained, that the larger the society, provided it lie within a practical sphere, the more duly capable it will be of self-government. And happily for the REPUBLICAN CAUSE, the practicable sphere may be carried to a very great extent, by a judicious modification and mixture of the FEDERAL PRINCIPLE.

A Freeman, III by Tench Coxe

Editor's Introduction:

Coxe concluded his "A Freeman" series by demonstrating that the Constitution did not created a consolidated government, that the Framers opposed consolidation, and that the States would not be annihilated if the Constitution was ratified. In fact, Coxe thought that that States would pass laws even more severe than those of the general government and would retain their independence in the new system in all areas not delegated to the central authority. Opponents of the Constitution focused much of their energy on the possible consolidation of the States, a prospect that the "friends" of the Constitution consistently refuted. That reliance on federalism formed the core of "originalism" and "strict construction."

A Freeman, III

February 6, 1788

By Tench Coxe of Pennsylvania

To the MINORITY of the CONVENTION of *Pennsylvania*

Gentlemen, In my former letters I endeavoured to point out certain provisions of the new Constitution, and several circumstances that must result from the proposed frame of government and the state constitutions, which might demonstrate, that there is no ground to apprehend a consolidation of the states, that shall join in the depending confederacy, into one government.

An observation of the honorable Mr. Wilson's has been adduced, among other arguments, to prove, that despotism would follow such a general government. I believe with him and with you that such would be the consequence of *a single national constitution, in which all the objects of society and government were so completely provided for, as to place the several states in the union on the footing of counties of the empire.*–But permit me to ask you, gentlemen, will such be the condition of the states? Where is the county that can independently train its own militia, appoint its civil and militia officers, establish *a peculiar system* of penal laws, issue criminal process *in its own name*, erect corporations, *impose direct taxes*, excises and duties, hold lands in its own right, *commence war* in any emergency, *regulate descents*, prescribe *the qualifications* of electors, alter its constitution or *the principles* of its government, divide itself into separate and *independent parts*, join itself to another state, issue writs for elections, and regulate the same, enact inspection laws, *erect courts*, appoint judges, *commission* all its officers, create new offices, sell and give away its lands, *erect fortifications*, and, in short where is the county in the union, or in the world, that can exercise in any instance *independent legislative, executive or judicial powers*?

Those three gentlemen who withheld their names from the act of the federal convention could not have apprehended the annihilation of the state governments, while that house was sitting, or they would, under the influence of such fear, certainly have pressed for a bill of rights. It appears they did not think one so necessary, as to concert a single motion to obtain it: A conclusive proof, in my mind, that they saw no symptoms of a design to consolidate in the framers of the plan, and that they had no apprehensions of the kind themselves.

The construction of the senate affords an absolute certainty, that the states will not lose their present share of separate powers. No state is to lose its voice therein without *its own consent*. Governor Randolph justly observed, that the force of the constitution of any state can only be lessened *by the absolute grant of its own citizens*. Whatever therefore is now possessed will remain, unless transferred by new grants. The state legislatures too being the immediate representatives and guardians of their *respective* constituents, and being the powerful creators of the senators, it cannot be apprehended, either that they will give away their own powers, or that they will chuse men who are unfriendly to them; nor is it at all probable that a senator would hazard the displeasure of the people, or the vengeance of so potent a body as a state legislature, by sacrificing their interests or powers. Rather may it be expected, that his interest and connexions in the state will too partially attach him to it, to the injury of national objects; or that he may neglect general concerns, from a desire to please a legislature or a people, who will be to him *the source of honors, emolument and power*.

So *independent* will the state governments remain, that their laws may, and in some instances will, be *severer* than those of the union. Treason against the United States, for instance, cannot be attended with confiscation and corruption of blood; but by the existing laws of all the states, *the unoffending families* of attainted persons, stripped of all hereditary rights, and condemned to the bitter portion of extreme poverty, are left without their friend and parent, to meet the trials of the world alone: an awful monument of *the sovereign and avenging power* of their native state. Let the Representative or Senator who may meditate the annihilation of the government of his state duly consider this, before it be too late.

You apprehend the power of Congress to lay direct taxes will tend to produce consolidation. But the several state possess that power also, and by an *early*, wise and faithful excise of it, can always supercede the use of it by Congress. For example; if ten thousand pounds were apportioned to Pennsylvania, to make up the interest on our foreign debts by the end of 1788, a tax for which would be laid in July, our legislature might proceed in the most easy and expeditious way to raise the money, against the time when the federal government must necessarily proceed, and by paying our quota into the federal treasury would fulfil the requisitions of the law. A federal government, that shall possess the least degree of policy or virtue, would never attempt to interfere with such honest, wise and effectual arrangements of any state. It cannot be reasonably feared that a federal legislature, chosen by *the equal voices* of all our citizens, *the poor, as well as the rich*, will ever wrest from the hands of the people and states, who respectively appoint them, powers so wisely placed and so honestly applied.

The check of the Senate on the appointment of officers will exceedingly favor the preservation of the state governments. Let us suppose an expedition on foot, which requires a number of general officers, whom a President might be inclined to appoint from the state to which he belongs, or for which several persons are nominated, that are too partially attached to the federal government, or desirous of lessening the powers of the separate states. *The Senate can reject them all*, and independently give their reasons to the people and the legislatures. That they will often do so, we cannot doubt, when we remember *where their private interests, affections and connexions lie*, to whom they will owe *their seats*–to whom they must look for *future favors* of the same kind.

The lordship of the soil is one of the most valuable and powerful appendages of sovereignty–This remains *in full perfection* with every state. From them must grants flow, to them must be paid *the annual acknowledgement*, whether it be a mere compliance with form in the rendering of a pepper corn, or *a solid revenue* in the payment of a quit-rent. To them also, as original and rightful proprietaries and *lords of the soil*, will the estates of extinct families revert.

Independent revenues and resources are indubitable proofs of *sovereignty*. The states will possess many of those which now exist, and which may hereafter be created. Taxes on state offices, fees for grants of lands, and various licences, tolls on rivers, canals, and roads not being post-roads, rents of public buildings, escheats, the mighty fund of quit-rents, and sales of lands; these and many others are (exclusively of Congress) within the power of the several states, besides their having access, in common with the federal government, to every source of revenue, but the duties on foreign merchandize and ships.

IMPEACHMENTS within the several states will afford them opportunities of exerting the most dignified and aweful powers of sovereignty. The people of every state, by their constitutional representatives, may impeach the public officer, however great or daring, that shall presume to violate their exclusive rights, or offend against the peace and dignity of their commonwealth, and may punish him, on conviction, by fine, imprisonment or death, without any possible interference of Congress.

But, Gentlemen, the subject is inexhaustible. Every section in the federal constitution, as we peruse it, affords new ideas opposed to consolidation: Every moment's reflexion, on the operation and tendency of the proposed government, adds to their number. I will not therefore trespass longer on your time. I will rest the matter on your own good sense and candor, confidently trusting that the removal of your apprehensions on this important point will render the new Constitution more agreeable to you. Thinking, as you did, consolidation was intended and would take place, and that it must produce a despotism, you would have been criminal in assenting to the plan proposed; but I will hope that the consideration of this point which we have taken together, will remove your fears, and open the door to comfortable hopes, rather than to apprehensions, from the great measure now waiting the Fiat of the people of the United States.

Marcus I by James Iredell

Editor's Introduction:

James Iredell was one of the most important members of the founding generation. Born in England in 1751, he emigrated the North America in 1767 after his father's merchant business collapsed. He studied law and was admitted to the North Carolina bar in 1771.

Iredell favored the patriot cause during the period leading to independence and at 23 drafted a political essay, *Principles of an American Whig*, that called for American independence. Iredell served as a judge during the American War for Independence and was later charged with revising the laws of North Carolina. He was an ardent proponent of the Constitution during the ratification period and was one of the first men appointed to the Supreme Court by George Washington. He died while on the federal bench.

Iredell was one of the leading voices in favor of ratification. His Marcus essays were intended to directly refute the most powerful voice against ratification, George Mason of Virginia. In a line by line attack on Mason's primary arguments, Iredell insisted that Mason and other opponents were mischaracterizing the powers of the general government, most importantly that the Constitution consolidated power and obliterated the States.

In this essay, he defends the omission of a bill of rights, the size of the House of Representatives, and the powers of the Senate. In each instance, he reasons that the Constitution expressly delegated a set of limited powers to the general government, and that if that government attempted to exercise a power beyond these limitations, it would be null and void. This is what makes Iredell one of the most important voices for originalism. As a future Supreme Court Justice, his position on the powers of the general government carries as much weight as that of Madison or Hamilton, perhaps even more so than in the case of Hamilton.

Marcus I

February 20, 1788

James Iredell of North Carolina

MR.M'LEAN, I beg the favour of you to publish in your paper, the following Answers to Mr. Mason's Objections to the New Constitution. Each objection is inserted in his own words (as taken from a printed newspaper) before the answer given to it, so that the merits of both will be fairly before the Public.–Nothing can be more easy than the business of objecting, and as mankind are generally much more apt to find fault than to approve its success is commonly proportionable; but I trust the good sense of America, at this awful period, will exert itself to judge coolly and impartially, especially as the dissenting gentlemen appear to differ as much from each other as from the respectable majority who have recommended the New Constitution to the public.–I am Sir, your very humble servant, The AUTHOR.

Answers to Mr. Mason's Objections to the New Constitution, Recommended by the late Convention at Philadelphia.

1st. Objection.

"There is no declaration of rights, and the laws of the general government being paramount to the laws and constitutions of the several States, the declarations of rights in the separate States are no security; nor are the people secured even in the enjoyment of the benefit of the common law, which stands here upon no other foundation than its having been adopted by the respective acts forming the constitutions of the several States."

Answer.

1. As to the want of a Declaration of Rights. The introduction of these in England, from which the idea was originally taken, was in consequence of usurpations of the Crown, contrary, as was conceived, to the principles of their government. But there, no original constitution is to be found, and the only meaning of a declaration of rights in that country is, that in certain particulars specified, the Crown had no authority to act. Could this have been necessary, had there been a Constitution in being, by which it could have been clearly discerned whether the Crown had such authority or not? Had the people by a solemn instrument delegated particular powers to the Crown at the formation of their government, surely the Crown which in that case could claim under that instrument only, could not have contended for more power than was conveyed by it. So it is in regard to the new Constitution here: The future government which may be formed under that authority, certainly cannot act beyond the warrant of that authority. As well might they attempt to impose a King upon America, as go one step in any other respect beyond the terms of their institution. The question then only is, whether more power will be vested in the future government than is necessary for the general purposes of the Union. This may occasion a ground of dispute–but after expressly defining the powers that are to be exercised, to say that

they shall exercise no other powers (either by a general or particular enumeration) would seem to me both nugatory and ridiculous. As well might a Judge when he condemns a man to be hanged, give strong injunctions to the Sheriff that he should not be beheaded.

2. As to the common law, it is difficult to know what is meant by that part of the objection. So far as the people are now entitled to the benefit of the common law, they certainly will have a right to enjoy it under the new constitution, till altered by the general Legislature, which even in this point has some cardinal limits assigned to it. What are most acts of Assembly but a deviation in some degree from the principles of the common law? The people are expressly secured (contrary to Mr. Mason's wishes) against ex post facto laws, so that the tenure of any property at any time held under the principles of the common law, cannot be altered by any act of the future general legislature. The principles of the common law, as they now apply, must surely always hereafter apply, except in those particulars in which express authority is given by this Constitution; in no other particular can the Congress have authority to change it, and I believe it cannot be shewn that any one power of this kind given is unnecessarily given, or that the power would answer its proper purpose if the Legislature was restricted from any innovations on the principles of the common law, which would not in all cases suit the vast variety of incidents that might arise out of it.

IId. Objection.

"In the House of Representatives there is not the substance but the shadow only of representation, which can never produce proper information in the Legislature, or inspire confidence in the people; the laws will therefore be generally made by men little concerned in, and unacquainted with, their effects and consequences."

Answer.

This is a mere matter of calculation. It is said the weight of this objection was in a great measure removed by altering the number of 40000 to 30000 constituents. To shew the discontented nature of man, some have objected to the number of representatives as being too large. I leave to every man's judgment whether the number is not sufficiently respectable, and whether if that number be sufficient it would have been right, in the very infancy of this government, to burthen the people with a great additional expence to answer no good purpose.

IIId. Objection.

"The Senate have the power of altering all money bills, and of originating appropriations of money, and the salaries of the officers of their own appointment, in conjunction with the President of the United States; although they are not the Representatives of the people, or amenable to them. These, with their other great powers (viz. their powers in the appointment of ambassadors and all public officers, in making treaties, and in trying all impeachments), their influence upon and connection with the Supreme Executive from these causes; their duration of office, and their being a constant existent body almost continually sitting, joined with their being one complete branch of the Legislature, will destroy any balance in the government, and enable them to accomplish what usurpations they please upon the rights and liberties of the people."

Answer.

This objection respecting the dangerous power of the Senate, is of that kind which may give rise to a great deal of gloomy prediction, without any solid foundation. An imagination indulging itself in chimerical fears, upon the disappointment of a favourite plan may point out danger arising from any system of government whatever, even if Angels were to have the administration of it; since I presume, none but the Supreme Being himself is altogether perfect, and of course every other species of beings may abuse any delegated portion of power. This sort of visionary scepticism therefore will lead us to this alternative, either to have no government at all, or to form the best system we can, making allowance for human imperfection. In my opinion, the fears as to the power of the Senate are altogether groundless, as to any probability of their being either able or willing to do any important mischief. My reasons are–1. Because tho' they are not immediately to represent the people, yet they are to represent the Representatives of the people, who are annually chosen, and it is therefore probable, the most popular, or confidential persons in each State, will be elected members of the Senate.

2. Because one third of the Senate are to be chosen as often as the immediate Representatives of the people, and as the President can act in no case from which any great danger can be apprehended without the concurrence of two-thirds, let us think ever so ill of the designs of the President, and the danger of a combination of power among a standing body generally associated with him, unless we suppose every one of them to be base and infamous (a supposition, thank God, bad as human nature is, not within the verge of the slightest probability), we have reason to believe that the one third newly introduced every second year, will bring with them from the immediate body of the people a sufficient portion of patriotism and independence to check any exorbitant designs of the rest.

3. Because in their legislative capacity they can do nothing without the concurrence of the House of Representatives, and we need look no further than England for a clear proof of the amazing consequence which Representatives of the people bear in a free government. There the King (who is hereditary, and therefore not so immediately interested, according to narrow views of interest which commonly govern

Kings, to consult the welfare of his people) has the appointment to almost every office in the government, many of which are of high dignity and great pecuniary value; has the creation of as many Peers as he pleases, is not restricted from bestowing places on the members of both Houses of Parliament, and has a direct negative on all bills, besides the power of dissolving the Parliament at his pleasure. In theory would not any one say this power was enormous enough to destroy any balance in the Constitution? Yet what does the history of that country tell us?–That so great is the natural power of the House of Commons (tho' a very imperfect representation of the people, and a large proportion of them actually purchasing their seats), that ever since the Revolution the Crown has continually aimed to corrupt them by the disposal of places and pensions; that without their hearty concurrence it found all the wheels of government perpetually clogged; and, that notwithstanding this, in great critical emergencies, the members have broke through the trammels of power and interest, and, by speaking the sense of the people (tho' so imperfectly representing them) either forced an alteration of measures, or made it necessary for the Crown to dissolve them. If their power under these circumstances, is so great, what would it be if their Representation was perfect and their members could hold no appointments, and at the same time had a security for their seats? The danger of a destruction of the balance would be perhaps on the popular side, notwithstanding the hereditary tenure and weighty prerogatives of the Crown, and the permanent station and great wealth and consequence of the Lords. Our Representatives therefore, being an adequate and fair representation of the people, and they being expressly excluded from the possession of any places, and not holding their existence upon any precarious tenure must have vast influence; and considering that in every popular government the danger of faction is often very serious and alarming, if such a danger could not be checked in its instant operation by some other power more independent of the immediate passions of the people, and capable therefore of thinking with more coolness, the government might be destroyed by a momentary impulse of passion, which the very members who indulged it might for ever afterwards in vain deplore. The institution of the Senate seems well calculated to answer this salutary purpose. Excluded as they are from places themselves, they appear to be as much above the danger of personal temptation as they can be. They have no permanent interest as a body to detach them from the general welfare, since six years is the utmost period of their existence, unless their respective legislatures are sufficiently pleased with their conduct to re-elect them. This power of re-election is itself a great check upon abuse, because if they have ambition to continue members of the Senate, they can only gratify this ambition by acting agreeably to the opinion of their constituents. The House of Representatives, as immediately representing the people, are to originate all money bills. This I think extremely right, and it is certainly a very capital acquisition to the popular Representative. But what harm can arise from the Senate, who are nearly a popular Representative also, proposing amendments when those amendments must be concurred with by the original proposers? The wisdom of the Senate may sometimes point out amendments, the propriety of which the other House may be very sensible of, though they had not occurred to themselves. There is no great danger of any body of men suffering by too eager an adoption of any amendment proposed to any system of their own. The probability is stronger of their being too tenacious of their original opinion, however erroneous, than of their profiting by the wise information of any other persons whatever. Human nature is so constituted, and therefore I think we may safely confide in the admission of a free intercourse of opinion on the detail of business, as well as to taxation as to other points.

Our House of Representatives surely could not have such reason to dread the power of a Senate circumstanced as ours must be, as the House of Commons in England the permanent authority of the Peers, and therefore a jealousy which may be well grounded in the one case, would be entirely ill directed in the other. For similar reasons, I dread not any power of originating appropriations of money as mentioned in the objection. While the concurrence of the other House must be had, and as that must necessarily be the most weighty in the government, I think no danger is to be apprehended. The Senate has no such authority as to awe or influence the House of Representatives, and it will be as necessary for one as for the other that proper active measures should be pursued. And in regard to appropriations of money, occasions for such appropriations may, on account of their concurrence with the executive power, occur to the Senate, which would not to the House of Representatives; and therefore if the Senate were precluded from laying any such proposals before the House of Representatives, the government might be embarrassed, and it ought ever to be remembered, that in our views of distant and chimerical dangers we ought not to hazard our very existence as a people, by proposing such restrictions as may prevent the exertion of any necessary power.–The power of the Senate in the appointment of Ambassadors, &c. is designed as a check upon the President.–They must be appointed in some manner. If the appointment was by the President alone, or by the President and a Privy Council (Mr. Mason's favourite plan), an objection to such a system would have appeared much more plausible. It would have been said that this was approaching too much towards Monarchical power, and if this new Privy Council had been like all I have ever heard of it would have afforded little security against an abuse of power in the President. It ought to be shewn by reason and probability (not bold assertion) how this concurrence of power with the President can make the Senate so dangerous. It is as good an argument to say that it will not, as that it will. The power of making treaties is so important, that it would have been highly dangerous to vest it in the Executive alone, and would have been the subject of much greater clamour. From the nature of the thing, it could not be vested in the popular Representative. It must therefore have been provided for, with the Senate's concurrence, or the concurrence of a Privy Council (a thing which I believe nobody has been mad enough to propose), or the power, the greatest Monarchical power that can be exercised, must have been vested in a manner that would have excited universal indignation, in the President alone. As to the power of trying impeachments, let Mr. Mason shew where this power could more properly have been placed. It is a necessary power in every free government, since even the Judges of the Supreme Court of Judicature themselves may require a trial, and other public officers might have too much influence before an ordinary and common Court. And what probability is there that such a Court acting in so solemn a manner, should abuse its power (especially as it is wisely provided that their sentences shall extend only to removal from office and incapacitation) more than any other Court? The argument as to the possible abuse of power, as I have before suggested, will reach all delegation of power whatever, since all power may be abused where fallible beings are to execute it; but we must take as much caution as we can, being careful at the same time not to be too wise to do any thing at all. The bold assertions at the end of this objection are mere declamation, and till some reason is assigned for them, I shall take the liberty to rely upon the reasons I have stated above, as affording a belief that the popular Representative must for ever be the most weighty in this government, and of course that apprehensions of danger from such a Senate are altogether ill founded.

(To be continued.)

Federalist No. 59 by Alexander Hamilton

Editor's Introduction:

Opponents of the Constitution regularly argued that the provision allowing the general government to alter the "times, places, and manner" of holding elections ensured that the States would never have control of federal elections. In their mind, this amounted to a federal veto of State elections laws. In *Federalist* No. 59, Hamilton reasoned that this power would only be used in extreme circumstances, namely if a State refused to hold an election for either a member of the House of Representatives or for the United States Senate. The general government had to have a power of preservation, and this portion of the Constitution provided the Congress the ability to maintain membership even if the States balked at sending members to the federal city. Hamilton relied on a "power of preservation" argument in several instances during his defense of the Constitution, most importantly in describing the powers of the executive branch.

Federalist No. 59

February 22, 1788

By Alexander Hamilton of New York

To the People of the State of New York:

THE natural order of the subject leads us to consider, in this place, that provision of the Constitution which authorizes the national legislature to regulate, in the last resort, the election of its own members. It is in these words: "The TIMES, PLACES, and MANNER of holding elections for senators and representatives shall be prescribed in each State by the legislature thereof; but the Congress may, at any time, by law, make or alter SUCH REGULATIONS, except as to the PLACES of choosing senators. "(a) This provision has not only been declaimed against by those who condemn the Constitution in the gross, but it has been censured by those who have objected with less latitude and greater moderation; and, in one instance it has been thought exceptionable by a gentleman who has declared himself the advocate of every other part of the system. I am greatly mistaken, notwithstanding, if there be any article in the whole plan more completely defensible than this. Its propriety rests upon the evidence of this plain proposition, that EVERY GOVERNMENT OUGHT TO CONTAIN IN ITSELF THE MEANS OF ITS OWN PRESERVATION. Every just reasoner will, at first sight, approve an adherence to this rule, in the work of the convention; and will disapprove every deviation from it which may not appear to have been dictated by the necessity of incorporating into the work some particular ingredient, with which a rigid conformity to the rule was incompatible. Even in this case, though he may acquiesce in the necessity, yet he will not cease to regard and to regret a departure from so fundamental a principle, as a portion of imperfection in the system which may prove the seed of future weakness, and perhaps anarchy.

It will not be alleged, that an election law could have been framed and inserted in the Constitution, which would have been always applicable to every probable change in the situation of the country;

and it will therefore not be denied, that a discretionary power over elections ought to exist somewhere. It will, I presume, be as readily conceded, that there were only three ways in which this power could have been reasonably modified and disposed: that it must either have been lodged wholly in the national legislature, or wholly in the State legislatures, or primarily in the latter and ultimately in the former. The last mode has, with reason, been preferred by the convention. They have submitted the regulation of elections for the federal government, in the first instance, to the local administrations; which, in ordinary cases, and when no improper views prevail, may be both more convenient and more satisfactory; but they have reserved to the national authority a right to interpose, whenever extraordinary circumstances might render that interposition necessary to its safety. Nothing can be more evident, than that an exclusive power of regulating elections for the national government, in the hands of the State legislatures, would leave the existence of the Union entirely at their mercy. They could at any moment annihilate it, by neglecting to provide for the choice of persons to administer its affairs. It is to little purpose to say, that a neglect or omission of this kind would not be likely to take place. The constitutional possibility of the thing, without an equivalent for the risk, is an unanswerable objection. Nor has any satisfactory reason been yet assigned for incurring that risk. The extravagant surmises of a distempered jealousy can never be dignified with that character.

If we are in a humor to presume abuses of power, it is as fair to presume them on the part of the State governments as on the part of the general government. And as it is more consonant to the rules of a just theory, to trust the Union with the care of its own existence, than to transfer that care to any other hands, if abuses of power are to be hazarded on the one side or on the other, it is more rational to hazard them where the power would naturally be placed, than where it would unnaturally be placed. Suppose an article had been introduced into the Constitution, empowering the United States to regulate the elections for the particular States, would any man have hesitated to condemn it, both as an unwarrantable transposition of power, and as a premeditated engine for the destruction of the State governments? The violation of principle, in this case, would have required no comment; and, to an unbiased observer, it will not be less apparent in the project of subjecting the existence of the national government, in a similar respect, to the pleasure of the State governments. An impartial view of the matter cannot fail to result in a conviction, that each, as far as possible, ought to depend on itself for its own preservation.

As an objection to this position, it may be remarked that the constitution of the national Senate would involve, in its full extent, the danger which it is suggested might flow from an exclusive power in the State legislatures to regulate the federal elections. It may be alleged, that by declining the appointment of Senators, they might at any time give a fatal blow to the Union; and from this it may be inferred, that as its existence would be thus rendered dependent upon them in so essential a point, there can be no objection to intrusting them with it in the particular case under consideration. The interest of each State, it may be added, to maintain its representation in the national councils, would be a complete security against an abuse of the trust. This argument, though specious, will not, upon examination, be found solid. It is certainly true that the State legislatures, by forbearing the appointment of senators, may destroy the national government. But it will not follow that, because they have a power to do this in one instance, they ought to have it in every other. There are cases in which the pernicious tendency of such a power may be far more decisive, without any motive equally cogent with that which must have regulated the conduct of the convention in respect to the formation of the Senate, to recommend their admission into the system.

So far as that construction may expose the Union to the possibility of injury from the State legislatures, it is an evil; but it is an evil which could not have been avoided without excluding the States, in their political capacities, wholly from a place in the organization of the national government. If this had been done, it would doubtless have been interpreted into an entire dereliction of the federal principle; and would certainly have deprived the State governments of that absolute safeguard which they will enjoy under this provision. But however wise it may have been to have submitted in this instance to an inconvenience, for the attainment of a necessary advantage or a greater good, no inference can be drawn from thence to favor an accumulation of the evil, where no necessity urges, nor any greater good invites. It may be easily discerned also that the national government would run a much greater risk from a power in the State legislatures over the elections of its House of Representatives, than from their power of appointing the members of its Senate. The senators are to be chosen for the period of six years; there is to be a rotation, by which the seats of a third part of them are to be vacated and replenished every two years; and no State is to be entitled to more than two senators; a quorum of the body is to consist of sixteen members.

The joint result of these circumstances would be, that a temporary combination of a few States to intermit the appointment of senators, could neither annul the existence nor impair the activity of the body; and it is not from a general and permanent combination of the States that we can have any thing to fear. The first might proceed from sinister designs in the leading members of a few of the State legislatures; the last would suppose a fixed and rooted disaffection in the great body of the people, which will either never exist at all, or will, in all probability, proceed from an experience of the inaptitude of the general government to the advancement of their happiness in which event no good citizen could desire its continuance. But with regard to the federal House of Representatives, there is intended to be a general election of members once in two years. If the State legislatures were to be invested with an exclusive power of regulating these elections, every period of making them would be a delicate crisis in the national situation, which might issue in a dissolution of the Union, if the leaders of a few of the most important States should have entered into a previous conspiracy to prevent an election. I shall not deny, that there is a degree of weight in the observation, that the interests of each State, to be represented in the federal councils, will be a security against the abuse of a power over its elections in the hands of the State legislatures. But the security will not be considered as complete, by those who attend to the force of an obvious distinction between the interest of the people in the public felicity, and the interest of their local rulers in the power and consequence of their offices.

The people of America may be warmly attached to the government of the Union, at times when the particular rulers of particular States, stimulated by the natural rivalship of power, and by the hopes of personal aggrandizement, and supported by a strong faction in each of those States, may be in a very opposite temper. This diversity of sentiment between a majority of the people, and the individuals who have the greatest credit in their councils, is exemplified in some of the States at the present moment, on the present question. The scheme of separate confederacies, which will always nultiply the chances of ambition, will be a never failing bait to all such influential characters in the State administrations as are capable of preferring their own emolument and advancement to the public weal. With so effectual a weapon in their hands as the exclusive power of regulating elections for the national government, a combination of a few such men, in a few of the most considerable States, where the temptation will always be the strongest, might accomplish the destruction of the Union, by seizing the opportunity of some casual dissatisfaction among the people (and which perhaps they may themselves have excited), to discontinue the choice of members for the federal House of Representatives. It ought never to be forgotten, that a firm union of this country, under an efficient government, will probably be an increasing object of jealousy to more than one nation of Europe; and that enterprises to subvert it will sometimes originate in the intrigues of foreign powers, and will seldom fail to be patronized and abetted by some of them. Its preservation, therefore ought in no case that can be avoided, to be committed to the guardianship of any but those whose situation will uniformly beget an immediate interest in the faithful and vigilant performance of the trust.

a 1st clause, 4th section, of the 1st article.

Federalist No. 60 by Alexander Hamilton

Editor's Introduction:

This essay in the *Federalist* is important for two reasons: First, Hamilton attempted to explain that the States still had control over elections and that unimpeded federal oversight would be a danger for the American federal republic, and second, the Union was too diverse to be forced into a situation where one faction, be it political or economic, could usurp power from other groups. States had to be able to control their own elections because of the sheer diversity of the Union. The merchant class could never overwhelm the agricultural class or vice versa because the Congress provided sufficient checks to prevent this from happening namely through the Senate. But Hamilton's discussion of the economic benefits of the Constitution gave credence to the progressive "economic" interpretation of the Constitution championed by Charles Beard in the early twentieth century.

Federalist No. 60

February 23, 1788

By Alexander Hamilton of New York

To the People of the State of New York:

WE HAVE seen, that an uncontrollable power over the elections to the federal government could not, without hazard, be committed to the State legislatures. Let us now see, what would be the danger on the other side; that is, from confiding the ultimate right of regulating its own elections to the Union itself. It is not pretended, that this right would ever be used for the exclusion of any State from its share in the representation. The interest of all would, in this respect at least, be the security of all. But it is alleged, that it might be employed in such a manner as to promote the election of some favorite class of men in exclusion of others, by confining the places of election to particular districts, and rendering it impracticable to the citizens at large to partake in the choice. Of all chimerical suppositions, this seems to be the most chimerical. On the one hand, no rational calculation of probabilities would lead us to imagine that the disposition which a conduct so violent and extraordinary would imply, could ever find its way into the national councils; and on the other, it may be concluded with certainty, that if so improper a spirit should ever gain admittance into them, it would display itself in a form altogether different and far more decisive.

The improbability of the attempt may be satisfactorily inferred from this single reflection, that it could never be made without causing an immediate revolt of the great body of the people, headed and directed by the State governments. It is not difficult to conceive that this characteristic right of freedom may, in certain turbulent and factious seasons, be violated, in respect to a particular class of citizens, by a victorious and overbearing majority; but that so fundamental a privilege, in a country so situated and enlightened, should be invaded to the prejudice of the great mass of the people, by the deliberate policy of the government, without occasioning a popular revolution, is altogether inconceivable and incredible.

In addition to this general reflection, there are considerations of a more precise nature, which forbid all apprehension on the subject. The dissimilarity in the ingredients which will compose the national government, and still more in the manner in which they will be brought into action in its various branches, must form a powerful obstacle to a concert of views in any partial scheme of elections. There is sufficient diversity in the state of property, in the genius, manners, and habits of the people of the different parts of the Union, to occasion a material diversity of disposition in their representatives towards the different ranks and conditions in society. And though an intimate intercourse under the same government will promote a gradual assimilation in some of these respects, yet there are causes, as well physical as moral, which may, in a greater or less degree, permanently nourish different propensities and inclinations in this respect. But the circumstance which will be likely to have the greatest influence in the matter, will be the dissimilar modes of constituting the several component parts of the government. The House of Representatives being to be elected immediately by the people, the Senate by the State legislatures, the President by electors chosen for that purpose by the people, there would be little probability of a common interest to cement these different branches in a predilection for any particular class of electors.

As to the Senate, it is impossible that any regulation of "time and manner," which is all that is proposed to be submitted to the national government in respect to that body, can affect the spirit which will direct the choice of its members. The collective sense of the State legislatures can never be influenced by extraneous circumstances of that sort; a consideration which alone ought to satisfy us that the discrimination apprehended would never be attempted. For what inducement could the Senate have to concur in a preference in which itself would not be included? Or to what purpose would it be established, in reference to one branch of the legislature, if it could not be extended to the other? The composition of the one would in this case counteract that of the other. And we can never suppose that it would embrace the appointments to the Senate, unless we can at the same time suppose the voluntary co-operation of the State legislatures. If we make the latter supposition, it then becomes immaterial where the power in question is placed whether in their hands or in those of the Union.

But what is to be the object of this capricious partiality in the national councils? Is it to be exercised in a discrimination between the different departments of industry, or between the different kinds of property, or between the different degrees of property? Will it lean in favor of the landed interest, or the moneyed interest, or the mercantile interest, or the manufacturing interest? Or, to speak in the fashionable language of the adversaries to the Constitution, will it court the elevation of "the wealthy and the well-born," to the exclusion and debasement of all the rest of the society?

If this partiality is to be exerted in favor of those who are concerned in any particular description of industry or property, I presume it will readily be admitted, that the competition for it will lie between landed men and merchants. And I scruple not to affirm, that it is infinitely less likely that either of them should gain an ascendant in the national councils, than that the one or the other of them should predominate in all the local councils. The inference will be, that a conduct tending to give an undue preference to either is much less to be dreaded from the former than from the latter.

The several States are in various degrees addicted to agriculture and commerce. In most, if not all of them, agriculture is predominant. In a few of them, however, commerce nearly divides its empire, and in most of them has a considerable share of influence. In proportion as either prevails, it will be conveyed into the national representation; and for the very reason, that this will be an emanation from a greater variety of interests, and in much more various proportions, than are to be found in any single State, it will be much less apt to espouse either of them with a decided partiality, than the representation of any single State.

In a country consisting chiefly of the cultivators of land, where the rules of an equal representation obtain, the landed interest must, upon the whole, preponderate in the government. As long as this interest prevails in most of the State legislatures, so long it must maintain a correspondent superiority in the national Senate, which will generally be a faithful copy of the majorities of those assemblies. It cannot therefore be presumed, that a sacrifice of the landed to the mercantile class will ever be a favorite object of this branch of the federal legislature. In applying thus particularly to the Senate a general observation suggested by the situation of the country, I am governed by the consideration, that the credulous votaries of State power cannot, upon their own principles, suspect, that the State legislatures would be warped from their duty by any external influence. But in reality the same situation must have the same effect, in the primative composition at least of the federal House of Representatives: an improper bias towards the mercantile class is as little to be expected from this quarter as from the other.

In order, perhaps, to give countenance to the objection at any rate, it may be asked, is there not danger of an opposite bias in the national government, which may dispose it to endeavor to secure a monopoly of the federal administration to the landed class? As there is little likelihood that the supposition of such a bias will have any terrors for those who would be immediately injured by it, a labored answer to this question will be dispensed with. It will be sufficient to remark, first, that for the reasons elsewhere assigned, it is less likely that any decided partiality should prevail in the councils of the Union than in those of any of its members. Secondly, that there would be no temptation to violate the Constitution in favor of the landed class, because that class would, in the natural course of things, enjoy as great a preponderancy as itself could desire. And thirdly, that men accustomed to investigate the sources of public prosperity upon a large scale, must be too well convinced of the utility of commerce, to be inclined to inflict upon it so deep a wound as would result from the entire exclusion of those who would best understand its interest from a share in the management of them. The importance of commerce, in the view of revenue alone, must effectually guard it against the enmity of a body which would be continually importuned in its favor, by the urgent calls of public necessity.

In the rather consult brevity in discussing the probability of a preference founded upon a discrimination between the different kinds of industry and property, because, as far as I understand the meaning of the objectors, they contemplate a discrimination of another kind. They appear to have in view, as the objects of the preference with which they endeavor to alarm us, those whom they designate by the description of "the wealthy and the well-born." These, it seems, are to be exalted to an odious pre-eminence over the rest of their fellow-citizens. At one time, however, their elevation is to be a necessary consequence of the smallness of the representative body; at another time it is to be effected by depriving the people at large of the opportunity of exercising their right of suffrage in the choice of that body.

But upon what principle is the discrimination of the places of election to be made, in order to answer the purpose of the meditated preference? Are "the wealthy and the well-born," as they are called, confined to particular spots in the several States? Have they, by some miraculous instinct or foresight, set apart in each of them a common place of residence? Are they only to be met with in the towns or cities?

Or are they, on the contrary, scattered over the face of the country as avarice or chance may have happened to cast their own lot or that of their predecessors? If the latter is the case, (as every intelligent man knows it to be,(a)) is it not evident that the policy of confining the places of election to particular districts would be as subversive of its own aim as it would be exceptionable on every other account? The truth is, that there is no method of securing to the rich the preference apprehended, but by prescribing qualifications of property either for those who may elect or be elected. But this forms no part of the power to be conferred upon the national government. Its authority would be expressly restricted to the regulation of the TIMES, the PLACES, the MANNER of elections. The qualifications of the persons who may choose or be chosen, as has been remarked upon other occasions, are defined and fixed in the Constitution, and are unalterable by the legislature.

Let it, however, be admitted, for argument sake, that the expedient suggested might be successful; and let it at the same time be equally taken for granted that all the scruples which a sense of duty or an apprehension of the danger of the experiment might inspire, were overcome in the breasts of the national rulers, still I imagine it will hardly be pretended that they could ever hope to carry such an enterprise into execution without the aid of a military force sufficient to subdue the resistance of the great body of the people. The improbability of the existence of a force equal to that object has been discussed and demonstrated in different parts of these papers; but that the futility of the objection under consideration may appear in the strongest light, it shall be conceded for a moment that such a force might exist, and the national government shall be supposed to be in the actual possession of it. What will be the conclusion? With a disposition to invade the essential rights of the community, and with the means of gratifying that disposition, is it presumable that the persons who were actuated by it would amuse themselves in the ridiculous task of fabricating election laws for securing a preference to a favorite class of men? Would they not be likely to prefer a conduct better adapted to their own immediate aggrandizement? Would they not rather boldly resolve to perpetuate themselves in office by one decisive act of usurpation, than to trust to precarious expedients which, in spite of all the precautions that might accompany them, might terminate in the dismission, disgrace, and ruin of their authors? Would they not fear that citizens, not less tenacious than conscious of their rights, would flock from the remote extremes of their respective States to the places of election, to overthrow their tyrants, and to substitute men who would be disposed to avenge the violated majesty of the people?

(a) Particularly in the Southern States and in this State.

Speeches at Edenton, N.C. by Hugh Williamson

Editor's Introduction:

Hugh Williamson was born in Pennsylvania in 1735, the son of a prominent merchant on the frontier of the State. He was sickly as a child, and so his family decided to invest in his education. He was graduated from the University of Pennsylvania first in his class in 1757. He decided to study theology at Princeton and eventually moved to Connecticut as a minister. Theological disputes with the New England clergy led him to abandon the ministry. He returned to Philadelphia, obtained a master's degree and was hired as a mathematics professor at his alma matter. He eventually took up the study of medicine and received a degree from the University of Utrecht in the Netherlands.

Williamson was gaining an international reputation in the 1770s, He was a highly respected man of science and was invited to the American Philosophical Society. During this time, Williamson became deeply interested in politics and actively supported the patriot cause. He witnessed the Boston Tea Party and was called to testify in London before the Privy Council on the American situation. He informed the Council that punitive measures would result in open rebellion and that the Parliament would do well to extend the rights of Englishman to their brothers across the Atlantic. His rock-ribbed advocacy for American rights and his interest in science and mathematics caught the attention of Benjamin Franklin. The two became friends and worked in concert to press for American interests in England. He was in the Netherlands publishing pamphlets in support the American cause when he learned that the colonies declared their independence. He rushed home to Philadelphia and offered his services as a doctor for the Continental Army. He was denied, and so he traveled to North Carolina where he opened a medical practice and helped smuggle medicine and other medical items through the British blockade. He was eventually appointed Surgeon General for the North Carolina militia, a position he held throughout the War.

Williamson endured the same hardships as the front-line soldiers during the difficult years of 1779 and 1780. His advice on diet and sanitation prevented widespread disease during the conflict, and as a result Williamson became one of the most respected men in his State.

He was sent to the Continental Congress and later attended the Annapolis Convention of 1786. Williamson was convinced that a stronger central government was necessary to shore up American finances. He represented North Carolina at the Philadelphia Convention in 1787 and lodged with Hamilton and Madison during the summer. His performance at the Convention included a steadfast defense of State powers and a verbal sparring match with New England delegates over the status of slaves for representation in the House. Williamson called them "rational beings" and thought they should be counted as one whole person toward representation. New England delegates disagreed.

He signed the Constitution and argued for its ratification, even before leaving Philadelphia. His "Letters of Sylvius" argued the new document would save the Union and preserve good government for both North Carolina and the federal republic. Williamson missed the first North Carolina ratifying convention due to his service in the Continental Congress but attended the second and voted for ratification. He was sent to Congress for a couple of terms. Williamson retired to New York City in 1793 and died over twenty years later. He spent the last years of his life studying medicine and science.

The following speeches echo much of what he said in his Letters of Sylvius. Williamson reassured his audience that the Constitution would strengthen the American economy but would not destroy the State courts or the federal structure. He insisted that, "The several States reserve every power that can be exercised for the particular use and comfort of the State. They do not yield a single power which is not purely of a national concern; nor do they yield a single power which is not absolutely necessary to the safety and prosperity of the nation, nor one that could be employed to any effect in the hands of particular States." These arguments were common among proponents of the document and form the backbone of originalism.

Speeches at Edenton, N.C.

February 25-27, 1788

By Hugh Williamson of North Carolina

[25 February] *The following Remarks on the New Plan of Government are handed us as the substance of Doctor* WILLIAMSON's *Address to the Freemen of Edenton and the County of Chowan, in North-Carolina, when assembled to instruct their Representatives.*

When Gentlemen are pleased to complain, that little power is left in the hands of the separate States; they should be advised to cast an eye upon the large code of laws, which have passed in this State since the peace. Let them consider how few of those laws have been framed, for the general benefit of the Nation. Nine out of ten of them, are domestic; calculated for the sole use of this State, or of particular citizens. There must still be use for such laws, though you should enable the Congress to collect a revenue for National purposes, and the collection of that revenue includes the chief of the new powers, which are now to be committed to the Congress.

Hitherto you have delegated certain powers to the Congress, and other powers to the Assemblies of the States. The portion that you have delegated to Congress is found to have been useless, because it is too small, and the powers that are committed to the assemblies of the several States, are also found to be absolutely ineffectual for national purposes, because they can never be so managed as to operate in concert. Of what use is that small portion of reserved power? It neither makes you respectable nor powerful. The consequence of such reservation is national contempt abroad, and a state of dangerous weakness at home. What avails the claim of power, which appears to be nothing better than the empty whistling of a name? The Congress will be chosen by yourselves, as your Members of Assembly are. They will be creatures of your hands, and subject to your advice. Protected and cherished by the small addition of power which you shall put into their hands, you may become a great and respectable nation.

[26 February] It is complained that the powers of the national Judiciary are too extensive. This objection appears to have the greatest weight in the eyes of gentlemen who have not carefully compared the powers which are to be delegated with those that had been formerly delegated to Congress. The powers that are now to be committed to the national Legislature, as they are detailed in the 8th section of the first article, have already been chiefly delegated to the Congress under one form or another, except those which are contained in the first paragraph of that section. And the objects that are now to be submitted to the Supreme Judiciary, or to the Inferior Courts, are those which naturally arise from the constitutional laws of Congress. If there is a single new case that can be exceptionable, it is that between a foreigner and a citizen, or that between the citizens of different States. These cases may come up by appeal. It is provided in this system that there shall be no fraudulent tender in the payments of debts. Foreigners, with whom we have treaties, will trust our citizens on the faith of this engagement. And the citizens of different States will do the same. If the Congress had a negative on the laws of the several States, they would certainly prevent all such laws as might endanger the honor or peace of the nation, by making a tender of base money; but they have no such power, and it is at least possible that some State may be found in this Union, disposed to break the Constitution, and abolish private debts by such tenders. In these cases the Courts of the offending States would probably decide according to its own laws. The foreigner would complain; and the nation might be involved in war for the support of such dishonest measures. Is it not better to have a Court of Appeals in which the Judges can only be determined by the laws of the nation? This Court is equally to be desired by the citizens of different States. But we are told that justice will be delayed, and the poor will be drawn away by the rich to a distant Court. The authors of this remark have not fully considered the question, else they must have recollected that the poor of this country have little to do with foreigners, or with the citizens of distant States. They do not consider that there may be an Inferior Court in every State; nor have they recollected that the appeals being *with such exceptions*, and *under such regulations* as Congress shall make, will never be permitted for trifling sums, or under trivial pretences, unless we can suppose that the national Legislature shall be composed of knaves and fools.

The line that separates the powers of the national Legislature from those of the several States is clearly drawn. The several States reserve every power that can be exercised for the particular use and comfort of the State. They do not yield a single power which is not purely of a national concern; nor do they yield a single power which is not absolutely necessary to the safety and prosperity of the nation, nor one that could be employed to any effect in the hands of particular States. The powers of Judiciary naturally arise from those of the Legislature. Questions that are of a national concern, and those cases which are determinable by the general laws of the nation, are to be referred to the national Judiciary, but they have not any thing to do with a single case either civil or criminal, which respects the private and particular concerns of a State or its citizens.

The possibility of keeping regular troops in the public service has been urged as another objection against the new Constitution. It is very remarkable that the same objection has not been made against the original Confederation, in which the same grievance obtained without the same guards. It is now provided, that no appropriation of money for the use of the army shall be for a longer time than two years. Provision is also made for having a powerful militia, in which case there never can be occasion for many regular troops. It has been objected in some of the Southern States, that the Congress, by a majority of votes, is to have the power to regulate trade. It is universally admitted that Congress ought to have this power, else our commerce, which is nearly ruined, can never be restored; but some gentlemen think that the concurrence of two thirds of the votes in Congress should have been required. By the sundry regulations of commerce, it will be in the power of Government not only to collect a vast revenue for the general benefit of the nation, but to secure the carrying trade in the hands of citizens in preference to strangers. It has been alledged that there are few ships belonging to the Southern States, and that the price of freight must rise in consequence of our excluding many foreign vessels: but when we have not vessels of our own, it is certainly proper that we should hire those of citizens in preference to strangers; for our revenue is promoted and the nation is strengthened by the profits that remain in the hands of citizens; we are injured by throwing it into the hands of strangers; and though the price of freight should rise for two or three years, this advantage is fully due to our brethren in the Eastern and middle States, who, with great and exemplary candor, have given us equal advantages in return. A small encrease in the price of freight would operate greatly in favor of the Southern States: it would promote the spirit of ship building; it would promote a nursery for native seamen, and would afford support to the poor who live near the sea coast; it would encrease the value of their lands, and at the same time it would reduce their taxes. It has finally been objected that the several States are not permitted to tax their exports for the benefit of their particular Treasuries. This strange objection has been occasionally repeated by citizens of this State. They must have transplanted it from another State, for it could not have been the growth of North-Carolina. Such have been the objections against the new Constitution.

Whilst the honest patriot, who guards with a jealous eye the liberties of his country, and apprehends danger under every form: the placeman in every State, who fears lest his office should pass into other hands; the idle, the factious, and the dishonest, who live by plunder or speculation on the miseries of their country; while these, assisted by a numerous body of secret enemies, who never have been reconciled to our Independence, are seeking for objections to this Constitution; it is a remarkable circumstance, and a very high encomium on the plan, that nothing more plausible has been offered against it; for it is an easy matter to find faults.

Let us turn our eyes to a more fruitful subject; let us consider the present condition of the United States, and the particular benefits that North Carolina must reap by the proposed form of Government. Without money, no Government can be supported; and Congress can raise no money under the present Constitution: They have not the power to make commercial treaties, because they cannot preserve them when made. Hence it is, that we are the prey of every nation: We are indulged in such foreign commerce, as must be hurtful to us: We are prohibited from that which might be profitable, and we are accordingly told, that on the last two years, the Thirteen States have hardly paid into the Treasury, as much as should have been paid by a single State. Intestine commotions in some of the States: Paper Money in others, a want of inclination in some, and a general suspicion throughout the Union, that the burthen is unequally laid; added to the general loss of trade have produced a general bankruptcy, and loss of honor. We have borrowed money of Spain-she demands the principal, but we cannot pay the interest. It is a circumstance perfectly humiliating, that we should remain under obligations to that nation: We are Considerably indebted to France but she is too generous to insist upon what she knows we cannot pay, either the principal or interest. In the hour of our distress, we borrowed money in Holland; not from the Government, but from private citizens. Those who are called the Patriots were our friends, and they are oppressed in their turn by hosts of enemies: They will soon have need of money: At this hour we are not able to pay the interests of their loan. What is to be done? Will you borrow money again from other citizens of that oppressed Republic, to pay the interest of what you borrowed from their brethren? This would be a painful expedient, but our want of

Government may render it necessary. You have two or three Ministers abroad; they must soon return home, for they cannot be supported. You have four or five hundred troops scattered along the Ohio to protect the frontier inhabitants, and give some value to your lands; those troops are ill paid, and in a fair way for being disbanded. There is hardly a circumstance remaining; hardly one external mark by which you can deserve to be called a nation. You are not in a condition to resist the most contemptible enemy. What is there to prevent an Algerine Pirate from landing on your coast, and carrying your citizens into slavery? You have not a single sloop of war. Does one of the States attempt to raise a little money by imposts or other commercial regu lations.–A neighboring State immediately alters her laws and defeats the revenue, by throwing the trade into a different channel. Instead of supporting or assisting, we are uniformly taking the advantage of one another. Such an assemblage of people are not a nation. Like a dark cloud, without cohesion or firmness, we are ready to be torn asunder and scattered abroad by every breeze of external violence, or internal commotion.

[27 February] Is there a man in this State who believes it possible for us to continue under such a Government?–Let us suppose but for a minute, that such a measure should be attempted.–Let us suppose that the several States shall be required and obliged to pay their several quotas according to the original plan. You know that North-Carolina, on the last four years, has not paid one dollar into the Treasury for eight dollars that she ought to have paid. We must encrease our taxes exceedingly, and those taxes must be of the most grievous kind; they must be taxes on lands and heads; taxes that cannot fail to grind the face of the poor; for it is clear that we can raise little by imports and exports. Some foreign goods are imported by water from the Northern States, such goods pay a duty for the benefit of those States, which is seldom drawn back; this operates as a tax upon our citizens. On this side, Virginia promotes her revenue to the amount of 25,000 dollars every year, by a tax on our tobacco that she exports: South-Carolina on the other side, may avail herself of similar opportunities. Two thirds of the foreign goods that are consumed in this State are imported by land from Virginia or South-Carolina; such goods pay a certain impost for the benefit of the importing States, but our Treasury is not profited by this commerce. By such means our citizens are taxed more than one hundred thousand dollars every year, but the State does not receive credit for a shilling of that money. Like a patient that is bleeding at both arms, North-Carolina must soon expire under such wasteful operations. Unless I am greatly mistaken, we have seen enough of the State of the Union, and of North-Carolina in particular, to be assured that another form of Government is become necessary. Is the form now proposed well calculated to give relief? To this, we must answer in the affirmative. All foreign goods that shall be imported into these States, are to pay a duty for the use of the nation. All the States will be on a footing, whether they have bad ports or good ones. No duties will be laid on exports; hence the planter will receive the true value of his produce, wherever it may be shipped. If excises are laid on wine, spirits, or other luxuries, they must be uniform throughout the States. By a careful management of imposts and excises, the national expences may be discharged without any other species of tax; but if a poll-tax, or land-tax shall ever become necessary, the weight must press equally on every part of the Union. For in all cases, such taxes must be according to the number of inhabitants. Is it not a pleasing consideration that North-Carolina, under all her natural disadvantages, must have the same facility of paying her share of the public debt as the most favored, or the most fortunate State? She gains no advantage by this plan, but she recovers from her misfortunes. She stands on the same footing with her sister States, and they are too generous to desire that she should stand on lower ground. When you consider those parts of the new System which are of the greatest import-those which respect the general question of liberty and safety, you will recollect that the States in Convention were unanimous; and you must remember that some of the members of that body have risqued their lives in defence of liberty; but the system does not require the help of such arguments; it will bear the most scrupulous examination.

When you refer the proposed system to the particular circumstances of North-Carolina, and consider how she is to be affected by this plan; you must find the utmost reason to rejoice in the prospect of better times-this is a sentiment that I have ventured with the greater confidence, because it is the general opinion of my late Honorable Colleagues, and I have the utmost reliance in their superior abilities. But if our constituents shall discover faults where we could not see any, or if they shall suppose that a plan is formed for abridging their liberties when we imagined that we had been securing both liberty and property on a more stable foundation; if they perceive that they are to suffer a loss where we thought they must rise from a misfortune; they will at least do us the justice to charge those errors to the head, and not to the heart.

The proposed system is now in your hands, and with it the fate of your country. We have a common interest, for we are embarked in the same vessel. At present she is in a sea of troubles, without sails, oars, or pilot; ready to be dashed into pieces by every flaw of wind. You may secure a port, unless you think it better to remain at sea. If there is any man among you that wishes for troubled times and fluctuating measures, that he may live by speculations, and thrive by the calamities of the State; this Government is not for him.

If there is any man who envies the prosperity of a native citizen, who wishes that we should remain without native merchants or seamen, without shipping, without manufactures, without commerce; poor and contemptible, the tributaries of a foreign country; this Government is not for him.

And if there is any man who has never been reconciled to our Independence, who wishes to see us degraded and insulted abroad, oppressed by anarchy at home, and torn into pieces by factions; incapable of resistance and ready to become a prey to the first invader; this Government is not for him.

But it is a Government, unless I am greatly mistaken, that gives the fairest promise of being firm and honorable; safe from Foreign Invasion or Domestic Sedition. A Government by which our commerce must be protected and enlarged; the value of our produce and of our lands must be encreased; the labourer and the mechanic must be encouraged and supported. It is a form of Government that is perfectly fitted for protecting Liberty and Property, and for cherishing the good Citizen and the Honest Man.

Marcus II by James Iredell

Editor's Introduction:

Iredell dedicated most of this essay to a discussion of the presidency. George Mason thought that the lack of a "privy council" would prevent the executive from having the requisite information necessary to be an effective executive. Iredell disagreed and used historical examples to show that a privy council did not always provide the proper checks on executive power.

Iredell also maintained that the federal judiciary would leave the State courts "uncontrolled as to all the affairs of" the State. Opponents of the Constitution worried that the federal court system would destroy the State courts by consolidating power in the center. As a future Supreme Court Justice and one of the most respected legal minds in his State, Iredell's defense of the federal system warrants attention, as does his insistence that the State courts would still have jurisdiction over the "internal concerns" of the State.

Marcus II

February 27, 1788

James Iredell of North Carolina

Answers to Mr. Mason's Objections to the New Constitution, Recommended by the late Convention at Philadelphia.

IVth. Objection.

"The Judiciary of the United States is so constructed and extended, as to absorb and destroy the Judiciaries of the several States; thereby rendering law as tedious, intricate and expensive; and justice as unattainable by a great part of the community as in England; and enabling the rich to oppress and ruin the poor."

Answer.

Mr. Mason has here asserted, "That the Judiciary of the United States is so constructed and extended, as to absorb and destroy the Judiciaries of the several States." How is this the case? Are not the State Judiciaries left uncontrouled as to all the affairs of that State only? In this, as in all other cases, where there is a wise distribution, power is commensurate to its object. With the mere internal concerns of a State, Congress are to have nothing to do. In no case but where the Union is in some measure concerned, are the Fœderal Courts to have any jurisdiction. The State Judiciary will be a satellite waiting upon its proper planet: That of the Union like the sun, cherishing and preserving a whole planetary system.

In regard to a possible ill construction of this authority, we must depend upon our future Legislature in this case, as well as others, in respect to which it is impracticable to define every thing; that it will be provided for so as to occasion as little expence and distress to individuals as can be. In parting with the coercive authority over the States, as States, there must be a coercion allowed as to individuals. The former power no man of common sense can any longer seriously contend for: The latter is the only alternative. Suppose an objection should be made, that the future Legislature should not ascertain salaries, because they might divide among themselves and their officers all the revenue of the Union:Will not every man see how irrational it is to expect that any government can exist, which is to be fettered in its most necessary operations, for fear of abuse?

Vth. Objection.

"The President of the United States, has no Constitutional Council (a thing unknown in any safe and regular government), he will therefore be unsupported by proper information and advice; and will generally be directed by minions and favorites--or he will become a tool to the Senate--or a Council of State will grow out of the principal officers of the great departments; the worst and most dangerous of all ingredients for such a Council in a free country; for they may be induced to join in any dangerous or oppressive measures; to shelter themselves, and prevent an enquiry into their own misconduct in office: Whereas, had a Constitutional Council been formed (as was proposed) of six Members, viz. two from the eastern, two from the middle, and two from the southern States; to be appointed by vote of the States in the House of Representatives, with the same duration and rotation of office as the Senate, the Executive would always have had safe and proper information and advice. The President of such a Council might have acted as Vice--President of the United States, pro tempore, upon any vacancy or disability of the Chief Magistrate; and long--continued Sessions of the Senate would, in a great measure have been prevented. From this fatal defect of a Constitutional Council, has arisen the improper power of the Senate, in the appointment of public officers, and the alarming dependence and connexion between that branch of the Legislature and the Supreme Executive. Hence also sprung that unnecessary and dangerous officer, the Vice--President; who, for want of other employment, is made President of the Senate; thereby dangerously blending the Executive and Legislative powers;

besides always giving to some of the States an unnecessary and unjust pre--eminence over the others."

Answer.

Mr. Mason here reprobates the omission of a particular Council for the President, as a thing contrary to the example of all safe and regular governments. Perhaps there are very few governments now in being, deserving of that character, if under the idea of safety, he means to include safety for a proper share of personal freedom, without which their safety and regularity in other respects would be of little consequence to a people so justly jealous of liberty as I hope the people in America ever will be. Since however Mr. Mason refers us to such authority, I think I cannot do better than to select for the subject of our enquiry in this particular, a government which must be universally acknowledged to be the most safe and regular of any considerable government now in being (though I hope, America will soon be able to dispute that pre--eminence). Every body must know I speak of Great--Britain; and in this I think I give Mr. Mason all possible advantage; since, in my opinion, it is most probable he had Great--Britain principally in his eye when he made this remark. And in the very height of our quarrel with that country, so wedded were our ideas to the institution of a Council, that the practice was generally, if not universally followed, at the formation of our governments, though we instituted councils of a quite different nature; and so far as the little experience of the writer goes, have very little benefited by it. My enquiry into this subject shall not be confined to the actual present practice of Great--Britain. I shall take the liberty to state the constitutional ideas of Councils in England, as derived from their ancient laws subsisting long before the Union, not omitting however to shew what the present practice really is.–By the laws of England(b)the King is said to have four Councils. 1. The High Court of Parliament. 2.

The Peers of the Realm. 3. His Judges. 4. His Privy Council.–By the first, I presume, is meant in regard to the making of laws; because the usual introductory expressions in most acts of Parliament, viz. "By the King's Most Excellent Majesty, by and with the advice and consent of the Lords Spiritual and Temporal, and Commons, &c." shew, that in a constitutional sense, they are deemed the King's laws, after a ratification in Parliament. The Peers of the Realm are, by their birth hereditary Counsellors of the Crown, and may be called upon for their advice either in time of Parliament, or when no Parliament is in being. They are called in some law books, Magnum Concilium Regis. (The King's Great Council). It is also considered the privilege of every particular Peer, to demand an audience of the King, and to lay before him any thing he may deem of public importance. The Judges, I presume, are called "A Council of the King," upon the same principle that the Parliament is, because the administration of justice is in his name, and the Judges are considered as his instruments in the distribution of it. We come now to the Privy Council, which I imagine, if Mr. Mason had any particular view towards England when he made this objection, was the one he intended as an example of a Constitutional Council in that kingdom. The Privy Council in that country is undoubtedly of very ancient institution; but it has one fixed property invariably annexed to it, that it is a mere creature of the Crown, dependent on its will both for number and duration, since the King may, whenever he thinks proper, discharge any particular Member, or the whole of it, and appoint another.(c)If this precedent is of moment to us, merely as a precedent, it should be followed in all its parts; and then what would there be in the regulation to prevent the President from being governed by "minions and favorites?" It would only be the means of rivetting them on constitutional ground. So far as precedents in England apply, the Peers being constitutionally the

Great Council of the King, tho' also a part of the Legislature, we have reason to hope, that there is by no means, such gross impropriety as has been suggested, in giving the Senate, tho' a branch of the Legislature, a strong controul over the Executive. The only difference in the two cases is, that the Crown may or may not give this consequence to the Peers at its own pleasure; and accordingly we find, that for a long time past, this Great Council has been very seldom consulted: Under our Constitution, the President is allowed no option in respect to certain points, wherein he cannot act without the Senate's concurrence. But we cannot infer from any example in England, that a concurrence between the Executive and a part of the Legislature is contrary to the maxims of their government, since their government allows of such a concurrence whenever the Executive pleases. The rule therefore from the example of the freest government in Europe, that the Legislative and Executive powers must be altogether distinct, is liable to exceptions. It does not mean that the Executive shall not form a part of the Legislature (for the King who has the whole Executive authority, is one entire branch of the Legislature; and this, Montesquieu,[2] who recognizes the general principle, declares is necessary): Neither can it mean (as the example above evinces) that the Crown must consult neither house as to any exercise of its Executive power: But its meaning must be, that one power shall not include both authorities: The King, for instance, shall not have the sole Executive, and sole Legislative authority also. He may have the former, but must participate the latter with the two Houses of Parliament. The rule also would be infringed were the three branches of the Legislature to share jointly the Executive power. But so long as the people's Representatives are altogether distinct from the Executive authority, the liberties of the people may be deemed secure. And in this point, surely there can be no manner of comparison between the provisions by which the independence of our

House of Representatives is guarded, and the condition in which the British House of Commons is left exposed to every species of corru ption.–But Mr. Mason says, for want of a Council, the President may become "a tool to the Senate." Why?–Because he cannot act without their concurrence. Would not the same reason hold for his being "a tool to the Council," if he could not act without their concurrence, supposing a Council was to be imposed upon him without his own nomination (according to Mr. Mason's plan)? As great care is taken to make him independent of the Senate; as I believe human precaution can provide. Whether the President will be a tool to any persons, will depend upon the man; and the same weakness of mind which would make him pliable to one body of controul, would certainly attend him with another. But Mr. Mason objects, if he is not directed by minions and favorites, nor becomes a tool of the Senate, "A Council of State will grow out of the principal officers of the great department[s], the worst and most dangerous of all ingredients for such a Council, in a free country; for they may be induced to join in any dangerous or oppressive measures to shelter themselves, and prevent an inquiry into their own misconduct in office." I beg leave again to carry him to my old authority, England, and ask him what efficient Council they have there, but one formed of their great officers? Notwithstanding their important constitutional Council, every body knows that the whole movements of their government, where a Council is consulted at all, are directed by their Cabinet Council, composed entirely of the principal officers of the great departments: That when a Privy Council is called, it is scarcely ever for any other purpose than to give a formal sanction to the previous determinations of the other; so much so that it is notorious that not one time in a thousand one Member of the Privy Council, except a known adherent of administration, is summoned to it. But though the President, under our Constitution, may have the aid of the "principal officers of the great departments," he is to have this aid, I think, in the most unexceptionable manner possible. He is not to be assisted by a Council, summoned to a jovial dinner perhaps, and giving their opinions according to the nod of the President--but the opinion is to be given with the utmost solemnity, in writing.3No after equivocation can explain it away. It must for ever afterwards speak for itself, and commit the character of the writer, in lasting colours either of fame or infamy, or neutral insignificance, to future ages, as well as the present. From those written reasons, weighed with care, surely the President can form as good a judgment as if they had been given by a dozen formal characters, carelessly met together on a slight appointment. And this further advantage would be derived from the proposed system (which would be wanting if he had constitutional advice to screen him) that the President must be personally responsible for every thing. For though an ingenious gentleman has proposed, that a Council should be formed, who should be responsible for their opinions; and the same sentiment of justice might be applied to these opinions of the great officers, I am persuaded it will in general be thought infinitely more safe, as well as more just, that the President who acts should be responsible for his conduct, following advice at his peril, than that there should be a danger of punishing any man for an erroneous opinion which might possibly be sincere. Besides the morality of this scheme, which may well be questioned, its inexpediency is glaring, since it would be so plausible an excuse, and the insincerity of it so difficult to detect; the hopes of impunity this avenue to escape, would afford, would nearly take away all dread of punishment. As to the temptations mentioned to the officers joining in dangerous or oppressive measures to shelter themselves, and prevent an enquiry into their own misconduct in office, this proceeds upon a supposition that the President and the great officers may form a very wicked combination to injure their country; a combination that in the first place it is utterly improbable, in a strong respectable government, should be formed for that purpose; and in the next, with such a government as this Constitution would give us, could have little chance of being successful, on account of the great superior strength, and natural and jealous vigilance of one at least, if not both the two weighty branches of Legislation. This evil however, of the possible depravity of all public officers, is one that can admit of no cure, since in every institution of government, the same danger in some degree or other must be risqued; it can only be guarded against by strong checks, and I believe it would be difficult for the objectors to our new Constitution, to provide stronger ones against any abuse of the Executive authority, than will exist in that. As to the Vice--President, it appears to me very proper he should be chosen much in the same manner as the President, in order that the States may be secure, upon any accidental loss by death or otherwise, of the President's service; of the services in the same important station of the man in whom they repose their second confidence. The complicated manner of election wisely prescribed, would necessarily occasion a considerable delay in the choice of another; and in the mean time the President of the Council, tho' very fit for the purpose of advising, might be very ill qualified, especially in a critical period, for an active executive department. I am concerned to see among Mr. Mason's other reasons, so trivial a one as the little advantage one State might accidentally gain by a Vice--President of their country having a seat, with merely a casting vote in the Senate. Such a reason is utterly unworthy that spirit of amity, and rejection of local views, which can alone save us from destruction. It was the glory of the late Convention, that by discarding such, they formed a general government upon principles that did as much honor to their hearts as to their understandings. God grant, that in all our deliberations, we may consider America as one body, and not divert our attention from so noble a prospect, to small considerations of partial jealousy and distrust. It is in vain to expect upon any system to secure an exact equilibrium of power for all the States. Some will occasionally have an advantage from the superior abilities of its Members; the field of emulation is however open to all. Suppose any one should now object to the superior influence of Virginia (and the writer of this is not a citizen of that State) on account of the high character of General Washington, confessedly the greatest man of the present age, and perhaps equal to any that has existed in any period of time: Would this be a reason for refusing a union with her, though the other States can scarcely hope for the consolation of ever producing his equal?

(To be continued.)

FEDERALIST NO. 62 BY JAMES MADISON

Editor's Introduction:

Madison covered the Senate in *Federalist* No. 62 and addressed several of the most acute accusations against that part of the general government, including the powers of the Senate and the size of the body. Madison, like other proponents of the document, insisted that the Senate would be the State check on the federal system, for it gave "to the State governments such an agency in the formation of the federal government as must secure the authority of the former, and may form a convenient link between the two systems." Having equal representation of the State maintained the federal structure of the general government, as under the Articles of Confederation, and Madison argued that the powers of the Senate would protect the federal republic from the "sudden and violent passions" of the people at large. Madison thought this anti-democratic body was a safeguard to liberty and good government.

Federalist No. 62

February 27, 1788

By James Madison of Virginia

To the People of the State of New York:

HAVING examined the constitution of the House of Representatives, and answered such of the objections against it as seemed to merit notice, I enter next on the examination of the Senate.

The heads into which this member of the government may be considered are:

I. The qualification of senators;

II. The appointment of them by the State legislatures;

III. The equality of representation in the Senate;

IV. The number of senators, and the term for which they are to be elected;

V. The powers vested in the Senate.

I. The qualifications proposed for senators, as distinguished from those of representatives, consist in a more advanced age and a longer period of citizenship. A senator must be thirty years of age at least; as a representative must be twenty-five. And the former must have been a citizen nine years; as seven years are required for the latter. The propriety of these distinctions is explained by the nature of the senatorial trust, which, requiring greater extent of information and ability of character, requires at the same time that the senator should have reached a period of life most likely to supply these advantages; and which, participating immediately in transactions with foreign nations, ought to be exercised by none who are not thoroughly weaned from the prepossessions and habits incident to foreign birth and education. The term of nine years appears to be a prudent mediocrity between a total exclusion of adopted citizens, whose merits and talents may claim a share in the public confidence, and an indiscriminate and hasty admission of them, which might create a channel for foreign influence on the national councils.

II. It is equally unnecessary to dilate on the appointment of senators by the State legislatures. Among the various modes which might have been devised for constituting this branch of the government, that which has been proposed by the convention is probably the most congenial with the public opinion. It is recommended by the double advantage of favoring a select appointment, and of giving to the State governments such an agency in the formation of the federal government as must secure the authority of the former, and may form a convenient link between the two systems.

III. The equality of representation in the Senate is another point, which, being evidently the result of compromise between the opposite pretensions of the large and the small States, does not call for much discussion. If indeed it be right, that among a people thoroughly incorporated into one nation, every district ought to have a PROPORTIONAL share in the government, and that among independent and sovereign States, bound together by a simple league, the parties, however unequal in size, ought to have an EQUAL share in the common councils, it does not appear to be without some reason that in a compound republic, partaking both of the national and federal character, the government ought to be founded on a mixture of the principles of proportional and equal representation. But it is superfluous to try, by the standard of theory, a part of the Constitution which is allowed on all hands to be the result, not of theory, but "of a spirit of amity, and that mutual deference and concession which the peculiarity of our political situation rendered indispensable." A common government, with powers equal to its objects, is called for by the voice, and still more loudly by the political situation, of America. A government founded on principles more consonant to the wishes of the larger States, is not likely to be obtained from the smaller States. The only option, then, for the former, lies between the proposed government and a government still more objectionable. Under this alternative, the advice of prudence must be to embrace the lesser evil; and, instead of indulging a fruitless anticipation of the possible mischiefs which may ensue, to contemplate rather the advantageous consequences which may qualify the sacrifice.

In this spirit it may be remarked, that the equal vote allowed to each State is at once a constitutional recognition of the portion of sovereignty remaining in the individual States, and an instrument for preserving that residuary sovereignty. So far the equality ought to be no less acceptable to the large than to the small States; since they are not less solicitous to guard, by every possible expedient, against an improper consolidation of the States into one simple republic.

Another advantage accruing from this ingredient in the constitution of the Senate is, the additional impediment it must prove against improper acts of legislation. No law or resolution can now be passed without the concurrence, first, of a majority of the people, and then, of a majority of the States. It must be acknowledged that this complicated check on legislation may in some instances be injurious as well as beneficial; and that the peculiar defense which it involves in favor of the smaller States, would be more rational, if any interests common to them, and distinct from those of the other States, would otherwise be exposed to peculiar danger. But as the larger States will always be able, by their power over the supplies, to defeat unreasonable exertions of this prerogative of the lesser States, and as the faculty and excess of law-making seem to be the diseases to which our governments are most liable, it is not impossible that this part of the Constitution may be more convenient in practice than it appears to many in contemplation.

IV. The number of senators, and the duration of their appointment, come next to be considered. In order to form an accurate judgment on both of these points, it will be proper to inquire into the purposes which are to be answered by a senate; and in order to ascertain these, it will be necessary to review the inconveniences which a republic must suffer from the want of such an institution.

First. It is a misfortune incident to republican government, though in a less degree than to other governments, that those who administer it may forget their obligations to their constituents, and prove unfaithful to their important trust. In this point of view, a senate, as a second branch of the legislative assembly, distinct from, and dividing the power with, a first, must be in all cases a salutary check on the government. It doubles the security to the people, by requiring the concurrence of two distinct bodies in schemes of usurpation or perfidy, where the ambition or corruption of one would otherwise be sufficient. This is a precaution founded on such clear principles, and now so well understood in the United States, that it would be more than superfluous to enlarge on it. I will barely remark, that as the improbability of sinister combinations will be in proportion to the dissimilarity in the genius of the two bodies, it must be politic to distinguish them from each other by every circumstance which will consist with a due harmony in all proper measures, and with the genuine principles of republican government.

Secondly. The necessity of a senate is not less indicated by the propensity of all single and numerous assemblies to yield to the impulse of sudden and violent passions, and to be seduced by factious leaders into intemperate and pernicious resolutions. Examples on this subject might be cited without number; and from proceedings within the United States, as well as from the history of other nations. But a position that will not be contradicted, need not be proved. All that need be remarked is, that a body which is to correct this infirmity ought itself to be free from it, and consequently ought to be less numerous. It ought, moreover, to possess great firmness, and consequently ought to hold its authority by a tenure of considerable duration.

Thirdly. Another defect to be supplied by a senate lies in a want of due acquaintance with the objects and principles of legislation. It is not possible that an assembly of men called for the most part from pursuits of a private nature, continued in appointment for a short time, and led by no permanent motive to devote the intervals of public occupation to a study of the laws, the affairs, and the comprehensive interests of their country, should, if left wholly to themselves, escape a variety of important errors in the exercise of their legislative trust. It may be affirmed, on the best grounds, that no small share of the present embarrassments of America is to be charged on the blunders of our governments; and that these have proceeded from the heads rather than the hearts of most of the authors of them. What indeed are all the repealing, explaining, and amending laws, which fill and disgrace our voluminous codes, but so many monuments of deficient wisdom; so many impeachments exhibited by each succeeding against each preceding session; so many admonitions to the people, of the value of those aids which may be expected from a well-constituted senate?

A good government implies two things: first, fidelity to the object of government, which is the happiness of the people; secondly, a knowledge of the means by which that object can be best attained. Some governments are deficient in both these qualities; most governments are deficient in the first. I scruple not to assert, that in American governments too little attention has been paid to the last. The federal Constitution avoids this error; and what merits particular notice, it provides for the last in a mode which increases the security for the first.

Fourthly. The mutability in the public councils arising from a rapid succession of new members, however qualified they may be, points out, in the strongest manner, the necessity of some stable institution in the government. Every new election in the States is found to change one half of the representatives. From this change of men must proceed a change of opinions; and from a change of opinions, a change of measures. But a continual change even of good measures is inconsistent with every rule of prudence and every prospect of success. The remark is verified in private life, and becomes more just, as well as more important, in national transactions.

V. To trace the mischievous effects of a mutable government would fill a volume. I will hint a few only, each of which will be perceived to be a source of innumerable others.

In the first place, it forfeits the respect and confidence of other nations, and all the advantages connected with national character. An individual who is observed to be inconstant to his plans, or perhaps to carry on his affairs without any plan at all, is marked at once, by all prudent people, as a speedy victim to his own unsteadiness and folly. His more friendly neighbors may pity him, but all will decline to connect their fortunes with his; and not a few will seize the opportunity of making their fortunes out of his. One nation is to another what one individual is to another; with this melancholy distinction perhaps, that the former, with fewer of the benevolent emotions than the latter, are under fewer restraints also from taking undue advantage from the indiscretions of each other. Every nation, consequently, whose affairs betray a want of wisdom and stability, may calculate on every loss which can be sustained from the more systematic policy of their wiser neighbors. But the best instruction on this subject is unhappily conveyed to America by the example of her own situation. She finds that she is held in no respect by her friends; that she is the derision of her enemies; and that she is a prey to every nation which has an interest in speculating on her fluctuating councils and embarrassed affairs.

The internal effects of a mutable policy are still more calamitous. It poisons the blessing of liberty itself. It will be of little avail to the people, that the laws are made by men of their own choice, if the laws be so voluminous that they cannot be read, or so incoherent that they cannot be understood; if they be repealed or revised before they are promulgated, or undergo such incessant changes that no man, who knows what the law is to-day, can guess what it will be to-morrow. Law is defined to be a rule of action; but how can that be a rule, which is little known, and less fixed?

Another effect of public instability is the unreasonable advantage it gives to the sagacious, the enterprising, and the moneyed few over the industrious and uniformed mass of the people. Every new regulation concerning commerce or revenue, or in any way affecting the value of the different species of property, presents a new harvest to those who watch the change, and can trace its consequences; a harvest, reared not by themselves, but by the toils and cares of the great body of their fellow-citizens. This is a state of things in which it may be said with some truth that laws are made for the FEW, not for the MANY.

In another point of view, great injury results from an unstable government. The want of confidence in the public councils damps every useful undertaking, the success and profit of which may depend on a continuance of existing arrangements. What prudent merchant will hazard his fortunes in any new branch of commerce when he knows not but that his plans may be rendered unlawful before they can be executed? What farmer or manufacturer will lay himself out for the encouragement given to any particular cultivation or establishment, when he can have no assurance that his preparatory labors and advances will not render him a victim to an inconstant government? In a word, no great improvement or laudable enterprise can go forward which requires the auspices of a steady system of national policy.

But the most deplorable effect of all is that diminution of attachment and reverence which steals into the hearts of the people, towards a political system which betrays so many marks of infirmity, and disappoints so many of their flattering hopes. No government, any more than an individual, will long be respected without being truly respectable; nor be truly respectable, without possessing a certain portion of order and stability.

Marcus IV by James Iredell

Editor's Introduction:

Marcus IV is arguably the most important of the five essays Iredell wrote in defense of the Constitution. He focused this essay on the "necessary and proper clause" and Mason's contention that it would be used to expand the power of the general government to the detriment of the States, the Union, and the American public. This is one of the reasons Mason insisted on a bill of rights. If the Congress had "implied powers," then a bill of rights would be necessary to ensure American civil liberties would be protected. Iredell forwarded the same arguments James Wilson made in October 1787, namely that if the Constitution did not expressly grant the power to the central government, then the power was unconstitutional. He cites trial by jury as an example. According to Article I, Section 8, Congress did not have any power over jury trials. The liberty of trail by jury, then, was not something the general government could infringe or disparage. Iredell was in effect making the case for strict construction in this essay.

March 12, 1788

By James Iredell of North Carolina

Answers to Mr. Mason's Objections to the New Constitution, Recommended by the late Convention at Philadelphia.

VIIIth. Objection.

"Under their own construction of the general clause at the end of the enumerated powers, the Congress may grant monopolies in trade and commerce, constitute new crimes, inflict unusual and severe punishments, and extend their power as far as they shall think proper; so that the State Legislatures have no security for the powers now presumed to remain to them, or the people for their rights. There is no declaration of any kind for preserving the Liberty of the Press–the Trial by Jury in civil cases–nor against the danger of standing armies in time of peace."

Answer. The general clause at the end of the enumerated powers is as follows:

–"To make all laws which shall be necessary and proper for carrying into execution the foregoing powers, and all other powers vested by this Constitution in the United States, or in any department or office thereof."

Those powers would be useless, except acts of Legislation could be exercised upon them. It was not possible for the Convention, nor is it for any human body, to foresee and provide for all contingent cases that may arise. Such cases must therefore be left to be provided for by the general Legislature, as they shall happen to come into existence. If Congress, under pretence of exercising the power delegated to them, should, in fact, by the exercise of any other power, usurp upon the rights of the different Legislatures, or of any private citizens, the people will be exactly in the same situation as if there had been an express provision against such power in particular, and yet they had presumed to exercise it. It would be an act of tyranny, against which no parchment stipulations can guard; and the Convention surely can be only answerable for the propriety of the powers given, not for the future virtues of all with whom those powers may be entrusted. It does not therefore appear to me, that there is any weight in this objection more than in others–but, that I may give it every fair advantage, I will take notice of every particular injurious act of power which Mr. Mason points out as exerciseable by the authority of Congress, under this general clause.

The first mentioned is, "That the Congress may grant monopolies in trade and commerce." Upon examining the Constitution, I find it expressly provided, "That no preference shall be given to the ports of one State over those of another;" and that "Citizens of each State shall be entitled to all privileges and immunities of citizens in the several States." These provisions appear to me to be calculated for the very purpose Mr. Mason wishes to secure. Can they be consistent with any monopoly in trade and commerce? I apprehend therefore, under this expression must be intended more than is expressed; and if I may conjecture from another publication of a gentleman of the same State and in the same party of opposition, I should suppose it arose from a jealousy of the Eastern States, very well known to be often expressed by some gentlemen of Virginia. They fear, that a majority of the States may establish regulations of commerce which will give great advantage to the carrying trade of America, and be a means of encouraging New England vessels rather than old England.–Be it so.–No regulations can give such advantage to New England vessels, which will not be enjoyed by all other American vessels, and many States can build as well as New England, tho' not at present perhaps in equal proportion. And what could conduce more to the preservation of the union, than allowing to every kind of industry in America a peculiar preference! Each State exerting itself in its own way, but the exertions of all contributing to the common security, and increasing the rising greatness of our country! Is it not the aim of every wise country to be as much the carriers of their own produce as can be? And would not this be the means in our own of producing a new source of activity among the people, giving to our own fellow citizens what otherwise must be given to strangers, and laying the foundation of an independent trade among ourselves, and of gradually raising a navy in America, which, however distant the prospect, ought certainly not to be out of our sight. There is no great probability however that our country is likely soon to enjoy so glorious an advantage. We must have treaties of commerce, because without them we cannot trade to other countries. We already have such with some nations–we have none with Great-Britain; which can be imputed to no other cause but our not having a strong respectable government to bring that nation to terms. And surely no man who feels for the honor of his country, but must view our present degrading commerce with that country with the highest indignation, and the most ardent wish to extricate ourselves from so disgraceful a situation. This only can be done by a powerful government, which can dictate conditions of advantage to ourselves, as an equivalent for advantages to them; and this could undoubtedly be easily done by such a government, without diminishing the value of any articles of our own produce; or if there was any diminution it would be too slight to be felt by any patriot in competition with the honor and interest of his country.

As to the constituting new crimes, and inflicting unusual and severe punishment, certainly the cases enumerated wherein the Congress are empowered either to define offences, or prescribe punishments, are such as are proper for the exercise of such authority in the general Legislature of the union. They only relate to "counterfeiting the securities and current coin of the United States; to piracies and felonies committed on the high seas, and offences against the law of nations, and to treason against the United States." These are offences immediately affecting the security, the honor or the interest of the United States at large, and of course must come within the sphere of the Legislative authority which is entrusted with their protection. Beyond these authorities Congress can exercise no other power of this kind, except in the enacting of penalties to enforce their acts of Legislation in the cases where express authority is delegated to them, and if they could not enforce such acts by the enacting of penalties, those powers would be altogether useless, since a legislative regulation without some sanction would be an absurd thing indeed. The Congress having, for these reasons, a just right to authority in the above particulars, the question is, whether it is practicable and proper to prescribe the limits to its exercise, for fear that they should inflict punishments unusual and severe? It may be observed in the first place, that a declaration against "cruel and unusual punishments," formed part of an article in the Bill of Rights at the Revolution in England, in 1688. The prerogative of the Crown having been grossly abused in some preceding reigns, it was thought proper to notice every grievance they had endured, and those declarations went to an abuse of power in the crown only, but were never intended to limit the authority of Parliament. Many of these articles of the Bill of Rights in England, without a due attention to the difference of the cases, were eagerly adopted when our Constitutions were formed, the minds of men then being so warmed with their exertions in the cause of liberty, as to lean too much perhaps towards a jealousy of power to repose a proper confidence in their own government. From these articles in the State Constitutions, many things were attempted to be transplanted into our new Constitution, which would either have been nugatory or improper: This is one of them. The expressions "unusual and severe," or "cruel and unusual," surely would have been too vague to have been of any consequence, since they admit of no clear and precise signification. If to guard against punishments being too severe, the Convention had enumerated a vast variety of cruel punishments, and prohibited the use of any of them, let the number have been ever so great, an inexhaustible fund must have been unmentioned, and if our government had been disposed to be cruel, their invention would only have been put to a little more trouble. If to avoid this difficulty, they had determined, not negatively, what punishments should not be exercised, but positively what punishments should, this must have led them into a labyrinth of detail which in the original constitution of a government would have appeared perfectly ridiculous, and not left a room for such changes according to circumstances, as must be in the power of every Legislature that is rationally formed. Thus, when we enter into particulars, we must be convinced that the proposition of such a restriction would have led to nothing useful, or to something dangerous, and therefore that its omission is not chargeable as a fault in the new Constitution. Let us also remember, that as those who are to make those laws must, themselves be subject to them, their own interest and feelings will dictate to them not to make them unnecessarily severe; and that in the case of treason, which usually in every country exposes men most to the avarice and rapacity of government, care is taken that the innocent family of the offender shall not suffer for the treason of their relation. This is the crime with respect to which a jealousy is of the most importance, and accordingly it is defined with great plainness and accuracy, and the temptations to abusive prosecutions guarded against as much as possible. I now proceed to the three great cases:–The Liberty of the Press–The Trial by Jury in civil cases, and a Standing Army in time of peace.

The Liberty of the Press is always a grand topic for declamation; but the future Congress will have no other authority over this than to secure to authors for a limited time the exclusive privilege of publishing their works. This authority has long been exercised in England, where the press is as free as among ourselves, or in any country in the world, and surely such an encouragement to genius is no restraint on the liberty of the press, since men are allowed to publish what they please of their own; and so far as this may be deemed a restraint upon others it is certainly a reasonable one, and can be attended with no danger of copies not being sufficiently multiplied, because the interest of the proprietor will always induce him to publish a quantity fully equal to the demand–besides, that such encouragement may give birth to many excellent writings which would otherwise have never appeared. If the Congress should exercise any other power over the press than this, they will do it without any warrant from this Constitution, and must answer for it as for any other act of tyranny.

In respect to the trial by jury in civil cases, it must be observed, it is a mistake to suppose, that such a trial takes place in all civil cases now. Even in the common law Courts, such a trial is only had where facts are disputed between the parties, and there are even some facts triable by other methods. In the Chancery and Admiralty Courts, in many of the States, I am told, they have no Juries at all. The States in these particulars differ very much in their practice from each other: A general declaration therefore to preserve the trial by Jury in all civil cases, would only have produced confusion, so that the Courts afterwards in a thousand instances would not have known how to have proceeded. If they had added "as heretofore accustomed," that would not have answered the purpose, because there has been no uniform custom about it. If therefore the Convention had interfered, it must have been by entering into a detail highly unsuitable to a fundamental constitution of government: If they had pleased some States, they must have displeased others, by innovating upon modes of administering justice perhaps endeared to them by habit, and agreeable to their settled conviction of propriety. As this was the case it appears to me it was infinitely better, rather than endanger every thing by attempting too much, to leave this complicated business of detail, to the regulation of the future Legislature, where it can be adjusted coolly and at ease, and upon full and exact information.–There is no danger of the trial by Jury being rejected, when so justly a favorite of the whole people. The Representatives of the people surely can have no interest in making themselves odious for the mere pleasure of being hated; and when a Member of the House of Representatives is only sure of being so for two years, but must continue a citizen all his life, his interest as a citizen, if he is a man of common sense, to say nothing of his being a man of common honesty, must ever be uppermost in his mind. We know the great influence of the monarchy in the British government, and upon what a different tenure the Commons there have their seats in Parliament, from that prescribed to our Representatives. We know also, they have a large standing army. It is in the power of the Parliament if they dare to exercise it, to abolish the trial by jury altogether–but woe be to the man who should dare to attempt it–it would undoubtedly produce an insurrection that would hurl every tyrant to the ground who attempted to destroy that great and just favorite of the English nation. We certainly shall be always sure of this guard at least, upon any such act of folly or insanity in our Representatives: They soon would be taught the consequence of sporting with the feelings of a free people. But when it is evident that such an attempt cannot be rationally apprehended, we have no reason to anticipate unpleasing emotions of that nature. There is indeed little probability, that any degree of tyranny which can be figured to the most discoloured imagination, as likely to arise out of our government, could find an interest in attacking the trial by Jury in civil cases; and in criminal ones, where no such difficulties intervened as in the other, and where there might be supposed temptations to violate the personal security of a citizen, it is sacredly preserved.

The subject of a standing army has been exhausted in so masterly a manner in two or three numbers of the Fœderalist(a work which I hope will soon be in every body's hands) that, but for the sake of regularity in answering Mr. Mason's objections, I should not venture upon the same topic; and shall only presume to do so, with a reference for fuller satisfaction to that able performance. It is certainly one of the most delicate and proper cases for the consideration of a free people, and so far as a jealousy of this kind leads to any degree of caution not incompatible with the public safety, it is undoubtedly to be commended. Our jealousy of this danger has descended to us from our British ancestors: In that country they have a monarch, whose power being limited, and at the same time his prerogatives very considerable, a constant jealousy of him is both natural and proper. The two last of the Stuarts having kept up a considerable body of standing forces in time of peace, for the clear and almost avowed purpose of subduing the liberties of the people, it was made an article of the Bill of Rights at the Revolution, "That the raising or keeping a standing army within the kingdom in time of peace, unless it be with the consent of Parliament, is against law;" but no attempt was made, or I dare say, ever thought of, to restrain the Parliament from the exercise of that right. An army has been since kept on foot annually by authority of Parliament, and I believe ever since the Revolution they have had some standing troops; disputes have frequently happened about the number, but I don't recollect any objection by the most zealous patriot, to the keeping up of any at all. At the same time, notwithstanding the above practice of an annual vote (arising from a very judicious caution) it is still in the power of Parliament to authorise the keeping up of any number of troops for any indefinite time, and to provide for their subsistence for any number of years: Considerations of prudence, not constitutional limits to their authority, alone restrain such an exercise of it. Our Legislature however will be strongly guarded, though that of Great Britain is without any check at all. No appropriations of money for military service can continue longer than two years. Considering the extensive services the general government may have to provide for upon this vast continent, no forces with any serious prospect of success, could be attempted to be raised for a shorter time. Its being done for so short a period, if there were any appearances of ill designs in the government, would afford time enough for the real friends of their country to sound an alarm; and when we know how easy it is to excite jealousy of any government, how difficult for the people to distinguish from their real friends, those factious men, who in every country are ready to disturb its peace for personal gratifications of their own, and those desperate ones to whom every change is welcome, we shall have much more reason to fear that the government may be overawed by groundless discontents, than that it should be able, if contrary to every probability such a government could be supposed willing, to effect any designs for the destruction of their own liberties, as well as those of their constituents: For surely we ought ever to remember, that there will not be a man in the government but who has been either mediately or immediately recently chosen by the people, and that for too limited a time to make any arbitrary designs, consistent with common sense, when every two years a new body of Representatives, with all the energy of popular feelings, will come to carry the strong force of a severe national controul, into every department of government; to say nothing of the one-third to compose the Senate, coming at the same time warm with popular sentiments from their respective Assemblies. Men may, to be sure, suggest dangers from any thing; but it may truly be said, that those who can seriously suggest the danger of a premeditated attack on the liberties of the people from such a government as this, could with ease assign reasons equally plausible for distrusting the integrity of any government formed in any manner whatever; and really it does seem to me, that all their reasons may be fairly carried to this position,–that in as much as any confidence in any men would be unwise, as we can give no power but what may be grossly abused, we had better give none at all, but continue as we are, or resolve into total anarchy at once, of which indeed, our present condition falls very little short. What sort of a government must that be, which, upon the most certain intelligence that hostilities were meditated against it, could take no method for its defence, till after a formal declaration, of war, or the enemy's standard was actually fixed upon the shore. The first has for some time been out of fashion; but if it had not, the restraint these gentlemen recommend, would certainly have brought it into disuse with every Power who meant to make war upon America. They would not be such fools as to give us the only warning we had informed them we would accept of, before we would take any steps to counteract their designs. The absurdity of our being prohibited from preparing to resist an invasion till after it had actually taken place, is so glaring that no man can consider it for a moment without being struck with astonishment, to see how rashly, and with how little consideration gentlemen, whose characters are certainly respectable, have suffered themselves to be led away by so delusive an idea. The example of other countries, so far from warranting any such limitation of power, is directly against it. That of England is particularly noticed. In our present articles of Confederation there is no such restriction. It has been observed by the Fœderalist, that Pennsylvania and North-Carolina appear to be the only States in the union, which have attempted any restraint of the Legislative authority in this particular, and that their restraint appears rather in the light of a caution than a prohibition; but, that notwithstanding that, Pennsylvania had been obliged to raise forces in the very face of that article of her Bill of Rights. That great writer, from the remoteness of his situation, did not know that North-Carolina had equally violated her Bill of Rights in a similar manner. The Legislature of that State, in November 1786, passed an act for raising 201 men for the protection of a County called Davidson County, against hostilities from the Indians; they were to continue for two years from the time of their first rendezvous, unless sooner disbanded by the Assembly; and were to be "subject to the same rules with respect to their government as were established in the time of the late war by the Congress of the United States, for the government of the Continental army:" These are the very words of the act. Thus, for the example of the only two countries in the world, that I believe ever attempted such a restriction, it appears to be a thing incompatible with the safety of government. Whether their restriction is to be considered as a caution or a prohibition, in less than five years after peace the caution has been disregarded, or the prohibition disobeyed. Can the most credulous or suspicious man, require stronger proof of the weakness and impolicy of such restraints?

(To be concluded in our next).

Federalist No. 69 by Alexander Hamilton

Editor's Introduction:

Federalist No. 69 is perhaps the best summary of original intent regarding executive powers during the ratification period. Hamilton contrasts the powers of the British king with those of the American president and leaves little doubt that the executive in America would neither be an elected king nor would have extensive powers over the purse and sword. The Constitution created a limited executive with concurrent powers over treaties, war, and appointments, and little to no legislative powers. Hamilton in fact argues that the president does not have any specific legislative authority other than a qualified veto. In the era of executive government, this is one essay that should be read and re-read to understand the Founders' executive.

Federalist No. 69

March 14, 1788

By Alexander Hamilton of New York

To the People of the State of New York:

I PROCEED now to trace the real characters of the proposed Executive, as they are marked out in the plan of the convention. This will serve to place in a strong light the unfairness of the representations which have been made in regard to it.

The first thing which strikes our attention is, that the executive authority, with few exceptions, is to be vested in a single magistrate. This will scarcely, however, be considered as a point upon which any comparison can be grounded; for if, in this particular, there be a resemblance to the king of Great Britain, there is not less a resemblance to the Grand Seignior, to the khan of Tartary, to the Man of the Seven Mountains, or to the governor of New York.

That magistrate is to be elected for FOUR years; and is to be re-eligible as often as the people of the United States shall think him worthy of their confidence. In these circumstances there is a total dissimilitude between HIM and a king of Great Britain, who is an HEREDITARY monarch, possessing the crown as a patrimony descendible to his heirs forever; but there is a close analogy between HIM and a governor of New York, who is elected for THREE years, and is re-eligible without limitation or intermission. If we consider how much less time would be requisite for establishing a dangerous influence in a single State, than for establishing a like influence throughout the United States, we must conclude that a duration of FOUR years for the Chief Magistrate of the Union is a degree of permanency far less to be dreaded in that office, than a duration of THREE years for a corresponding office in a single State.

The President of the United States would be liable to be impeached, tried, and, upon conviction of treason, bribery, or other high crimes or misdemeanors, removed from office; and would afterwards be liable to prosecution and punishment in the ordinary course of law. The person of the king of Great Britain is sacred and inviolable; there is no constitutional tribunal to which he is amenable; no punishment to which he can be subjected without involving the crisis of a national revolution. In this delicate and important circumstance of personal responsibility, the President of Confederated America would stand upon no better ground than a governor of New York, and upon worse ground than the governors of Maryland and Delaware.

The President of the United States is to have power to return a bill, which shall have passed the two branches of the legislature, for reconsideration; and the bill so returned is to become a law, if, upon that reconsideration, it be approved by two thirds of both houses. The king of Great Britain, on his part, has an absolute negative upon the acts of the two houses of Parliament. The disuse of that power for a considerable time past does not affect the reality of its existence; and is to be ascribed wholly to the crown's having found the means of substituting influence to authority, or the art of gaining a majority in one or the other of the two houses, to the necessity of exerting a prerogative which could seldom be exerted without hazarding some degree of national agitation. The qualified negative of the President differs widely from this absolute negative of the British sovereign; and tallies exactly with the revisionary authority of the council of revision of this State, of which the governor is a constituent part. In this respect the power of the President would exceed that of the governor of New York, because the former would possess, singly, what the latter shares with the chancellor and judges; but it would be precisely the same with that of the governor of Massachusetts, whose constitution, as to this article, seems to have been the original from which the convention have copied.

The President is to be the "commander-in-chief of the army and navy of the United States, and of the militia of the several States, when called into the actual service of the United States. He is to have power to grant reprieves and pardons for offenses against the United States, EXCEPT IN CASES OF IMPEACHMENT; to recommend to the consideration of Congress such measures as he shall judge necessary and expedient; to convene, on extraordinary occasions, both houses of the legislature, or either of them, and, in case of disagreement between them WITH RESPECT TO THE TIME OF ADJOURNMENT, to adjourn them to such time as he shall think proper; to take care that the laws be faithfully executed; and to commission all officers of the United States." In most of these particulars, the power of the President will resemble equally that of the king of Great Britain and of the governor of New York. The most material points of difference are these:

First. The President will have only the occasional command of such part of the militia of the nation as by legislative provision may be called into the actual service of the Union. The king of Great Britain and the governor of New York have at all times the entire command of all the militia within their several jurisdictions. In this article, therefore, the power of the President would be inferior to that of either the monarch or the governor.

Secondly. The President is to be commander-in-chief of the army and navy of the United States. In this respect his authority would be nominally the same with that of the king of Great Britain, but in substance much inferior to it. It would amount to nothing more than the supreme command and direction of the military and naval forces, as first General and admiral of the Confederacy; while that of the British king extends to the DECLARING of war and to the RAISING and REGULATING of fleets and armies, all which, by the Constitution under consideration, would appertain to the legislature. The governor of New York, on the other hand, is by the constitution of the State vested only with the command of its militia and navy. But the constitutions of several of the States expressly declare their governors to be commanders-in-chief, as well of the army as navy;

and it may well be a question, whether those of New Hampshire and Massachusetts, in particular, do not, in this instance, confer larger powers upon their respective governors, than could be claimed by a President of the United States.

Thirdly. The power of the President, in respect to pardons, would extend to all cases, EXCEPT THOSE OF IMPEACHMENT. The governor of New York may pardon in all cases, even in those of impeachment, except for treason and murder. Is not the power of the governor, in this article, on a calculation of political consequences, greater than that of the President? All conspiracies and plots against the government, which have not been matured into actual treason, may be screened from punishment of every kind, by the interposition of the prerogative of pardoning. If a governor of New York, therefore, should be at the head of any such conspiracy, until the design had been ripened into actual hostility he could insure his accomplices and adherents an entire impunity. A President of the Union, on the other hand, though he may even pardon treason, when prosecuted in the ordinary course of law, could shelter no offender, in any degree, from the effects of impeachment and conviction. Would not the prospect of a total indemnity for all the preliminary steps be a greater temptation to undertake and persevere in an enterprise against the public liberty, than the mere prospect of an exemption from death and confiscation, if the final execution of the design, upon an actual appeal to arms, should miscarry? Would this last expectation have any influence at all, when the probability was computed, that the person who was to afford that exemption might himself be involved in the consequences of the measure, and might be incapacitated by his agency in it from affording the desired impunity? The better to judge of this matter, it will be necessary to recollect, that, by the proposed Constitution, the offense of treason is limited "to levying war upon the United States, and adhering to their enemies, giving them aid and comfort"; and that by the laws of New York it is confined within similar bounds.

Fourthly. The President can only adjourn the national legislature in the single case of disagreement about the time of adjournment. The British monarch may prorogue or even dissolve the Parliament. The governor of New York may also prorogue the legislature of this State for a limited time; a power which, in certain situations, may be employed to very important purposes.

The President is to have power, with the advice and consent of the Senate, to make treaties, provided two thirds of the senators present concur. The king of Great Britain is the sole and absolute representative of the nation in all foreign transactions. He can of his own accord make treaties of peace, commerce, alliance, and of every other description. It has been insinuated, that his authority in this respect is not conclusive, and that his conventions with foreign powers are subject to the revision, and stand in need of the ratification, of Parliament. But I believe this doctrine was never heard of, until it was broached upon the present occasion. Every jurist of that kingdom, and every other man acquainted with its Constitution, knows, as an established fact, that the prerogative of making treaties exists in the crown in its utomst plentitude; and that the compacts entered into by the royal authority have the most complete legal validity and perfection, independent of any other sanction. The Parliament, it is true, is sometimes seen employing itself in altering the existing laws to conform them to the stipulations in a new treaty; and this may have possibly given birth to the imagination, that its co-operation was necessary to the obligatory efficacy of the treaty. But this parliamentary interposition proceeds from a different cause: from the necessity of adjusting a most artificial and intricate system of revenue and commercial laws, to the changes made in them by the operation of the treaty; and of adapting new provisions and precautions to the new state of things, to keep the machine from running into disorder. In this respect, therefore, there is no comparison between the intended power of the President and the actual power of the British sovereign. The one can perform alone what the other can do only with the concurrence of a branch of the legislature. It must be admitted, that, in this instance, the power of the federal Executive would exceed that of any State Executive. But this arises naturally from the sovereign power which relates to treaties. If the Confederacy were to be dissolved, it would become a question, whether the Executives of the several States were not solely invested with that delicate and important prerogative.

The President is also to be authorized to receive ambassadors and other public ministers. This, though it has been a rich theme of declamation, is more a matter of dignity than of authority. It is a circumstance which will be without consequence in the administration of the government; and it was far more convenient that it should be arranged in this manner, than that there should be a necessity of convening the legislature, or one of its branches, upon every arrival of a foreign minister, though it were merely to take the place of a departed predecessor.

The President is to nominate, and, WITH THE ADVICE AND CONSENT OF THE SENATE, to appoint ambassadors and other public ministers, judges of the Supreme Court, and in general all officers of the United States established by law, and whose appointments are not otherwise provided for by the Constitution. The king of Great Britain is emphatically and truly styled the fountain of honor. He not only appoints to all offices, but can create offices. He can confer titles of nobility at pleasure; and has the disposal of an immense number of church preferments. There is evidently a great inferiority in the power of the President, in this particular, to that of the British king;

nor is it equal to that of the governor of New York, if we are to interpret the meaning of the constitution of the State by the practice which has obtained under it. The power of appointment is with us lodged in a council, composed of the governor and four members of the Senate, chosen by the Assembly. The governor CLAIMS, and has frequently EXERCISED, the right of nomination, and is ENTITLED to a casting vote in the appointment. If he really has the right of nominating, his authority is in this respect equal to that of the President, and exceeds it in the article of the casting vote. In the national government, if the Senate should be divided, no appointment could be made; in the government of New York, if the council should be divided, the governor can turn the scale, and confirm his own nomination. If we compare the publicity which must necessarily attend the mode of appointment by the President and an entire branch of the national legislature, with the privacy in the mode of appointment by the governor of New York, closeted in a secret apartment with at most four, and frequently with only two persons; and if we at the same time consider how much more easy it must be to influence the small number of which a council of appointment consists, than the considerable number of which the national Senate would consist, we cannot hesitate to pronounce that the power of the chief magistrate of this State, in the disposition of offices, must, in practice, be greatly superior to that of the Chief Magistrate of the Union.

Hence it appears that, except as to the concurrent authority of the President in the article of treaties, it would be difficult to determine whether that magistrate would, in the aggregate, possess more or less power than the Governor of New York. And it appears yet more unequivocally, that there is no pretense for the parallel which has been attempted between him and the king of Great Britain. But to render the contrast in this respect still more striking, it may be of use to throw the principal circumstances of dissimilitude into a closer group.

The President of the United States would be an officer elected by the people for FOUR years; the king of Great Britain is a perpetual and HEREDITARY prince. The one would be amenable to personal punishment and disgrace; the person of the other is sacred and inviolable. The one would have a QUALIFIED negative upon the acts of the legislative body; the other has an ABSOLUTE negative. The one would have a right to command the military and naval forces of the nation; the other, in addition to this right, possesses that of DECLARING war, and of RAISING and REGULATING fleets and armies by his own authority. The one would have a concurrent power with a branch of the legislature in the formation of treaties; the other is the SOLE POSSESSOR of the power of making treaties. The one would have a like concurrent authority in appointing to offices; the other is the sole author of all appointments. The one can confer no privileges whatever; the other can make denizens of aliens, noblemen of commoners; can erect corporations with all the rights incident to corporate bodies. The one can prescribe no rules concerning the commerce or currency of the nation; the other is in several respects the arbiter of commerce, and in this capacity can establish markets and fairs, can regulate weights and measures, can lay embargoes for a limited time, can coin money, can authorize or prohibit the circulation of foreign coin. The one has no particle of spiritual jurisdiction; the other is the supreme head and governor of the national church! What answer shall we give to those who would persuade us that things so unlike resemble each other? The same that ought to be given to those who tell us that a government, the whole power of which would be in the hands of the elective and periodical servants of the people, is an aristocracy, a monarchy, and a despotism.

Publicola: An Address to the Freemen of North Carolina by Archibald Maclaine

Editor's Introduction:

Archibald Maclaine was a well-respected lawyer and jurist in North Carline. He was born in Ireland in 1728 and emigrated to the British North American colonies in 1750, first arriving in Philadelphia and then in the Carolinas in 1752. He apprenticed in a mercantile shop in Ireland and continued the trade in the colonies. He eventually studied law and became one of the most respected legal minds in the State of North Carolina. Thought tied to several loyalists through marriage, he nevertheless supported the patriot cause during the American War for Independence though he also spoke of the need to protect loyalist property. He helped draft the North Carolina Bill of Rights and was nominated to the North Carolina Supreme Court, though he declined the appointment.

Maclaine attended the first ratification convention for North Carolina and promoted ratification. His Publicola essays echoed other supporters of the document, particularly their insistence that the Constitution would not produce a consolidated government and that the States would be as free to legislate for their immediate domestic concerns as they had enjoyed under the Articles of Confederation. Maclaine shaded toward nationalism more than other proponents of the document from his State and region, but he never forgot that he was a North Carolinian first, and he believed that ratifying the document would allow North Carolina to prosper within a stronger Union of States.

Maclaine died in 1790, just two years after the Constitution was ratified.

Publicola: An Address to the Freemen of North Carolina

March 20, 1788

By Archibald Maclaine of North Carolina

To the Freemen of the state of North-Carolina.

The constitution proposed by the late general Convention, being in some states opposed with great warmth, and uncommon perseverance; and among ourselves being a common topic of discussion, tho' apparently little understood; it becomes the duty of every citizen who conceives he can throw any light upon the subject, to communicate his sentiments to you.

We have among us some characters who have uniformly opposed giving Congress any additional powers–what idea such persons have of a government, which by its constitution is empowered to make treaties, contract debts and to demand monies from the several states, without being able to raise a single shilling, or inforce obedience to any one of its acts, they would do well to inform us. They had better acknowledge with candour, what they avow in principle, that we have no occasion for a federal government. Congress, in its present state of imbecility, is a considerable expence to the states. If it cannot be rendered more useful, we had much better keep the money among ourselves, than part with it to so little purpose. Our present form of federal government (for it is no more) is the only one in the known world altogether without energy.

There are others who acknowledge that a reform is necessary, but at the same time start numerous objections to the remedy proposed. These objections are indeed so various and contradictory, that they destroy themselves–Scarcely any two of those who oppose the new constitution agree together; nor is there among the whole any thing proposed to substitute in the place of that which they reject. It is evident from this, that whatever may be their professions, they do not wish for any reform–Their strength lies in cavilling; convinced that if they can successfully oppose the proposed government, nothing better can be substituted in its place.

I very sincerely believe that there are many averse from the new constitution upon principle. They conceive that some parts of it may prove dangerous to liberty–It is to such I would wish to offer my remarks; for as to those who are opposed, without reasoning upon, or even reading, what they condemn, I consider them as incorrigible; and however respectable they may appear from station or capacity, I cannot view their conduct without discovering some degree of contempt for their selfish meanness.

Every man of common understanding, and common honesty, will readily acknowledge that something more than a bare federal union is necessary to make us a great and respectable nation–Mixed governments are universally acknowledged to be the best, as partaking of the different forms which are necessary for securing the rights of the people, and at the same time for promoting that dispatch and energy which is necessary for defence against enemies. The new government is partly federal, and partly national. The confederation still subsists, where it is not altered by the new form. To prove this, if it should be doubted, take part of the preamble to the latter: "We the people of the United States in order to form a more perfect union." The constitution of the respective states, and the rights of the people, are to remain as under the confederation, excepting such parts as interfere with the express powers given to Congress by the new constitution. All the clamour therefore, which has been raised about the trial by jury, and the liberty of the press, might have been spared, as altogether unfounded. To those who wish to trust themselves under separate state-governments, which may, as they have hitherto done, disregard the recommendations and requisitions of the union, I would recommend an attentive perusal of history, and as they do not seem to place any dependance on the reasoning of their fellow citizens, learn to be wise from the experience of past ages. They will find that in all countries, a strict union among the people, has been the only means of preserving liberty. Spain, composed of a number of kingdoms, principalities and provinces, which in the beginning of the reign of the Emperor Charles the Fifth, the first sovereign of that united country, enjoyed more liberty than any other country in Europe; but for want of union among the people, lost the whole; and their Kings from being the most limited, became in a few years to be some of the most absolute monarchs in Europe. At this day, there is not the shadow of liberty among them–every species of tyranny, which could be devised, has reduced the people to the most abject slavery. When people enter into society, they must, in order to obtain protection, give up some part of their natural liberty, in order to secure the rest–the more we retain in our hands, consistent with that protection, which is necessary for society, will be so much the better, and this is called civil liberty–In small states, the people generally retain more than in those which are extensive; but at the same time, they are more subject to violence and oppression, from their powerful neighbours. There is no possible way of uniting the force of a number of small states, but under one head. If each one is left to its own deliberations, it may determine, for want of knowing what is most salutary for the whole, contrary to the general interest; and thus defeat the purposes of the union–In all events, the very time taken in deliberating may prove fatal.–Instead of searching for objections against the new constitution, something should be proposed that will better answer the purpose, and at the same time secure the liberties of the people.–There are no powers granted by the new constitution, but what are necessary in all governments, and if we cannot entrust them in the hands of our own citizens; persons of our own choice, and whom we may remove at stated, and short periods, we must be contented to live without any effective government–We must be contented to remain at the mercy of the first foreign invader who may think us worth subduing; or, what will unquestionably be much worse, to fall into civil wars, and at last become the prey of the most daring desperado among ourselves. There is scarcely an objection made to the new constitution, but what will operate with equal force against any form of government that can be devised.

It is very remarkable that the principal opponents among us, are either those whose private interest may be affected by the proposed constitution; or those who conceive that their importance may be lessened by the intended change. Had the interested and ambitious acted honestly, and taken as much pains to explain and elucidate, as they have done to prevent; those among you, who have little or no means of information but from your wealthy, or dignified neighbours, would not at this day have raised your voices against a work that does honour, even to the most celebrated of those names who assisted in forming it. The new constitution is not pretended to be a work of perfection–such is not to be expected from imperfect beings; but it is perfect, compared to what we had reason to expect, from the jarring interests, and dissonant opinions of those who composed it–It is not a work intended for this, or that state, but for the whole body of the union. But were it completely adapted to our present situation, so as to be unexceptionable to all, time would render it defective–Improvements in commerce and manufactures, in arts and sciences; an increase in population, and an alteration in manners, would render amendments to the new constitution necessary–nothing in this world can be permanent; but it has been truly and elegantly observed by one of the framers of the new constitution, that the seeds of reformation are sown in the work itself–there is express provision made for amendments, when its defects and imperfections shall be discovered in its operation.

There is reason to believe that those who are predetermined against the new constitution, have insidiously endeavoured to poison your minds so far, as to prevail on many of you to make it a previous condition with your representatives, to vote against it;–those who will take the trouble to reflect upon the consequences of such a measure, must be convinced of the absurdity, as well as the fatal tendency of it. It is putting a negative upon the proposed constitution before debate; and should your delegates be convinced hereafter, that it is worthy of adoption, they will be embarrassed with your instructions. The greatest part of you have not the means of information, and being unaccustomed to think of government, few of you are competent judges of it. Why do the people chuse representatives but to decide for them? Why do the representatives want instructions, but to give them a plausible pretext for voting against the conviction of their own minds? It must be a bad cause that will not admit of a free investigation. Instructions to reject the new constitution, defeats the very purpose for which the Convention is to meet. We are, by the resolves of the Congress and Assembly, to elect persons "for the purpose of deliberating and determining on the said constitution;" not for the purpose either of adoption or rejection, without deliberation and debate. Were that to be the case, the members of the Convention would have no more to do than to examine all the different instructions; to count noses, and by that summary method, to adopt, or reject. This method, if not the most rational, that might be adopted, will at least be equal to the throw of a die, or any other species of gaming; though by some persons it may not be thought altogether so eligible as that, which is authorised; of collecting the united wisdom of the state in order, to deliberate and determine.

The arguments which mislead you are as weak as they are dishonest. You are told that by adopting the new constitution, the dignity of the state will be lost; that you will be drained of your money by foreign taxes (for so the taxes of Congress are as modestly as wisely called) and be obliged to attend foreign Courts, at a great distance, and an enormous expence; whereas, say the objectors, we are able to support our own state; the taxes imposed by our legislature, will be consumed among ourselves; and we can have justice as well administered at home, as at six or seven hundred miles distance, and at a much cheaper rate. To those who do not look further, but consider this state, not only as the guardian of our liberties, but as bulwark of defence, these are flattering arguments; and when they are applied to a man heated with zeal, he will be apt to set all the powers of Europe at defiance. If however he should happen to recollect that a handful of men during the late war, took possession of one of the principal ports of the state, and kept possession of it ten months, even when a body of militia, three times their number, advanced against them; and that, that very handful of men, marched a hundred miles through the country unmolested, and plundered a principal seaport before their return, it is possible he may begin to doubt his own prowess, and even question whether the state can be depended upon for a guard against the depredations of a single privateer. It is not material what resources we have–experience may teach us, that under our present government, we cannot make a proper use of them. The United States are, and for some years have been, without any national character–Foreigners say, and they say truly, that we have no government–Even in this state, our policy is so wretched, that we have lost all credit, the very soul of commerce. No foreigner, no not an individual of any of our sister states, will trust us with a shilling. Our paper money, and our judicial decisions, banish all confidence; and the former has banished all gold and silver–Let paper money be no longer a tender, and justice be done to those who have transactions with us, and I will venture to assert that we shall soon have among us, a pound value in gold and silver, for every shilling in paper which we now possess. Wherever depreciated money is a lawful tender, that which is good vanishes, as if by inchantment.

I am astonished to hear that appeals are held up as a bugbear by men of understanding, if indeed they are in earnest. It is well known to every one who has looked into the new constitution, with any degree of attention, that the federal courts can have nothing to do with suits between citizens of the same state, unless where they claim lands under grants of different states. This [is] a power reserved by the confederation, and it is necessary for the purpose of giving each party a fair and impartial trial, before Judges who may be supposed indifferent to both states–The citizen of this state will have the benefit of this regulation, when he claims land in another state, either under a grant of that state, or his own. Appeals will be regulated by your own representatives in Congress, and will undoubtedly be confined to suits where the value contended for, will bear the expence and trouble. This is a sufficient security for us, as a great majority of the states must necessarily be at a considerable distance from the seat of government; and in framing laws the members will be attentive to the interest of their respective constituents. But I find some people are so strangely infatuated, as to think that Congress can, and therefore will, usurp powers not given them by the states, and do any thing, however oppressive and tyrannical. I know no good grounds for such a supposition, but this, that the legislative and judicial powers of the state have too often stepped over the bounds prescribed for them by the constitution; and yet, strange to tell, few of those, whose arguments I am now considering, think such measures censurable–The conclusion to be drawn here is obvious–The objectors hope to enjoy the same latitude of doing evil with impunity, and they are fearful of being restricted, if an efficient government takes place. But in truth many of the arguments used against the new constitution are utterly unaccountable; such for instance, that taxes are to be levied at the point of the bayonet–I would be glad to know the reason for this extraordinary assertion–Who has informed those worthy objectors all over the United States (for they catch at the arguments of each other) that the people would refuse to pay taxes for the support of the union? For to make soldiers necessary in the collection, resistance in the people is pre-supposed. That the people in this state should raise any objections to federal courts, and to appeals, is to me past all comprehension. After complaining for some years past, of the delays in our own courts, and of frequent decisions which have given great offence to the people in general, it would naturally occur that some reform should be thought necessary, and that any scheme that would effect such a salutary purpose, would readily be adopted. All criminal matters must be tried, and finally determined, in the state where the offence may be committed, even if it should be treason against the United States; and though the federal courts must be confined to some particular cases specified in the new constitution, yet the rules of their conduct will have a powerful influence upon the courts of the state. If business is transacted in the former upon settled and uniform principles, and without unnecessary delays, the latter will be ashamed to neglect their duty. I am informed that our Judges see clearly that this will be one of the consequences of adopting the new constitution, and one of them, fearful of being restricted to do what is right, expressed his apprehensions, that the great federal courts would overshadow the courts of the state: So unwilling are men possessed of absolute power to relinquish any part of it. For this, and several reasons, altogether as good, our Judges are decidedly opposed to the new constitution. But I suppose no good citizen will think it any degradation to the state, that our courts should undergo a reform from the example of the courts of the union (of which we are a part) or even from the example of the courts of any other country. The apprehensions of paying taxes for the support of the union, should not influence our conduct in deciding whether we shall receive the new constitution–We should have paid them long since, towards discharging the interest of our debts, and had our government been judiciously conducted, we might have done it with ease. Taxes are necessary for the support of every government, and though we shall always have a state establishment to support, the taxes for the union will be applied for our protection and defence from foreign enemies–Besides they will be rated by our own immediate representatives, and they and their families will be equally liable with ourselves. But it is not probable, in our present situation, that the federal government will want any direct taxes from the states, for a considerable time to come–I am persuaded that nothing but a rupture with some foreign power will make taxation necessary; and if we are enabled to make good our past engagements, there will be little or no danger of a war on our parts–But if it should be unavoidable, it is certainly better for us to pay a moderate tax, in order to be prepared to repel an enemy, than to suffer the country to be invaded and plundered. We have had sufficient experience of that already, and no good man wishes for a repetition of it.–But the sale of the western territory, and the duties arising from imposts, will, in all probability, be more than equal to our wants while we continue in peace–These last will increase yearly beyond all exception, and our exports in proportion; so that every succeeding year we shall be the better able to pay. Much of the sums collected at the different ports will center among ourselves. The different federal departments must be supported, and commerce will make us ample returns for whatever monies may be drawn from us. Exclusive of the advantages of a general trade, we must supply many, and might in time supply almost all of the materials necessary for equiping a navy.

Fabius I by John Dickinson

Editor's Introduction:

No founder has been more unjustly neglected than John Dickinson of Delaware. He was the author of the Articles of Confederation, served at virtually every important event leading to independence and in the early federal republic, and personified the conservative spirit of the founding period.

He was born in 1732 on the family tobacco plantation in Maryland and spent most of his youth at the new family planation near Dover, Delaware, a structure that still stands to this day. He was privately educated, studied law, and became one of the top attorneys in the American colonies. He was elected to serve in both the Delaware and Pennsylvania legislatures and during the years leading to the American War for Independence urged a moderate tone. His *Letters from a Farmer in Pennsylvania* earned him the nickname "The Penman of the Revolution," but while Dickinson pressed for the recognition of American rights, he shied away from independence. He was sent to the Continental Congress where his *Declaration of the Causes of Taking up Arms* defended the right of armed resistance to British "tyranny."

Yet, Dickinson refused to vote for the Declaration of Independence and privately hoped for a reconciliation between the Crown and the colonies.

When war came, he actively fought for independence in both Delaware and Pennsylvania. The British burned his property in Philadelphia in retaliation. Dickinson served in the Second Continental Congress and as president of both Delaware and Pennsylvania concurrently in the 1780s.

He attended the Philadelphia Convention in 1787 and helped moderate the "innovations" of men like Madison. More than anything, Dickinson resisted the call for a national government. He was an erstwhile federalist who believed in the sovereignty of the States and the blessings of the Union. He retired from public life after the Philadelphia Convention and lived out his years as a planter. He proposed the gradual abolition of slavery in Delaware and ultimately freed his slaves. When the Federalist faction distorted the original intent of the Constitution by centralizing power, Dickinson became an active proponent of the Jeffersonian faction in American politics. He died in 1808.

His Fabius letters were as important as the *Federalist*, and as such deserve a close reading. Dickinson wrote eight installments throughout April 1788, each designed to answer critics and draw attention to the benefits of the new Constitution. As he stated in Fabius I, Dickison thought the Union was the "political rock of our salvation." Fabius I serves as an introduction to the general themes and tone of the series.

Fabius I

April 12, 1788

By John Dickinson of Delaware

OBSERVATIONS on the CONSTITUTION

proposed by the FEDERAL CONVENTION

The Constitution proposed by the Federal Convention now engages the fixed attention of America.

Every person appears to be affected. Those who wish the adoption of the plan, consider its rejection as the source of endless contests, confusions, and misfortunes; and they also consider a resolution to alter, without previously adopting it, as a rejection.

Those who oppose the plan, are influenced by different views. Some of them are friends, others of them are enemies, to the United States. The latter are of two classes; either men without principles or fortunes, who think they may have a chance to mend their circumstances, with impunity, under a weak government, or in public convulsions, but cannot make them worse even by the last-or men who have been always averse to the revolution; and though at first confounded by that event, yet, their hopes reviving with the declension of our affairs, have since persuaded themselves, that at length the people, tired out with their continued distresses, will return to their former connection with Great Britain. To argue with these opposers, would be vain-The other opposers of the plan deserve the highest respect.

What concerns all, should be considered by all; and individuals may injure a whole society, by not declaring their sentiments. It is therefore not only their right, but their duty, to declare them. Weak advocates of a good cause or artful advocates of a bad one, may endeavour to stop such communications, or to discredit them by clamor and calumny. This, however, is not the age for such tricks of controversy. Men have suffered so severely by being deceived upon subjects of the highest import, those of religion and freedom, that truth becomes infinitely valuable to them, not as a matter of curious speculation, but of beneficial practice-A spirit of enquiry is excited, information diffused, judgment strengthened.

Before this tribunal, let everyone freely speak, what he really thinks, but with so sincere a reverence for the cause he ventures to discuss as to use the utmost caution, lest he should lead into errors, upon a point of such sacred concern as the public happiness.

It is not the design of this address, to describe the present derangement of our affairs, the mischief that must ensue from its continuance, the horrors of a total dissolution of the union, or the division of it into partial confederacies. Nor is it intended to describe the evils that will result from pursuing the plan of another Federal Convention; as if a better temper of conciliation, or a more satisfactory harmony of decisions, could be expected from men, after their minds are agitated with disgust and disappointments, than before they were thus disturbed; though from an uncontradicted assertion it appears, that without such provocations, the difficulty of reconciling the interests of the several states was so near to INSUPERABLE, in the late Convention, that after many weeks spent in the most faithful labors to promote concord, the members were upon the very point of dispersing in the utmost disorder, jealousy and resentment, and leaving the states exposed to all the tempests of passions, that have been so fatal to confederacies of democratical republics.

All these things have been laid before the public in a much better manner, than the writer of this address is capable of and to repeat what has been said, he means not. What he wishes, is to simplify the subject, so as to facilitate the enquiries of his fellow citizens.

Many are the objections made to the system proposed. They should be distinguished. Some may be called local, because they spring from the supposed interests of individual states. Thus, for instance, some inhabitants of large states may desire the system to be so altered, that they may possess more authority in the decisions of the government; or some inhabitants of commercial states may desire it to be so altered, that the advantages of their trade may center almost wholly among themselves; and this predilection they may think compatible with the common welfare. Their judgment being thus warped at the beginning of their deliberation, objections are accumulated as very important, that, without this prepossession, would never have obtained their approbation. Certain it is, that strong understandings may be so influenced by this insulated patriotism, as to doubt, whether general benefits can be communicated by a general government.

Probably nothing would operate so much for the correction of these errors, as a perusal of the accounts transmitted to us by the ancients, of the calamities occasioned in Greece by a conduct founded on similar errors. They are expressly ascribed to this cause that each city meditated apart on its own profit and ends-insomuch that those who seemed to contend for union, could never relinquish their own interests and advancement, while they deliberated for the public.

Heaven grant! that our countrymen may pause in time—duly estimate the present moment—and solemnly reflect—whether their measures may not tend to draw down the same distractions upon us, that desolated Greece.

They may now tolerably judge from the proceedings of the Federal Convention and of other Conventions, what are the sentiments of America upon her present and future prospects. Let the voice of her distress be venerated—and adhering to the generous Virginian declaration, let them resolve to CLING TO UNION AS THE POLITICAL ROCK OF OUR SALVATION.

Fabius II by John Dickinson

Editor's Introduction:

Dickinson insisted in this essay that the States would remain sovereign under the new Constitution. He argued that Senators represented the "sovereignties of the several states" and argued that the Union maintained a "strong confederation of the States." He believed members of Congress held their seats for the correct amount of time and thought the indirect election of president would result in the best candidate for office. He considered the clear language of the Constitution to be a strength and scoffed at the notion that the document would create a monarchy or oligarchy.

Fabius II

April 15, 1788

By John Dickinson of Delaware

OBSERVATIONS ON THE CONSTITUTION proposed by the FEDERAL CONVENTION.

But besides the objections originating from the before mentioned cause, that have been called local, there are other objections that are supposed to arise from the maxims of liberty and policy.–

Hence it is inferred, that the proposed system has such inherent vices, as must necessarily produce a bad administration, and at length the oppression of a monarchy or an aristocracy in the federal officers.

The writer of this address being convinced by as exact an investigation as he could make, that such mistakes may lead to the perdition of his country, esteems it his indispensable duty, strenuously to contend, that–THE POWER OF THE PEOPLE pervading the proposed system, together with the STRONG CONFEDERATION OF THE STATES, forms an adequate security against every danger that has been apprehended.

If this single assertion can be supported by facts and arguments, there will be reason to hope, that painful anxieties will be removed from the minds of some citizens, who are truely devoted to the interests of America , and who have been thrown into afflictive perplexities, by the never-ending mazes of multiplied, intricate, and contrariant disquisitions. The objectors agree, that the confederation of the states will be strong, according to the system proposed, and so strong, that many of them loudly complain of that strength. On this part of the assertion, there is no dispute: But some of the objections that have been published, strike at another part of the principle assumed, and deny, that the system is sufficiently founded on the power of the people. The course of regular enquiry demands, that these objections should be considered in the first place. If they are removed, then all the rest of the objections, concerning unnecessary taxations, standing armies, the abolishment of trials by jury, the liberty of the press, the freedom of commerce, the judicial, executive, and legislative authorities of the several states, & the rights of citizens, and the other abuses of federal government, must, of consequence, be rejected, if the principle contains the salutary, purifying, and preserving qualities attributed to it. The question then will be-Not what may be done when the government shall be turned into a tyranny but, how the government can be so turned?

Thus unembarrassed by subordinate discussions, we may come fairly to the contemplation of that superior point, and be better enabled to discover, whether our attention to it will afford any lights, whereby we may be conducted to peace, liberty, and safety.

The objections, denying that the system proposed is sufficiently founded on the power of the people, state, that the number of the federal trustees or officers, is too small, and that they are to hold their offices too long.

One would really have supposed, that smallness of number could not be termed a cause of danger, as influence must encrease with enlargement. If this is a fault, it will soon be corrected, as an addition will be often made to the number of the senators, and, almost every year, to that of the representatives; and in all probability much sooner, than we shall be able and willing to bear the expence of the addition.

As to the senate, it never can be, and it never ought to be large, if it is to possess the powers, which almost all the objectors seem inclined to allot to it, as will be evident to every intelligent person, who considers those powers.

Tho' small, let it be remembered, that it is to be created by the sovereignties of the several states; that is, by the persons, whom the people of each state shall judge to be most worthy, and who, surely, will be religiously attentive to making a selection, in which the interest and honour of their state will be so extensively concerned. It should be remembered too, that this is the same manner, in which the members of Congress are now appointed; and that herein, the sovereignties of the states are so intimately involved, that however a renunciation of part of these powers may be desired by some of the states, it NEVER will be obtained from the rest of them. Peaceable, fraternal, and benevolent as these are, they think, the concessions they have made, ought to satisfy all.

That the senate may always be kept full, without the interference of Congress, it is provided that if vacancies happen by resignation or otherwise, during the recess of the legislature of any state, the executive thereof may make temporary appointments, until the next meeting of the legislature, which shall then fill up such vacancies.

As to the house representatives, it is to consist of a number of persons, not exceeding one for every thirty thousand. Thus, every member of that house will be elected by a majority of the electors of a whole state; or, by a majority of electors, among thirty thousand persons. These electors will reside, widely dispersed, over an extensive country. Cabal and corruption will be as impracticable, as, on such occasions, human institutions can render them. The will of freemen, thus circumstanced, will give the fiat. The purity of election thus obtained, will amply compensate for the supposed defect representation; and the members, thus chosen, will be most apt to harmonize in their proceedings, with the general interests, feelings, and sentiments of the people.

Allowing such an increase of population as, from experience and a variety of causes, may be expected, the representatives, in a short period, will amount to several hundreds, and most probably long before any change of manners for the worse, that might tempt or encourage our rulers to mal-administration, will take place on this continent.

That this house may always be kept full, without the interference of Congress, it is provided in the system, that when vacancies happen in any state, the executive authority thereof shall issue writs of election to fill such vacancies.

But, it seems, the number of the federal officers is not only too small: They are to hold their offices too long.

This objection surely applies not to the house representatives, who are to be chosen every two years, especially if the extent of empire, and the vast variety and importance of their deliberations, be considered. In that view, they and the senate will actually be not only legislative but also diplomatic bodies, perpetually engaged in the arduous task of reconciling, in their determinations, the interests of several sovereign states, not to insist on the necessity of a competent knowledge of foreign affairs, relative to the states.

They who desire the representatives to be chosen every year, should exceed Newton in calculations, if they attempt to evince, that the public business would, in that case, be better transacted, than when they are chosen every two years. The idea, however, should be excused for the zeal that prompted it.

Is monarchy or aristocracy to be produced, without the consent of the people, by a house ofrepresentatives, thus constituted? It has been unanimously agreed by the friends of liberty, that FREQUENT ELECTIONS OF THE REPRESENTATIVES OF THE PEOPLE, ARE THE MOST SOVEREIGN REMEDY OF ALL GRIEVANCES IN A FREE GOVERNMENT. Let us pass on to the senate.

At the end of two years after the first election, one third is to be elected for six years. Of the remaining thirds, one will constantly have but four years, and the other but two years to continue in office. The whole number at first will amount but to twenty-six, must ever continue very small, will be regularly renovated by the biennial election of one third, and will be overlooked, and overawed by the house representatives, nearly three times more numerous at the beginning, rapidly and vastly augmenting, and more enabled to overlook & overawe them, by holding their offices for two years, as thereby they will acquire better information, respecting national affairs. These representatives will also command the public purse, as all bills for raising revenue, must originate in their house.

As in the Roman armies, when the Principes and Hastati had failed, there were still the Triarii, who generally put things to rights, so we shall be supplied with another resource.

We are to have a president, to superintend, and if he thinks the public weal requires it, to controul any act of the representatives and senate.

This president is to be chosen, not by the people at large, because it may not be possible, that all the freemen of the empire should always have the necessary information, for directing their choice of such an officer; nor by Congress, lest it should disturb the national councils; nor BY ANY ONE BODY WHATEVER, for fear of undue influence.

He is to be chosen in the following manner. Each state shall appoint, as the legislature thereof may direct, a number of electors, equal to the whole number of senators and representatives, to which the state shall be entitled in Congress: but no senator or representative, or person holding an office of trust or profit under the United States, shall be appointed an elector. As these electors are to be appointed, as the legislature of each state may direct, of course they will be appointed by the people of the state, if such be the pleasure of the people. Thus, the fairest, freest opening is given, for each state to chuse such electors for this purpose, as shall be most signally qualified to fulfil the trust.

To guard against undue influence these electors, thus chosen, are to meet in their respective states, and vote by ballot; and still further to guard against it, Congress may determine the time of chusing the electors, and the day on which they shall give their votes-WHICH DAY SHALL BE THE SAME THROUGHOUT THE UNITED STATES. All the votes from the several states are to be transmitted to Congress, and therein counted. The president is to hold his office for four years. When these electors meet in their respective states, utterly vain will be the unreasonable suggestions derived from partiality. The electors may throw away their votes, mark, with public disappointment, some person improperly favoured by them, or justly revering the duties of their office, dedicate their votes to the best interests of their country.

This president will be no dictator. two thirds of the representatives and the senate may pass any law, notwithstanding his dissent; and he is removable and punishable for misbehaviour.

Can the limited, fluctuating senate, placed amidst, such powers, if it should become willing, ever become able, to make America pass under its yoke? The senators will generally be inhabitants of places very distant one from another. They can scarcely be acquainted till they meet. Few of them can ever act together for any length of time, unless their good conduct recommends them to a re-election; and then there will be frequent changes in a body dependent upon the choice of other bodies, the legislatures of the several states, that are altering every year. Machiavel and Cesar Borgia together could not form a conspiracy in such a senate, dangerous to any but themselves and their accomplices.

It is essential to every good government, that there should be some council, permanent enough to get a due knowledge of affairs internal and external; so constituted, that by some deaths or removals, the current of information should not be impeded or disturbed; and so regulated, as to be responsible to, and controulable by the people. Where can the authority for combining these advantages, be more safely, beneficially or satisfactorily, lodged, than in the senate, to be formed according to the plan proposed? Shall parts of the trust be committed to the president, with counsellors who shall subscribe their advices? If assaults upon liberty are to be guarded against, and surely they ought to be with sleepless vigilance, why should we depend more on the commander in chief of the army and navy of the United States, and of the militia of the several states, and on his counsellors, whom he may secretly influence, than on the senate to be appointed by the persons exercising, the sovereign authority of the several states? In truth, the objections against the powers of the senate originated from a desire to have them, or at least some of them, vested in a body, in which the several states should be represented, in proportion to the number of inhabitants, as in the house of representatives. This method is UNATTAINABLE, and the wish for it should be dismissed from every mind, that desires the existence of a confederation.

What assurance can be given, or what probability be assigned, that a board of councillors would continue honest, longer than the senate? Or, that they would possess more useful information, respecting all the states, then the senators of all the states? It appears needless to pursue this argument any further.

How varied, ballanced, concordant, and benign, is the system proposed to us? To secure the freedom, and promote the happiness of these and future states, by giving THE WILL OF THE PEOPLE a decisive influence over the whole, and over all the parts, with what a comprehensive arrangement does it embrace different modes of representation, from an election by a county to an election by an empire? What are the complicated ballot, and all the refined devices of Venice for maintaining her aristocracy, when compared with this plain dealing work for diffusing the blessings of equal liberty and common prosperity over myriads of the human race?

All the foundations before mentioned, of the federal government, are by the proposed system to be established, in the most clear, strong, positive, unequivocal expressions, of which our language is capable. Magna charta, or any other law, never contained clauses more decisive and emphatic. While the people of these states have sense, they will understand them; and while they have spirit, they will make them to be observed.

Fabius III by John Dickinson

Editor's Introduction:

Fabius III offered a philosophical and theological exposition on the nature of power, sovereignty, and liberty. Dickinson's Quaker rearing and devout Christian beliefs often dictated his public course. His advocacy of the Constitution was no different. Dickinson argued that men had to surrender a portion of their rights to live in a complex civilization, and that man, as a naturally social creation made in the image of God, could not thrive nor find happiness unless he existed in a society. "Contributing" his rights for the good the whole created "security" which led to freedom. This is similar to the Puritan belief in the liberty of the community over individual liberty, and like the Puritans, Dickinson grounded his arguments in Scripture.

He then expanded this view to include the federal republic. Yet, just as with individual citizens, the center could not abuse any part of the system, as the rest of the system would view it as an unjust and illegal infringement on the liberty of the whole and stamp out this type of usurpation. Dickinson maintained his belief in real federalism even when arguing that some liberties or rights had to be delegated to the center for the good of the whole.

Fabius III

April 17, 1788

By John Dickinson of Delaware

OBSERVATIONS ON THE CONSTITUTION proposed by the FEDERAL CONVENTION

The Writer of this Address hopes, that he will now be thought so disengaged from the objections against the part of the principle assumed, concerning the power of the people, that he may be excused for recurring to his assertion, that-the power of the people pervading the proposed system, together with the strong confederation of the states, will form an adequate security against every danger that has been apprehended.

It is a mournful, but may be a useful truth, that the liberty of single republics has generally been destroyed by some of the citizens, and of confederated republics, by some of the associated states.

It is more pleasing, and may be more profitable to reflect, that, their tranquility and prosperity have commonly been promoted, in proportion to the strength of their government for protecting the worthy against the licentious.

As in forming political society, each individual contributes some of his rights, in order that he may, from a common stock of rights, derive greater benefits, than he could from merely his own; so, in forming confederation, each political society should contribute such a share of their rights, as will, from a common stock of rights, produce the largest quantity of benefits for them.

But, what is that share? and, how to be managed? Momentous questions! Here, flattery is treason; and error, destruction.

Are they unanswerable? No. Our most gracious Creator does not condemn us to sigh for unattainable blessedness: But one thing he demands-that we should seek for it in his way, and not in our own.

Humility and benevolence must take place of pride and overweening selfishness. Reason, then rising above these mists, will discover to us, that we cannot be true to ourselves, without being true to others-that to be solitary, is to be wretched-that to love our neighbours as ourselves, is to love ourselves in the best manner-that is to give, is to gain-and, that we never consult our own happiness more effectually, than when we most endeavour to correspond with the Divine designs, communicating happiness, as much as we can, to our fellow creatures. INESTIMABLE TRUTH! sufficient, if they do not barely ask what it is, to melt tyrants into men, and soothe] the inflamed minds of a multitude into mildness-sufficient to overflow this earth with unknown - felicity)INESTIMABLE TRUTH! which our Maker, in his providence, enables us, not only to talk and write about, but to adopt in practice of vast extent, and of instructive example.

Let us now enquire, if there be not some principle, simple as the laws of nature in other instances, from which, as from a source, the many benefits of society are deduced.

We may with reverence say, that our Creator designed men for society, because otherwise they could not be happy. They cannot be happy without freedom; nor free without security; that is, without the absence of fear nor thus secure, without society. The conclusion is strictly syllogistic-that men cannot be free without society. Of course, they can not be equally free without society, which freedom produces the greatest happiness.

As these premises are invincible, we have advanced a considerable way in our enquiry upon this deeply interesting subject If we can determine, what share of his rights, every individual must contribute to the common stock of rights in forming society, for obtaining equal freedom, we determine at the same time, what share of their rights each political society must contribute to the common stock of rights informing confederation, which is only a larger society, for obtaining equal freedom: For, if the deposit be not proportioned to the magnitude of the association in the latter case, it will generate the same mischief among the component parts of it, from their inequality, that would result from a defective contribution to association in the former case, among the component parts of it, from their inequality.

Each individual then must contribute such a share of his rights, as is necessary for attaining that SECURITY that is essential to freedom; and he is bound to make this contribution by the law of his nature; that is, by the command of his creator; therefore, he must submit his will, in what concerns all, to the will of the whole society. What does he lose by this submission? The power of doing injuries to others-the dread of suffering injuries from them-and, the in commodities of mental or bodily weakness-What does he gain by it? The aid of those associated with him-protection against injuries from them or others-a capacity of enjoying his undelegated rights to the best advantage-a repeal of his fears-and tranquility of mind or, in other words, that perfect liberty better described in the Holy Scriptures, than any where else, in these expressions-"When everyman shall sit under his vine, and under his fig-tree, and NONE SHALL MAKE HIM AFRAID."

The like submission, with a correspondent expansion and accommodation, must be made between states, for obtaining the like benefits in a confederation. Men are the materials of both. As the largest number is but a junction of units a confederation is but an assembly of individuals. The sanction of that law of his nature, upon which the happiness of a man depends in society, must attend him in confederation, or he becomes unhappy; for confederation should promote the happiness of individuals, or it does not answer the intended purpose. Herein there is a progression, not a contradiction. As man, he becomes a citizen; as a citizen, he becomes a fœderalist. The generation of one, is not the destruction of the other. He carries into society his naked rights: These thereby improved, he carries into confederation. If that sacred law before mentioned, is not here observed, the confederation would not be real, but pretended. He would confide, and be deceived.

The dilemma is inevitable. There must either be one will, or several wills. If but one will, all the people are concerned; if several wills, few comparatively are concerned. Surprizing! that this doctrine should be contended for by those, who declare, that the constitution is not founded on a bottom broad enough; and, though THE WHOLE PEOPLE of the United States are to be TREBLY represented in it in THREE DIFFERENT MODES of representation, and their servants will have the most advantageous situation and opportunities of acquiring all requisite information for the welfare of the whole union, yet insist for a privilege of opposing obstructing, and confounding their measures taken with common consent for the general weal, by the delays, negligences, rivalries, or other selfish views of parts of the union.

Thus, while one state should be relied upon by the union for giving aid, upon a recommendation of Congress, to another in distress, the latter might be ruined; and the state relied upon, might suppose, it would gain by such an event.

When any persons speak of a confederation, do they, or do they not acknowledge, that the whole is interested in the safety of every part-in the agreement of parts-in the relation of parts to one another-to the whole-or, to other societies? If they do-then, the authority of the whole, must be co-extensive with its interests-and if it is, the will of the whole must and ought in such cases to govern.

If they do not acknowledge, that the whole is thus interested, the conversation should cease. Such persons mean not a confederation, but something else.

As to the idea, that this superintending sovereign will must of consequence destroy the subordinate sovereignties of the several states, it is begging concession of the question, by inferring that a manifest and great usefulness must necessarily end in abuse; and not only so, but it requires an extinction of the principle of all society: for, the subordinate sovereignties, or, in other words, the undelegated rights of the several states, in a confederation, stand upon the very same foundation with the undelegated rights of individuals in a society, the federal sovereign will being composed of the subordinate sovereign wills of the several confederated states. If as some persons seem to think, a bill of rights is the best security of rights, the sovereignties of the several states have this best security by the proposed constitution, & more than this best security, for they are not barely declared to be rights, but are taken into it as component parts, for their perpetual preservation by themselves. In short, the government of each State is, and is to be, sovereign and supreme in all matters that relate to each state only. It is to be subordinate barely in those matters that relate to the whole; and it will be their own faults, if the several states suffer the federal sovereignty to interfere in things of their respective jurisdictions. An instance of such interference with regard to any single state, will be a dangerous precedent as to all, and therefore will be guarded against by all, as the trustees or servants of the several states will not dare, if they retain their senses, so to violate the independent sovereignty of their respective states, that justly darling object of American affections, to which they are responsible, besides being endeared by all the charities of life.

The common sense of mankind agrees to the devolution of individual wills in society; and if it has not been as universally assented to in confederation, the reasons are evident, & worthy of being retained in remembrance by Americans. They were, want opportunities, or the loss of them, through defects of knowledge and virtue. The principle however has been sufficiently vindicated in imperfect combinations, as their prosperity has generally been commensurate to its operation.

How beautifully and forcibly does the inspired Apostle Saint Paul, argue upon a sublimer subject, with a train of reasoning strictly applicable to the present ? His words are-"If the foot shall say, because I am not the hand, I am not of the body; is it therefore not of the body? and if the ear shall say, because I am not the eye, I am not of the body; is it therefore not of the body?" As plainly inferring, as could be done in that allegorical manner, the strongest censure of such partial discontents and dissentions, especially, as his meaning is enforced by his description of the benefits of union in these expressions-"But, now they are many members, yet but one body: and the eye CANNOT say to the hand, I have no need of thee; nor again, the head to the feet, I have no need of you."

When the commons of Rome upon a rupture with the senate, seceded in arms upon the Mons sacer, Menenius Agrippa used the like allusion to the human body, in his famous apologue of a quarrel among some of the members. The unpolished but honest-hearted Romans of that day, understood him, and were appeased. They returned to the city, and-the world was conquered.

Another comparison has been made by statesmen and the learned, between a natural and a political body; and no wonder indeed, when the title of the latter was borrowed from the resemblance. It has therefore been justly observed, that if a mortification takes place in one or some of the limbs, and the rest of the body is sound, remedies maybe applied, and not only the contagion prevented from spreading, but the diseased part or parts saved by the connection with the body, & restored to former usefulness. When general putrefaction prevails, death is to be expected. History sacred and prophane tells us, that, CORRUPTION OF MANNERS IS THE VERY BASIS OF SLAVERY.

Fabius IV by John Dickison

Editor's Introduction:

Dickinson insisted in Fabius IV that liberty could only be preserved by the people who had a "duty to watch and...right to take care that the Constitution be preserved." He conceded that a good constitution may not always produced a good government, but he had faith in the established checks and in the American public that tyranny could be adequately resisted. He reiterated that the Senate represented "the sovereignties of the several states" and that the president and supreme court would dually represent the "sovereignties of the several states and the people of the whole union." Dickinson believed that when the document was reviewed with a clear mind, no reasonable man would determine that it was not the best system that could be devised for "United America."

Fabius IV

April 19, 1788

By John Dickinson of Delaware

OBSERVATIONS ON THE CONSTITUTION proposed by the FEDERAL CONVENTION.

Another question remains. How are the contributed rights to be managed? The resolution has been in great measure anticipated, by what has been said concerning the system proposed. Some few reflections may perhaps finish it.

If it can be considered separately, [a] Constitution is the organization of the contributed rights in society. Government is certainly the exercise of them. It is intended for the benefit of the governed; of course can have no just powers but what conduce to that end: & the awefulness of the trust is demonstrated in this—that it is founded on the nature of man, that is, on the will of his MAKER, and is therefore sacred.

Let the reader be pleased to consider the writer, as treating of equal liberty with reference to the people and states of United America, and their meditated confederation.

If the organization of a constitution be defective, it may be amended.

A good constitution promotes, but not always produces a good administration.

The government must never be lodged in a single body. From such an one, with an unlucky composition of its parts, rash, partial, illegal, and when intoxicated with success, even cruel, insolent, &contemptible edicts, may at times be expected. By these, if other mischiefs do not follow, the national dignity may be impaired.

Several inconveniences might attend a division of the government into two bodies, that probably would be avoided in another arrangement.

The judgment of the most enlightened among mankind, confirmed by multiplied experiments, points out the propriety of government being committed to such a number of great departments, as can be introduced without confusion, distinct in office, and yet connected in operation. It seems to be agreed, that three or four of these departments are a competent number.

Such a repartition appears well calculated, to encrease the safety and repose of the governed, which, with the advancement of their happiness in other respects, are the objects of government; as thereby there will be more obstructions interposed, against errors, feuds, and frauds, in the administration, and the interference of the people need be less frequent. Thus, wars, tumults, and uneasinesses, are avoided. The departments so constituted, may therefore be said to be balanced.

But, notwithstanding, it must be granted, that a bad administration may take place. What is then to be done? The answer is instantly found—Let the Fasces be lowered before—not the Majesty, it is not a term fit for mortals—but, before the supreme sovereignty of the people. IT IS THEIR DUTY TO WATCH, AND THEIR RIGHT TO TAKE CARE, THAT THE CONSTITUTION BE PRESERVED; or in the Roman phrase on perilous occasions—To PROVIDE, THAT THE REPUBLIC RECEIVE NO DAMAGE.

Political bodies are properly said to be balanced, with respect to this primary origination and ultimate destination, not to any intrinsic or constitutional properties. It is the power from which they proceed, and which they serve, that truly and of right balances them.

But, as a good constitution not always produces a good administration, a defective one not always excludes it. Thus, in governments very different from those of United America, general manners and customs, improvement in knowledge, and the education and disposition of princes, not unfrequently soften the features, and qualify the defects. Jewels of value are substituted, in the place of the rare and genuine orient of highest price and brightest lustre: and though the sovereigns cannot even in their ministers, be brought to account by the governed, yet there are instances of their conduct indicating veneration for the rights of the people, and an internal conviction of the guilt that attends their violation. Some of them appear to be fathers of their countries. Revered princes! Friends of mankind! May peace be in their lives, and hope sit smiling in their beds of death.

By this animating, presiding will of the people, is meant a reasonable, not a distracted will. When frensy seizes the mass, it would be madness to think of their happiness, that is, of their freedom. They will infallibly have a Philip or a Cesar, to bleed them into soberness of mind. At present we are cool; and let us attend to our business.

Our government under the proposed confederation, will be guarded by a repetition of the strongest cautions against excesses. In the senate the sovereignties of the several states will be equally represented; in the house representatives, the people of the whole union will be equally represented; and, in the president, and the federal independent judges, so much concerned in the execution of the laws, and in the determination of their constitutionality, the sovereignties of the several states and the people of the whole union, will be conjointly represented.

Where was there ever or where is there now upon the face of the earth, a government so diversified and at tempered? If a work formed with so much deliberation, so respectful and affectionate an attention to the interests, feelings, and sentiments of all United America, will not satisfy, what would satisfy all United America?

It seems highly probable, that those who would reject this labour of public love, would also have rejected the Heaven-taught institution of trial by jury, had they been consulted upon its establishment. Would they not have cried out, that there never was framed so detestable, so paltry, and so tyrannical a device for extinguishing freedom, and throwing unbounded domination into the hands of the king and barons, under a contemptible pretence of preserving it? What! Can freedom be preserved by imprisoning its guardians? Can freedom be preserved, by keeping twelve men closely confined without meat, drink, fire, or candle, until they unanimously agree, and this to be infinitely repeated? Can freedom be preserved, by thus delivering up a number of freemen to a monarch and an aristocracy, fortified by dependant and obedient judges and officers, to be shut up, until under duress they speak as they are ordered? Why can't the twelve jurors separate, after hearing the evidence, return to their respective homes, and there take time, and think of the matter at their ease? Is there not a variety of ways, in which causes have been, and can be tried, without this tremendous, unprecedented inquisition? Why then is it insisted on; but because the fabricators of it know that it will, and intend that it shall reduce the people to slavery? Away with it-Freemen will never be enthralled by so insolent, so execrable, so pitiful a contrivance.

Happily for us our ancestors thought otherwise. They were not so over-nice &curious, as to refuse blessings, because, they might possibly be abused.

They perceived, that the uses included were great and manifest. Perhaps they did not foresee, that from this acorn, as it were, would grow up oaks, that changing their native soil for another element, would bound over raging mountains of waters, bestow and receive benefits around the globe, and secure the just liberties of the nation for a long succession of ages. As to abuses, they trusted to their own spirit for preventing or correcting them: And worthy is it of deep consideration by every friend of freedom, that abuses that seem to be but "trifles may be attended by fatal consequences. What can be "trifling," that diminishes or detracts from the only defence, that ever was found against "open attacks and secret machinations) It originates from a knowledge of human nature. With a superior force, wisdom, and benevolence united, it rives the difficulties that have distressed, or destroyed the rest of mankind. It reconciles contradictions, immensity of power, with safety of private station. It is ever new & always the same.

Trial by jury and the dependance of taxation upon representation, those corner stones of liberty, were not obtained by a bill of rights, or any other records, and have not been and cannot be preserved by them. They and all other rights must be preserved, by soundness of sense and honesty of heart. Compared with these, what are a bill of rights, or any characters drawn upon paper or parchment, those frail remembrancers? Do we want to be reminded, that the sun enlightens, warms, invigorates, and cheers? or how horrid it would be, to have his blessed beams intercepted, by our being thrust into mines or dungeons? Liberty is the sun of freemen, and the beams are their rights.

"It is the duty which everyman owes to his country, his friends, his posterity, and himself, to maintain to the utmost of his power this valuable palladium in all its rights; to restore it to its antient dignity, if at all impaired by the different value of property, or otherwise deviated - from its first institution; to amend it, wherever it is defective; and above all, to guard with the most jealous circumspection against the new and arbitrary methods of trial, which, under a variety of plausible pretences, may in time imperceptibly undermine this best preservative of liberty." trial by jury is our birthright; and tempted to his own ruin, by some seducing spirit, must be the man, who in opposition to the genius of United America, shall dare to attempt its subversion.

In the proposed confederation, it is preserved inviolable in criminal cases, and cannot be altered in other respects, but when the genius of United America demands it.

There seems to be a disposition in men to find fault, no difficult matter, rather than to do right. The works of creation itself have been objected to: and one learned prince declared, that if he had been consulted, they would have been improved. With what book has so much fault been found, as with the Bible? Perhaps, principally, because it so clearly and strongly enjoins men to do right. How many, how plausible objections have been made against it, with how much ardor, with how much pains? Yet, the book has done an immensity of good in the world; would do more, if duly regarded; and might lead the objectors themselves and their posterity to perpetual happiness, if they would value it as they ought.

When objections are made to a system of high import, should they not be weighed against the benefits? Are these great, positive, immediate? Is there a chance endangering them by rejection or delay? May they not be attained without admitting the objections, supposing the objections to be well founded? If the objections are well founded, may they not be hereafter admitted, without danger disgust, or inconvenience? Is the system so formed, that they may be thus admitted? May they not be of less efficacy, than they are thought to be by their authors? Are they not designed to hinder evils, which are generally deemed to be sufficiently provided against? May not the admission of them prevent benefits, that might otherwise be obtained? In political affairs, is it not more safe and advantageous, for all to agree in measures that may not be best, than to quarrel among themselves, what are best?

When questions of this kind with regard to the plan proposed, are calmly considered, it seems reasonable to hope, that every faithful citizen of United America, will make up his mind, with much satisfaction to himself, and advantage to his country.

Fabius VIII by John Dickison

Editor's Introduction:

Dickinson concluded his Fabius series with a series of questions designed to force the reader to consider the benefits of the Constitution. To Dickinson, the Constitution would protect the "states of America" and would "communicate equal liberty and assure just protection to them." He always regarded the Union as a confederacy of States, and in fact called it a "confederacy of republics." He also provided arguably the best summary of originalism when he wrote, "America is, and will be, divided into several sovereign states, each possessing every power proper for governing within its own limits for its own purposes, and also for acting as a member of the union." That was a nail in the coffin of nationalism, the "one nation of people" thesis advanced by nationalists after the Constitution was ratified. Dickinson never sold the document on those terms, nor did anyone else. Dickinson thought that amendments could and should be proposed as time and circumstances dictated. This would be the only legal way of making the Constitution a "living document." Regardless, Dickinson judged the Constitution to be a blessing and a benefit to the continued prosperity of "United America," a confederation of "sovereign states."

Fabius VIII

April 29, 1788

By John Dickinson of Delaware

OBSERVATIONS ON THE CONSTITUTION proposed by the FEDERAL CONVENTION.

The proposed confederation offers to us a system of diversified representation in the legislative, executive, and judicial departments, as essentially necessary to the good government of an extensive republican empire. Every argument to recommend it, receives new force, by contemplating events, that must take place. The number of states in America will encrease. If not united to the present, the consequences are evident. If united, it must be by a plan that will communicate equal liberty and assure just protection to them. These ends can never be attained, but by a close combination of the several states.

It has been asserted, that a very extensive territory cannot be ruled by a government of republican form. What is meant by this proposition? Is it intended to abolish all ideas of connection, and to precipitate us into the miseries of division, either as single states, or partial confederacies? To stupify us into despondence, that destruction may certainly seize us? The fancy of poets never feign'd so dire a Metamorphosis, as is now held up to us. The Egis of their Minerva was only said to turn men into stones. This spell is to turn "a band of brethren into a monster, preying upon itself and prey'd upon by all its enemies.

If hope is not to be abandoned, common sense teaches us to attempt the best means of preservation. This is all that men can do, and this they ought to do. Will it be said, that any kind of disunion, or a connection tending to it, is preferable to a firm union? Or, is there any charm in that despotism, which is said, to be alone competent to the rule of such an empire? There is no evidence of fact, nor any deduction of reason, that justifies the assertion. It is true, that extensive territory has in general been arbitrarily governed; and it is as true, that a number of republics, in such territory, loosely connected, must inevitably rot into despotism. Such territory has never been governed by a confederacy of republics. Granted. But, Where was there ever a confederacy of republics, in such territory, united, as these states are to be by the proposed constitution? Where was there ever a confederacy, in which, the sovereignty of each state was equally represented in one legislative body, the people of each state equally represented in another, and the sovereignties & people of all the states conjointly represented in a third branch? Or, in which, no law could be made, but by the agreement of three such branches? Or, in which, the appointment to federal offices was vested in a chief magistrate chosen as our president is to be, with the concurrence of a senate elected by the sovereignties of each state? Or, in which, the other acts of the executive department were regulated, as they are to be with us? Or, in which, the federal judges were to hold their offices independently and during good behaviour? Or, in which, the authority over the militia and troops was so distributed and controuled, as it is to be with us? Or, in which, the people were so drawn together by religion, blood, language, manners and customs, undisturbed by former feuds or prejudices? Or, in which, the affairs relating to the whole union, were to be managed by an assembly of several representative bodies, invested with different powers that became efficient only in concert, without their being embarrassed by attention to other business? Or, in which, a provision was made for the federal revenue, without recurring to coertion, the miserable expedient of every other confederacy that has existed, an expedient always attended with odium, & often with a delay productive of irreparable damage? Where was there ever a confederacy, that thus adhered to the first principle of society, obliging by its direct authority every individual, to contribute, when the public good necessarily required it, a just proportion of aid to the support of the commonwealth protecting him-without disturbing him in the discharge of the duties owing by him to the state of which he is an inhabitant; and at the same time so amply, so anxiously provided, for bringing the interests, and even the wishes of every sovereignty and of every person of the union, under all their various modifications and impressions, into their full operation and efficacy in the national councils? The instance never existed. The conclusion ought not to be made. It is without premises.

It has been said, that the varied representation of sovereignties and people in the legislature, was a mere compromise.

This is a great and dangerous mistake. The equal representation of each state in one branch of the legislature, was an original substantive proposition, as the writer is instructed, made in Convention, very soon after the draft offered by Virginia, to which state United America is much indebted not only in other respects, but for her merit in the origination and prosecution of this momentous business.

The proposition was expressly made upon this principle, that a territory of such extent as that of United America, could not be safely and advantageously governed, but by a combination of republics, each retaining - all the rights of supreme sovereignty, excepting such as ought to be contributed to the union; that for the securer preservation of these sovereignties, they ought to be represented in a body by themselves, and with equal suffrage; and that they would be annihilated, if both branches of the legislature were to be formed representatives of the people, in proportion to the number of inhabitants in each state.

The principle appears to be well founded in reason. Why cannot a very extensive territory be ruled by a government of republican form? Because, its power must languish through distance of parts. Granted, if it be not a "body by joints and bands having nourishment ministered and knit together." If it be such a body, the objection is removed. Instead of such a perfect body, framed upon the principle that commands men to associate, and societies to confederate; that which by communicating and extending happiness, corresponds with the gracious intentions of our maker towards us his creatures; what is proposed? Truly, that the natural legs and arms of this body should be cut off because they are too weak, and their places supplied by stronger limbs of wood and iron.

Arbitrary princes rule extensive territories, by sending viceroys to govern certain districts.

America is, and will be, divided into several sovereign states, each possessing every power proper for governing within its own limits for its own purposes, and also for acting as a member of the union.

They will be civil and military stations, conveniently planted throughout the empire, with lively and regular communications. A stroke, a touch upon any part, will be immediately felt by the whole. Rome famed for imperial arts, had a glimpse of this great truth; and endeavoured, as well as her hard hearted policy would permit, to realize it in her COLONIES. They were miniatures of the capital: But wanted the vital principle of sovereignty, and were too small. They were melted down into, or overwhelmed by the nations around them. Were they now existing, they might be called, little statues-something like to our living originals. These will bear a remarkable resemblance to the mild features of patriarchal government, in which each son ruled his own houshold, and in other matters the whole family was directed by the common ancestor.

Will a people thus happily situated, and attached as they will naturally be, with an ardor of affection to their own state, ever desire to exchange their condition, for subjection to an absolute ruler, or can they ever look but with veneration, or act but with deference to that union, that alone can, under providence, preserve them from such subjection?

Can any government be devised, that will be more suited to citizens, who wish for equal freedom and common prosperity? better calculated for preventing corruption of manners? for advancing the improvements that endear or adorn life? or that can be more conformed to the nature and understanding, to the best and the last end of man? What harvests of happiness may grow from the seeds of liberty that are now sowing? The cultivation will indeed demand continual care, unceasing diligence, and frequent conflicts with difficulties. This too is consonant to the laws of our nature. As we pass through night in today, so we do through trouble into joy. Generally, the higher the prize, the deeper the suffering. We die into immortality. To object against the benefits offered to us by our Creator, by excepting to the terms annexed, is a crime to be equalled only by its folly.

Delightful are the prospects that will open to the view of United America-her sons well prepared to defend their own happiness, and ready to relieve the misery of others-her fleets formidable, but only to the unjust-her revenue sufficient, yet unoppressive-her commerce affluent, without debasing-peace and plenty within her borders and the glory that arises from a proper use of power, encircling them.

Whatever regions may be destined for servitude, let us hope, that some portions of this land may be blessed with liberty; let us be convinced, that nothing short of such an union as has been proposed, can preserve the blessing; and therefore let us be resolved to adopt it.

As to alterations, a little experience will cast more light upon the subject, than a multitude of debates. Whatever qualities are possessed by those who object, they will have the candor to confess, that they will be encountered by opponents, not in any respect inferior, and yet differing from them in judgment, upon every point they have mentioned.

Such untired industry to serve their country, did the delegates to the federal convention exert, that they not only laboured to form the best plan they could, but, provided for making at any time amendments on the authority of the people, without shaking the stability of the government. For this end, the Congress, whenever two thirds of both houses shall deem it necessary, shall propose amendments to the constitution, or, on the application of the legislatures of two thirds of the several states, SHALL call a convention for proposing amendments, which, in either case, shall be valid to all intents and purposes, as part of the constitution, when ratified by the legislatures of three-fourths of the several states, or by conventions in three-fourths thereof as one or the other mode of ratification may be proposed by Congress.

Thus, by a gradual progress, as has been done in England, we may from time to time introduce every improvement in our constitution, that shall be suitable to our situation. For this purpose, it may perhaps be adviseable, for every state, as it sees occasion, to form with the utmost deliberation, drafts of alterations respectively required by them, and to enjoin their representatives, to employ every proper method to obtain a ratification.

In this way of proceeding the undoubted sense of every state, collected - in the coolest manner, not the sense of individuals, will be laid before the whole union in Congress, and that body will be enabled with the clearest light that can be afforded by every part of it, and with the least occasion of irritation, to compare and weigh the sentiments of all United America; forthwith to adopt such alterations as are recommended by general unanimity; by degrees to devise modes of conciliation upon contradictory propositions; and to give the revered advice of our common country, upon those, if any such there should be, that in her judgment are inadmissible, because they are incompatible with the happiness of these states.

It cannot be with reason apprehended, that Congress will refuse to act upon any articles calculated to promote the common welfare, tho' they may be unwilling to act upon such as are designed to advance PARTIAL interests: but, whatever their sentiments may be, they MUST call a Convention for proposing amendments, on applications of two-thirds of the legislatures of the several states.

May those good citizens, who have sometimes turned their thoughts towards a second Convention, be pleased to consider, that there are men who speak as they do, yet do not mean as they do. These borrow the sanction of their respected names, to conceal desperate designs. May they also consider, whether persisting in the suggested plan, in preference to the constitutional provision, may not kindle flames of jealousy and discord, which all their abilities and virtues can never extinguish.

FEDERALIST NO. 78 BY ALEXANDER HAMILTON

Editor's Introduction:

Hamilton published the last eight essays of the *Federalist* on the same day, May 28, 1788. Most of these essays focus on the judicial branch, and two, *Federalist* No. 78 and *Federalist* No. 81, are among the most cited documents by the Supreme Court. Hamilton's defense of the federal judiciary began with an assessment of the independency of federal judges and included an explanation of what became known as "judicial review." John Marshall, in fact, cited No. 78 in the landmark case of *Marbury v. Madison* and used it in support of his decision to invalidate a portion of the Judiciary Act. It must be noted that Hamilton wasn't alone in believing that the Supreme Court would invalidate unconstitutional federal legislation. Other proponents of the document made similar statements and even Patrick Henry hoped the Supreme Court would provide a check on bad legislation. But because of Hamilton's role in the general government, his stature as one of the leading members of the founding generation, and the fame of the *Federalist* papers, No. 78 is the most studied and best known explanation of judicial review during the ratification period.

Federalist No. 78

May 28, 1788

By Alexander Hamilton of New York

To the People of the State of New York:

WE PROCEED now to an examination of the judiciary department of the proposed government.

In unfolding the defects of the existing Confederation, the utility and necessity of a federal judicature have been clearly pointed out. It is the less necessary to recapitulate the considerations there urged, as the propriety of the institution in the abstract is not disputed; the only questions which have been raised being relative to the manner of constituting it, and to its extent. To these points, therefore, our observations shall be confined.

The manner of constituting it seems to embrace these several objects: 1st. The mode of appointing the judges. 2d. The tenure by which they are to hold their places. 3d. The partition of the judiciary authority between different courts, and their relations to each other.

First. As to the mode of appointing the judges; this is the same with that of appointing the officers of the Union in general, and has been so fully discussed in the two last numbers, that nothing can be said here which would not be useless repetition.

Second. As to the tenure by which the judges are to hold their places; this chiefly concerns their duration in office; the provisions for their support; the precautions for their responsibility.

According to the plan of the convention, all judges who may be appointed by the United States are to hold their offices DURING GOOD BEHAVIOR; which is conformable to the most approved of the State constitutions and among the rest, to that of this State. Its propriety having been drawn into question by the adversaries of that plan, is no light symptom of the rage for objection, which disorders their imaginations and judgments. The standard of good behavior for the continuance in office of the judicial magistracy, is certainly one of the most valuable of the modern improvements in the practice of government. In a monarchy it is an excellent barrier to the despotism of the prince; in a republic it is a no less excellent barrier to the encroachments and oppressions of the representative body. And it is the best expedient which can be devised in any government, to secure a steady, upright, and impartial administration of the laws.

Whoever attentively considers the different departments of power must perceive, that, in a government in which they are separated from each other, the judiciary, from the nature of its functions, will always be the least dangerous to the political rights of the Constitution; because it will be least in a capacity to annoy or injure them. The Executive not only dispenses the honors, but holds the sword of the community. The legislature not only commands the purse, but prescribes the rules by which the duties and rights of every citizen are to be regulated. The judiciary, on the contrary, has no influence over either the sword or the purse; no direction either of the strength or of the wealth of the society; and can take no active resolution whatever. It may truly be said to have neither FORCE nor WILL, but merely judgment; and must ultimately depend upon the aid of the executive arm even for the efficacy of its judgments.

This simple view of the matter suggests several important consequences. It proves incontestably, that the judiciary is beyond comparison the weakest of the three departments of power; that it can never attack with success either of the other two; and that all possible care is requisite to enable it to defend itself against their attacks. It equally proves, that though individual oppression may now and then proceed from the courts of justice, the general liberty of the people can never be endangered from that quarter; I mean so long as the judiciary remains truly distinct from both the legislature and the Executive. For I agree, that "there is no liberty, if the power of judging be not separated from the legislative and executive powers." And it proves, in the last place, that as liberty can have nothing to fear from the judiciary alone, but would have every thing to fear from its union with either of the other departments; that as all the effects of such a union must ensue from a dependence of the former on the latter, notwithstanding a nominal and apparent separation; that as, from the natural feebleness of the judiciary, it is in continual jeopardy of being overpowered, awed, or influenced by its co-ordinate branches; and that as nothing can contribute so much to its firmness and independence as permanency in office, this quality may therefore be justly regarded as an indispensable ingredient in its constitution, and, in a great measure, as the citadel of the public justice and the public security.

The complete independence of the courts of justice is peculiarly essential in a limited Constitution. By a limited Constitution, I understand one which contains certain specified exceptions to the legislative authority; such, for instance, as that it shall pass no bills of attainder, no ex-post-facto laws, and the like. Limitations of this kind can be preserved in practice no other way than through the medium of courts of justice, whose duty it must be to declare all acts contrary to the manifest tenor of the Constitution void. Without this, all the reservations of particular rights or privileges would amount to nothing.

Some perplexity respecting the rights of the courts to pronounce legislative acts void, because contrary to the Constitution, has arisen from an imagination that the doctrine would imply a superiority of the judiciary to the legislative power. It is urged that the authority which can declare the acts of another void, must necessarily be superior to the one whose acts may be declared void. As this doctrine is of great importance in all the American constitutions, a brief discussion of the ground on which it rests cannot be unacceptable.

There is no position which depends on clearer principles, than that every act of a delegated authority, contrary to the tenor of the commission under which it is exercised, is void. No legislative act, therefore, contrary to the Constitution, can be valid. To deny this, would be to affirm, that the deputy is greater than his principal; that the servant is above his master; that the representatives of the people are superior to the people themselves; that men acting by virtue of powers, may do not only what their powers do not authorize, but what they forbid.

If it be said that the legislative body are themselves the constitutional judges of their own powers, and that the construction they put upon them is conclusive upon the other departments, it may be answered, that this cannot be the natural presumption, where it is not to be collected from any particular provisions in the Constitution. It is not otherwise to be supposed, that the Constitution could intend to enable the representatives of the people to substitute their WILL to that of their constituents. It is far more rational to suppose, that the courts were designed to be an intermediate body between the people and the legislature, in order, among other things, to keep the latter within the limits assigned to their authority. The interpretation of the laws is the proper and peculiar province of the courts. A constitution is, in fact, and must be regarded by the judges, as a fundamental law. It therefore belongs to them to ascertain its meaning, as well as the meaning of any particular act proceeding from the legislative body. If there should happen to be an irreconcilable variance between the two, that which has the superior obligation and validity ought, of course, to be preferred; or, in other words, the Constitution ought to be preferred to the statute, the intention of the people to the intention of their agents.

Nor does this conclusion by any means suppose a superiority of the judicial to the legislative power. It only supposes that the power of the people is superior to both; and that where the will of the legislature, declared in its statutes, stands in opposition to that of the people, declared in the Constitution, the judges ought to be governed by the latter rather than the former. They ought to regulate their decisions by the fundamental laws, rather than by those which are not fundamental.

This exercise of judicial discretion, in determining between two contradictory laws, is exemplified in a familiar instance. It not uncommonly happens, that there are two statutes existing at one time, clashing in whole or in part with each other, and neither of them containing any repealing clause or expression. In such a case, it is the province of the courts to liquidate and fix their meaning and operation. So far as they can, by any fair construction, be reconciled to each other, reason and law conspire to dictate that this should be done; where this is impracticable, it becomes a matter of necessity to give effect to one, in exclusion of the other. The rule which has obtained in the courts for determining their relative validity is, that the last in order of time shall be preferred to the first. But this is a mere rule of construction, not derived from any positive law, but from the nature and reason of the thing. It is a rule not enjoined upon the courts by legislative provision, but adopted by themselves, as consonant to truth and propriety, for the direction of their conduct as interpreters of the law. They thought it reasonable, that between the interfering acts of an EQUAL authority, that which was the last indication of its will should have the preference.

But in regard to the interfering acts of a superior and subordinate authority, of an original and derivative power, the nature and reason of the thing indicate the converse of that rule as proper to be followed. They teach us that the prior act of a superior ought to be preferred to the subsequent act of an inferior and subordinate authority; and that accordingly, whenever a particular statute contravenes the Constitution, it will be the duty of the judicial tribunals to adhere to the latter and disregard the former.

It can be of no weight to say that the courts, on the pretense of a repugnancy, may substitute their own pleasure to the constitutional intentions of the legislature. This might as well happen in the case of two contradictory statutes; or it might as well happen in every adjudication upon any single statute. The courts must declare the sense of the law; and if they should be disposed to exercise WILL instead of JUDGMENT, the consequence would equally be the substitution of their pleasure to that of the legislative body. The observation, if it prove any thing, would prove that there ought to be no judges distinct from that body.

If, then, the courts of justice are to be considered as the bulwarks of a limited Constitution against legislative encroachments, this consideration will afford a strong argument for the permanent tenure of judicial offices, since nothing will contribute so much as this to that independent spirit in the judges which must be essential to the faithful performance of so arduous a duty.

This independence of the judges is equally requisite to guard the Constitution and the rights of individuals from the effects of those ill humors, which the arts of designing men, or the influence of particular conjunctures, sometimes disseminate among the people themselves, and which, though they speedily give place to better information, and more deliberate reflection, have a tendency, in the meantime, to occasion dangerous innovations in the government, and serious oppressions of the minor party in the community. Though I trust the friends of the proposed Constitution will never concur with its enemies, in questioning that fundamental principle of republican government, which admits the right of the people to alter or abolish the established Constitution, whenever they find it inconsistent with their happiness, yet it is not to be inferred from this principle, that the representatives of the people, whenever a momentary inclination happens to lay hold of a majority of their constituents, incompatible with the provisions in the existing Constitution, would, on that account, be justifiable in a violation of those provisions; or that the courts would be under a greater obligation to connive at infractions in this shape, than when they had proceeded wholly from the cabals of the representative body. Until the people have, by some solemn and authoritative act, annulled or changed the established form, it is binding upon themselves collectively, as well as individually; and no presumption, or even knowledge, of their sentiments, can warrant their representatives in a departure from it, prior to such an act. But it is easy to see, that it would require an uncommon portion of fortitude in the judges to do their duty as faithful guardians of the Constitution, where legislative invasions of it had been instigated by the major voice of the community.

But it is not with a view to infractions of the Constitution only, that the independence of the judges may be an essential safeguard against the effects of occasional ill humors in the society. These sometimes extend no farther than to the injury of the private rights of particular classes of citizens, by unjust and partial laws. Here also the firmness of the judicial magistracy is of vast importance in mitigating the severity and confining the operation of such laws. It not only serves to moderate the immediate mischiefs of those which may have been passed, but it operates as a check upon the legislative body in passing them; who, perceiving that obstacles to the success of iniquitous intention are to be expected from the scruples of the courts, are in a manner compelled, by the very motives of the injustice they meditate, to qualify their attempts. This is a circumstance calculated to have more influence upon the character of our governments, than but few may be aware of. The benefits of the integrity and moderation of the judiciary have already been felt in more States than one; and though they may have displeased those whose sinister expectations they may have disappointed, they must have commanded the esteem and applause of all the virtuous and disinterested. Considerate men, of every description, ought to prize whatever will tend to beget or fortify that temper in the courts: as no man can be sure that he may not be to-morrow the victim of a spirit of injustice, by which he may be a gainer to-day. And every man must now feel, that the inevitable tendency of such a spirit is to sap the foundations of public and private confidence, and to introduce in its stead universal distrust and distress.

That inflexible and uniform adherence to the rights of the Constitution, and of individuals, which we perceive to be indispensable in the courts of justice, can certainly not be expected from judges who hold their offices by a temporary commission. Periodical appointments, however regulated, or by whomsoever made, would, in some way or other, be fatal to their necessary independence. If the power of making them was committed either to the Executive or legislature, there would be danger of an improper complaisance to the branch which possessed it; if to both, there would be an unwillingness to hazard the displeasure of either; if to the people, or to persons chosen by them for the special purpose, there would be too great a disposition to consult popularity, to justify a reliance that nothing would be consulted but the Constitution and the laws.

There is yet a further and a weightier reason for the permanency of the judicial offices, which is deducible from the nature of the qualifications they require. It has been frequently remarked, with great propriety, that a voluminous code of laws is one of the inconveniences necessarily connected with the advantages of a free government. To avoid an arbitrary discretion in the courts, it is indispensable that they should be bound down by strict rules and precedents, which serve to define and point out their duty in every particular case that comes before them; and it will readily be conceived from the variety of controversies which grow out of the folly and wickedness of mankind, that the records of those precedents must unavoidably swell to a very considerable bulk, and must demand long and laborious study to acquire a competent knowledge of them. Hence it is, that there can be but few men in the society who will have sufficient skill in the laws to qualify them for the stations of judges. And making the proper deductions for the ordinary depravity of human nature, the number must be still smaller of those who unite the requisite integrity with the requisite knowledge. These considerations apprise us, that the government can have no great option between fit character; and that a temporary duration in office, which would naturally discourage such characters from quitting a lucrative line of practice to accept a seat on the bench, would have a tendency to throw the administration of justice into hands less able, and less well qualified, to conduct it with utility and dignity. In the present circumstances of this country, and in those in which it is likely to be for a long time to come, the disadvantages on this score would be greater than they may at first sight appear; but it must be confessed, that they are far inferior to those which present themselves under the other aspects of the subject.

Upon the whole, there can be no room to doubt that the convention acted wisely in copying from the models of those constitutions which have established GOOD BEHAVIOR as the tenure of their judicial offices, in point of duration; and that so far from being blamable on this account, their plan would have been inexcusably defective, if it had wanted this important feature of good government. The experience of Great Britain affords an illustrious comment on the excellence of the institution.

FEDERALIST NO. 80 BY ALEXANDER HAMILTON

Editor's Introduction:

Hamilton outlines the limits of federal judicial authority in *Federalist* No. 80. He aims to reassure opponents that the powers of the judicial branch were both necessary and clearly defined by the document, meaning that they could not be abused and were essential to the proposed plan of Union. He thinks the new judicial branch would solve some of the glaring weaknesses in the Articles of Confederation, most importantly the role of the federal government in dealing with international disputes. Hamilton also narrowly describes what federal laws would come under the jurisdiction of the federal court system, i.e. those that are expressly denied by Article I, Section 10. He concludes by contending that if the federal judiciary abused its power, the legislature would have the authority to limit federal court jurisdiction.

Federalist No. 80

May 28, 1788

By Alexander Hamilton of New York

To the People of the State of New York:

To JUDGE with accuracy of the proper extent of the federal judicature, it will be necessary to consider, in the first place, what are its proper objects.

It seems scarcely to admit of controversy, that the judicary authority of the Union ought to extend to these several descriptions of cases: 1st, to all those which arise out of the laws of the United States, passed in pursuance of their just and constitutional powers of legislation; 2d, to all those which concern the execution of the provisions expressly contained in the articles of Union; 3d, to all those in which the United States are a party; 4th, to all those which involve the PEACE of the CONFEDERACY, whether they relate to the intercourse between the United States and foreign nations, or to that between the States themselves; 5th, to all those which originate on the high seas, and are of admiralty or maritime jurisdiction; and, lastly, to all those in which the State tribunals cannot be supposed to be impartial and unbiased.

The first point depends upon this obvious consideration, that there ought always to be a constitutional method of giving efficacy to constitutional provisions. What, for instance, would avail restrictions on the authority of the State legislatures, without some constitutional mode of enforcing the observance of them? The States, by the plan of the convention, are prohibited from doing a variety of things, some of which are incompatible with the interests of the Union, and others with the principles of good government. The imposition of duties on imported articles, and the emission of paper money, are specimens of each kind. No man of sense will believe, that such prohibitions would be scrupulously regarded, without some effectual power in the government to restrain or correct the infractions of them. This power must either be a direct negative on the State laws, or an authority in the federal courts to overrule such as might be in manifest contravention of the articles of Union. There is no third course that I can imagine.

The latter appears to have been thought by the convention preferable to the former, and, I presume, will be most agreeable to the States.

As to the second point, it is impossible, by any argument or comment, to make it clearer than it is in itself. If there are such things as political axioms, the propriety of the judicial power of a government being coextensive with its legislative, may be ranked among the number. The mere necessity of uniformity in the interpretation of the national laws, decides the question. Thirteen independent courts of final jurisdiction over the same causes, arising upon the same laws, is a hydra in government, from which nothing but contradiction and confusion can proceed.

Still less need be said in regard to the third point. Controversies between the nation and its members or citizens, can only be properly referred to the national tribunals. Any other plan would be contrary to reason, to precedent, and to decorum.

The fourth point rests on this plain proposition, that the peace of the WHOLE ought not to be left at the disposal of a PART. The Union will undoubtedly be answerable to foreign powers for the conduct of its members. And the responsibility for an injury ought ever to be accompanied with the faculty of preventing it. As the denial or perversion of justice by the sentences of courts, as well as in any other manner, is with reason classed among the just causes of war, it will follow that the federal judiciary ought to have cognizance of all causes in which the citizens of other countries are concerned. This is not less essential to the preservation of the public faith, than to the security of the public tranquillity. A distinction may perhaps be imagined between cases arising upon treaties and the laws of nations and those which may stand merely on the footing of the municipal law. The former kind may be supposed proper for the federal jurisdiction, the latter for that of the States. But it is at least problematical, whether an unjust sentence against a foreigner, where the subject of controversy was wholly relative to the lex loci, would not, if unredressed, be an aggression upon his sovereign, as well as one which violated the stipulations of a treaty or the general law of nations. And a still greater objection to the distinction would result from the immense difficulty, if not impossibility, of a practical discrimination between the cases of one complexion and those of the other. So great a proportion of the cases in which foreigners are parties, involve national questions, that it is by far most safe and most expedient to refer all those in which they are concerned to the national tribunals.

The power of determining causes between two States, between one State and the citizens of another, and between the citizens of different States, is perhaps not less essential to the peace of the Union than that which has been just examined. History gives us a horrid picture of the dissensions and private wars which distracted and desolated Germany prior to the institution of the Imperial Chamber by Maximilian, towards the close of the fifteenth century; and informs us, at the same time, of the vast influence of that institution in appeasing the disorders and establishing the tranquillity of the empire. This was a court invested with authority to decide finally all differences among the members of the Germanic body.

A method of terminating territorial disputes between the States, under the authority of the federal head, was not unattended to, even in the imperfect system by which they have been hitherto held together. But there are many other sources, besides interfering claims of boundary, from which bickerings and animosities may spring up among the members of the Union. To some of these we have been witnesses in the course of our past experience. It will readily be conjectured that I allude to the fraudulent laws which have been passed in too many of the States. And though the proposed Constitution establishes particular guards against the repetition of those instances which have heretofore made their appearance, yet it is warrantable to apprehend that the spirit which produced them will assume new shapes, that could not be foreseen nor specifically provided against. Whatever practices may have a tendency to disturb the harmony between the States, are proper objects of federal superintendence and control.

It may be esteemed the basis of the Union, that "the citizens of each State shall be entitled to all the privileges and immunities of citizens of the several States." And if it be a just principle that every government OUGHT TO POSSESS THE MEANS OF EXECUTING ITS OWN PROVISIONS BY ITS OWN AUTHORITY, it will follow, that in order to the inviolable maintenance of that equality of privileges and immunities to which the citizens of the Union will be entitled, the national judiciary ought to preside in all cases in which one State or its citizens are opposed to another State or its citizens. To secure the full effect of so fundamental a provision against all evasion and subterfuge, it is necessary that its construction should be committed to that tribunal which, having no local attachments, will be likely to be impartial between the different States and their citizens, and which, owing its official existence to the Union, will never be likely to feel any bias inauspicious to the principles on which it is founded.

The fifth point will demand little animadversion. The most bigoted idolizers of State authority have not thus far shown a disposition to deny the national judiciary the cognizances of maritime causes. These so generally depend on the laws of nations, and so commonly affect the rights of foreigners, that they fall within the considerations which are relative to the public peace. The most important part of them are, by the present Confederation, submitted to federal jurisdiction.

The reasonableness of the agency of the national courts in cases in which the State tribunals cannot be supposed to be impartial, speaks for itself. No man ought certainly to be a judge in his own cause, or in any cause in respect to which he has the least interest or bias. This principle has no inconsiderable weight in designating the federal courts as the proper tribunals for the determination of controversies between different States and their citizens. And it ought to have the same operation in regard to some cases between citizens of the same State. Claims to land under grants of different States, founded upon adverse pretensions of boundary, are of this description. The courts of neither of the granting States could be expected to be unbiased. The laws may have even prejudged the question, and tied the courts down to decisions in favor of the grants of the State to which they belonged. And even where this had not been done, it would be natural that the judges, as men, should feel a strong predilection to the claims of their own government.

Having thus laid down and discussed the principles which ought to regulate the constitution of the federal judiciary, we will proceed to test, by these principles, the particular powers of which, according to the plan of the convention, it is to be composed. It is to comprehend "all cases in law and equity arising under the Constitution, the laws of the United States, and treaties made, or which shall be made, under their authority; to all cases affecting ambassadors, other public ministers, and consuls; to all cases of admiralty and maritime jurisdiction; to controversies to which the United States shall be a party; to controversies between two or more States; between a State and citizens of another State; between citizens of different States; between citizens of the same State claiming lands and grants of different States; and between a State or the citizens thereof and foreign states, citizens, and subjects." This constitutes the entire mass of the judicial authority of the Union. Let us now review it in detail. It is, then, to extend:

First. To all cases in law and equity, ARISING UNDER THE CONSTITUTION and THE LAWS OF THE UNITED STATES. This corresponds with the two first classes of causes, which have been enumerated, as proper for the jurisdiction of the United States. It has been asked, what is meant by "cases arising under the Constitution," in contradiction from those "arising under the laws of the United States"? The difference has been already explained. All the restrictions upon the authority of the State legislatures furnish examples of it. They are not, for instance, to emit paper money; but the interdiction results from the Constitution, and will have no connection with any law of the United States. Should paper money, notwithstanding, be emited, the controversies concerning it would be cases arising under the Constitution and not the laws of the United States, in the ordinary signification of the terms. This may serve as a sample of the whole.

It has also been asked, what need of the word "equity." What equitable causes can grow out of the Constitution and laws of the United States? There is hardly a subject of litigation between individuals, which may not involve those ingredients of FRAUD, ACCIDENT, TRUST, or HARDSHIP, which would render the matter an object of equitable rather than of legal jurisdiction, as the distinction is known and established in several of the States. It is the peculiar province, for instance, of a court of equity to relieve against what are called hard bargains: these are contracts in which, though there may have been no direct fraud or deceit, sufficient to invalidate them in a court of law, yet there may have been some undue and unconscionable advantage taken of the necessities or misfortunes of one of the parties, which a court of equity would not tolerate. In such cases, where foreigners were concerned on either side, it would be impossible for the federal judicatories to do justice without an equitable as well as a legal jurisdiction. Agreements to convey lands claimed under the grants of different States, may afford another example of the necessity of an equitable jurisdiction in the federal courts. This reasoning may not be so palpable in those States where the formal and technical distinction between LAW and EQUITY is not maintained, as in this State, where it is exemplified by every day's practice.

The judiciary authority of the Union is to extend:

Second. To treaties made, or which shall be made, under the authority of the United States, and to all cases affecting ambassadors, other public ministers, and consuls. These belong to the fourth class of the enumerated cases, as they have an evident connection with the preservation of the national peace.

Third. To cases of admiralty and maritime jurisdiction. These form, altogether, the fifth of the enumerated classes of causes proper for the cognizance of the national courts.

Fourth. To controversies to which the United States shall be a party. These constitute the third of those classes.

Fifth. To controversies between two or more States; between a State and citizens of another State; between citizens of different States. These belong to the fourth of those classes, and partake, in some measure, of the nature of the last.

Sixth. To cases between the citizens of the same State, CLAIMING LANDS UNDER GRANTS OF DIFFERENT STATES. These fall within the last class, and ARE THE ONLY INSTANCES IN WHICH THE PROPOSED CONSTITUTION DIRECTLY CONTEMPLATES THE COGNIZANCE OF DISPUTES BETWEEN THE CITIZENS OF THE SAME STATE.

Seventh. To cases between a State and the citizens thereof, and foreign States, citizens, or subjects. These have been already explained to belong to the fourth of the enumerated classes, and have been shown to be, in a peculiar manner, the proper subjects of the national judicature.

From this review of the particular powers of the federal judiciary, as marked out in the Constitution, it appears that they are all conformable to the principles which ought to have governed the structure of that department, and which were necessary to the perfection of the system. If some partial inconviences should appear to be connected with the incorporation of any of them into the plan, it ought to be recollected that the national legislature will have ample authority to make such EXCEPTIONS, and to prescribe such regulations as will be calculated to obviate or remove these inconveniences. The possibility of particular mischiefs can never be viewed, by a wellinformed mind, as a solid objection to a general principle, which is calculated to avoid general mischiefs and to obtain general advantages.

FEDERALIST NO. 81 BY ALEXANDER HAMILTON

Editor's Introduction:

Federalist No. 81 is one of the most cited essays by the Supreme Court in the collection, only surpassed by numbers 78 and 42. Hamilton compares the judiciary under the Constitution to the British model—a model he finds defective—explains that the federal judiciary will never "encroach" on the legislative power (some that has happened frequently in the twentieth century), and applauds the Framers for allowing for the creation of inferior courts, a prospect that he thinks would make the judicial branch more efficient. He also argues that States, like any sovereignty, cannot be sued without their consent. This is called "state sovereign immunity" and was eventually codified by the Eleventh Amendment. Hamilton concludes by arguing that the Constitution does not abolish trial by jury, one of the key arguments against the document during the ratification period.

Federalist No. 81

May 28, 1788

By Alexander Hamilton of New York

To the People of the State of New York:

LET US now return to the partition of the judiciary authority between different courts, and their relations to each other, "The judicial power of the United States is" (by the plan of the convention) "to be vested in one Supreme Court, and in such inferior courts as the Congress may, from time to time, ordain and establish."

That there ought to be one court of supreme and final jurisdiction, is a proposition which is not likely to be contested. The reasons for it have been assigned in another place, and are too obvious to need repetition. The only question that seems to have been raised concerning it, is, whether it ought to be a distinct body or a branch of the legislature. The same contradiction is observable in regard to this matter which has been remarked in several other cases. The very men who object to the Senate as a court of impeachments, on the ground of an improper intermixture of powers, advocate, by implication at least, the propriety of vesting the ultimate decision of all causes, in the whole or in a part of the legislative body.

The arguments, or rather suggestions, upon which this charge is founded, are to this effect: "The authority of the proposed Supreme Court of the United States, which is to be a separate and independent body, will be superior to that of the legislature. The power of construing the laws according to the SPIRIT of the Constitution, will enable that court to mould them into whatever shape it may think proper; especially as its decisions will not be in any manner subject to the revision or correction of the legislative body. This is as unprecedented as it is dangerous. In Britain, the judical power, in the last resort, resides in the House of Lords, which is a branch of the legislature; and this part of the British government has been imitated in the State constitutions in general. The Parliament of Great Britain, and the legislatures of the several States, can at any time rectify, by law, the exceptionable decisions of their respective courts. But the errors and usurpations of the Supreme Court of the United States will be uncontrollable and remediless." This, upon examination, will be found to be made up altogether of false reasoning upon misconceived fact.

In the first place, there is not a syllable in the plan under consideration which DIRECTLY empowers the national courts to construe the laws according to the spirit of the Constitution, or which gives them any greater latitude in this respect than may be claimed by the courts of every State. I admit, however, that the Constitution ought to be the standard of construction for the laws, and that wherever there is an evident opposition, the laws ought to give place to the Constitution. But this doctrine is not deducible from any circumstance peculiar to the plan of the convention, but from the general theory of a limited Constitution; and as far as it is true, is equally applicable to most, if not to all the State governments. There can be no objection, therefore, on this account, to the federal judicature which will not lie against the local judicatures in general, and which will not serve to condemn every constitution that attempts to set bounds to legislative discretion.

But perhaps the force of the objection may be thought to consist in the particular organization of the Supreme Court; in its being composed of a distinct body of magistrates, instead of being one of the branches of the legislature, as in the government of Great Britain and that of the State. To insist upon this point, the authors of the objection must renounce the meaning they have labored to annex to the celebrated maxim, requiring a separation of the departments of power. It shall, nevertheless, be conceded to them, agreeably to the interpretation given to that maxim in the course of these papers, that it is not violated by vesting the ultimate power of judging in a PART of the legislative body. But though this be not an absolute violation of that excellent rule, yet it verges so nearly upon it, as on this account alone to be less eligible than the mode preferred by the convention.

From a body which had even a partial agency in passing bad laws, we could rarely expect a disposition to temper and moderate them in the application. The same spirit which had operated in making them, would be too apt in interpreting them; still less could it be expected that men who had infringed the Constitution in the character of legislators, would be disposed to repair the breach in the character of judges. Nor is this all. Every reason which recommends the tenure of good behavior for judicial offices, militates against placing the judiciary power, in the last resort, in a body composed of men chosen for a limited period. There is an absurdity in referring the determination of causes, in the first instance, to judges of permanent standing; in the last, to those of a temporary and mutable constitution. And there is a still greater absurdity in subjecting the decisions of men, selected for their knowledge of the laws, acquired by long and laborious study, to the revision and control of men who, for want of the same advantage, cannot but be deficient in that knowledge. The members of the legislature will rarely be chosen with a view to those qualifications which fit men for the stations of judges; and as, on this account, there will be great reason to apprehend all the ill consequences of defective information, so, on account of the natural propensity of such bodies to party divisions, there will be no less reason to fear that the pestilential breath of faction may poison the fountains of justice. The habit of being continually marshalled on opposite sides will be too apt to stifle the voice both of law and of equity.

These considerations teach us to applaud the wisdom of those States who have committed the judicial power, in the last resort, not to a part of the legislature, but to distinct and independent bodies of men. Contrary to the supposition of those who have represented the plan of the convention, in this respect, as novel and unprecedented, it is but a copy of the constitutions of New Hampshire, Massachusetts,

Pennsylvania, Delaware, Maryland, Virginia, North Carolina, South Carolina, and Georgia; and the preference which has been given to those models is highly to be commended.

It is not true, in the second place, that the Parliament of Great Britain, or the legislatures of the particular States, can rectify the exceptionable decisions of their respective courts, in any other sense than might be done by a future legislature of the United States. The theory, neither of the British, nor the State constitutions, authorizes the revisal of a judicial sentence by a legislative act. Nor is there any thing in the proposed Constitution, more than in either of them, by which it is forbidden. In the former, as well as in the latter, the impropriety of the thing, on the general principles of law and reason, is the sole obstacle. A legislature, without exceeding its province, cannot reverse a determination once made in a particular case; though it may prescribe a new rule for future cases. This is the principle, and it applies in all its consequences, exactly in the same manner and extent, to the State governments, as to the national government now under consideration. Not the least difference can be pointed out in any view of the subject.

It may in the last place be observed that the supposed danger of judiciary encroachments on the legislative authority, which has been upon many occasions reiterated, is in reality a phantom. Particular misconstructions and contraventions of the will of the legislature may now and then happen; but they can never be so extensive as to amount to an inconvenience, or in any sensible degree to affect the order of the political system. This may be inferred with certainty, from the general nature of the judicial power, from the objects to which it relates, from the manner in which it is exercised, from its comparative weakness, and from its total incapacity to support its usurpations by force. And the inference is greatly fortified by the consideration of the important constitutional check which the power of instituting impeachments in one part of the legislative body, and of determining upon them in the other, would give to that body upon the members of the judicial department. This is alone a complete security. There never can be danger that the judges, by a series of deliberate usurpations on the authority of the legislature, would hazard the united resentment of the body intrusted with it, while this body was possessed of the means of punishing their presumption, by degrading them from their stations. While this ought to remove all apprehensions on the subject, it affords, at the same time, a cogent argument for constituting the Senate a court for the trial of impeachments.

Having now examined, and, I trust, removed the objections to the distinct and independent organization of the Supreme Court, I proceed to consider the propriety of the power of constituting inferior courts, and the relations which will subsist between these and the former.

The power of constituting inferior courts is evidently calculated to obviate the necessity of having recourse to the Supreme Court in every case of federal cognizance. It is intended to enable the national government to institute or AUTHORUZE, in each State or district of the United States, a tribunal competent to the determination of matters of national jurisdiction within its limits.

But why, it is asked, might not the same purpose have been accomplished by the instrumentality of the State courts? This admits of different answers. Though the fitness and competency of those courts should be allowed in the utmost latitude, yet the substance of the power in question may still be regarded as a necessary part of the plan, if it were only to empower the national legislature to commit to them the cognizance of causes arising out of the national Constitution. To confer the power of determining such causes upon the existing courts of the several States, would perhaps be as much "to constitute tribunals," as to create new courts with the like power. But ought not a more direct and explicit provision to have been made in favor of the State courts? There are, in my opinion, substantial reasons against such a provision: the most discerning cannot foresee how far the prevalency of a local spirit may be found to disqualify the local tribunals for the jurisdiction of national causes; whilst every man may discover, that courts constituted like those of some of the States would be improper channels of the judicial authority of the Union. State judges, holding their offices during pleasure, or from year to year, will be too little independent to be relied upon for an inflexible execution of the national laws. And if there was a necessity for confiding the original cognizance of causes arising under those laws to them there would be a correspondent necessity for leaving the door of appeal as wide as possible. In proportion to the grounds of confidence in, or distrust of, the subordinate tribunals, ought to be the facility or difficulty of appeals. And well satisfied as I am of the propriety of the appellate jurisdiction, in the several classes of causes to which it is extended by the plan of the convention. I should consider every thing calculated to give, in practice, an UNRESTRAINED COURSE to appeals, as a source of public and private inconvenience.

I am not sure, but that it will be found highly expedient and useful, to divide the United States into four or five or half a dozen districts; and to institute a federal court in each district, in lieu of one in every State. The judges of these courts, with the aid of the State judges, may hold circuits for the trial of causes in the several parts of the respective districts. Justice through them may be administered with ease and despatch; and appeals may be safely circumscribed within a narrow compass. This plan appears to me at present the most eligible of any that could be adopted; and in order to it, it is necessary that the power of constituting inferior courts should exist in the full extent in which it is to be found in the proposed Constitution.

These reasons seem sufficient to satisfy a candid mind, that the want of such a power would have been a great defect in the plan. Let us now examine in what manner the judicial authority is to be distributed between the supreme and the inferior courts of the Union. The Supreme Court is to be invested with original jurisdiction, only "in cases affecting ambassadors, other public ministers, and consuls, and those in which A STATE shall be a party." Public ministers of every class are the immediate representatives of their sovereigns. All questions in which they are concerned are so directly connected with the public peace, that, as well for the preservation of this, as out of respect to the sovereignties they represent, it is both expedient and proper that such questions should be submitted in the first instance to the highest judicatory of the nation. Though consuls have not in strictness a diplomatic character, yet as they are the public agents of the nations to which they belong, the same observation is in a great measure applicable to them. In cases in which a State might happen to be a party, it would ill suit its dignity to be turned over to an inferior tribunal. Though it may rather be a digression from the immediate subject of this paper, I shall take occasion to mention here a supposition which has excited some alarm upon very mistaken grounds. It has been suggested that an assignment of the public securities of one State to the citizens of another, would enable them to prosecute that State in the federal courts for the amount of those securities; a suggestion which the following considerations prove to be without foundation.

It is inherent in the nature of sovereignty not to be amenable to the suit of an individual WITHOUT ITS CONSENT. This is the general sense, and the general practice of mankind; and the exemption, as one of the attributes of sovereignty, is now enjoyed by the government of every State in the Union. Unless, therefore, there is a surrender of this immunity in the plan of the convention, it will remain with the States, and the danger intimated must be merely ideal. The circumstances which are necessary to produce an alienation of State sovereignty were discussed in considering the article of taxation, and need not be repeated here. A recurrence to the principles there established will satisfy us, that there is no color to pretend that the State governments would, by the adoption of that plan, be divested of the privilege of paying their own debts in their own way, free from every constraint but that which flows from the obligations of good faith. The contracts between a nation and individuals are only binding on the conscience of the sovereign, and have no pretensions to a compulsive force. They confer no right of action, independent of the sovereign will. To what purpose would it be to authorize suits against States for the debts they owe? How could recoveries be enforced? It is evident, it could not be done without waging war against the contracting State; and to ascribe to the federal courts, by mere implication, and in destruction of a pre-existing right of the State governments, a power which would involve such a consequence, would be altogether forced and unwarrantable.

Let us resume the train of our observations. We have seen that the original jurisdiction of the Supreme Court would be confined to two classes of causes, and those of a nature rarely to occur. In all other cases of federal cognizance, the original jurisdiction would appertain to the inferior tribunals; and the Supreme Court would have nothing more than an appellate jurisdiction, "with such EXCEPTIONS and under such REGULATIONS as the Congress shall make."

The propriety of this appellate jurisdiction has been scarcely called in question in regard to matters of law; but the clamors have been loud against it as applied to matters of fact. Some well-intentioned men in this State, deriving their notions from the language and forms which obtain in our courts, have been induced to consider it as an implied supersedure of the trial by jury, in favor of the civil-law mode of trial, which prevails in our courts of admiralty, probate, and chancery. A technical sense has been affixed to the term "appellate," which, in our law parlance, is commonly used in reference to appeals in the course of the civil law. But if I am not misinformed, the same meaning would not be given to it in any part of New England. There an appeal from one jury to another, is familiar both in language and practice, and is even a matter of course, until there have been two verdicts on one side. The word "appellate," therefore, will not be understood in the same sense in New England as in New York, which shows the impropriety of a technical interpretation derived from the jurisprudence of any particular State. The expression, taken in the abstract, denotes nothing more than the power of one tribunal to review the proceedings of another, either as to the law or fact, or both. The mode of doing it may depend on ancient custom or legislative provision (in a new government it must depend on the latter), and may be with or without the aid of a jury, as may be judged advisable. If, therefore, the re-examination of a fact once determined by a jury, should in any case be admitted under the proposed Constitution, it may be so regulated as to be done by a second jury, either by remanding the cause to the court below for a second trial of the fact, or by directing an issue immediately out of the Supreme Court.

But it does not follow that the re-examination of a fact once ascertained by a jury, will be permitted in the Supreme Court. Why may not it be said, with the strictest propriety, when a writ of error is brought from an inferior to a superior court of law in this State, that the latter has jurisdiction of the fact as well as the law? It is true it cannot institute a new inquiry concerning the fact, but it takes cognizance of it as it appears upon the record, and pronounces the law arising upon it. This is jurisdiction of both fact and law; nor is it even possible to separate them. Though the common-law courts of this State ascertain disputed facts by a jury, yet they unquestionably have jurisdiction of both fact and law; and accordingly when the former is agreed in the pleadings, they have no recourse to a jury, but proceed at once to judgment. I contend, therefore, on this ground, that the expressions, "appellate jurisdiction, both as to law and fact," do not necessarily imply a re-examination in the Supreme Court of facts decided by juries in the inferior courts.

The following train of ideas may well be imagined to have influenced the convention, in relation to this particular provision. The appellate jurisdiction of the Supreme Court (it may have been argued) will extend to causes determinable in different modes, some in the course of the COMMON LAW, others in the course of the CIVIL LAW. In the former, the revision of the law only will be, generally speaking, the proper province of the Supreme Court; in the latter, the re-examination of the fact is agreeable to usage, and in some cases, of which prize causes are an example, might be essential to the preservation of the public peace. It is therefore necessary that the appellate jurisdiction should, in certain cases, extend in the broadest sense to matters of fact. It will not answer to make an express exception of cases which shall have been originally tried by a jury, because in the courts of some of the States ALL CAUSES are tried in this mode; and such an exception would preclude the revision of matters of fact, as well where it might be proper, as where it might be improper. To avoid all inconveniencies, it will be safest to declare generally, that the Supreme Court shall possess appellate jurisdiction both as to law and FACT, and that this jurisdiction shall be subject to such EXCEPTIONS and regulations as the national legislature may prescribe. This will enable the government to modify it in such a manner as will best answer the ends of public justice and security.

This view of the matter, at any rate, puts it out of all doubt that the supposed ABOLITION of the trial by jury, by the operation of this provision, is fallacious and untrue. The legislature of the United States would certainly have full power to provide, that in appeals to the Supreme Court there should be no re-examination of facts where they had been tried in the original causes by juries. This would certainly be an authorized exception; but if, for the reason already intimated, it should be thought too extensive, it might be qualified with a limitation to such causes only as are determinable at common law in that mode of trial.

The amount of the observations hitherto made on the authority of the judicial department is this: that it has been carefully restricted to those causes which are manifestly proper for the cognizance of the national judicature; that in the partition of this authority a very small portion of original jurisdiction has been preserved to the Supreme Court, and the rest consigned to the subordinate tribunals; that the Supreme Court will possess an appellate jurisdiction, both as to law and fact, in all the cases referred to them, both subject to any EXCEPTIONS and REGULATIONS which may be thought advisable; that this appellate jurisdiction does, in no case, ABOLISH the trial by jury; and that an ordinary degree of prudence and integrity in the national councils will insure us solid advantages from the establishment of the proposed judiciary, without exposing us to any of the inconveniences which have been predicted from that source.

Federalist No. 82 by Alexander Hamilton

Editor's Introduction:

Hamilton continues his discussion of jurisdiction in this essay, mainly to argue that the State courts would not be destroyed by the federal courts. That was a popular accusation among opponents of the document, and Hamilton insists that the State courts will "retain all PRE-EXISTING authorities" which were not "exclusively" granted to the general government. Decisions of State courts could be appealed to the Supreme Court, but only when the State courts and the federal courts had concurrent jurisdiction. In other words, cases that were strictly under the jurisdiction of the State could not be appealed to the federal bench. This issue became a major rub between Virginia and the general government in the early nineteenth century and eventually resulted in two Supreme Court cases, the most important being *Cohens v. Virginia* of 1821. In that case, Chief Justice John Marshall broadly interpreted the appellate power of the federal courts and struck down attempts by the State of Virginia to eliminate what had become a federal veto of State law.

Federalist No. 82

May 28, 1788

By Alexander Hamilton of New York

To the People of the State of New York:

THE erection of a new government, whatever care or wisdom may distinguish the work, cannot fail to originate questions of intricacy and nicety; and these may, in a particular manner, be expected to flow from the establishment of a constitution founded upon the total or partial incorporation of a number of distinct sovereignties. 'Tis time only that can mature and perfect so compound a system, can liquidate the meaning of all the parts, and can adjust them to each other in a harmonious and consistent WHOLE.

Such questions, accordingly, have arisen upon the plan proposed by the convention, and particularly concerning the judiciary department. The principal of these respect the situation of the State courts in regard to those causes which are to be submitted to federal jurisdiction. Is this to be exclusive, or are those courts to possess a concurrent jurisdiction? If the latter, in what relation will they stand to the national tribunals? These are inquiries which we meet with in the mouths of men of sense, and which are certainly entitled to attention.

The principles established in a former paper teach us that the States will retain all PRE-EXISTING authorities which may not be exclusively delegated to the federal head; and that this exclusive delegation can only exist in one of three cases: where an exclusive authority is, in express terms, granted to the Union; or where a particular authority is granted to the Union, and the exercise of a like authority is prohibited to the States; or where an authority is granted to the Union, with which a similar authority in the States would be utterly incompatible. Though these principles may not apply with the same force to the judiciary as to the legislative power, yet I am inclined to think that they are, in the main, just with respect to the former, as well as the latter.

And under this impression, I shall lay it down as a rule, that the State courts will RETAIN the jurisdiction they now have, unless it appears to be taken away in one of the enumerated modes.

The only thing in the proposed Constitution, which wears the appearance of confining the causes of federal cognizance to the federal courts, is contained in this passage: "The JUDICIAL POWER of the United States SHALL BE VESTED in one Supreme Court, and in SUCH inferior courts as the Congress shall from time to time ordain and establish." This might either be construed to signify, that the supreme and subordinate courts of the Union should alone have the power of deciding those causes to which their authority is to extend; or simply to denote, that the organs of the national judiciary should be one Supreme Court, and as many subordinate courts as Congress should think proper to appoint; or in other words, that the United States should exercise the judicial power with which they are to be invested, through one supreme tribunal, and a certain number of inferior ones, to be instituted by them. The first excludes, the last admits, the concurrent jurisdiction of the State tribunals; and as the first would amount to an alienation of State power by implication, the last appears to me the most natural and the most defensible construction.

But this doctrine of concurrent jurisdiction is only clearly applicable to those descriptions of causes of which the State courts have previous cognizance. It is not equally evident in relation to cases which may grow out of, and be PECULIAR to, the Constitution to be established; for not to allow the State courts a right of jurisdiction in such cases, can hardly be considered as the abridgment of a pre-existing authority. I mean not therefore to contend that the United States, in the course of legislation upon the objects intrusted to their direction, may not commit the decision of causes arising upon a particular regulation to the federal courts solely, if such a measure should be deemed expedient; but I hold that the State courts will be divested of no part of their primitive jurisdiction, further than may relate to an appeal; and I am even of opinion that in every case in which they were not expressly excluded by the future acts of the national legislature, they will of course take cognizance of the causes to which those acts may give birth. This I infer from the nature of judiciary power, and from the general genius of the system. The judiciary power of every government looks beyond its own local or municipal laws, and in civil cases lays hold of all subjects of litigation between parties within its jurisdiction, though the causes of dispute are relative to the laws of the most distant part of the globe. Those of Japan, not less than of New York, may furnish the objects of legal discussion to our courts. When in addition to this we consider the State governments and the national governments, as they truly are, in the light of kindred systems, and as parts of ONE WHOLE, the inference seems to be conclusive, that the State courts would have a concurrent jurisdiction in all cases arising under the laws of the Union, where it was not expressly prohibited.

Here another question occurs: What relation would subsist between the national and State courts in these instances of concurrent jurisdiction? I answer, that an appeal would certainly lie from the latter, to the Supreme Court of the United States. The Constitution in direct terms gives an appellate jurisdiction to the Supreme Court in all the enumerated cases of federal cognizance in which it is not to have an original one, without a single expression to confine its operation to the inferior federal courts. The objects of appeal, not the tribunals from which it is to be made, are alone contemplated. From this circumstance, and from the reason of the thing, it ought to be construed to extend to the State tribunals. Either this must be the case, or the local courts must be excluded from a concurrent jurisdiction in matters of national concern, else the judiciary authority of the

Union may be eluded at the pleasure of every plaintiff or prosecutor. Neither of these consequences ought, without evident necessity, to be involved; the latter would be entirely inadmissible, as it would defeat some of the most important and avowed purposes of the proposed government, and would essentially embarrass its measures. Nor do I perceive any foundation for such a supposition. Agreeably to the remark already made, the national and State systems are to be regarded as ONE WHOLE. The courts of the latter will of course be natural auxiliaries to the execution of the laws of the Union, and an appeal from them will as naturally lie to that tribunal which is destined to unite and assimilate the principles of national justice and the rules of national decisions. The evident aim of the plan of the convention is, that all the causes of the specified classes shall, for weighty public reasons, receive their original or final determination in the courts of the Union. To confine, therefore, the general expressions giving appellate jurisdiction to the Supreme Court, to appeals from the subordinate federal courts, instead of allowing their extension to the State courts, would be to abridge the latitude of the terms, in subversion of the intent, contrary to every sound rule of interpretation.

But could an appeal be made to lie from the State courts to the subordinate federal judicatories? This is another of the questions which have been raised, and of greater difficulty than the former. The following considerations countenance the affirmative. The plan of the convention, in the first place, authorizes the national legislature "to constitute tribunals inferior to the Supreme Court." It declares, in the next place, that "the JUDICIAL POWER of the United States SHALL BE VESTED in one Supreme Court, and in such inferior courts as Congress shall ordain and establish"; and it then proceeds to enumerate the cases to which this judicial power shall extend. It afterwards divides the jurisdiction of the Supreme Court into original and appellate, but gives no definition of that of the subordinate courts. The only outlines described for them, are that they shall be "inferior to the Supreme Court," and that they shall not exceed the specified limits of the federal judiciary. Whether their authority shall be original or appellate, or both, is not declared. All this seems to be left to the discretion of the legislature. And this being the case, I perceive at present no impediment to the establishment of an appeal from the State courts to the subordinate national tribunals; and many advantages attending the power of doing it may be imagined. It would diminish the motives to the multiplication of federal courts, and would admit of arrangements calculated to contract the appellate jurisdiction of the Supreme Court. The State tribunals may then be left with a more entire charge of federal causes; and appeals, in most cases in which they may be deemed proper, instead of being carried to the Supreme Court, may be made to lie from the State courts to district courts of the Union.

Federalist No. 84 by Alexander Hamilton

Editor's Introduction:

Hamilton transitions away from a discussion of the judicial branch to an evaluation of what he considers miscellaneous subjects, the most important being a call for a bill of rights. Hamilton, like other proponents of the document, considers a bill of rights to be both unnecessary and dangerous. The Constitution protected those civil liberties established by the Magna Charta and prohibited the establishment of monarchy. Hamilton's assertion that a bill of rights would be dangerous upholds the principle of federalism, for if an enumerated list of rights were added to the document, then designing men could assume that the Constitution possessed powers that were not expressly delegated to that government. In other words, a bill of rights opened the door to implied powers. He asks explicitly, "For why declare that things shall not be done which there is no power to do?" He also argues that the general government under the new Constitution will be no more expensive than that under the Articles of Confederation. Most of the departments already existed, and others would simply be transferred from State to federal control, meaning expenses would not increase.

Federalist No. 84

May 28, 1788

By Alexander Hamilton of New York

To the People of the State of New York:

IN THE course of the foregoing review of the Constitution, I have taken notice of, and endeavored to answer most of the objections which have appeared against it. There, however, remain a few which either did not fall naturally under any particular head or were forgotten in their proper places. These shall now be discussed; but as the subject has been drawn into great length, I shall so far consult brevity as to comprise all my observations on these miscellaneous points in a single paper.

The most considerable of the remaining objections is that the plan of the convention contains no bill of rights. Among other answers given to this, it has been upon different occasions remarked that the constitutions of several of the States are in a similar predicament. I add that New York is of the number. And yet the opposers of the new system, in this State, who profess an unlimited admiration for its constitution, are among the most intemperate partisans of a bill of rights. To justify their zeal in this matter, they allege two things: one is that, though the constitution of New York has no bill of rights prefixed to it, yet it contains, in the body of it, various provisions in favor of particular privileges and rights, which, in substance amount to the same thing; the other is, that the Constitution adopts, in their full extent, the common and statute law of Great Britain, by which many other rights, not expressed in it, are equally secured.

To the first I answer, that the Constitution proposed by the convention contains, as well as the constitution of this State, a number of such provisions.

Independent of those which relate to the structure of the government, we find the following: Article 1, section 3, clause 7 "Judgment in cases of impeachment shall not extend further than to removal from office, and disqualification to hold and enjoy any office of honor, trust, or profit under the United States; but the party convicted shall, nevertheless, be liable and subject to indictment, trial, judgment, and punishment according to law." Section 9, of the same article, clause 2 "The privilege of the writ of habeas corpus shall not be suspended, unless when in cases of rebellion or invasion the public safety may require it." Clause 3 "No bill of attainder or ex-post-facto law shall be passed." Clause 7 "No title of nobility shall be granted by the United States; and no person holding any office of profit or trust under them, shall, without the consent of the Congress, accept of any present, emolument, office, or title of any kind whatever, from any king, prince, or foreign state." Article 3, section 2, clause 3 "The trial of all crimes, except in cases of impeachment, shall be by jury; and such trial shall be held in the State where the said crimes shall have been committed; but when not committed within any State, the trial shall be at such place or places as the Congress may by law have directed." Section 3, of the same article "Treason against the United States shall consist only in levying war against them, or in adhering to their enemies, giving them aid and comfort. No person shall be convicted of treason, unless on the testimony of two witnesses to the same overt act, or on confession in open court." And clause 3, of the same section "The Congress shall have power to declare the punishment of treason; but no attainder of treason shall work corruption of blood, or forfeiture, except during the life of the person attainted."

It may well be a question, whether these are not, upon the whole, of equal importance with any which are to be found in the constitution of this State. The establishment of the writ of habeas corpus, the prohibition of ex-post-facto laws, and of TITLES OF NOBILITY, TO WHICH WE HAVE NO CORRESPONDING PROVISION IN OUR CONSTITUTION, are perhaps greater securities to liberty and republicanism than any it contains. The creation of crimes after the commission of the fact, or, in other words, the subjecting of men to punishment for things which, when they were done, were breaches of no law, and the practice of arbitrary imprisonments, have been, in all ages, the favorite and most formidable instruments of tyranny. The observations of the judicious Blackstone, in reference to the latter, are well worthy of recital: "To bereave a man of life, says he or by violence to confiscate his estate, without accusation or trial, would be so gross and notorious an act of despotism, as must at once convey the alarm of tyranny throughout the whole nation; but confinement of the person, by secretly hurrying him to jail, where his sufferings are unknown or forgotten, is a less public, a less striking, and therefore A MORE DANGEROUS ENGINE of arbitrary government." And as a remedy for this fatal evil he is everywhere peculiarly emphatical in his encomiums on the habeas-corpus act, which in one place he calls "the BULWARK of the British Constitution."

Nothing need be said to illustrate the importance of the prohibition of titles of nobility. This may truly be denominated the corner-stone of republican government; for so long as they are excluded, there can never be serious danger that the government will be any other than that of the people.

To the second that is, to the pretended establishment of the common and state law by the Constitution, I answer, that they are expressly made subject "to such alterations and provisions as the legislature shall from time to time make concerning the same." They are therefore at any moment liable to repeal by the ordinary legislative power, and of course have no constitutional sanction. The only use of the declaration was to recognize the ancient law and to remove doubts which might have been occasioned by the Revolution. This consequently can be considered as no part of a declaration of rights, which under our constitutions must be intended as limitations of the power of the government itself.

It has been several times truly remarked that bills of rights are, in their origin, stipulations between kings and their subjects, abridgements of prerogative in favor of privilege, reservations of rights not surrendered to the prince. Such was MAGNA CHARTA, obtained by the barons, sword in hand, from King John. Such were the subsequent confirmations of that charter by succeeding princes. Such was the PETITION OF RIGHT assented to by Charles I., in the beginning of his reign. Such, also, was the Declaration of Right presented by the Lords and Commons to the Prince of Orange in 1688, and afterwards thrown into the form of an act of parliament called the Bill of Rights. It is evident, therefore, that, according to their primitive signification, they have no application to constitutions professedly founded upon the power of the people, and executed by their immediate representatives and servants. Here, in strictness, the people surrender nothing; and as they retain every thing they have no need of particular reservations. "WE, THE PEOPLE of the United States, to secure the blessings of liberty to ourselves and our posterity, do ORDAIN and ESTABLISH this Constitution for the United States of America." Here is a better recognition of popular rights, than volumes of those aphorisms which make the principal figure in several of our State bills of rights, and which would sound much better in a treatise of ethics than in a constitution of government.

But a minute detail of particular rights is certainly far less applicable to a Constitution like that under consideration, which is merely intended to regulate the general political interests of the nation, than to a constitution which has the regulation of every species of personal and private concerns. If, therefore, the loud clamors against the plan of the convention, on this score, are well founded, no epithets of reprobation will be too strong for the constitution of this State. But the truth is, that both of them contain all which, in relation to their objects, is reasonably to be desired.

I go further, and affirm that bills of rights, in the sense and to the extent in which they are contended for, are not only unnecessary in the proposed Constitution, but would even be dangerous. They would contain various exceptions to powers not granted; and, on this very account, would afford a colorable pretext to claim more than were granted. For why declare that things shall not be done which there is no power to do? Why, for instance, should it be said that the liberty of the press shall not be restrained, when no power is given by which restrictions may be imposed? I will not contend that such a provision would confer a regulating power; but it is evident that it would furnish, to men disposed to usurp, a plausible pretense for claiming that power. They might urge with a semblance of reason, that the Constitution ought not to be charged with the absurdity of providing against the abuse of an authority which was not given, and that the provision against restraining the liberty of the press afforded a clear implication, that a power to prescribe proper regulations concerning it was intended to be vested in the national government. This may serve as a specimen of the numerous handles which would be given to the doctrine of constructive powers, by the indulgence of an injudicious zeal for bills of rights.

On the subject of the liberty of the press, as much as has been said, I cannot forbear adding a remark or two: in the first place, I observe, that there is not a syllable concerning it in the constitution of this State; in the next, I contend, that whatever has been said about it in that of any other State, amounts to nothing. What signifies a declaration, that "the liberty of the press shall be inviolably preserved"? What is the liberty of the press? Who can give it any definition which would not leave the utmost latitude for evasion? I hold it to be impracticable; and from this I infer, that its security, whatever fine declarations may be inserted in any constitution respecting it, must altogether depend on public opinion, and on the general spirit of the people and of the government. And here, after all, as is intimated upon another occasion, must we seek for the only solid basis of all our rights.

There remains but one other view of this matter to conclude the point. The truth is, after all the declamations we have heard, that the Constitution is itself, in every rational sense, and to every useful purpose, A BILL OF RIGHTS. The several bills of rights in Great Britain form its Constitution, and conversely the constitution of each State is its bill of rights. And the proposed Constitution, if adopted, will be the bill of rights of the Union. Is it one object of a bill of rights to declare and specify the political privileges of the citizens in the structure and administration of the government? This is done in the most ample and precise manner in the plan of the convention; comprehending various precautions for the public security, which are not to be found in any of the State constitutions. Is another object of a bill of rights to define certain immunities and modes of proceeding, which are relative to personal and private concerns? This we have seen has also been attended to, in a variety of cases, in the same plan. Adverting therefore to the substantial meaning of a bill of rights, it is absurd to allege that it is not to be found in the work of the convention. It may be said that it does not go far enough, though it will not be easy to make this appear; but it can with no propriety be contended that there is no such thing. It certainly must be immaterial what mode is observed as to the order of declaring the rights of the citizens, if they are to be found in any part of the instrument which establishes the government. And hence it must be apparent, that much of what has been said on this subject rests merely on verbal and nominal distinctions, entirely foreign from the substance of the thing.

Another objection which has been made, and which, from the frequency of its repetition, it is to be presumed is relied on, is of this nature: "It is improper say the objectors to confer such large powers, as are proposed, upon the national government, because the seat of that government must of necessity be too remote from many of the States to admit of a proper knowledge on the part of the constituent, of the conduct of the representative body." This argument, if it proves any thing, proves that there ought to be no general government whatever. For the powers which, it seems to be agreed on all hands, ought to be vested in the Union, cannot be safely intrusted to a body which is not under every requisite control. But there are satisfactory reasons to show that the objection is in reality not well founded. There is in most of the arguments which relate to distance a palpable illusion of the imagination. What are the sources of information by which the people in Montgomery County must regulate their judgment of the conduct of their representatives in the State legislature? Of personal observation they can have no benefit. This is confined to the citizens on the spot. They must therefore depend on the information of intelligent men, in whom they confide; and how must these men obtain their information? Evidently from the complexion of public measures, from the public prints, from correspondences with their representatives, and with other persons who reside at the place of their deliberations. This does not apply to Montgomery County only, but to all the counties at any considerable distance from the seat of government.

It is equally evident that the same sources of information would be open to the people in relation to the conduct of their representatives in the general government, and the impediments to a prompt communication which distance may be supposed to create, will be overbalanced by the effects of the vigilance of the State governments. The executive and legislative bodies of each State will be so many sentinels over the persons employed in every department of the national administration; and as it will be in their power to adopt and pursue a regular and effectual system of intelligence, they can never be at a loss to know the behavior of those who represent their constituents in the national councils, and can readily communicate the same knowledge to the people. Their disposition to apprise the community of whatever may prejudice its interests from another quarter, may be relied upon, if it were only from the rivalship of power. And we may conclude with the fullest assurance that the people, through that channel, will be better informed of the conduct of their national representatives, than they can be by any means they now possess of that of their State representatives.

It ought also to be remembered that the citizens who inhabit the country at and near the seat of government will, in all questions that affect the general liberty and prosperity, have the same interest with those who are at a distance, and that they will stand ready to sound the alarm when necessary, and to point out the actors in any pernicious project. The public papers will be expeditious messengers of intelligence to the most remote inhabitants of the Union.

Among the many curious objections which have appeared against the proposed Constitution, the most extraordinary and the least colorable is derived from the want of some provision respecting the debts due TO the United States. This has been represented as a tacit relinquishment of those debts, and as a wicked contrivance to screen public defaulters. The newspapers have teemed with the most inflammatory railings on this head; yet there is nothing clearer than that the suggestion is entirely void of foundation, the of spring of extreme ignorance or extreme dishonesty. In addition to the remarks I have made upon the subject in another place, I shall only observe that as it is a plain dictate of common-sense, so it is also an established doctrine of political law, that "STATES NEITHER LOSE ANY OF THEIR RIGHTS, NOR ARE DISCHARGED FROM ANY OF THEIR OBLIGATIONS, BY A CHANGE IN THE FORM OF THEIR CIVIL GOVERNMENT." The last objection of any consequence, which I at present recollect, turns upon the article of expense. If it were even true, that the adoption of the proposed government would occasion a considerable increase of expense, it would be an objection that ought to have no weight against the plan.

The great bulk of the citizens of America are with reason convinced, that Union is the basis of their political happiness. Men of sense of all parties now, with few exceptions, agree that it cannot be preserved under the present system, nor without radical alterations; that new and extensive powers ought to be granted to the national head, and that these require a different organization of the federal government a single body being an unsafe depositary of such ample authorities. In conceding all this, the question of expense must be given up; for it is impossible, with any degree of safety, to narrow the foundation upon which the system is to stand. The two branches of the legislature are, in the first instance, to consist of only sixty-five persons, which is the same number of which Congress, under the existing Confederation, may be composed. It is true that this number is intended to be increased; but this is to keep pace with the progress of the population and resources of the country. It is evident that a less number would, even in the first instance, have been unsafe, and that a continuance of the present number would, in a more advanced stage of population, be a very inadequate representation of the people.

Whence is the dreaded augmentation of expense to spring? One source indicated, is the multiplication of offices under the new government. Let us examine this a little.

It is evident that the principal departments of the administration under the present government, are the same which will be required under the new. There are now a Secretary of War, a Secretary of Foreign Affairs, a Secretary for Domestic Affairs, a Board of Treasury, consisting of three persons, a Treasurer, assistants, clerks, etc. These officers are indispensable under any system, and will suffice under the new as well as the old. As to ambassadors and other ministers and agents in foreign countries, the proposed Constitution can make no other difference than to render their characters, where they reside, more respectable, and their services more useful. As to persons to be employed in the collection of the revenues, it is unquestionably true that these will form a very considerable addition to the number of federal officers; but it will not follow that this will occasion an increase of public expense. It will be in most cases nothing more than an exchange of State for national officers. In the collection of all duties, for instance, the persons employed will be wholly of the latter description. The States individually will stand in no need of any for this purpose. What difference can it make in point of expense to pay officers of the customs appointed by the State or by the United States? There is no good reason to suppose that either the number or the salaries of the latter will be greater than those of the former.

Where then are we to seek for those additional articles of expense which are to swell the account to the enormous size that has been represented to us? The chief item which occurs to me respects the support of the judges of the United States. I do not add the President, because there is now a president of Congress, whose expenses may not be far, if any thing, short of those which will be incurred on account of the President of the United States. The support of the judges will clearly be an extra expense, but to what extent will depend on the particular plan which may be adopted in regard to this matter. But upon no reasonable plan can it amount to a sum which will be an object of material consequence.

Let us now see what there is to counterbalance any extra expense that may attend the establishment of the proposed government. The first thing which presents itself is that a great part of the business which now keeps Congress sitting through the year will be transacted by the President. Even the management of foreign negotiations will naturally devolve upon him, according to general principles concerted with the Senate, and subject to their final concurrence. Hence it is evident that a portion of the year will suffice for the session of both the Senate and the House of Representatives; we may suppose about a fourth for the latter and a third, or perhaps half, for the former. The extra business of treaties and appointments may give this extra occupation to the Senate. From this circumstance we may infer that, until the House of Representatives shall be increased greatly beyond its present number, there will be a considerable saving of expense from the difference between the constant session of the present and the temporary session of the future Congress.

But there is another circumstance of great importance in the view of economy. The business of the United States has hitherto occupied the State legislatures, as well as Congress. The latter has made requisitions which the former have had to provide for. Hence it has happened that the sessions of the State legislatures have been protracted greatly beyond what was necessary for the execution of the mere local business of the States. More than half their time has been frequently employed in matters which related to the United States. Now the members who compose the legislatures of the several States amount to two thousand and upwards, which number has hitherto performed what under the new system will be done in the first instance by sixty-five persons, and probably at no future period by above a fourth or fifth of that number. The Congress under the proposed government will do all the business of the United States themselves, without the intervention of the State legislatures, who thenceforth will have only to attend to the affairs of their particular States, and will not have to sit in any proportion as long as they have heretofore done. This difference in the time of the sessions of the State legislatures will be clear gain, and will alone form an article of saving, which may be regarded as an equivalent for any additional objects of expense that may be occasioned by the adoption of the new system.

The result from these observations is that the sources of additional expense from the establishment of the proposed Constitution are much fewer than may have been imagined; that they are counter-balanced by considerable objects of saving; and that while it is questionable on which side the scale will preponderate, it is certain that a government less expensive would be incompetent to the purposes of the Union.

Federalist No. 85 by Alexander Hamilton

Editor's Introduction:

Hamilton concludes the *Federalist* with an appeal to Union. By May, it became clear that ratification was going to be a difficult sell in New York and Virginia. Hamilton knew it which is why he insists that the Union was necessary for the security, stability, and prosperity of the United States. Hamilton also argues that the remaining States should ratify the document *as is* and then propose amendments as needed. This would avoid the delicate problem of forcing the States that already ratified to consider an amended Constitution before it was promulgated. He contends that those who sought this course were determined to defeat the document and had no interest in maintaining the Union.

Federalist No. 85

May 28, 1788

By Alexander Hamilton of New York

To the People of the State of New York:

ACCORDING to the formal division of the subject of these papers, announced in my first number, there would appear still to remain for discussion two points: "the analogy of the proposed government to your own State constitution," and "the additional security which its adoption will afford to republican government, to liberty, and to property." But these heads have been so fully anticipated and exhausted in the progress of the work, that it would now scarcely be possible to do any thing more than repeat, in a more dilated form, what has been heretofore said, which the advanced stage of the question, and the time already spent upon it, conspire to forbid.

It is remarkable, that the resemblance of the plan of the convention to the act which organizes the government of this State holds, not less with regard to many of the supposed defects, than to the real excellences of the former. Among the pretended defects are the re-eligibility of the Executive, the want of a council, the omission of a formal bill of rights, the omission of a provision respecting the liberty of the press. These and several others which have been noted in the course of our inquiries are as much chargeable on the existing constitution of this State, as on the one proposed for the Union; and a man must have slender pretensions to consistency, who can rail at the latter for imperfections which he finds no difficulty in excusing in the former. Nor indeed can there be a better proof of the insincerity and affectation of some of the zealous adversaries of the plan of the convention among us, who profess to be the devoted admirers of the government under which they live, than the fury with which they have attacked that plan, for matters in regard to which our own constitution is equally or perhaps more vulnerable.

The additional securities to republican government, to liberty and to property, to be derived from the adoption of the plan under consideration, consist chiefly in the restraints which the preservation of the Union will impose on local factions and insurrections, and on the ambition of powerful individuals in single States, who may acquire credit and influence enough, from leaders and favorites, to become the despots of the people; in the diminution of the opportunities to foreign intrigue, which the dissolution of the Confederacy would invite and facilitate; in the prevention of extensive military establishments, which could not fail to grow out of wars between the States in a disunited situation; in the express guaranty of a republican form of government to each; in the absolute and universal exclusion of titles of nobility; and in the precautions against the repetition of those practices on the part of the State governments which have undermined the foundations of property and credit, have planted mutual distrust in the breasts of all classes of citizens, and have occasioned an almost universal prostration of morals.

Thus have I, fellow-citizens, executed the task I had assigned to myself; with what success, your conduct must determine. I trust at least you will admit that I have not failed in the assurance I gave you respecting the spirit with which my endeavors should be conducted. I have addressed myself purely to your judgments, and have studiously avoided those asperities which are too apt to disgrace political disputants of all parties, and which have been not a little provoked by the language and conduct of the opponents of the Constitution. The charge of a conspiracy against the liberties of the people, which has been indiscriminately brought against the advocates of the plan, has something in it too wanton and too malignant, not to excite the indignation of every man who feels in his own bosom a refutation of the calumny. The perpetual changes which have been rung upon the wealthy, the well-born, and the great, have been such as to inspire the disgust of all sensible men. And the unwarrantable concealments and misrepresentations which have been in various ways practiced to keep the truth from the public eye, have been of a nature to demand the reprobation of all honest men. It is not impossible that these circumstances may have occasionally betrayed me into intemperances of expression which I did not intend; it is certain that I have frequently felt a struggle between sensibility and moderation; and if the former has in some instances prevailed, it must be my excuse that it has been neither often nor much.

Let us now pause and ask ourselves whether, in the course of these papers, the proposed Constitution has not been satisfactorily vindicated from the aspersions thrown upon it; and whether it has not been shown to be worthy of the public approbation, and necessary to the public safety and prosperity. Every man is bound to answer these questions to himself, according to the best of his conscience and understanding, and to act agreeably to the genuine and sober dictates of his judgment. This is a duty from which nothing can give him a dispensation. 'T is one that he is called upon, nay, constrained by all the obligations that form the bands of society, to discharge sincerely and honestly. No partial motive, no particular interest, no pride of opinion, no temporary passion or prejudice, will justify to himself, to his country, or to his posterity, an improper election of the part he is to act. Let him beware of an obstinate adherence to party; let him reflect that the object upon which he is to decide is not a particular interest of the community, but the very existence of the nation; and let him remember that a majority of America has already given its sanction to the plan which he is to approve or reject.

I shall not dissemble that I feel an entire confidence in the arguments which recommend the proposed system to your adoption, and that I am unable to discern any real force in those by which it has been opposed. I am persuaded that it is the best which our political situation, habits, and opinions will admit, and superior to any the revolution has produced.

Concessions on the part of the friends of the plan, that it has not a claim to absolute perfection, have afforded matter of no small triumph to its enemies. "Why," say they, "should we adopt an imperfect thing? Why not amend it and make it perfect before it is irrevocably established?" This may be plausible enough, but it is only plausible. In the first place I remark, that the extent of these concessions has been greatly exaggerated. They have been stated as amounting to an admission that the plan is radically defective, and that without material alterations the rights and the interests of the community cannot be safely confided to it. This, as far as I have understood the meaning of those who make the concessions, is an entire perversion of their sense. No advocate of the measure can be found, who will not declare as his sentiment, that the system, though it may not be perfect in every part, is, upon the whole, a good one; is the best that the present views and circumstances of the country will permit; and is such an one as promises every species of security which a reasonable people can desire.

I answer in the next place, that I should esteem it the extreme of imprudence to prolong the precarious state of our national affairs, and to expose the Union to the jeopardy of successive experiments, in the chimerical pursuit of a perfect plan. I never expect to see a perfect work from imperfect man. The result of the deliberations of all collective bodies must necessarily be a compound, as well of the errors and prejudices, as of the good sense and wisdom, of the individuals of whom they are composed. The compacts which are to embrace thirteen distinct States in a common bond of amity and union, must as necessarily be a compromise of as many dissimilar interests and inclinations. How can perfection spring from such materials?

The reasons assigned in an excellent little pamphlet lately published in this city, are unanswerable to show the utter improbability of assembling a new convention, under circumstances in any degree so favorable to a happy issue, as those in which the late convention met, deliberated, and concluded. I will not repeat the arguments there used, as I presume the production itself has had an extensive circulation. It is certainly well worthy the perusal of every friend to his country. There is, however, one point of light in which the subject of amendments still remains to be considered, and in which it has not yet been exhibited to public view. I cannot resolve to conclude without first taking a survey of it in this aspect.

It appears to me susceptible of absolute demonstration, that it will be far more easy to obtain subsequent than previous amendments to the Constitution. The moment an alteration is made in the present plan, it becomes, to the purpose of adoption, a new one, and must undergo a new decision of each State. To its complete establishment throughout the Union, it will therefore require the concurrence of thirteen States. If, on the contrary, the Constitution proposed should once be ratified by all the States as it stands, alterations in it may at any time be effected by nine States. Here, then, the chances are as thirteen to nine in favor of subsequent amendment, rather than of the original adoption of an entire system.

This is not all. Every Constitution for the United States must inevitably consist of a great variety of particulars, in which thirteen independent States are to be accommodated in their interests or opinions of interest. We may of course expect to see, in any body of men charged with its original formation, very different combinations of the parts upon different points. Many of those who form a majority on one question, may become the minority on a second, and an association dissimilar to either may constitute the majority on a third. Hence the necessity of moulding and arranging all the particulars which are to compose the whole, in such a manner as to satisfy all the parties to the compact; and hence, also, an immense multiplication of difficulties and casualties in obtaining the collective assent to a final act. The degree of that multiplication must evidently be in a ratio to the number of particulars and the number of parties.

But every amendment to the Constitution, if once established, would be a single proposition, and might be brought forward singly. There would then be no necessity for management or compromise, in relation to any other point no giving nor taking. The will of the requisite number would at once bring the matter to a decisive issue. And consequently, whenever nine, or rather ten States, were united in the desire of a particular amendment, that amendment must infallibly take place. There can, therefore, be no comparison between the facility of affecting an amendment, and that of establishing in the first instance a complete Constitution.

In opposition to the probability of subsequent amendments, it has been urged that the persons delegated to the administration of the national government will always be disinclined to yield up any portion of the authority of which they were once possessed. For my own part I acknowledge a thorough conviction that any amendments which may, upon mature consideration, be thought useful, will be applicable to the organization of the government, not to the mass of its powers; and on this account alone, I think there is no weight in the observation just stated. I also think there is little weight in it on another account. The intrinsic difficulty of governing thirteen States at any rate, independent of calculations upon an ordinary degree of public spirit and integrity, will, in my opinion constantly impose on the national rulers the necessity of a spirit of accommodation to the reasonable expectations of their constituents. But there is yet a further consideration, which proves beyond the possibility of a doubt, that the observation is futile. It is this that the national rulers, whenever nine States concur, will have no option upon the subject. By the fifth article of the plan, the Congress will be obliged "on the application of the legislatures of two thirds of the States “which at present amount to nine,” to call a convention for proposing amendments, which shall be valid, to all intents and purposes, as part of the Constitution, when ratified by the legislatures of three fourths of the States, or by conventions in three fourths thereof." The words of this article are peremptory. The Congress "shall call a convention." Nothing in this particular is left to the discretion of that body. And of consequence, all the declamation about the disinclination to a change vanishes in air. Nor however difficult it may be supposed to unite two thirds or three fourths of the State legislatures, in amendments which may affect local interests, can there be any room to apprehend any such difficulty in a union on points which are merely relative to the general liberty or security of the people. We may safely rely on the disposition of the State legislatures to erect barriers against the encroachments of the national authority.

If the foregoing argument is a fallacy, certain it is that I am myself deceived by it, for it is, in my conception, one of those rare instances in which a political truth can be brought to the test of a mathematical demonstration. Those who see the matter in the same light with me, however zealous they may be for amendments, must agree in the propriety of a previous adoption, as the most direct road to their own object.

The zeal for attempts to amend, prior to the establishment of the Constitution, must abate in every man who is ready to accede to the truth of the following observations of a writer equally solid and ingenious: "To balance a large state or society,” says he, “whether monarchical or republican, on general laws, is a work of so great difficulty, that no human genius, however comprehensive, is able, by the mere dint of reason and reflection, to effect it. The judgments of many must unite in the work; experience must guide their labor; time must bring it to perfection, and the feeling of inconveniences must correct the mistakes which they INEVITABLY fall into in their first trials and experiments." These judicious reflections contain a lesson of moderation to all the sincere lovers of the Union, and ought to put them upon their guard against hazarding anarchy, civil war, a perpetual alienation of the States from each other, and perhaps the military despotism of a victorious demagogue, in the pursuit of what they are not likely to obtain, but from time and experience. It may be in me a defect of political fortitude, but I acknowledge that I cannot entertain an equal tranquility with those who affect to treat the dangers of a longer continuance in our present situation as imaginary. A nation, without a national government, is, in my view, an awful spectacle. The establishment of a Constitution, in time of profound peace, by the voluntary consent of a whole people, is a prodigy, to the completion of which I look forward with trembling anxiety. I can reconcile it to no rules of prudence to let go the hold we now have, in so arduous an enterprise, upon seven out of the thirteen States, and after having passed over so considerable a part of the ground, to recommence the course. I dread the more the consequences of new attempts, because I know that powerful individuals, in this and in other States, are enemies to a general national government in every possible shape.

Speech Before the Virginia Ratifying Convention by Edmund Randolph

Editor's Introduction:

Edmund Randolph's first speech at the Virginia Ratifying Convention was in many respects a *mea culpa*. He famously refused the sign the Constitution while a delegate to the Philadelphia Convention and then wrote a lengthy explanation of his decision after the fact in a stinging indictment of the document. But things had changed by June 1788. Virginia was in the position of being the ninth State to ratify the document, meaning that it might determine if the Union stayed together or if Virginia would resume its status as a "free and independent State." Randolph argues that he still had reservations about the Constitution, and that he would still refuse to sign the document, but he thinks that the Union was more important than trifling objections and so at this juncture he would support ratification without amendments in the interest of the Union. This was a major concession. Randolph placed the Union in high esteem than any power or civil liberty that the document lacked, and he hoped that the men of Virigina would avoid the disaster of disunion by agreeing to ratify the Constitution. Both George Mason—who also refused to sign the Constitution—and Patrick Henry, the leading voices against ratification, viewed Randolph's move as a betrayal.

Randolph's support was not taken lightly. He was the incumbent Governor of Virginia, a son of one of the most important families in the State, an aid-de-camp to George Washington during the War for Independence, the former Attorney General of Virginia, and a highly respected legal mind. The State sent him to the Annapolis Convention in 1786 and as a result naturally chose him to take part in the Philadelphia Convention in 1787. He presented James Madison's "Virginia Plan" at the Convention but became disillusioned with the final product. Nevertheless, Randolph had always favored a stronger central government, and once the Constitution was ratified was appointed the first Attorney General of the United States. He later accepted the position of Secretary of State after fellow Virginian Thomas Jefferson resigned in 1793.

Randolph resigned as Secretary of State in 1795 and returned to Virginia to practice law. His last high-profile case was as lead defense attorney in Aaron Burr's treason trial in 1807. Randolph died in 1813.

Speech Before the Virginia Ratifying Convention

June 4, 1788

By Edmund Randolph of Virginia

Gov. RANDOLPH. Mr. Chairman, had the most enlightened statesman whom America has yet seen, foretold, but a year ago, the crisis which has now called us together, he would have been confronted by the universal testimony of history; for never was it yet known, that, in so short a space, by the peaceable working of events, without a war, or even the menace of the smallest force, a nation has been brought to agitate a question, an error in the issue of which may blast their happiness. It is, therefore, to be feared, lest to this trying exigency the best wisdom should be unequal; and here (if it were allowable to lament any ordinance of nature) might it be deplored that, in proportion to the magnitude of a subject, is the mind intemperate. Religion, the dearest of all interests, has too often sought proselytes by fire rather than by reason; and politics, the next in rank, is too often nourished by passion, at the expense of the understanding. Pardon me, however, for expecting one exception to the tendency of mankind from the dignity of this Convention — a mutual toleration, and a persuasion that no man has a right to impose his opinions on others. Pardon me, too, sir, if I am particularly sanguine in my expectations from the chair: it well knows what is order, how to command obedience, and that political opinions may be as honest on one side as on the other. Before I press into the body of the argument, I must take the liberty of mentioning the part I have already borne in this great question; but let me not here be misunderstood. I come not to apologize to any individual within these walls, to the Convention as a body, or even to my fellow-citizens at large. Having obeyed the impulse of duty, having satisfied my conscience, and, I trust, my God, I shall appeal to no other tribunal: nor do I come a candidate for popularity; my manner of life has never yet betrayed such a desire. The highest honors and emoluments of this commonwealth are a poor compensation for the surrender of personal independence. The history of England from the revolution, and that of Virginia for more than twenty years past, show the vanity of a hope that general favor should ever follow the man who, without partiality or prejudice, praises or disapproves the opinions of friends or of foes: nay, I might enlarge the field, and declare, from the great volume of human nature itself, that to be moderate in politics forbids an ascent to the summit of political fame. But I come hither, regardless of allurements, to continue as I have begun; to repeat my earnest endeavors for a firm, energetic government; to enforce my objections to the Constitution, and to concur in any practical scheme of amendments; but I never will assent to any scheme that will operate a dissolution of the Union, or any measure which may lead to it.

This conduct may possibly be upbraided as injurious to my own views; if it be so, it is, at least, the natural offspring of my judgment. I refused to sign, and if the same were to return, again would I refuse. Wholly to adopt, or wholly to reject, as proposed by the Convention, seemed too hard an alternative to the citizens of America, whose servants we were, and whose pretensions amply to discuss the means of their happiness were undeniable. Even if adopted under the terror of impending anarchy, the government must have been without the safest bulwark — the hearts of the people; and, if rejected because the chance for amendments was cut off, the Union would have been irredeemably lost. This seems to have been verified by the event in Massachusetts; but our Assembly have removed these inconveniences, by propounding the Constitution to our full and free inquiry When I withheld my subscription, I had not even the glimpse of the genius of America, relative to the principles of the new Constitution. Who, arguing from the preceding history of Virginia, could have divined that she was prepared for the important change? In former times, indeed, she transcended every colony in professions and practices of loyalty; but she opened a perilous war, under a democracy almost as pure as representation would admit; she supported it under a constitution which subjects all rule, authority, and power, to the legislature; every attempt to alter it had been baffled; the increase of Congressional power had always excited an alarm. I therefore would not bind myself to uphold the new Constitution, before I had tried it by the true touchstone; especially, too, when I foresaw that even the members of the general Convention might be instructed by the comments of those who were without doors. But I had, moreover, objections to the

Constitution, the most material of which, too lengthy in detail, I have as yet barely stated to the public, but shall explain when we arrive at the proper points. Amendments were consequently my wish; these were the grounds of my repugnance to subscribe, and were perfectly reconcilable with my unalterable resolution to be regulated by the spirit of America, if, after our best efforts for amendments, they could not be removed. I freely indulge those who may think this declaration too candid, in believing that I hereby depart from the concealment belonging to the character of a statesman. Their censure would be more reasonable, were it not for an unquestionable fact, that the spirit of America depends upon a combination of circumstances which no individual can control, and arises not from the prospect of advantages which may be gained by the arts of negotiation, but from deeper and more honest causes.

As with me the only question has ever been between previous and subsequent amendments, so will I express my apprehensions, that the postponement of this Convention to so late a day has extinguished the probability of the former without inevitable ruin to the Union, and the Union is the anchor of our political salvation; and I will assent to the lopping of this limb, (meaning his arm,) before I assent to the dissolution of the Union. I shall now follow the honorable gentleman (Mr. Henry) in his inquiry. Before the meeting of the federal Convention, says the honorable gentleman, we rested in peace; a miracle it was, that we were so: miraculous must it appear to those who consider the distresses of the war, and the no less afflicting calamities which we suffered in the succeeding peace. Be so good as to recollect how we fared under the Confederation. I am ready to pour forth sentiments of the fullest gratitude to those gentlemen who framed that system. I believe they had the most enlightened heads in this western hemisphere. Notwithstanding their intelligence, and earnest solicitude for the good of their country, this system proved totally inadequate to the purpose for which it was devised. But, sir, this was no disgrace to them. The subject of confederations was then new, and the necessity of speedily forming some government for the states, to defend them against the pressing dangers, prevented, perhaps, those able statesmen from making that system as perfect as more leisure and deliberation might have enabled them to do. I cannot otherwise conceive how they could have formed a system that provided no means of enforcing the powers which were nominally given it. Was it not a political farce to pretend to vest powers, without accompanying them with the means of putting them in execution? This want of energy was not a greater solecism than the blending together, and vesting in one body, all the branches of government. The utter inefficacy of this system was discovered, the moment the danger was over, by the introduction of peace; the accumulated public misfortunes that resulted from its inefficacy rendered an alteration necessary: this necessity was obvious to all America: attempts have accordingly been made for this purpose.

I have been a witness to this business from its earliest beginning. I was honored with a seat in the small Convention held at Annapolis. The members of that Convention thought, unanimously, that the control of commerce should be given to Congress, and recommended to their states to extend the improvement to the whole system. The members of the general Convention were particularly deputed to meliorate the Confederation. On a thorough contemplation of the subject, they found it impossible to amend that system. What was to be done? The dangers of America, which will be shown at another time by particular enumeration, suggested the expedient of forming a new plan. The Confederation has done a great deal for us, we all allow; but it was the danger of a powerful enemy, and the spirit of America, sir, and not any energy in that system, that carried us through that perilous war: for what were its best arms? The greatest exertions were made when the danger was most imminent. This system was not signed till March, 1781; Maryland having not acceded to it before, yet the military achievements and other exertions of America, previous to that period, were as brilliant, effectual, and successful, as they could have been under the most energetic government. This clearly shows that our perilous situation was the cement of our union. How different the scene when this peril vanished, and peace was restored! The demands of Congress were treated with neglect. One state complained that another had not paid its quotas as well as itself; public credit gone — for I believe, were it not for the private credit of individuals, we should have been ruined long before that time; commerce languishing; produce falling in value, and justice trampled under foot. We became contemptible in the eyes of foreign nations; they discarded us as little wanton bees, who had played for liberty, but had no sufficient solidity or wisdom to secure it on a permanent basis, and were therefore unworthy of their regard. It was found that Congress could not even enforce the observance of treaties. That treaty under which we enjoy our present tranquillity was disregarded. Making no difference between the justice of paying debts due to people here, and that of paying those due to people on the other side of the Atlantic, I wished to see the treaty complied with, by the payment of the British debts, but have not been able to know why it has been neglected. What was the reply to the demands and requisitions of Congress? — You are too contemptible; we will despise and disregard you.

I shall endeavor to satisfy the gentleman's political curiosity. Did not our compliance with any demand of Congress depend on our own free will? If we refused, I know of no coercive force to compel a compliance. After meeting in Convention, the deputies from the states communicated their information to one another. On a review of our critical situation, and of the impossibility of introducing any degree of improvement into the old system, what ought they to have done? Would it not have been treason to return without proposing some scheme to relieve their distressed country? The honorable gentleman asks why we should adopt a system that shall annihilate and destroy our treaties with France and other nations. I think the misfortune is, that these treaties are violated already, under the honorable gentleman's favorite system. I conceive that our engagements with foreign nations are not at all affected by this system; for the 6th article expressly provides that "all debts contracted, and engagements entered into, before the adoption of this Constitution, shall be as valid against the United States under this Constitution as under the Confederation." Does this system, then, cancel debts due to or from the continent? Is it not a well-known maxim that no change of situation can alter an obligation once rightly entered into? He also objects because nine states are sufficient to put the government in motion. What number of states ought we to have said? Ought we to have required the concurrence of all the thirteen? Rhode Island — in rebellion against integrity — Rhode Island plundered all the world by her paper money; and, notorious for her uniform opposition to every federal duty, would then have it in her power to defeat the Union; and may we not judge with absolute certainty, from her past conduct, that she would do so? Therefore, to have required the ratification of all the thirteen states would have been tantamount to returning without having done any thing. What other number would have been proper? Twelve? The same spirit that has actuated me in the whole progress of the business, would have prevented me from leaving it in the power of any one state to dissolve the Union; for would it not be lamentable that nothing could be done, for the defection of one state? A majority of the whole would have been too few. Nine states therefore seem to be a most proper number.

The gentleman then proceeds, and inquires why we assumed the language of "We, the people." I ask, Why not? The government is for the people; and the misfortune was, that the people had no agency in the government before. The Congress had power to make peace and war under [29] the old Confederation. Granting passports, by the law of nations, is annexed to this power; yet Congress was reduced to the humiliating condition of being obliged to send deputies to Virginia to solicit a passport. Notwithstanding the exclusive power of war given to Congress, the second article of the Confederation was interpreted to forbid that body to grant a passport for tobacco, which, during the war, and in pursuance of engagements made at Little York, was to have been sent into New York. What harm is there in consulting the people on the construction of a government by which they are to be bound? Is it unfair? Is it unjust? If the government is to be binding on the people, are not the people the proper persons to examine its merits or defects? I take this to be one of the least and most trivial objections that will be made to the Constitution; it carries the answer with itself. In the whole of this business, I have acted in the strictest obedience to the dictates of my conscience, in discharging what I conceive to be my duty to my country. I refused my signature, and if the same reasons operated on my mind, I would still refuse; but as I think that those eight states which have adopted the Constitution will not recede, I am a friend to the Union.

Speech Before the Virginia Ratifying Convention by George Nicholas

Editor's Introduction:

George Nicholas never held any prominent position in the United States federal government. His brother married into Thomas Jefferson's family (and ultimately bankrupt Jefferson's estate), was governor of Virginia and served in the United States Congress. Not so for George. He served in the Virginia House of Delegates and after removing to Kentucky served as attorney general for that State. He was also the first professor of law at Transylvania University.

He had a respected legal mind and was good friends with James Madison. That didn't stop Madison from uncontrollably laughing when someone described the portly Nicholas as "plum pudding with legs." His physique may not have inspired confidence, but Nicholas showed that he could match wits with the best Virginia had to offer during the ratifying Convention.

In this speech, Nicholas defended the legislative branch of the new Constitution, most importantly the House of Representatives as a better example of representative government than the House of Commons. Nicholas particularly focused on the mode of election and the fear that Congressional ability to regulate elections would destroy the State governments. Nicholas rejected this argument and thought it would only be used in extraordinary circumstances. He also praised the Constitution for its limitation on power rather than an extensive grant. Nicholas considered the document to be an improvement over the Articles of Confederation and attacks against it as warrantless fearmongering.

Speech Before the Virginia Ratifying Convention

June 4, 1788

By George Nicholas of Virginia

Mr. NICHOLAS. Mr. Chairman, the time being now come when this state is to decide on this important question, of rejecting or receiving this plan of government, it gave me great pleasure, yesterday, when the Convention determined to proceed with the fullest deliberation on the subject; as every gentleman will, in the course of the discussion, have an opportunity to urge every objection that may arise in his mind against this system. I beg gentlemen to offer all their objections here, and that none may be insisted on elsewhere; and I hope nothing urged without these walls will influence the mind of any one. If this part of the plan now under consideration be materially defective, I will readily agree it ought to be wholly rejected, because representation is the corner-stone on which the whole depends; but if, on investigation, it should be found to be otherwise, the highest gratitude should be shown to those gentlemen who framed it: although some small defects may appear in it, yet its merits, I hope, will amply cover those defects.

I shall take it into consideration, 1st, as it affects the qualifications of the electors; 2dly, as it affects the qualifications of the elected; 3dly, as to their number; 4thly, the time of their continuance in office; 5thly, their powers; and 6thly, whether this power be sufficient to enable them to discharge their duty without diminishing the security of the people — or, in other words, their responsibility.

I will consider it first, then, as to the qualifications of the electors. The best writers on government agree that, in a republic, those laws which fix the right of suffrage are fundamental. If, therefore, by the proposed plan, it is left uncertain in whom the right of suffrage is to rest, or if it has placed that right in improper hands, I shall admit that it is a radical defect; but in this plan there is a fixed rule for determining the qualifications of electors, and that rule the most judicious that could possibly have been devised, because it refers to a criterion which cannot be changed. A qualification that gives a right to elect representatives for the state legislatures, gives also, by this Constitution, a right to choose representatives for the general government. As the qualifications of electors are different in the different states, no particular qualifications, uniform through the states, would have been politic, as it would have caused a great inequality in the electors, resulting from the situation and circumstances of the respective states. Uniformity of qualifications would greatly affect the yeomanry in the states, as it would either exclude from this inherent right some who are entitled to it by the laws of some states at present, or be extended so universally as to defeat the admirable end of the institution of representation.

Secondly, as it respects the qualifications of the elected. It has ever been considered a great security to liberty, that very few should be excluded from the right of being chosen to the legislature. This Constitution has amply attended to this idea. We find no qualifications required except those of age and residence, which create a certainty of their judgment being matured, and of being attached to their state. It has been objected, that they ought to be possessed of landed estates; but, sir, when we reflect that most of the electors are landed men, we must suppose they will fix on those who are in a similar situation with themselves. We find there is a decided majority attached to the landed interest; consequently, the landed interest must prevail in the choice. Should the state be divided into districts, in no one can the mercantile interest by any means have an equal weight in the elections; therefore, the former will be more fully represented in the Congress; and men of eminent abilities are not excluded for the want of landed property. There is another objection which has been echoed from one end of the continent to the other — that Congress may alter the time, place, and manner of holding elections; that they may direct the place of elections to be where it will be impossible for those who have a right to vote, to attend; for instance, that they may order the freeholders of Albemarle to vote in the county of Princess Anne, or vice versa; or regulate elections, otherwise, in such a manner as totally to defeat their purpose, and lay them entirely under the influence of Congress. I flatter myself, that, from an attentive consideration of this power, it will clearly appear that it was essentially necessary to give it to Congress, as, without it, there could have been no security for the general government against the state legislatures. What, Mr. Chairman, is the danger apprehended in this case? If I understand it right, it must be, that Congress might cause the elections to be held in the most inconvenient places, and at so inconvenient a time, and in such a manner, as to give them the most undue influence over the choice, nay, even to prevent the elections from being held at all, — in order to perpetuate themselves. But what would be the consequence of this measure? It would be this, sir, — that Congress would cease to exist; it would destroy the Congress itself; it would absolutely be an act of suicide; and therefore it can never be expected. This alteration, so much apprehended, must be made by law; that is, with the concurrence of both branches of the legislature. Will the House of Representatives, the members of which are chosen only for two years, and who depend on the people for their reelection, agree to such an alteration? It is unreasonable to suppose it.

But let us admit, for a moment, that they will: what would be the consequence of passing such a law? It would be, sir, that, after the expiration of the two years, at the next election they would either choose such men as would alter the law, or they would resist the government. An enlightened people will never suffer what was established for their security to be perverted to an act of tyranny. It may be said, perhaps, that resistance would then become vain; Congress are vested with the power of raising an army; to which I say, that if ever Congress shall have an army sufficient for their purpose, and disposed to execute their unlawful commands, before they would act under this disguise, they would pull off the mask, and declare themselves absolute. I ask, Mr. Chairman, is it a novelty in our government? Has not our state legislature the power of fixing the time, places, and manner of holding elections? The possible abuse here complained of never can happen as long as the people of the United States are virtuous. As long as they continue to have sentiments of freedom and independence, should the Congress be wicked enough to harbor so absurd an idea as this objection supposes, the people will defeat their attempt by choosing other representatives, who will alter the law. If the state legislature, by accident, design, or any other cause, would not appoint a place for holding elections, then there might be no election till the time was past for which they were to have been chosen; and as this would eventually put an end to the Union, it ought to be guarded against; and it could only be guarded against by giving this discretionary power, to the Congress, of altering the time, place, and manner of holding the elections. It is absurd to think that Congress will exert this power, or change the time, place, and manner established by the states, if the states will regulate them properly, or so as not to defeat the purposes of the Union. It is urged that the state legislature ought to be fully and exclusively possessed of this power. Were this the case, it might certainly defeat the government. As the powers vested by this plan in Congress are taken from the state legislatures, they would be prompted to throw every obstacle in the way of the general government. It was then necessary that Congress should have this power.

Another strong argument for the necessity of this power is, that, if it was left solely to the states, there might have been as many times of choosing as there are states. States having solely the power of altering or establishing the time of election, it might happen that there should be no Congress. Not only by omitting to fix a time, but also by the elections in the states being at thirteen different times, such intervals might elapse between the first and last election, as to prevent there being a sufficient number to form a house; and this might happen at a time when the most urgent business rendered their session necessary; and by this power, this great part of the representation will be always kept full, which will be a security for a due attention to the interest of the community; and also the power of Congress to make the times of elections uniform in all the states, will destroy the continuance of any cabal, as the whole body of representatives will go out of office at once.

I come now, sir, to consider that part of the Constitution which fixes the number of representatives. It is first necessary for us to establish what the number of representatives is to be. At present it only consists of sixty-five; but let us consider that it is only to continue at that number till the actual enumeration shall be made, which is to be within three years after the first meeting of Congress; and that the number of representatives will be ascertained, and the proportion of taxes fixed, within every subsequent term of ten years. Till this enumeration be made, Congress will have no power to lay direct taxes: as there is no provision for this purpose, Congress cannot impose it; as direct taxation and representation are to be regulated by the enumeration there directed, therefore they have no power of laying direct taxes till the enumeration be actually made. I conceive no apportionment can be made before this enumeration, there being no certain data to go on. When the enumeration shall be made, what will be the consequence? I conceive there will be always one for every thirty thousand. Many reasons concur to lead me to this conclusion. By the Constitution, the allotment now made will only continue till the enumeration be made; and as a new enumeration will take place every ten years, I take it for granted that the number of representatives will be increased, according to the progressive increase of population, at every respective enumeration; and one for every thirty thousand will amount to one hundred representatives, if we compute the number of inhabitants to be only three millions in the United States, which is a very moderate calculation. The first intention was only to have one for every forty thousand, which was afterwards estimated to be too few, and, according to this proportion, the present temporary number is fixed; but as it now stands, we readily see that the proportion of representatives is sufficiently numerous to answer every purpose of federal legislation, and even soon to gratify those who wish for the greatest number. I take it that the number of representatives will be proportioned to the highest number we are entitled to; and that it never will be less than one for every thirty thousand. I formed this conclusion from the situation of those who will be our representatives. They are all chosen for two years; at the end of which term they are to depend on the people for their reelection. This dependence will lead them to a due and faithful discharge of their duty to their constituents: the augmentation of their number will conciliate the affections of the people at large; for the more the representatives increase in number, the greater the influence of the people in the government, and the greater the chance of reelection to the representatives.

But it has been said, that the Senate will not agree to any augmentation of the number of representatives. The Constitution will entitle the House of Representatives to demand it. Would the Senate venture to stand out against them? I think they would not, sir. Were they ready to recede from the evident sense of the Constitution, and grasp at power not thereby given them, they would be compelled to desist. But, that I may not be charged with urging suppositions, let us see what ground this stands upon, and whether there be any real danger to be apprehended. The first objection that I shall consider is, that, by paucity of numbers, they will be more liable to depart from their duty, and more subject to influence. I apprehend that the fewer the number of representatives, the freer the choice, and the greater the number of electors, the less liable to the unworthy acts of the candidates will they be; and thus their suffrage, being free, will probably fall on men of the most merit. The practice of that country, which is situated more like America than any other country in the world, will justify this supposition. The British House of Commons consists, I believe, of five hundred and fifty-eight members; yet the greater number of these are supposed to be under the undue influence of the crown. A single fact from the British history illustrates these observations, — viz., that there is scarcely an instance, for a century past, of the crown's exercising its undoubted prerogative of rejecting a bill sent up to it by the two houses of Parliament: it is no answer to say, that the king's influence is sufficient to prevent any obnoxious bills passing the two houses; there are many instances, in that period, not only of bills passing the two houses, but even receiving the royal assent, contrary to the private wish and inclination of the prince.

It is objected, however, as a defect in the Constitution, that it does not prohibit the House of Representatives from giving their powers, particularly that respecting the support &c., of armies, out of their hands for a longer term than two years. Here, I think, the enemies to the plan reason unfairly; they first suppose that Congress, from a love of power natural to all, will, in general, abuse that with which they are invested; and then they would make us apprehend that the House of Representatives, notwithstanding their love of power, (and it must be supposed as great in a branch of Congress as in the whole,) will give out of their hands the only check which can insure to them the continuance of the participation of the powers lodged in Congress in general. In England, there is no restraint of this kind on the Parliament; and yet there is no instance of a money bill being passed for a longer term than one year; the proposed plan, therefore, when it declares that no appropriation for the support of an army shall be made for a longer term than two years, introduces a check unknown to the English constitution, and one which will be found very powerful when we reflect that, if the House of Representatives could be prevailed on to make an appropriation for an army for two years, at the end of that time there will be a new choice of representatives. Thus I insist that security does not depend on the number of representatives: the experience of that country also shows that many of their counties and cities contain a greater number of souls than will be entitled to a representation in America; and yet the representatives chosen in those places have been the most strenuous advocates of liberty, and have exerted themselves in the defence of it, even in opposition to those chosen by much smaller numbers. Many of the senatorial districts in Virginia also contain a greater number of souls; and yet I suppose no gentleman within these walls will pay the senators chosen by them so poor a compliment as to attribute less wisdom and virtue to them than to the delegates chosen from single counties; and as there is greater probability that the electors in a large district will be more independent, so I think the representatives chosen in such districts will be more so too; for those who have sold themselves to their representatives will have no right to complain, if they, in their turn, barter away their rights and liberties; but those who have not themselves been bought, will never consent to be sold. Another objection made to the small number of representatives, is, that, admitting they were sufficient to secure their integrity, yet they cannot be acquainted with the local situation and circumstances of their constituents. When we attend to the object of their jurisdiction, we find this objection insupportable. Congress will superintend the great national interests of the Union. Local concerns are left to the state legislatures. When the members compare and communicate to one another their knowledge of their respective districts and states, their collective intelligence will sufficiently enable them to perform the objects of their cognizance. They cannot extend their influence or agency to any objects but those of a general nature; the representatives will, therefore, be sufficiently acquainted with the interests of their states, although chosen by large districts. As long as the people remain virtuous and uncorrupted, so long, we may fairly conclude, will their representatives, even at their present number, guard their interests, and discharge their duty with fidelity and zeal: when they become otherwise, no government can possibly secure their freedom.

I now consider the time of their continuance in office. A short continuance in office, and a return of the officers to the mass of the people, there to depend solely on their former good conduct for their reelection, is of the highest security to public liberty. Let the power of the persons elected be what it may, they are only the trustees, and not the masters, of the people; yet the time ought not to be so short that they could not discharge their duty with ability. Considering this, a term of two years is short enough in this case. Many will have a considerable distance to travel from the places of their abode to the seat of the general government. They must take time to consider the situation of the Union, make themselves acquainted with the circumstances of our finances, and the relative situation of, and our connections with, foreign nations, and a variety of other objects of importance. Would it not be the height of impolicy that they should go out of their office just as they began to know something of the nature of their duty? Were this the case, the interest of their constituents could never be sufficiently attended to. Our representatives for the state legislature are chosen for one year, and it has never been thought too long a term. If one year be not too long to elect a state representative, give me leave to say, that two years ought not to be considered as too long for the election of the members of the general legislature. The objects of the former are narrow, and limited to state and local affairs; the objects of the latter are coextensive with the continent. In England, at the time they were most jealous of the prerogative of the king, triennial elections were their most ardent wish; they would have thought themselves perfectly happy in this acquisition; nor did they think of a shorter term of elections. Let gentlemen recollect that it is to septennial elections we owe our liberties. The elections were for seven years in most of the states before the late revolution.

I now consider their weight and power, and whether these will be sufficient to give them, as the representatives of the people, their due weight in the government. By the Constitution, they are one entire branch of the legislature, without whose consent no law can be passed; — all money bills are to originate in their house; — they are to have the sole power of impeachment; — their consent is necessary to all acts or resolutions for the appropriation of the public money; to all acts for laying and collecting duties, imposts, and excises; for borrowing money on the credit of the United States; for creating all officers, and fixing their salaries; for coining money; for raising and supporting armies; for raising and maintaining a navy; and for establishing rules for the government of the land and naval forces: these are the powers which will be fixed in the House of Representatives.

Hence, it appears, our representatives have more comparative power in the scale of government than the commons of England; and yet, in that country, the commons, possessing less powers, opposed with success much greater powers than our representatives have to encounter. In that country, the king is one entire branch of the legislature, and an hereditary monarch; can prorogue or dissolve, call or dismiss, the two houses at his pleasure. Besides his judicial influence, he is head of the church, fountain of honor, generalissimo of the forces by sea or land, may raise what fleets and armies he pleases, is rendered personally sacred by the constitutional maxim that he can do no wrong; and, besides several other great powers, has a grand revenue settled on him, sufficient to answer the ordinary ends of government; it being established as a custom, at the accession of every new king, to settle such a revenue on him for life; and can increase the House of Lords at any time, and thereby extend his legislative influence. Notwithstanding the enormity of these powers, it has been found that the House of Commons, with powers greatly inferior to those of our representatives, is a match for both the king and the nobles. This superiority resulted from their having the power of withholding or granting supplies. What will put this in a still clearer point of view, is, that the House of Commons were not originally possessed of these powers. The history of the English Parliament will show that the great degree of power which they now possess was acquired from beginnings so small, that nothing but the innate weight of the power of the people, when lodged with their representatives, could have effected it. In the reign of Edward I., in the year 1295, the House of Commons were first called by legal authority; they were then confined to giving their assent barely to supplies to the crown. In the reign of Edward II., they first annexed petitions to the bills by which they granted subsidies. Under Edward III., they declared they would not in future acknowledge any law to which they had not consented: in the same reign, they impeached and brought to punishment some of the ministers of the crown. Under Henry IV., they refused supplies until an answer had been given to their petitions; and have increased their powers, in succeeding reigns, to such a degree, that they entirely control the operation of government, even in those cases where the king's prerogative gave him, nominally, the sole direction.

Let us here consider the causes to which this uncommon weight and influence may be assigned. The government being divided into branches, executive and legislative, in all contests between them the people have divided into the favorers of one or the other. From their dread of the executive, and affection to their representatives, they have always sided with the legislature. This has rendered the legislature successful. The House of Commons have succeeded also by withholding supplies; they can, by this power, put a stop to the operations of government, which they have been able to direct as they pleased. This power has enabled them to triumph over all obstacles; it is so important that it will in the end swallow up all others. Any branch of government that depends on the will of another for supplies of money, must be in a state of subordinate dependence, let it have what other powers it may. Our representatives, in this case, will be perfectly independent, being vested with this power fully. Another source of superiority is the power of impeachment. In England, very few ministers have dared to bring on themselves an accusation by the representatives of the people, by pursuing means contrary to their rights and liberties. Few ministers will ever run the risk of being impeached, when they know the king cannot protect them by a pardon. This power must have much greater force in America, where the President himself is personally amenable for his mal-administration; the power of impeachment must be a sufficient check on the President's power of pardoning before conviction. I think we may fairly conclude, that, if the House of Commons, in England, have been able to oppose, with success, a powerful hereditary nobility, and an hereditary monarch, with all the appendages of royalty, and immense powers and revenues, our federal House of Representatives will be able to oppose, with success, all attempts by a President, only chosen for four years, by the people, with a small revenue, and limited powers, sufficient only for his own support; and a Senate chosen only for six years, (one third of whom vacate their seats every two years,) accountable to the state legislatures, and having no separate interest from them or the people.

I now come to consider their responsibility to the people at large. The probability of their consulting most scrupulously the interests of their constituents must be self-evident; this probability will result from their biennial elections, whether they wish to be reelected or not. If they wish to be reelected, they will know that on their good conduct alone their reelection will depend: if they wish not to be reelected, they will not enter into a fixed combination against the people, because they return to the mass of the people, where they will participate in the disadvantages of bad laws. By the publication of the yeas and nays, the votes of the individual members will be known; they will act, therefore, as if under the eyes of their constituents. The state legislatures, also, will be a powerful check on them: every new power given to Congress is taken from the state legislatures; they will be, therefore, very watchful over them; for, should they exercise any power not vested in them, it will be a usurpation of the rights of the different state legislatures, who would sound the alarm to the people. Upon such an appeal from the states to the people, nothing but the propriety of their conduct would insure the Congress any chance of success. Should a struggle actually ensue, it would terminate to the disadvantage of the general government, as Congress would be the object of the fears, and the state legislatures the object of the affections, of the people. One hundred and sixty members, chosen in this state legislature, must, on any dispute between Congress and the state legislature, have more influence than ten members of Congress. One representative to Congress will be chosen by eight or ten counties; his influence and chance of reelection will be very small when opposed by twenty men of the best interests in the district: when we add to this the influence of the whole body of the state officers, I think I may venture to affirm that every measure of Congress would be successfully opposed by the states. The experience of this state legislature hath fully satisfied me that this reasoning is just. The members of our Senate have never ventured to oppose any measure of the House of Delegates; and if they had, their chance of being reelected, when opposed by the delegates of the different counties, would be small. But what demonstrates that there is sufficient responsibility in the representatives to the people, and what must satisfy the committee, is this — that it will be their own interest to attend to that of the people at large. They can pass no law but what will equally affect their own persons, their families, and property. This will be an additional influence to prevail with them to attend to their duty, and more effectually watch and check the executive. Their consequence as members will be another inducement. If they will individually signalize themselves in support of their constituents, and in curbing the usurpations of the executive, it will best recommend them to the people, secure their reelection, and enhance their consequence. They therefore will become watchful guardians of the interests of the people.

The Constitution has wisely interposed another check, to wit: — that no person holding an office of trust or profit under the United States shall be a member of either house during his continuance in office. No powers ought to be vested in the hands of any who are not representatives of the people, and amenable to them. A review of the history of those countries with which I am acquainted, will show, that, for want of representation and responsibility, power has been exercised with an intention to advance the interest of a few, and not to remove the grievances of the many. At the time the Romans expelled their kings, the executive authority was given to consuls, and the people did not gain by the change; for the plebeian interest declined, while that of the patricians rapidly advanced, till the oppressions of the latter caused the former to retire to the Sacred Mount; and even this struggle terminated only in the creation of the tribunes of the people. Another struggle produced only the advantage of their admission to the consular dignity, and permission to intermarry into patrician families; so that every success on the side of the people only produced a change in their tyrants. Under Louis XI., in France, a war took place between the king and his barons, professedly for the public good only; and, they being successful, a treaty was made for the securing that public good; but it contained stipulations only in favor of a few lords, — not a word in favor of the people. But in England, where the people had delegated all their power to a few representatives, all contests have terminated in favor of the people. One contest produced Magna Charta, containing stipulations for the good of the whole. This Great Charter was renewed, enlarged, and confirmed, by several succeeding kings: the Habeas Corpus under Charles II., and Declaration of Rights under William and Mary, — the latter limiting the prerogative of the crown, the former establishing the personal liberty of the subject, — were also in favor of the whole body of the people. Every revolution terminated differently in Rome and in England; in the first they only caused a change in their masters, in the second they ended in a confirmation of their liberties. The powerful influence of the people in gaining an extension of their liberties will appear more forcibly, and our confidence in our House of Representatives must be increased, when we come to consider the manner in which the House of Commons in England are elected. They consist of five hundred and fifty-eight members, two hundred of whom are chosen by about seven thousand freeholders in the counties, out of eight millions of people: the rest are chosen by towns, several of which, though small, elect five members; and even there are instances of two representatives being chosen by one elector. The most baneful elections procure seats; one half of the candidates purchase them: yet the people in England have ever prevailed when they persisted in any particular purpose. If, then, they have prevailed there when opposed by two other powerful branches of the legislature, and when elected so unduly, what may we not expect from our House of Representatives, fairly chosen by the people? If the people there prevail with septennial elections, what may we not expect from our representatives, chosen only for two years, and who only have to encounter the feeble power of the President, and a Senate whose interest will lead them to do their duty? The opposers of this plan of government dread the exercise of the most necessary, the most indispensable powers, and exercised by their own representatives. Magna Charta, and Declaration of Rights, only say that such powers shall not be exercised but with consent of Parliament; and experience has proved that the making their consent necessary has sufficiently secured a proper exercise of those powers. The best writers also agree that such powers may always be lodged with representatives.

We have all the security which a people sensible and jealous of their liberties can wish for. Experience has evinced that mankind can trust those who have similar rights with themselves. Power lodged in the hands of representatives, chosen as ours must be, cannot be abused. The truth of this cannot but strike every gentleman in the committee: and still the people can, when they please, change the government, being possessed of the supreme power.

Speech Before the Virginia Ratifying Convention by Edmund Pendleton

Editor's Introduction:

Few men were held in higher esteem among Virginia society than Edmund Pendleton. He counted among his personal friends George Washington and Patrick Henry, and he was so respected his peers selected him to preside over both the convention that declared Virginia independence in 1776 and the Virginia Ratifying Convention in 1788.

Pendleton was born in 1721 in Caroline County, Virginia. His father died before he was born, and he was reared for a time by his material grandmother. He was admitted to the Virginia bar in 1741 and established a reputation as a fine attorney. He tutored both his nephew John Penn, a signatory to the Declaration of Independence, and John Taylor of Caroline, the conservative Jeffersonian statesman. Pendleton was elected to the House of Burgesses and later to the First Continental Congress with Washington and Henry. Like John Dickinson and other "moderate" members of American society, Pendleton opposed a break with Great Britain until the move seemed necessary.

He was de facto governor of Virginia for about a year and was later appointed first Chief Justice of the Virginia Supreme Court, a position he held until his death in 1803.

Pendelton's June 5 speech emphasized that the Constitution was nearly a proposal without power until the States ratified the document. In essence, the men who debated the document gave it meaning and validity, a position James Madison would later echo. He agreed with Henry that if the document created a consolidated government, it would be impracticable and dangerous to the American political system, but Pendleton argued that the Constitution maintained the federal republic. The States, he insisted, retained all powers not delegated to the general government, and he questioned how anyone could read the Constitution and conclude that the general government could exceed those powers granted in Article I, Section 8. He concluded that, "When, therefore, the federal government is, in so many respects, so absolutely dependent on the state governments, I wonder how any gentleman, reflecting on the subject, could have conceived an idea of a possibility of the former destroying the latter."

Speech Before the Virginia Ratifying Convention

June 5, 1788

By Edmund Pendleton of Virginia

Mr. PENDLETON. Mr. Chairman, my worthy friend (Mr. Henry) has expressed great uneasiness in his mind, and informed us that a great many of our citizens are also extremely uneasy, at the proposal of changing our government; but that, a year ago, before this fatal system was thought of, the public mind was at perfect repose. It is necessary to inquire whether the public mind was at ease on the subject, and if it be since disturbed, what was the cause. What was the situation of this country before the meeting of the federal Convention? Our general government was totally inadequate to the purpose of its institution; our commerce decayed; our finances deranged; public and private credit destroyed: these and many other national evils rendered necessary the meeting of that Convention. If the public mind was then at ease, it did not result from a conviction of being in a happy and easy situation: it must have been an inactive, unaccountable stupor. The federal Convention devised the paper on your table as a remedy to remove our political diseases. What has created the public uneasiness since? Not public reports, which are not to be depended upon; but mistaken apprehensions of danger, drawn from observations on government which do not apply to us. When we come to inquire into the origin of most governments of the world, we shall find that they are generally dictated by a conqueror, at the point of the sword, or are the offspring of confusion, when a great popular leader, taking advantage of circumstances, if not producing them, restores order at the expense of liberty, and becomes the tyrant over the people. It may well be supposed that, in forming a government of this sort, it will not be favorable to liberty: the conqueror will take care of his own emoluments, and have little concern for the interest of the people. In either case, the interest and ambition of a despot, and not the good of the people, have given the tone to the government. A government thus formed must necessarily create a continual war between the governors and governed.

Writers consider the two parties (the people and tyrants) as in a state of perpetual warfare, and sound the alarm to the people. But what is our case? We are perfectly free from sedition and war: we are not yet in confusion: we are left to consider our real happiness and security: we want to secure these objects: we know they cannot be attained without government. Is there a single man, in this committee, of a contrary opinion? What was it that brought us from a state of nature to society, but to secure happiness? And can society be formed without government? Personify government: apply to it as a friend to assist you, and it will grant your request. This is the only government founded in real compact. There is no quarrel between government and liberty; the former is the shield and protector of the latter. The war is between government and licentiousness, faction, turbulence, and other violations of the rules of society, to preserve liberty. Where is the cause of alarm? We, the people, possessing all power, form a government, such as we think will secure happiness: and suppose, in adopting this plan, we should be mistaken in the end; where is the cause of alarm on that quarter? In the same plan we point out an easy and quiet method of reforming what may be found amiss. No, but, say gentlemen, we have put the introduction of that method in the hands of our servants, who will interrupt it from motives of self-interest. What then? We will resist, did my friend say? conveying an idea of force. Who shall dare to resist the people? No, we will assemble in Convention; wholly recall our delegated powers, or reform them so as to prevent such abuse; and punish those servants who have perverted powers, designed for our happiness, to their own emolument. We ought to be extremely cautious not to be drawn into dispute with regular government, by faction and turbulence, its natural enemies. Here, then, sir, there is no cause of alarm on this side; but on the other side, rejecting of government, and dissolving of the Union, produce confusion and despotism.

But an objection is made to the form: the expression, We, the people, is thought improper. Permit me to ask the gentleman who made this objection, who but the people can delegate powers? Who but the people have a right to form government? The expression is a common one, and a favorite one with me. The representatives of the people, by their authority, is a mode wholly inessential. If the objection be, that the Union ought to be not of the people, but of the state governments, then I think the choice of the former very happy and proper. What have the state governments to do with it? Were they to determine, the people would not, in that case, be the judges upon what terms it was adopted.

But the power of the Convention is doubted. What is the power? To propose, not to determine. This power of proposing was very broad; it extended to remove all defects in government: the members of that Convention, who were to consider all the defects in our general government, were not confined to any particular plan. Were they deceived? This is the proper question here. Suppose the paper on your table dropped from one of the planets; the people found it, and sent us here to consider whether it was proper for their adoption; must we not obey them? Then the question must be between this government and the Confederation. The latter is no government at all. It has been said that it has carried us, through a dangerous war, to a happy issue. Not that Confederation, but common danger, and the spirit of America, were bonds of our union: union and unanimity, and not that insignificant paper, carried us through that dangerous war. "United, we stand — divided, we fall!" echoed and reechoed through America — from Congress to the drunken carpenter — was effectual, and procured the end of our wishes, though now forgotten by gentlemen, if such there be, who incline to let go this stronghold, to catch at feathers; for such all substituted projects may prove.

This spirit had nearly reached the end of its power when relieved by peace. It was the spirit of America, and not the Confederation, that carried us through the war: thus I prove it. The moment of peace showed the imbecility of the federal government: Congress was empowered to make war and peace; a peace they made, giving us the great object, independence, and yielding us a territory that exceeded my most sanguine expectations. Unfortunately, a single disagreeable clause, not the object of the war, has retarded the performance of the treaty on our part. Congress could only recommend its performance, not enforce it; our last Assembly (to their honor be it said) put this on its proper grounds — on honorable grounds; it was as much as they ought to have done. This single instance shows the imbecility of the Confederation; the debts contracted by the war were unpaid; demands were made on Congress; all that Congress was able to do was to make an estimate of the debt, and proportion it among the several states; they sent on the requisitions, from time to time, to the states, for their respective quotas. These were either complied with partially, or not at all. Repeated demands on Congress distressed that honorable body; but they were unable to fulfil those engagements, as they so earnestly wished. What was the idea of other nations respecting America? What was the idea entertained of us by those nations to whom we were so much indebted? The inefficacy of the general government warranted an idea that we had no government at all. Improvements were proposed, and agreed to by twelve states; but were interrupted, because the little state of Rhode Island refused to accede to them. This was a further proof of the imbecility of that government. Need I multiply instances to show that it is wholly ineffectual for the purposes of its institution? Its whole progress since the peace proves it.

Shall we then, sir, continue under such a government, or shall we introduce that kind of government which shall produce the real happiness and security of the people? When gentlemen say that we ought not to introduce this new government, but strengthen the hands of Congress, they ought to be explicit. In what manner shall this be done? If the union of the states be necessary, government must be equally so; for without the latter, the former cannot be effected. Government must then have its complete powers, or be ineffectual; a legislature to fix rules, impose sanctions, and point out the punishment of the transgressors of these rules; an executive to watch over officers, and bring them to punishment; a judiciary, to guard the innocent, and fix the guilty, by a fair trial. Without an executive, offenders would not be brought to punishment; without a judiciary, any man might be taken up, convicted, and punished without a trial. Hence the necessity of having these three branches. Would any gentleman in this committee agree to vest these three powers in one body — Congress? No. Hence the necessity of a new organization and distribution of those powers. If there be any feature in this government which is not republican, it would be exceptionable. From all the public servants responsibility is secured, by their being representatives, mediate or immediate, for short terms, and their powers defined. It is, on the whole complexion of it, a government of laws, not of men.

But it is represented to be a consolidated government, annihilating that of the states — a consolidated government, which so extensive a territory as the United States cannot admit of, without terminating in despotism. If this be such a government, I will confess, with my worthy friend, that it is inadmissible over such a territory as this country. Let us consider whether it be such a government or not. I should understand a consolidated government to be that which should have the sole and exclusive power, legislative, executive, and judicial, without any limitation. Is this such a government? Or can it be changed to such a one? It only extends to the general purposes of the Union. It does not intermeddle with the local, particular affairs of the states. Can Congress legislate for the state of Virginia? Can they make a law altering the form of transferring property, or the rule of descents, in Virginia? In one word, can they make a single law for the individual, exclusive purpose of any one state? It is the interest of the federal to preserve the state governments; upon the latter the existence of the former depends: the Senate derives its existence immediately from the state legislatures; and the representatives and President are elected under their direction and control; they also preserve order among the citizens of their respective states, and without order and peace no society can possibly exist. Unless, therefore, there be state legislatures to continue the existence of Congress, and preserve order and peace among the inhabitants, this general government, which gentlemen suppose will annihilate the state governments, must itself be destroyed. When, therefore, the federal government is, in so many respects, so absolutely dependent on the state governments, I wonder how any gentleman, reflecting on the subject, could have conceived an idea of a possibility of the former destroying the latter. But the power of laying direct taxes is objected to. Government must be supported; this cannot be done without a revenue: if a sufficient revenue be not otherwise raised, recurrence must be had to direct taxation; gentlemen admit this, but insist on the propriety of first applying to the state legislatures.

Let us consider the consequence that would result from this. In the first place, time would be lost by it. Congress would make requisitions in December; our legislature do not meet till October; here would be a considerable loss of time, admitting the requisitions to be fully complied with. But suppose the requisitions to be refused; would it not be dangerous to send a collector, to collect the Congressional taxes, after the state legislature had absolutely refused to comply with the demands of Congress? Would not resistance to collectors be the probable consequence? Would not this resistance terminate in confusion, and a dissolution of the Union? The concurrent power of two different bodies laying direct taxes, is objected to. These taxes are for two different purposes, and cannot interfere with one another. I can see no danger resulting from this; and we must suppose that a very small sum more than the impost would be sufficient. But the representation is supposed too small. I confess, I think with the gentleman who opened the debate (Mr. Nicholas) on this subject; and I think he gave a very satisfactory answer to this objection, when he observed that, though the number might be insufficient to convey information of necessary local interests to a state legislature, yet it was sufficient for the federal legislature, who are to act only on general subjects, in which this state is concerned in common with other states. The apportionment of representation and taxation by the same scale is just; it removes the objection, that, while Virginia paid one sixth part of the expenses of the Union, she had no more weight in public counsels than Delaware, which paid but a very small portion. By this just apportionment she is put on a footing with the small states, in point of representation and influence in councils. I cannot imagine a more judicious principle than is here fixed by the Constitution — the number shall not exceed one for every thirty thousand. But it is objected that the number may be less. If Virginia sends in that proportion, I ask, Where is the power in Congress to reject them? States might incline to send too many; they are therefore restrained: but can it be doubted that they will send the number they are entitled to? We may be therefore sure, from this principle unequivocally fixed in the Constitution, that the number of our representatives will be in proportion to the increase or decrease of our population. I can truly say that I am of no party, nor actuated by any influence, but the true interest and real happiness of those whom I represent; and my age and situation, I trust, will sufficiently demonstrate the truth of this assertion. I cannot conclude without adding, that I am perfectly satisfied with this part of the system.

Speech Before the Virginia Ratifying Convention by Edmund Randolph

Editor's Introduction:

Randolph's June 6 speech continued to press the importance of Union for Virginia. He listed several reasons why he thought Virginia could not be an independent State, but he anchored them on economics and safety. Virginia, he contended, would be alone, unable to defend itself against foreign invasion or internecine warfare. Virginia could not afford to pay its debts and its economy would stagnate without the support of the Union. This was arguably the best pro-Union speech of the ratification period. By making this speech, Randolph implicitly recognized that the States *could* "secede" from the Union and that the American War for Independence established each State as a sovereign political entity. He thought secession would be political suicide, but nevertheless recognized its legality. He also contended that opponents of the document read the Baron de Montesquieu incorrectly. Randolph argued that republican government could exist over large territories—as in the case of Virginia—if the people chose their representatives. That was the key. Montesquieu did not think *democracy* could work over a substantial territory, but republican government could.

Speech Before the Virginia Ratifying Convention

June 6, 1788

By Edmund Randolph of Virginia

Gov. RANDOLPH. Mr. Chairman, I am a child of the revolution. My country, very early indeed, took me under its protection, at a time when I most wanted it, and, by a succession of favors and honors, gratified even my most ardent wishes. I feel the highest gratitude and attachment to my country; her felicity is the most fervent prayer of my heart. Conscious of having exerted my faculties to the utmost in her behalf, if I have not succeeded in securing the esteem of my countrymen, I shall reap abundant consolation from the rectitude of my intentions: honors, when compared to the satisfaction accruing from a conscious independence and rectitude of conduct, are no equivalent. The unwearied study of my life shall be to promote her happiness. As a citizen, ambition and popularity are no objects with me. I expect, in the course of a year, to retire to that private station which I most sincerely and cordially prefer to all others. The security of public justice, sir, is what I most fervently wish, as I consider that object to be the primary step to the attainment of public happiness. I can declare to the whole world, that, in the part I take in this very important question, I am actuated by a regard for what I conceive to be our true interest. I can also, with equal sincerity, declare that I would join heart and hand in rejecting this system, did I not conceive it would promote our happiness; but, having a strong conviction on my mind, at this time, that by a disunion we shall throw away all those blessings we have so earnestly fought for, and that a rejection of the Constitution will operate disunion, pardon me if I discharge the obligation I owe to my country, by voting for its adoption. We are told that the report of dangers is false. The cry of peace, sir, is false: say peace, when there is peace; it is but a sudden calm. The tempest growls over you: look round — wheresoever you look, you see danger. Where there are so many witnesses in many parts of America, that justice is suffocated, shall peace and happiness still be said to reign? Candor, sir, requires an undisguised representation of our situation. Candor, sir, demands a faithful exposition of facts. Many citizens have found justice strangled and trampled under foot, through the course of jurisprudence in this country. Are those who have debts due to them satisfied with your government? Are not creditors wearied with the tedious procrastination of your legal process — a process obscured by legislative mists? Cast your eyes to your seaports; see how commerce languishes. This country, so blessed, by nature, with every advantage that can render commerce profitable, through defective legislation is deprived of all the benefits and emoluments she might otherwise reap from it. We hear many complaints on the subject of located lands; a variety of competitors claiming the same lands under legislative acts, public faith prostrated, and private confidence destroyed. I ask you if your laws are reverenced. In every well-regulated community, the laws command respect. Are yours entitled to reverence? We not only see violations of the constitution, but of national principles in repeated instances. How is the fact? The history of the violations of the constitution extends from the year 1776 to this present time — violations made by formal acts of the legislature: every thing has been drawn within the legislative vortex.

There is one example of this violation in Virginia, of a most striking and shocking nature — an example so horrid, that, if I conceived my country would passively permit a repetition of it, dear as it is to me, I would seek means of expatriating myself from it. A man, who was then a citizen, was deprived of his life thus: from a mere reliance on general reports, a gentleman in the House of Delegates informed the house, that a certain man (Josiah Philips) had committed several crimes, and was running at large, perpetrating other crimes. He therefore moved for leave to attaint him; he obtained that leave instantly; no sooner did he obtain it, than he drew from his pocket a bill ready written for that effect; it was read three times in one day, and carried to the Senate. I will not say that it passed the same day through the Senate; but he was attainted very speedily and precipitately, without any proof better than vague reports. Without being confronted with his accusers and witnesses, without the privilege of calling for evidence in his behalf, he was sentenced to death, and was afterwards actually executed. Was this arbitrary deprivation of life, the dearest gift of God to man, consistent with the genius of a republican government? Is this compatible with the spirit of freedom? This, sir, has made the deepest impression on my heart, and I cannot contemplate it without horror. There are still a multiplicity of complaints of the debility of the laws. Justice, in many instances, is so unattainable that commerce may, in fact, be said to be stopped entirely. There is no peace, sir, in this land. Can peace exist with injustice, licentiousness, insecurity, and oppression? These considerations, independent of many others which I have not yet enumerated, would be a sufficient reason for the adoption of this Constitution, because it secures the liberty of the citizen, his person and property, and will invigorate and restore commerce and industry. An additional reason to induce us to adopt it is that excessive licentiousness which has resulted from the relaxation of our laws, and which will be checked by this government. Let us judge from the fate of more ancient nations: licentiousness has produced tyranny among many of them: it has contributed as much (if not more) as any other cause whatsoever to the loss of their liberties. I have respect for the integrity of our legislatures; I believe them to be virtuous; but as long as the defects of the Constitution exist, so long will laws be imperfect.

The honorable gentleman went on further, and said that the accession of eight states is not a reason for our adoption. Many other things have been alleged out of order; instead of discussing the system regularly, a variety of points are promiscuously debated, in order to make temporary impression on the members. Sir, were I convinced of the validity of their arguments, I would join them heart and hand. Were I convinced that the accession of eight states did not render our accession also necessary to preserve the Union, I would not accede to it till it should be previously amended; but, sir, I am convinced that the Union will be lost by our rejection. Massachusetts has adopted it; she has recommended subsequent amendments; her influence must be very considerable to obtain them. I trust my countrymen have sufficient wisdom and virtue to entitle them to equal respect. Is it urged that, being wiser, we ought to prescribe amendments to the other states? I have considered this subject deliberately; wearied myself in endeavoring to find a possibility of preserving the Union, without our unconditional ratification; but, sir, in vain; I find no other means. I ask myself a variety of questions applicable to the adopting states, and I conclude, Will they repent of what they have done? Will they acknowledge themselves in an error? Or will they recede, to gratify Virginia? My prediction is, that they will not. Shall we stand by ourselves, and be severed from the Union, if amendments cannot be had? I have every reason for determining within myself that our rejection must dissolve the Union; and that that dissolution will destroy our political happiness. The honorable gentleman was pleased to draw out several other arguments out of order, — that this government would destroy the state governments, the trial by jury, &c. &c., — and concluded by an illustration of his opinion by a reference to the confederacy of the Swiss. Let us argue with unprejudiced minds. They say that the trial by jury is gone. Is this so? Although I have declared my determination to give my vote for it, yet I shall freely censure those parts which appear to me reprehensible.

The trial by jury in criminal cases is secured; in civil cases it is not so expressly secured as I should wish it; but it does not follow that Congress has the power of taking away this privilege, which is secured by the constitution of each state, and not given away by this Constitution. I have no fear on this subject. Congress must regulate it so as to suit every state. I will risk my property on the certainty that they will institute the trial by jury in such manner as shall accommodate the conveniences of the inhabitants in every state. The difficulty of ascertaining this accommodation was the principal cause of its not being provided for. It will be the interest of the individuals composing Congress to put it on this convenient footing. Shall we not choose men respectable for their good qualities? Or can we suppose that men tainted with the worst vices will get into Congress? I beg leave to differ from the honorable gentleman in another point. He dreads that great inconveniences will ensue from the federal court; that our citizens will be harassed by being carried thither. I cannot think that this power of the federal judiciary will necessarily be abused; the inconvenience here suggested being of a general nature, affecting most of the states, will, by general consent of the states, be removed: and, I trust, such regulations shall be made in this case as will accommodate the people in every state. The honorable gentleman instanced the Swiss cantons, as an example, to show us the possibility, if not expediency, of being in amicable alliance with the other states, without adopting this system. Sir, references to history will be fatal in political reasons unless well guarded. Our mental ability is often so contracted, and powers of investigation so limited, that sometimes we adduce as an example in our favor what in fact militates against us. Examine the situation of that country comparatively to us: the extent and situation of that country is totally different from ours; their country is surrounded by powerful, ambitious, and reciprocally jealous nations; their territory small, and soil not very fertile. The peculiarity, sir, of their situation, has kept them together, and not that system of alliance to which the gentleman seems to attribute the durability and felicity of their connection.

[Here his excellency quoted some passages from Stanyard, illustrating his argument, and largely commented upon it; the effect of which was, that the narrow confines of that country rendered it very possible for a system of confederacy to accommodate those cantons, that would not suit the United States; that it was the fear of the ambitious and warlike nations that surrounded them, and the reciprocal jealousy of the other European powers, that rendered their union so desirable; and that, notwithstanding these circumstances, and their being a hardy race of people, yet such was the injudicious construction of their confederacy, that very considerable broils interrupted their harmony sometimes.]

His excellency then continued: I have produced this example to show that we ought not to be amused with the historical references which have no kind of analogy to the points under our consideration. We ought to confine ourselves to those points, solely, which have an immediate and strict similitude to the subject of our discussion. The reference made by the honorable gentleman over the way is extremely inapplicable to us. Are the Swiss cantons circumstanced as we are? Are we surrounded by formidable nations? Or are we situated in any manner like them? We are not, sir. Then it naturally results, that no such friendly intercourse as he flattered himself with could take place, in a case of a dissolution of our union. We are remotely situated from powerful nations, the dread of whose attack might impel us to unite firmly with one another; nor are we situated in an inaccessibly strong position; we have to fear much from one another. We must soon feel the fatal effects of an imperfect system of union. The honorable gentleman attacks the Constitution, as he thinks it is contrary to our bill of rights. Do we not appeal to the people, by whose authority all government is made? That bill of rights is of no validity, because, I conceive, it is not formed on due authority. It is not a part of our Constitution; it has never secured us against any danger; it has been repeatedly disregarded and violated. But we must not discard the Confederation, for the remembrance of its past services. I am attached to old servants. I have regard and tenderness for this old servant; but when reason tells us, that it can no longer be retained without throwing away all that it has gained us, and running the risk of losing every thing dear to us, must we still continue our attachment? Reason and my duty tell me not. Other gentlemen may think otherwise.

But, sir, is it not possible that men may differ in sentiments, and still be honest? We have an inquisition within ourselves, that leads us not to offend so much against charity. The gentleman expresses a necessity of being suspicious of those who govern. I will agree with him in the necessity of political jealousy to a certain extent; but we ought to examine how far this political jealousy ought to be carried. I confess that a certain degree of it is highly necessary to the preservation of liberty; but it ought not to be extended to a degree which is degrading and humiliating to human nature; to a degree of restlessness, and active disquietude, sufficient to disturb a community, or preclude the possibility of political happiness and contentment. Confidence ought also to be equally limited. Wisdom shrinks from extremes, and fixes on a medium as her choice. Experience and history, the least fallible judges, teach us that, in forming a government, the powers to be given must be commensurate to the object. A less degree will defeat the intention, and a greater will subject the people to the depravity of rulers, who, though they are but the agents of the people, pervert their powers to their emoluments and ambitious views.

Mr. Chairman, I am sorry to be obliged to detain the house; but the relation of a variety of matters renders it now unavoidable. I informed the house yesterday, before rising, that I intended to show the necessity of having a national government in preference to the Confederation; also to show the necessity of conceding the power of taxation, and distinguishing between its objects; and I am the more happy that I possess materials of information for that purpose. My intention, then, is to satisfy the gentlemen of this committee that a national government is absolutely indispensable, and that a confederacy is not eligible, in our present situation: the introductory step to this will be, to endeavor to convince the house of the necessity of the Union, and that the present Confederation is actually inadequate and unamendable. The extent of the country is objected, by the gentleman over the way, as an insurmountable obstacle to the establishing a national government in the United States. It is a very strange and inconsistent doctrine, to admit the necessity of the Union, and yet urge this last objection, which I think goes radically to the existence of the Union itself. If the extent of the country be a conclusive argument against a national government, it is equally so against a union with the other states. Instead of entering largely into a discussion of the nature and effect of the different kinds of government, or into an inquiry into the particular extent of country that may suit the genius of this or that government, I ask this question — Is this government necessary for the safety of Virginia? Is the union indispensable for our happiness? I confess it is imprudent for any nation to form alliance with another whose situation and construction of government are dissimilar to its own. It is impolitic and improper for men of opulence to join their interest with men of indigence and chance. But we are now inquiring particularly whether Virginia, as contradistinguished from the other states, can exist without the union — a hard question, perhaps, after what has been said. I will venture, however, to say, she cannot. I shall not rest contented with asserting — I shall endeavor to prove.

Look at the most powerful nations on earth. England and France have had recourse to this expedient. Those countries found it necessary to unite with their immediate neighbors, and this union has prevented the most lamentable mischiefs. What divine preëminence is Virginia possessed of above other states? Can Virginia send her navy and thunder to bid defiance to foreign nations? And can she exist without a union with her neighbors, when the most potent nations have found such a union necessary, not only to their political felicity, but their national existence? Let us examine her ability. Although it be impossible to determine with accuracy what degree of internal strength a nation ought to possess to enable it to stand by itself, yet there are certain sure facts and circumstances which demonstrate that a particular nation cannot stand singly. I have spoken with freedom, and I trust I have done it with decency; but I must also speak the truth. If Virginia can exist without the union, she must derive that ability from one or other of these sources, — viz., from her natural situation, or because she has no reason to fear from other nations. What is her situation? She is not inaccessible: she is not a petty republic, like that of St. Marino, surrounded by rocks and mountains, with a soil not very fertile, nor worthy the envy of surrounding nations. Were this, sir, her situation, she might, like that petty state, subsist separated from all the world. On the contrary, she is very accessible: the large, capacious Bay of Chesapeake, which is but too excellently adapted for the admission of enemies, renders her very vulnerable.

I am informed — and I believe rightly, because I derive my information from those whose knowledge is most respectable — that Virginia is in a very unhappy position with respect to the access of foes by sea, though happily situated for commerce. This being her situation by sea, let us look at land. She has frontiers adjoining the states of Pennsylvania, Maryland, and North Carolina. Two of those states have declared themselves members of the Union: will she be inaccessible to the inhabitants of those states? Cast your eyes to the western country, that is inhabited by cruel savages, your natural enemies. Besides their natural propensity to barbarity, they may be excited, by the gold of foreign enemies, to commit the most horrid ravages on your people. Our greatly-increasing population is one remedy to this evil; but being scattered thinly over so extensive a country, how difficult is it to collect their strength, or defend the country! This is one point of weakness. I wish, for the honor of my countrymen, that it was the only one. There is another circumstance which renders us more vulnerable. Are we not weakened by the population of those whom we hold in slavery? The day may come when they may make impression upon us. Gentlemen who have been long accustomed to the contemplation of the subject, think there is a cause of alarm in this case: the number of those people, compared to that of the whites, is an immense proportion: their number amounts to 236,000 — that of the whites only to 352,000. Will the American spirit, so much spoken of, repel an invading enemy, or enable you to obtain an advantageous peace? Manufactures and military stores may afford relief to a country exposed: have we these at present? Attempts have been made to have these here. If we shall be separated from the Union, shall our chance of having these be greater? — or will not the want of these be more deplorable?

We shall be told of the exertions of Virginia under the Confederation — her achievements when she had no commerce. These, sir, were necessary for her immediate safety; nor would these have availed without the aid of the other states. Those states, then our friends, brothers, and supporters, will, if disunited from us, be our bitterest enemies. If, then, sir, Virginia, from her situation, is not inaccessible or invulnerable, let us consider if she be protected by having no cause to fear from other nations. Has she no cause to fear? You will have cause to fear, as a nation, if disunited; you will not only have this cause to fear from yourselves, from that species of population I before mentioned, and your once sister states, but from the arms of other nations. Have you no cause of fear from Spain, whose dominions border on your country? Every nation, every people, in our circumstances, have already had abundant cause to fear. Let us see the danger to be apprehended from France. Let us suppose Virginia separated from the other states; as part of the former confederated states, she will owe France a very considerable sum. Will France be as magnanimous as ever? France, by the law of nations, will have a right to demand the whole of her, or of the others. If France were to demand it, what would become of the property of America? Could she not destroy what little commerce we have? Could she not seize our ships, and carry havoc and destruction before her on our shores? The most lamentable desolation would take place. We owe a debt to Spain also: do we expect indulgence from that quarter? That nation has a right to demand the debt due to it, and power to enforce that right. Will the Dutch be silent about the debt due to them? Is there any one who pretends that any of these nations will be patient? The debts due the British are also very considerable; these debts have been withheld contrary to treaty: if Great Britain will demand the payment of these debts peremptorily, what will be the consequence? Can we pay them if demanded? Will no danger result from a refusal? Will the British nation suffer their subjects to be stripped of their property? Is not that nation amply able to do her subjects justice? Will the resentment of that powerful and supercilious nation sleep forever? If we become one sole nation, uniting with our sister states, our means of defence will be greater; the indulgence for the payment of those debts will be greater, and the danger of an attack less probable. Moreover, vast quantities of lands have been sold by citizens of this country to Europeans, and these lands cannot be found. Will this fraud be countenanced or endured? Among so many causes of danger, shall we be secure, separated from our sister states? Weakness itself, sir, will invite some attack upon your country. Contemplate our situation deliberately, and consult history; it will inform you that people in our circumstances have ever been attacked, and successfully: open any page, and you will there find our danger truly depicted. If such a people had any thing, was it not taken? The fate which will befall us, I fear, sir, will be, that we shall be made a partition of. How will these our troubles be removed? Can we have any dependence on commerce? Can we make any computation on this subject? Where will our flag appear? So high is the spirit of commercial nations, that they will spend five times the value of the object, to exclude their rivals from a participation in commercial profits; they seldom regard any expenses. If we should be divided from the rest of the states, upon what footing would our navigation in the Mississippi be? What would be the probable conduct of France and Spain? Every gentleman may imagine, in his own mind, the natural consequences. To these considerations I might add many others of a similar nature. Were I to say that the boundary between us and North Carolina is not yet settled, I should be told that Virginia and that state go together. But what, sir, will be the consequence of the dispute that may arise between us and Maryland, on the subject of Potomac River? It is thought Virginia has a right to an equal navigation with them in that river. If ever it should be decided on grounds of prior right, their charter will inevitably determine it in their favor. The country called the Northern Neck will probably be severed from Virginia: there is not a doubt but the inhabitants of that part will annex themselves to Maryland, if Virginia refuse to accede to the Union. The recent example of those regulations lately made respecting that territory will illustrate that probability. Virginia will also be in danger of a conflict with Pennsylvania, on the subject of boundaries. I know that some gentlemen are thoroughly persuaded that we have a right to those disputed boundaries: if we have such a right, I know not where it is to be found.

Are we not borderers on states that will be separated from us? Call to mind the history of every part of the world, where nations bordered on one another, and consider the consequences of our separation from the Union. Peruse those histories, and you find such countries to have ever been almost a perpetual scene of bloodshed and slaughter — the inhabitants of one escaping from punishment into the other — protection given them — consequent pursuit — robbery, cruelty, and murder. A numerous standing army, that dangerous expedient, would be necessary, but not sufficient, for the defence of such borders. Every gentleman will amplify the scene in his own mind.

If you wish to know the extent of such a scene, look at the history of England and Scotland before the union; you will see their borderers continually committing depredations, and cruelties of the most calamitous and deplorable nature, on one another. Mr. Chairman, were we struck off from the Union, and disputes of the back lands should be renewed, which are of the most alarming nature, and which must produce uncommon mischiefs, can you inform me how this great subject would be settled? Virginia has a large, unsettled country; she has at last quieted it. But there are great doubts whether she has taken the best way to effect it. If she has not, disagreeable consequences may ensue. I have before hinted at some other causes of quarrel between the other states and us; particularly the hatred that would be generated by commercial competitions. I will only add, on that subject, that controversies may arise concerning the fisheries, which may terminate in wars. Paper money may also be an additional source of disputes. Rhode Island has been in one continued train of opposition to national duties and integrity; they have defrauded their creditors by their paper money. Other states have also had emissions of paper money, to the ruin of credit and commerce. May not Virginia, at a future day, also recur to the same expedient? Has Virginia no affection for paper money, or disposition to violate contracts? I fear she is as fond of these measures as most other states in the Union. The inhabitants of the adjacent states would be affected by the depreciation of paper money, which would assuredly produce a dispute with those states. This danger is taken away by the present Constitution, as it provides "that no state shall emit bills of credit." Maryland has counteracted the policy of this state frequently, and may be meditating examples of this kind again. Before the revolution, there was a contest about those back lands, in which even government was a party; it was put an end to by the war. Pennsylvania was ready to enter into a war with us, for the disputed lands near the boundaries, and nothing but the superior prudence of the man who was at the head of affairs in Virginia could have prevented it.

I beg leave to remind you of the strength of Massachusetts and other states to the north; and what would their conduct be to us, if disunited from them? In case of a conflict between us and Maryland, or Pennsylvania, they would be aided by the whole strength of the more northern states; in short, by that of the adopting states. For these reasons, I conceive that, if Virginia supposes she has no cause of apprehension, she will find herself in a fatal error.

Suppose the American spirit in the fullest vigor in Virginia; what military preparations and exertions is she capable of making? The other states have upwards of 330,000 men capable of bearing arms: this will be a good army, or they can very easily raise a good army out of so great a number. Our militia amounts to 50,000: even stretching it to the improbable amount (urged by some) of 60,000, — in case of an attack, what defence can we make? Who are militia? Can we depend solely upon these? I will pay the last tribute of gratitude to the militia of my country: they performed some of the most gallant feats during the last war, and acted as nobly as men inured to other avocations could be expected to do; but, sir, it is dangerous to look to them as our sole protectors. Did ever militia defend a country? Those of Pennsylvania were said to differ very little from regulars; yet these, sir, were insufficient for the defence of that state. The militia of our country will be wanted for agriculture. On this noblest of arts depend the virtue and the very existence of a country; if it be neglected, every thing else must be in a state of ruin and decay. It must be neglected if those hands which ought to attend to it are occasionally called forth on military expeditions. Some also will be necessary for manufactures, and those mechanic arts which are necessary for the aid of the farmer and planter. If we had men sufficient in number to defend ourselves, it could not avail without other requisites. We must have a navy, to be supported in time of peace as well as war, to guard our coasts and defend us against invasions. The impossibility of building and equipping a fleet in short time constitutes the necessity of having a certain number of ships of war always ready in time of peace: the maintaining a navy will require money; and where, sir, can we get money for this and other purposes? How shall we raise it? Review the enormity of the debts due by this country. The amount of the debt we owe to the continent for bills of credit, rating at forty for one, will amount to between 6 and 700,000 pounds. There is also due the continent the balance of requisitions due by us; and, in addition to this proportion of the old Continental debt, there are the foreign, domestic, state, military, and loan-office debts; to which when you add the British debt, where is the possibility of finding money to raise an army or navy? Review, then, your real ability. Shall we recur to loans? Nothing can be more impolitic; they impoverish a nation. We, sir, have nothing to repay them; nor, sir, can we procure them. Our numbers are daily increasing by immigration; but this, sir, will not relieve us when our credit is gone and it is impossible to borrow money. If the imposts and duties in Virginia, even on the present footing, be very unproductive, and not equal to our necessity, what would they be if we were separated from the Union? From the first of September to the first of June, the amount put into the treasury is only £59,000, or a little more. But, sir, if smuggling be introduced in consequence of high duties, or otherwise, and the Potomac should be lost, what hope is there of getting money there? Shall we be asked if the impost would be bettered by the Union? I answer that it will, sir. Credit being restored, and confidence diffused in the country, merchants and men of wealth will be induced to come among us, immigration will increase, and commerce will flourish; the impost will therefore be more sure and productive.

Under these circumstances, can you find men to defend you? If not men, where can you have a navy? It is an old observation, that he who commands the sea will command the land; and it is justified by modern experience in war. The sea can only be commanded by commercial nations. The United States have every means, by nature, to enable them to distribute supplies mutually among one another; to supply other nations with many articles, and to carry for other nations. Our commerce would not be kindly received by foreigners, if transacted solely by ourselves. As it is the spirit of commercial nations to engross as much as possible the carrying trade, this makes it necessary to defend our commerce. But how shall we compass this end? England has arisen to the greatest height, in modern times, by her navigation act, and other excellent regulations. The same means would produce the same effects. We have inland navigation. Our last exports did not exceed £1,000,000. Our export trade is entirely in the hands of foreigners. We have no manufactures — depend for supplies on other nations — and so far are we from having any carrying trade, that, as I have already said, our exports are in the hands of foreigners. Besides the profit that might be made by our natural materials, much greater gains would accrue from their being first wrought before they were exported. England has reaped immense profits by this, nay, even by purchasing and working up those materials which their country did not afford: her success in commerce is generally ascribed to her navigation act. Virginia would not, encumbered as she is, agree to have such an act. Thus, for the want of a navy, are we deprived of the multifarious advantages of our natural situation; nor is it possible that, if the Union was dissolved, we ever should have a navy sufficient either for our defence or the extension of our trade.

I beg gentlemen to consider these things — our inability to raise and man a navy, and the dreadful consequences of the dissolution of the Union. I will close this catalogue of the evils of the dissolution of the Union by recalling to your mind what passed in the year 1781. Such was the situation of our affairs then, that the power of dictator was given to the commander-in-chief, to save us from destruction. This shows the situation of the country to have been such as to make it ready to embrace an actual dictator. At some future period, will not our distresses impel us to do what the Dutch have done — throw all power into the hands of a stadtholder? How infinitely more wise and eligible than this desperate alternative, is a union with our American brethren! I feel myself so abhorrent to any thing that will dissolve our Union, that I cannot prevail with myself to assent to it directly or indirectly. If the Union is to be dissolved, what step is to be taken? Shall we form a partial confederacy? Or is it expected that we shall successfully apply to foreign alliance for military aid? This last measure, sir, has ruined almost every nation that used it: so dreadful an example ought to be most cautiously avoided; for seldom has a nation recurred to the expedient of foreign succor, without being ultimately crushed by that succor. We may lose our liberty and independence by an injudicious scheme of policy. Admitting it to be a scheme replete with safety, what nation shall we solicit? — France? She will disdain a connection with a people in our predicament. I would trust every thing to the magnanimity of that nation; but she would despise a people who had, like us, so imprudently separated from their brethren; and, sir, were she to accede to our proposal, with what facility could she become mistress of our country! To what nation, then, shall we apply? To Great Britain? Nobody has as yet trusted that idea. An application to any other must be either fruitless or dangerous. To those who advocate local confederacies, and at the same time preach up for republican liberty, I answer that their conduct is inconsistent: the defence of such partial confederacies will require such a degree of force and expense as will destroy every feature of republicanism. Give me leave to say, that I see nought but destruction in a local confederacy. With what state can we confederate but North Carolina? — North Carolina, situated worse than ourselves. Consult your own reason; I beseech gentlemen most seriously to reflect on the consequences of such a confederacy; I beseech them to consider whether Virginia and North Carolina, both oppressed with debts and slaves, can defend themselves externally, or make their people happy internally. North

Carolina, having no strength but militia, and Virginia, in the same situation, will make, I fear, but a despicable figure in history. Thus, sir, I hope that I have satisfied you that we are unsafe without a union; and that in union alone safety consists.

I come now, sir, to the great inquiry, whether the Confederation be such a government as we ought to continue under — whether it be such a government as can secure the felicity of any free people. Did I believe the Confederation was a good thread, which might be broken without destroying its utility entirely, I might be induced to concur in putting it together; but I am so thoroughly convinced of its incapacity to be mended or spliced, that I would sooner recur to any other expedient.

When I spoke last, I endeavored to express my sentiments concerning that system, and to apologize (if an apology was necessary) for the conduct of its framers; that it was hastily devised to enable us to repel a powerful enemy, that the subject was novel, and that its inefficacy was not discovered till requisitions came to be made by Congress. In the then situation of America, a speedy remedy was necessary to ward off the danger, and this sufficiently answered that purpose; but so universally is its imbecility now known, that it is useless for me to exhibit it at this time. Has not Virginia, as well as every other state, acknowledged its debility, by sending delegates to the general Convention? The Confederation is, of all things, the most unsafe, not only to trust to in its present form, but even to amend.

The object of a federal government is to remedy and strengthen the weakness of its individual branches, whether that weakness arises from situation or from any external cause. With respect to the first, is it not a miracle that the Confederation carried us through the last war? It was our unanimity, sir, that carried us through it. That system was not ultimately concluded till the year 1781. Although the greatest exertions were made before that time, when came requisitions for men and money, — its defects then were immediately discovered: the quotas of men were readily sent; not so those of money. One state feigned inability; another would not comply till the rest did; and various excuses were offered: so that no money was sent into the treasury — not a requisition was fully complied with. Loans were the next measure fallen upon: upwards of 80,000,000 of dollars were wanting, beside the emissions of dollars forty for one. These show the impossibility of relying on requisitions.

[Here his excellency enumerates the different delinquencies of different states, and the consequent distresses of Congress.] If the American spirit is to be depended upon, I call him to awake, to see how his Americans have been disgraced; but I have no hopes that things will be better hereafter. I fully expect things will be as they have been, and that the same derangement will produce similar miscarriages. Will the American spirit produce money or credit, unless we alter our system? Are we not in a contemptible situation? Are we not the jests of other nations?

But it is insinuated by the honorable gentleman, that we want to be a grand, splendid, and magnificent people: we wish not to become so: the magnificence of a royal court is not our object. We want a government, sir — a government that will have stability, and give us security; for our present government is destitute of the one and incapable of producing the other. It cannot, perhaps, with propriety, be denominated a government, being void of that energy requisite to enforce sanctions. I wish my country not to be contemptible in the eyes of foreign nations. A well-regulated community is always respected. It is the internal situation, the defects of government, that attract foreign contempt: that contempt, sir, is too often followed by subjugation. Advert to the contemptuous manner in which a shrewd politician speaks of our government.

[Here his excellency quoted a passage from Lord Sheffield, the purport of which was, that Great Britain might engross our trade on her own terms; that the imbecility and inefficacy of our general government were such, that it was impossible we could counteract her policy, however rigid or illiberal towards us her commercial regulations might be.]

Reflect but a moment on our situation. Does it not invite real hostility? The conduct of the British ministry to us is the natural effect of our unnerved government. Consider the commercial regulations between us and Maryland. Is it not known to gentlemen that the states have been making reprisals on each other — to obviate a repetition of which, in some degree, these regulations have been made? Can we not see, from this circumstance, the jealousy, rivalship, and hatred that would subsist between them, in case this state was out of the Union? They are importing states, and importing states will ever be competitors and rivals. Rhode Island and Connecticut have been on the point of war, on the subject of their paper money; Congress did not attempt to interpose. When Massachusetts was distressed by the late insurrection, Congress could not relieve her. Who headed that insurrection? Recollect the facility with which it was raised, and the very little ability of the ring-leader, and you cannot but deplore the extreme debility of our merely nominal government. We are too despicable to be regarded by foreign nations. The defects of the Confederation consisted principally in the want of power: it had nominally powers, powers on paper, which it could not use. The power of making peace and war is expressly delegated to Congress; yet the power of granting passports, though within that of making peace and war, was considered by Virginia as belonging to herself. Without adequate powers vested in Congress, America cannot be respectable in the eyes of other nations. Congress, sir, ought to be fully vested with power to support the Union, protect the interests of the United States, maintain their commerce, and defend them from external invasions and insults, and internal insurrections; to maintain justice, and promote harmony and public tranquillity among the states.

A government not vested with these powers will ever be found unable to make us happy or respectable. How far the Confederation is different from such a government, is known to all America. Instead of being able to cherish and protect the states, it has been unable to defend itself against the encroachments made upon it by the states. Every one of them has conspired against it; Virginia as much as any. This fact could be proved by reference to actual history. I might quote the observations of an able modern author, not because he is decorated with the name of author, but because his sentiments are drawn from human nature, to prove the dangerous impolicy of withholding necessary powers from Congress; but I shall at this time fatigue the house as little as possible. What are the powers of Congress? They have full authority to recommend what they please; this recommendatory power reduces them to the condition of poor supplicants. Consider the dignified language of the members of the American Congress. May it please your high mightinesses of Virginia to pay your just proportionate quota of our national debt: we humbly supplicate that it may please you to comply with your federal duties. We implore, we beg your obedience! Is not this, sir, a fair representation of the powers of Congress? Their operations are of no validity when counteracted by the states. Their authority to recommend is a mere mockery of government. But the amendability of the Confederation seems to have great weight on the minds of some gentlemen. To what point will the amendments go? What part makes the most important figure? What part deserves to be retained? In it one body has the legislative, executive, and judicial powers; but the want of efficient powers has prevented the dangers naturally consequent on the union of these. Is this union consistent with an augmentation of their power? Will you, then, amend it by taking away one of these three powers? Suppose, for instance, you only vested it with the legislative and executive powers, without any control on the judiciary; what must be the result? Are we not taught by reason, experience, and governmental history, that tyranny is the natural and certain consequence of uniting these two powers, or the legislative and judicial powers, exclusively, in the same body? If any one denies it, I shall pass by him as an infidel not to be reclaimed. Whenever any two of these three powers are vested in one single body, they must, at one time or other, terminate in the destruction of liberty. In the most important cases, the assent of nine states is necessary to pass a law. This is too great a restriction, and whatever good consequences it may, in some cases, produce, yet it will prevent energy in many other cases. It will prevent energy, which is most necessary on some emergencies, even in cases wherein the existence of the community depends on vigor and expedition. It is incompatible with that secrecy which is the life of execution and despatch. Did ever thirty or forty men retain a secret? Without secrecy no government can carry on its operations on great occasions; this is what gives that superiority in action to the government of one. If any thing were wanting to complete this farce, it would be, that a resolution of the Assembly of Virginia, and the other legislatures, should be necessary to confirm and render of any validity the Congressional acts; this would openly discover the debility of the general government to all the world. But, in fact, its imbecility is now nearly the same as if such acts were formally requisite. An act of the Assembly of Virginia, controverting a resolution of Congress, would certainly prevail. I therefore conclude that the Confederation is too defective to deserve correction. Let us take farewell of it, with reverential respect, as an old benefactor. It is gone, whether this house says so or not. It is gone, sir, by its own weakness.

I am afraid I have tired the patience of this house; but I trust you will pardon me, as I was urged by the importunity of the gentleman in calling for the reasons of laying the groundwork of this plan. It is objected by the honorable gentleman over the way (Mr. George Mason) that a republican government is impracticable in an extensive territory, and the extent of the United States is urged as a reason for the rejection of this Constitution. Let us consider the definition of a republican government, as laid down by a man who is highly esteemed. Montesquieu, so celebrated among politicians, says, that "a republican government is that in which the body, or only a part, of the people is possessed of the supreme power; a monarchical, that in which a single person governs by fixed and established laws; a despotic government, that in which a single person, without law and without rule, directs every thing by his own will and caprice." This author has not distinguished a republican government from a monarchy by the extent of its boundaries, but by the nature of its principles. He, in another place, contradistinguishes it as a government of laws, in opposition to others which he denominates a government of men.

The empire or government of laws, according to that phrase, is that in which the laws are made with the free-will of the people; hence, then, if laws be made by the assent of the people, the government may be deemed free. When laws are made with integrity, and executed with wisdom, the question is, whether a great extent of country will tend to abridge the liberty of the people. If defensive force be necessary in proportion to the extent of country, I conceive that, in a judiciously-constructed government, be the country ever so extensive, its inhabitants will be proportionably numerous, and able to defend it. Extent of country, in my conception, ought to be no bar to the adoption of a good government. No extent on earth seems to be too great, provided the laws be wisely made and executed. The principles of representation and responsibility may pervade a large as well as small territory; and tyranny is as easily introduced into a small as into a large district. If it be answered, that some of the most illustrious and distinguished authors are of a contrary opinion, I reply, that authority has no weight with me till I am convinced; that not the dignity of names, but the force of reasoning, gains my assent.

I intended to show the nature of the powers which ought to have been given to the general government, and the reason of investing it with the power of taxation; but this would require more time than my strength, or the patience of the committee, would now admit of. I shall conclude with a few observations, which come from my heart. I have labored for the continuance of the Union — the rock of our salvation. I believe that, as sure as there is a God in heaven, our safety, our political happiness and existence, depend on the union of the states; and that without this union, the people of this and the other states will undergo the unspeakable calamities which discord, faction, turbulence, war, and bloodshed, have produced in other countries. The American spirit ought to be mixed with American pride, to see the Union magnificently triumphant. Let that glorious pride, which once defied the British thunder, reanimate you again. Let it not be recorded of Americans, that, after having performed the most gallant exploits, after having overcome the most astonishing difficulties, and after having gained the admiration of the world by their incomparable valor and policy, they lost their acquired reputation, their national consequence and happiness, by their own indiscretion. Let no future historian inform posterity that they wanted wisdom and virtue to concur in any regular, efficient government. Should any writer, doomed to so disagreeable a task, feel the indignation of an honest historian, he would reprehend and criminate our folly with equal severity and justice. Catch the present moment — seize it with avidity and eagerness — for it may be lost, never to be regained! If the Union be now lost, I fear it will remain so forever. I believe gentlemen are sincere in their opposition, and actuated by pure motives; but, when I maturely weigh the advantages of the Union, and dreadful consequences of its dissolution; when I see safety on my right, and destruction on my left; when I behold respectability and happiness acquired by the one, but annihilated by the other, — I cannot hesitate to decide in favor of the former. I hope my weakness, from speaking so long, will apologize for my leaving this subject in so mutilated a condition. If a further explanation be desired, I shall take the liberty to enter into it more fully another time.

Speech Before the Virginia Ratifying Convention by James Madison

Editor's Introduction:

Maidson's June 6 speech at the Virginia Ratifying Convention is remarkable only for its summary of several points he made in the *Federalist* essays. He wondered aloud how Patrick Henry could believe that the States and the people thereof enjoyed any stability and prosperity under the Articles of Confederation and worried that men like Henry would ultimately destroy the Union. He warned against factions, of the tyranny of the majority, and he reiterated his position that the Constitution produced a "mixed" government, meaning partly federal and party "consolidated." Yet, he also emphasized that the powers of the central authority were circumscribed by the text of the Constitution: "If Virginia was separated from all the states, her power and authority would extend to all cases: in like manner, were all powers vested in the general government, it would be a consolidated government; but the powers of the federal government are enumerated; it can only operate in certain cases; it has legislative powers on defined and limited objects, beyond which it cannot extend its jurisdiction." To Madison, then, Virginia was an "independent State" that delegated some of its powers to the center for the general purposes of Union but retained all else as if it were a free State. That is, at its core, originalism.

Speech Before the Virginia Ratifying Convention

June 6, 1788

By James Madison of Virginia

Mr. MADISON then arose — [but he spoke so low that his exordium could not be heard distinctly.] I shall not attempt to make impressions by any ardent professions of zeal for the public welfare. We know the principles of every man will, and ought to be, judged, not by his professions and declarations, but by his conduct; by that criterion I mean, in common with every other member, to be judged; and should it prove unfavorable to my reputation, yet it is a criterion from which I will by no means depart. Comparisons have been made between the friends of this Constitution and those who oppose it: although I disapprove of such comparisons, I trust that, in point of truth, honor, candor, and rectitude of motives, the friends of this system, here and in other states, are not inferior to its opponents. But professions of attachment to the public good, and comparisons of parties, ought not to govern or influence us now. We ought, sir, to examine the Constitution on its own merits solely: we are to inquire whether it will promote the public happiness: its aptitude to produce this desirable object ought to be the exclusive subject of our present researches. In this pursuit, we ought not to address our arguments to the feelings and passions, but to those understandings and judgments which were selected by the people of this country, to decide this great question by a calm and rational investigation. I hope that gentlemen, in displaying their abilities on this occasion, instead of giving opinions and making assertions, will condescend to prove and demonstrate, by a fair and regular discussion. It gives me pain to hear gentlemen continually distorting the natural construction of language; for it is sufficient if any human production can stand a fair discussion. Before I proceed to make some additions to the reasons which have been adduced by my honorable friend over the way, I must take the liberty to make some observations on what was said by another gentleman, (Mr. Henry.) He told us that this Constitution ought to be rejected because it endangered the public liberty, in his opinion, in many instances. Give me leave to make one answer to that observation: Let the dangers which this system is supposed to be replete with be clearly pointed out: if any dangerous and unnecessary powers be given to the general legislature, let them be plainly demonstrated; and let us not rest satisfied with general assertions of danger, without examination. If powers be necessary, apparent danger is not a sufficient reason against conceding them. He has suggested that licentiousness has seldom produced the loss of liberty; but that the tyranny of rulers has almost always effected it. Since the general civilization of mankind, I believe there are more instances of the abridgment of the freedom of the people by gradual and silent encroachments of those in power, than by violent and sudden usurpations; but, on a candid examination of history, we shall find that turbulence, violence, and abuse of power, by the majority trampling on the rights of the minority, have produced factions and commotions, which, in republics, have, more frequently than any other cause, produced despotism. If we go over the whole history of ancient and modern republics, we shall find their destruction to have generally resulted from those causes. If we consider the peculiar situation of the United States, and what are the sources of that diversity of sentiment which pervades its inhabitants, we shall find great danger to fear that the same causes may terminate here in the same fatal effects which they produced in those republics. This danger ought to be wisely guarded against. Perhaps, in the progress of this discussion, it will appear that the only possible remedy for those evils, and means of preserving and protecting the principles of republicanism, will be found in that very system which is now exclaimed against as the parent of oppression.

I must confess I have not been able to find his usual consistency in the gentleman's argument on this occasion. He informs us that the people of the country are at perfect repose, — that is, every man enjoys the fruits of his labor peaceably and securely, and that every thing is in perfect tranquillity and safety. I wish sincerely, sir, this were true. If this be their happy situation, why has every state acknowledged the contrary? Why were deputies from all the states sent to the general Convention? Why have complaints of national and individual distresses been echoed and reechoed throughout the continent? Why has our general government been so shamefully disgraced, and our Constitution violated? Wherefore have laws been made to authorize a change, and wherefore are we now assembled here? A federal government is formed for the protection of its individual members. Ours has attacked itself with impunity. Its authority has been disobeyed and despised. I think I perceive a glaring inconsistency in another of his arguments. He complains of this Constitution, because it requires the consent of at least three fourths of the states to introduce amendments which shall be necessary for the happiness of the people. The assent of so many he urges as too great an obstacle to the admission of salutary amendments, which, he strongly insists, ought to be at the will of a bare majority. We hear this argument, at the very moment we are called upon to assign reasons for proposing a constitution which puts it in the power of nine states to abolish the present inadequate, unsafe, and pernicious Confederation! In the first case, he asserts that a majority ought to have the power of altering the government, when found to be inadequate to the security of public happiness. In the last case, he affirms that even three fourths of the community have not a right to alter a government which experience has proved to be subversive of national felicity! nay, that the most necessary and urgent alterations cannot be made without the absolute unanimity of all the states! Does not the thirteenth article of the Confederation expressly require that no alteration shall be made without the unanimous consent of all the states? Could any thing in theory be more perniciously improvident and injudicious than this submission of the will of the majority to the most trifling minority? Have not experience and practice actually manifested this theoretical inconvenience to be extremely impolitic? Let me mention one fact, which I conceive must carry conviction to the mind of any one: the smallest state in the Union has obstructed every attempt to reform the government; that little member has repeatedly disobeyed and counteracted the general authority; nay, has even supplied the enemies of its country with provisions. Twelve states had agreed to certain improvements which were proposed, being thought absolutely necessary to preserve the existence of the general government; but as these improvements, though really indispensable, could not, by the Confederation, be introduced into it without the consent of every state, the refractory dissent of that little state prevented their adoption. The inconveniences resulting from this requisition, of unanimous concurrence in alterations in the Confederation, must be known to every member in this Convention; it is therefore needless to remind them of them. Is it not self-evident that a trifling minority ought not to bind the majority? Would not foreign influence be exerted with facility over a small minority? Would the honorable gentleman agree to continue the most radical defects in the old system, because the petty state of Rhode Island would not agree to remove them?

He next objects to the exclusive legislation over the district where the seat of government may be fixed. Would he submit that the representatives of this state should carry on their deliberations under the control of any other member of the Union? If any state had the power of legislation over the place where Congress should fix the general government, this would impair the dignity, and hazard the safety, of Congress. If the safety of the Union were under the control of any particular state, would not foreign corruption probably prevail, in such a state, to induce it to exert its controlling influence over the members of the general government? Gentlemen cannot have forgotten the disgraceful insult which Congress received some years ago. When we also reflect that the previous cession of particular states is necessary before Congress can legislate exclusively any where, we must, instead of being alarmed at this part, heartily approve of it.

But the honorable member sees great danger in the provision concerning the militia. This I conceive to be an additional security to our liberty, without diminishing the power of the states in any considerable degree. It appears to me so highly expedient that I should imagine it would have found advocates even in the warmest friends of the present system. The authority of training the militia, and appointing the officers, is reserved to the states. Congress ought to have the power to establish a uniform discipline throughout the states, and to provide for the execution of the laws, suppress insurrections, and repel invasions: these are the only cases wherein they can interfere with the militia; and the obvious necessity of their having power over them in these cases must convince any reflecting mind. Without uniformity of discipline, military bodies would be incapable of action: without a general controlling power to call forth the strength of the Union to repel invasions, the country might be overrun and conquered by foreign enemies: without such a power to suppress insurrections, our liberties might be destroyed by domestic faction, and domestic tyranny be established.

The honorable member then told us that there was no instance of power once transferred being voluntarily renounced. Not to produce European examples, which may probably be done before the rising of this Convention, have we not seen already, in seven states, (and probably in an eighth state,) legislatures surrendering some of the most important powers they possessed? But, sir, by this government, powers are not given to any particular set of men; they are in the hands of the people; delegated to their representatives chosen for short terms: to representatives responsible to the people, and whose situation is perfectly similar to their own. As long as this is the case we have no danger to apprehend. When the gentleman called our recollection to the usual effects of the concession of powers, and imputed the loss of liberty generally to open tyranny, I wish he had gone on farther. Upon his review of history, he would have found that the loss of liberty very often resulted from factions and divisions; from local considerations, which eternally lead to quarrels; he would have found internal dissensions to have more frequently demolished civil liberty, than a tenacious disposition in rulers to retain any stipulated powers.

[Here Mr. Madison enumerated the various means whereby nations had lost their liberties.]

The power of raising and supporting armies is exclaimed against as dangerous and unnecessary. I wish there were no necessity of vesting this power in the general government. But suppose a foreign nation to declare war against the United States; must not the general legislature have the power of defending the United States? Ought it to be known to foreign nations that the general government of the United States of America has no power to raise and support an army, even in the utmost danger, when attacked by external enemies? Would not their knowledge of such a circumstance stimulate them to fall upon us? If, sir, Congress be not invested with this power, any powerful nation, prompted by ambition or avarice, will be invited, by our weakness, to attack us; and such an attack, by disciplined veterans, would certainly be attended with success, when only opposed by irregular undisciplined militia. Whoever considers the peculiar situation of this country, the multiplicity of its excellent inlets and harbors, and the uncommon facility of attacking it, — however much he may regret the necessity of such a power, cannot hesitate a moment in granting it. One fact may elucidate this argument. In the course of the late war, when the weak parts of the Union were exposed, and many states were in the most deplorable situation by the enemy's ravages, the assistance of foreign nations was thought so urgently necessary for our protection, that the relinquishment of territorial advantages was not deemed too great a sacrifice for the acquisition of one ally. This expedient was admitted with great reluctance, even by those states who expected advantages from it. The crisis, however, at length arrived, when it was judged necessary for the salvation of this country to make certain cessions to Spain; whether wisely or otherwise is not for me to say; but the fact was, that instructions were sent to our representative at the court of Spain, to empower him to enter into negotiations for that purpose. How it terminated is well known. This fact shows the extremities to which nations will go in cases of imminent danger, and demonstrates the necessity of making ourselves more respectable. The necessity of making dangerous cessions, and of applying to foreign aid, ought to be excluded.

The honorable member then told us that there are heart-burnings in the adopting states, and that Virginia may, if she does not come into the measure, continue in amicable confederacy with the adopting states. I wish as seldom as possible to contradict the assertions of gentlemen; but I can venture to affirm, without danger of being in an error, that there is the most satisfactory evidence that the satisfaction of those states is increasing every day, and that, in that state where it was adopted only by a majority of nineteen, there is not one fifth of the people dissatisfied. There are some reasons which induce us to conclude that the grounds of proselytism extend every where; its principles begin to be better understood; and the inflammatory violence wherewith it was opposed by designing, illiberal, and unthinking minds, begins to subside. I will not enumerate the causes from which, in my conception, the heart-burnings of a majority of its opposers have originated. Suffice it to say, that in all they were founded on a misconception of its nature and tendency. Had it been candidly examined and fairly discussed, I believe, sir, that but a very inconsiderable minority of the people of the United States would have opposed it. With respect to the Swiss, whom the honorable gentleman has proposed for our example, as far as historical authority may be relied on, we shall find their government quite unworthy of our imitation. I am sure, if the honorable gentleman had adverted to their history and government, he never would have quoted their example here; he would have found that, instead of respecting the rights of mankind, their government (at least of several of their cantons) is one of the vilest aristocracies that ever was instituted: the peasants of some of their cantons are more oppressed and degraded than the subjects of any monarch in Europe; nay, almost as much so as those of any Eastern despot. It is a novelty in politics, that from the worst of systems the happiest consequences should ensue. Their aristocratical rigor, and the peculiarity of their situation, have so long supported their union: without the closest alliance and amity, dismemberment might follow; their powerful and ambitious neighbors would immediately avail themselves of their least jarrings. As we are not circumstanced like them, no conclusive precedent can be drawn from their situation. I trust the gentleman does not carry his idea so far as to recommend a separation from the adopting states. This government may secure our happiness; this is at least as probable as that it shall be oppressive. If eight states have, from a persuasion of its policy and utility, adopted it, shall Virginia shrink from it, without a full conviction of its danger and inutility? I hope she will never shrink from any duty: I trust she will not determine without the most serious reflection and deliberation.

I confess to you, sir, were uniformity of religion to be introduced by this system, it would, in my opinion, be ineligible; but I have no reason to conclude that uniformity of government will produce that of religion. This subject is, for the honor of America, perfectly free and unshackled. The government has no jurisdiction over it: the least reflection will convince us there is no danger to be feared on this ground.

But we are flattered with the probability of obtaining previous amendments. This calls for the most serious attention of this house. If amendments are to be proposed by one state, other states have the same right, and will also propose alterations. These cannot but be dissimilar, and opposite in their nature. I beg leave to remark, that the governments of the different states are in many respects dissimilar in their structure; their legislative bodies are not similar; their executive are more different. In several of the states, the first magistrate is elected by the people at large; in others, by joint ballot of the members of both branches of the legislature; and in others, in other different manners. This dissimilarity has occasioned a diversity of opinion on the theory of government, which will, without many reciprocal concessions, render a concurrence impossible. Although the appointment of an executive magistrate has not been thought destructive to the principles of democracy in many of the states, yet, in the course of the debate, we find objections made to the federal executive: it is urged that the President will degenerate into a tyrant. I intended, in compliance with the call of the honorable member, to explain the reasons of proposing this Constitution, and develop its principles; but I shall postpone my remarks till we hear the supplement which, he has informed us, he intends to add to what he has already said.

Give me leave to say something of the nature of the government, and to show that it is safe and just to vest it with the power of taxation. There are a number of opinions; but the principal question is, whether it be a federal or consolidated government. In order to judge properly of the question before us, we must consider it minutely in its principal parts. I conceive myself that it is of a mixed nature; it is in a manner unprecedented; we cannot find one express example in the experience of the world. It stands by itself. In some respects it is a government of a federal nature; in others, it is of a consolidated nature. Even if we attend to the manner in which the Constitution is investigated, ratified, and made the act of the people of America, I can say, notwithstanding what the honorable gentleman has alleged, that this government is not completely consolidated, nor is it entirely federal. Who are parties to it? The people — but not the people as composing one great body; but the people as composing thirteen sovereignties. Were it, as the gentleman asserts, a consolidated government, the assent of a majority of the people would be sufficient for its establishment; and, as a majority have adopted it already, the remaining states would be bound by the act of the majority, even if they unanimously reprobated it. Were it such a government as is suggested, it would be now binding on the people of this state, without having had the privilege of deliberating upon it. But, sir, no state is bound by it, as it is, without its own consent. Should all the states adopt it, it will be then a government established by the thirteen states of America, not through the intervention of the legislatures, but by the people at large. In this particular respect, the distinction between the existing and proposed governments is very material. The existing system has been derived from the dependent derivative authority of the legislatures of the states; whereas this is derived from the superior power of the people. If we look at the manner in which alterations are to be made in it, the same idea is, in some degree, attended to. By the new system, a majority of the states cannot introduce amendments; nor are all the states required for that purpose; three fourths of them must concur in alterations; in this there is a departure from the federal idea. The members to the national House of Representatives are to be chosen by the people at large, in proportion to the numbers in the respective districts. When we come to the Senate, its members are elected by the states in their equal and political capacity. But had the government been completely consolidated, the Senate would have been chosen by the people in their individual capacity, in the same manner as the members of the other house. Thus it is of a complicated nature; and this complication, I trust, will be found to exclude the evils of absolute consolidation, as well as of a mere confederacy. If Virginia was separated from all the states, her power and authority would extend to all cases: in like manner, were all powers vested in the general government, it would be a consolidated government; but the powers of the federal government are enumerated; it can only operate in certain cases; it has legislative powers on defined and limited objects, beyond which it cannot extend its jurisdiction.

But the honorable member has satirized, with peculiar acrimony, the powers given to the general government by this Constitution. I conceive that the first question on this subject is, whether these powers be necessary; if they be, we are reduced to the dilemma of either submitting to the inconvenience or losing the Union. Let us consider the most important of these reprobated powers; that of direct taxation is most generally objected to. With respect to the exigencies of government, there is no question but the most easy mode of providing for them will be adopted. When, therefore, direct taxes are not necessary, they will not be recurred to. It can be of little advantage to those in power to raise money in a manner oppressive to the people. To consult the conveniences of the people will cost them nothing, and in many respects will be advantageous to them. Direct taxes will only be recurred to for great purposes What has brought on other nations those immense debts, under the pressure of which many of them labor? Not the expenses of their governments, but war. If this country should be engaged in war, — and I conceive we ought to provide for the possibility of such a case, — how would it be carried on? By the usual means provided from year to year? As our imports will be necessary for the expenses of government and other common exigencies, how are we to carry on the means of defence? How is it possible a war could be supported without money or credit? And would it be possible for a government to have credit without having the power of raising money? No; it would be impossible for any government, in such a case, to defend itself. Then, I say, sir, that it is necessary to establish funds for extraordinary exigencies, and to give this power to the general government; for the utter inutility of previous requisitions on the states is too well known. Would it be possible for those countries, whose finances and revenues are carried to the highest perfection, to carry on the operations of government on great emergencies, such as the maintenance of a war, without an uncontrolled power of raising money? Has it not been necessary for Great Britain, notwithstanding the facility of the collection of her taxes, to have recourse very often to this and other extraordinary methods of procuring money? Would not her public credit have been ruined, if it was known that her power to raise money was limited? Has not France been obliged, on great occasions, to use unusual means to raise funds? It has been the case in many countries, and no government can exist unless its powers extend to make provisions for every contingency. If we were actually attacked by a powerful nation, and our general government had not the power of raising money, but depended solely on requisitions, our condition would be truly deplorable: if the revenue of this commonwealth were to depend on twenty distinct authorities, it would be impossible for it to carry on its operations. This must be obvious to every member here; I think, therefore, that it is necessary, for the preservation of the Union, that this power shall be given to the general government.

But it is urged that its consolidated nature, joined to the power of direct taxation, will give it a tendency to destroy all subordinate authority; that its increasing influence will speedily enable it to absorb the state governments. I cannot think this will be the case. If the general government were wholly independent of the governments of the particular states, then, indeed, usurpation might be expected to the fullest extent. But, sir, or whom does this general government depend? It derives its authority from these governments, and from the same sources from which their authority is derived. The members of the federal government are taken from the same men from whom those of the state legislatures are taken. If we consider the mode in which the federal representatives will be chosen, we shall be convinced that the general will never destroy the individual governments; and this conviction must be strengthened by an attention to the construction of the Senate. The representatives will be chosen probably under the influence of the members of the state legislatures; but there is not the least probability that the election of the latter will be influenced by the former. One hundred and sixty members represent this commonwealth in one branch of the legislature, are drawn from the people at large, and must ever possess more influence than the few men who will be elected to the general legislature.

The reasons offered on this subject, by a gentleman on the same side, (Mr. Nicholas,) were unanswerable, and have been so full that I shall add but little more on the subject. Those who wish to become federal representatives must depend on their credit with that class of men who will be the most popular in their counties, who generally represent the people in the state governments; they can, therefore, never succeed in any measure contrary to the wishes of those on whom they depend. It is almost certain, therefore, that the deliberations of the members of the federal House of Representatives will be directed to the interest of the people of America. As to the other branch, the senators will be appointed by the legislatures; and, though elected for six years, I do not conceive they will so soon forget the source from whence they derive their political existence. This election of one branch of the federal by the state legislatures, secures an absolute dependence of the former on the latter. The biennial exclusion of one third will lessen the facility of a combination, and may put a stop to intrigues. I appeal to our past experience, whether they will attend to the interests of their constituent states. Have not those gentlemen, who have been honored with seats in Congress, often signalized themselves by their attachment to their seats? I wish this government may answer the expectation of its friends, and foil the apprehension of its enemies. I hope the patriotism of the people will continue, and be a sufficient guard to their liberties. I believe its tendency will be, that the state governments will counteract the general interest, and ultimately prevail. The number of the representatives is yet sufficient for our safety, and will gradually increase; and, if we consider their different sources of information, the number will not appear too small.

Speech Before the Virginia Ratifying Convention by Francis Corbin

Editor's Introduction:

Francis Corbin was a middling member of Virginia society, a man who was respected but not as successful as other political giants in the Commonwealth. He married into the wealthy Beverley family and his brother-in-law, Carter Braxton, signed the Declaration of Independence. Corbin was in Europe during the American War for Independence, and while he was elected to the Virginia legislature for ten consecutive one year terms when he returned home in 1783, he never reached the status of a first rate Virginia statesmen. He failed several times for election to the United States Congress, and he eventually retired to Caroline County and focused on his life as a planter. He was uneasy with slavery and discussed moving to New England several times to rid himself of the institution. He died of gout in 1821 at the age of 61.

Corbin ardently supported the Constitution. He proposed the first resolution for calling for a State ratification convention in 1787 and voted for the document without amendments. His June 7 speech focused on several points Patrick Henry made in opposition to the document, from his castigation of the phrase "We the People," to his insistence that the Articles of Confederation were a "perfect" system. Like Madison, Corbin worried about the problems of "faction," but he disagreed with Madison on the structure of the central government under the Constitution. Corbin labeled it "a representative federal republic, as contradistinguished from a confederacy. The former is more wisely constructed than the latter; it places the remedy in the hands which feel the disorder: the other places the remedy in those hands which cause the disorder." In other words, Corbin thought the word "representative" added the spirit of democracy to the federal structure and placed the government more readily in the hands of the people. It was not a pure democracy, but it allowed the people the ability to control the system. Like Randolph, Corbin believed that the spirit of Union should be the highest order of the Convention, and that the Union was more important than any petty disagreements over structure. He concluded by stating, "By union alone can we exist: by no other means can we be happy. Union must be the object of every gentleman here."

Speech Before the Virginia Ratifying Convention

June 7, 1788

By Francis Corbin of Virginia

Mr. CORBIN. Mr. Chairman, permit me to make a few observations on this great question. It is with great difficulty I prevail on myself to enter into the debate, when I consider the great abilities of those gentlemen who have already spoken on the subject. But as I am urged by my duty to my constituents, and as I conceive that the different manner of treating the subject may make different impressions, I shall offer my observations with diffident respect, but with firmness and independence. I will promise my acknowledgments to those honorable gentlemen who were in the federal Convention, for the able and satisfactory manner in which they discharged their duty to their country. The introductory expression of "We, the people," has been thought improper by the honorable gentleman. I expected no such objection as this. Ought not the people, sir, to judge of that government whereby they are to be ruled? We are, sir, deliberating on a question of great consequence to the people of America, and to the world in general. We ought, therefore, to decide with extreme caution and circumspection: it is incumbent upon us to proceed without prejudice or prepossession. No member of the committee entertains a greater regard than myself for the gentleman on the other side, who has placed himself in the front of opposition, (Mr. Henry.) No man admires more than I do his declamatory talents; but I trust that neither declamation nor elegance of periods will mislead the judgment of any member here, and that nothing but the force of reasoning will operate conviction. He has asked, with an air of triumph, whether the Confederation was not adequate to the purposes of the federal government: permit me to say, No. If, sir, perfection existed in that system, why was the federal Convention called? Why did every state except Rhode Island send deputies to that Convention?

Was it not from a persuasion of its inefficacy? If this be not sufficient to convince him, let me call the recollection of the honorable gentleman to other circumstances. Let him go into the interior parts of the country, and inquire into the situation of the farmers. He will be told that tobacco, and other produce, are miserably low, merchandise dear, and taxes high. Let him go through the United States. He will perceive appearances of ruin and decay every where. Let him visit the sea-coast — go to our ports and inlets. In those ports, sir, where we had every reason to see the fleets of all nations, he will behold but a few trifling little boats; he will every where see commerce languish; the disconsolate merchant, with his arms folded, ruminating, in despair, on the wretched ruins of his fortune, and deploring the impossibility of retrieving it. The West Indies are blocked up against us. Not the British only, but other nations, exclude us from those islands; our fur trade gone to Canada; British sentinels within our own territories; our posts withheld. To these distresses we may add the derangement of our finances: yet the honorable gentleman tells us they are not sufficient to justify so radical a change. Does he know the consequences of deranged finances? What confusions, disorders, and even revolutions, have resulted from this cause, in many nations! Look at France at this time: that kingdom is almost convulsed; ministers of state, and first princes of the blood, banished; manufacturers and merchants become bankrupt, and the people discontented; all owing to the derangement of their finances.

The honorable gentleman must be well acquainted with the debts due by the United States, and how much is due to foreign nations. Has not the payment of these been shamefully withheld? How long, sir, shall we be able, by fair promises, to satisfy these creditors? How long can we amuse, by idle words, those who are amply possessed of the means of doing themselves justice? No part of the principal is paid to those nations; nor has even the interest been paid as honorably and punctually as it ought. Nay, we were obliged to borrow money last year to pay the interest. What! borrow money to discharge the interest of what was borrowed, and continually augment the amount of the public debt! Such a plan would destroy the richest country on earth. What is to be done? Compel the delinquent states to pay requisitions to Congress? How are they to be compelled? By the instrumentality of such a scheme as was proposed to be introduced in the year 1784? Is this cruel mode of compulsion eligible? Is it consistent with the spirit of republicanism? This savage mode, which could be made use of under the Confederation, leads directly to civil war and destruction. How different is this from the genius of the proposed Constitution! By this proposed plan, the public money is to be collected by mild and gentle means; by a peaceable and friendly application to the individuals of the community: whereas, by the other scheme, the public treasury must be supplied through the medium of the sword, by desolation and murder — by the blood of the citizens. Yet we are told that there is too much energy in this system. Coercion is necessary in every government. Justice, sir, cannot be done without it. It is more necessary in federal governments than any other, because of the natural imbecility of such governments.

The honorable gentleman is possessed of much historical knowledge. I appeal to that knowledge therefore. Will he not agree that there was a coercive power in the federal government of the Amphictyonics? The coercive power of the Amphictyonic council was so great as to enable it to punish disobedience and refractory behavior in the most severe manner. Is there not an instance of its carrying fire and sword through the territories, and levelling to the ground the towns, of those who disobeyed it? [Here Mr. Corbin mentions particular instances.] Is there no coercion in the Germanic body? This body, though composed of three hundred different component sovereignties, principalities, and cities, and divided into nine circles, is controlled by one superintending power, the emperor. Is there no coercive power in the confederate government of the Swiss? In the alliance between them and France, there is a provision whereby the latter is to interpose and settle differences that may arise among them; and this interposition has been more than once used. Is there none in Holland? What is the stadtholder? This power is necessary in all governments; a superintending coercive power is absolutely indispensable. This does not exist under the present Articles of Confederation. To vest it with such a power, on its present construction, without any alteration, would be extremely dangerous, and might lead to civil war. Gentlemen must, before this, have been convinced of the necessity of an alteration. Our state vessel has sprung a leak; we must embark in a new bottom, or sink into perdition.

The honorable gentleman has objected to the Constitution, on the old worn-out idea that a republican government is best calculated for a small territory. If a republic, sir cannot be accommodated to an extensive country, let me ask, How small must a country be to suit the genius of republicanism? In what particular extent of country can a republican government exist? If contracted into as small a compass as you please, it must labor under many disadvantages. Too small an extent will render a republic weak, vulnerable, and contemptible. Liberty, in such a petty state, must be on a precarious footing; its existence must depend on the philanthropy and good nature of its neighbors. Too large an extent, it is said, will produce confusion and tyranny. What has been so often deprecated will be removed by this plan. The extent of the United States cannot render this government oppressive. The powers of the general government are only of a general nature, and their object is to protect, defend, and strengthen the United States; but the internal administration of government is left to the state legislatures, who exclusively retain such powers as will give the states the advantages of small republics, without the danger commonly attendant on the weakness of such governments.

There are controversies even about the name of this government. It is denominated by some a federal, by others a consolidated government. The definition given of it by my honorable friend (Mr. Madison) is, in my opinion, accurate. Let me, however, call it by another name — a representative federal republic, as contradistinguished from a confederacy. The former is more wisely constructed than the latter;

it places the remedy in the hands which feel the disorder: the other places the remedy in those hands which cause the disorder. The evils that are most complained of in such governments (and with justice) are faction, dissension, and consequent subjection of the minority to the caprice and arbitrary decisions of the majority, who, instead of consulting the interest of the whole community collectively, attend sometimes to partial and local advantages. To avoid this evil is perhaps the great desideratum of republican wisdom; it may be termed the philosopher's stone. Yet, sir, this evil will be avoided by this Constitution: faction will be removed by the system now under consideration, because all the causes which are generally productive of faction are removed. This evil does not take its flight entirely; for were jealousies and divisions entirely at an end, it might produce such lethargy as would ultimately terminate in the destruction of liberty, to the preservation of which, watchfulness is absolutely necessary. It is transferred from the state legislatures to Congress, where it will be more easily controlled. Faction will decrease in proportion to the diminution of counsellors. It is much easier to control it in small than in large bodies. Our state legislature consists of upwards of one hundred and sixty, which is a greater number than Congress will consist of at first. Will not more concord and unanimity exist in one than in thirteen such bodies? Faction will more probably decrease, or be entirely removed, if the interest of a nation be entirely concentrated, than if entirely diversified. If thirteen men agree, there will be no faction. Yet if opposite, and of heterogeneous dispositions, it is impossible that a majority of such clashing minds can ever concur to oppress the minority. It is impossible that this government, which will make us one people, will have a tendency to assimilate our situations, and is admirably calculated to produce harmony and unanimity, can ever admit of an oppressive combination by one part of the Union against the other.

A confederate government is, of all others, best calculated for an extensive country. Its component individual governments are, of all others, best calculated for an extensive country. Its component individual governments administer and afford all the local conveniences that the most compact governments can do; and the strength and energy of the confederacy may be equal to those of any government. A government of this kind may extend to all the western world; nay, I may say, ad infinitum. But it is needless to dwell any longer on this subject; for the objection that an extensive territory is repugnant to a republican government applies against this and every state in the Union, except Delaware and Rhode Island. Were the objection well founded, a republican government could exist in none of the states, except those two. Such an argument goes to the dissolution of the Union, and its absurdity is demonstrated by our own experience.

But an objection is urged against this government because of its power of laying direct taxes. Let me ask the honorable gentleman who opposes it on this ground, if he reflects whether this power be indispensable or not. Sir, if it be not vested with the power of commanding all the resources of the state when necessary, it will be trifling. Wars are as much (and more) carried on by the length of the purse, as by that of the sword. They cannot be carried on without money. Unless this power be given to Congress, foreign nations may crush you. The concession of this power is necessary to do Virginia justice, by compelling the delinquent states to pay as well as she: while she paid her quotas, and her citizens were much distressed to pay their taxes, other states most shamefully neglected or refused to pay their proportions. I trust gentlemen need not be alarmed on the subject of taxation, nor intimidated by the idea of double collectors, who, they tell us, will oppress and ruin the people. From our attention to our situation, we shall see that this mode of levying money, though indispensably necessary on great emergencies, will be but seldom recurred to. Let us attend to the finances of this country.

Mr. CORBIN then stated the probable annual amount of duties on imported articles throughout the continent, including West India produce, which, he said, from the best calculation he could procure, would exceed the annual expenses of the administration of the general government, including the civil list, contingent charges, and the interest of the foreign and domestic debts, by eighty or ninety thousand pounds; that, he said, would enable the United States to discharge, in a few years, the principal debts due to foreign nations; that, in the course of thirty years, that surplus would enable the United States to perform the most splendid enterprises. He then concluded that no danger was to be apprehended from the power of direct taxation, since there was every reason to believe it would be very seldom used. He then made an estimate of the state debt, and clearly proved that, with economical regulations, all the demands of the internal administration of government would be paid with facility and ease from the different resources of the state; and that there would also be a considerable surplus, which, with prudence and economy, might answer many valuable purposes.

Mr. Corbin then continued as follows: The honorable gentleman declared in the most solemn manner, that, if he could see one single trait in that government to secure liberty, he would not object to it. I meet him on this ground. Liberty is secured, sir, by the limitation of its powers, which are clearly and unequivocally defined, and which are to be exercised by our own representatives freely chosen. What power is given that will endanger liberty? I consider all the traits of this system as having a tendency to the security of our liberty. I consider all its powers necessary, and only given to avoid greater evils; and if this conclusion of mine be well founded, let me ask if public liberty is not secured by bars and adamantine bolts — secured by the strongest guards and checks which human ingenuity can invent. Will this dread power of taxation render liberty insecure? Sir, without this power, other powers will answer no purpose. Government cannot exist without the means of procuring money. My honorable friend told us he considered this clause as the vitals of the Constitution. I will change the phrase, and say that I consider this part as the lungs of the Constitution. If it be sick, the whole system is consumptive, and must soon decay; and this power can never be dangerous if the principles of equal and free representation be fully attended to. While the right of suffrage is secured, we have little to fear. This government, sir, fully secures us this noble privilege, on the purest and simplest principles of equality. That number which, in any one part of the country, has a right to send a representative, has the same right in another part. What does the Constitution say? That thirty thousand shall have one representative, no matter where. If this be not equal representation, what, in the name of God, is equal representation? But, says the honorable gentleman, the Constitution may be satisfied by one from each state. I conceive there is no fear of this. There is not a power to diminish the number. Does it not say that representatives shall be apportioned according to the number of the people, and that direct taxes shall be regulated by the same rules? Virginia, in the first instance, will have ten times as many as Delaware, and afterwards in proportion to their numbers. What is the criterion of representation? Do the people wish land only to be represented? They have their wish: for the qualifications which the laws of the states require to entitle a man to vote for a state representative are the qualifications required by this plan to vote for a representative to Congress; and in this state, and most of the others, the possession of a freehold is necessary to entitle a man to the privilege of a vote. Do they wish persons to be represented? Here also they are indulged; for the number of representatives is determined by the number of people: this idea is so well attended to, that even three fifths of those who are not free are included among those of whom thirty thousand shall have a right to elect one representative; so that, in either point of view, their wish is gratified. Is not liberty secured on this foundation? If it be not secured by one or the other mode, or by both, I am totally without reason. Liberty seems intrenched on this ground.

But the gentleman objects that the number is not sufficient. My opinion, with deference to that gentleman, and others who may be of different opinion from me, is, that it is fully sufficient. Being delegated solely for general purposes, a few intelligent men will suffice; at least one for every thirty thousand, aided by the Senate, seems sufficient. Are combinations, or factions, so often formed in small as in numerous bodies? Are laws better made in large than in small assemblies? Is not the influence of popular declaimers less in small than in great bodies? Would not a more numerous representation be very expensive? Is economy of no consideration? We ought, sir, to attend to the situation of the people; and our measures should be as economical as possible, without extending, however, our parsimony to a dangerous length. Objections should be founded on just and real grounds, and ought not to be urged out of a mere obstinacy. Besides, it is by no means certain that a very numerous body is more independent, or upright, than a small one. Why should the number of our representatives be greater, Mr. Chairman? The county of Middlesex, in England, which includes the cities of London and Westminster, contains upwards of nine hundred and ninety thousand souls, and yet sends to Parliament no more than eight members. Among all the clamors of the people there, it never entered into the brain of any of them that these eight were not enough. They complain that the boroughs of Old Sarum, Newton, and Gatton, and other such places, should send each two members to Parliament, although without houses or inhabitants, while the richest city sends but four. They also complain of the influence of the landed interest in some cases; that the county of Cornwall sends forty members to Parliament, although it pays but eighteen parts, out of five hundred and thirteen, to the subsidy and land tax, when the county of Middlesex, which is calculated to pay two hundred and fifty parts out of five hundred and thirteen, sends but eight members. In that country, it has been uniformly found that those members, who are chosen by numerous respectable electors, make the greatest opposition to oppression and corruption, and signalize themselves for the preservation of liberty. The collective body of the commons there have generally exerted themselves in the defence of freedom, and have been successful in their exertions, notwithstanding the inequality of their election. Our representatives are chosen in the fairest manner; their election is founded in absolute equality. Is the American spirit so degenerated, notwithstanding these advantages, that the love of liberty is more predominant and warm in the breast of a Briton than in that of an American? When liberty is on a more solid foundation here than in Britain, will Americans be less ready to maintain and defend it than Britons? No, sir; the spirit of liberty and independence of the people of this country, at present, is such that they could not be enslaved under any government that could be described. What danger is there, then, to be apprehended from a government which is theoretically perfect, and the possible blemishes of which can only be demonstrated by actual experience?

The honorable gentleman then urges an objection respecting the militia, who, he tells us, will be made the instruments of tyranny to deprive us of our liberty. Your militia, says he, will fight against you. Who are the militia? Are we not militia? Shall we fight against ourselves? No, sir; the idea is absurd. We are also terrified by the dread of a standing army. It cannot be denied that we ought to have the means of defence, and be able to repel an attack.

If some of the community are exclusively inured to its defence, and the rest attend to agriculture, the consequence will be, that the arts of war and defence, and of cultivating the soil, will be understood. Agriculture will flourish, and military discipline will be perfect. If, on the contrary, our defence be solely intrusted to militia, ignorance of arms and negligence of farming will ensue: the former plan is, in every respect, more to the interest of the state. By it we shall have good farmers and soldiers; by the latter we shall have neither. If the inhabitants be called out on sudden emergencies of war, their crops, the means of their subsistence, may be destroyed by it. If we are called in the time of sowing seed, or of harvest, the means of subsistence might be lost; and the loss of one year's crop might have been prevented by a trivial expense, if appropriated to the purpose of supporting a part of the community, exclusively occupied in the defence of the whole. I conceive that this idea, if it be a new one, is yet founded on solid and very substantial reasons. But, sir, we are told of the expediency and propriety of previous amendments. What end would it answer to attempt it? Will the states which have adopted the Constitution rescind their adopting resolutions? Had we adopted it, would we recede from it to please the caprice of any other state? Pride, sir, revolts at the idea. Admitting this state proposes amendments previous to her adoption, must there not be another federal convention? Must there not be also a convention in each state? Suppose some of our proposed conditions to be rejected; will not our exclusion out of the Union be the consequence? Or would other conventions again be called, and would be eternally revolving and devising expedients, without coming to a final decision? The loss of the union, sir, must be the result of a pertinacious demand of precedent conditions. My idea is, that we should go hand in hand with Massachusetts: adopt it first, and then propose amendments of a general nature; for local ones cannot be expected. Consider the situation of Massachusetts, commanding the north, and the importance and respectability of Virginia to the south. These, sir, are the two most populous, wealthy, and powerful states in the Union. Is it not very probable that their influence would have very great weight in carrying any amendments? Would any gentleman turn a deaf ear to their solicitations? By union alone can we exist: by no other means can we be happy. Union must be the object of every gentleman here. I never yet have heard any gentleman so wild and frantic in his opposition as to avow an attachment to partial confederacies. By previous adoption, the union will be preserved; by insisting on alterations previous to our adoption, the union may be lost, and our political happiness destroyed by internal dissensions. I trust, therefore, that this Convention, after deliberate discussion, will not hesitate to determine on a previous ratification of a system which, even in its present form, seems competent to the perpetual preservation of our security and happiness.

Speech Before the Virginia Ratifying Convention by Edmund Randolph

Editor's Introduction:

Randolph focused more intently on the powers of the general government in his June 10 speech. He attempted to bring the debate back to order and review the Constitution clause by clause. The Convention adopted that method when it opened the previous week, but Patrick Henry hijacked the proceedings and almost every speech focused on his criticisms of the Constitution. Randolph thought the people had nothing to fear from the executive branch because it was far less powerful than the King of Great Britain, that the elections were securely in the hands of the States, and that the powers of the general government were limited by the text. For example, Randolph insisted that the general government did not have any control over religion as it was not delegated to the central authority. The "sweeping clauses" granted no new powers, and he argued that, "No sophistry will be permitted to be used to explain away any of those powers; nor can they possibly assume any other power, but what is contained in the Constitution, without absolute usurpation. Another security is that, if they attempt such a usurpation, the influence of the state governments will nip it in the bud of hope." In short, implied powers did not exist and the States could block any unconstitutional legislation. This would later be called "nullification."

Speech Before the Virginia Ratifying Convention

June 10, 1788

By Edmund Randolph of Virginia

Gov. RANDOLPH. Mr. Chairman, I was restrained yesterday, by the lateness of the day, from making those observations which I intended to make in answer to the honorable gentleman who had gone before me. I shall now resume that subject. I hope we shall come at last to a decision. I shall not forever wander from the point, or transgress the rules of this house; but, after making answer to him, shall go on in regular order.

He observed that the only question was, with respect to previous and subsequent amendments. Were this the only question, sir, I am sure this inconsiderable matter would not long retard a decision. I conceive the preservation of the Union to be a question of great magnitude. This must be a peculiar object of my attention, unless I depart from that rule which has regulated my conduct since the introduction of federal measures. Suppose, contrary to my expectation, this Convention should propose certain amendments previous to its ratification, — mild and pliant as those states may be who have received it unanimously; flexible as those may be who have adopted it by a majority; I had rather argue, from human nature, that they will not recede from their resolutions, to accommodate our caprice. Is there no jealousy existing between the states? They discover no superiority, in any one state, of arrogating to itself a right to dictate what ought to be done. They would not see the reasons of such amendments, for some amendments in themselves are really dangerous. The same reasons could not be impressed on all the states. I shall mention one example: I shall suppose, for instance, that we shall propose, as an amendment, that the President shall have a council. I conceive a council to be injurious to the executive. The counsellors will either impede or clog the President; or, if he be a man of dexterity, they will be governed by him. They will also impair his responsibility. Is it probable that all the other states would think alike on the subject, or agree to such an alteration? As there is a mode in the Constitution itself to procure amendments, not by reference to the people, but by the interposition of the state legislatures, will the people of Virginia bind themselves not to enter into the Union till amendments shall have been obtained? I refer it to any gentleman here, whether this may not entirely exclude us from the Union.

The honorable gentleman then told us, that Maryland held out, and that there can be no danger from our holding out of the Union; that she refused to come into the Confederation until the year 1781, when she was pressed by the then Congress. Is this a proper comparison? The fear of the British army and navy kept the states together. This fear induced that state to come into the Union then, otherwise the Union would have been destroyed. We are also told that Vermont held out. His information is inaccurate. Pardon me for saying that it is not to be found in the history of those times. The right to that territory was long in dispute between New York and Connecticut. The inhabitants took that opportunity of erecting themselves into a state. They pressed Congress for admission into the Union. Their solicitations were continually opposed till the year 1781, when a kind of assent was given. Can it be said, from this, that the people of Vermont held out against the Confederation of twelve states? Were they sufficiently wealthy and numerous to do so? Virginia is said to be able to stand by herself. From her situation she has cause to fear. She has also cause to fear from her inability to raise an army, a navy, or money. I contend that she is not able to stand by herself. I am sure that every man who comes from the exposed parts of this country is well convinced of this truth. As these have been enumerated, it would be useless to go over them again. He then told us that an error in government never can be removed. I will acknowledge, with him, that there are governments in Europe, whereof the defects have a long time been unaltered, and are not easily changed.

We need not go farther than the war to find a willing relinquishment of power. Look at the Confederation: you will find there such a voluntary relinquishment. View the convention at Annapolis: the object of its delegation involved in its nature some relinquishment of power. It produced this effect — all the states, except Rhode Island, agreed to call a general Convention, to revise the Confederation, and invest Congress with more power. A general Convention has been called; it has proposed a system which concedes considerable powers to Congress. Eight states have already assented to this concession. After this, can we say that men will not voluntarily relinquish power? Contrast this country with Scotland, blessed with union. The circumstances of the two countries are not dissimilar. View Scotland: that country is greatly benefited by union. It would not be now in its present flourishing situation without the auspices of England. This observation brings us to the necessity of union.

Were we not to look to futurity, have we nothing to fear from the present state of Europe? We are exposed at sea. The honorable gentleman tells us we have no hostility to fear from that quarter; that our ambassador at Paris would have informed us if there were any combustibles preparing. If he has not done any such thing, it is no conclusive evidence of safety. Nations have passions like men. It is the disposition of nations to attack where there is a demonstrable weakness. Are you weak? Go to history; it will tell you, you will be insulted. One insult will produce another, till at last it produces a partition. So, when they tell us there is no storm gathering, they ought to support their allegations by some probable evidence. The honorable gentleman then told us that armies do not collect debts; but armies make reprisals. If the debts which we owe continue on the disgraceful footing they have been on hitherto, without even the payment of interest, we may well expect such reprisals. The seizure of our vessels in foreign ports must be the certain consequence of the continuance of such a disgraceful conduct. He then informed us that no danger was to be apprehended from Spain — that she trembles for Mexico and Peru. That nation, sir, is a powerful nation, and has immense resources. What will she be when united with France and other nations who have cause of complaint against us? Mr. Chairman, Maryland seems, too, to be disregarded. The loss of the Union would not bring her arms upon our heads: — look at the Northern Neck! If the Union is dissolved, will it adhere to Virginia? Will the people of that place sacrifice their safety for us? How are we to retain them? By force of arms? Is this the happy way he proposes for leaving us out of the Union?

We are next informed that there is no danger from the borders of Maryland and Pennsylvania, and that my observations upon the frontiers of England and Scotland are inapplicable. He distinguishes republican from monarchical borderers, and ascribes pacific meekness to the former, and barbarous ferocity to the latter. There is as much danger, sir, from republican borderers as from any other. The danger results from the situation of borderers, and not from the nature of the government under which they live. History will show that as much barbarity and cruelty have been committed upon one another by republican borderers as by any other. We are borderers upon three states, two of which are ratifying states. I therefore repeat, sir, that we have danger to apprehend from this quarter.

As to the people's complaints of the government, the gentleman must either have misunderstood me, or went over very slightly what I said of the Confederation. He spoke of the Constitution of Virginia, concerning which I said nothing. The Confederation, sir, on which we are told we ought to trust our safety, is totally void of coercive power and energy. Of this the people of America have been long convinced; and this conviction has been sufficiently manifested to the world. Of this I spoke, and now I repeat, that if we trust to it, we shall be defenceless. The general government ought to be vested with powers competent to our safety, or else the necessary consequence must be, that we shall be defenceless.

The honorable gentleman tells us that, if the project at Albany for the colonial consolidation, as he terms it, had been completed, it would have destroyed all union and happiness. What has that to do with this paper? It tells us what the present situation of America is. Can any man say he could draw a better picture of our situation than that paper? He says that, by the completion of that project, the king of Great Britain might have bound us so tight together, that resistance would have been ineffectual. Does it not tell us that union is necessary? Will not our united strength be more competent to our defence, against any assault, than the force of a part? If, in their judgment alone who could decide on it, it was judged sufficient to secure their happiness and prosperity, why say that that project would have destroyed us? But the honorable gentleman again recurs to his beloved requisitions, on which he advises us to trust our happiness. Can any thing be more imprudent than to put the general government on so humiliating and disgraceful a footing? What are they but supplications and entreaties to the states to do their duty? Shall we rely on a system of which every man knows the inefficacy? One cannot conceive any thing more contemptible than a government which is forced to make humble applications to other governments for the means of its common support — which is driven to apply for a little money to carry on its administration a few months. After the total incapacity of the Confederation to secure our happiness has been fully experienced, what will be the consequence if we reject this Constitution? Shall we recur to separate confederacies? The honorable gentleman acknowledges them to be evils which ought not to be resorted to but on the last necessity — they are evils of the first magnitude.

Permit me to extract out of the confederation of Albany a fact of the highest authority, because drawn from human nature, which clearly demonstrates the fatal impolicy of separate confederacies. [Here he made a quotation to that effect.] If there is a gentleman here who harbors in his mind the idea of a separate confederacy, I beg him to consider the consequence. Where shall we find refuge in the day of calamity? The different confederacies will be rivals in power and commerce, and therefore will soon be implacable enemies of one another. I ask if there be any objection to this system, that will not come with redoubled energy against any other plan. See the defects in this Constitution, and examine if they do not appear with tenfold force in separate confederacies. After having acknowledged the evil tendency of separate confederacies, he recurs to this — that this country is too extensive for the system. If there be an executive dependent for his election on the people, a judiciary which will administer the laws with justice, no extent of country will be too great for a republic.

Where is there a precedent to prove that this country is too extensive for a government of this kind? America cannot find a precedent to prove this. Theoretic writers have adopted a position that extensive territories will not admit of a republican government. These positions were laid down before the science of government was as well understood as it is now. Where would America look for a precedent to warrant her adoption of that position? If you go to Europe, before arts and sciences had arrived at their present perfection, no example worthy of imitation can be found. The history of England, from the reign of Henry VII.; of Spain, since that of Charles V.; and of France, since that of Francis I., prove that they have greatly improved in the science of politics since that time. Representation, the source of American liberty and English liberty, was a thing not understood in its full extent till very lately.

The position I have spoken of was founded upon an ignorance of the principles of representation. Its force must be now done away, as this principle is so well understood. If laws are to be made by the people themselves, in their individual capacities, it is evident that they cannot conveniently assemble together, for this purpose, but in a very limited sphere; but if the business of legislation be transacted by representatives, chosen periodically by the people, it is obvious that it may be done in any extent of country. The experience of this commonwealth, and of the United States, proves this assertion.

Mr. Chairman, I am astonished that the rule of the house to debate regularly has not been observed by gentlemen. Shall we never have order? I must transgress that rule now, not because I think the conduct of the gentleman deserves imitation, but because the honorable gentleman ought to be answered. In that list of facts with which he would touch our affections, he has produced a name (Mr. Jefferson) which will ever be remembered with gratitude by this commonwealth. I hope that his life will be continued, to add, by his future actions, to the brilliancy of his character. Yet I trust that his name was not mentioned to influence any member of this house. Notwithstanding the celebrity of his character, his name cannot be used as authority against the Constitution. I know not his authority. I have had no letter from him. As far as my information goes, it is only a report circulated through the town, that he wished nine states to adopt, and the others to reject it, in order to get amendments. Which is the ninth state to introduce the government? That illustrious citizen tells you, that he wishes the government to be adopted by nine states, to prevent a schism in the Union. This, sir, is my wish. I will go heart and hand to obtain amendments, but I will never agree to the dissolution of the Union. But unless a ninth state will accede, this must inevitably happen. No doubt he wished Virginia to adopt. I wish not to be bound by any man's opinion; but, admitting the authority which the honorable gentleman has produced to be conclusive, it militates against himself. Is it right to adopt? He says, no; because there is a President. I wish he was eligible after a given number of years.

I wish also some other changes to be made in the Constitution. But am I therefore obliged to run the risk of losing the Union, by proposing amendments previously, when amendments without that risk can be obtained afterwards? Am I to indulge capricious opinions so far as to lose the Union? The friends of the Union will see how far we carry our attachment to it, and will therefore concur with our amendments. The honorable gentleman has told us, that Holland is ruined by a stadtholder and a stadtholder's wife. I believe this republic is much indebted to that execrated stadtholder for her power and wealth. Recur to the history of Holland, and you will find that country never could have resisted Spain, had it not been for the stadtholder. At those periods when they had no stadtholder, their government was weak and their public affairs deranged. Why has this been mentioned? Was it to bias our minds against the federal executive? Are we to have no executive at all, or are we to have eight or ten? An executive is as necessary, for the security of liberty and happiness, as the two other branches of government. Every state in the Union has an executive.

Let us consider whether the federal executive be wisely constructed. This is a point in which the constitution of every state differs widely as to the mode of electing their executives, and as to the time of continuing them in office. In some states the executive is perpetually eligible. In others he is rendered ineligible after a given period. They are generally elected by the legislature. It cannot be objected to the federal executive that the power is executed by one man. All the enlightened part of mankind agree that the superior despatch, secrecy, and energy, with which one man can act, render it more politic to vest the power of executing the laws in one man, than in any number of men. How is the President elected? By the people — on the same day throughout the United States — by those whom the people please. There can be no concert between the electors. The votes are sent sealed to Congress. What are his powers? To see the laws executed. Every executive in America has that power. He is also to command the army: this power also is enjoyed by the executives of the different states. He can handle no part of the public money except what is given him by law. At the end of four years, he may be turned out of his office. If he misbehaves he may be impeached, and in this case he will never be reelected. I cannot conceive how his powers can be called formidable. Both houses are a check upon him. He can do no important act without the concurrence of the Senate. In England, the sword and purse are in different hands. The king has the power of the sword, and the purse is in the hands of the people alone. Take a comparison between this and the government of England.

It will prove in favor of the American principle. In England, the king declares war. In America, Congress must be consulted. In England, Parliament gives money. In America, Congress does it. There are consequently more powers in the hands of the people, and greater checks upon the executive here, than in England. Let him pardon me, when I say he is mistaken in passing a eulogium on the English government to the prejudice of this plan. Those checks which he says are to be found in the English government, are also to be found here. Our government is founded upon real checks. He ought to show there are no checks in it. Is this the case? Who are your representatives? They are chosen by the people for two years. Who are your senators? They are chosen by the legislatures, and a third of them go out of the Senate at the end of every second year. They may also be impeached. There are no better checks upon earth. Are there better checks in the government of Virginia? There is not a check in the one that is not in the other. The difference consists in the length of time, and in the nature of the objects. Any man may be impeached here — so he may there. If the people of Virginia can remove their delegates for misbehavior, by electing other men at the end of the year, so, in like manner, the federal representatives may be removed at the end of two, and the senators at the end of six years.

The honorable gentleman has praised the Virginia government. We can prove that the federal Constitution is equally excellent. The legislature of Virginia may conceal their transactions as well as the general government. There is no clause in the Constitution of Virginia to oblige its legislature to publish its proceedings at any period. The clause in this Constitution which provides for a periodical publication, and which the honorable gentleman reprobates so much, renders the federal Constitution superior to that of Virginia in this respect. The expression, from time to time, renders us sufficiently secure: it will compel them to publish their proceedings as often as it can conveniently and safely be done; and must satisfy every mind, without an illiberal perversion of its meaning. His bright ideas are very much obscured by torturing the explication of words. His interpretation of elections must be founded on a misapprehension. The Constitution says, that "the times, places, and manner of holding elections for senators and representatives, shall be prescribed in each state by the legislature thereof; but the Congress may at any time, by law, make or alter such regulation, except as to the place of choosing senators." It says, in another place, "that the electors in each state shall have the qualifications requisite for electors of the most numerous branch of the state legislature." Who would have conceived it possible to deduce, from these clauses, that the power of election was thrown into the hands of the rich? As the electors of the federal representatives are to have the same qualifications with those of the representatives of this state legislature, — or, in other words, as the electors of the one are to be electors of the other, — this suggestion is unwarrantable, unless he carries his supposition farther, and says that Virginia will agree to her own suicide, by modifying elections in such manner as to throw them into the hands of the rich. The honorable gentleman has not given us a fair object to be attacked; he has not given us any thing substantial to be examined.

It is also objected that the trial by jury, the writ of habeas corpus, and the liberty of the press, are insecure. But I contend that the habeas corpus is at least on as secure and good a footing as it is in England. In that country, it depends on the will of the legislature. That privilege is secured here by the Constitution, and is only to be suspended in cases of extreme emergency. Is this not a fair footing? After agreeing that the government of England secures liberty, how do we distrust this government? Why distrust ourselves? The liberty of the press is supposed to be in danger. If this were the case, it would produce extreme repugnancy in my mind. If it ever will be suppressed in this country, the liberty of the people will not be far from being sacrificed.

Where is the danger of it? He says that every power is given to the general government that is not reserved to the states. Pardon me if I say the reverse of the proposition is true. I defy any one to prove the contrary. Every power not given it by this system is left with the states. This being the principle, from what part of the Constitution can the liberty of the press be said to be in danger?

[Here his excellency read the 8th section of the 1st article, containing all the powers given to Congress.]

Go through these powers, examine every one, and tell me if the most exalted genius can prove that the liberty of the press is in danger. The trial by jury is supposed to be in danger also. It is secured in criminal cases, but supposed to be taken away in civil cases. It is not relinquished by the Constitution; it is only not provided for. Look at the interest of Congress to suppress it. Can it be in any manner advantageous for them to suppress it? In equitable cases, it ought not to prevail, nor with respect to admiralty causes; because there will be an undue leaning against those characters, of whose business courts of admiralty will have cognizance. I will rest myself secure under this reflection — that it is impossible for the most suspicious or malignant mind to show that it is the interest of Congress to infringe on this trial by jury.

Freedom of religion is said to be in danger. I will candidly say, I once thought that it was, and felt great repugnance to the Constitution for that reason. I am willing to acknowledge my apprehensions removed; and I will inform you by what process of reasoning I did remove them. The Constitution provides that "the senators and representatives before mentioned, and the members of the several state legislatures, and all executive and judicial officers, both of the United States and of the several states, shall be found, by oath or affirmation, to support this Constitution; but no religious test shall ever be required as a qualification to any office or public trust under the United States." It has been said that, if the exclusion of the religious test were an exception from the general power of Congress, the power over religion would remain. I inform those who are of this opinion, that no power is given expressly to Congress over religion. The senators and representatives, members of the state legislatures, and executive and judicial officers, are bound, by oath or affirmation, to support this Constitution. This only binds them to support it in the exercise of the powers constitutionally given it. The exclusion of religious tests is an exception from this general provision, with respect to oaths or affirmations. Although officers, &c., are to swear that they will support this Constitution, yet they are not bound to support one mode of worship, or to adhere to one particular sect. It puts all sects on the same footing. A man of abilities and character, of any sect whatever, may be admitted to any office or public trust under the United States. I am a friend to a variety of sects, because they keep one another in order. How many different sects are we composed of throughout the United States! How many different sects will be in Congress! We cannot enumerate the sects that may be in Congress! And there are now so many in the United States, that they will prevent the establishment of any one sect, in prejudice to the rest, and will forever oppose all attempts to infringe religious liberty. If such an attempt be made, will not the alarm be sounded throughout America? If Congress should be as wicked as we are foretold they will be, they would not run the risk of exciting the resentment of all, or most, of the religious sects in America.

The judiciary is drawn up in terror. Here I have an objection of a different nature. I object to the appellate jurisdiction as the greatest evil in it. But I look at the Union — the object which guides me. When I look at the Union, objects of less consideration vanish, and I hope that the inconvenience will be redressed, and that Congress will prohibit the appeal with respect to matters of fact. When it respects only matters of law, no danger can possibly arise from it. Can Congress have any interest in continuing appeals of fact? If Pennsylvania has an interest in continuing it, will not Georgia, North Carolina, South Carolina, Virginia, New York, and the Eastern States, have an interest in discontinuing it? What advantage will its continuance be to Maryland, New Jersey, or Delaware? Is there not unanimity against it in Congress almost? Kentucky will be equally opposed to it. Thus, sir, all these will be opposed to one state. If Congress wish to aggrandize themselves by oppressing the people, the judiciary must first be corrupted! No man says any thing against them; they are more independent than in England.

But they say that the adoption of this system will occasion an augmentation of taxes. To object to it on this ground, is as much as to say, No Union — stand by yourselves! An increase of taxes is a terror that no friend to the Union ought to be alarmed at. The impost must produce a great sum. The contrary cannot be supposed. I conceive the particular expense of particular states will be diminished, and that diminution will, to a certain extent, support the Union. Either disunion, or separate confederacies, will enhance the expense. A union of all the states will be, even on economical principles, more to the interest of the people of Virginia than either separate confederacies or disunion. Had the states complied with the obligations imposed upon them by the Confederation, this attempt would never have been made. The unequivocal experience we have had of their inefficacy renders this change necessary. If union be necessary for our safety, we ought not to address the avarice of this house. I am confident that not a single member of this committee would be moved by such unworthy considerations. We are told that the people do not understand this government. I am persuaded that they do not — not for the want of more time to understand it, but to correct the misrepresentations of it. When I meditated an opposition to previous amendments, I marked the number of what appeared to me to be errors, and which I wished to be subsequently removed. But its real errors have been exaggerated; it has not met with a fair decision. It must be candidly acknowledged that there are some evils in it which ought to be removed. But I am confident that such gross misrepresentations have been made of it, that, if carried before any intelligent men, they would wonder at such glaring attempts to mislead, or at such absolute misapprehension of the subject. Though it be not perfect, any government is better than the risk which gentlemen wish us to run.

Another construction he gives is, that it is exclusively in the power of Congress to arm the militia, and that the states could not do it if Congress thought proper to neglect it. I am astonished how this idea could enter into the gentleman's mind, whose acuteness no man doubts. How can this be fairly deduced from the following clause? — "To provide for the organizing, arming, and disciplining the militia, and for governing such part of them as may be employed in the service of the United States, reserving to the states respectively the appointment of the officers, and the authority of training the militia, according to the discipline prescribed by Congress." He complains much of implication; but in this case he has made use of it himself, for his construction of this clause cannot possibly be supported without it. It is clear and self-evident that the pretended danger cannot result from the clause. Should Congress neglect to arm or discipline the militia, the states are fully possessed of the power of doing it; for they are restrained from it by no part of the Constitution.

The sweeping clause, as it is called, is much dreaded. I find that I differ from several gentlemen on this point. This formidable clause does not in the least increase the powers of Congress. It is only inserted for greater caution, and to prevent the possibility of encroaching upon the powers of Congress. No sophistry will be permitted to be used to explain away any of those powers; nor can they possibly assume any other power, but what is contained in the Constitution, without absolute usurpation. Another security is that, if they attempt such a usurpation, the influence of the state governments will nip it in the bud of hope. I know this government will be cautiously watched. The smallest assumption of power will be sounded in alarm to the people, and followed by bold and active opposition. I hope that my countrymen will keep guard against every arrogation of power. I shall take notice of what the honorable gentleman said with respect to the power to provide for the general welfare. The meaning of this clause has been perverted, to alarm our apprehensions. The whole clause has not been read together. It enables Congress "to lay and collect taxes, duties, imposts, and excises; to pay the debts and provide for the common defence and general welfare of the United States; but all duties, imposts, and excises, shall be uniform throughout the United States." The plain and obvious meaning of this is, that no more duties, taxes, imposts, and excises, shall be laid, than are sufficient to pay the debts, and provide for the common defence and general welfare, of the United States.

If you mean to have a general government at all, ought it not to be empowered to raise money to pay the debts, and advance the prosperity, of the United States, in the manner that Congress shall think most eligible? What is the consequence of the contrary? You give it power by one hand, and take it away from it by the other. If it be defective in some parts, yet we ought to give due credit to those parts which are acknowledged to be good. Does not the prohibition of paper money merit our approbation? I approve of it because it prohibits tender-laws, secures the widows and orphans, and prevents the states from impairing contracts. I admire that part which forces Virginia to pay her debts. If we recur to the bill of rights, which the honorable gentleman speaks so much of, we shall find that it recommends justice. Had not this power been given, my affection for it would not have been so great. When it obliges us to tread in the path of virtue, when it takes away from the most influential man the power of directing our passions to his own emolument, and of trampling upon justice, I hope to be excused when I say, that, were it more objectionable than it is, I should vote for the Union.

Speech Before the Virginia Ratifying Convention by George Nicholas

Editor's Introduction:

No speech better identified the key argument for originalism than this June 10 offering from George Nicholas. He began his discussion with a summary of why the Union was necessary for the security of his home state, namely, to better facilitate foreign relations and to keep both foreign aggression and civil war at bay. But the end of the speech contains the real gems. Nicholas argued that the "general welfare" clause contained no new power and was simply a restatement of the same language in the Articles of Confederation. If this was true, then it carried the same meaning, and if the power was limited in the Articles, then it was as limited in the Constitution. He swept aside fear "necessary and proper clause" by contending that it granted no new powers, only those already delegated in Article I, Section 8. And finally, Nicholas nearly provided the direct language for the future Tenth Amendment to the Constitution when he argued a bill of rights was unnecessary. "Where, by the Constitution, the general government has general powers for any purpose, its powers are absolute. Where it has powers with some exceptions, they are absolute only as to those exceptions. In either case, the people retain what is not conferred on the general government, as it is by their positive grant that it has any of its powers....In disputes between Congress and the people, the reverse of the proposition holds. Is the disputed right enumerated? If not, Congress cannot meddle with it." That is originalism. He then outlined what has become known as nullification "They [the people of the States] also know that they retain every thing else, and have a right to resume what they have given up, if it be perverted from its intended object." A right to resume means they can tell the general government, "no."

Speech Before th Virginia Ratifying Convention
June 10, 1788
By George Nicholas of Virginia

Mr. GEORGE NICHOLAS, in reply to Mr. Harrison, observed, that the turpitude of a man's character was not a sufficient reason to deprive him of his life without a trial; that such a doctrine as that was a subversion of every shadow of freedom; that a fair trial was necessary to determine whether accusations against men's characters were well-founded or not; and that no person would be safe, were it once adopted as a maxim, that a man might be condemned without a trial. Mr. Nicholas then proceeded: Although we have sat eight days, so little has been done, that we have hardly begun to discuss the question regularly. The rule of the house to proceed clause by clause has been violated. Instead of doing this, gentlemen alarm us by declamations without reason or argument — by bold assertions that we are going to sacrifice our liberties. It is a fact known to many members within my hearing, that several members have tried their interest without doors to induce others to oppose this system. Every local interest that could affect their minds has been operated upon.

Can it be supposed that gentlemen elected, for their ability and integrity, to represent the people of Virginia in this Convention, to determine on this important question, whether or not we shall be connected with the other states in the Union — can it be thought, I say, that gentlemen in a situation like this will be influenced by motives like these? An answer which has been given is, that, if this Constitution be adopted, the western countries will be lost. It is better that a few countries should be lost, than all America. But, sir, no such consequence can follow from its adoption. They will be much more secure than they are at present. This Constitution, sir, will secure the equal liberty and happiness of all. It will do immortal honor to the gentlemen who formed it. I shall show the inconsistency of the gentleman who entertained us so long, (Mr. Henry.) He insisted that subsequent amendments would go to a dissolution of the Union; that Massachusetts was opposed to it in its present state. Massachusetts has absolutely ratified it, and has gone further, and said that such and such amendments shall be proposed by their representatives.

But such was the attachment of that respectable state to the Union, that, even at that early period, she ratified it unconditionally, and depended on the probability of obtaining amendments hereafter. Can this be a dissolution of the Union? Does this indicate an aversion to the Union on the part of that state? or can an imitation of her conduct injure us? He tells us that our present government is strong. How can that government be strong which depends on humble supplications for its support? Does a government which is dependent for its existence on others, and which is unable to afford protection to the people, deserve to be continued? But the honorable gentleman has no objections to see little storms in republics; they may be useful in the political as well as in the natural world. Every thing the great Creator has ordained in the natural world is founded on consummate wisdom: but let him tell us what advantages convulsions, dissensions, and bloodshed, will produce in the political world. Can disunion be the means of securing the happiness of the people in this political hemisphere? The worthy member has enlarged on our bill of rights.

Let us see whether his encomiums on the bill of rights be consistent with his other arguments. Our declaration of rights says that all men are by nature equally free and independent. How comes the gentleman to reconcile himself to a government wherein there are an hereditary monarch and nobility? He objects to this change, although our present federal system is totally without energy. He objects to this system, because he says it will prostrate your bill of rights. Does not the bill of rights tell you that a majority of the community have an indubitable right to alter any government which shall be found inadequate to the security of the public happiness? Does it not say "that no free government, or the blessings of liberty, can be preserved to any people, but by a firm adherence to justice, moderation, temperance, frugality, and virtue, and by frequent recurrence to fundamental principles"? Have not the inadequacy of the present system, and repeated flagrant violations of justice, and the other principles recommended by the bill of rights, been amply proved? As this plan of government will promote our happiness and establish justice, will not its adoption be justified by the very principles of your bill of rights?

But he has touched on a string which will have great effect. The western country is not safe if this plan be adopted. What do they stand in need of? Do they want protection from enemies? The present weak government cannot protect them. But the exercise of the congressional powers, proposed by this Constitution, will afford them ample security, because the general government can command the whole strength of the Union, to protect any particular part. There is another point wherein this government will set them right. I mean the western posts. This is a subject with which every gentleman here is acquainted. They have been withheld from us, since the peace, by the British. The violation of the treaty on our part authorizes this detention in some degree. The answer of the British minister to our demand of surrendering the posts was, that, as soon as America should show a disposition to comply with the treaty on her part, Great Britain would do the same. By this Constitution, treaties will be the supreme law of the land. The adoption of it, therefore, is the only chance we have of getting the western posts.

As to the navigation of the Mississippi, it is one of the most unalienable rights of the people, and which ought to be relinquished on no consideration. The strength of the western people is not adequate to its retention and enjoyment. They can receive no aid from the Confederation. This navigation can only be secured by one of two ways — by force or by treaty. As to force, I apprehend that the new government will be much more likely to hold it than the old. It will be also more likely to retain it be means of treaties; because, as it will be more powerful and respectable, it will be more feared; and as they will have more power to injure Spain, Spain will be more inclined to do them justice, by yielding it, or by giving them an adequate compensation.

It was said that France and Spain would not be pleased to see the United States united in one great empire. Shall we remain feeble and contemptible to please them? Shall we reject our own interest to protect theirs? We shall be more able to discharge our engagements. This may be agreeable to them. There are many strong reasons to expect that the adoption of this system will be beneficial to the back country, and that their interest will be much better attended to under the new than under the old government. There are checks in this Constitution which will render the navigation of the Mississippi safer than it was under the Confederation. There is a clause which, in my opinion, will prohibit the general government from relinquishing that navigation. The 5th clause of the 9th section of the 1st article provides "that no preference shall be given, by any regulation of commerce or revenue, to the ports of one state over those of another." If Congress be expressly prohibited to give preference to the ports of one state over those of another, there is a strong implication that they cannot give preference to the ports of any foreign nation over those of a state. This will render it unconstitutional to give Spain a preference to the western country in the navigation of that river. They may say that this is a constrained construction, but it appears to me rational. It would be a violation of true policy to give such a preference. It would be a departure from natural construction to suppose that an advantage withheld from the states should be given to a foreign nation.

Under the Confederation, Congress cannot make a treaty without the consent of nine states. Congress, by the proposed plan, cannot make a treaty without the consent of two thirds of the senators present, and of the President. Two thirds will amount to nine states, if the senators from all the states be present. Can it be candidly and fairly supposed that they will not all, or nearly all, be present when so important a subject as a treaty is to be agitated? The consent of the President is a very great security. He is elected by the people at large. He will not have the local interests which the members of Congress may have. If he deviates from his duty, he is responsible to his constituents. He will be degraded, and will bring on his head the accusation of the representatives of the people — an accusation which has ever been, and always will be, very formidable. He will be absolutely disqualified to hold any place of profit, honor, or trust, and liable to further punishment if he has committed such high crimes as are punishable at common law. From the summit of honor and esteem he will be precipitated to the lowest infamy and disgrace. Although the representatives have no immediate agency in treaties, yet, from their influence in the government, they will direct every thing. They will be a considerable check on the Senate and President. Those from small states will be particularly attentive, to prevent a sacrifice of territory.

The people of New England have lately purchased great quantities of lands in the western country. Great numbers of them have moved thither. Every one has left his friends, relations, and acquaintances, behind him. This will prevent those states from adopting a measure that would so greatly tend to the injury of their friends. Has not Virginia, in the most explicit terms, asserted her right to that navigation? Can she ever enjoy it under so feeble a government as the present? This is one reason why she should assent to ratify this system. A strong argument offered by the gentleman last up, against the concession of direct taxation, is, that the back lands and impost will be sufficient for all the exigencies of government, and calculates the impost as a considerable amount. The impost will be affected by this business. The navigation of that river will increase the impost. Are not the United States as much interested as the people of Kentucky to retain that navigation? Congress will have as much interest in it as any inhabitant of that country, and must exert themselves for it. Kentucky will have taxes to pay.

How can they pay them without navigation? It will be to their interest to have it in their power to navigate the Mississippi, and raise money by imposts. It will be to the interest of all the states, as it will increase the general resources of the united community. Considering Kentucky as an independent state, she will, under the present system, and without the navigation of that river, be furnished with the articles of her consumption through the medium of the importing states. She will, therefore, be taxed by every importing state. If the new Constitution takes place, the amounts of duties on imported articles will go into the general treasury, by which means Kentucky will participate an equal advantage with the importing states. It will, then, be clearly to the advantage of the inhabitants of that country that it should take place. He tells us that he prays for union. What kind of union? A union of the whole, I suppose, if it could be got on his terms. If on such terms, he will adopt it. If not, he will recur to partial confederacies. He will attempt amendments. If he cannot obtain them, then he will choose a partial confederacy. Now, I beg every gentleman in this committee, who would not sacrifice the union, to attend to the situation in which they are about to place themselves.

I beg gentlemen seriously to reflect on this important business. They say amendments may be previously obtained, but acknowledged to be difficult. Will you join in an opposition that so directly tends to disunion? Can any member here think of disunion, or a partial confederacy, without horror? Yet both are expressly preferred to union, unless this system be amended previously. But, says the worthy member, why should not previous amendments be obtained? Will they not be agreed to, as the eight adopting states are friends to the union? But what follows? If they are so, they will agree to subsequent amendments. If you recommend alterations after ratifying, the friendship of the adopting states to the union, and the desires of several of them to have amendments, will lead them to gratify every reasonable proposal. By this means you secure the government and union. But if you reject the Constitution, and say you must have alterations as the previous condition of adoption, you sacrifice the union, and all the valuable parts of it.

Can we trust, says he, our liberty to the President — to the Senate — to the House of Representatives? We do not trust our liberty to a particular branch: one branch has not the whole power. One branch is a check on the other. The representatives have a controlling power over the whole. He then told us that republican borderers are not disposed to quarrels. This controverts the uniform evidence of history. I refer the gentleman to the history of Greece. Were not the republics of that country, which bordered on one another, almost perpetually at war? Their confederated republics, as long as they were united, were continually torn by domestic factions. This was the case with the Amphictyons. They called to their assistance the Macedonian monarch, and were subjected themselves by that very prince. This was the fate of the other Grecian republics. Dissensions among themselves rendered it necessary for them to call for foreign aid, and this expedient ultimately ended in their own subjugation. This proves the absolute necessity of the union.

There is a country which affords strong examples, which may be of great utility to us: I mean Great Britain. England, before it was united to Scotland, was almost constantly at war with that part of the island. The inhabitants of the north and south parts of the same island were more bitter enemies to one another than to the nations on the Continent. England and Scotland were more bitter enemies, before the union, than England and France have ever been, before or since. Their hatred and animosities were stimulated by the interference of other nations. Since the union, both countries have enjoyed domestic tranquillity, the greatest part of the time, and both countries have been greatly benefited by it. This is a convincing proof that union is necessary for America, and that partial confederacies would be productive of endless dissensions, and unceasing hostilities between the different parts.

The gentleman relies much on the force of requisitions. I shall mention two examples which will show their inutility. They are fruitless without the coercion of arms. If large states refuse, a complete civil war, or dissolution of the confederacy, will result. If small states refuse, they will be destroyed, or obliged to comply. From the history of the United Netherlands, the inutility of requisitions, without recurring to force, may be proved. The small provinces refused to comply. Holland, the most powerful, marched into their territories with an army, and compelled them to pay. The other example is from the New England confederacy. Massachusetts, the most wealthy and populous state, refused to contribute her share. The rest were unable to compel her, and the league was dissolved. Attend to a resolution of the Assembly of Virginia in the year 1784.

[Here Mr. Nicholas read a resolution of that year, to enable Congress to compel a compliance with requisitions.]

I am sure that the gentleman recognizes his child. Is not this a conclusive evidence of the utter inefficacy of requisitions? This expedient of coercion is a dreadful alternative. It confounds those who are innocent, and willing to pay, with those who refuse. How are they to be discriminated, if a state is to be attacked for the refusal of its legislature? I am sure there is not a man in the committee who does not see the impolicy and danger of such an expedient.

We are next terrified with the thought of excises. In some countries excises are terrible. In others, they are not only harmless, but useful. In our sister states, they are excised without any inconvenience. They are a kind of tax on manufactures. Our manufactures are few in proportion to those of other states. We may be assured that Congress will make such regulations as shall make excises convenient and easy for the people.

Another argument made use of is, that ours is the largest state, and must pay in proportion to the other states. How does that appear? The proportion of taxes are fixed by the number of inhabitants, and not regulated by the extent of territory, or fertility of soil. If we be wealthier, in proportion, than other states, it will fall lighter upon us than upon poorer states. They must fix the taxes so that the poorest states can pay; and Virginia, being richer; will bear it easier.

The honorable gentleman says that the first collections are to go to Congress, and that the state legislatures must bear all deficiencies. How does this appear? Does he prove it? Nothing of it appears in the plan itself. The Congress and the state legislatures have concurrent jurisdictions in laying and collecting taxes. There is no rule that shows that Congress shall have the first collections. Each is independent of the other.

Another argument against this disingenuous construction is drawn from that clause which regulates representation, which is conclusive from the words themselves: "Representatives and direct taxes shall be apportioned among the several states which may be included within this Union, according to their respective numbers." Each state will know, from its population, its proportion of any general tax. As it was justly observed by the gentleman over the way, (Mr. Randolph,) they cannot possibly exceed that proportion: they are limited and restrained expressly to it. The state legislatures have no check of this kind. Their power is uncontrolled. This excludes the danger of interference. Each collects its own taxes, and bears its own deficiencies; and officers are accountable to each government for the different collections.

I deny, on my part, what he says with respect to the general welfare. He tells you that, under pretence of providing for the general welfare, they may lay the most enormous taxes. There is nothing in the clause which warrants this suggestion.

It provides "that Congress shall have the power to lay and collect taxes, duties, imposts, and excises; to pay the debts, and provide for the common defence and general welfare, of the United States." The debts of the Union ought to be paid. Ought not the common defence to be provided for? Is it not necessary to provide for the general welfare? It has been fully proved that this power could not be given to another body. The amounts to be raised are confined to these purposes solely. Will oppressive burdens be warranted by this clause? They are not to raise money for any other purpose. It is a power which is drawn from his favorite Confederation, the 8th article of which provides "that all charges of war, and all other expenses that shall be incurred for the common defence or general welfare, and allowed by the United States, in Congress assembled, shall be defrayed out of a common treasury, which shall be supplied by the several states, in proportion to the value of all lands, within each state, granted to or surveyed for any person, as such land, and the building and improvement thereon, shall be estimated, according to such mode as the United States, in Congress assembled, shall, from time to time, direct and appoint.

"The taxes for paying that proportion shall be laid and levied, by the authority and direction of the legislatures of the several states, within the time agreed upon by the United States, in Congress assembled." Now, sir, by a comparison of this article with the clause in the Constitution, we shall find them to be nearly the same. The common defence and general welfare are the objects expressly mentioned to be provided for, in both systems. The power in the Confederation to secure and provide for those objects was constitutionally unlimited. The requisitions of Congress are binding on the states, though, from the imbecility of their nature, they cannot be enforced. The same power is intended by the Constitution. The only difference between them is, that Congress is, by this plan, to impose the taxes on the people, whereas, by the Confederation, they are laid by the states. The amount to be raised, and the power given to raise it, is the same in principle. The mode of raising only is different, and this difference is founded on the necessity of giving the government that energy without which it cannot exist. The power has not been reprobated in the Confederation. It ought not to be blamed in the proposed plan of government.

The gentleman has adverted to what he calls the sweeping clause, &c., and represents it as replete with great dangers. This dreaded clause runs in the following words: "To make all laws which shall be necessary and proper for carrying into execution the foregoing powers, and all other powers vested by this Constitution in the government of the United States, or in any department or officer thereof." The committee will perceive that the Constitution had enumerated all the powers which the general government should have, but did not say how they were to be exercised. It therefore, in this clause, tells how they shall be exercised. Does this give any new power? I say not. Suppose it had been inserted, at the end of every power, that they should have power to make laws to carry that power into execution; would this have increased their powers? If, therefore, it could not have increased their powers, if placed at the end of each power, it cannot increase them at the end of all. This clause only enables them to carry into execution the powers given to them, but gives them no additional power.

But it is objected to for want of a bill of rights. It is a principle universally agreed upon, that all powers not given are retained. Where, by the Constitution, the general government has general powers for any purpose, its powers are absolute. Where it has powers with some exceptions, they are absolute only as to those exceptions. In either case, the people retain what is not conferred on the general government, as it is by their positive grant that it has any of its powers. In England, in all disputes between the king and people, recurrence is had to the enumerated rights of the people, to determine. Are the rights in dispute secured? Are they included in Magna Charta, Bill of Rights, &c.? If not, they are, generally speaking, within the king's prerogative. In disputes between Congress and the people, the reverse of the proposition holds. Is the disputed right enumerated? If not, Congress cannot meddle with it.

Which is the most safe? The people of America know what they have relinquished for certain purposes. They also know that they retain every thing else, and have a right to resume what they have given up, if it be perverted from its intended object. The king's prerogative is general, with certain exceptions. The people are, therefore, less secure than we are. Magna Charta, Bill of Rights, &c., secure their liberty. Our Constitution itself contains an English Bill of Rights. The English Bill of Rights declares that Parliaments shall be held frequently. Our Constitution says that Congress shall sit annually. The English Declaration of Rights provides that no laws shall be suspended. The Constitution provides that no laws shall be suspended, except one, and that in time of rebellion or invasion, which is the writ of habeas corpus. The Declaration of Rights says that there should be no army in time of peace without the consent of Parliament. Here we cannot have an army even in time of war, with the approbation of our representatives, for more than two years.

The liberty of the press is secured. What secures it in England? Is it secured by Magna Charta, the Declaration of Rights, or by any other express provision? It is not. They have no express security for the liberty of the press. They have a reliance on Parliament for its protection and security. In the time of King William, there passed an act for licensing the press. That was repealed. Since that time, it has been looked upon as safe. The people have depended on their representatives. They will not consent to pass an act to infringe it, because such an act would irritate the nation. It is equally secure with us. As to the trial by jury, consider in what situation it is by the state

Constitution. It is not on a better footing. It is by implication under the control of the legislature, because it has left particular cases to be decided by the legislature. Here it is secured in criminal cases, and left to the legislatures in civil cases. One instance will prove the evil tendency of fixing it in the Constitution. It will extend to all cases. Causes in chancery, which, strictly speaking, never are, nor can be, well tried by a jury, would then be tried by that mode, and could not be altered, though found to be inconvenient.

But taxes are to be increased, we are told. I think they will not. I am clearly of opinion that the deduction in the civil list of the states will be equal to the increase of that of the general government. Then the increase of custom-house officers is dreaded. The present custom-house officers will be sufficient in the hands of Congress; so that as much as economy will take place, so far the revenues will be increased. Mr. Nicholas concluded by making a few observations on the general structure of the government, and its probable happy operation. He said that it was a government calculated to suit almost any extent of territory. He then quoted the opinion of the celebrated Montesquieu, from vol. i., book 9, where that writer speaks of a confederate republic as the only safe means of extending the sphere of a republican government to any considerable degree.

Speech Before the Virginia Ratifying Convention by George Nicholas

Editor's Introduction:

The brief speech by George Nicholas reemphasized his position on the "necessary and proper clause." Nicholas correctly opined that the words could have been added to the end of every power in Article I, Section 8, and that the phrase was neither an open ended grant of power nor a "sweeping clause," but simply a way for the Constitution to grant authority to the Congress to pass legislation putting the express power into effect. And, he concluded, "After granting some powers, the rest must remain with the people."

Speech Before Virginia Ratifying Convention

June 16, 1788

By George Nicholas of Virginia

Mr. GEORGE NICHOLAS, in reply to the gentlemen opposed to the clause under debate, went over the same grounds, and developed the same principles, which Mr. Pendleton and Mr. Madison had done. The opposers of the clause, which gave the power of providing for the general welfare, supposed its dangers to result from its connection with, and extension of, the powers granted in the other clausfes. He endeavored to show the committee that it only empowered Congress to make such laws as would be necessary to enable them to pay the public debts and provide for the common defence; that this general welfare was united, not to the general power of legislation, but to the particular power of laying and collecting taxes, imposts, and excises, for the purpose of paying the debts and providing for the common defence, — that is, that they could raise as much money as would pay the debts and provide for the common defence, in consequence of this power. The clause which was affectedly called the sweeping clause contained no new grant of power. To illustrate this position, he observed that, if it had been added at the end of every one of the enumerated powers, instead of being inserted at the end of all, it would be obvious to any one that it was no augmentation of power. If, for instance, at the end of the clause granting power to lay and collect taxes, it had been added that they should have power to make necessary and proper laws to lay and collect taxes, who could suspect it to be an addition of power? As it would grant no new power if inserted at the end of each clause, it could not when subjoined to the whole.

He then proceeded thus: But, says he, who is to determine the extent of such powers? I say, the same power which, in all well-regulated communities, determines the extent of legislative powers. If they exceed these powers, the judiciary will declare it void, or else the people will have a right to declare it void. Is this depending on any man? But, says the gentleman, it may go to any thing. It may destroy the trial by jury; and they may say it is necessary for providing for the general defence. The power of providing for the general defence only extends to raise any sum of money they may think necessary, by taxes, imposts, &c. But, says he, our only defence against oppressive laws consists in the virtue of our representatives. This was misrepresented. If I understand it right, no new power can be exercised. As to those which are actually granted, we trust to the fellow-feelings of our representatives; and if we are deceived, we then trust to altering our government. It appears to me, however, that we can confide in their discharging their powers rightly, from the peculiarity of their situation, and connection with us. If, sir, the powers of the former Congress were very inconsiderable, that body did not deserve to have great powers.

It was so constructed that it would be dangerous to invest it with such. But why were the articles of the bill of rights read? Let him show us that those rights are given up by the Constitution. Let him prove them to be violated. He tells us that the most worthy characters of the country differ as to the necessity of a bill of rights. It is a simple and plain proposition. It is agreed upon by all that the people have all power. If they part with any of it, is it necessary to declare that they retain the rest? Liken it to any similar case. If I have one thousand acres of land, and I grant five hundred acres of it, must I declare that I retain the other five hundred? Do I grant the whole thousand acres, when I grant five hundred, unless I declare that the five hundred I do not give belong to me still? It is so in this case. After granting some powers, the rest must remain with the people.

Speech Before the Virginia Ratifying Convention by John Marshall

Editor's Introduction:

John Marshall is one of the most important men in American history. No man did more to codify the nationalist interpretation of the Constitution than Marshall. His over three decades as United States Supreme Court Chief Justice provided a path for Marshall to undermine those who believed the Constitution as ratified required "strict construction" and limited central authority. Marshall knew as much. He sat through the entire Virginia Ratifying Convention where men like George Nicholas, James Madison, Francis Corbin, Edmund Pendleton, and Edmund Randolph made those very arguments. Even Marshall himself made similar statements the times he spoke before the convention.

Marshall was born in 1755 on the frontier of Virginia. His mother was from the powerful Randolph family but was ostracized because she eloped with a man below her station. Marshall's father made a good living as a surveyor, but like most frontier families, Marshall grew up in a log cabin around country people with simple homespun ways.

He joined the fighting during the American War for Independence, but unlike other Americans who found loyalty to their State more important than an "American nation," Marshall's experience fortified a sense of national pride. He studied law during the War and was eventually elected to the Virginia House of Delegates. Marshall's political career in Virginia was unremarkable, though he aligned himself with the more conservative element in Richmond, and in time, Richmond became his favorite place. He drank, gambled, dabbled in slavery and other investments, and eventually exhausted his finances. His supported the ratification of the Constitution and practiced law, but when John Adams tapped him as a diplomat to France, Marshall jumped at the opportunity. A federal job nearly doubled his income. He was eventually elected to the Congress and then served as Secretary of State for a few years, but just before Adams left office, he nominated Marshall as Chief Justice of the Supreme Court to stymie President-Elect Thomas Jefferson the opportunity of remaking the Supreme Court.

Marshall relished the chance and destroying the "republican" agenda from the federal bench. He considered Jefferson's followers to be "terrorists" and worried about a French reign of terror in America. He also knocked down almost every effort to hogtie federal authority, a process that included going back on promises he made during ratification. Among them a promise that the federal courts would not invalidate State laws that were outside of the jurisdiction of the federal court system. Marshall did just that, twice. Jefferson complained loudly that Marshall was ruling by decree without any real legal justification. Marshall telegraphed some of his moves in this June 20 speech before the Virginia Ratifying Convention, which makes it an important "originalist" document.

Speech Before the Virginia Ratifying Convention

June 20, 1788

By John Marshall of Virginia

Mr. JOHN MARSHALL. Mr. Chairman, this part of the plan before us is a great improvement on that system from which we are now departing. Here are tribunals appointed for the decision of controversies which were before either not at all, or improperly, provided for. That many benefits will result from this to the members of the collective society, every one confesses. Unless its organization be defective, and so constructed as to injure, instead of accommodating, the convenience of the people, it merits our approbation. After such a candid and fair discussion by those gentlemen who support it, — after the very able manner in which they have investigated and examined it, — I conceived it would be no longer considered as so very defective, and that those who opposed it would be convinced of the impropriety of some of their objections. But I perceive they still continue the same opposition. Gentlemen have gone on an idea that the federal courts will not determine the causes which may come before them with the same fairness and impartiality with which other courts decide. What are the reasons of this supposition? Do they draw them from the manner in which the judges are chosen, or the tenure of their office? What is it that makes us trust our judges? Their independence in office, and manner of appointment. Are not the judges of the federal court chosen with as much wisdom as the judges of the state governments? Are they not equally, if not more independent? If so, shall we not conclude that they will decide with equal impartiality and candor? If there be as much wisdom and knowledge in the United States as in a particular state, shall we conclude that the wisdom and knowledge will not be equally exercised in the selection of judges?

The principle on which they object to the federal jurisdiction seems, to me, to be founded on a belief that there will not be a fair trial had in those courts. If this committee will consider it fully, they will find it has no foundation, and that we are as secure there as any where else. What mischief results from some causes being tried there? Is there not the utmost reason to conclude that judges, wisely appointed, and independent in their office, will never countenance any unfair trial? What are the subjects of its jurisdiction? Let us examine them with an expectation that causes will be as candidly tried there as elsewhere, and then determine. The objection which was made by the honorable member who was first up yesterday (Mr. Mason) has been so fully refuted that it is not worth while to notice it. He objected to Congress having power to create a number of inferior courts, according to the necessity of public circumstances. I had an apprehension that those gentlemen who placed no confidence in Congress would object that there might be no inferior courts. I own that I thought those gentlemen would think there would be no inferior courts, as it depended on the will of Congress, but that we should be dragged to the centre of the Union. But I did not conceive that the power of increasing the number of courts could be objected to by any gentleman, as it would remove the inconvenience of being dragged to the centre of the United States. I own that the power of creating a number of courts is, in my estimation, so far from being a defect, that it seems necessary to the perfection of this system. After having objected to the number and mode, he objected to the subject matter of their cognizance. [Here Mr. Marshall read the 2d section.]

These, sir, are the points of federal jurisdiction to which he objects, with a few exceptions. Let us examine each of them with a supposition that the same impartiality will be observed there as in other courts, and then see if any mischief will result from them. With respect to its cognizance in all cases arising under the Constitution and the laws of the United States, he says that, the laws of the United States being paramount to the laws of the particular states, there is no case but what this will extend to. Has the government of the United States power to make laws on every subject? Does he understand it so? Can they make laws affecting the mode of transferring property, or contracts, or claims, between citizens of the same state? Can they go beyond the delegated powers? If they were to make a law not warranted by any of the powers enumerated, it would be considered by the judges as an infringement of the Constitution which they are to guard. They would not consider such a law as coming under their jurisdiction. They would declare it void. It will annihilate the state courts, says the honorable gentleman. Does not every gentleman here know that the causes in our courts are more numerous than they can decide, according to their present construction? Look at the dockets. You will find them crowded with suits, which the life of man will not see determined. If some of these suits be carried to other courts, will it be wrong? They will still have business enough.

Then there is no danger that particular subjects, small in proportion, being taken out of the jurisdiction of the state judiciaries, will render them useless and of no effect. Does the gentleman think that the state courts will have no cognizance of cases not mentioned here? Are there any words in this Constitution which exclude the courts of the states from those cases which they now possess? Does the gentleman imagine this to be the case? Will any gentleman believe it? Are not controversies respecting lands claimed under the grants of different states the only controversies between citizens of the same state which the federal judiciary can take cognizance of? The case is so clear, that to prove it would be a useless waste of time. The state courts will not lose the jurisdiction of the causes they now decide. They have a concurrence of jurisdiction with the federal courts in those cases in which the latter have cognizance.

How disgraceful is it that the state courts cannot be trusted! says the honorable gentleman. What is the language of the Constitution? Does it take away their jurisdiction? Is it not necessary that the federal courts should have cognizance of cases arising under the Constitution, and the laws, of the United States? What is the service or purpose of a judiciary, but to execute the laws in a peaceable, orderly manner, without shedding blood, or creating a contest, or availing yourselves of force? If this be the case, where can its jurisdiction be more necessary than here?

To what quarter will you look for protection from an infringement on the Constitution, if you will not give the power to the judiciary? There is no other body that can afford such a protection. But the honorable member objects to it, because he says that the officers of the government will be screened from merited punishment by the federal judiciary. The federal sheriff, says he, will go into a poor man's house and beat him, or abuse his family, and the federal court will protect him. Does any gentleman believe this? Is it necessary that the officers will commit a trespass on the property or persons of those with whom they are to transact business? Will such great insults on the people of this country be allowable? Were a law made to authorize them, it would be void. The injured man would trust to a tribunal in his neighborhood. To such a tribunal he would apply for redress, and get it. There is no reason to fear that he would not meet that justice there which his country will be ever willing to maintain. But, on appeal, says the honorable gentleman, what chance is there to obtain justice? This is founded on an idea that they will not be impartial. There is no clause in the Constitution which bars the individual member injured from applying to the state courts to give him redress. He says that there is no instance of appeals as to fact in common-law cases. The contrary is well known to you, Mr. Chairman, to be the case in this commonwealth. With respect to mills, roads, and other cases, appeals lie from the inferior to the superior court, as to fact as well as law. Is it a clear case, that there can be no case in common law in which an appeal as to fact might be proper and necessary? Can you not conceive a case where it would be productive of advantages to the people at large to submit to that tribunal the final determination, involving facts as well as law? Suppose it should be deemed for the convenience of the citizens that those things which concerned foreign ministers should be tried in the inferior courts; if justice could be done, the decision would satisfy all. But if an appeal in matters of facts could not be carried to the superior court, then it would result that such cases could not be tried before the inferior courts, for fear of injurious and partial decisions.

But, sir, where is the necessity of discriminating between the three cases of chancery, admiralty, and common law? Why not leave it to Congress? Will it enlarge their powers? Is it necessary for them wantonly to infringe your rights? Have you any thing to apprehend, when they can in no case abuse their power without rendering themselves hateful to the people at large? When this is the case, something may be left to the legislature freely chosen by ourselves, from among ourselves, who are to share the burdens imposed upon the community, and who can be changed at our pleasure. Where power may be trusted, and there is no motive to abuse it, it seems to me to be as well to leave it undetermined as to fix it in the Constitution.

With respect to disputes between a state and the citizens of another state, its jurisdiction has been decried with unusual vehemence. I hope that no gentleman will think that a state will be called at the bar of the federal court. Is there no such case at present? Are there not many cases in which the legislature of Virginia is a party, and yet the state is not sued? It is not rational to suppose that the sovereign power should be dragged before a court. The intent is, to enable states to recover claims of individuals residing in other states. I contend this construction is warranted by the words. But, say they, there will be partiality in it if a state cannot be defendant — if an individual cannot proceed to obtain judgment against a state, though he may be sued by a state. It is necessary to be so, and cannot be avoided. I see a difficulty in making a state defendant, which does not prevent its being plaintiff. If this be only what cannot be avoided, why object to the system on that account? If an individual has a just claim against any particular state, is it to be presumed that, on application to its legislature, he will not obtain satisfaction? But how could a state recover any claim from a citizen of another state, without the establishment of these tribunals?

The honorable member objects to suits being instituted in the federal courts, by the citizens of one state, against the citizens of another state. Were I to contend that this was necessary in all cases, and that the government without it would be defective, I should not use my own judgment. But are not the objections to it carried too far? Though it may not in general be absolutely necessary, a case may happen, as has been observed, in which a citizen of one state ought to be able to recur to this tribunal, to recover a claim from the citizen of another state. What is the evil which this can produce? Will he get more than justice there? The independence of the judges forbids it. What has he to get? Justice. Shall we object to this, because the citizen of another state can obtain justice without applying to our state courts? It may be necessary with respect to the laws and regulations of commerce, which Congress may make. It may be necessary in cases of debt, and some other controversies. In claims for land, it is not necessary, but it is not dangerous. In the court of which state will it be instituted? said the honorable gentleman. It will be instituted in the court of the state where the defendant resides, where the law can come at him, and nowhere else. By the laws of which state will it be determined? said he.

By the laws of the state where the contract was made. According to those laws, and those only, can it be decided. Is this a novelty? No; it is a principle in the jurisprudence of this commonwealth. If a man contracted a debt in the East Indies, and it was sued for here, the decision must be consonant to the laws of that country. Suppose a contract made in Maryland, where the annual interest is at six per centum, and a suit instituted for it in Virginia; what interest would be given now, without any federal aid? The interest of Maryland most certainly; and if the contract had been made in Virginia, and suit brought in Maryland, the interest of Virginia must be given, without doubt. It is now to be governed by the laws of that state where the contract was made. The laws which governed the contract at its formation govern it in its decision. To preserve the peace of the Union only, its jurisdiction in this case ought to be recurred to. Let us consider that, when citizens of one state carry on trade in another state, much must be due to the one from the other, as is the case between North Carolina and Virginia. Would not the refusal of justice to our citizens, from the courts of North Carolina, produce disputes between the states? Would the federal judiciary swerve from their duty in order to give partial and unjust decisions?

The objection respecting the assignment of a bond to a citizen of another state has been fully answered. But suppose it were to be tried, as he says; what would be given more than was actually due in the case he mentioned? It is possible in our courts, as they now stand, to obtain a judgment for more than justice. But the court of chancery grants relief. Would it not be so in the federal court? Would not depositions be taken to prove the payments; and if proved, would not the decision of the court be accordingly?

He objects, in the next place, to its jurisdiction in controversies between a state and a foreign state. Suppose, says he, in such a suit, a foreign state is cast; will she be bound by the decision? If a foreign state brought a suit against the commonwealth of Virginia, would she not be barred from the claim if the federal judiciary thought it unjust? The previous consent of the parties is necessary; and, as the federal judiciary will decide, each party will acquiesce. It will be the means of preventing disputes with foreign nations. On an attentive consideration of these points, I trust every part will appear satisfactory to the committee.

The exclusion of trial by jury, in this case, he urged to prostrate our rights. Does the word court only mean the judges? Does not the determination of a jury necessarily lead to the judgment of the court? Is there any thing here which gives the judges exclusive jurisdiction of matters of fact? What is the object of a jury trial? To inform the court of the facts. When a court has cognizance of facts, does it not follow that they can make inquiry by a jury? It is impossible to be otherwise. I hope that in this country, where impartiality is so much admired, the laws will direct facts to be ascertained by a jury. But, says the honorable gentleman, the juries in the ten miles square will be mere tools of parties, with which he would not trust his person or property; which, he says, he would rather leave to the court. Because the government may have a district of ten miles square, will no man stay there but the tools and officers of the government? Will nobody else be found there? Is it so in any other part of the world, where a government has legislative power? Are there none but officers, and tools of the government of Virginia, in Richmond? Will there not be independent merchants, and respectable gentlemen of fortune, within the ten miles square? Will there not be worthy farmers and mechanics? Will not a good jury be found there, as well as any where else? Will the officers of the government become improper to be on a jury? What is it to the government whether this man or that man succeeds? It is all one thing. Does the Constitution say that juries shall consist of officers, or that the Supreme Court shall be held in the ten miles square? It was acknowledged, by the honorable member, that it was secure in England. What makes it secure there? Is it their constitution? What part of their constitution is there that the Parliament cannot change? As the preservation of this right is in the hands of Parliament, and it has ever been held sacred by them, will the government of America be less honest than that of Great Britain? Here a restriction is to be found. The jury is not to be brought out of the state. There is no such restriction in that government; for the laws of Parliament decide every thing respecting it. Yet gentlemen tell us that there is safety there, and nothing here but danger. It seems to me that the laws of the United States will generally secure trials by a jury of the vicinage, or in such manner as will be most safe and convenient for the people.

But it seems that the right of challenging the jurors is not secured in this Constitution. Is this done by our own Constitution, or by any provision of the English government? Is it done by their Magna Charta, or bill of rights? This privilege is founded on their laws. If so, why should it be objected to the American Constitution, that it is not inserted in it? If we are secure in Virginia without mentioning it in our Constitution, why should not this security be found in the federal court?

The honorable gentleman said much about the quitrents in the Northern Neck. I will refer it to the honorable gentleman himself. Has he not acknowledged that there was no complete title? Was he not satisfied that the right of the legal representatives of the proprietor did not exist at the time he mentioned? If so, it cannot exist now. I will leave it to those gentlemen who come from that quarter. I trust they will not be intimidated, on this account, in voting on this question. A law passed in 1782, which secures this. He says that many poor men may be harassed and injured by the representatives of Lord Fairfax. If he has no right, this cannot be done. If he has this right, and comes to Virginia, what laws will his claims be determined by? By those of this state. By what tribunals will they be determined? By our state courts. Would not the poor man, who was oppressed by an unjust prosecution, be abundantly protected and satisfied by the temper of his neighbors, and would he not find ample justice? What reason has the honorable member to apprehend partiality or injustice? He supposes that, if the judges be judges of both the federal and state courts, they will incline in favor of one government. If such contests should arise, who could more properly decide them than those who are to swear to do justice? If we can expect a fair decision any where, may we not expect justice to be done by the judges of both the federal and state governments? But, says the honorable member, laws may be executed tyrannically. Where is the independency of your judges? If a law be exercised tyrannically in Virginia, to what can you trust? To your judiciary. What security have you for justice? Their independence. Will it not be so in the federal court?

Gentlemen ask, What is meant by law cases, and if they be not distinct from facts? Is there no law arising on cases of equity and admiralty? Look at the acts of Assembly. Have you not many cases where law and fact are blended? Does not the jurisdiction in point of law as well as fact, find itself completely satisfied in law and fact? The honorable gentleman says that no law of Congress can make any exception to the federal appellate jurisdiction of facts as well as law. He has frequently spoken of technical terms, and the meaning of them. What is the meaning of the term exception? Does it not mean an alteration and diminution? Congress is empowered to make exceptions to the appellate jurisdiction, as to law and fact, of the Supreme Court. These exceptions certainly go as far as the legislature may think proper for the interest and liberty of the people. Who can understand this word, exception, to extend to one case as well as the other? I am persuaded that a reconsideration of this case will convince the gentleman that he was mistaken. This may go to the cure of the mischief apprehended. Gentlemen must be satisfied that this power will not be so much abused as they have said.

The honorable member says that he derives no consolation from the wisdom and integrity of the legislature, because we call them to rectify defects which it is our duty to remove. We ought well to weigh the good and evil before we determine. We ought to be well convinced that the evil will be really produced before we decide against it. If we be convinced that the good greatly preponderates, though there be small defects in it, shall we give up that which is really good, when we can remove the little mischief it may contain, in the plain, easy method pointed out in the system itself?

I was astonished when I heard the honorable gentleman say that he wished the trial by jury to be struck out entirely. Is there no justice to be expected by a jury of our fellow-citizens? Will any man prefer to be tried by a court, when the jury is to be of his countrymen, and probably of his vicinage? We have reason to believe the regulations with respect to juries will be such as shall be satisfactory. Because it does not contain all, does it contain nothing? But I conceive that this committee will see there is safety in the case, and that there is no mischief to be apprehended.

He states a case, that a man may be carried from a federal to an anti-federal corner, (and vice versa) where men are ready to destroy him. Is this probable? Is it presumable that they will make a law to punish men who are of different opinions in politics from themselves? Is it presumable that they will do it in one single case, unless it be such a case as must satisfy the people at large? The good opinion of the people at large must be consulted by their representatives; otherwise, mischiefs would be produced which would shake the government to its foundation. As it is late, I shall not mention all the gentleman's argument, but some parts of it are so glaring that I cannot pass them over in silence. He says that the establishment of these tribunals, and more particularly in their jurisdiction of controversies between citizens of these states and foreign citizens and subjects, is like a retrospective law. Is there no difference between a tribunal which shall give justice and effect to an existing right, and creating a right that did not exist before? The debt or claim is created by the individual. He has bound himself to comply with it. Does the creation of a new court amount to a retrospective law?

We are satisfied with the provision made in this country on the subject of trial by jury. Does our Constitution direct trials to be by jury? It is required in our bill of rights, which is not a part of the Constitution. Does any security arise from hence? Have you a jury when a judgment is obtained on a replevin bond, or by default? Have you a jury when a motion is made for the commonwealth against an individual; or when a motion is made by one joint obligor against another, to recover sums paid as security? Our courts decide in all these cases, without the intervention of a jury; yet they are all civil cases. The bill of rights is merely recommendatory. Were it otherwise, the consequence would be that many laws which are found convenient would be unconstitutional. What does the government before you say? Does it exclude the legislature from giving a trial by jury in civil cases? If it does not forbid its exclusion, it is on the same footing on which your state government stands now. The legislature of Virginia does not give a trial by jury where it is not necessary, but gives it wherever it is thought expedient. The federal legislature will do so too, as it is formed on the same principles.

The honorable gentleman says that unjust claims will be made, and the defendant had better pay them than go to the Supreme Court. Can you suppose such a disposition in one of your citizens, as that, to oppress another man, he will incur great expenses? What will he gain by an unjust demand? Does a claim establish a right? He must bring his witnesses to prove his claim. If he does not bring his witnesses, the expenses must fall upon him. Will he go on a calculation that the defendant will not defend it, or cannot produce a witness? Will he incur a great deal of expense, from a dependence on such a chance? Those who know human nature, black as it is, must know that mankind are too well attached to their interest to run such a risk. I conceive that this power is absolutely necessary, and not dangerous; that, should it be attended by little inconveniences, they will be altered, and that they can have no interest in not altering them. Is there any real danger? When I compare it to the exercise of the same power in the government of Virginia, I am persuaded there is not. The federal government has no other motive, and has every reason for doing right which the members of our state legislature have. Will a man on the eastern shore be sent to be tried in Kentucky, or a man from Kentucky be brought to the eastern shore to have his trial? A government, by doing this, would destroy itself. I am convinced the trial by jury will be regulated in the manner most advantageous to the community.

Speech Before the New York Ratifying Convention by Alexander Hamilton

Editor's Introduction:

Hamilton's nearly singular defense of the Constitution in the New York Ratifying Convention followed similar themes from the *Federalist* papers. In this speech, he castigates those who would wish to remain under the Articles of Confederation while admitting that the system did not work. He argued that the central government needed a compulsory power and that if the general government remained a unicameral legislature without other branches to check its power, it would become the most miserable despotism in the history of the Western world. He also explained that because of the diversity in the Union, i.e., States with different economic, political, and social institutions, a singular national government would have been ineffective. Hence, the number of compromises and limited scope of federal power. He defended the three-fifths compromise as a means of preserving the Union and also insisted it was inserted to help protect the Southern States from being plundered by the North. In fact, he thought it would help *Northern* States more than Southern States because unlike the North, the South did not get to count its entire population when determining representation in Congress.

Speech Before the New York Ratifying Convention

June 20, 1788

By Alexander Hamilton of New York

The Hon. Mr. HAMILTON then rose. Mr. Chairman, the honorable member who spoke yesterday went into an explanation of a variety of circumstances, to prove the expediency of a change in our national government, and the necessity of a firm union. At the same time, he described the great advantages which this state, in particular, receives from the confederacy, and its peculiar weaknesses when abstracted from the Union. In doing this, he advanced a variety of arguments, which deserve serious consideration. Gentlemen have this day come forward to answer him. He has been treated as having wandered in the flowery fields of fancy; and attempts have been made to take off from the minds of the committee that sober impression which might be expected from his arguments. I trust, sir, that observations of this kind are not thrown out to cast a light air on this important subject, or to give any personal bias on the great question before us. I will not agree with gentlemen who trifle with the weaknesses of our country, and suppose that they are enumerated to answer a party purpose, and to terrify with ideal dangers. No. I believe these weaknesses to be real, and pregnant with destruction. Yet, however weak our country may be, I hope we never shall sacrifice our liberties. If, therefore, on a full and candid discussion, the proposed system shall appear to have that tendency, for God's sake, let us reject it! But let us not mistake words for things, nor accept doubtful surmises as the evidence of truth. Let us consider the Constitution calmly and dispassionately, and attend to those things only which merit consideration.

No arguments drawn from embarrassment or inconvenience ought to prevail upon us to adopt a system of government radically bad; yet it is proper that these arguments, among others, should be brought into view. In doing this, yesterday, it was necessary to reflect upon our situation; to dwell upon the imbecility of our union; and to consider whether we, as a state, could stand alone. Although I am persuaded this Convention will be resolved to adopt nothing that is bad, yet I think every prudent man will consider the merits of the plan in connection with the circumstances of our country, and that a rejection of the Constitution may involve most fatal consequences. I make these remarks to show that, though we ought not to be actuated by unreasonable fear, yet we ought to be prudent.

This day, sir, one gentleman has attempted to answer the arguments advanced by my honorable friend; another has treated him as having wandered from the subject. This being the case, I trust I shall be indulged in reviewing the remarks that have been made.

Sir, it appears to me extraordinary, that, while gentlemen in one breath acknowledge that the old Confederation requires many material amendments, they should in the next deny that its defects have been the cause of our political weakness, and the consequent calamities of our country. I cannot but infer from this, that there is still some lurking favorite imagination, that this system, with correctness, might become a safe and permanent one. It is proper that we should examine this matter. We contend that the radical vice in the old Confederation is, that the laws of the Union apply only to states in their corporate capacity. Has not every man who has been in our legislature experienced the truth of this position? It is inseparable from the disposition of bodies, who have a constitutional power of resistance, to examine the merits of a law. This has ever been the case with the federal requisitions. In this examination, not being furnished with those lights which directed the deliberations of the general government, and incapable of embracing the general interests of the Union, the states have almost uniformly weighed the requisitions by their own local interests, and have only executed them so far as answered their particular convenience or advantage. Hence there have ever been thirteen different bodies to judge of the measures of Congress, and the operations of government have been distracted by their taking different courses. Those which were to be benefited have complied with the requisitions; others have totally disregarded them. Have not all of us been witnesses to the unhappy embarrassments which resulted from these proceedings? Even during the late war, while the pressure of common danger connected strongly the bond of our union, and incited to vigorous exertion, we have felt many distressing effects of the important system. How have we seen this state, though most exposed to the calamities of the war, complying, in an unexampled manner, with the federal requisitions, and compelled by the delinquency of others to bear most unusual burdens! Of this truth we have the most solemn proof on our records. In 1779 and '80, when the state, from the ravages of war, and from her great exertions to resist them, became weak, distressed, and forlorn, every man avowed the principle which we now contend for — that our misfortunes, in a great degree, proceeded from the want of vigor in the Continental government. These were our sentiments when we did not speculate, but feel. We saw our weakness, and found ourselves its victims. Let us reflect that this may again, in all probability, be our situation. This is a weak state, and its relative state is dangerous. Your capital is accessible by land, and by sea is exposed to every daring invader; and on the north-west you are open to the inroads of a powerful foreign nation. Indeed, this state, from its situation, will, in time of war, probably be the theatre of its operations.

Gentlemen have said that the non-compliance of the states had been occasioned by their sufferings. This may in part be true. But has this state been delinquent? Amidst all our distresses, we have fully complied. If New York could comply wholly with the requisitions, is it not to be supposed that the other states could in part comply? Certainly every state in the Union might have executed them in some degree. But New Hampshire, which has not suffered at all, is totally delinquent. North Carolina is totally delinquent. Many others have contributed in a very small proportion. And Pennsylvania and New York are the only states which have perfectly discharged their federal duty.

From the delinquency of those states which have suffered little by the war, we naturally conclude, that they have made no efforts; and a knowledge of human nature will teach us that their ease and security have been a principal cause of their want of exertion. While danger is distant, its impression is weak; and while it affects only our neighbors, we have few motives to provide against it. Sir, if we have national objects to pursue, we must have national revenues. If you make requisitions, and they are not complied with, what is to be done? It has been observed, to coerce the states is one of the maddest projects that was ever devised. A failure of compliance will never be confined to a single state. This being the case, can we suppose it wise to hazard a civil war? Suppose Massachusetts, or any large state, should refuse, and Congress should attempt to compel them, would they not have influence to procure assistance, especially from those states which are in the same situation as themselves? What picture does this idea present to our view? A complying state at war with a non-complying state; Congress marching the troops of one state into the bosom of another; this state collecting auxiliaries, and forming, perhaps, a majority against its federal head. Here is a nation at war with itself. Can any reasonable man be well disposed towards a government which makes war and carnage the only means of supporting itself — a government that can exist only by the sword? Every such war must involve the innocent with the guilty. This single consideration should be sufficient to dispose every peaceable citizen against such a government.

But can we believe that one state will ever suffer itself to be used as an instrument of coercion? The thing is a dream; it is impossible. Then we are brought to this dilemma — either a federal standing army is to enforce the requisitions, or the federal treasury is left without supplies, and the government without support. What, sir, is the cure for this great evil? Nothing, but to enable the national laws to operate on individuals, in the same manner as those of the states do. This is the true reasoning upon the subject, sir. The gentlemen appear to acknowledge its force; and yet, while they yield to the principle, they seem to fear its application to the government.

What, then, shall we do? Shall we take the old Confederation, as the basis of a new system? Can this be the object of the gentlemen? Certainly not. Will any man, who entertains a wish for the safety of his country, trust the sword and the purse with a single assembly organized on principles so defective — so rotten? Though we might give to such a government certain powers with safety, yet to give them the full and unlimited powers of taxation and the national forces, would be to establish a despotism; the definition of which is, a government in which all power is concentred in a single body. To take the old Confederation, and fashion it upon these principles, would be establishing a power which would destroy the liberties of the people. These considerations show clearly that a government totally different must be instituted. They had weight in the Convention who formed the new system. It was seen that the necessary powers were too great to be trusted to a single body; they therefore formed two branches, and divided the powers, that each might be a check upon the other. This was the result of their wisdom; and I presume that every reasonable man will agree to it. The more this subject is explained, the more clear and convincing it will appear to every member of this body. The fundamental principle of the old Confederation is defective; we must totally eradicate and discard this principle before we can expect an efficient government. The gentlemen who have spoken to-day have taken up the subject of the ancient confederacies; but their view of them has been extremely partial and erroneous. The fact is, the same false and impracticable principle ran through the ancient governments. The first of these governments that we read of, was the Amphictyonic confederacy. The council which managed the affairs of this league possessed powers of a similar complexion to those of our present Congress. The same feeble mode of legislation in the head, and the same power of resistance in the members, prevailed. When a requisition was made, it rarely met a compliance; and a civil war was the consequence. Those that were attacked called in foreign aid to protect them; and the ambitious Philip, under the mask of an ally to one, invaded the liberties of each, and finally subverted the whole.

The operation of this principle appears in the same light in the Dutch republics. They have been obliged to levy taxes by an armed force. In this confederacy, one large province, by its superior wealth and influence, is commonly a match for all the rest; and when they do not comply, the province of Holland is obliged to compel them. It is observed, that the United Provinces have existed a long time; but they have been constantly the sport of their neighbors, and have been supported only by the external pressure of the surrounding powers. The policy of Europe, not the policy of their government, has saved them from dissolution. Besides, the powers of the stadtholder have given energy to the operations of this government, which is not to be found in ours. This prince has a vast personal influence; he has independent revenues; he commands an army of forty thousand men.

The German confederacy has also been a perpetual source of wars. They have a diet, like our Congress, who have authority to call for supplies. These calls are never obeyed; and in time of war, the imperial army never takes the field till the enemy are returning from it. The emperor's Austrian dominions, in which he is an absolute prince, alone enable him to make head against the common foe. The members of this confederacy are ever divided and opposed to each other. The king of Prussia is a member; yet he has been constantly in opposition to the emperor. Is this a desirable government?

I might go more particularly into the discussion of examples, and show that, wherever this fatal principle has prevailed, even as far back as the Lycian and Achæan leagues, as well as the Amphictyonic confederacy, it has proved the destruction of the government. But I think observations of this kind might have been spared. Had they not been entered into by others, I should not have taken up so much of the time of the committee. No inference can be drawn from these examples, that republics cannot exist: we only contend that they have hitherto been founded on false principles. We have shown how they have been conducted, and how they have been destroyed. Weakness in the head has produced resistance in the members; this has been the immediate parent of civil war: auxiliary force has been invited; and foreign power has annihilated their liberties and name. Thus Philip subverted the Amphictyonic, and Rome the Achæan republic.

We shall do well, sir, not to deceive ourselves with the favorable events of the late war. Common danger prevented the operation of the ruinous principle, in its full extent; but, since the peace, we have experienced the evils; we have felt the poison of the system in its unmingled purity.

Without dwelling any longer on this subject, I shall proceed to the question immediately before the committee.

In order that the committee may understand clearly the principles on which the general Convention acted, I think it necessary to explain some preliminary circumstances. Sir, the natural situation of this country seems to divide its interests into different classes. There are navigating and non-navigating states. The Northern are properly navigating states: the Southern appear to possess neither the means nor the spirit of navigation. This difference of situation naturally produces a dissimilarity of interests and views respecting foreign commerce. It was the interest of the Northern States that there should be no restraints on their navigation, and they should have full power, by a majority in Congress, to make commercial regulations in favor of their own, and in restraint of the navigation of foreigners. The Southern States wish to impose a restraint on the Northern, by requiring that two thirds in Congress should be requisite to pass an act in regulation of commerce. They were apprehensive that the restraints of a navigation law would discourage foreigners, and, by obliging them to employ the shipping of the Northern States, would probably enhance their freight. This being the case, they insisted strenuously on having this provision ingrafted in the Constitution; and the Northern States were as anxious in opposing it. On the other hand, the small states, seeing themselves embraced by the Confederation upon equal terms, wished to retain the advantages which they already possessed. The large states, on the contrary, thought it improper that Rhode Island and Delaware should enjoy an equal suffrage with themselves. From these sources a delicate and difficult contest arose. It became necessary, therefore, to compromise, or the Convention must have dissolved without effecting any thing. Would it have been wise and prudent in that body, in this critical situation, to have deserted their country? No.

Every man who hears me, every wise man in the United States, would have condemned them. The Convention were obliged to appoint a committee for accommodation. In this committee, the arrangement was formed as it now stands, and their report was accepted. It was a delicate point, and it was necessary that all parties should be indulged. Gentlemen will see that, if there had not been a unanimity, nothing could have been done; for the Convention had no power to establish, but only to recommend, a government. Any other system would have been impracticable. Let a convention be called to-morrow; let them meet twenty times, — nay, twenty thousand times; they will have the same difficulties to encounter, the same clashing interests to reconcile.

But, dismissing these reflections, let us consider how far the arrangement is in itself entitled to the approbation of this body. We will examine it upon its own merits.

The first thing objected to is that clause which allows a representation for three fifths of the negroes. Much has been said of the impropriety of representing men who have no will of their own. Whether this be reasoning or declamation, I will not presume to say. It is the unfortunate situation of the Southern States to have a great part of their population, as well as property, in blacks. The regulation complained of was one result of the spirit of accommodation which governed the Convention; and without this indulgence no union could possibly have been formed. But, sir, considering some peculiar advantages which we derive from them, it is entirely just that they should be gratified. The Southern States possess certain staples, — tobacco, rice, indigo, &c., — which must be capital objects in treaties of commerce with foreign nations; and the advantages which they necessarily procure in those treaties will be felt throughout all the states. But the justice of this plan will appear in another view. The best writers on government have held that representation should be compounded of persons and property. This rule has been adopted, as far as it could be, in the constitution of New York. It will, however, by no means be admitted that the slaves are considered altogether as property. They are men, though degraded to the condition of slavery. They are persons known to the municipal laws of the states which they inhabit, as well as to the laws of nature. But representation and taxation go together, and one uniform rule ought to apply to both. Would it be just to compute these slaves in the assessment of taxes, and discard them from the estimate in the apportionment of representatives? Would it be just to impose a singular burden, without conferring some adequate advantage?

Another circumstance ought to be considered. The rule we have been speaking of is a general rule, and applies to all the states. Now, you have a great number of people in your state, which are not represented at all, and have no voice in your government. These will be included in the enumeration — not two fifths, nor three fifths, but the whole. This proves that the advantages of the plan are not confined to the Southern States, but extend to other parts of the Union.

I now proceed to consider the objection with regard to the number of representatives, as it now stands. I am persuaded the system, in this respect, stands on a better footing than the gentlemen imagine.

It has been asserted that it will be in the power of Congress to reduce the number. I acknowledge that there are no direct words of prohibition, but contend that the true and genuine construction of the clause gives Congress no power whatever to reduce the representation below the number as it now stands. Although they may limit, they can never diminish the number. One representative for every thirty thousand inhabitants is fixed as the standard of increase; till, by the natural course of population, it shall become necessary to limit the ratio. Probably, at present, were this standard to be immediately applied, the representation would considerably exceed sixty-five. In three years, it would exceed one hundred. If I understand the gentlemen, they contend that the number may be enlarged, or may not. I admit that this is in the discretion of Congress; and I submit to the committee whether it be not necessary and proper. Still, I insist that an immediate limitation is not probable, nor was it in the contemplation of the Convention. But, sir, who will presume to say to what precise point the representation ought to be increased? This is a matter of opinion, and opinions are vastly different upon the subject. A proof of this is drawn from the representations in the state legislatures. In Massachusetts, the Assembly consists of about three hundred; in South Carolina, of nearly one hundred; in New York, there are sixty-five. It is observed generally that the number ought to be large; let the gentlemen produce their criterion. I confess it is difficult for me to say what number may be said to be sufficiently large. On one hand, it ought to be considered that a small number will act with more facility, system, and decision; on the other, that a large one may enhance the difficulty of corruption. The Congress is to consist, at first, of ninety-one members. This, to a reasonable man, may appear as near the proper medium as any number whatever, at least for the present. There is one source of increase, also, which does not depend upon any constructions of the Constitution; it is the creation of new states. Vermont, Kentucky, and Franklin, will probably become independent. New members of the Union will also be formed from the unsettled tracts of western territory.

These must be represented, and will all contribute to swell the federal legislature. If the whole number in the United States be, at present, three millions, as is commonly supposed, according to the ratio of one for thirty thousand, we shall have, on the first census, a hundred representatives. In ten years, thirty more will be added; and in twenty-five years, the number will be double. Then, sir, we shall have two hundred, if the increase goes on in the same proportion. The Convention of Massachusetts, who made the same objections, have fixed upon this number as the point to which they chose to limit the representation. But can we pronounce, with certainty, that it will not be expedient to go beyond this number? We cannot. Experience alone must determine. This matter may, with more safety, be left to the discretion of the legislature, as it will be the interest of the large and increasing states of Massachusetts, New York, Pennsylvania, &c., to augment the representation. Only Connecticut, Rhode Island, Delaware, and Maryland, can be interested in limiting it. We may, therefore, safely calculate upon a growing representation, according to the advance of population, and the circumstances of the country.

The state governments possess inherent advantages, which will ever give them an influence and ascendency over the national government, and will forever preclude the possibility of federal encroachments. That their liberties, indeed, can be subverted by the federal head, is repugnant to every rule of political calculation. Is not this arrangement, then, sir, a most wise and prudent one? Is not the present representation fully adequate to our present exigencies, and sufficient to answer all the purposes of the Union? I am persuaded that an examination of the objects of the federal government will afford a conclusive answer.

Many other observations might be made on this subject, but I cannot now pursue them; for I feel myself not a little exhausted. I beg leave, therefore, to waive, for the present, the further discussion of the question.

Speech Before the New York Ratifying Convention by John Jay

Editor's Introduction:

John Jay focused on representation in this brief speech before the New York Ratifying Convention. Most important, he emphasized that because the Constitution formed a general government for general purposes, the men who represented each State did not need to be concerned with the local conditions of their constituents. Jay considered foreign policy to be the most important role of the general government: "What are the objects of our state legislatures? Innumerable things of small moment occupy their attention; matters of a private nature, which require much minute and local information. The objects of the general government are not of this nature. They comprehend the interests of the states in relation to each other, and in relation to foreign powers. Surely there are men in this state fully informed of the general interests of its trade, its agriculture, its manufactures. Is any thing more than this necessary? Is it requisite that our representatives in Congress should possess any particular knowledge of the local interests of the county of Suffolk, distinguished from those of Orange and Ulster?" He considered the number of representatives ideal for resisting corruption and conducting the business of the Union.

Speech Before the New York Ratifying Convention

June 23, 1788

By John Jay of New York

The Hon. Mr. JAY. I will make a few observations on this article, Mr. Chairman, though I am sensible it may not appear very useful to travel over the field which has been already so fully explored.

Sir, it seems to be, on all sides, agreed that a strong, energetic federal government is necessary for the United States.

It has given me pleasure to hear such declarations come from all parts of the house. If gentlemen are of this opinion, they give us to understand that such a government is the favorite of their desire; and also that it can be instituted; that, indeed, it is both necessary and practicable; or why do they advocate it?

The gentleman last on the floor has informed us that, according to his idea of a complete representation, the extent of our country is too great for it. [Here he called on Mr. Smith, to know if he had mistaken him; who replied, My idea is not that a proper representation for a strong federal government is unattainable; but that such a representation, under the proposed Constitution, is impracticable.] Sir, continued Mr. Jay, I now understand the gentleman in a different sense: however, what I shall say will reach equally his explanation. I take it that no federal government is worth having, unless it can provide for the general interests of the United States. If this Constitution be so formed as to answer these purposes, our object is obtained. The providing for the general interests of the Union requires certain powers in government, which the gentleman seems to be willing it should possess; that is, the important powers of war and peace. These powers are peculiarly interesting; their operation reaches objects the most dear to the people; and every man is concerned in them; yet, for the exercise of these powers the gentleman does not think a very large representation necessary. But, sir, if the proposed Constitution provides for a representation adequate to the purposes I have described, why not adequate to all other purposes of a federal government? The adversaries of the plan seem to consider the general government as possessing all the minute and local powers of the state governments. The direct inference from this, according to their principle, would be, that the federal representation should be proportionably large. In this state, as the gentleman says, we have sixty-five. If the national representation is to be extended in proportion, what an unwieldy body shall we have! If the United States contain three millions of inhabitants, in this ratio, the Congress must consist of more than eight hundred. But, sir, let us examine whether such a number is necessary or reasonable. What are the objects of our state legislatures? Innumerable things of small moment occupy their attention; matters of a private nature, which require much minute and local information. The objects of the general government are not of this nature. They comprehend the interests of the states in relation to each other, and in relation to foreign powers. Surely there are men in this state fully informed of the general interests of its trade, its agriculture, its manufactures. Is any thing more than this necessary? Is it requisite that our representatives in Congress should possess any particular knowledge of the local interests of the county of Suffolk, distinguished from those of Orange and Ulster? The Senate is to be composed of men appointed by the state legislatures: they will certainly choose those who are most distinguished for their general knowledge. I presume they will also instruct them, that there will be a constant correspondence supported between the senators and the state executives, who will be able, from time to time, to afford them all that particular information which particular circumstances may require. I am in favor of large representations: yet, as the minds of the people are so various on this subject, I think it best to let things stand as they are. The people in Massachusetts are satisfied with two hundred: many others suppose either number unnecessarily large. There is no point on which men's opinions vary more materially. If the matter be doubtful, — and much may be rationally said on both sides, — gentlemen ought not to be very strenuous on such points. The Convention who decided this question took all these different opinions into consideration, and were directed by a kind of necessity of mutual accommodation, and by reasons of expediency; it would therefore be unfair to censure them. Were I asked if the number corresponds exactly with my own private judgment, I should answer, No. But I think it is best, under our present circumstances, to acquiesce. Yet, sir, if I could be convinced that danger would probably result from so small a number, I should certainly withhold my acquiescence. But whence will this danger arise? Sir, I am not fearful of my countrymen: we have yet known very little of corruption: we have already experienced great distresses and difficulties; we have seen perilous times, when it was the interest of Great Britain to hold out the most seducing temptations to every man worth gaining. I mention this as a circumstance to show that, in case of a war with any foreign power, there can be little fear of corruption; and I mention it to the honor of the American character. At the time I allude to, how many men had you in Congress? Generally fewer than sixty-five.

Sir, all the arguments offered on the other side serve to show that it will be easier to corrupt under the old than under the new government: such arguments, therefore, do not seem to answer the gentleman's purpose. In the federal government, as it now stands, there are but thirteen votes, though there may be sixty or seventy voices.

Now, what is the object of corruption? To gain votes. In the new government there are to be ninety-one votes. Is it easier to buy many than a few? In the present Congress, you cannot declare war, make peace, or do any other important act, without the concurrence of nine states. There are rarely more than nine present. A full Congress is an extraordinary thing. Is it necessary to declare war, or pass a requisition of money to support it? A foreign prince says, this will be against my interest; I must prevent it. How? By having recourse to corruption. If there are eleven states on the floor, it will be necessary to corrupt three. What measure shall I take? Why, it is common for each state to have no more than two members in Congress. I will take off one, and the vote of that state is lost. I will take off three, and their most important plan is defeated. Thus, in the old government, it is only necessary to bribe the few; in the new government, it is necessary to corrupt the many. Where lies the greater security? The gentleman says, the election is annual, and you may recall your delegate when you please. But how are you to form your opinion of his conduct? He may excuse himself from acting without giving any reason. Nay, on a particular emergency, he has only to go home, for which he may have a thousand plausible reasons to offer, and you have no mode of compelling his attendance. To detect corruption is at all times difficult, but, under these circumstances, it appears almost impossible. I give out these hints to show that, on the score of corruption, we have much the best chance under the new Constitution; and that, if we do not reach perfection, we certainly change for the better. But, sir, suppose corruption should infect one branch of the government, — for instance, the House of Representatives; what a powerful check you have in the Senate! You have a double security; you have two chances in your favor to one against you. The two houses will naturally be in a state of rivalship: this will make them always vigilant, quick to discern a bad measure, and ready to oppose it. Thus the chance of corruption is not only lessened by an increase of the number, but vastly diminished by the necessity of concurrence. This is the peculiar excellence of a division of the legislature.

Sir, I argue from plain facts. Here is no sophistry, no construction, no false glosses, but simple inferences from the obvious operation of things. We did not come here to carry points. If the gentleman will convince me I am wrong, I will submit. I mean to give my ideas frankly upon the subject. If my reasoning is not good, let them show me the folly of it. It is from this reciprocal interchange of ideas that the truth must come out. My earnest wish is, that we may go home attended with the pleasing consciousness that we have industriously and candidly sought the truth, and have done our duty. I cannot conclude without repeating that, though I prefer a large representation, yet, considering our present situation, I see abundant reason to acquiesce in the wisdom of the general Convention, and to rest satisfied that the representation will increase in a sufficient degree to answer the wishes of the most zealous advocate for liberty.

SPEECH BEFORE THE NEW YORK RATIFYING CONVENTION BY ALEXANDER HAMILTON

Editor's Introduction:

This speech almost led to a duel. Hamilton spent a considerable amount of time defending the powers of the States. This was logical. Opponents of the document had made great strides in getting a large percentage of the people of New York to believe that the Constitution would destroy the States. Hamilton had to respond and refute the charge, even if he did not necessarily believe it. He explained that the "leading objects" of the federal government were commerce and defense, a position echoed by nearly every proponent of the Constitution from New Hampshire to Georgia. While he argued that the powers of the government were "numerous, extensive, and important," he insisted that they were never intended to either annihilate the States or exceed the limits proscribed by the Constitution. He labeled the States the constituent members of the Union, and said, "The blow aimed at the members must give a fatal wound to the head; and the destruction of the states must be at once a political suicide." This was Hamilton's most "State's Rights" speech during the ratification period.

John Lansing thought Hamilton was lying. He recalled Hamilton's June 1787 speech before the Philadelphia Convention where he labeled the States mere corporate entities of the central authority. This made the States the creature of the general government. Hamilton denied that he said it, so Lansing called on Robert Yates to produce his notes. Yates generally agreed with Hamilton, though the evidence clearly showed that Hamilton did call for the reduction of the States to mere "corporate powers." Lansing decline to pursue the matter and the Convention adjourned for the day.

Speech Before the New York Ratifying Convention
June 27, 1788
By Alexander Hamilton of New York

The Hon. Mr. HAMILTON. This is one of those subjects, Mr. Chairman, on which objections very naturally arise, and assume the most plausible shape. Its address is to the passions, and its first impressions create a prejudice, before cool examination has an opportunity for exertion. It is more easy for the human mind to calculate the evils than the advantages of a measure; and vastly more natural to apprehend the danger than to see the necessity of giving powers to our rulers. Hence I may justly expect that those who hear me will place less confidence in those arguments which oppose, than in those which favor, their prepossessions.

After all our doubts, our suspicions, and speculations, on the subject of government, we must return at last to this important truth — that, when we have formed a constitution upon free principles, when we have given a proper balance to the different branches of administration, and fixed representation upon pure and equal principles, we may, with safety, furnish it with all the powers necessary to answer, in the most ample manner, the purposes of government. The great desiderata are, free representation and mutual checks. When these are obtained, all our apprehensions of the extent of power are unjust and imaginary. What, then, is the structure of this Constitution? One branch of the legislature is to be elected by the people — by the same people who choose your state representatives. Its members are to hold their offices two years, and then return to their constituents. Here, sir, the people govern; here they act by their immediate representatives. You have also a Senate, constituted by your state legislatures, by men in whom you place the highest confidence, and forming another representative branch. Then, again, you have an executive magistrate, created by a form of election which merits universal admiration. In the form of this government, and in the mode of legislation, you find all the checks which the greatest politicians and the best writers have ever conceived. What more can reasonable men desire? Is there any one branch in which the whole legislative and executive powers are lodged? No. The legislative authority is lodged in three distinct branches, properly balanced; the executive is divided between two branches; and the judicial is still reserved for an independent body, who hold their office during good behavior. This organization is so complex, so skilfully contrived, that it is next to impossible that an impolitic or wicked measure should pass the scrutiny with success. Now, what do gentlemen mean by coming forward and declaiming against this government? Why do they say we ought to limit its power, to disable it, and to destroy its capacity of blessing the people? Has philosophy suggested, has experience taught, that such a government ought not to be trusted with every thing necessary for the good of society? Sir, when you have divided and nicely balanced the departments of government; when you have strongly connected the virtue of your rulers with their interest; when, in short, you have rendered your system as perfect as human forms can be, — you must place confidence; you must give power.

We have heard a great deal of the sword and the purse. It is said our liberties are in danger, if both are possessed by Congress. Let us see what is the true meaning of this maxim, which has been so much used, and so little understood. It is, that you shall not place these powers either in the legislative or executive, singly; neither one nor the other shall have both, because this would destroy that division of powers on which political liberty is founded, and would furnish one body with all the means of tyranny. But where the purse is lodged in one branch, and the sword in another, there can be no danger. All governments have possessed these powers: they would be monsters without them, and incapable of exertion. What is your state government? Does not your legislature command what money it pleases? Does not your executive execute the laws without restraint? These distinctions between the purse and the sword have no application to the system, but only to its separate branches. Sir, when we reason about the great interests of a free people, it is high time that we dismiss our prejudices, and banish declamation. In order to induce us to consider the powers given by this Constitution as dangerous, in order to render plausible an attempt to take away the life and spirit of the most important power in government, the gentleman complains that we shall not have a true and safe representation. I asked him what a safe representation was; and he has given no satisfactory answer. The Assembly of New York has been mentioned as a proper standard; but if we apply this standard to the general government, our Congress will become a mere mob, exposed to every irregular impulse, and subject to every breeze of faction. Can such a system afford security? Can you have confidence in such a body? The idea of taking the ratio of representation, in a small society, for the ratio of a great one, is a fallacy which ought to be exposed. It is impossible to ascertain to what point our representation will increase; it may vary from one, to two, three, or four hundred: it depends upon the progress of population. Suppose it to rest at two hundred; is not this number sufficient to secure it against corruption? Human nature must be a much more weak and despicable thing than I apprehend it to be, if two hundred of our fellow-citizens can be corrupted in two years. But suppose they are corrupted; can they, in two years, accomplish their designs? Can they form a combination, and even lay a foundation for a system of tyranny, in so short a period? It is far from my intention to wound the feelings of any gentleman; but I must, in this most interesting discussion, speak of things as they are, and hold up opinions in the light in which they ought to appear; and I maintain that all that has been said of corruption, of the purse and the sword, and of the danger of giving powers, is not supported by principles or fact; that it is mere verbiage and idle declamation. The true principle of government is this — make the system complete in its structure, give a perfect proportion and balance to its parts, and the powers you give it will never affect your security. The question, then, of the division of powers between the general and state governments, is a question of convenience: it becomes a prudential inquiry, what powers are proper to be reserved to the latter; and this immediately involves another inquiry into the proper objects of the two governments. This is the criterion by which we shall determine the just distribution of powers.

The great leading objects of the federal government, in which revenue is concerned, are to maintain domestic peace, and provide for the common defence. In these are comprehended the regulation of commerce, — that is, the whole system of foreign intercourse, — the support of armies and navies, and of the civil administration. It is useless to go into detail. Every one knows that the objects of the general government are numerous, extensive, and important. Every one must acknowledge the necessity of giving powers, in all respects, and in every degree, equal to these objects. This principle assented to, let us inquire what are the objects of the state governments. Have they to provide against foreign invasion? Have they to maintain fleets and armies? Have they any concern in the regulation of commerce, the procuring alliances, or forming treaties of peace? No. Their objects are merely civil and domestic — to support the legislative establishment, and to provide for the administration of the laws.

Let any one compare the expense of supporting the civil list in a state with the expense of providing for the defence of the Union. The difference is almost beyond calculation. The experience of Great Britain will throw some light on this subject. In that kingdom, the ordinary expenses of peace to those of war are as one to fourteen. But there they have a monarch, with his splendid court, and an enormous civil establishment, with which we have nothing in this country to compare. If, in Great Britain, the expenses of war and peace are so disproportioned, how wide will be their disparity in the United States! How infinitely wider between the general government and each individual state! Now, sir, where ought the great resources to be lodged? Every rational man will give an immediate answer. To what extent shall these resources be possessed? Reason says, As far as possible exigencies can require; that is, without limitation. A constitution cannot set bounds to a nation's wants; it ought not, therefore, to set bounds to its resources. Unexpected invasions, long and ruinous wars, may demand all the possible abilities of the country. Shall not your government have power to call these abilities into action? The contingencies of society are not reducible to calculations. They cannot be fixed or bounded, even in imagination. Will you limit the means of your defence, when you cannot ascertain the force or extent of the invasion? Even in ordinary wars, a government is frequently obliged to call for supplies, to the temporary oppression of the people.

Sir, if we adopt the idea of exclusive revenues, we shall be obliged to fix some distinguished line, which neither government shall overpass. The inconvenience of this measure must appear evident on the slightest examination. The resources appropriated to one may diminish or fail, while those of the other may increase beyond the wants of government. One may be destitute of revenues, while the other shall possess an unnecessary abundance; and the Constitution will be an eternal barrier to a mutual intercourse and relief. In this case, will the individual state stand on so good a ground as if the objects of taxation were left free and open to the embrace of both the governments? Possibly, in the advancement of commerce, the imposts may increase to such a degree as to render direct taxes unnecessary. These resources, then, as the Constitution stands, may be occasionally relinquished to the states; but on the gentleman's idea of prescribing exclusive limits, and precluding all reciprocal communication, this would be entirely improper. The laws of the states must not touch the appropriated resources of the United States, whatever may be their wants. Would it not be of much more advantage to the states to have a concurrent jurisdiction, extending to all the sources of revenue, than to be confined to such a small resource, as, on calculation of the objects of the two governments, should appear to be their due proportion? Certainly you cannot hesitate on this question. The gentleman's plan would have a further ill effect; it would tend to dissolve the connection and correspondence of the two governments, to estrange them from each other, and to destroy that mutual dependence which forms the essence of union.

Sir, a number of arguments have been advanced by an honorable member from New York, which to every unclouded mind must carry conviction. He has stated that, in certain emergencies, it may be necessary to borrow; and that it is impossible to borrow, unless you have funds to pledge for the payment of your debts. Limiting the powers of government to certain resources, is rendering the fund precarious; and obliging the government to ask, instead of empowering them to command, is to destroy all confidence and credit. If the power of taxing is restricted, the consequence is, that, on the breaking out of a war, you must divert the funds, appropriated to the payment of debts, to answer immediate exigencies. Thus you violate your engagements, at the very time you increase the burden of them. Besides, sound policy condemns the practice of accumulating debts. A government, to act with energy, should have the possession of all its revenues to answer present purposes. The principle for which I contend is recognized in all its extent by our old constitution. Congress is authorized to raise troops, to call for supplies without limitation, and to borrow money to any amount. It is true they must use the form of recommendations and requisitions; but the states are bound by the solemn ties of honor, of justice, of religion, to comply without reserve.

Mr. Chairman, it has been advanced as a principle, that no government but a despotism can exist in a very extensive country. This is a melancholy consideration indeed. If it were founded on truth, we ought to dismiss the idea of a republican government, even for the state of New York. This idea has been taken from a celebrated writer, who, by being misunderstood, has been the occasion of frequent fallacies in our reasoning on political subjects. But the position has been misapprehended; and its application is entirely false and unwarrantable: it relates only to democracies, where the whole body of the people meet to transact business, and where representation is unknown. Such were a number of ancient and some modern independent cities. Men who read without attention have taken these maxims respecting the extent of country, and, contrary to their meaning, have applied them to republics in general. This application is wrong in respect to all representative governments, but especially in relation to a confederacy of states, in which the supreme legislature has only general powers, and the civil and domestic concerns of the people are regulated by the laws of the several states. This distinction being kept in view, all the difficulty will vanish, and we may easily conceive that the people of a large country may be represented as truly as those of a small one. An assembly constituted for general purposes may be fully competent to every federal regulation, without being too numerous for deliberate conduct. If the state governments were to be abolished, the question would wear a different face; but this idea is inadmissible. They are absolutely necessary to the system. Their existence must form a leading principle in the most perfect constitution we could form.

I insist that it never can be the interest or desire of the national legislature to destroy the state governments. It can derive no advantage from such an event; but, on the contrary, would lose an indispensable support, a necessary aid in executing the laws, and conveying the influence of government to the doors of the people. The Union is dependent on the will of the state governments for its chief magistrate, and for its Senate. The blow aimed at the members must give a fatal wound to the head; and the destruction of the states must be at once a political suicide. Can the national government be guilty of this madness? What inducements, what temptations, can they have? Will they attach new honors to their station? Will they increase the national strength? Will they multiply the national resources? Will they make themselves more respectable in the view of foreign nations, or of their fellow-citizens, by robbing the states of their constitutional privileges? But imagine, for a moment, that a political frenzy should seize the government; suppose they should make the attempt. Certainly, sir, it would be forever impracticable. This has been sufficiently demonstrated by reason and experience. It has been proved that the members of republics have been, and ever will be, stronger than the head. Let us attend to one general historical example: in the ancient feudal governments of Europe, there were, in the first place, a monarch; subordinate to him, a body of nobles; and subject to these, the vassals, or the whole body of the people. The authority of the kings was limited, and that of the barons considerably independent. A great part of the early wars in Europe were contests between the king and his nobility. In these contests, the latter possessed many advantages derived from their influence, and the immediate command they had over the people; and they generally prevailed. The history of the feudal wars exhibits little more than a series of successful encroachments on the prerogatives of monarchy. Here, sir, is one great proof of the superiority which the members in limited governments possess over their head. As long as the barons enjoyed the confidence and attachment of the people, they had the strength of the country on their side, and were irresistible. I may be told that, in some instances, the barons were overcome; but how did this happen? Sir, they took advantage of the depression of the royal authority, and the establishment of their own power, to oppress and tyrannize over the vassals. As commerce enlarged, and as wealth and civilization increased, the people began to feel their own weight and consequence: they grew tired of their oppressions, united their strength with that of the prince, and threw off the yoke of aristocracy. These very instances prove what I contend for. They prove that in whatever direction the popular weight leans, the current of power will flow; wherever the popular attachments lie, there will rest the political superiority. Sir, can it be supposed that the state will become the oppressors of the people? Will they forfeit their affections? Will they combine to destroy the liberties and happiness of their fellow-citizens, for the sole purpose of involving themselves in ruin? God forbid! The idea, sir, is shocking. It outrages every feeling of humanity, and every dictate of common sense.

There are certain social principles in human nature, from which we may draw the most solid conclusion with respect to the conduct of individuals and of communities. We love our families more than our neighbors; we love our neighbors more than our countrymen in general. The human affections, like the solar heat, lose their intensity as they depart from the centre, and become languid in proportion to the expansion of the circle in which they act. On these principles, the attachment of the individual will be first and forever secured by the state governments: they will be a mutual protection and support. Another source of influence, which has already been pointed out, is the various official connections in the states. Gentlemen endeavor to evade the force of this by saying that these officers will be insignificant. This is by no means true. The state officers will ever be important, because they are necessary and useful. Their powers are such as are extremely interesting among the people; such as affect their property, their liberty, and life. What is more important than the administration of justice and the execution of the civil and criminal laws? Can the state governments become insignificant while they have the power of raising money independently, and without control? If they are really useful, if they are calculated to promote the essential interests of the people, they must have their confidence and support. The states can never lose their powers till the whole people of America are robbed of their liberties. These must go together; they must support each other, or meet one common fate. On the gentleman's principle we may safely trust the state governments, though we have no means of resisting them; but we cannot confide in the national government, though we have an effectual constitutional guard against every encroachment.

This is the essence of their argument, and it is false and fallacious beyond conception.

With regard to the jurisdiction of the two governments, I shall certainly admit that the Constitution ought to be so formed as not to prevent the states from providing for their own existence; and I maintain that it is so formed, and that their power of providing for themselves is sufficiently established. This is conceded by one gentleman, and in the next breath the concession is retracted. He says, Congress have but one exclusive right in taxation — that of duties on imports; certainly, then, their other powers are only concurrent. But, to take off the force of this obvious conclusion, he immediately says that the laws of the United States are supreme; and that where there is one supreme, there cannot be concurrent authority; and further, that where the laws of the Union are supreme, those of the states must be subordinate, because there cannot be two supremes. This is curious sophistry. That two supreme powers cannot act together, is false. They are inconsistent only when they are aimed at each other, or at one indivisible object. The laws of the United States are supreme, as to all their proper, constitutional objects: the laws of the states are supreme in the same way. These supreme laws may act on different objects without clashing, or they may operate on different parts of the same object, with perfect harmony. Suppose both governments should lay a tax of a penny on a certain article: had not each an independent and uncontrollable power to collect its own tax? The meaning of the maxim, there cannot be two supremes, is simply this — two powers cannot be supreme over each other. This meaning is entirely perverted by the gentleman. But it is said, disputes between collectors are to be referred to the federal courts. This is again wandering in the field of conjecture. But suppose the fact certain; is it not to be presumed that they will express the true meaning of the Constitution and the laws?

Will they not be bound to consider the concurrent jurisdiction; to declare that both the taxes shall have equal operation; that both the powers, in that respect, are sovereign and coextensive? If they transgress their duty, we are to hope that they will be punished. Sir, we can reason from probabilities alone. When we leave common sense, and give ourselves up to conjecture, there can be no certainty, no security in our reasonings.

I imagine I have stated to the committee abundant reasons to prove the entire safety of the state governments and of the people. I would go into a more minute consideration of the nature of the concurrent jurisdiction, and the operation of the laws, in relation to revenue; but at present I feel too much indisposed to proceed. I shall, with the leave of the committee, improve another opportunity of expressing to them more fully my ideas on this point. I wish the committee to remember that the Constitution under examination is framed upon truly republican principles; and that, as it is expressly designed to provide for the common protection and the general welfare of the United States, it must be utterly repugnant to this Constitution to subvert the state governments, or oppress the people.

Speech Before the North Carolina Ratifying Convention by William Richardson Davie

Editor's Introduction:

William Richardson Davie personified the conservative Southern gentleman. His parents emigrated to the United States from Great Britain when Davie was around eight and settled in the up-country of South Carolina. His parents sent him to the College of New Jersey for a university education, and Davie was graduated in 1776. He immediately joined the cause for independence and quickly earned a fine reputation as an "unorthodox" frontier partisan leader. His name was mentioned with such heroes as Francis Marion and Thomas Sumter of South Carolina. Davie was wounded in 1779, and while convalescing he studied law. He rejoined the war effort in 1780, this time as a regular in the Continental Army as Nathanael Greene's commissary general.

He married into the politically powerful Jones family after the war—his uncle by marriage was the arch anti-federalist Willie Jones—and became a planter. He loved horse racing, politics, and education. Davie, in fact, owned one of the most celebrated thoroughbreds in the history of the sport, Sir Archie, where he put him to stud. Davie also helped found the University of North Carolina.

He served as a diplomat to France and as Governor of North Carolina, but he spent most of his life engaged as a planter and attorney. Davie attended the Philadelphia Convention but was home on business and did not sign the document. He fervently supported ratification and proposed the final resolution for North Carolina's ratification in 1789. In 1788, however, opponents of the document outnumber supporters, and so Davie, along with James Iredell and Archibald Maclaine, did their best to defend the document in the hostile Hillsborough Convention. His July 24 speech explained the defects of the Articles of Confederation, the purposes of a central government for the Union, and the necessity of a true federal republic with enhanced powers. Davie emphasized during this speech that, "the state governments are the pillars upon which this government is extended over such an immense territory, and are essential to its existence." He believed it, as did most of the honest proponents of the Constitution.

Speech Before the North Carolina Ratifying Convention
July 24, 1788
By William Richardson Davie of North Carolina

Mr. DAVIE. Mr. Chairman, the observation of the reverend gentleman is grounded, I suppose, on a supposition that the Federal Convention exceeded their powers. This objection has been industriously circulated; but I believe, on a candid examination, the prejudice on which this error is founded will be done away. As I had the honor, sir, to be a member of the Convention, it may be expected I would answer an objection personal in its nature, and which contains rather a reflection on our conduct, than an objection to the merits of the Constitution. After repeated and decisive proofs of the total inefficiency of our general government, the states deputed the members of the Convention to revise and strengthen it. And permit me to call to your consideration that, whatever form of confederate government they might devise, or whatever powers they might propose to give this new government, no part of it was binding until the whole Constitution had received the solemn assent of the people. What was the object of our mission? "To decide upon the most effectual means of removing the defects of our federal union." This is a general, discretional authority to propose any alteration they thought proper or necessary. Were not the state legislatures afterwards to review our proceedings? Is it not immediately through their recommendation that the plan of the Convention is submitted to the people? And this plan must still remain a dead letter, or receive its operation from the fiat of this Convention. Although the Federal Convention might recommend the concession of the most extensive powers, yet they could not put one of them into execution. What have the Convention done that can merit this species of censure? They have only recommended a plan of government containing some additional powers to those enjoyed under the present feeble system; amendments not only necessary, but which were the express object of the deputation. When we investigate this system candidly and accurately, and compare all its parts with one another, we shall find it absolutely necessary to confirm these powers, in order to secure the tranquillity of the states and the liberty of the people. Perhaps it would be necessary, to form a true judgment of this important question, to state some events, and develop some of those defects, which gave birth to the late Convention, and which have produced this revolution in our federal government. With the indulgence of the committee, I will attempt this detail with as much precision as I am capable of. The general objects of the union are, 1st, to protect us against foreign invasion; 2d, to defend us against internal commotions and insurrections; 3d, to promote the commerce, agriculture, and manufactures, of America. These objects are requisite to make us a safe and happy people, and they cannot be attained without a firm and efficient system of union.

As to the first, we cannot obtain any effectual protection from the present Confederation. It is indeed universally acknowledged, that its inadequacy in this case is one of its greatest defects. Examine its ability to repel invasion. In the late glorious war, its weakness was unequivocally experienced. It is well known that Congress had a discretionary right to raise men and money; but they had no power to do either. In order to preclude the necessity of examining the whole progress of its imbecility, permit me to call to your recollection one single instance. When the last great stroke was made which humbled the pride of Britain, and put us in possession of peace and independence, so low were the finances and credit of the United States, that our army could not move from Philadelphia, until the minister of his most Christian majesty was prevailed upon to draw bills to defray the expense of the expedition. These were not obtained on the credit or interest of Congress, but by the personal influence of the commander-in-chief.

Had this great project miscarried, what fatal events might have ensued! It is a very moderate presumption, that what has once happened may happen again. The next important consideration, which is involved in the external powers of the Union, are treaties. Without a power in the federal government to compel the performance of our engagements with foreign nations, we shall be perpetually involved in destructive wars. The Confederation is extremely defective in this point also. I shall only mention the British treaty as a satisfactory proof of this melancholy fact. It is well known that, although this treaty was ratified in 1784, it required the sanction of a law of North Carolina in 1787; and that our enemies, presuming on the weakness of our federal government, have refused to deliver up several important posts within the territories of the United States, and still hold them, to our shame and disgrace. It is unnecessary to reason on facts, the perilous consequences of which must in a moment strike every mind capable of reflection.

The next head under which the general government may be considered, is the regulation of commerce. The United States should be empowered to compel foreign nations into commercial regulations that were either founded on the principles of justice or reciprocal advantages. Has the present Confederation effected any of these things? Is not our commerce equally unprotected abroad by arms and negotiation? Nations have refused to enter into treaties with us. What was the language of the British court on a proposition of this kind? Such as would insult the pride of any man of feeling and independence. — "You can make engagements, but you cannot compel your citizens to comply with them. We derive greater profits from the present situation of your commerce than we could expect under a treaty; and you have no kind of power that can compel us to surrender any advantage to you." This was the language of our enemies; and while our government remains as feeble as it has been, no nation will form any connection with us that will involve the relinquishment of the least advantage. What has been the consequence? A general decay of trade, the rise of imported merchandise, the fall of produce, and an uncommon decrease of the value of lands. Foreigners have been reaping the benefits and emoluments which our citizens ought to enjoy. An unjustifiable perversion of justice has pervaded almost all the states, and every thing presented to our view a spectacle of public poverty and private wretchedness!

While this is a true representation of our situation, can our general government recur to the ordinary expedient of loans? During the late war, large sums were advanced to us by foreign states and individuals. Congress have not been enabled to pay even the interest of these debts, with honor and punctuality. The requisitions made on the states have been every where unproductive, and some of them have not paid a stiver. These debts are a part of the price of our liberty and independence — debts which ought to be regarded with gratitude and discharged with honor. Yet many of the individuals who lent us money in the hour of our distress, are now reduced to indigence in consequence of our delinquency. So low and hopeless are the finances of the United States, that, the year before last. Congress were obliged to borrow money even to pay the interest of the principal which we had borrowed before. This wretched resource of turning interest into principal, is the most humiliating and disgraceful measure that a nation could take, and approximates with rapidity to absolute ruin. Yet it is the inevitable and certain consequence of such a system as the existing Confederation.

There are several other instances of imbecility in that system. It cannot secure to us the enjoyment of our own territories, or even the navigation of our own rivers. The want of power to establish a uniform rule for naturalization through the United States is also no small defect, as it must unavoidably be productive of disagreeable controversies with foreign nations. The general government ought in this, as in every other instance, to possess the means of preserving the peace and tranquillity of the Union. A striking proof of the necessity of this power recently happened in Rhode Island: A man who had run off with a vessel and cargo, the property of some merchants in Holland, took sanctuary in that place: application was made for him as a citizen of the United Netherlands by the minister, but, as he had taken the oath of allegiance, the state refused to deliver him up, and protected him in his villany. Had it not been for the peculiar situation of the states at that time, fatal consequences might have resulted from such a conduct, and the contemptible state of Rhode Island might have involved the whole Union in a war.

The encroachments of some states on the rights of others, and of all on those of the Confederacy, are incontestable proofs of the weakness and imperfection of that system. Maryland lately passed a law granting exclusive privileges to her own vessels, contrary to the Articles of the Confederation. Congress had neither power nor influence to alter it; all they could do was to send a contrary recommendation. It is provided, by the 6th Article of the Confederation, that no compact shall be made between two or more states without the consent of Congress; yet this has been recently violated by Virginia and Maryland, and also by Pennsylvania and New Jersey. North Carolina and Massachusetts have had a considerable body of forces on foot, and those in this state raised for two years, notwithstanding the express provision in the Confederation that no force should be kept up by any state in time of peace.

As to internal tranquillity, — without dwelling on the unhappy commotions in our own back counties, — I will only add that, if the rebellion in Massachusetts had been planned and executed with any kind of ability, that state must have been ruined; for Congress were not in a situation to render them any assistance.

Another object of the federal union is, to promote the agriculture and manufactures of the states — objects in which we are so nearly concerned. Commerce, sir, is the nurse of both. The merchant furnishes the planter with such articles as he cannot manufacture himself, and finds him a market for his produce. Agriculture cannot flourish if commerce languishes; they are mutually dependent on each other.

Our commerce, as I have before observed, is unprotected abroad, and without regulation at home, and in this and many of the states ruined by partial and iniquitous laws — laws which, instead of having a tendency to protect property and encourage industry, led to the depreciation of the one, and destroyed every incitement to the other — laws which basely warranted and legalized the payment of just debts by paper, which represents nothing, or property of very trivial value.

These are some of the leading causes which brought forward this new Constitution. It was evidently necessary to infuse a greater portion of strength into the national government. But Congress were but a single body, with whom it was dangerous to lodge additional powers. Hence arose the necessity of a different organization. In order to form some balance, the departments of government were separated, and as a necessary check, the legislative body was composed of two branches. Steadiness and wisdom are better insured when there is a second branch, to balance and check the first. The stability of the laws will be greater when the popular branch, which might be influenced by local views, or the violence of party, is checked by another, whose longer continuance in office will render them more experienced, more temperate, and more competent to decide rightly.

The Confederation derived its sole support from the state legislatures. This rendered it weak and ineffectual. It was therefore necessary that the foundations of this government should be laid on the broad basis of the people. Yet the state governments are the pillars upon which this government is extended over such an immense territory, and are essential to its existence. The House of Representatives are immediately elected by the people. The senators represent the sovereignty of the states; they are directly chosen by the state legislatures, and no legislative act can be done without their concurrence. The election of the executive is in some measure under the control of the legislatures of the states, the electors being appointed under their direction.

The difference, in point of magnitude and importance, in the members of the confederacy, was an additional reason for the division of the legislature into two branches, and for establishing an equality of suffrage in the Senate. The protection of the small states against the ambition and influence of the larger members, could only be effected by arming them with an equal power in one branch of the legislature. On a contemplation of this matter, we shall find that the jealousies of the states could not be reconciled any other way. The lesser states would never have concurred unless this check had been given them, as a security for their political existence, against the power and encroachments of the great states. It may be also proper to observe, that the executive is separated in its functions from the legislature, as well as the nature of the case would admit, and the judiciary from both.

Another radical vice in the old system, which was necessary to be corrected, and which will be understood without a long deduction of reasoning, was, that it legislated on states, instead of individuals; and that its powers could not be executed but by fire or by the sword — by military force, and not by the intervention of the civil magistrate. Every one who is acquainted with the relative situation of the states, and the genius of our citizens, must acknowledge that, if the government was to be carried into effect by military force, the most dreadful consequences would ensue. It would render the citizens of America the most implacable enemies to one another. If it could be carried into effect against the small states, yet it could not be put in force against the larger and more powerful states. It was therefore absolutely necessary that the influence of the magistrate should be introduced, and that the laws should be carried home to individuals themselves.

In the formation of this system, many difficulties presented themselves to the Convention.

Every member saw that the existing system would ever be ineffectual, unless its laws operated on individuals, as military coercion was neither eligible nor practicable. Their own experience was fortified by their knowledge of the inherent weakness of all confederate governments. They knew that all governments merely federal had been short lived, or had existed from principles extraneous from their constitutions, or from external causes which had no dependence on the nature of their governments. These considerations determined the Convention to depart from that solecism in politics — the principle of legislation for states in their political capacities.

The great extent of country appeared to some a formidable difficulty; but a confederate government appears, at least in theory, capable of embracing the various interests of the most extensive territory. Founded on the state governments solely, as I have said before, it would be tottering and inefficient. It became, therefore, necessary to bottom it on the people themselves, by giving them an immediate interest and agency in the government. There was, however, some real difficulty in conciliating a number of jarring interests, arising from the incidental but unalterable difference in the states in point of territory, situation, climate, and rivalship in commerce. Some of the states are very extensive, others very limited: some are manufacturing states, others merely agricultural: some of these are exporting states, while the carrying and navigation business are in the possession of others. It was not easy to reconcile such a multiplicity of discordant and clashing interests. Mutual concessions were necessary to come to any concurrence. A plan that would promote the exclusive interests of a few states would be inturious to others. Had each state obstinately insisted on the security of its particular local advantages, we should never have come to a conclusion. Each, therefore, amicably and wisely relinquished its particular views. The Federal Convention have told you, that the Constitution which they formed "was the result of a spirit of amity, and of that mutual deference and concession which the peculiarity of their political situation rendered indispensable." I hope the same laudable spirit will govern this Convention in their decision on this important question.

The business of the Convention was to amend the Confederation by giving it additional powers. The present form of Congress being a single body, it was thought unsafe to augment its powers, without altering its organization. The act of the Convention is but a mere proposal, similar to the production of a private pen. I think it a government which, if adopted, will cherish and protect the happiness and liberty of America; but I hold my mind open to conviction. I am ready to recede from my opinion if it be proved to be ill-founded. I trust that every man here is equally ready to change an opinion he may have improperly formed. The weakness and inefficiency of the old Confederation produced the necessity of calling the Federal Convention. Their plan is now before you; and I hope, on a deliberate consideration, every man will see the necessity of such a system. It has been the subject of much jealousy and censure out of doors. I hope gentlemen will now come forward with their objections, and that they will be thrown out and answered with candor and moderation.

Speeches Before the North Carolina Ratifying Convention by James Iredell

Editor's Introduction:

James Iredell focused most of his July 25 speech on the importance of the Senate. He had elaborated on other topics in the Marcus essays, but in this speech, Iredell explained the benefits and powers of the Senate in more detail. In short, Iredell considered the Senate as the key component of the Constitution. It was to be the check on every branch in the government, and as the representatives of the States, the Senate protected the federal nature of the general government. He did not, however, lose sight of the fact that the House of Representatives also relied on the States for its existence. As the members of the House were to be chosen in the same manner of the "most numerous branch of the state legislature," if you abolish the States, you abolished the general government. This was a popular argument for ratification in several States.

Speeches Before the North Carolina Ratifying Convention

July 25, 1788

By James Iredell of North Carolina

Mr. IREDELL. Mr. Chairman, I have waited for some time in hopes that a gentleman better qualified than myself would explain this part. Every objection to every part of this Constitution ought to be answered as fully as possible.

I believe, sir, it was the general sense of all America, with the exception only of one state, in forming their own state constitutions, that the legislative body should be divided into two branches, in order that the people might have a double security. It will often happen that, in a single body, a bare majority will carry exceptionable and pernicious measures. The violent faction of a party may often form such a majority in a single body, and by that means the particular views or interests of a part of the community may be consulted, and those of the rest neglected or injured. Is there a single gentleman in this Convention, who has been a member of the legislature, who has not found the minority in the most important questions to be often right? Is there a man here, who has been in either house, who has not at some times found the most solid advantages from the cooperation or opposition of the other? If a measure be right, which has been approved of by one branch, the other will probably confirm it; if it be wrong, it is fortunate that there is another branch to oppose or amend it. These principles probably formed one reason for the institution of a Senate, in the form of government before us. Another arose from the peculiar nature of that government, as connected with the government of the particular states.

The general government will have the protection and management of the general interests of the United States. The local and particular interests of the different states are left to their respective legislatures. All affairs which concern this state only are to be determined by our representatives coming from all parts of the state; all affairs which concern the Union at large are to be determined by representatives coming from all parts of the Union. Thus, then, the general government is to be taken care of, and the state governments to be preserved. The former is done by a numerous representation of the people of each state, in proportion to its importance. The latter is effected by giving each state an equal representation in the Senate. The people will be represented in one house, the state legislatures in the other.

Many are of the opinion that the power of the Senate is too great; but I cannot think so, considering the great weight which the House of Representatives will have. Several reasons may be assigned for this. The House of Representatives will be more numerous than the Senate. They will represent the immediate interests of the people. They will originate all money bills, which is one of the greatest securities in any republican government. The respectability of their constituents, who are the free citizens of America, will add great weight to the representatives; for a power derived from the people is the source of all real honor, and a demonstration of confidence which a man of any feeling would be more ambitious to possess, than any other honor or any emolument whatever. There is, therefore, always a danger of such a house becoming too powerful, and it is necessary to counteract its influence by giving great weight and authority to the other. I am warranted by well-known facts in my opinion that the representatives of the people at large will have more weight than we should be induced to believe from a slight consideration.

The British government furnishes a very remarkable instance to my present purpose. In that country, sir, is a king, who is hereditary — a man, who is not chosen for his abilities, but who, though he may be without principles or abilities, is by birth their sovereign, and may impart the vices of his character to the government. His influence and power are so great, that the people would bear a great deal before they would attempt to resist his authority. He is one complete branch of the legislature — may make as many peers as he pleases, who are immediately members of another branch; he has the disposal of almost all offices in the kingdom, commands the army and navy, is head of the church, and has the means of corrupting a large proportion of the representatives of the people, who form the third branch of the legislature. The House of Peers, which forms the second branch, is composed of members who are hereditary, and, except as to money bills, (which they are not allowed either to originate or alter,) hath equal authority with the other house. The members of the House of Commons, who are considered to represent the people, are elected for seven years, and they are chosen by a small proportion of the people, and, I believe I may say, a large majority of them by actual corruption. Under these circumstances, one would suppose their influence, compared to that of the king and the lords, was very inconsiderable. But the fact is, that they have, by degrees, increased their power to an astonishing degree, and, when they think proper to exert it, can command almost any thing they please. This great power they enjoy, by having the name of representatives of the people, and the exclusive right of originating money bills. What authority, then, will our representatives not possess, who will really represent the people, and equally have the right of originating money bills?

The manner in which our Senate is to be chosen gives us an additional security. Our senators will not be chosen by a king, nor tainted by his influence. They are to be chosen by different legislatures in the Union. Each is to choose two. It is to be supposed that, in the exercise of this power, the utmost prudence and circumspection will be observed. We may presume that they will select two of the most respectable men in the state, two men who had given the strongest proofs of attachment to the interests of their country. The senators are not to hold estates for life in the legislature, nor to transmit them to their children. Their families, friends, and estates, will be pledges for their fidelity to their country. Holding no office under the United States, they will be under no temptation of that kind to forget the interest of their constituents. There is every probability that men elected in this manner will, in general, do their duty faithfully. It may be expected, therefore, that they will cooperate in every laudable act, but strenuously resist those of a contrary nature. To do this to effect, their station must have some permanency annexed to it.

As the representatives of the people may probably be more popular, and it may be sometimes necessary for the Senate to prevent factious measures taking place, which may be highly injurious to the real interests of the public, the Senate should not be at the mercy of every popular clamor. Men engaged in arduous affairs are often obliged to do things which may, for the present, be disapproved of, for want of full information of the case, which it is not in every man's power immediately to obtain. In the mean time, every one is eager to judge, and many to condemn; and thus many an action is for a time unpopular, the true policy and justice of which afterwards very plainly appear. These observations apply even to acts of legislation concerning domestic policy: they apply much more forcibly to the case of foreign negotiations, which will form one part of the business of the Senate. I hope we shall not be involved in the labyrinths of foreign politics. But it is necessary for us to watch the conduct of European powers, that we may be on our defence and ready in case of an attack. All these things will require a continued attention; and, in order to know whether they were transacted rightly or not, it must take up a considerable time.

A certain permanency in office is, in my opinion, useful for another reason. Nothing is more unfortunate for a nation than to have its affairs conducted in an irregular manner. Consistency and stability are necessary to render the laws of any society convenient for the people.

If they were to be entirely conducted by men liable to be called away soon, we might be deprived, in a great measure, of their utility; their measures might be abandoned before they were fully executed, and others, of a less beneficial tendency, substituted in their stead. The public also would be deprived of that experience which adds so much weight to the greatest abilities.

The business of a senator will require a great deal of knowledge, and more extensive information than can be acquired in a short time. This can be made evident by facts well known. I doubt not the gentlemen of this house, who have been members of Congress, will acknowledge that they have known several instances of men who were members of Congress, and were there many months before they knew how to act, for want of information of the real state of the Union. The acquisition of full information of this kind must employ a great deal of time; since a general knowledge of the affairs of all the states, and of the relative situation of foreign nations, would be indispensable. Responsibility, also, would be lessened by a short duration; for many useful measures require a good deal of time, and continued operations, and no man should be answerable for the ill success of a scheme which was taken out of his hands by others.

For these reasons, I hope it will appear that six years are not too long a duration for the Senate. I hope, also, it will be thought that, so far from being injurious to the liberties and interest of the public, it will form an additional security to both, especially when the next clause is taken up, by which we shall see that one third of the Senate is to go out every second year, and two thirds must concur in the most important cases; so that, if there be only one honest man among the two thirds that remain, added to the one third which has recently come in, this will be sufficient to prevent the rights of the people being sacrificed to any unjust ambition of that body.

I was in hopes some other gentleman would have explained this paragraph, because it introduces an entire change in our system; and every change ought to be founded on good reasons, and those reasons made plain to the people. Had my abilities been greater, I should have answered the objection better. I have, however, done it in the best manner in my power, and I hope the reasons I have assigned will be satisfactory to the committee.

****

Mr. IREDELL. Mr. Chairman, I am glad to see so much candor and moderation. The liberal sentiments expressed by the honorable gentleman who spoke last command my respect. No time can be better employed than in endeavoring to remove, by fair and just reasoning, every objection which can be made to this Constitution. I apprehend that the honorable gentleman is mistaken as to the extent of the operation of this clause. He supposes that the control of the general government over elections looks forward to a consolidation of the states, and that the general word time may extend to twenty, or any number of years. In my humble opinion, this clause does by no means warrant such a construction. We ought to compare other parts with it. Does not the Constitution say that representatives shall be chosen every second year? The right of choosing them, therefore, reverts to the people every second year. No instrument of writing ought to be construed absurdly, when a rational construction can be put upon it. If Congress can prolong the election to any time they please, why is it said that representatives shall be chosen every second year? They must be chosen every second year; but whether in the month of March, or January, or any other month, may be ascertained, at a future time, by regulations of Congress. The word time refers only to the particular month and day within the two years. I heartily agree with the gentleman, that, if any thing in this Constitution tended to the annihilation of the state government, instead of exciting the admiration of any man, it ought to excite the resentment and execration. No such wicked intention ought to be suffered. But the gentlemen who formed the Constitution had no such object; nor do I think there is the least ground for that jealousy. The very existence of the general government depends on that of the state governments. The state legislatures are to choose the senators. Without a Senate there can be no Congress. The state legislatures are also to direct the manner of choosing the President. Unless, therefore, there are state legislatures to direct that manner, no President can be chosen. The same observation may be made as to the House of Representatives, since, as they are to be chosen by the electors of the most numerous branch of each state legislature, if there are no state legislatures, there are no persons to choose the House of Representatives. Thus it is evident that the very existence of the general government depends on that of the state legislatures, and of course, that their continuance cannot be endangered by it.

An occasion may arise when the exercise of this ultimate power in Congress may be necessary; as, for instance, if a state should be involved in war, and its legislature could not assemble, (as was the case of South Carolina, and occasionally of some other states, during the late war;) it might also be useful for this reason — lest a few powerful states should combine, and make regulations concerning elections which might deprive many of the electors of a fair exercise of their rights, and thus injure the community, and occasion great dissatisfaction. And it seems natural and proper that every government should have in itself the means of its own preservation. A few of the great states might combine to prevent any election of representatives at all, and thus a majority might be wanting to do business; but it would not be so easy to destroy the government by the non-election of senators, because one third only are to go out at a time, and all the states will be equally represented in the Senate. It is not probable this power would be abused; for, if it should be, the state legislatures would immediately resent it, and their authority over the people will always be extremely great. These reasons induce me to think that the power is both necessary and useful. But I am sensible great jealousy has been entertained concerning it; and as perhaps the danger of a combination, in the manner I have mentioned, to destroy or distress the general government, is not very probable, it may be better to incur the risk, than occasion any discontent by suffering the clause to continue as it now stands. I should, therefore, not object to the recommendation of an amendment similar to that of other states — that this power in Congress should only be exercised when a state legislature neglected or was disabled from making the regulations required.

Speech Before the North Carolina Ratifying Convention by William Richardson Davie

Editor's Introduction:

This brief speech by William Richardson Davie supported the general argument that the States were an essential component of the general system of government. Davie, in fact, thought that States could withhold their Senators and destroy the general government. He called the States, "the foundation on which this government was raised, and without which it cannot possibly exist." At the same time, he argued that federal control over elections would only be used in extraordinary circumstances but was essential to preserve the general government. He considered this an advantage rather than a defect and maintained that the States were the "massy pillars on which this political fabric was to be extended and supported."

Speech Before the North Carolina Ratifying Convention

July 25, 1788

By William Richardson Davie

Mr. DAVIE. Mr. Chairman, a consolidation of the states is said by some gentlemen to have been intended. They insinuate that this was the cause of their giving this power of elections. If there were any seeds in this Constitution which might, one day, produce a consolidation, it would, sir, with me, be an insuperable objection, I am so perfectly convinced that so extensive a country as this can never be managed by one consolidated government. The Federal Convention were as well convinced as the members of this house, that the state governments were absolutely necessary to the existence of the federal government. They considered them as the great massy pillars on which this political fabric was to be extended and supported; and were fully persuaded that, when they were removed, or should moulder down by time, the general government must tumble into ruin. A very little reflection will show that no department of it can exist without the state governments.

Let us begin with the House of Representatives. Who are to vote for the federal representatives? Those who vote for the state representatives. If the state government vanishes, the general government must vanish also. This is the foundation on which this government was raised, and without which it cannot possibly exist.

The next department is the Senate. How is it formed? By the states themselves. Do they not choose them? Are they not created by them? And will they not have the interest of the states particularly at heart? The states, sir, can put a final period to the government, as was observed by a gentleman who thought this power over elections unnecessary. If the state legislatures think proper, they may refuse to choose senators, and the government must be destroyed.

Is not this government a nerveless mass, a dead carcase, without the executive power? Let your representatives be the most vicious demons that ever existed; let them plot against the liberties of America; let them conspire against its happiness, — all their machinations will not avail if not put in execution. By whom are their laws and projects to be executed? By the President. How is he created? By electors appointed by the people under the direction of the legislatures — by a union of the interest of the people and the state governments. The state governments can put a veto, at any time, on the general government, by ceasing to continue the executive power. Admitting the representatives or senators could make corrupt laws, they can neither execute them themselves, nor appoint the executive. Now, sir, I think it must be clear to every candid mind, that no part of this government can be continued after the state governments lose their existence, or even their present forms. It may also be easily proved that all federal governments possess an inherent weakness, which continually tends to their destruction. It is to be lamented that all governments of a federal nature have been short-lived.

Such was the fate of the Achæan league, the Amphictyonic council, and other ancient confederacies; and this opinion is confirmed by the uniform testimony of all history. There are instances in Europe of confederacies subsisting a considerable time; but their duration must be attributed to circumstances exterior to their government. The Germanic confederacy would not exist a moment, were it not for fear of the surrounding powers, and the interest of the emperor. The history of this confederacy is but a series of factions, dissensions, bloodshed, and civil war. The confederacies of the Swiss, and United Netherlands, would long ago have been destroyed, from their imbecility, had it not been for the fear, and even the policy, of the bordering nations. It is impossible to construct such a government in such a manner as to give it any probable longevity. But, sir, there is an excellent principle in this proposed plan of federal government, which none of these confederacies had, and to the want of which, in a great measure, their imperfections may be justly attributed — I mean the principle of representation. I hope that, by the agency of this principle, if it be not immortal, it will at least be long-lived. I thought it necessary to say this much to detect the futility of that unwarrantable suggestion, that we are to be swallowed up by a great consolidated government. Every part of this federal government is dependent on the constitution of the state legislatures for its existence. The whole, sir, can never swallow up its parts. The gentleman from Edenton (Mr. Iredell) has pointed out the reasons of giving this control over elections to Congress, the principal of which was, to prevent a dissolution of the government by designing states. If all the states were equally possessed of absolute power over their elections, without any control of Congress, danger might be justly apprehended where one state possesses as much territory as four or five others; and some of them, being thinly peopled now, will daily become more numerous and formidable. Without this control in Congress, those large states might successfully combine to destroy the general government. It was therefore necessary to control any combination of this kind.

Another principal reason was, that it would operate, in favor of the people, against the ambitious designs of the federal Senate. I will illustrate this by matter of fact. The history of the little state of Rhode Island is well known. An abandoned faction have seized on the reins of government, and frequently refused to have any representation in Congress. If Congress had the power of making the law of elections operate throughout the United States, no state could withdraw itself from the national councils, without the consent of a majority of the members of Congress. Had this been the case, that trifling state would not have withheld its representation. What once happened may happen again; and it was necessary to give Congress this power, to keep the government in full operation. This being a federal government, and involving the interests of several states, and some acts requiring the assent of more than a majority, they ought to be able to keep their representation full. It would have been a solecism, to have a government without any means of self-preservation. The Confederation is the only instance of a government without such means, and is a nerveless system, as inadequate to every purpose of government as it is to the security of the liberties of the people of America. When the councils of America have this power over elections, they can, in spite of any faction in any particular state, give the people a representation. Uniformity in matters of election is also of the greatest consequence. They ought all to be judged by the same law and the same principles, and not to be different in one state from what they are in another. At present, the manner of electing is different in different states. Some elect by ballot, and others viva voce. It will be more convenient to have the manner uniform in all the states. I shall now answer some observations made by the gentleman from Mecklenburg. He has stated that this power over elections gave to Congress power to lengthen the time for which they were elected. Let us read this clause coolly, all prejudice aside, and determine whether this construction be warrantable. The clause runs thus: "The times places, and manner, of holding elections for senators and representatives, shall be prescribed in each state by the legislature thereof; but the Congress may at any time, by law, make or alter such regulations, except as to the place of choosing senators." I take it as a fundamental principle, which is beyond the reach of the general or individual governments to alter, that the representatives shall be chosen every second year, and that the tenure of their office shall be for two years; that senators be chosen every sixth year, and that the tenure of their office be for six years. I take it also as a principle, that the electors of the most numerous branch of the state legislatures are to elect the federal representatives. Congress has ultimately no power over elections, but what is primarily given to the state legislatures. If

Congress had the power of prolonging the time, &c., as gentlemen observe, the same powers must be completely vested in the state legislatures. I call upon every gentleman candidly to declare, whether the state legislatures have the power of altering the time of elections for representatives from two to four years, or senators from six to twelve; and whether they have the power to require any other qualifications than those of the most numerous branch of the state legislatures; and also whether they have any other power over the manner of elections, any more than the mere mode of the act of choosing; or whether they shall be held by sheriffs, as contradistinguished from any other officer; or whether they shall be by votes, as contradistinguished from ballots, or any other way. If gentlemen will pay attention, they will find that, in the latter part of this clause, Congress has no power but what was given to the states in the first part of the same clause. They may alter the manner of holding the election, but cannot alter the tenure of their office. They cannot alter the nature of the elections; for it is established, as fundamental principles, that the electors of the most numerous branch of the state legislature shall elect the federal representatives, and that the tenure of their office shall be for two years; and likewise, that the senators shall be elected by the legislatures, and that the tenure of their office shall be for six years. When gentlemen view the clause accurately, and see that Congress have only the same power which was in the state legislature, they will not be alarmed. The learned doctor on my right (Mr. Spencer) has also said that Congress might lengthen the time of elections. I am willing to appeal to grammatical construction and punctuation. Let me read this, as it stands on paper. [Here he read the clause different ways, expressing the same sense.] Here, in the first part of the clause, this power over elections is given to the states, and in the latter part the same power is given to Congress, and extending only to the time of holding, the place of holding, and the manner of holding, the elections. Is this not the plain, literal, and grammatical construction of the clause? Is it possible to put any other construction on it, without departing from the natural order, and without deviating from the general meaning of the words, and every rule of grammatical construction? Twist it, torture it, as you may, sir, it is impossible to fix a different sense upon it. The worthy gentleman from New Hanover, (whose ardor for the liberty of his country I wish never to be damped,) has insinuated that high characters might influence the members on this occasion. I declare, for my own part, I wish every man to be guided by his own conscience and understanding, and by nothing else. Every man has not been bred a politician, nor studied the science of government; yet, when a subject is explained, if the mind is unwarped by prejudice, and not in the leading-strings of other people, gentlemen will do what is right. Were this the case, I would risk my salvation on a right decision.

Speeches Before the North Carolina Ratifying Convention by Archibald Maclaine

Editor's Introduction:

Archibald Maclaine's July 28 and 29 speeches were aimed at those who argued the Constitution produced a consolidation of the States. He argued the States courts would still function, that the jurisdiction of the federal judiciary was limited by the language of the Constitution, and that "the powers of Congress are limited and enumerated. We say we have given them those powers, but we do not say we have given them more. We retain all those rights which we have not given away to the general government." This point had been made in several State ratifying conventions. To the charge that the States should have been agents to the compact, Maclaine argued that the government had to be formed by the people, because the people had the power to "[form] their state governments, and can alter them at pleasure. Their transcendent power is competent to form this or any other government which they think promotive of their happiness." That would be the "principles of 1776."

Speeches Before the North Carolina Ratifying Convention July 28-29, 1788

By Archibald Maclaine of North Carolina

Mr. MACLAINE. Mr. Chairman, I hoped that some gentleman more capable than myself would have obviated the objections to this part. The objections offered by the gentleman appear to me totally without foundation. He told us that these clauses tended to a consolidation of the states. I cannot see how the states are to be consolidated by establishing these two clauses. He enumerated a number of cases which would be involved within the cognizance of the federal courts; customs, excises, duties, stamp duties — a stamp on every article, on every contract — in order to bring all persons into the federal court; and said that there would be necessarily courts in every district and county, which would be attended with enormous and needless expense, for that the state courts could do every thing. He went on further, and said that there would be a necessity of having sheriffs and other officers in these inferior departments. A wonderful picture indeed, drawn up in a wonderful manner! I will venture to say that the gentleman's suggestions are not warranted by any reasonable construction of the Constitution. The laws can, in general, be executed by the officers of the states. State courts and state officers will, for the most part, probably answer the purpose of Congress as well as any other. But the gentleman says that the state courts will be swallowed up by the federal courts. This is only a general assertion, unsupported by any probable reasons or arguments. The objects of each are separate and distinct. I suppose that whatever courts there may be, they will be established according to the convenience of the people. This we must suppose from the mode of electing and appointing the members of the government. State officers will as much as possible be employed, for one very considerable reason — I mean, to lessen the expense. But he imagines that the oath to be taken by officers will tend to the subversion of our state governments and of our liberty. Can any government exist without fidelity in its officers? Ought not the officers of every government to give some security for the faithful discharge of their trust? The officers are only to be sworn to support the Constitution, and therefore will only be bound by their oath so far as it shall be strictly pursued. No officer will be bound by his oath to support any act that would violate the principles of the Constitution.

The gentleman has wandered out of his way to tell us — what has so often been said out of doors — that there is no declaration of rights; that consequently all our rights are taken away. It would be very extraordinary to have a bill of rights, because the powers of Congress are expressly defined; and the very definition of them is as valid and efficacious a check as a bill of rights could be, without the dangerous implication of a bill of rights. The powers of Congress are limited and enumerated. We say we have given them those powers, but we do not say we have given them more. We retain all those rights which we have not given away to the general government. The gentleman is a professional man. If a gentleman had made his last will and testament, and devised or bequeathed to a particular person the sixth part of his property, or any particular specific legacy, could it be said that that person should have the whole estate? If they can assume powers not enumerated, there was no occasion for enumerating any powers. The gentleman is learned. Without recurring to his learning, he may only appeal to his common sense; it will inform him that, if we had all power before, and give away but a part, we still retain the rest. It is as plain a thing as possibly can be, that Congress can have no power but what we expressly give them. There is an express clause which, however disingenuously it has been perverted from its true meaning, clearly demonstrates that they are confined to those powers which are given them. This clause enables them to "make all laws which shall be necessary and proper for carrying into execution the foregoing powers, and all other powers vested by this Constitution in the government of the United States, or any department or officers thereof." This clause specifies that they shall make laws to carry into execution all the powers vested by this Constitution; consequently, they can make no laws to execute any other power. This clause gives no new power, but declares that those already given are to be executed by proper laws. I hope this will satisfy gentlemen.

****

Mr. MACLAINE. Mr. Chairman, I beg leave to make a few observations. One of the gentleman's objections to the Constitution now under consideration is, that it is not the act of the states, but of the people; but that it ought to be the act of the states; and he instances the delegation of power by the states to the Confederation, at the commencement of the war, as a proof of this position. I hope, sir, that all power is in the people, and not in the state governments. If he will not deny the authority of the people to delegate power to agents, and to devise such a government as a majority of them thinks will promote their happiness, he will withdraw his objection. The people, sir, are the only proper authority to form a government. They, sir, have formed their state governments, and can alter them at pleasure. Their transcendent power is competent to form this or any other government which they think promotive of their happiness. But the gentleman contends that there ought to be a bill of rights, or something of that kind — something declaring expressly, that all power not expressly given to the Constitution ought to be retained by the states; and he produces the Confederation as an authority for its necessity. When the Confederation was made, we were by no means so well acquainted with the principles of government as we are now. We were then jealous of the power of our rulers, and had an idea of the British government when we entertained that jealousy. There is no people on earth so well acquainted with the nature of government as the people of America generally are. We know now that it is agreed upon by most writers, and men of judgment and reflection, that all power is in the people, and immediately derived from them. The gentleman surely must know that, if there be certain rights which never can, nor ought to, be given up, these rights cannot be said to be given away, merely because we have omitted to say that we have not given them up. Can any security arise from declaring that we have a right to what belongs to us? Where is the necessity of such a declaration? If we have this inherent, this unalienable, this indefeasible title to those rights, if they are not given up, are they not retained? If Congress should make a law beyond the powers and the spirit of the Constitution, should we not say to Congress, "You have no authority to make this law. There are limits beyond which you cannot go. You cannot exceed the power prescribed by the Constitution. You are amenable to us for your conduct. This act is unconstitutional. We will disregard it, and punish you for the attempt."

But the gentleman seems to be most tenacious of the judicial power of the states. The honorable gentleman must know, that the doctrine of reservation of power not relinquished, clearly demonstrates that the judicial power of the states is not impaired. He asks, with respect to the trial by jury, "When the cause has gone up to the superior court, and the verdict is set aside, what benefit arises from having had a jury trial in the inferior court?" I would ask the gentleman, "What is the reason, that, on a special verdict or case agreed, the decision is left to the court?" There are a number of cases where juries cannot decide. When a jury finds the fact specially, or when it is agreed upon by the parties, the decision is referred to the court. If the law be against the party, the court decides against him; if the law be for him, the court judges accordingly. He, as well as every gentleman here, must know that, under the Confederation, Congress set aside juries. There was an appeal given to Congress: did Congress determine by a jury? Every party carried his testimony in writing to the judges of appeal, and Congress determined upon it.

The distinction between matters of law and of fact has not been sufficiently understood, or has been intentionally misrepresented. On a demurrer in law, in which the facts are agreed upon by the parties, the law arising thereupon is referred to the court. An inferior court may give an erroneous judgment; an appeal may be had from this court to the Supreme Federal Court, and a right decision had. This is an instance wherein it can have cognizance of matter of law solely. In cases where the existence of facts has been first disputed by one of the parties, and afterwards established as in a special verdict, the consideration of these facts, blended with the law, is left to the court. In such cases, inferior courts may decide contrary to justice and law, and appeals may be had to the Supreme Court. This is an instance wherein it may be said they have jurisdiction both as to law and fact. But where facts only are disputed, and where they are once established by a verdict, the opinion of the judges of the Supreme Court cannot, I conceive, set aside these facts; for I do not think they have the power so to do by this Constitution.

The federal court has jurisdiction only in some instances. There are many instances in which no court but the state courts can have any jurisdiction whatsoever, except where parties claim land under the grant of different states, or the subject of dispute arises under the

Constitution itself. The state courts have exclusive jurisdiction over every other possible controversy that can arise between the inhabitants of their own states; nor can the federal courts intermeddle with such disputes, either originally or by appeal. There is a number of other instances, where, though jurisdiction is given to the federal court, it is not taken away from the state courts. If a man in South Carolina owes me money, I can bring suit in the courts of that state, as well as in any inferior federal court. I think gentlemen cannot but see the propriety of leaving to the general government the regulation of the inferior federal tribunals. This is a power which our own state legislature has. We may trust Congress as well as them.

INDEX

www.ingramcontent.com/pod-product-compliance
Lightning Source LLC
LaVergne TN
LVHW010709061126
851857LV00014B/1111
9781734950427